PAMPA GRANDE AND THE MOCHICA CULTURE

Izumi Shimada

Pampa Grande and the Mochica Culture

UNIVERSITY OF TEXAS PRESS   AUSTIN

Library of Congress Cataloging-in-Publication
Data

Shimada, Izumi.
    Pampa Grande and the Mochica culture /
Izumi Shimada.
        p.   cm.
    Includes bibliographical references and index.
    ISBN 0-292-77674-8 (alk. paper)
    1. Pampa Grande Site (Peru)   2. Mochica
Indians—Urban residence.   3. Mochica
Indians—Art.   4. Mochica Indians—
Antiquities.   5. Land settlement patterns—
Peru—Lambayeque (Dept.)   6. Lambayeque
(Peru : Dept.)—Antiquities.   I. Title.
F3430.1.M6S55   1994
985′.1401—dc20   93-26108

Contents

Preface

This book has two aims. The first is to provide an archaeologically based synthesis of the prominent Regional Developmental Mochica (or Moche) culture that flourished on the North Coast of Peru during the first millennium of our era. This provides the background for the second aim, which is to provide a case study of the city of Pampa Grande, the last capital of this culture.

Many books in different languages have attempted to present comprehensive pictures of the Mochica culture. In reality, however, many have focused on interpreting representational ceramic art. Often one gets an impression that "Mochica archaeology" is a mere supplement to iconographic studies. There are various basic problems with the reading of narrative art on funerary vessels in reconstructing cultural realities other than those pertaining to religion and cosmology.

This book is intended to add to, rather than challenge or replace, art historical visions of the Mochica world. In this book, Mochica art is neither accorded special status nor treated in isolation; rather, art is regarded as an integral part of the cultural system, its stylistic and iconographic changes mirroring important changes in the natural and/or cultural worlds (Shi-

mada 1991a). Overall, the book integrates insights and information from various complementary disciplines such as art history, ethnography, ethnohistory, geography, and geology. Thus, the Mochica prehistory presented in this book is a synthesis of extant archaeological and related knowledge and to a large degree reflects the research priorities and idiosyncracies of the methods and theories adopted by archaeologists.

In regard to the second aim of the book, Pampa Grande remains to date one of the few pre-Hispanic cities in South America for which we have sufficient chronological control and excavation data on a wide range of contexts to allow a detailed, comprehensive, synchronic reconstruction of pre-Hispanic urbanism. The city was rapidly established at the end of the sixth century and abandoned ca. A.D. 700–750. This was a turbulent period when much of the Peruvian Andes was experiencing major environmental and cultural upheavals leading to the demise of various regional cultures and the emergence of the "Wari Empire" centered in the Central Highlands of Peru. In other words, in examining the conditions and processes underlying its emergence and demise, this case study of pre-Hispanic urbanism offers insights into broader processes and issues that affected the entire Andes.

The potential significance of Pampa Grande with its immense, multilevel adobe platform mound of Huaca Fortaleza (also known as Huaca Grande) was recognized in the early part of this century by Heinrich Brüning (Schaedel 1988: 17), a German ethnologist, who photographed the site in 1907. Starting in the late 1940's, the site was visited by a series of foreign scholars as part of their regional or even pan-Andean settlement surveys (e.g., P. Kosok, H. and P. Reichlen, R. Schaedel, First University of Tokyo Expedition to the Andes [see Ishida]), and by the beginning of the 1950's, the extensive Mochica occupation of the site was firmly established. However, no systematic surveys or excavations were carried out until 1971, when the Royal Ontario Museum of Toronto, Canada, initiated its multiyear investigation into the origin and nature of Mochica urbanism at Pampa Grande under the direction of Kent C. Day.

In 1973, as a graduate student looking for doctoral thesis material, I joined Day in Lambayeque. Together, we carried out four months of intensive surface survey and collection, plane-table mapping of Pampa Grande, and intermittent site surveys in the Lambayeque and adjacent valleys of La Leche and Zaña to the north and south. The architectural and artifactual patterns discerned at the site, in turn, formed the basis for generating specific research questions addressed during the 1975 season and for establishing appropriate methodologies.

The yearlong field season in 1975 took on a more intense and diversified character with the addition of seven new members from different universities in Canada, Peru, and the United States. Following some two months of additional survey and mapping at the site, the remainder of the field season was devoted to large scale excavation and artifact analysis.

Originally, there was a plan to publish an edited book on Pampa Grande with an accompanying volume of plane-table maps covering an estimated 25 percent of the standing architecture at the site. This plan was never implemented, as the project ceased to exist in 1976. Yet there has been

increasing recognition of the overall significance of the site and time period. Publications by former project members do exist but are limited to their specific research topics, and a holistic vision of Moche V Pampa Grande cannot be readily gained from them. Thus, one of the basic aims of this book is to describe as much as possible the data generated by our project and offer a coherent synthesis.

Though this book retains some of the basic views regarding socioeconomic organization presented in my doctoral thesis (Shimada 1976), overall it only partially resembles it. Differences have resulted primarily from reassessment of the assumptions underlying the analysis and interpretations presented in the thesis and from the availability of new data on both Pampa Grande and its time period. In response to my requests, fellow members of the Pampa Grande project have generously offered me the opportunity to study and incorporate both published and unpublished data, easily doubling the amount of data compared to my thesis.

Additional data on Pampa Grande were acquired from a series of small excavations carried out in July–August of 1978 (I. Shimada 1982; Shimada and Shimada 1981), as well as from various subsequent visits. An inspection made shortly after the disastrous 1982–1983 rains and floods was informative as well as saddening. The enormous Huaca Fortaleza, which had towered over the site for some 1,400 years, was badly eroded down to its foundation in places, exposing previously unseen construction features (Shimada in press 1; Shimada and Cavallaro 1986, in press).

In retrospect, it is obvious that before and during the project we did not clearly perceive and appreciate the specific and general significance of what was encompassed by Pampa Grande and its time period. We were overly focused on Pampa Grande without proper regional perspective and examination of broader conditions and long-term developments. Genuine appreciation of its significance has gradually emerged over the past dozen years due to a series of complementary and follow-up investigations in the Lambayeque and other regions of the Central Andes.

The past decade saw a notable concentration of archaeological and ethnohistorical investigations in the Lambayeque region that had been long awaited (Shimada 1985a). For example, the Sicán Archaeological Project under my direction in the Batán Grande region of the La Leche Valley has yielded much new relevant data over the past twelve seasons (e.g., Shimada 1990a). This project was an outgrowth of the Pampa Grande research in that, among other aims, it attempted to elucidate regional cultural developments before, during, and after Moche V Pampa Grande. Survey by J. Nolan (1980) clarified Mochica settlement patterns and associated irrigation systems that linked the Lambayeque Valley and the Zaña Valley to the south. Ongoing excavation of sumptuous Mochica burials at Sipán in the mid-Lambayeque Valley by W. Alva (1988, 1990) and his team have not only brought worldwide attention to the Lambayeque region and Mochica archaeology but have also generated new research questions, particularly in regard to the early phases of Mochica cultural evolution and sociopolitical organization. The ongoing survey of the north bank of the Lambayeque Valley by members of the Sicán Archaeological Project attempts to answer these new questions.

Concurrent fieldwork elsewhere in the Central Andes has helped to place Pampa Grande in an even broader context. For example, the University of Tokyo expeditions to the Cajamarca Basin in the North Highlands of Peru has firmly established the contemporaneity of the Middle Cajamarca culture with Moche IV and V (Matsumoto 1988; Terada and Matsumoto 1985), raising the distinct possibility of strong competition over control of certain areas on the northern North Coast. Similarly, we now have a significant new perspective on the establishment of Pampa Grande with the recent discovery that it coincided closely with a prolonged period of environmental degradation, including a thirty-two-year-long drought, the severest documented for the past 1,500 years (Schaaf 1988; Shimada et al. 1991a,b).

Overall, these recent developments have helped to rectify the most serious drawback of the single-site, single-period orientation of the Royal Ontario Museum project at Pampa Grande by allowing the placement of Moche V Pampa Grande in proper diachronic, regional, and interregional contexts. Thus, in addition to being a case study of pre-Hispanic urbanism, Pampa Grande can be also seen as a study of creative responses to severe external stresses, both cultural and natural. In essence, Pampa Grande is seen here as the product of creative, systemic responses to (1) a prolonged period of climatic anomalies that spanned much of the sixth century A.D., (2) pressure from the encroaching highland powers of the Cajamarca and Wari cultures during the seventh century, and (3) the political and social instability within the urban population brought together under climatic stress.

Chapter 1 summarizes the developmental trajectory and major achievements of the Mochica culture to define its significance within Andean civilization. It also sets out the major theoretical issues addressed in the book. Chapter 2 describes the growth of Mochica archaeology, including its idiosyncrasies and intellectual underpinnings, to allow the reader to evaluate better the weaknesses and strengths of the synthesis offered in this book. In this context, the early and continuing predominance of iconographic studies points to the need for holistic, more broadly based cultural syntheses. Chapter 3 describes the environmental setting of the Mochica culture, emphasizing its dynamic and multifaceted character as well as some creative cultural responses to its potential and its limitations.

Chapters 4 and 5 together offer a comprehensive synthesis of over five hundred years of antecedent Mochica cultural evolution, highlighting the long-term trends and major achievements that were to shape Pampa Grande. Chapter 4 summarizes the difficulties in defining the origins of the Mochica culture and chronicles the evolution of its hegemony over the North Coast of Peru. Chapter 5 focuses on the internal organization and structure and antecedent developments that may have contributed to the Moche V urbanism and state posited for Pampa Grande. In the process, it elucidates the pros and cons of different views

on the nature of Mochica sociopolitical organization and urbanism.

Against this backdrop, Chapter 6 defines the extraordinary circumstances and forces responsible for the Moche IV–V transformation and attendant establishment of Pampa Grande. Explanations invoking climatic anomaly and other alternatives are scrutinized.

Chapter 7 describes the planned urban landscape and how topographic and architectural features were used effectively to bipartition the site both physically and socially. It also tackles the sociopolitical significance of architectural organization and variation. Gigantic Huaca Fortaleza was much more than the symbolic and physical center of the emergent city; its construction is believed to have played a critical role in the establishment of new social and administrative rules and forms culminating in the state and the city. Chapter 8 characterizes Moche V urban subsistence and various forms of craft production that satisfied the day-to-day needs of its urban population, as well as the political economy of the Moche V state. In addition, evidence indicating the redistributive nature of the urban economy is discussed. Chapter 9 shows how traditional Mochica iconography and rituals were selectively retained, sometimes with modified usages and significance, suggesting some fundamental ideological reassessment concurrent with the Moche IV–V transformation.

Chapter 10 describes the violent end of Mochica occupation at Pampa Grande and assesses the relative merits of competing explanations for the Moche V demise. The final chapter summarizes the book and discusses the long-term significance of the Moche V culture and Pampa Grande in Andean prehistory.

Certain terms used in this book need to be clarified. The archaeological culture about which this book is written is called Mochica or Moche. We do not know the original name of the culture or how well the archaeological culture corresponds to the natives' perception of their culture (cf. Lanning 1967: 29–30). This book follows the pioneering scholars Rafael Larco Hoyle and Alfred L. Kroeber in using the term *Mochica* to refer to the archaeological culture. This culture is most commonly identified by a distinct "corporate" (elite/ ritual) art style, which emphasized naturalistic representations by means of sculptural treatment of volume and bichrome painting (dark red on cream background or vice versa) and pictorial composition. Usage of the term *Moche* is restricted (except in quotes) to the type site, the valley of that name, and the five phases (Moche I–V) of the Mochica culture.

The disappearance of this art style does not mean that the population that developed it died out or migrated elsewhere; rather, it reflects a significant transformation or displacement of the earlier dominant political and/or religious group together with the media of expression that served to diffuse its dogma. In addition, osteological analyses of human remains and the continuity in "folk" (utilitarian/ domestic) style ceramics argue for the basic biological continuity of populations on the pre-Hispanic North Coast (see Moseley 1978a; Newman 1948). R. Schaedel (1985a, 1987, 1988) sees the Mochica culture as defined here as the first "cultural climax" of the single, long cultural tradition of the *Muchik* people whose cultural substratum still remains viable. I concur largely, but not entirely, with this view.

Though the term *pyramid* is employed in the literature, strictly speaking, the Mochica did not construct pyramids. While the designation *truncated pyramids* is a better approximation, their mounds are in reality multilevel trapezoidal platforms. In this book the designation *platform mound* replaces *pyramid*.

Moche I–V are classificatory units primarily defined by observed changes in the form of stirrup-spout bottles (Larco Hoyle 1948). Limited stratigraphic data (e.g., Strong and Evans 1952) and independent seriations (e.g., Donnan 1965; Klein 1967) show that they constitute a viable relative chronology at least in the southern Mochica stronghold of the Chicama, Moche, and Virú valleys. The boundary between any two successive phases is arbitrarily drawn and, with the exception of Moche V, the absolute dates bracketing each phase should be considered educated guesses based on a small number of inconclusive radiocarbon dates. Further, these dates are approximate in the sense that the ceramic

vessel forms were unlikely to have changed appreciably overnight or even synchronously throughout the extensive Mochica domain. Table 1 (in Chapter 1) summarizes the Mochica cultural chronology and its relationship to the widely used periodization scheme of the Central Andes. According to this scheme, the long evolution of the Mochica culture spanned much of the Early Intermediate Period and the first portion of the Middle Horizon.

Table 2 (also in Chapter 1) summarizes relevant radiocarbon dates. Whenever available, each is accompanied by (1) an assessment of the sample and its relationship with the event or material remains to be dated, and (2) its corresponding computer-calibrated calendrical date. Due to variation in the amount of atmospheric carbon isotopes, radiocarbon years are not a uniform measure of time. To put it another way, conversion of radiocarbon to calendrical dates is neither simple nor linear; the exclusive use of radiocarbon dates deters meaningful chronological comparisons. Until recently, many archaeologists insisted on the exclusive use of uncalibrated radiocarbon dates (5568 half-life radiocarbon age B.P. minus 1950, represented by lowercase b.c./a.d. dates). However, with the recent establishment of high-precision calibration tables as the international standard (Pearson and Stuiver 1986; Stuiver and Pearson 1986) and the ready availability of computer calibration software (e.g., Stuiver and Reimer 1986), calibrated dates (represented by uppercase B.C./A.D. years) should be concurrently utilized, as is done in this book.

In regard to bibliographic citations in the text, the date of original publication appears in parentheses, while the date of the edition used in this book, if different, appears in brackets.

I received generous support and collaboration from numerous colleagues and institutions in the preparation and writing of this book. First and foremost, I am grateful to Kent C. Day for a helpful introduction to North Coast archaeology and for providing me the opportunity and support for my dissertation research at Pampa Grande. A. D. Tushingham, the chief archaeologist of the Royal Ontario Museum during the span of the Pampa Grande project, has continued to encourage me toward the completion of this book. I extend my gratitude to my fellow project members, the late Martha B. Anders, Jonathan Haas, Andrew Ignatieff, Hans Knapp, Melody J. Shimada, and Luis Watanabe, for their companionship and collaboration in and out of the field. Andrew and Hans generously allowed me free use of their unpublished data. Some of their unpublished drawings were redrawn to illustrate the text here.

In writing my doctoral thesis and this book, I benefited from substantive and theoretical critiques, sharing of data, and/ or editorial suggestions made by Walter Alva, Garth Bawden, Duccio Bonavia, Kate Cleland, Kent Day, Carlos Elera, Patricia Lyon, Adriana Maguiña, Ryozo Matsumoto, Dorothy Menzel, Michael Moseley, Allison Paulsen, Victor Pimentel, Colin Renfrew, Glenn Russell, Jeremy Sabloff, Richard Schaedel, Anne-Louise Schaffer, Hartmut and Marianne Tschauner, Segundo Vásquez, David Wilcox, and David Wilson. Yoshitake Suzuki shared with me his recollections and photos from the 1940's, when he photographed excavations under the direction of Rafael Larco Hoyle in the Hacienda Chiclín in the Chicama Valley and artifacts thus recovered. My wife, Melody, as always, has spent many hours reading, commenting on, and editing the manuscript for this book. Without her assistance, this book would not have been feasible. Also, I thank Ulrich Menge for his permission to read and cite a few passages of Max Uhle's unpublished final report of his excavation at the site of Moche, kept at the Ibero-Amerikanisches Institut in Berlin. In all cases, I alone am responsible for factual errors or misinterpretations.

Funding for my participation in the Pampa Grande project in 1973 was made possible by the Shirley William Fulton Memorial Scholarship of the University of Arizona. The 1975 season was supported by funds from the Canada Council and the Royal Ontario Museum. My 1978 fieldwork at Pampa Grande was carried out with a Princeton University Faculty Research Grant. The Sicán Archaeological Project has received generous support from the National Geographic Society, National Science Foundation, Shibusawa Foundation for Ethnological Studies, and Princeton and Harvard universities.

Some of the drawings in this book were partially or wholly prepared by Genaro Barr, German Ocas, Japhet Rosell, César Samillán, and Charles Sternberg. Some photographs were expertly taken by Yutaka Yoshii of Lima. For providing photographs and/or allowing us to photograph objects for this volume, I thank the Amano Museum, the Museo de la Nación, the National Museum of Anthropology and Archaeology, the Central Reserve Bank of Peru Museum, the Rafael Larco Herrera Museum, the National Air Photographic Service of Peru, Eugenio Nicolini, and Raúl Apesteguía, all in Lima; the Brüning National Archaeological Museum, Lambayeque; the Museum of Ethnology, Berlin; the Peabody Museum of Archaeology and Ethnology, Cambridge, Mass.; the Metropolitan Museum of Art, New York; the Field Museum of Natural History, Chicago; and the National Geographic Society, Washington, D.C. The following colleagues made available photographs and/or drawings for this book: Raffael Cavallaro, William Conklin, Alan Craig, Kent Day, Jonathan Haas, Andrew Ignatieff, Hans Knapp, Crystal Schaaf, Lonnie Thompson, and James Vreeland.

MAY, 1992

PAMPA GRANDE AND THE MOCHICA CULTURE

1

The Mochica
and Pampa Grande in
Andean Prehistory

The Central Andes, roughly corresponding to modern Peru, was the setting for a series of complex pre-Hispanic cultures, including the Inca, who had built the largest native political system in the New World by the time the Spaniards arrived in 1532. Yet, by a time over a thousand years earlier, a number of remarkable regional cultures had already achieved artistic, technological, and organizational features that compared favorably to or even remained unsurpassed by the Inca.

One such culture was the Mochica, which emerged on the arid North Coast of Peru (Fig. 1.1; Tables 1, 2) sometime around the time of Christ. Evolving out of earlier indigenous cultures known as Cupisnique and Salinar, and coexisting or competing with the contemporaneous Gallinazo (North Coast) and Cajamarca and Recuay cultures (both in the North Highlands), the Mochica grew in productive capacity, sociopolitical complexity, and territorial extent for over half a millennium. However, the processes and timing of their formation and expansion are in many ways still unclear. The traditional view is that the Mochica polity with its capital at the site of Moche began its expansion out of its heartland (the Chicama-Moche region) during Moche III (ca. A.D.

200). It was previously thought that by ca. A.D. 500 (Moche IV) the Mochica had, at least in part by military conquest, established hegemony over the entire North Coast, a stretch of over 350 km encompassing ten contiguous coastal river valleys (Fig. 1.2). The extent of Mochica trade and its sphere of interaction appears to have stretched from the South Coast of Peru, where the Nasca culture flourished, north to the Ecuadorian coast, where valuable tropical shells were gathered.

The recent discoveries of sumptuous early Mochica burials (Moche I–III; they may warrant the label, *royal tombs*) at the sites of Loma Negra/Vicús, Sipán, and La Mina in the upper Piura, Lambayeque, and Jequetepeque valleys, respectively, have forced us to reconsider some basic aspects of the above scenario and underlying premises. Traditionally, the apparent stylistic homogeneity found along the North Coast was assumed to indicate political unity achieved by a single Mochica polity based at the "capital" of Moche. The data now available raise the distinct possibility that, at least for the span of Moche I to early IV, two or even more regional polities that shared the art style we call Mochica held sway over different regions of the North Coast (see Donnan 1990a; cf. Klein 1967).

At the same time, there were other polities on the North Coast identified by a distinct style called Gallinazo. During Moche III (or perhaps slightly earlier), the polity based at Moche began its southward military expansion by conquering the Gallinazo polities. North of the Chicama-Moche region, there is no clear evidence of a similar, concurrent forcible expansion, perhaps due to the presence of powerful local Mochica polities in the Jequetepeque and Lambayeque valleys. In fact, in the mid-Lambayeque Valley, the Gallinazo and Mochica polities may have coexisted until both were incorporated into the expanding polity out of Moche around A.D. 500 (late Moche IV; see Schaedel 1985a: 448; Shimada 1981: 421).

Overall, instead of viewing North Coast prehistory in terms of a single dominant political center in the Chicama-Moche region, the revised perspective for Moche I to early IV postulates a parallel political development of Lambayeque-centered "northern Mochica" and Moche-based "southern Mochica" polities, each with a number of conquered and allied local Gallinazo and Mochica polities. Further, it is argued in this book that sometime in Moche IV, the southern Mochica polity eclipsed its northern counterpart, creating a short-lived pan–North Coast hegemony. With the Moche IV–V transformation ca. A.D. 550–600, the balance of power shifted to the north, with the Lambayeque region emerging as the seat of Moche V geopolitics. The cultural differences between the northern (Motupe to Jequetepeque) and southern (Chicama to Nepeña) North Coast that Kroeber (1930) recognized for Chimú times now appear to date back to the beginning of Mochica times or earlier.

Why the Mochica polity centered at Moche began its southward expansion has not yet been fully determined, though the acquisition of additional agricultural lands and tribute has been often cited as the basic motive (e.g., Carneiro 1970; Wilson

Table 1. Summary of Mochica cultural chronology and its relationship to the widely used periodization scheme.

Relationships with Contemporaneous Cultures	Major Events and Processes	Phases and Dates	Major Sites
Pressure from Wari and Middle Cajamarca B Peer interaction with final Maranga/Nievería and late Guangala	Establishment of the Moche V capital at Pampa Grande and northern shift of Mochica geopolitics; abandonment of Moche and the Southern Sector	V (A.D. 550–650/700)	MIDDLE HORIZON Pampa Grande, Galindo, Pacatnamú, San José de Moro, Huaca Soledad
	Three-decade drought Major El Niño event?	Drought (A.D. 562–594)	
	Brief integration of the northern and southern Mochica by the polity centered at Moche	VI-B (A.D. 500–550) VI-A (A.D. 450–500)	EARLY INTERMEDIATE Moche, Mocollope, Huaca El Brujo, Huancaco, Pampa de los Incas, Pañamarca
Peer interaction with late Nasca Middle Cajamarca A	Forceful expansion and dominance of the Southern Sector by the southern Mochica; "horizontality" and economic self-sufficiency; agricultural maximization	III-C (A.D. 400–450?) III-B (A.D. 300–400?) III-A (A.D. 200–300?)	Moche, Huaca El Brujo, Sipán, Huaca Santa Rosa, Huancaco
Conflict and/or tense coexistence with Recuay and Late Gallinazo	Semi-autonomous Mochica polities centered in the Chicama-Moche, Lambayeque, Jequetepeque, and perhaps upper Piura valleys	I/II (A.D. 1–200?)	Loma Negra, La Mina, Sipán, Moche

Figure 1.1. Map of the Central Andes with major "Regional Developmental Cultures" that flourished during the Early Intermediate Period.

1983). The Mochica intrusion as signaled by the abrupt supplanting of local- by Mochica-style ceramics was accompanied by major changes in the regional settlement system. Most scholars agree on the imposition of an administrative hierarchy in each of the subjugated valleys. The regional centers are symbolized by monumental adobe platform mounds that are said to have followed the architectural canons expressed at the Huaca del Sol[1] and its sister mound of Huaca de la Luna at Moche (Conklin and Moseley 1988: 150). Even though Colonial looting removed over two-thirds of its mass, Huaca del Sol at the site of Moche (Fig. 1.3), built with over 143 million adobe bricks and at least 342 by 159 m and some 40–41 m high (Hastings and Moseley 1975), staggers visitors to this day. This and other Mochica mounds were essentially built using the widespread traditional North Coast technique of juxtaposed, standardized columns of adobe bricks. This technique, together with the marking of a certain portion of constituent bricks with simple geometric designs that began perhaps sometime before Moche III, has been interpreted as indicating the presence of a corvée labor tax much like the *mit'a* system in the Inca Empire.

However, the specific changes seen in regional settlement systems differ considerably from one valley to the next (cf. Conrad 1978; Proulx 1973; Wilson 1988), and, in addition to the maximization of agricultural production, we must consider other contributing factors in explaining the Mochica dominance of the southern North Coast. These factors include the thwarting of the coastward expansion of the contemporaneous North Highland Recuay polities, the buildup of competing Gallinazo polities on the coast, and the securing of overland and maritime trade routes.

Related to the above debate is one surrounding the nature of Mochica sociopolitical integration: did the Mochica polity (either Moche- or Lambayeque-based) attain the level of "state"? This issue has been hotly debated since the 1940's without a satisfactory resolution. We see a wide range of competing views stemming in part from the lack of a consensus in regard to the

Table 2. Relevant radiocarbon dates for the Mochica and contemporary North Coast cultures.

Context and Material	Lab No.	C-14 Age (BP ± 1∂; ad)	Calibrated Date (AD)
PAMPA GRANDE (LAMBAYEQUE VALLEY)			
burnt wooden post atop platform mound (Huaca 18), Sector H; Moche V	A-1704	1280 ± 70 BP; ad 690	AD 740 ± 80
charred cotton, floor of elite compound ("Deer House"; Unit 14); Moche V	SMU-399	1300 ± 60 BP; ad 650	AD 710 ± 60
charred cotton, floor of burnt platform mound in rectangular enclosure (Unit 16); Moche V	SMU-644	1250 ± 50 BP; ad 650	AD 770 ± 70
burnt cane, roof of *Spondylus* workshop, rectangular compound (Unit 15); Moche V	SMU-682	1380 ± 40 BP; ad 570 f	AD 650 ± 20
carbonized corn kernels in an urn placed in the floor of Structure 43, Unit 45, Sector H; Moche V	A-1705	1380 ± 70 BP; ad 570 not corrected for C=12/13 fractionation	AD 650 ± 50
HUACA SOLEDAD (LA LECHE VALLEY)			
charcoal from a firepit, Test Pit 3, Cut A, Southern Cemetery stratigraphically pre–Moche IV intrusion and is associated with Late Gallinazo ceramics	SMU-897	1570 ± 40 BP; ad 380 f	AD 490 ± 60
charcoal from "protective organic layer" covering Phase I construction, Mound II; associated with Moche V (?) burnished blackware bowl fragments	SMU-833	1410 ± 60 BP; ad 540	AD 630 ± 40
HUACA DEL PUEBLO BATAN GRANDE (LA LECHE VALLEY)			
Trench 1/2-'79 charcoal from firepit near the sterile sand, Stratum XII, Level N; associated with Moche IV ceramics	SMU-873	1540 ± 60 BP; ad 410	AD 520 ± 70
charcoal from firepit in the sandy Stratum XII, Level D/E; Moche V	SMU-901	1430 ± 60 BP; ad 520 f	AD 620 ± 40
charcoal from buried, discolored, and sooted vessel near the top of Stratum XII; Moche V	SMU-876	1410 ± 60 BP; ad 540	AD 650 ± 40
SIPAN (LAMBAYEQUE VALLEY)			
"Fragments of roofing beams" (Alva 1988: 524) of the burial chamber of the Lord of Sipán; Moche III		"about AD 290"	
PACATNAMU (JEQUETEPEQUE VALLEY)			
three different charcoal samples each taken from over a square yard from a deep layer at the northwest corner of Huaca 31 mound; a "period when Mochica and Gallinazo pottery was used concurrently as grave offering" (Ubbelohde-Doering 1967: 22); associated cemetery contains Moche II, IV, and V burials	Heidelberg University	1465 ± 50–100 BP; ad 485	
GALINDO (MOCHE VALLEY)			
wood charcoal from "pre-primary" room in the south court razed in order to construct the foundation of the Huaca Galindo; end of Moche IV or the onset of Moche V	GX-3256	1415 ± 185 BP; ad 535	
wood charcoal from "post-primary" squatter occupation at the Huaca Galindo compound, immediately after Moche V	GX-3257	1325 ± 165 BP; ad 625	
Ash level, ceramic workshop; Moche V	K4649-RC14-5	1260 ± 140 BP; ad 690	
Hearth, Structure 18; Moche V; unacceptably old	K4649	2335 ± 175 BP; 385 bc	
HUACA DEL SOL, MOCHE (MOCHE VALLEY)			
ash mixed with bones from a layer beneath Huaca del Sol mound; associated with Moche I sherds; unacceptably old	C-382	2823 ± 500 BP; 873 bc	

Table 2. (continued)

Context and Material	Lab No.	C-14 Age (BP ± 1∂; ad)	Calibrated Date (AD)
HUACA DE LA CRUZ (VIRU VALLEY)			
piece of sedge rope that tied the coffin of the Warrior-Priest; Moche IV; unacceptably old	C-619	1838 ± 190 BP; ad 112	
fragment of textile associated with Burial 3; Moche IV; seems somewhat too young	L-335A	1300 ± 80 BP; ad 650	
fragment of basket associated with Burial 10; late Moche IV	L-335B	1300 ± 80 BP; ad 650	
V-66 (VIRU VALLEY)			
Puerto Moorin (Salinar) occupation	UCLA (1975A)	2035 ± 60; 85 bc	
Late Gallinazo occupation	UCLA (1975B)	1600 ± 60; ad 350	
V-434 (VIRU VALLEY)			
Puerto Moorin (Salinar) occupation	UCLA (1974B)	1950 ± 60; ad 1	
Puerto Moorin (Salinar) occupation	UCLA (1974C)	1890 ± 70; ad 60	
Late Puerto Moorin (Salinar)/Early Gallinazo occupation	UCLA (1974A)	1870 ± 70; ad 80	
Late Gallinazo occupation	UCLA (1974D)	1600 ± 60; ad 350	
CERRO SAJINO (LA LECHE VALLEY)			
a sample of carbonized beam from the burnt adobe storage structure (full of charred maize) atop of the Cerro; associated with Late Gallinazo ceramics.	SMU-2612	1680 ± 50 BP; a.d. 270	AD 360 ± 50
SITES IN THE SANTA VALLEY			
textile fragment excavated from habitation refuse at 156 P4L1 #27; Moche IV; unacceptably young	UCLA 1801	1060 ± 60 BP; ad 890	
textile fragment excavated from habitation refuse at 92 P2L2 #170; Moche IV	UCLA 1802	1550 ± 110 BP; ad 400	
textile fragment excavated from habitation refuse at 156 P1L3 #2; Moche IV	UCLA 1803	1390 ± 60 BP; ad 560	
textile fragment excavated from habitation refuse at 161 P1L1 #63; Moche III	UCLA 1804	1450 ± 140 BP; ad 500	
textile fragment excavated from habitation refuse at 161 P1L4 #93; Moche III	UCLA 1805	1870 ± 50 BP; ad 80	
textile fragment excavated from habitation refuse at 161 P1L1 #71; Moche III; unacceptably young	UCLA 1806	1220 ± 70 BP; ad 730	
VICUS (UPPER PIURA VALLEY)			
sample (unspecified) from Site 3C-VI-1; associated with gilded copper object of early Mochica style (Moche I–II?)	GX-216	2030 ± 105 BP; 280 bc	

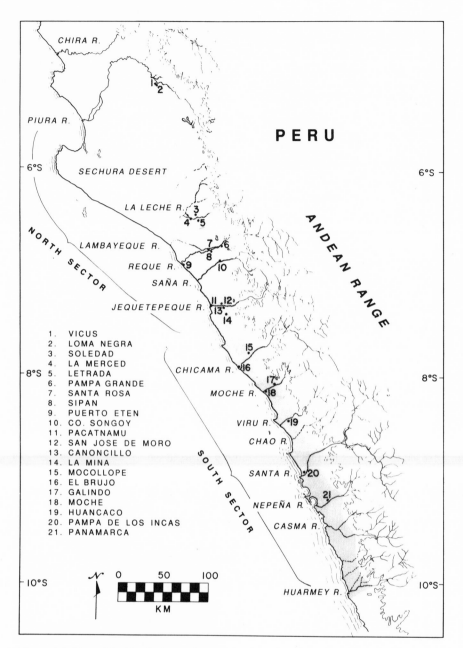

PERU

1. VICUS
2. LOMA NEGRA
3. SOLEDAD
4. LA MERCED
5. LETRADA
6. PAMPA GRANDE
7. SANTA ROSA
8. SIPAN
9. PUERTO ETEN
10. CO. SONGOY
11. PACATNAMU
12. SAN JOSE DE MORO
13. CANONCILLO
14. LA MINA
15. MOCOLLOPE
16. EL BRUJO
17. GALINDO
18. MOCHE
19. HUANCACO
20. PAMPA DE LOS INCAS
21. PANAMARCA

Figure 1.2. Map of the North Coast of Peru showing river valleys, major Mochica sites, and maximum extent of the Mochica culture around A.D. 500. Contour lines are at 1000 meters.

definition of *state*, differential emphasis placed on various relevant data, and insufficient excavation data. For example, Schaedel (1972, 1985b; also Kutscher 1955a, 1967) characterized the Mochica polity as a confederation of chiefdoms or a "super-chiefdom" and posited that the first state-level administration on the North Coast was introduced by the inferred Wari invaders.[2] Steward and Faron (1959: 86, 92) saw the polity as an established state structured along status differentiation and occupational specialization, while Larco Hoyle (1939: 132, 138) described it as a state-level theocratic dynasty assisted by powerful military chiefs. Kosok (1965: 111) was less committed, suggesting that it was in a transitional stage between a theocratic chiefdom and a secular state. A few (Conklin and Moseley 1988: 151) even go so far as to call it an empire, a dubious characterization. Many contemporary scholars view the Mochica polity as the first true secular or expansionist state to emerge on the Pacific coast of South America (e.g., Carneiro 1970; Moseley 1983a: 222; T. Topic 1982: 270–273; Wilson 1988: 332–342).

Evidence in support of a secular Mochica state is wide-ranging but not unequivocal. For example, the increasing number of explicit depictions of armed combat and warriors in Mochica ceramic art during Moche III–IV is usually interpreted as indicating the importance of warfare as a means of sociopolitical integration and territorial expansion. Mochica iconography, however, has a clearly religious character, and extracting secular meaning is not a simple matter. Also, many scholars argue that the capture of sacrificial victims was the motive for warfare (e.g., Kutscher 1955a).

Figure 1.3. Impressive Huaca del Sol (Pyramid of the Sun) at the site of Moche as seen from the east. It is evident that this edifice is not a pyramid but rather a multilevel platform. Holes near the base were made by looters. Photo R-6065. Courtesy of the Servicio Aerofotográfico Nacional del Perú.

Figure 1.4. Moche IV example of a "portrait vessel." Raúl Apesteguía Collection, Lima. Photo by Y. Yoshii.

Both sides of this debate recognize the dynamic character of Mochica leadership during its long existence; the question is whether secular, military leaders superseded theocratic elite control within this time span.

In contrast to the above debate, there is a good consensus regarding the impressive achievements of the Mochica in the arts and crafts. The technical and artistic mastery and sophistication seen in ceramics, metalwork, and textiles befit earlier characterizations such as the Mastercraftsman or Regional Classic culture. Its naturalistic, representational art style has been long appreciated worldwide and ranks among the great narrative arts of the world. There is nothing comparable in Andean civilization to this sort of narrative "visual text." Mochica art tells us a good deal about significant events and features of the Mochica world, both real and mythological. Tens of thousands of realistically painted and modeled ceramic vessels depicting a broad spectrum of subject matter and scenes (Figs. 1.4, 1.5) are a genuine source of fascination and information for both the general public and the academic community. Mochica ceramic art developed pictorial composition to a singular level among numerous pre-Hispanic Andean art styles.

At the same time, the breadth and depth of information to be extracted from Mochica ceramics may have lulled scholars into a false sense of complacency. We must be aware that these ceramics were overwhelmingly derived from funerary contexts, and their decorations have strong religious tones. Further, in spite of many years of research, the meaning of the iconography remains elusive.

Like their ceramics, the basic features of the Mochica metallurgy followed earlier North Coast developments. Their artisans, however, took Cupisnique metallurgy emphasizing copper and gold sheet metal to new heights; in fact, the artistic virtuosity and technological sophistication of Mochica metallurgy is in many ways unparalleled in the New World and remarkable for its innovative qualities (Figs. 1.6, 1.7; see Jones 1979; Lechtman 1979, 1988). The spectacular gold, silver, copper, and gold-plated copper objects, many decorated with fine repoussé work, that accompany deceased Mochica elite unearthed at the site of Sipán (Alva 1988, 1990; Alva et al. 1989) amply demonstrate this point.

Textiles are usually not well preserved on the North Coast. However, some that have survived show that, as with the case of the metallurgy, they are of high artistic and

Figure 1.5. Moche IV stirrup-spout bottle that effectively combines modeling and fine-line drawing to illustrate the gathering of landsnails. Museo de la Nación, Lima. Photo by Y. Yoshii.

Figure 1.6. Mochica headdress plaque fashioned out of hammered gold alloy sheet. Facial features are done in repoussé. Rafael Larco Herrera Museum, Lima. Photo by Y. Yoshii.

technical qualities, possessing their own consistent and diagnostic structural features that had long-lasting influence on the textiles of subsequent cultures (Conklin 1979; Reid 1988).

The Mochica achievements outlined above must be seen within the opportunities and limitations of the North Coast environment. At least from the time of the Cupisnique culture during the first millennium B.C., the North Coast river valleys have constituted one of the two main breadbaskets of the Central Andes. Together with the relatively low gradients and extensiveness of the coastal alluvial plains, large amounts of runoff from regular seasonal rainfall in the adjacent North Highlands supported large-scale irrigation agriculture of maize, beans, squash, cotton, and other native crops.

Figure 1.7. Early Mochica style gilded copper ornament 12 cm high, representing a "warrior" from a looted tomb in Loma Negra near Cerro Vicús in the upper Piura Valley. Gift of Jane Costello Goldberg from the Collection of Arnold I. Goldberg, 1981 (1981.459.32). Courtesy of the Metropolitan Museum of Art, New York.

The riches of the Pacific complemented the agricultural products. Many fish, shellfish, crustaceans, sea mammals, and other marine resources are abundant, readily exploitable, and available year-round. In fact, the cold Peru (or Humboldt) Current is often thought of as the richest fishing ground in the world.

This dual subsistence base was quite productive. Furthermore, available climatic data (e.g., Cardich 1985; Thompson et al. 1985; Shimada et al. 1991a,b) indicate that for much of its duration, the Mochica culture was blessed with relative abundance of rainfall in the highlands. Most likely, these factors contributed to a significant increase in Mochica population. Various major features of the Mochica culture, such as the strong coastal orientation in their territorial expansion and trade, seem to have been designed to sustain the dual economic pillars.

Whatever we choose to call the late Mochica sociopolitical form and complexity just prior to Pampa Grande, many of their organizational, material, and symbolic features and achievements were impressive, autogenous, and unprecedented in the Andes. The significance of the Mochica culture in Andean civilization can also be gauged by long-term impacts. For example, Mochica icons and stylistic features were repeatedly revived or imitated by Mochica descendants on the North Coast. As a whole, the Mochica can be characterized as the primary cultural development on the Peruvian coast during the first millennium.

The history of many cultures, including that of the Mochica, features periods of seeming tranquility interspersed with those of "upheaval," with brief periods that seem extraordinary in the scope and magnitude of changes that transpired. The period of some one hundred to one hundred fifty years starting ca. A.D. 550 was just such an era for much of the Central Andes. This period spans the end of the Early Intermediate Period and the beginning of the Middle Horizon (Tables 1, 2) and saw the decline and eventual demise of Regional Developmental cultures and the initiation of the "First Round of Empire Building" (Lanning 1967) in the Peruvian Andes.

For the Mochica culture on the North Coast, the onset of this turbulent period marked the major transition from Moche IV to V that included abandonment of both their "paramount" site of Moche and the southern half of the Mochica hegemony. The planned inland city of Pampa Grande, occupying the neck of the large Lambayeque Valley approximately 165 km north of Moche and 55 km from the coast, emerged as the dominant center of Moche V society. With the gigantic Huaca Fortaleza (Fig. 1.8) at its physical and symbolic center, the site, covering some 6 km^2, was one of the largest settlements on the Peruvian coast for its time, boasting an estimated population of ten to fifteen thousand.

The northward shift of the Mochica seat of power and population nucleation at a few valley neck sites was accompanied by major changes in many aspects of Mochica culture and society (Shimada 1982, 1991a, in press 1). Moche V culture and Pampa Grande were by no means a predictable outgrowth of the preceding five-hundred-year Mochica cultural tradition. Traditional values and institutions were reassessed and transformed, accompanied by a myriad of innovations. New and revived ceramic forms, often in black or grey wares, emerged, while fine traditional painted wares manifested new iconographic emphases. Even burial position and ritual paraphernalia changed during Moche V. The imposing Huaca Fortaleza was probably built within one or two generations by combining the traditional technique of standardized vertical segments of stacked adobe bricks with the innovative technique of refuse-filled adobe chambers.

Pampa Grande and the contemporaneous site of Galindo in the Moche Valley have been argued as constituting autogenous North Coast cities (e.g., Bawden 1982a; Shimada 1978). However, some researchers question their city status (Schaedel 1985b), the autogenous origin of major architectural forms, or even their urbanism (ibid.; McEwan 1990). The origin of urbanism on the Peruvian coast has been a controversial issue at least since the time of the Virú Valley Project in the late 1940's (see Chapter 2) when it was noted that the disappearance of Mochica-style

Figure 1.8. Oblique-angle airphoto of the site of Pampa Grande with the gigantic Huaca Fortaleza platform mound situated at the center. Much of the site is still densely covered by standing architecture.

ceramics seemed to correlate with the appearance of new intrusive ceramic styles, architectural forms, and settlement types (e.g., see Willey 1953). In particular, the Virú Valley Project noted the new emphasis on planned, more secular Rectangular Enclosure Compounds supplanting earlier Mochica emphasis on religious monumental platform mounds. Their "Virú Valley model" essentially saw North Coast cities as having been introduced by the Wari conquerors.

Though some specific Moche V features, such as refuse-filled adobe chambers and certain ceramic forms and techniques, are likely to have originated out of the Central Coast of Peru (e.g., Late Lima or Early Nievería culture; Shimada 1991b: il) and coastal Ecuador, we do not see evidence of the inferred Wari conquest at Pampa Grande, where traditional Mochica political and religious symbolism, such as representational art and monumental platform mounds, persisted.

Also, this model does not adequately account for the valley neck locations and population nucleation at Galindo and Pampa Grande. The model further suffers from imprecise chronological control; it subsumes a series of major events and processes within a single phase called Tomaval (no subphase divisions) that probably spanned upwards of three to four hundred years (at least ca. A.D. 700–1000). The earliest Tomaval ceramics appear to be stylistically contemporaneous with those of Moche V (Middle Horizon Epoch 1B), which appear to predate the rare Provincial Wari (Middle Horizon Epoch 2A) ceramics. Thus, it is not clear whether the inferred Wari invasion and attendant emergence of new community types came before, during, or after the Moche IV–V transition. Any causal linkage among the major events remains obscure.

The exogenous origin theory was challenged in the 1970's by members of the Chan Chan–Moche Valley Project, which attempted to show direct cultural continuity between the Moche V and the later Chimú Kingdom without any significant interruption by the inferred Wari invaders (see Table 1.1 in Moseley and Day 1982: 8; Mackey 1982; T. Topic 1982). Mackey (1982: 322) rejected the Wari introduction theory for North Coast cities in favor of an indigenous origin: "urbanism did not suddenly arise without antecedents but shows a continuous indigenous development." In their zeal, researchers did not properly assess evidence relevant to documenting Wari influence or invasion, such as Provincial Wari ceramics at Huaca del Sol in Moche (see Menzel 1977), in this region of the North Coast.

Major changes during the Moche IV–V transition were explained by this project in terms of environmental factors: catastrophic flooding and coastal uplift, resulting in sand sheet movement and downcutting by rivers, together disrupted the irrigation systems (e.g., Moseley and Deeds 1982; Nials et al. 1979a,b). Though this view may account for the observed inland population movements, it does not precisely date relevant events and processes or adequately account for the establishment of the new capital so far to the north.

This book offers an alternative explanation based on a recent multidisciplinary investigation of a 1,500-year precipitation record. This record revealed a thirty-two-year-long drought, the most severe during this span, during the late sixth century (Shimada et al. 1991a,b). Pampa Grande is seen as a case of relatively short-lived urbanism based on the integration of populations brought together by unique stressful cultural and natural conditions through the organizational framework of the earlier urban Mochica ceremonial-civic centers. In a basic sense, Pampa Grande was the Mochicas' collective effort to survive a stressful period and revive the former glory and power of the Lambayeque-based northern Mochica polity. The establishment of the capital at Pampa Grande was clearly planned with Huaca Fortaleza serving as the hub of physical growth and of the bipartitioned social organization of the emerging city. Most of the commoners were massed together in the physically segregated southern portion of the city, while the elite were on the northern and western sides of Huaca Fortaleza within walled enclosures or other structures. The construction of Huaca Fortaleza served not only to symbolize the viability of the Mochica polity and religion but also, perhaps fortuitously, to underlay the foundation of urbanism at Pampa Grande with the permanence of a large labor force. It was a truly unprecedented time for the Mochica elite, who faced the complex task of managing the needs and desires of a relocated and expanding population of varied skills, social positions, and ethnicities. It was this unique, dynamic condition that led to the creation of new social forms and relations, which in turn necessitated increasingly complex control measures and hierarchies that characterize the state.

At the same time, as this city and state grew, the social and administrative institutions and constituent populations that earlier had been vital in the formative stage of the city gradually lost their original purpose and became too costly to maintain. In the long run, this condition is seen to have created sociopolitical instability, eventually preconditioning the sudden, violent collapse of the Moche V polity that, at least in time, coincided with the second wave of Wari expansion (Middle Horizon Epoch 2A).

Though the second half of the book focuses on the internal structure and workings of Pampa Grande as the Moche V urban capital, the conditions and processes underlying its establishment and demise are relevant to the Central Andes as a whole.

2

Archaeology of the Mochica Culture: Growth and Characteristics

The archaeology of the Mochica culture has a long and distinguished history. If *prehistory* is defined as the synthesis of extant archaeological knowledge, it is well worth considering the intellectual traditions that, together with the intrinsic qualities of the Mochica culture, have given rise to the synthesis presented here. In other words, a historical review of Mochica archaeology allows us to understand how certain assumptions, approaches, and concepts, as well as any resultant unevenness in our knowledge of Mochica culture and society, have come to be. It also provides a proper perspective for understanding how our Pampa Grande research contributes to advances in Mochica and, more broadly, New World archaeology.

1. Early Scholarship

The voluminous documentation on the Inca Empire following the Spanish conquest ca. A.D. 1532–1535 has been a mixed blessing for students of Andean civilization. Official chronicles and ecclesiastic, legal, and administrative writings preserved abundant information on nonmaterial aspects of the Empire that would be difficult to reconstruct archaeologically, a fact that is of particular importance be-

cause no Andean culture developed writing as we know it. However, the impressive achievements and glory of the Empire, together with the sheer amount of written data, have had the long-lasting effect of hindering recognition and serious study of pre-Inca cultures, such as the Mochica. Even today, archaeologists implicitly depend on detailed and voluminous Colonial writings on the Incas and their culture to interpret pre-Inca cultures. However, without clear demonstration of continuity, analogy to Inca features and patterns is of limited or questionable value. Further, many historical documents were written from a sixteenth-century European perspective, describing much of Andean prehistory in terms of Old World models, particularly Biblical history.

During the sixteenth and seventeenth centuries, only a few writers recognized pre-Inca cultures. Those early writers who described the indigenous populations of the North Coast of Peru focused on the Kingdom of Chimor or Chimú (see Table 1) and its enormous capital of Chan Chan (Fig. 1.2). It was natural that the Kingdom received much attention, as it controlled the Peruvian coast from Tumbes near the Ecuadorian border to just north of Lima and had been a formidable rival until conquered by the Incas around A.D. 1460–1470 (Rowe 1945, 1948a,b). Also accounting for the early recognition of Chimú was the founding (in 1535 by Francisco Pizarro) and rapid growth of the city of Trujillo just east of Chan Chan, which was known as a veritable gold mine among Colonial looters.

The physical destruction and disruption of native societies brought about by the Spaniards' insatiable quest for gold and silver throughout the Andes is well known. The North Coast, with its prominent Mochica and later Sicán and Chimú cultures (Table 1), suffered greatly from wanton looting, which was neither illicit nor concealed. Lorenzo (1981: 192–193) describes the legal basis for this activity: "If there was anything resembling archaeology in the Spanish colonies in the sixteenth century, it was the licenses issued by the Spanish Crown to private parties to excavate the tombs of chiefs in exchange for one-fifth of the gold, silver and precious stones found." One commercial company established in the Moche Valley in the late sixteenth century systematically "mined" buried treasure (mostly from pre-Hispanic graves) until the early nineteenth century (Holstein 1927; Rivero and Tschudi 1855). In 1602, another group of Spaniards diverted the Moche River to wash away two-thirds of the Huaca del Sol at the site of Moche (Fig. 1.3) just outside of Trujillo; they recovered some 2,800 kg—nearly 6,000 lb—of precious metals (Kosok 1965: 93; Lothrop 1938: 67).

Serious intellectual interest in pre-Inca cultures of the North Coast evolved quite slowly. Publications on these earlier cultures were sparse and, with a few notable exceptions, did not form a coherent intellectual tradition until the late nineteenth century.

The Jesuit priest Antonio de la Calancha (1638 [1976]) extensively recorded the customs and beliefs of the Chimú, while Fernando de la Carrera (1644 [1939]) compiled a dictionary of *Yunga* or *Muchik,* the presumed native language of the Chimú and earlier Mochica, while there were still some speakers alive. Studying pre-Hispanic toponymy together with dictionaries has been helpful for delineating territorial divisions and social frontiers of the sixteenth and perhaps fifteenth centuries (e.g., Netherly 1977; Ramírez 1985a).

Perhaps the first serious study of the cultural and natural history of the North Coast was carried out by Baltazar Jaime Martínez de Compañón (1782–1788 [1978–1991]; see also Schaedel 1949), Bishop of the Diocese of Trujillo. He produced a nine-volume treatise and a series of accurate, detailed maps of ruins near Trujillo, including the first map of the Huaca del Sol, which was by then already two-thirds destroyed. He also made a collection of Chimú ceramics, many of which he carefully illustrated in color. Most of his paintings are of Chimú blackware vessels, although some appear to be of different styles, including Mochica. It is understandable that the Bishop did not differentiate Chimú and Mochica styles, since the Chimú often adopted earlier Mochica ceramic motifs and forms (see Chapter 11). A progressive thinker for his time, he inferred social status based on differences in funerary treatment and offerings, which he carefully painted and inventoried according to category and substance. Unfortunately most of his written documentation remains to be published. Martínez de Compañón's lead was not followed for another hundred years.

With the reign of Charles III of Spain in the mid- to late eighteenth century, which Lorenzo (1981: 195) characterizes as an era of "enlightened despotism," we see the first serious field explorations and natural history studies of the Andes, in particular by the noted German geographer and naturalist Baron Alexander von Humboldt (1814). During the eighteenth century and the first half of the nineteenth century, there were few advances made in the study of ancient Peruvian monuments and cultures. This situation was due partly to Eurocentric conceptions of human progress and nature and partly to inadequate fieldwork often dependent on unreliable secondhand information. A comparative study of Peruvian (mostly Inca) and Egyptian civilizations by Alcides D'Orbigny (1839) illustrates this failure to perceive pre-Hispanic Peruvian cultures on their own terms.

2. Emergence of Peruvian and Peruvianist Scholarship and the Recognition of Pre-Inca Cultures

During the nineteenth century there was a significant upsurge in field exploration and publications (including various popular travelogues) about the Andes by people of diverse nationalities and backgrounds (including businessmen and diplomats), such as Adolf Bastian, Francis Comte de Castelnau, Thomas J. Hutchinson, Ernest W. Middendorf, Antonio Raimondi, Ephraim George Squier, W. B. Stevenson, Johann Jakob von Tschudi, and Charles Wiener. Willey and Sabloff (1980: 34) characterize the New World archaeology of 1840–1914 as emphasizing "the description of archaeological materials, especially architecture and monuments, and rudimentary classification of these materials." This heightened interest in the Andes reflects that period's romanticism and fascination with the exotic, a philosophical shift toward positivism, and the growing prestige of science, as well as increasing formalization and widening areal coverage of fledgling archaeology in western Europe and the United States. In short, we are speaking of the emergence of "Peruvianist" (as opposed to "Peruvian") scholarship (Schaedel and Shimada 1982). The cosmopolitan character of Mochica and North Coast archaeology today has its roots in this period.

During this time, Mariano Eduardo de Rivero, a Peruvian scholar and the first director of the National Museum in Lima, together with the Peruvianist von Tschudi, published what may be the first formal textbook on Peruvian archaeology. *Antigüedades Peruanas,* published in 1851 and promptly translated into English (1855), helped to promote interest in Peruvian prehistory and archaeology within and outside of Peru. The book has been justifiably criticized as offering only superficial or limited firsthand knowledge of ruins and failing to explore prehistory beyond the historically reconstructed Inca dynasty (Hutchinson 1873: 250–251; Uhle 1903: 8). Rivero was nevertheless important, as he was a Peruvian working in an era when those who were interested in Peruvian prehistory were mainly Europeans or Americans, many of whom made collections for foreign museums and left few, if any, graphic or written descriptions of ruins and artifacts in Peru for Peruvian scholars and the public.

During the second half of the nineteenth century there was greater emphasis on empiricism and ethnological observations, as well as clear recognition of the greater antiquity of various pre-Inca cultures. Although more Peruvianists traveled through northern Peru describing its archaeological wonders, various pre-Inca cultures were not documented until the arrival of the German scholar Max Uhle, who carried out stratigraphic excavation and seriation of excavated gravelots at the end of the century.

The work of E. G. Squier (1877) is crucial to understanding these important changes. Following his term as Diplomatic Commissioner of the United States in Peru, he retraced the path of the well-known sixteenth-century writer Pedro Cieza de León. Cieza de León arrived in Peru in 1548 as an infantryman of the Spanish royal troops and traveled through the former dominion of the Inca Empire, eventually compiling the highly regarded *Chronicle of Peru* (Cieza de León 1554[1984]). Squier's methodology was quite simple, based on direct field observation of architecture supplemented by occasional studies of artifact collections and examination of pits dug by grave looters. With only a compass, a tape measure, stakes, and a camera, he produced accurate maps of various ruins such as the Huaca del Sol and the major Mochica platform mound at Pañamarca in the Nepeña Valley.

Perhaps the most important aspect of his work was in demonstrating the importance of methodological rigor, and of cultivating critical acumen in archaeological fieldwork and observations, over artistic or literary descriptions and interpretations. Squier also affirmed the indigenous character of ancient Peruvian civilization and the existence of various pre-Inca cultures. It is no surprise that Squier is often regarded as the father of scientific archaeology in Peru (e.g., Porras 1963: 62; Ravines 1970: 32).

Squier was soon followed by other Peruvianists who reiterated the antiquity and variability of pre-Inca cultures. Valuable firsthand field observations abounded during the latter part of the nineteenth century (e.g., Markham 1892; Middendorf 1893–1895), though romanticism and dependence on hearsay lingered on (e.g., Wiener 1880). The British Consul and amateur archaeologist, Hutchinson (1873), rejected much of sixteenth- and seventeenth-century writers' claims of barbaric pre-Inca and non-Inca peoples and argued instead that the Incas undid many of the accomplishments of pre-Inca cultures. He traveled to various parts of the North Coast, including the site of Patapo, across from Pampa Grande in the Lambayeque Valley. In his effort to demonstrate the existence and antiquity of pre-Inca cultures, he suggested application of the stratigraphic principle employed by Heinrich Schliemann in his excavations in search of the ancient city of Ilium (Hutchinson 1873: 264–265).

The sorts of insights long sought and anticipated by Squier, Hutchinson, and others were realized with the arrival in Peru of Max Uhle (1892), who was equipped with advanced archaeological knowledge and training. Through his association with Alphonso Stübel,[3] and reading of works of Schliemann and W. M. Flinders Petrie, Uhle helped transform American archaeology, shifting its focus from description and rudimentary classification to chronology or time-ordering of events (Willey and Sabloff 1980: 73).

Much of Uhle's success in defining pre-Inca cultures stems from his shrewd selection of excavation sites. Rowe (1954: 7) notes that among the various sites around Trujillo that Uhle visited, the site of Moche showed the best promise of yielding early materials. During the latter months of 1899 and on through February of 1900, Uhle (1913, n.d.; see Menzel 1977: 37–41) excavated at the top of Cerro Blanco, a conical peak that overlooks the site of Moche, and on and around the Huaca del Sol and Huaca de la Luna (Fig. 2.1). The thirty-two graves excavated from Cemetery or Site F at the west foot of the Huaca de la Luna were fundamental to the first chronological and stylistic definition of the Mochica culture. The gravelots from this excavation remain the type or diagnostic collection for the Mochica style.

Yet during his some two decades of active fieldwork in the Andes, Uhle published only a brief preliminary report of his excavation at Moche.[4] A. L. Kroeber and his students and colleagues at Berkeley deserve credit for making Uhle's materials accessible and meaningful by analyzing and publishing gravelots and their associations (e.g., Donnan 1965; Kroeber 1925; Menzel 1977).

Uhle discovered graves and cache offerings with "Tiahuanaco-influenced" (now known to be primarily Wari) and Chimú styles at other excavation loci at Moche, including the south platform of the Huaca del Sol (Menzel 1977: 37–40). Primarily using stylistic analogies from his landmark excavations at Pachacamac (Uhle 1903), a famed religious center just south of Lima, he correctly seriated funerary ceramics excavated at Moche from Mochica to "Tiahuanaco-influenced" to Chimú (early to late). This chronology has since been independently confirmed by a number of seriation studies and stratigraphic excavations in various North Coast valleys.[5]

The above tripartite sequence formed the basis for the more general four-part chronology, applicable to much of ancient Peru, that Uhle eventually formulated. The sequence is as follows: (1) early regional styles, such as Mochica;[6] (2) "Tiahuanaco-influenced" styles, such as Sicán (which represents fusion of the preceding Mochica style with "Tiahuanaco"); (3) late regional styles, such as Chimú; and (4) Inca and Inca-influenced styles. In sum, by the turn of the century, the relative antiquity and distinctiveness of the Mochica culture were firmly established.

3. Systematization and Modern Trends

A. Establishment and Character of Collections

The generation of archaeologists who followed Uhle during the first half of this century systematized Mochica archaeology by amassing large artifact (primarily ceramics) collections, which allowed chronological and iconographic studies to be undertaken. During this period Peruvian input, particularly from Rafael Larco Hoyle and from Julio C. Tello and his students, came to match that of Peruvianists, notably

North American and German scholars.

One of the principal Peruvianists involved in this systematization was A. L. Kroeber, whose interest in Peruvian archaeology began when he came into contact with the work and collections of Uhle housed at the Robert Lowie Museum at Berkeley. Kroeber's (1925; also see 1944) analysis of Uhle's unpublished field notes and collections from the sites of Moche and Cerro Blanco clarified gravelot associations and chronological relationships of the various loci excavated by Uhle within these sites. The analysis was based on systematic classification of the funerary vessels into stylistically defined units. Kroeber (1963) properly insisted that a clear and basic analytical separation be made between *time* and *style*, concerns which had often been ignored in Andean archaeology.

Probably reflecting his general interest in the interrelationship between natural environments and cultural developments, Kroeber turned our attention to the environmental setting of the Mochica and succeeding North Coast cultures. His bipartition of the North Coast (Kroeber 1930) is still sound and useful. He recognized the northern North Coast, the Moche V heartland, as a separate cultural and geographical subarea composed of the contiguous Motupe, La Leche, Lambayeque, Zaña, and Jequetepeque valleys (Fig. 1.2). These valleys are more open, merging imperceptibly into one another as the Andean foothills recede considerably farther inland, in contrast to the repetitive, triangular circumscribed valleys of the southern North Coast (Kroeber 1930: 56–57). In cultural terms, he noted (1930: 63) that adobe mounds in the northern subarea are freestanding within or just outside cultivation fields, as opposed to constructed against the sides or on the summits of hills, the predominant pattern in the southern subarea. In addition, northern mounds are characterized by steep sides, long zigzag ramps, and the frequent use of refuse-filled chambers.

At many of the Mochica monumental constructions he visited, Kroeber documented preserved friezes, variation in the size and form of adobe bricks, and the "segmentary" construction technique of juxtaposed vertical columns of adobe bricks. These observations, together with

his incisive comments regarding their possible social and chronological significance, were instrumental in the establishment of a tradition of innovative architectural analyses on the North Coast.

Tello's role in Peruvian scholarship paralleled Kroeber's leadership and contributions to the Peruvianist tradition. Kroeber (quoted by Lothrop 1948a: 51) admiringly described Tello as a "human dynamo" knowing "as much Peruvian archaeology as the rest of us put together." Until his death in 1947, Tello's charisma, national eminence, wide field experience, and archaeological knowledge provided a major boost to Peruvian scholarship. However, Tello favored highland and eastern Andean cultures and did not recognize the Mochica culture as the primary autogenous cultural development on the Peruvian coast during the first millennium (Tello 1942). Nevertheless, he inspired many Peruvian scholars, including E. Yacovleff and F. L. Herrera (1934–1935; also Herrera 1942), who utilized Mochica and other ceramic representations together with field observations and sixteenth- and seventeenth-century writings in their comprehensive study of ancient Andean utilization of plant resources.

The idea of extracting "ethnographic" information about the Mochica through their representational art occurred much earlier and is, in fact, one of the distinguishing features of Mochica archaeology. Scholars familiar with narrative Western art were naturally attracted to similarly narrative Mochica art. The superficial search for conventional meanings in Mochica art based on the literal reading of its paintings and sculptural modeling can be seen as early as the late nineteenth century. For example, Squier (1877: 180–181) inferred class differentiation based on Mochica and Chimú painted and modeled ceramics. Frequent representations depicting "combat" between "warriors" in different dress were interpreted by T. A. Joyce (1912: 155) as contests between men of different Mochica clans.

Recognizing the importance of documenting originality, mastery, and variability in Mochica art, Uhle's contemporary compatriot, Arthur Baessler, published the first major compilation of Mochica

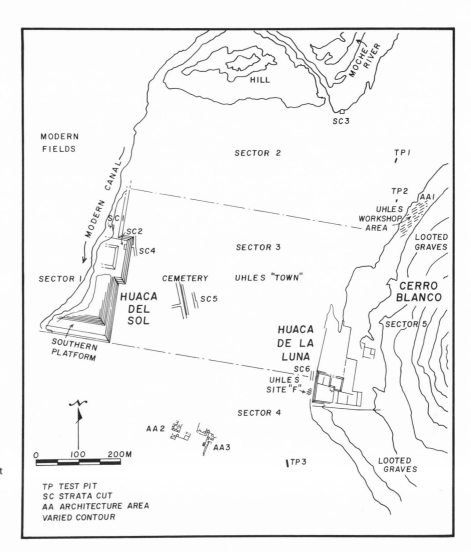

Figure 2.1. Site of Moche with locations of major structures and excavations carried out by Max Uhle and the Chan Chan–Moche Valley Project. Compiled from Map 5 in Donnan and Mackey 1978: 56 and Fig. 11.1 in T. Topic 1982: 264.

painted and modeled ceramics in his four-volume *Ancient Peruvian Art* (1902–1903). Through systematic examination of his large collection of effigy vessels and vase paintings, Baessler explored the "deeper meaning" behind the realism of Mochica ceramic art, perhaps for the first time. The basic approach pioneered by Baessler is followed today, though considerably more rigorously.

Rafael Larco Hoyle, a Peruvian collector and amateur archaeologist, enthusiastically continued this "ethnographic" interpretation of Mochica art from the late 1930's until his death in 1966. Based on the tens of thousands of vessels he excavated and purchased, together with his personal knowledge of traditional customs retained by contemporary North Coast inhabitants,

Larco Hoyle (1938, 1939) published two volumes of a planned comprehensive eight-volume study of the Mochica people and culture. Although his work is weakened by some serious methodological flaws discussed later, he showed the potential breadth of information to be gleaned from Mochica ceramics.[7]

Three basic features of Mochica ceramic art provide the key to the continuing success and importance of the ethnographic approach (Kutscher 1967: 116–117):

First and foremost, Mochica art is the only true pre-Hispanic narrative art south of the Maya territory in Mesoamerica. The narration is made effective by the naturalistic rendering of the subject matter (both painting and modeling). The full sculptural modeling found on ceramic vessels was unsurpassed in the pre-Hispanic Andes, with the possible exception of earlier Cupisnique examples. Mochica painted ceramics may be characterized as the painted Greek vases of the New World in that both are representational in nature, telling us stories about significant features and historical events in the real or mythical world (see Figs. 1.4, 2.2). Though primarily limited to bichrome slip painting (Figs. 2.3, 2.4),[8] Mochica artists were able to capture the most easily identifiable aspects of the subject matter by effectively combining profile and frontal views with formalized conventions for showing depth of field, background, and relative importance of the subject matters (Figs. 1.4, 2.4). Thus, precise taxonomic identification of many natural subjects is feasible; Figure 2.5 speaks for itself. Larco Hoyle (1938) identified sixteen mammal, thirty-four bird, five amphibian and reptile, twenty-one shell and other invertebrates, and twelve fish species. Dunn (1979) identified nineteen races of maize (*Zea mays L.*) from thirty-five Mochica ceramic jars with mold-impressed maize representations. These findings are testimony to the observational powers of Mochica artisans, as well as the diversity of domesticated and wild resources that were valued for food and religious reasons. There is, in fact, good correspondence between the inventory of faunal remains recovered from modern excavations at Mochica sites and Larco's list (see Chapter 8).

The second basic feature of Mochica ceramic art is the diversity of subject matter depicted. "Nothing seems to have been too low, vulgar, or revolting, nothing too high or sublime, that it was not depicted" (Kutscher 1967: 116). Indeed, the subjects include all manner of sexual acts, human sacrifice, combat, craft production, hunting, plants and animals of economic or religious significance, deities, burial ceremonies, childbirth, dancing, and feasting. However, this apparent diversity bears further scrutiny. For example, in spite of frequent depictions of economically significant plants and inferred "agricultural fertility" and "water" cults, representations of planting and irrigation are curiously missing (Kutscher 1967: 118). In fact, Donnan (1978: 158) observes that, in contrast to the general impression that Mochica ceramic art depicts "an almost infinite variety of subjects, . . . it is limited to the representation of a very small number of basic themes," perhaps fewer than fifteen. The subject matter depicted was apparently defined by formal and ideological structures. Debate as to the secular versus sacred nature of Mochica art will be discussed later.

The third feature important to the ethnographic approach, the sheer volume of decorated ceramic vessels available for study, together with the diversity of the subject matter, creates an unmatched research opportunity. Consider, for example, the total size of collections assembled by various members of the Larco family at the Hacienda Chiclín in the Chicama Valley during the early to mid-twentieth century. The large collection made by Rafael Larco Herrera from 1903–1924 was donated to the Archaeological Museum in Madrid in 1924 with the exception of one fine Mochica "portrait" vessel. His son, Rafael Larco Hoyle, inherited a small second collection from his father in 1925 and began assembling what later became the largest Mochica ceramic collection in the world (Evans 1968: 233). Larco Hoyle's collection expanded rapidly through excavations he personally directed and recorded, and the purchase of various private collections from all over the North Coast. Using his own workers, Larco Hoyle conducted excavations in and outside of his extensive

Figure 2.3. Moche IV stirrup-spout bottle with fineline drawing of "runners" each carrying a bag containing beans. Note that the runner at the top has arrived at his destination to reveal the beans in his bag to a waiting figure. Museum of the Banco Central de Reserva, Lima. Photo by Y. Yoshii.

Figure 2.2. Larco (1943: 291) interpreted this Mochica fineline drawing as representing "the supreme divinity deciphering beans." Redrawn from upper figure in Larco 1943: 291.

hacienda. Although his field observations and methodology have never been described in print, he maintained detailed written and photographic records of excavations and excavated materials (Yoshitake Suzuki, pers. com. 1980).[9] The primary focus of his excavations was burials, which provided a wide range of often differentially distributed, well-preserved funerary offerings with good chronological control. These categories of information and materials were crucial to Larco Hoyle's Mochica "ethnography."

At the time of his death in 1966, Larco Hoyle and his family had amassed a collection that included forty thousand complete ceramic vessels (mostly Mochica) and thousands of metal, textile, wood, and other artifacts (Evans 1968: 234). The collection is now housed in the Rafael Larco

Figure 2.4. Fine example of Moche IV naturalistic fineline drawing. Note how the elaborately dressed figure at the center is drawn larger than the other figures. The whole scene represents the capture of "enemy" warriors stripped of armor and weapons. Ropes are tied around the necks of naked prisoners. A severed head and hand hang from a nearby "fence." Orange paint was used to highlight the victors' armor. Museo Nacional de Antropología y Arqueología, Lima. Photo by Y. Yoshii.

Figure 2.5. Moche I stirrup-spout bottle said to have come from the Chicama Valley. Note the naturalistic rendering and effective use of the vessel shape to best show the condor (*Vultur gryphus*). Condors are still occasionally seen on the North Coast. Raúl Apesteguía Collection, Lima. Photo by Y. Yoshii.

Herrera Museum in Lima. The total number of whole Mochica ceramic vessels in private and public collections scattered throughout the world probably exceeds eighty thousand. The value of systematic analysis of this immense corpus is apparent.

At the same time, it should be noted that the clear majority of known Mochica artifacts was *recovered unscientifically by huaqueros* (grave looters). Further, whether scientifically excavated or looted, the overwhelming portion of known Mochica artifacts was derived from *funerary contexts in the presumed heartland* of the Chicama, Moche, and Virú valleys. This skewed sample must be kept in mind throughout this book.

Archaeological synthesis is inherently biased toward the best-preserved and most visible components of a culture: technology, subsistence, and the rich and powerful. In this respect, Mochica archaeology has a definite advantage in having that culture's own artistic representations of their world—cultural and natural, real and mythical, elite and popular. However, Mochica archaeology has involved surprisingly little fieldwork to augment and verify these artistic representations. Hardly any residential settlements, particularly those of Moche I–III, have been excavated. We see, instead, the continued over-sampling of burials and monumental and ceremonial architecture. Steward and Faron (1959: 68) voiced a similar concern many years ago regarding the "almost exclusive" concern with spectacular materials and "overshadowing importance" attached to funerary ceramics as having led to a de-emphasis of other cultural features that "from a broad social science point of view, are more important."

B. Relative Chronology

Gravelot studies, nonetheless, have made significant contributions to Mochica archaeology, particularly in regard to its relative chronology. Analysis of undisturbed gravelots allows identification of contemporaneous variation. Thus, a systematic analysis of different gravelots (ideally from stratified settings) will eventually reveal how style and form change through time. Larco Hoyle (1948) established the first relative chronology of Mochica funerary ceramics (Fig. 2.6). This five-phase chronology was based on stratigraphic data collected through his excavations of Mochica burials, many within the same cemeteries, and insights gained through studying morphological variation in painted and modeled funerary stirrup-spout bottles. He felt stirrup-spout and chamber forms were sensitive time indicators.

Detailed stylistic and/or morphological analyses have refined Larco Hoyle's scheme. For example, in analyzing gravelots excavated by Uhle at Moche, C. Donnan (1965) was able to bipartition Moche III into A and B, and today three (A–C) subphases are recognized, presumably with corresponding temporal differences (Menzel 1977: 59–60). Another important refinement was the stylistic seriation of red slip paint "fineline drawings" decorating vessel bodies (Klein 1967: 78–116; also see Donnan 1976: 54–58). The tradition of fineline representations was firmly established by early Moche III, and as artisans gained greater control over this decorative mode, they gradually shifted from silhouette to ever more flowing, expressive, finer line drawings to decorate the vessels. Moche III drawings are "relatively large, . . . painted with broad line, and the representation generally involves a considerable amount of solid area or silhouette" (Donnan 1976: 57). During Moche IV, with improved fineline technique, drawings show more small figures, details, and open area. In general, Moche IV fineline drawings emphasize complex representational scenes of action and multiple figures (Figs. 1.5, 2.3, 2.4). In Moche V, the trend toward greater detail and complexity reaches its extreme; complex action scenes with many figures and fillers often literally cover the entire vessel surface (Fig. 2.7).

Larco Hoyle's, Klein's, and Donnan's seriations offer operational ease and reliability not available for other styles in the Andes. At the same time, we still do not know the rate at which vessel form changed over time or the degree of homogeneity in form and iconography for any given time period over a wide area. The samples used for the establishment as well as subsequent verification and refinement of existing seriations were funerary ceramics (particularly the last three phases) from the presumed Mochica heartland. The applicability of these seriations for nonceramic artifacts and for ceramics in nonfunerary settings, particularly those in more peripheral areas of the Mochica domain, has not been adequately tested. Likewise, the duration of each phase or subphase needs to be established and refined.

Fine painted ceramics occur in residential sites but seem to be relatively uncommon and unevenly distributed. We need large samples from controlled excavations of such sites (particularly stratified sites containing Moche I–III) for assessment of the degree and nature of correspondence between funerary and nonfunerary ceramics. Precise dating of murals, textiles, and metal and wooden objects is also quite difficult. For example, sumptuary objects of hammered gold (Fig. 1.6) or *tumbaga* (copper-gold alloys) may have been pace-setters of Mochica art, exhibiting more exclusive and perhaps innovative stylistic and iconographic features. Thus, there may well have been a temporal gap between stylistic expressions on these precious metal objects and ceramics (Donnan, quoted in Lechtman, Erlij, and Barry 1982: 3; see Chapter 4).

The Mochica style is too often perceived as homogeneous in space. This perception underlies the view *assuming* Mochica political unification of the North Coast (see Moseley 1975a). Yet this very premise remains to be verified, particularly for the first three phases. The looting in the 1960's of numerous fine ceramic and metal objects of Moche I and II styles from deep shafttombs in the Loma Negra area of the upper Piura Valley region (Figs. 1.7, 2.8; see Chapter 4), far north of the Chicama and Moche valleys, raised basic questions regarding the geographical origins and sociopolitical significance of the Mochica style. Attempting to explain this discovery, Larco Hoyle (1963, 1967) himself raised the possibility that the Mochica culture evolved in the Vicús region. These questions have not yet been answered; rather the urgency of resolving them has been driven home by the recent discoveries of sumptuous early Mochica elite burials at Sipán (see Chapter 4) and La Mina in the Jequetepeque-Chicama border region (Donnan 1990a).

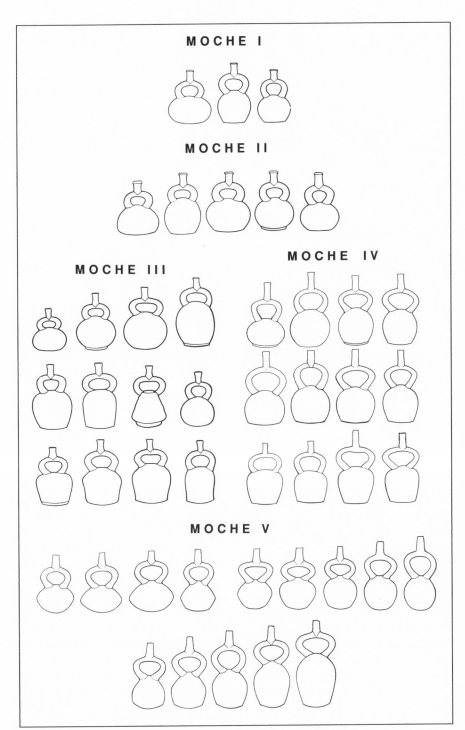

Figure 2.6. Seriation of Mochica stirrup-spout bottles developed by Rafael Larco Hoyle based primarily on his sample from the Chicama Valley. Based on Figs. 50–179 in Klein 1967: 78–99 and Figs. 25–28a, 29a, and 30a in Donnan 1976: 45–50.

Figure 2.7. A Moche V stirrup-spout bottle with fineline representation of a mythical personage holding what seems to be a rattle. Perched on the shoulder of the stirrup is an opposing pair of monkeys. Many Moche V stirrup-spout bottles have similarly placed monkeys, and later Chimú style bottles further popularized the custom of adorning stirrup-spouts with monkey ornaments. The custom was most likely adopted from northern North Coast potters. This bottle may well have been looted from the site of San José de Moro. Museo de la Nación, Lima. Courtesy of the National Geographic Society.

Figure 2.8. Early Mochica style gilded copper "fox head" ornament, 8.2 cm long, from a looted tomb in Loma Negra near Cerro Vicús in the upper Piura Valley. Gift of Jane Costello Goldberg from the Collection of Arnold I. Goldberg, 1982 (1982.392.6). Courtesy of the Metropolitan Museum of Art, New York.

We now face not only the question of the applicability of Larco Hoyle's five-phase seriation in the area north of the presumed heartland, but also the more basic question of the significance of observed stylistic and morphological variation. Do the established phases truly have chronological significance? Or, do they reflect political or ethnic subdivisions? Variability in space also might mean that the Mochica style as defined today originated out of a composite of roughly contemporaneous regional styles sharing the same broad cultural substratum, as opposed to having evolved out of one local style in the presumed heartland. Such variability would weaken the argument for a strong centralized Mochica state and strengthen the alternative view of a confederation of semi-autonomous chiefdoms or city-states like that of the Classic Maya (e.g., see Culbert 1988). In any case, the answers to these basic issues will not readily come from the existing archaeological predilection for excavating burials.

The five-phase Mochica chronology also has a serious problem in regard to precision. We do not know the duration of most of the phases, and if our educated guesses are taken at face value, then each phase spans too much time (approxi-

mately one to two hundred years) for any meaningful synchronic cultural reconstruction (Shimada 1990b, 1991a). Some studies even lump Moche III and IV ceramics together, covering a time period of up to three hundred years. For example, without extensive excavation it would be difficult to ascertain whether Moche III expansion involved a single successful conquest or a much more complex situation that required a series of reconquests over a span of several generations.

Overall, we need systematic studies of ceramic variability in space based on samples with specific, reliable provenience, and we need to continue improving our dating in both precision (duration of chronological divisions) and accuracy (stratigraphic verification and interregional testing).

C. Iconographic Studies

Given the three features outlined above, it is understandable that Mochica archaeology has seemed synonymous with iconography. An impressive body of literature on Mochica iconography has been published since the early twentieth century by scholars from some dozen countries. In fact, the number of such publications overshadows the number of those based on archaeological excavations focusing on nonartistic and nonfunerary aspects of the Mochica culture.

The overwhelming majority of recent iconographic studies have been carried out by Peruvianists. Monographs such as *The Mochica* by E. P. Benson (1972; also see 1974), *Moche: Gods, Warriors, Priests* by E. K. de Bock (1988), *Moche Art of Ancient Peru* by C. B. Donnan (1978), and *Iconografía Mochica* by A. M. Hocquenghem (1987) are excellent testimony to the continuing development of appropriate methodologies and increasing methodological rigor employed in the analysis of Mochica art (see Lyon 1983). The level and scope of analysis and interpretation, however, remain quite variable.

Several generations of German scholars[10] have undertaken time-consuming basic documentation of Mochica iconography. This long-term effort finds a recent parallel in the Moche Archive established in the Museum of Cultural History at the University of California, Los Angeles, by its director, Christopher B. Donnan. The archive, with over 125,000 photos of some 10,000 objects, is the world's largest single repository of Mochica art.

Considering the undeniable importance of iconographic studies in providing insights and generating questions about the Mochica culture, let's examine the various methodologies and philosophies underlying modern Mochica iconographic studies.

In theory, iconographic studies bridge the fields of archaeology and art history, although they are, in fact, often carried out with little integration of archaeological data. At the same time, their liminal position has fostered a variety of approaches, each influenced by such factors as different conceptions of iconography and of the relationship between art and its broader cultural setting. No one current methodology stands as *the* approach to Mochica art.

Most contemporary approaches blend ethnographic/historical analogy with the conventional art historical approach of examining the contexts and organizational structures of component motifs. The first seeks understanding based on what is known about a similar historical or existing culture on the assumption that the present can explain the past. The second

treats ancient iconography in terms of itself and derives meaning through understanding internal structural relationships.

Larco Hoyle's "Mochica ethnography" exemplifies the first approach. He assumed that strong cultural, biological, and environmental continuities exist between prehistoric and historic times, and that artistic renderings are accurate representations of reality. Although these are not unreasonable assumptions given the archaeological and historical data (e.g., Gillin 1947; Schaedel 1985a), continuity, nonetheless, was assumed and not proven. Although this problematical approach still resurfaces from time to time (e.g., Dobkin de Rios 1977, 1982), recent uses of ethnographic and historical analogies are much more circumscribed in scope and careful to specify what is being compared and how the analogies are to be assessed (e.g., Sharon and Donnan 1977; cf. Schaedel 1985a: 458).

One of the major objections to this analogy-based methodology is what has been called the "disjunction of meaning" (e.g., Panofsky 1962; Kubler 1970); i.e., a given motif may remain the same in form over time but change in meaning. In addition, this methodology does not treat iconography as a functioning semantic system, and organizational structure is imposed by the investigator. Meaning is inferred by referring to similar features in historic or modern cultures or by establishing boundaries to limit possible interpretations. The crucial assumption here is that the total "meaning" of a motif can be extracted from the individual units that compose it without understanding the systemic relationships among those units or, for that matter, among the motifs of a cultural system. However, it is highly questionable whether the individual units add up to a meaningful whole.

Consider the massive interlocking "feline" canines of the personage in Figure 2.9. Larco Hoyle (1946: 171; cf. Lyon 1983) identified this personage as *Ai-apaec*, or the supreme divinity of the Mochica pantheon (which he saw as essentially monotheistic) after a similar, later Chimú deity known by this name. Larco Hoyle regarded it as the personification of a divinity variously shown as an agriculturalist, fisher-

man, curer, musician, and hunter, imposing his own conception of the Mochica religion and interpreting the iconography from this base but without considering disjuncture of meaning from form.

The preceding discussion points to the need to study Mochica iconography within the context of its organizational structure, on its own terms. This philosophy has led to a number of alternative approaches.

Kutscher (1955a, 1967) saw Mochica vessels as having much more than iconographic information and encompassing both sacred and secular domains; he regarded them as anthropological specimens amenable for activity and social analyses. This conception of Mochica art derived from his belief in the *integrated* nature of (1) sacred and secular domains, (2) cultural, social, and natural spheres, and (3) iconographic elements and their broader organizational themes. On this basis, Kutscher argued for the systematic analysis of representational contexts (i.e., ways in which specific motifs appear in isolation and in combination) in elucidating the underlying symbolic values and the meanings of specific motifs and themes in Mochica art, and began a systematic compilation of ceramic representations (Kutscher 1983).

Perhaps the most influential figure in modern iconographic studies is Erwin Panofsky (1955, 1962), who developed his methodology based on historical Western art rather than on nonliterate pre-Hispanic Andean art. Panofsky also argued for a structural/contextual approach, as the artists' values may have been unconsciously expressed and therefore difficult to discern through the study of isolated motifs. More specifically, he recommended a three-step procedure for iconographic interpretation: (1) a "pre-iconographic description," or objective, comprehensive description of the primary subject matter, including determination of interrelationships among constituent motifs and contexts of their occurrences; (2) "iconographic analysis," or definition of the conventional meaning or concept underlying and unifying motifs (e.g., a consistent association of the fanged *Ai-apaec* with cultivated plants and decapitation may imply his power over "life forces"); and (3) search for the "intrinsic" meaning of the art, the basic philosophy or cosmovision of the culture that underlies the conventional meanings.

Though some scholars may be optimistic about the prospects for ferreting out "intrinsic meaning," others refrain from inferring meaning. Though acknowledging that an outline of how Mochica symbolism worked may be elucidated, Benson (1972), for example, is cautious about our chances of determining specific original meanings. She points out (1972: 89) that any attempt at social reconstruction is limited by the fact that the figures depicted on the pots, even if they are perfectly human in form, probably had religious (including supernatural) association.

One modern scholar who has wholeheartedly embraced Panofsky's methodology in exploring the intrinsic meaning of Mochica art is A. M. Hocquenghem (see particularly 1987: 19–45). In her effort to present a comprehensive interpretive model of Mochica iconography, she has combined Panofskian and analogy-based methodologies. She uses extensive ethnohistorical and ethnographic data from a wide region of the Ecuadorian and Peruvian highlands to buttress her view that Mochica art was an extension of the cos-

movision that defined their relationship with the natural and supernatural worlds. In her conception, Mochica art narrates astrological and agricultural/seasonal life cycles and calendars that regulated the activities and roles of inhabitants in these two parallel worlds. Real-world scenes show only natural creatures, while mythical-world scenes contain only supernatural creatures.

Hocquenghem sees known ecological and cultural differences between the coast and highlands as being of little consequence, based on her belief that both areas shared "pan-Andean" structural principles and religious ideologies. For example, she cites widespread dual and quadripartite social divisions and similar methods of time reckoning in support of this basic premise. However, she considers neither "disjunction of meaning" nor the potential role of post-Mochica expansions of the Wari and Inca cultures in establishing these institutions and customs. The actual existence in the Mochica culture of the calendars, institutions, and customs found in ethnographic and historical cultures needs to be verified independently.

Kubler's "configurational" or "structural linguistic" approach (1967) deals with the first two of the three tasks defined by Panofsky and avoids problems associated with the analogy-based approach. In his analysis, images are seen to be structured in much the same fashion as language, and one studies patterns of motif clusters for similarities between motifs from different contexts to identify the internal organizational principles. Kubler's repeated cautions about the "disjunction of meaning" from form imply that his approach is best used in synchronic situations. In addition, as this approach emphasizes systematic contextual analysis of motifs, it is most useful in the analysis of complex, flat representations such as those in Mochica murals and painted vessels.

The thematic approach advocated by Donnan builds upon the above linguistic model. He argues that systematic examination of the seemingly infinite diversity of subject matter in Mochica art reveals consistent correlation of motifs that can be subsumed into fifteen or so themes. Hocquenghem (1987: 21) recognizes nineteen basic themes in Mochica art.[11] Specific representations of a given theme, however,

Figure 2.9. Moche IV stirrup-spout bottle that shows the fanged deity that Larco Hoyle called *Ai-apaec* emerging out of a *Strombus* shell. He is holding spear throwers and spears. Benson (1972: 28) differentiates passive and active deities with prominent fangs, calling the former "creator" or "supreme god" and the latter "'fanged deity,' because the feline essence is probably most powerful." The creator deity usually wears a "sunrise" headdress. These deities commonly have snake earrings. Rafael Larco Herrera Museum, Lima. Photo by Y. Yoshii.

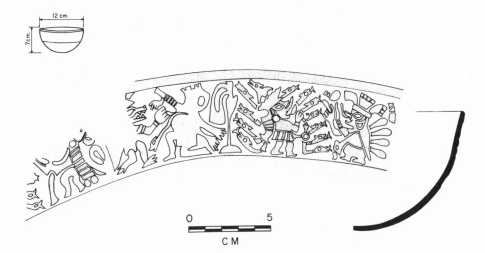

Figure 2.10. A roll-out drawing of the Presentation Theme that decorated a small bowl excavated in Sector H. Drawing by Genaro Barr.

vary as artists exercise their creativity within the boundaries set by cultural expectations and rules. Nonetheless, these representations share a certain number of symbolic elements—and their interrelationships—to maintain the compositional integrity of the theme. It is argued that in settings where the same cultural knowledge is widely shared, even abbreviated depictions of the symbolic elements would be enough to invoke images of the complete themes in the mind of the observer.

An analogy in Western art would be works that depict the "Nativity Theme" with a specific set of characteristic symbolic elements such as the Christ child and Virgin Mary (Donnan 1978: 158). One of the basic Mochica themes, according to Donnan, is the "Presentation Theme," which shows the "presentation of a goblet," perhaps containing human blood from prisoners, to a major mythical figure (Fig. 2.10). Many examples of this theme are known, ranging from the famed murals at the Mochica southern frontier center of Pañamarca in the Nepeña Valley to painted and modeled ceramic vessels. In Moche V, a "Funerary Theme" showing elaborate funerary preparation becomes quite common (see Chapter 9). In general, themes are believed to illustrate important aspects of Mochica beliefs regarding their cosmos, deities, and associated rituals.

The basic advantage of this approach in Donnan's (1978: 172) own words is that it "allows us to understand a great many examples of Moche art which would otherwise have little meaning. It also demonstrates the way Moche artists chose to represent a given theme; namely, by illustrating one of its symbolic units alone or showing two or more of them in various combinations." *Meaning* here refers both to the conventional meaning and to an understanding of the structural principles or grammar governing thematic representations.

Because of the inherent tendency of the thematic approach to create a compartmentalized and static view of iconography, understanding of interrelationships among themes is not readily forthcoming. Bonavia (1985: 64) comments, "It strikes me as still too speculative to pronounce so firmly on the limited number of basic themes in the Moche scenic world. Nor am I entirely sure that the components of each theme appear only in that particular context and not mixed with others, in which case we would have a great many possibilities, immensely enlarging the small universe posited by Donnan." Donnan has not yet adequately described all of his themes or their interrelationships.

In addition, there are various questions regarding the extent and nature of shared cultural knowledge. How widely or evenly was such knowledge shared by different segments of Mochica society? By whom and how was the dissemination of knowledge controlled? To what extent and in what ways do funerary context ceramics reflect access to and control and sharing of such knowledge in real life?

For all approaches discussed above, the relevant data were drawn from a rather restricted range of sources and contexts—essentially funerary and ceremonial. Impressive Mochica polychrome murals described as having ceremonial or religious significance have been recorded only at structures and sites themselves characterized as ceremonial or religious.[12] These identifications may be accurate but essentially based on circular reasoning; conclusions based on such a limited data base may have equally limited utility. Did Mochica artists consciously differentiate between religious and vernacular, funerary and living, or elite and folk art? Does an overgeneralized view of the sacred nature of Mochica art mask actual differences? The pitfall of this "sacred art" view is that it becomes *both* the analytical base and the interpretive base. Unless we expand significantly the scope of our data base to include habitational sites of the Mochica populace, we will continue to have difficulty verifying the sacred nature of Mochica art.

There is no single method of capturing the total meaning of a particular motif, theme, act, or artifact. Consider the various ways of characterizing a book: content, size, shape, color, typeface, cost, etc. A given depiction at one analytical level may be studied with other lines of evidence for useful material and behavioral data, and only at a more abstract level may an iconographic study seek to define the original meaning of the artisans.

We cannot ignore the distinct possibility that a specific activity or object may have had different manifest (overt) and latent (covert) functions, and that Mochica artisans depicted only the culturally defined manifest functions. However, a given symbolic act, whether or not the performer is cognizant of it, may serve another purpose. A major advantage of archaeology is that its material analysis elucidates nonsymbolic aspects of a specific act or object. Take, for example, Mochica scenes of sea-lion hunts, which typically have men clubbing animals shown with round objects in or in front of their mouths, believed to be gastric stones. Gillin (1947: 124; also Rost-

worowski 1981: 113) observed the use of "stones" removed from sea lions for folk-curing practices in the village of Moche. Donnan (1978: 136) sees the sea lion as a "significant animal in Moche art," often painted or modeled in ceramics, and, following the above ethnographic data, suggests that these "stones" were earlier used in Mochica curing practices. At the same time, there are indications that sea lions served other purposes. Larco Hoyle (1938: 97) reports their teeth accompanying human burials, while other excavators have unearthed sea-lion bones, some with butcher marks, in refuse at Mochica sites (see Chapter 8), suggesting their use as food. The preceding illustrates how excavation data enrich the understanding of Mochica art obtained from iconographic studies.

Certainly, the preceding discussion is not an exhaustive review of Mochica iconographic studies. The Russian scholar Yuri Berezkin, for one, is critical of how the Mochica mythological system has been studied. He urges accurate identification of individual mythological personages, including their hierarchical positions and functions, as well as their changing character over time, for basic understanding of the system and subjects of the myths (oral traditions). He posits that the hierarchy and different functions of supernatural beings in some ways reflect Mochica social reality. Thus, opposing tribes of "warrior-people" and "shaman people," each with their own deity in the Mochica mythical world, are believed to be indicative of asymmetrical upper and lower moieties (also see Hocquenghem 1987: 27–33; Netherly 1977, 1990) within the Mochica society. He further suggests that the Mochica plural pantheon seen in Moche III and IV transformed to one dominated by a competing dyad or triad of principal deities during Moche V. This change, he believes, reflects a concurrent transformation to statehood with a significant shift in modes of production and increasing consolidation and hierarchization of sociopolitical groups.

Berezkin is one of very few to explore the dynamic aspects of the Mochica pantheon and ideology as reflected through its iconography. Most scholars focusing on the structural aspects of Mochica art recognize changes in its form (style) over time, but tend to treat the content (iconography) as stable through time and space. As we will see in Chapter 9, Moche V art serves as an excellent illustration that such treatment is not warranted.

In sum, while these iconographic studies are fascinating and provide many insights into Mochica beliefs, the dynamic aspects of the iconography and its relationships to broader cultural and natural processes await further examination (see Shimada 1991a). Furthermore, inferences derived from iconographic studies must be independently verified with physical evidence from archaeological fieldwork.

D. Defining Environmental and Architectural Settings: Settlement-Pattern and Related Studies

Paralleling these advances in chronological and iconographic studies were settlement-pattern and related studies to elucidate the spatial extent and organization of the Mochica population and its adaptation to its natural and cultural settings. The most significant research in these studies was the Virú Valley Project carried out in 1946 under the sponsorship of the Institute of Andean Research. The project, which built upon the earlier work of W. Bennett (e.g., 1939), H. Horkheimer (1944), Kroeber (e.g., 1930, 1944), and Larco Hoyle, has had a long-lasting impact on Mochica and, more broadly, New World archaeology.[13] The ambitious goal of this project was to study the entire cultural history of the small Virú Valley by bringing together archaeologists and specialists from allied disciplines such as geography, ethnobotany, and ethnography (Willey 1946). Professionals and graduate students from American and Peruvian institutions were involved. The project introduced various innovative methodologies and theoretical perspectives, and verified and refined cultural chronologies and inferences put forth by Uhle and Larco Hoyle, among others.

The project's numerous accomplishments include stratigraphic excavations and seriation of surface-collected ceramics, which demonstrated Moche III intrusion into the Virú Valley of the Mochica polity based in the neighboring Moche and Chicama valleys. This intrusion ended the local, contemporaneous Gallinazo polity and style (Collier 1955; Ford 1949; Strong and Evans 1952; Willey 1953). As a result, a conception of the Mochica as a predatory, expanding multi-valley polity began to take root. The well-publicized discovery of the sumptuous burial of a Mochica "Warrior-Priest" (most likely a regional lord) atop the Huaca de la Cruz ("Pyramid of the Cross"; Strong 1947; Strong and Evans 1952) captured the public's imagination. In addition to twenty-seven fine ceramic vessels, the adult male was accompanied by a child and a wooden staff with carvings showing a standing adult anthropomorphic creature flanked by a child, much like the burial.

One of the project's most significant contributions was the settlement-pattern study, which attempted to elucidate the nature and organization of human activities in their social and natural environments through analysis of architecture at various levels and scale (Willey 1953, 1974). This development, together with the contemporary work of P. Kosok (1965) and R. Schaedel (1951a,b) emphasizing airphoto interpretation[14] and sketch cartography at a multi-valley level, provided a major thrust to the functional and chronological analysis of architecture at varied levels of organization and in different environmental settings. Willey's study showed how the conquering Mochica reorganized the local Virú Valley population into a smaller number of larger settlements. The resultant settlement pattern and hierarchy has been more recently interpreted as focusing on strategic control of irrigation water, agricultural lands, and communication routes (Conrad 1978; T. Topic 1982). Further, from a diachronic perspective, Collier (1962a) and Willey (1953; also see Schaedel 1966a,b) documented the trend toward urbanization on the North Coast. The shift in corporate construction from monumental, "sacred" platform mounds to more "secular" Great Rectangular Enclosure Compounds following the termination of the Mochica domination of the Virú and nearby valleys was credited to Wari invaders.

The settlement survey, though intended to locate all sites, was biased toward larger and more accessible sites (Willey 1974) and did not adequately clarify the factors and forces that affected the condition and visibility of archaeological sites, e.g., flash flood erosion and sand dune coverage (e.g., Moseley 1978b, 1983b; Moseley, Feldman, and Ortloff 1981). It is likely that numerous localized and small-scale Mochica occupations and sites went undetected.

Willey's study, together with contemporaneous macroregional surveys by Kosok and Schaedel, stimulated similar studies all over the New World. For some subsequent projects on the North Coast, the settlement-pattern study became the first basic task, though one that varied greatly in the thoroughness of the survey and the definition and size of the survey area (e.g., Donnan 1973a; Moseley and Deeds 1982; Proulx 1973). The necessary relative chronology is either developed using ceramics collected during survey or adopted from a nearby valley (e.g., Wilson 1988). Either way, the chronology requires stratigraphic verification and/or refinement in the latter case to avoid perpetuating any problems inherent in the adopted chronology (Shimada 1990b). In the Virú Valley Project, which lasted only one season, Willey depended on the ceramic seriation being established concurrently by J. Ford (1949) and stratigraphically verified by other members (Strong and Evans 1952; also Collier 1955). Prior research by W. C. Bennett and Larco Hoyle in the late 1930's in this and adjacent valleys provided additional data. These collaborative works took care of many of the tasks accompanying the survey.

However, the Virú Valley Project was unique in having many professional archaeologists working toward the same set of research goals. More recent settlement surveys in Peru have been carried out by individual archaeologists working with students and local workers. Too often these surveys have failed to carry out the necessary post-survey excavations that test and refine chronological and functional inferences. Instead, the archaeologists often leave their study areas to initiate new fieldwork elsewhere. Andean archaeology would be better served if more archaeological fieldwork took on a regional approach and long-term commitment to the same study area (Shimada 1990b).

For better or for worse, the Virú Valley Project also established the individual coastal river valley as the geographical unit of study, what geographers call "study area" (I. Shimada 1982). The way one delimits the size and shape of the study area affects the settlement patterns one finds (Pinder, Shimada, and Gregory 1982), and the individual valley studies carried out thus far on the North Coast have been neither all contiguous nor comparable in intensity. The single-valley approach is too constricting for holistic study of the Mochica polity with its multi-valley territorial base. Problems with the notion of the Virú Valley as a microcosm of the Central Andes and the associated evolutionary schemes have already been discussed elsewhere (Rowe 1962; Schaedel and Shimada 1982).

In respect to the problem of study area, the multi-valley studies of Kosok (e.g., 1965) during the 1940's and 1950's (often in collaboration with Schaedel [e.g., 1951a, 1966a]), are particularly important. This multi-valley approach, however, was a means toward an end. Kosok (1940, 1965: 1–5) concurred with K. Wittfogel (1957; also Steward 1949) in recognizing the critical relationship between socioeconomic and political development on the one hand and the construction and maintenance of large-scale irrigation on the other. Kosok felt that fieldwork on the North Coast would reveal critical aspects of the transformation of primitive, theocratic societies into early civilizations with emerging class structures and secular rulers. In fact, he considered control of water and the irrigation system to be the power base of the Mochica aristocratic priest-warriors (1965: 10–13).

Given his interest in water management and the presence of various intervalley canals on the North Coast, a multi-valley perspective was necessary for fieldwork. The immense size of the area to be surveyed and the nature of archaeological remains he sought (primarily canals and cultivation fields) led to a heavy dependence on airphoto interpretation complemented by field checks by jeep and horseback.

The Kosok-Schaedel surveys of North Coast valleys do not appear to have been as systematic or ambitious as Willey's Virú Valley study, varying in intensity and extent of coverage from valley to valley (Schaedel 1951a: 240). Synchronic settlement system reconstruction throughout valleys (as opposed to within valleys) would be difficult from their data. Also, post-survey excavation for chronological and functional verification or refinement was limited. Yet Kosok (1965: 143, 151) reports that within the hydrologically interlinked valleys of Motupe, La Leche, Lambayeque, and Zaña, they located and mapped some 280 settlements, walls, roads, cultivation fields, and irrigation canals.

The data thus gathered allowed Kosok and Schaedel to project the agricultural potentials and carrying capacities of different valleys in different periods. Kosok (1959: 56, 1965: 88; also Schaedel 1972: 27) estimated that the amount of land under modern cultivation on much of the North Coast had decreased by 30–50 percent since the inferred pre-Hispanic maximum around A.D. 1000–1200. Another study puts the figure around 30–40 percent (see Table 2.1 in Moseley and Deeds 1982: 52–53). These figures should be considered in light of cultivated crops (critical pollen data are scant), water management practices (furrow forms, prehistoric use of "overflow water," etc.), and amount of water available (see Chapters 3 and 6).

One important insight that emerged from the Kosok-Schaedel multi-valley approach is the pairing of small and large river valleys in the growth of complex cultures on the North Coast (Schaedel 1951a). The La Leche and Lambayeque were hydrologically linked by the Antigua Taymi and Raca Rumi canals, and the Moche and Chicama by the La Cumbre. The smaller La Leche and Moche were the settings for the major political and religious centers. The Lambayeque and Chicama valleys, with considerably more reliable and ample water supplies and larger cultivation areas, served as the regional breadbaskets. It is apparent that developments in each valley could not have been understood on their own, as these contiguous valleys were parts of unified hydrological and political systems during certain pre-Hispanic periods.

In sum, while most archaeologists of Kosok's time did little more than mention the general importance of irrigation and note some related features, Kosok documented through his fieldwork the dependence of the Mochica and their North Coast descendants on irrigation. As Nolan (1980: 112) observed, because Kosok worked largely in isolation from archaeologists (with the notable exception of Schaedel) and died before the publication of the vast quantity of data he had amassed, "the study of irrigation as played out in Peru . . . [did not receive] the intensity of interest which the subject and the area merit" until the 1970's (see Rodríguez 1970 as an exception). However, Kosok's posthumously published *Life, Land and Water in Ancient Peru* (1965) has had a major impact in directing our attention toward this subject. While the book remains one of the most informative sources on North Coast cultural ecology and archaeology, its multi-valley approach has been rarely adopted in recent decades, and the single-valley perspective enjoys continuing popularity.

Related to the above discussion is the coast-centric nature of fieldwork pertaining to the Mochica culture. Different scholars define the valleys in which they work based on different criteria, and there is no "operational definition" of the coastal river valley that approaches a consensus (I. Shimada 1982: 186–187; see Chapter 3). Thus, how far one surveys along the river toward its headwaters among Andean peaks will consequently affect how one views the Mochicas' territory and interactions with highland neighbors. In fact, Mochica archaeology has been overly coast-centric in its perspective. For much of the history of Mochica archaeology, the Mochica culture was viewed from and within the North Coast with no east-west transects examining coterminous cultural developments in contiguous coastal and highland areas.

At the same time, we cannot ignore the precocity of Mochica archaeology in comparison with that of the surrounding highland regions. However, with the recent surge in archaeological research on contemporaneous neighboring highland cultures (Cajamarca, Huamachuco, and Recuay), the Mochica culture is now being examined in a broader setting. Although little material evidence of contact has been found, we will see in Chapter 4 that the ebb and flow of the Mochica polity was paralleled by those of the Cajamarca polity early in their evolution and inversely mirrored during the final phase of the Mochica culture, as reflected in the distribution and technical and stylistic coherence of their respective ceramics.

E. Other Modern Advances

Paralleling American input in timing but not in scale, a succession of German scholars since the days of Uhle have contributed to the advancement of Mochica archaeology.

In 1937–1938, H. Ubbelohde-Doering (e.g., 1967) excavated Mochica burials (primarily Moche V) at the "ceremonial city" of Pacatnamú overlooking the mouth of the Jequetepeque River. We are gaining some understanding of the importance of this site through the recent posthumous publication of his excavation results (Ubbelohde-Doering 1983; Hecker and Hecker 1983), a complementary mapping project and ceramic analysis by G. and W. Hecker (1984, 1985, 1987), architectural analysis by R. Keatinge (1977, 1982; Keatinge et al. 1975), and most recently, excavations by the Pacatnamú Project under the direction of C. B. Donnan and G. A. Cock (1986). In addition, Ubbelohde-Doering's work in the Jequetepeque Valley showed the considerable overlap in time and space of Gallinazo and Mochica ceramics, a fact that was not previously well appreciated for understanding the origin and meaning of the Mochica style.

The discovery toward the end of the 1950's of a distinct ceramic style called Vicús and the alleged association of fine Moche I and II ceramics in looted shafttombs around Cerro Vicús in the upper Piura Valley (Fig. 1.2; Guzmán and Casafranca 1964: 7–8, 1967; Horkheimer 1965) stirred considerable interest among Peruvian and Peruvianist scholars. Though R. Matos's survey (1965–1966) suggested the presence there of Moche I through V ceramics, excavations to establish their chronological and functional contexts and verify looters' information regarding the association of Vicús- and Mochica-style ceramics have met with little success.[15] For example, the seven tombs excavated by Hans Disselhoff

(1971, 1972) contained only Vicús-style ceramics. His radiocarbon dates (1969) suggest, however, that the Vicús style may have lasted up to if not well into the Middle Horizon, making it essentially contemporaneous with the total span of Mochica.

What really awakened general archaeological and public interest in the upper Piura, however, was the discovery of large caches of artistically and technically outstanding Mochica-style copper, silver, and gold objects at Loma Negra, locally known as Tierra Dura, southeast of Cerro Vicús.[16]

Lechtman, Erlij, and Barry (1982) have suggested that some of the Loma Negra Mochica copper objects may have been gilded using a highly sophisticated electro-chemical replacement plating that deposited a uniform layer of gold only one micron thick. In general, Lechtman has been largely responsible for recent advances in Andean archaeometallurgy. Taking the pioneering leads provided by P. Bergsøe (1937, 1938), E. R. Caley (1973; Caley and Shank 1971), Patterson (1971), and Root (1949, 1951), she has shown that the copper-based Mochica metallurgy formed the core of the North Peruvian metallurgical tradition, one of the two major metallurgical traditions of the New World.

4. The Chan Chan–Moche Valley Project

A new era of Mochica archaeology arrived in 1968 with initiation of the Chan Chan–Moche Valley Project (1968–1976) under the direction of M. E. Moseley and C. Mackey. With substantial funding and many participants, this "mega-project" aimed at elucidating the historical antecedents and cultural and natural contexts of the emergence and functioning of Chan Chan, the capital of the Chimú Kingdom (ca. A.D. 1200–1470). Advocating a strong functionalist orientation, coverage of all pre-Hispanic human existence within a single valley, and the autogenous nature of cultural developments, this project is a modern-day counterpart of the Virú Valley Project. At the same time, within this project some of the research issues and directions outlined above that had received little attention from either Peruvian or Peruvianist archaeologists were revived and given new impetus.

The Mochica culture was regarded as the immediate predecessor to the Chimú Kingdom, which was the culmination of an autogenous and continuous North Coast cultural tradition. The developmental trends and achievements of the Mochica culture were to be documented by excavation programs at the principal sites of Moche and Galindo, as well as at a series of small habitational sites.

Excavations at small sites presumably with fewer activities that fit into a more discretely organized repertoire (Bankes 1971, 1972; Kroeber 1963; Moseley and Mackey 1972) were aimed at identification of activity areas and their organization within larger sites. In addition, these investigations were intended to counterbalance the heavy emphasis on elite, monumental, urban, and ceremonial settings. However, in reality this idealized feedback of information was quite ineffectual, as small-site excavations were limited in scale and in depth of analysis. Work at the site of Moche, in retrospect, seems to have contributed to the "snowballing process" of biases in Mochica archaeology.

The disproportionate attention the site of Moche has received over time is not coincidental. Easy access from the bustling city of Trujillo and the impressive size of the Huaca del Sol and Huaca de la Luna have attracted attention since the days of Colonial looting. Also, the proximity of Larco's plantation in Chiclín in the Chicama Valley just to the north and the influential Virú Valley Project to the south meant findings could be readily applied to the Moche Valley.

Uhle's pioneering excavation at Moche had revealed architectural buildup (what he called a "town") and unlooted Mochica cemeteries in the sand-covered area between the two main Huacas (Fig. 2.1). The Chan Chan–Moche Valley Project's monthlong bulldozer excavation of four major trenches, some well over 50 m long and 5–6 m wide, sought intact burials (Maps 5–6 in Donnan and Mackey 1978: 71; T. Topic 1977: 20–22). The trenches revealed Moche I, III, and IV burials (a total of thirty-three), as well as several Salinar and Gallinazo burials. One trench near the east base of the Huaca del Sol exposed over 6 m of stratified deposits (Donnan and

Mackey 1978: 59). Reconstructed burial drawings have been published (ibid.), although without crucial stratigraphic data or profiles.

Excavations atop the Sol and Luna mounds, as well as in the intervening sand-filled area ("plaza"), helped to clarify the history and nature of Mochica occupation at this inferred capital. For example, excavations in and around the plaza revealed differentiated clusters of domestic structures, suggesting socially stratified residents (T. Topic 1977, 1982). It was also found that Mochica occupation largely ceased by the end of Moche IV (Mackey and Hastings 1982; Uceda 1992), though the two *huacas* apparently retained some ceremonial importance well into Moche V and beyond (Menzel 1977). It is significant that the site of Galindo, which emerged during Moche V as the dominant settlement in the valley, was urban in character and situated inland at the valley neck on the north bank (Bawden 1977, 1982a,b, 1983).

The project also elaborated the detailed analysis of Mochica architecture that began with Kroeber's (1926, 1930) pioneering work. Moseley's analysis of the segmentary construction of Mochica mounds (Fig. 2.11) and canals, and a related study of marked adobe bricks (Hastings and Moseley 1975; Moseley 1975b), pushed Kroeber's earlier observations and inferences to a new level. Marking on adobe bricks at the Huaca del Sol and its possible significance was first discussed by Uhle (n.d.). Efforts to document temporal and spatial variability in patterns of marking bricks, and to unravel their meaning, continue to this day.[17]

Several views of considerable interest to this book were forcefully advocated by the project: (1) that the Mochica polity represented the first multi-valley predatory state on the Peruvian coast, (2) that the major Moche V settlements of Pampa Grande and Galindo were true cities based on an independent North Coast urban tradition, and (3) that a local Moche V culture formed the basic substratum of the subsequent Chimú culture without any significant intervening disruption or external input, thereby rejecting any significant impact from Wari expansion. Overall, the project came to espouse views on state and

Figure 2.11. Photograph showing segmentary construction (contiguous columns of adobe bricks) exposed on the south face of the South Platform of the Huaca del Sol platform mound at the site of Moche. Photo R-6061. Courtesy of the Servicio Aerofotográfico Nacional del Perú.

city formation and Wari invasion into the North Coast that squarely challenged or otherwise noticeably differed from conventional wisdom dating back to the 1940's. The debate is considered in depth in Chapters 5 and 6.

To provide empirical support for the primacy of demographic and technological-ecological variables in cultural developments, the Chan Chan–Moche Valley Project and its outgrowth, the *Programa Riego Antiguo* (Ancient Irrigation Program), carried out a series of in-depth studies on various facets of the regional agricultural production and environment. For the first time since Kosok's work, these studies brought irrigation and an attendant multi-valley perspective to the forefront of North Coast archaeology. Moseley and his

colleagues carried out detailed surveys and excavations of the La Cumbre Intervalley Canal (Chicama to Moche valleys) and attendant cultivation fields near Chan Chan. J. Kus (1972), for example, documented variability in the form and organization of furrows and the possible relationship of this variability to cultivated crops. Though the La Cumbre Canal, which exhibits a technical sophistication unrivaled in the world for its time of construction (e.g., Ortloff, Feldman, and Moseley 1985; Ortloff, Moseley, and Feldman 1982, 1983), was commonly attributed to Mochica engineering, it is now known to be a product of the Chimú state. In the process, this team also documented a series of geologically recent tectonic and associated sand movements that altered regional gradients

and contours, which, in turn, may have forced abandonment and/or reconstruction of Mochica canals and cultivation fields (cf. Farrington 1983; Pozorski and Pozorski 1982).

In the Jequetepeque Valley, Eling (1987) combined archaeological observations with pollen and geomorphological data to identify Mochica cultivation fields in what are now sand-covered areas. Nolan's (1980) examination of the Collique Canal, which took water from the Lambayeque Valley south to the adjacent Zaña Valley, is crucial to understanding the location of Pampa Grande and its rural hinterland, as we will see later in more detail.

Complementing these studies of Mochica agricultural production were analyses of excavated food remains by S. Pozorski (e.g., 1976, 1979) and M. Shimada (Shimada and Shimada 1981, 1985), who documented late Mochica subsistence, including the dietary importance of llamas. Though there had been a string of studies identifying Mochica subsistence items, the studies by Pozorski and Shimada differed because both plant and animal remains were examined and because they themselves were actively involved in recovering them; organic analysis had become an integral part of field research (cf. Towle 1952, 1961).

Ongoing multidisciplinary documentation of traditional North Coast agriculture (including environmental perception, water management, and native cultigens) jointly headed by Rodríguez Suy Suy, Schaedel, and J. Vreeland promises to shed much light on the specifics and underlying logic of ancient Mochica subsistence strategies.[18]

5. The Royal Ontario Museum Pampa Grande Project

The Pampa Grande project directed by Kent C. Day was fundamentally an outgrowth of the Chan Chan–Moche Valley Project in terms of the research interests and interpretive models brought to bear. Through an intensive functional/structural study of the Moche V site of Pampa Grande, the project aimed at testing the hypothesis that this was the first indigenous North Coast city. The long-term and broader aim of the Royal Ontario Museum project at Pampa Grande was to demonstrate strong evolutionary linkage between the expected model of Mochica urbanism (Pampa Grande and Galindo) and the emergent model of Chimú urbanism.

Within this general research framework, each project member focused on a separate topic. M. Anders (1977, 1981) excavated the inferred formal storage facilities (found mostly in the central portion of the site) and their surroundings to determine their contents, organization, and administration, while J. Haas (1985) excavated atop Huaca Fortaleza to elucidate the nature of the Moche V leadership. Day, seeking Mochica antecedents to the *Ciudadelas* (large, walled "royal" compounds found at Chan Chan) and the related architectural

symbolism of power, excavated a large adobe compound and also excavated structures atop Huaca 2, the second largest platform mound at the site. L. Watanabe provided comparative data for Day with his excavation of a large nearby masonry compound. A. Ignatieff sampled varied architectural settings in a central sector to clarify the manner and context of articulation between ruler and ruled. H. Knapp examined variation in adobe bricks, including presence or absence of intentional markings, in order to elucidate Mochica construction techniques and associated labor organization (Shimada 1990a, in press 1; Shimada and Cavallaro 1986, in press). M. Shimada (Shimada and Shimada 1981, 1985) analyzed organic remains excavated by herself and other project members to define urban subsistence and management of natural resources. My basic concern was the organization of craft production and how it related to the social organization and political economy (e.g., I. Shimada 1976, 1978, 1982).

Perhaps the project's most important contribution to archaeology was the establishment of a fine-grained, comprehensive functional/structural model of pre-Hispanic urbanism based on (1) delineation of architectural organization through clearing of wall corners and access, plus accompanying plane-table mapping of an estimated 25 percent of all standing architecture; (2) tight temporal control by focusing on the last occupational floor (Moche V) and taking advantage of good preservation and minimal post–Moche V abandonment deposits; and (3) subsequent multistage excavations of mapped areas, including extensive excavations of interlinked architectural settings of varied form, size, and location. This excavation strategy, together with the diverse research topics of project members, effectively sampled much of the architectural and artifactual variability identified at the site and generated a large corpus of data for comprehensive reconstruction of Moche V urbanism "from the ground up." The degree of temporal control attained through the tracing of plastered floors from one room to the next over a large area is unique among pre-Columbian urban studies. In essence, this broad-spectrum approach to

Moche V urbanism helped to rectify the long-standing bias of Mochica archaeology toward burials and monumental architecture.

The project also represented the first serious archaeological attention given to the Lambayeque Valley, one of the largest river valleys on the Peruvian coast, since the pioneering work of H. Brüning (1922; Schaedel 1988), J. Ford (unpublished), Kroeber, Kosok, H. and P. Reichlen (unpublished), and Schaedel. It is difficult to explain this notable hiatus in light of the general recognition of the valley's ongoing economic and demographic significance and in the light of the presence of hundreds of archaeological sites, many boasting monumental structures. The distance from Lima, the capital of Peru, may be partially responsible. A stronger influence, I suspect, was the widespread Culture Area approach that viewed the Lambayeque as marginal to the culture core area of the Moche and Chicama valleys to the south (e.g., Willey 1971). Recent documentation of early Mochica elite burials at Sipán and nearby contemporaneous sites (Tschauner and Tschauner 1992), and the florescence of the Moche V in the Lambayeque region, is forcing a major revision of conventional views of Mochica sociopolitical organization and dynamics. For the span of Moche I to early IV, this book posits parallel development of Lambayeque-based "northern Mochica" and Moche-based "southern Mochica" polities. Much as Kutscher (1955a) and Schaedel (1972) have argued, the notion of confederation(s) or competing regional chiefdoms sharing the art style and symbolism we call Mochica must be seriously considered.

6. Retrospect and Prospect

Mochica archaeology, reflecting the intrinsic qualities of the subject, local environment, particular historical and political contexts in which it has grown, and personal qualities of major scholars involved, has come to possess certain features crucial to proper appreciation of the cultural synthesis presented here. It has had a long and illustrious history with various colorful personalities and a series of major projects that have given rise to an impression that the North Coast has been the scene of the most active archaeological research in South America. Relatively good preservation of archaeological remains, ready access from major modern settlements, and the favorable social and economic climate of the North Coast have contributed to Peruvianists' enthusiasm. Uhle provided a head start toward scientific status, and Larco Hoyle, Kroeber, the Virú Valley Project, and Donnan provided a generally reliable and readily applicable chronology. The Chan Chan–Moche Valley Project was like the Virú Valley Project in that it provided a comprehensive understanding of human occupation in a single valley by bringing together specialists from different disciplines and a structural/functional orientation. It also revived Kosok's concern with irrigation and agricultural production.

Nevertheless, various problematical features have become entrenched. The Mochica archaeology of recent decades has had only partial success in breaking out of the limits and biases of earlier eras and data bases. There remains disproportionate emphasis on the elite and on burials and major sites, including Pampa Grande. There have been too few concurrent studies of residential and smaller specialized settlements, in spite of the fact that Peruvian archaeology from the days of Kroeber has espoused small-site methodology as one of the primary field strategies. The single-valley approach has become quite popular. At the same time, the multi-valley approach of Kosok and Schaedel countered the tendency of such studies to overemphasize the importance and representativeness of their valley in understanding the Mochica culture with its pan–North Coast extension. The weakness of the single-valley approach was highlighted by a series of recent discoveries of early Mochica elite burials at La Mina and Sipán, north of the presumed Mochica heartland.

Problems surrounding large urban sites, however, still await resolution. Enough new evidence was unearthed in the sand-filled area at Moche confirming the presence of the "town" about which Uhle spoke to warrant additional documentation of its architectural organization and functional differentiation. Is there direct

evolutionary linkage between the urban character of Moche and the later sites of Galindo and Pampa Grande, or do we need to look for an external origin and cause or a unique formative circumstance? We attempt to deal with this question in Chapters 5 and 9.

Though we have a five-phase relative chronology, it is still inadequate for any detailed cultural reconstruction, as each phase spans too much time. The nature and cultural significance of variability in style, form, and iconography have yet to be fully studied. Archaeologists have been too hasty in equating the stylistic homogeneity found in primarily funerary objects with political unification. Similarly, the applicability of this chronology in peripheral areas of the Mochica territory has not been satisfactorily established. Absolute chronology is beginning to emerge, but with the exception of Moche V it is still woefully inadequate. There is a distinct possibility that certain successive phases in different valleys may have overlapped in absolute time, and that some phases (particularly Moche I–III) may have had sociopolitical rather than temporal significance (i.e., they represented regional ethnic polities within the North Coast cultural substratum). The current emphases on burials and monumental architecture are not suited for testing these alternative views. Excavation of stratified sites, particularly those encompassing Moche I–III, development of alternative (e.g., quantitative) seriations, and additional settlement-pattern studies are urgently needed. The last has particular urgency as the rapidly expanding coastal populations establish settlements or cultivation in unoccupied areas that inevitably have archaeological remains. Such studies, however, should heed the associated problems discussed earlier.

The immense amount of data extracted from narrative Mochica art has been long and intensely used by scholars from many countries for detailed cultural reconstructions of ideological and social domains, perhaps to the detriment of the development of what should be complementary archaeological fieldwork. We need more comprehensive and balanced sampling of the Mochica archaeological universe. At least in Moche V ceramics, there is a definite possibility that the themes and motifs found on funerary-context vessels differ significantly from those excavated from habitational settlements (see Chapter 9). Inferences derived from these two data sources would differ but together should flesh out our picture of the Mochica world. It is evident that we need to enlarge our secular-context samples and systematically compare them with the presently available funerary objects to define the degree and nature of their correspondence. It is encouraging that there is more collaboration between traditional archaeological and iconographic studies, a trend that we hope will intensify.

Peruvian/Peruvianist collaboration has been quite limited. Since the days of the Virú Valley Project, the Peruvianists, particularly Americans and to a lesser extent Germans, seem to have dominated Mochica and North Coast archaeology in general. The Virú Valley Project, though in many ways a classic in New World archaeology, was not exemplary in Peruvian/Peruvianist collaboration and in disseminating its results in Peru. Peruvian participation in and out of the field was minimal and tended to be obscured by notable American participants and their accomplishments.

Over the past decade, however, there has been a sharp decline in fieldwork by Peruvianists, with the slack effectively taken up by teams from the University of Trujillo and the National Institute of Culture, Trujillo branch (which often work in collaboration). There is clear interest among Peruvian archaeologists to carry out locally funded and directed projects (both re-

search and emergency rescue operations). They have already produced some important results in Mochica archaeology (e.g., Uceda 1988, 1990; Uceda, Carcelen, and Pimentel 1990). Most notable is the documentation of long construction sequences and associated well-preserved high-relief painted friezes at Huaca de la Luna (Moche; Uceda 1992) and Huaca El Brujo (lower Chicama Valley; Correa 1992). In addition, there are complementary investigations at various Gallinazo sites (e.g., Barr 1991; Salinas 1991; also Maguiña 1992) that should help clarify the origins of the Mochica style and polity. These are highly commendable accomplishments given the extant economic and political problems. At the same time, these projects tend to be site-specific without complementary regional surveys, and to overemphasize technical and cultural-historical issues.

In nearly all cases of Peruvianist research on the North Coast, invaluable assistance by local Peruvian experts and patrons such as Jorge Rondón (Lambayeque), Oscar Lostanau and José Ramírez (Jequetepeque), Rafael Larco Hoyle (Chicama), and Víctor Antonio Rodríguez Suy Suy (Moche) must be clearly acknowledged. The recently instituted practice among foreign archaeological projects of designating a Peruvian co-director and incorporating Peruvian students for on-site training should foster broader, more spontaneous interaction between Peruvianist and Peruvian scholars. We also need better communication of another sort—intervalley comparisons of the type once carried out

by Kosok and Schaedel, concomitant with ever more intensive valley-wide surveys using the individual-valley approach. In addition, coast/highland interaction (even extending to the eastern side of the Andes) deserves further investigation as our understanding of the contemporary polities in the North Highlands, such as Recuay and Cajamarca, rapidly improves. The survey by Topic and Topic (1982, 1983) of routes and fortification on the cis-Andean[19] slope between the Huamachuco Basin in the North Highlands and the Moche Valley on the coast serves as a model for such investigation. The Sicán Archaeological Project's (Matsumoto and Kimura 1991, 1992; Tschauner and Tschauner 1992) ongoing transect survey, covering the Huambos region in the North Highlands down to the Pacific coast, attempts to elucidate both intervalley (Lambayeque and La Leche) and coast/highland relationships among contemporaneous Mochica, Gallinazo, and Cajamarca polities. The Chongoyape area in the lower reaches of the *chaupiyunga* zone (characterized by year-round warmth) is hypothesized as the cultural frontier between the coastal and highland-based polities (I. Shimada 1982).

With the widespread renewed interest in Early Intermediate Period cultures among Peruvian and Peruvianist archaeologists over the past decade, it is likely that we will soon see major advances in Mochica archaeology. Improved communication and collaboration between these two groups will have a significant impact on how well we advance.

3

Mochica Land and Culture

As part of our aim of achieving a holistic understanding of the Mochica culture, we now turn to its environmental setting, starting with the Central Andes, gradually narrowing our scope to the North Coast[20] and eventually focusing on the Lambayeque Valley where Pampa Grande is situated. Our primary concern in this chapter is understanding how the Mochica interacted with their environment in a creative and dynamic manner not just for subsistence but for general enrichment of their lives. This requires an understanding of the physical reality as well as how the Mochica perceived its potentials and limitations. Thus, whenever possible, the Andean environment is described in terms of both "scientific understanding" and the indigenous rationale and perceptions as inferred from sixteenth-century Spanish writings and archaeological investigations.

By the beginning of the sixth century, Mochica hegemony reached its greatest extent, stretching from the north bank of the La Leche River in the north to the south bank of the Huarmey River to the south, a linear distance of some 470 km encompassing fourteen contiguous coastal river valleys (Figs. 1.1, 1.2). With long-suspected Mochica occupation in the Casma Valley finally documented (Wilson 1991), it is now clear that there was no gap between the Nepeña and Huarmey valleys (cf. I. Shimada 1982, 1987a). In addition, we anticipate eventual documentation that the territory probably extended to the upper Piura Valley on the Far North Coast, an additional distance of over 300 km, as explained in Chapter 4. In essence, Mochica territory covered roughly a third of the entire Peruvian coast.

1. The Central Andes

The Central Andes is one of the subjective tripartite divisions of the Andean mountain chain, which flanks the entire Pacific coast of South America. Essentially the Central Andes coincide with the western half of modern Peru where the mountain chain stretches in a gentle northwest-southeast arc. Mochica territory occupied the northwest corner of the Central Andes. The North Andes curve notably to the east and recede further inland, narrowing and breaking up into lower, shorter segments. They are close to the equator, receive much more rain, have lush vegetational coverage, and are not affected by the cold Peru Current. The boundary between the North and Central Andes traditionally has been conceived of as lying immediately north of the

Sechura Desert or between Tumbes and Piura (e.g., Bennett 1948; Lanning 1967; Willey 1971), which coincided with the northern frontier of Mochica territory. However, the boundary is essentially dynamic. From Moche V through Sicán and Chimú times, the North Coast populations maintained close contact with those on the Far North Coast and the Ecuadorian coast (Shimada 1988a; cf. Burger 1984a; Collier 1948).

South of Lake Titicaca, the Andes turn westward and are oriented north-south. The high and unbroken eastern cordillera effectively removes moisture from the air mass coming from Amazonia. Thus, the *altiplano* or high plateau that links the widely separated eastern and western cordilleras of the Andes is quite arid. It extends southward well beyond the Tropic of Capricorn.

Many years of field research by environmental scientists, particularly German and French geographers, has shown that the Central Andes possess other distinctive and important features that set this area apart from other areas of the Andes and the world.[21] Unlike most other alpine regions, much of the total elevational span (0–6,768 m) of the Central Andes is densely occupied and/or cultivated, largely due to the climatic benefits of its proximity to the equator. Though it has a considerable latitudinal span (from roughly 5° south to 17° south), the whole area is under the same basic climatic regime characterized by contrasting dry and wet seasons.

At the same time, traveling across the Central Andes at almost any latitude, one is overwhelmed by the tremendous ecological variability resulting from horizontally compacted extreme elevational differences. Such differences are variously labeled as "ecological," "vegetational," "production," or "life" zones. Just as the sheer presence of the Andes is dominating and pervasive, there are ubiquitous and relentless reminders of the climatic and economic significance of the nearby Pacific, particularly the cold Peru Current. There are other features much more sporadic in time and space, visually less impressive but with long-term and varied effects on Andean life and landscape. These include the widespread distribution of the multipurpose llama, the principal domesticated Andean camelid, and unpredictable and often catastrophic "quirks" of the Central Andean range and the Pacific, such as droughts, earthquakes, and the El Niño Countercurrent and associated torrential rains.

The above broad-stroke characterization emphasizes the dynamic aspects of the Central Andean environment. The area has seen both ephemeral and long-term environmental changes, many brought about by human activity that, although localized, may have had widespread systemic effect. Indigenous perceptions and utilization of the environment have been correspondingly flexible. In this regard, the often heard "Three Worlds of the Andes" (coast, highland, and jungle or *selva*) oversimplify the physical and cultural realities and impose a static image of what is in reality a dynamic and continuous situation (I. Shimada 1982, 1985b; also see Netherly 1977). Andean peoples have continuously crosscut these "Worlds" in their resource exploitation and territorial expansion.

Yet our current understanding of microenvironmental variation and variability—often of greater concern to local inhabitants than general characteristics—remains inadequate. The situation is often aggravated by archaeologists' misleading or erroneous interpretations and analyses of environmental data (see Craig 1984 for examples and cautions). In our eagerness to invoke long-distance trade, hasty assumptions have been made that particular natural resources (e.g., feathers, minerals) were not indigenous to the area under study. Even in some areas for which we have detailed environmental pictures, it is uncertain how modern or "scientific" understanding relates to prehistoric cultural perceptions of the same environment or resource.

2. Mochica Land in Central Andean Context

A. The Diversity of Vertically Differentiated Microenvironments

Perhaps most important to Andean inhabitants was accessibility to an impressive range of microenvironments and resources largely created by *horizontally condensed extreme altitudinal differences.* In many parts of the Central Andes, traveling eastward from the extremely arid desert along the Pacific coast within a horizontal distance of 200 to 250 km, one ascends rugged, typically treeless cis-Andean peaks and foothills, temperate and fertile intermontane basins, moist short grassland or *puna,* and majestic peaks (many over 6,000 m high) with glaciers or permanent snow. Continuing east down the rugged eastern escarpment, one rapidly descends to hot, humid tropical rainforests that may begin as high as 2,500 m above sea level. The precipitous eastern slope of the Andes has highly condensed environmental zones ("condensed verticality," Brush 1977), and an elevational difference of 30 m or less may mean a different set of cultivars and fallowing pattern (e.g., Brush 1982; Camino, Recharte, and Bidegaray 1981; Webster 1971; Yamamoto 1982). Adaptation to this fine vertical zonation has led to an impressive variety of maize and tubers or root crops (such as potatoes) and the complex agricultural calendars found in many highland regions. The famous Andean terraces, called *andenes,* not only reduced soil erosion but also increased cultivation areas. It is understandable that the Andean highlanders' view of the world is typically expansive and vertical, given the increase in range, quality, and quantity of desired resources typically achieved by moving up and down the slopes (Murra 1972, 1984).

On the basis of the environmental potentials and characteristics described above, some argue an inherent "downward thrust" to territorial expansion or population migration in the Andes (Moseley 1983a: 195–196). Other scholars have emphasized the opposite; Murra (1968: 58; also Cardich 1985) noted that "in the course of human settlements in the Andes demographic pressure was directed upward. It was a matter of taming the altitude and the *puna.*"

In the North Highlands of Peru, where extensive *puna* gives way to more dissected, moister *jalca* grassland,[22] upward expansion would have been much more restricted. Certain tuber crops in Cajamarca (Figs. 1.1, 1.2) today are cultivated to about 3,700 m, with the prehistoric maximum ca. 3,900 m; corresponding figures for the central and southern highlands of Peru are 4,000 m or higher (Cardich 1979: 92). These considerations regarding areas of potential exploitation must be kept in mind when examining interaction between contemporaneous Mochica and Cajamarca polities in the following chapter.

One environmental zone attractive to both highland and coastal inhabitants is the *yunga* or *chaupiyunga* found on both the eastern and western slopes of the Andes. The *yunga* is characterized (as denoted by this Quechua word) by year-round sunshine and warmth (typical daily temperature range of 20°–27° C), allowing a wide range of cultigens including highly valued fruits and hot, spicy chili peppers. Important hallucinogens such as coca (*Erythroxylum novogranatense* var. *truxillense*), San Pedro cactus (*Trichocereus pachanoi*), and *espingo* (*Quararibea* sp.?) are also found here. The cis-Andean slopes also yield minerals (e.g., copper and iron oxides and silver) used for pigments and smelting by the Mochica (Lechtman 1976; Netherly 1977; Shimada 1985c, 1987b, 1988b). In northern Peru, the cis-Andean *yunga* penetrates up to ca. 2,500 m, and available evidence indicates that contemporaneous Mochica, Recuay, and Cajamarca populations contested its control (Proulx 1982; I. Shimada 1982; Topic and Topic 1983). The presence of Sicán and Chimú ceramics and toponyms of North Coast derivation in the eastern *yunga* of northern Peru (e.g., at Gran Pajatén, Bonavia 1968; at Uchucmarca, Thompson 1976; in the Jaén–San Ignacio area, R. Shady, pers. com. 1991; in the Cajamarca area, Rostworowski 1985) suggests that certain North Coast pre-Hispanic polities may have established their own colonies there to cultivate highly valued crops such as coca and maize and exploit local resources such as bird feathers, timber, medicinal and aromatic plants, and gold nuggets.

Perhaps the most important reason to control the cis-Andean *yunga* was access to the principal intakes for the "mother" or "Maximum Elevation Canals" (MECs). By virtue of being the highest and usually the largest canals, these fed secondary and tertiary canals lower down, determining the extent of irrigation within the coastal valley (Moseley and Deeds 1982; I. Shimada 1982).

The inland-most location of the MEC intake is basic to our definition of the coastal river valley. While the western boundary of the valley is clearly the Pacific, the eastern boundary is the inland-most intake of the north- or south-bank MEC (Shimada 1982: 185–187). In the case of the Lambayeque Valley, the intake is over 50 km inland from the Pacific and ca. 180 m above sea level (Fig. 3.1). Above this location the Andean foothills close in and rise sharply, and cultivation of the mountain slopes becomes increasingly dependent on regular annual rainfall, supplemented by relatively small independent irrigation networks. In a real sense the MECs define the extent and nature of cultivation and occupation in the coastal valleys, and their control was of overriding concern. In the arid coastal valleys of Peru, "irrigation has always been the *sine qua non* of agricultural production. Without it, life would be impossible. It is true at present—it was true in the past" (Kosok 1965: 10). Ethnohistorical research has shown that in late pre-Hispanic times, the territories of provincial polities within each valley were demarcated using valley edges and major waterways, including canals (Netherly 1977, 1984).

In the preceding chapter we noted that the way one delimits a study area or valley can influence the settlement patterns that emerge. For meaningful settlement-pattern analysis, we need to gain an idea of the physical world as it was perceived by the culture under study. MECs changed in location and extent in accordance with a given culture's worldview, organizational skills, technology, population pressure, interaction with neighbors, and amount and pattern of water flow. Thus, a valley defined by MECs is culturally meaningful, can be readily identified in the field, is relevant to the geographical reality, and is dynamic in conception.

The coastal region is essentially rainless, with the exception of rare intrusions of the warm El Niño Countercurrent. Andean mountains were of the utmost importance to the Mochica and other coastal dwellers in part due to the fact that water necessary for their very existence derived from regular seasonal (around November to April) rainfall in the highlands. Reinhard (1985: 13) explains the reason for the widespread mountain worship on the coast and in the highlands:

Throughout the Andes, mountain deities are perceived as the controllers of meteorological phenomena (rain, hail, frost, clouds, lightning, etc.). . . . As controllers of water, they were closely associated with lakes, and what was perceived as the ultimate source of water, the ocean. . . . For this reason sea water and sea shells [especially the thorny oyster, *Spondylus princeps,* and conch shell, *Strombus galetaus,* and *Conus fergusoni* from the warm waters off coastal Ecuador] played an important role in the worship of mountains for rain throughout the Andes. . . . By controlling meteorological phenomena, not only the fertility of crops, but also the fertility of livestock [especially llamas and alpacas] was dependent upon the mountain deities.

It is quite likely that the Mochica saw the Andean mass and nearby Pacific in complementary opposition. The Pacific offered a stable, year-round, abundant supply of fish, shellfish and mammals, unlike agriculture, which was affected by seasonal fluctuations in the water supply. Their perception of this complementarity probably extended to climate and cosmology as holding the key to life, water, and the dynamic forces of the universe. The intermediate coast reaps the benefits and suffers the havoc of their interplay. The very essence of coastal life was interwoven with their dynamics and products, and it is understandable that Mochica art is replete with explicit and implicit signs of the reverence the coastal inhabitants held toward the sea and mountains.

Benson (1972: 27) has argued that the "fanged god" (Larco's *Ai-apaec*), the inferred supreme deity of the Mochica with huge feline fangs and semicircular "sunrise" headdress, dwelt in the mountains (Fig. 2.9). According to her, the fanged god as the sun rises every morning over the mountain and at night sets in the sea where he fights with fish and crab monsters.

Mochica ceramic art also includes modeled representations of three, five, or seven "mountain peaks" accompanied by scenes

of "rituals," including a figure draped over the central peak with long hair flowing downslope. Donnan (1978: 148, 151) suggests the figures in the Mochica mountain scenes may well be guardian spirits and the long, flowing hair "a vital link with the life force." The last may be interpreted as lifegiving water. Hocquenghem (1977a, 1979a,b) sees the importance of mountains for the Mochica in relation to ancestral worship. For modern folk healers of the Trujillo and Lambayeque regions mountains offer magical herbs, lagoons for initiation, a means of cleansing and revitalizing themselves, homes for guardian spirits, passages to "enchanted lands," and water for the coast (Sharon 1978).

In spite of minimal elevational differences within the alluvial plains of coastal river valleys, there is significant environmental and seasonal variability.[23] Much of the observed variation in plant cover, for example, is due to variation in soil quality and moisture availability, which are, in turn, related to location within the valley and seasonal fluctuations in river discharge volume or, in some rare cases, coastal rains. The coastal gradient, while slight, varies sufficiently within and between valleys to have important implications for irrigation.

Seasonal differences on the coast are not as marked as in the highlands, but there are, nonetheless, some important differences. The discharge volumes of coastal rivers show marked seasonal differences reflecting the seasonal rainfall pattern in the adjacent highlands (Fig. 3.2). The majority of rain in the highlands falls during the summer wet season. In the North Highlands of Peru, seasonal rainfall commonly starts in the spring around October or November (accompanied by a gradual increase in warmth), with March being the rainiest month (Johnson 1976). The rains largely stop by May. In the highland regions farther south, the peak rainfall month comes earlier, between January and February.

Coastal irrigation agriculture is dictated by the above rainfall patterns. If rainfall starts late, different crops or varieties of crops may be needed. Most irrigated land on the coast yields one crop per year, although land close to intakes with year-round access to water allows two crops. In

this regard, the demarcation of late pre-Hispanic North Coast provincial polities described earlier assured them access to roughly the same range of production zones (Netherly 1977, 1984). These wedge-shaped territories included fertile valley bottomland yielding two crops at the apex, and Pacific coast out to offshore islands.

There is a surprising degree of environmental diversity to be found in the Andean foothills that circumscribe these coastal plains. For example, on the cis-Andean slopes overlooking the Zaña Valley there is a dense, lush subtropical evergreen forest supported by fine nightly rains (e.g., Dillehay and Netherly 1983). This is believed to "represent remnants of a 'life zone' that was formerly much more extensive along the cis-Andean foothills when it was established during pluvial intervals of the Late Pleistocene" (Craig 1985: 26). At the beginning of the Holocene the forest is believed to have extended somewhat lower and wider (Craig 1985: 26). Farther north at this elevation, drier but still dense evergreen forests are found. Netherly (1977: 32) emphasizes the significance of these forests for increasing available moisture in the catchment areas of coastal rivers, which would stabilize runoff, prolonging the period of relatively high discharge and extending the period of maximum irrigation. In addition, these forests offer a range of resources such as bird feathers, monkeys, and tropical hardwoods that have often been assumed to be imports from the eastern forest (see below).

B. Proximity to the Equator: Altitude-Latitude Interplay and Ramifications of Tropical Alpine Conditions

The preceding might suggest that differences in altitude are far more important than latitude. However, the fact that the Central Andes is a tropical alpine region close to the equator is of equal import. Braun-Blanquet (1950: 363) has observed that the diversity of vegetation zones "increases with the elevation of the mountains and with the proximity to the Equator." High average diurnal temperatures have allowed extensive human occupation (Troll 1958, 1968; Rhoades and Thompson 1975: 544–545) and cultivation of the highlands, up to 4,600 m (Cardich 1984/85: 63) and

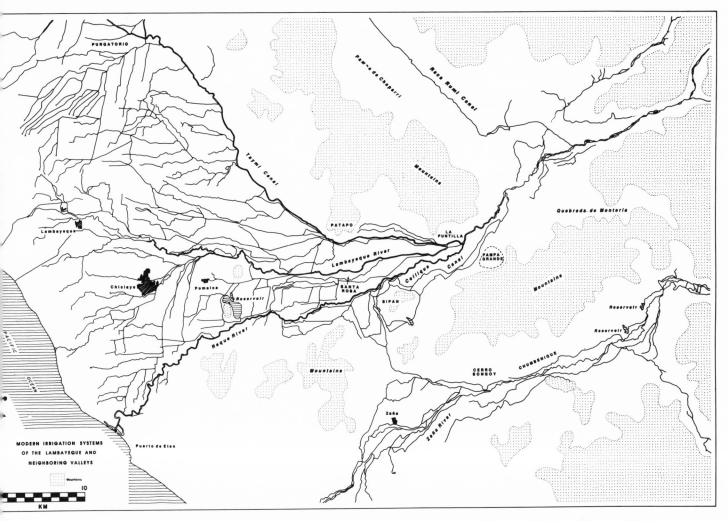

Figure 3.1. Topographic map of the Lambayeque Valley showing the extent of modern irrigation and the locations of major Mochica and modern settlements, as well as the colonial tripartite division of cultivated lands.

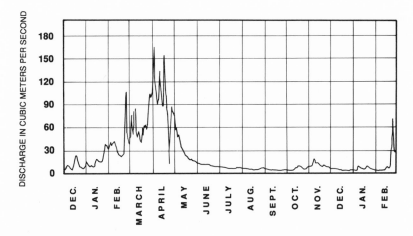

Figure 3.2. Chart showing daily discharge volume of the Chicama River. Redrawn from ONERN 1973: 202, Gráfico No. 3.

TOTAL ANNUAL DISCHARGE: 768,956,000 M³   MAXIMUM MONTHLY DISCHARGE: 163.07 M³/SEC
AVERAGE MONTHLY DISCHARGE: 24.32 M³/SEC   MINIMUM MONTHLY DISCHARGE: 2.80 M³/SEC

even up to 5,200 m in the case of isolated herders (Bowman 1938: 39). In fact, the percentage of habitation and cultivation of land over 2,800 m in elevation in Peru (ca. 60 percent) is the highest for all alpine regions of the world (Cardich 1980: 8).

The significance of latitude and its interrelationship with altitude in Central Andean cultural ecology can be effectively illustrated by a series of east-west transects cut at various latitudes along the Andean range (Fig. 3.3 D-D' and E-E'). In the southernmost transect through the *altiplano*, the western slope of the Andean range is quite steep and reaches close to the Pacific. This steep gradient, together with relatively limited precipitation on the cis-Andean slope, has resulted in small, mostly seasonal and often downcutting rivers which, in turn, give rise to poorly developed coastal alluvial plains and limited agricultural productivity. Perennial shortage of water places a premium not only on sophisticated water management and technology (including the *pukios*, networks of underground galleries to tap filtration water for irrigation; Schreiber and Lancho 1988; cf. Barnes and Fleming 1991) but also on nonagricultural resources, such as labor services (e.g., trading), minerals, and marine and craft products.

The adjacent *altiplano* achieved impressive pre-Hispanic productivity and population size largely based on a set of hardy tubers and grains (what Lumbreras [1974: 197] calls the "Cordilleran Complex"), lacustrine resources, domesticated camelids (e.g., Browman 1980; Mujica 1985; Murra 1968), and technologies such as "freeze-drying" and "raised fields."[24] This is in spite of marked diurnal temperature variation, wet (ca. November–April) and dry (ca. May–October) seasons, nearly year-round frost, unpredictable spells of drought or conversely floods and hail, and soil low in organic nutrients.

A transect through the North Coast (Fig. 3.3 A-A' and B-B'; ca. 9° south) shows major differences with important cultural ramifications. Here, Andean foothills are often lower, farther inland, and broken up; in general, the farther north along the coast, the less "circumscribed" the river valley. Also, the more gradual, longer cis-Andean slope, called "extended

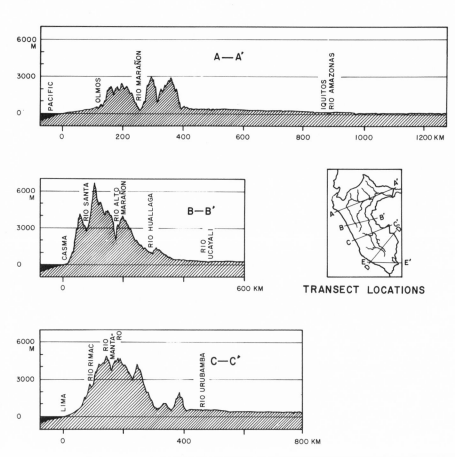

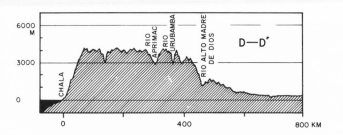

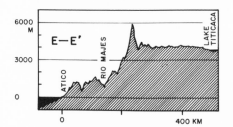

VERTICAL SCALE   1
HORIZONTAL SCALE   40

Figure 3.3. Five east-west transects through Peru illustrating significant horizontal and vertical differences. Redrawn from figure in Pulgar Vidal 1987: 25.

verticality" (Brush 1977), reaches only ca. 4,500 m or less above sea level. The continental divide is well over 100 km inland for the northern North Coast (Fig. 1.2). In essence, at this latitude, the humid air and moderating influence of the Pacific reaches considerably farther inland (up to 50 km) than in areas to the south. Many of the vegetational zones recognized along the coast farther south are found at lower elevations here (Koepcke 1954: 19). In addition, the extensive, low-gradient coastal valleys are blessed with thick, fertile alluvia watered by large perennial rivers.

Though slight in absolute terms, gradient variability within the coastal valley is crucial to how efficiently water can be tapped and distributed. Various favorable natural conditions of the North Coast allowed canals to approximate theoretical maximum distributional efficiency and extent (Fig. 3.4; e.g., Moseley 1983b; Moseley et al. 1983). These conditions include the typically high annual volume and high minimum discharge volume of North Coast rivers (i.e., stable flow), and low, consistent gradients such as those found in the extensive valley bottomlands of the Lambayeque (1.1 percent gradient, a rise of about 150 m over a distance of approximately 58 km from the mouth of the Chancay-Reque River; see Table 3), Jequetepeque, and Chicama valleys. Overall, the North Coast, particularly the northern half, offers highly favorable conditions for extensive irrigation and large-scale cultivation (e.g., Kroeber 1930; Kosok 1959; Moseley 1983b). It is no surprise that the largest irrigation systems in the pre-Hispanic New World developed here.

In considering intervalley irrigation, we must examine the demographic and political significance of the pairing of small valleys with limited runoff and large valleys with large, stable (high minimum) runoff. Kroeber (1930: 75–76) noted the disproportionate importance of small coastal valleys in Peruvian prehistory but without suggesting why this was the case. Schaedel (1951a: 240) later argued that the small La Leche and Moche valleys with their notable urban developments and/or concentration of massive constructions served as the seats of political power while the large adjacent Lambayeque and Chicama valleys

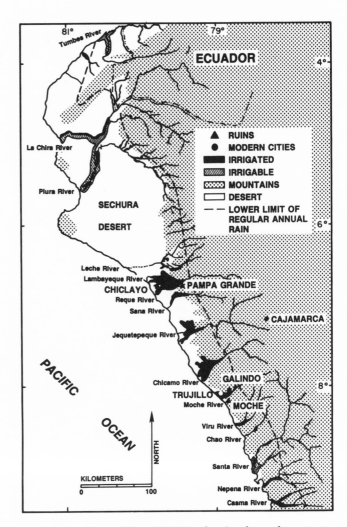

Figure 3.4. Map showing the modern extent of irrigated land on the North Coast and the locations of the sites of Galindo, Moche, and Pampa Grande. Modified from Plate XIV in Kroeber 1930.

became the breadbaskets. Kosok (1965: 88) suggested that such asymmetry developed as the small valleys were more "*advantageous in size* for developing the greatest amount of *intravalley economic, social and political centralization.*" Based on his recent research in the Moche Valley, Moseley (1982; Moseley and Deeds 1982) reached the same conclusion; in the early growth phases of the Mochica polity, the Moche-Chicama pairing may have played an important role. In light of this view, the establishment of the Moche V capital of Pampa Grande in the large Lambayeque Valley is curious.

The adjacent North Highlands receive more rain than the Central or South Highlands, as these relatively narrow, low mountains do not effectively remove the moisture that the trade winds bring from the Amazonian Basin. Thus, the northern sector around Cajamarca supports *jalca,* and the fertile, temperate intermontane basins, though limited in extent, sustained the Cajamarca and Recuay cultures (Fig. 1.1).

Overall, the northern and southern transects contrast sharply; the crucial economic and demographic potential of the North Coast (particularly the Lambayeque area) seems superior to that of the adjacent

Table 3. Annual minimum and maximum discharge volumes of major North Coast rivers. Figures in part A are taken from Table 1 in Moseley 1983b: 785. Figures in part B are taken from Kroeber 1930: 76.

A

River	Drainage Basin Size (km²)	Irrigated Area (km²)	Length (km)	Flow Volume (m³ × 10⁶)	150 m Elevation (km from mouth)	% Gradient (1000·0 masl)
Chancay	3,375	523.42	194	701	58	1.1
Zaña	1,125	191.13	119	202	51	1.0
Jequetepeque	4,050	295.78	154	945	30	1.1
Chicama	3,004	403.71	164	783	27	1.1
Moche	1,562	200.26	105	320	19	2.1
Virú	1,308	164.05	89	105	24	2.2
Chao	600	NA	78	NA	22	2.4
Santa	11,250	86.43	332	4,594	27	0.9

B

River	Class	Basin, Km²	Within Rain Zone, Km²	Under Irrigation, H	In Actual Cultivation, H
Jequetepeque	1	5,800	4,000	30,000	c. 15,000
Chicama	1	4,800	2,200	35,000	c. 17,000
Moche	1	1,950	800	10,000	c. 5,000 −
Virú	2	1,500	900	5,000	c. 2,500
Chao	2	1,300	600	500	300
Santa	1	10,500[a]		5,000[b]	3,000[b]
Lacramarca	3	800	200	100	
Nepeña	2	2,500	1,200	8,000	4,000
Casma	2	2,600	1,300	c. 10,000	
Culebra	3	950	100	250	
Huarmey	2	2,700	1,700	2,000	c. 2,000

[a]Whole drainage; basin below confluence of Huaraz and Chuquicara, 800 km² only.
[b]Below confluence of Huaraz and Chuquicara.

North Highlands, while the balance between coast and highlands tips in favor of the latter in the south. In terms of material achievements (e.g., monumental public structures), most of the impressive pre-Hispanic Andean cultures do seem to have emerged on the North Coast (Cupisnique, Mochica, Sicán, and Chimú) and the circum–Lake Titicaca region (Pucará, Tiahuanaco [Tiwanaku], and Inca). Certainly the Spaniards recognized and quickly exploited the favorable conditions of the North Coast: mild, sunny climate, potential seaport sites, high agricultural productivity, and large native population accustomed to labor tribute under powerful, stratified, pre-Hispanic polities (e.g., Ramírez 1985b). By the late sixteenth century, the North Coast was one of the most urban and economically active regions of the entire Viceroyalty of Peru (ibid.). The long distinction stands to this day.

At a very general level, much of the 2,400-km Peruvian coast may be described as a series of monotonous, treeless, arid deserts, interrupted by the lush green of roughly triangular, irrigated bottomlands watered by some forty perennial rivers. The monotony is also broken by scattered patches (some covering 5–10 km² or more) of *lomas*[25] on seaside mountain slopes between the river valleys. Some have characterized the coastal river valleys as homogeneous and repetitive, juxtaposed with adjacent linear and vertical highlands (e.g., Patterson 1973). Accordingly, the Mochicas' impressive coastwise territorial expansion, together with the surprising paucity of Mochica artifacts in the adjacent North Highlands, has been interpreted as reflecting their attempt to gain "more of the same" critical resources of cultivable land and water (e.g., Carneiro 1970).

In reality, on the North Coast alone there is a surprisingly wide range of resources and microenvironments. It is still not properly appreciated that llamas, colorful feathers, *espingo* seeds (today used in magic and curing), and even gold nuggets and arsenic-bearing ores valued by the Mochica and typically attributed to the adjacent highlands or Amazonian jungle (e.g., Donnan 1978; Lechtman 1976; O'Neil 1984) were and still are present in appreciable quantities on the North Coast (Koepcke 1954; Netherly 1977; Shimada 1985b,c). The extensive semitropical thorny forest dominated by *algarrobo* (*Prosopis chilensis, juliflora,* and *limensis*), *faique* (*Acacia macracantha*), *vichayo* (*Capparis ovalifolia*), *zapote* (*Capparis angulata*), and *palo verde* (*Parkinsonia aculeata*) in the central La Leche Valley and to the north (Fig. 3.5) is densely inhabited by birds of all colors (e.g., parrot, *Aratinga wagleri*), together with anteaters (*Tamandua* sp.), pumas (*Felis concolor*), iguanas (Fig. 3.6; *Iguana iguana*), squirrels (*Sciurus straminaus*), boa constrictors (*Boa constrictor*), and foxes (*Dusicyon sechurae*) (I. Shimada 1982: 183; see Suárez 1985). The forests of Colán and Chaparrí in the upper reaches of the same valley boast im-

Figure 3.5. Panoramic view of extensive subtropical thorny evergreen forest in the Poma National Archaeological and Ecological Reserve in the central La Leche Valley.

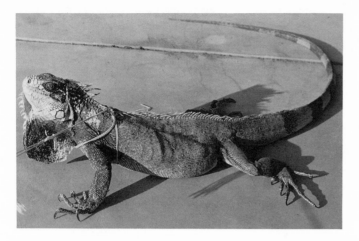

Figure 3.6. Iguana found in the Poma National Archaeological and Ecological Reserve, central La Leche Valley. It is also found in the subtropical evergreen thorny forest in the upper Piura Valley.

pressive stands of *espingo* trees and provide habitats for deer (*Odocoileus virginianus*), spectacled bears (*Tremarctos ornatus*), peccaries (*Tayassu tajacu*), pumas, and other animals. Although the well-known placer gold sources are rivers on the eastern Andean slopes (e.g., Chinchipe and Negro; Craig 1973; I. Shimada 1982: 181), practically all cis-Andean rivers carry some gold nuggets. At Cerro Morro de Eten in the Lambayeque Valley, gold may have been prehistorically mined (Fig. 3.7; Shimada 1981: 433). Arsenopyrite and its common weathering product, scorodite, are available at a number of coastal mines in the Lambayeque region (Fig. 3.8; see Merkel and Shimada 1988; Shimada and Merkel 1991; cf. Lechtman 1976, 1991; Netherly 1977). Scorodite could well have been used as a source of arsenic for the arsenical copper that appears to have been smelted in small amounts by Mochica metallurgists (Lechtman 1979; Patterson 1971). Coastal breeding and herding of llamas is discussed later. Overall, before we look to the highlands and jungle as the provenience of a given product, we need to keep in mind that our knowledge of North Coast resources is still inadequate.

C. Proximity and Importance of the Pacific Ocean

Another major characteristic of Central Andean geography of particular importance to North Coast inhabitants is the proximity and overall climatic and economic importance of the Pacific Ocean. Proximity should be gauged in terms of not only physical distance but also mental attitude. The vertical and expansive worldview mentioned earlier encompassed both the Pacific and offshore islands that dot much of the Peruvian coast. An excellent illustration of this point is seen among modern Indians of the south Peruvian highlands, who journey down to the coast typically with llamas to collect and carry back edible marine algae for their own consumption and/or use in trade, a pattern most likely of considerable antiquity (Masuda 1985). North Highlanders similarly travel down to collect seaweed and shellfish (I. Shimada 1982: 188; see Matsuzawa 1978: 670). The shells are heated to produce lime, which is used in coca chewing to release the alkaloid known as cocaine.

The cultural and climatic significance of the Pacific and its renewable resources to past and present Andean peoples cannot be overemphasized. The Peru Current, which slowly flows (0.2–0.3 knots) northward from Antarctica along much of the western

South American coast up to the region of Cabo Blanco in northern Peru (where it veers westward and loses its identity), is the largest cold current of the world. Water temperatures immediately offshore between Salaverry (near the city of Trujillo) and Cabo Blanco vary between 16° and 18° C in winter and a couple of degrees higher in summer, in contrast to corresponding figures of over 25° C for water out at sea (Collin 1984: 19; Posner 1954: 67). Farther south, it can be as cold as 10° C (Idyll 1973: 22).

Damp air masses that have been effectively cooled moving over the cold Peru Current are pushed inland; that is, the heating of the land mass causes a strong afternoon sea breeze to develop, which moves inland to fill the convection lows (e.g., see Howell 1954; Johnson 1976). This warming, together with a low temperature gradient, has the important effect of raising the capacity of the air masses to hold on to their relatively high moisture content. Consequently, the captured moisture is not released as rain until the masses come into contact with the coastal Andean range farther inland and higher up. The South Pacific anticyclone, an area of high barometric pressure, drives the Peru Current northward and imposes pockets of high pressure over the coast (Johnson 1976). The combined effects leave the coast rainless for many years at a time, barring the intrusion of the warm El Niño Countercurrent.

The cold current and associated cloud cover, simply by their presence, also keep coastal air temperatures relatively stable and cool in spite of proximity to the equator. Thus, the city of Chiclayo at a latitude of about 6°48′ south, with abundant sunshine year-round, has an average annual air temperature near 22° C (a high of ca. 35° and low of 10° C) and annual average humidity of about 76 percent. The city of Lima, some 800 km farther south, has an average annual air temperature of approximately 19° C. The temperature difference between these two cities is largely a function of their distance from the equator. Even the cold Peru Current is gradually heated as it travels northward, and it consequently loses cloud cover (warmer air masses). A typical winter day in Lima is chilly, damp, and rarely sunny due to the thick cloud cover, while Chiclayo on the same day is likely to be considerably warmer, drier, and sunnier. Overall, the Peruvian coastal deserts, unlike the stereotypical image of hot, dry deserts in other parts of the world, are damp and clammy.

It seems anomalous to have a cold tropical current. The widely accepted explanation for the coldness and biotic richness of the Peru Current is that the prevailing southerly winds create an "Ekmann spiral" that shears off the surface waters, allowing cold water low in dissolved oxygen but high in phosphorus and nitrogen to rise to the surface from depths of 300 m (Cane 1983, 1986; Collin 1984). The high concentration of nutrient salts maintained by this slow, constant upwelling (20–100 m upward per month) sustains a tremendous population of minute floating plants called phytoplankton, which in turn form the base of an immensely populous ecological pyramid that includes impressive arrays of fish, shellfish, and sea animals and birds that ancient and modern fishermen have intensely exploited.

The economic importance of the Peru Current is effectively illustrated by the fact that, though accounting for only a tiny fraction of global sea surface, it produced fully 22 percent by weight of all fish caught throughout the world in the early 1970's (Idyll 1973: 22). It is perhaps the richest fishing ground in the world. Anchovies, which gather by the billion near the shore close to the surface, are preyed upon by the largest concentration of guano-producing cormorants (*Phalacrocorax bougainvillii*), boobies (*Sula variegata*), and pelicans (*Pelicanus thagus*) in the world. More recently the modern Peruvian fishing industry has exploited anchovies for the production of

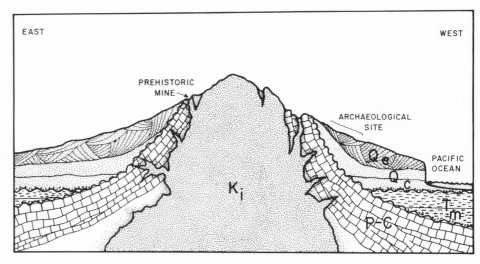

CRETACEOUS   GRANODIORITE INTRUSIVE

PERMO-CARBONIFEROUS LIMESTONE   WITH   CONTACT METAMORPHISM

TERTIARY   MARINE   SANDY   SHALES

QUATERNARY   SANDY   CONGLOMERATES AND   CROSS-BEDDED   EOLIAN   SANDS

Figure 3.7. Geological profile of the Cerro Morro de Eten, which includes a pre-Hispanic gold mine. Redrawn from the original by Alan K. Craig.

Figure 3.8. Pre-Hispanic copper mine of Barranco Colorado just south of the village of Batán Grande, La Leche Valley. Prehistoric miners cut a meter-wide trench at the apex of the mountain following the vein. They carefully removed only the highest-grade copper oxide ores, generating little gangue and talus.

fish meal (used to enrich livestock feed), fish oil, and other lesser products. In the peak year of 1970, 12.3 million tons of anchovies were caught (Idyll 1973: 26), and many feel overfishing caused the collapse of this industry.

The seabirds that nest on rocky offshore islands are estimated to consume on an annual basis some 2.5 million metric tons of fish (overwhelmingly anchovies), as much as the total commercial catch of all U.S. fisheries in the early 1950's (Posner 1954: 66; Idyll 1973: 27). This "feasting" results in an important by-product, guano,[26] an excellent natural fertilizer rich in nitrogen and phosphorus and formerly much in demand throughout the world. Deposits of guano are widespread features of the coast and offshore islands. Also, for every drop deposited on land a dozen fall into the Pacific, "returning" nutrients back to the sea. Millions of birds over millennia have created guano deposits as thick as 60 m, as in the case of the Chincha Islands off the Peruvian South Coast (Kubler 1948).

The Peruvian government annually "mines" some 5,000 tons of guano (Posner 1954: 66), continuing a long tradition that began in pre-Hispanic times and intensified in the Colonial era (e.g., Julien 1985). In southern Peru, where soil is often depleted of organic nutrients, guano doubled or even tripled maize yields during the Incaic and Colonial periods, and people traveled considerable distances to procure it (Diez de San Miguel 1964: 245; Cieza de León 1554 [1932]: 232–233). On the North Coast, where the soil is quite fertile, guano may have been used to expand cultivation to "marginal areas" of poor soil. Guano on offshore islands may well have been mined for agricultural fertilizer, as suggested by the Quechua origin of the word (wanu) and by Colonial descriptions of its late pre-Hispanic mining for agricultural use on the North Coast (Netherly 1977: 50). Further, Larco Hoyle (1944c: 13) illustrates a possible Moche III vessel believed to represent workers mining guano on an island. Kubler (1948: 40–41) went so far as to claim that "the success of the Mochica cultural pattern may have depended in part upon a technique of guano fertilization of arid coastal valleys." Guano miners had to contend with treacherous

footing, foul odors, and rock-hard deposits, as well as exposure to cold, damp winds. Mining may well have been intermittent in accordance with the agricultural calendar and demand, carried out by corvée laborers from agricultural communities that received a portion of what they mined. In spite of these lines of evidence pointing to the Mochica use of guano as agricultural fertilizer, we have no independent confirmation from studies of cultivation fields.

Guano islands were fishing/processing (salting and/or drying) bases as well as hunting grounds for penguins, seals, and sea lions, whose bones with butchering marks were excavated at Pampa Grande (Shimada and Shimada 1981: 30–31). In addition, they held considerable religious importance as a resting place for the deceased ancestors of coastal populations, as well as the setting for human sacrifices and other offerings for agricultural fertility (Hocquenghem 1987: 131; Netherly 1977: 51–53). They were sanctuaries for different "ethnic groups or social divisions" (Netherly 1977: 45; also Murphy 1925). Hocquenghem (1979; also Netherly 1977: 51–53) interprets Mochica scenes of naked "prisoners" and cargo on boats as offerings destined for the guano islands (Fig. 3.9) at the opening of the fishing season to ensure an abundance of fish and guano for crops. Three of the eight or nine Mochica-style wooden figures discovered in 1871 nearly 20 m deep in guano deposits on North Macabí Island off the Chicama Valley depict naked "prisoners" (Kubler 1948: 44). Finds from these islands include ceremonial items such as necklaces, Spondylus shells, and headless mummies.

Spondylus, Strombus, and Conus shells (Figs. 2.9, 3.10) held symbolic significance related to all-important life-giving water for both the coastal and highland inhabitants of the Central Andes before and after the Spanish Conquest (e.g., Marcos 1980; Murra 1975).[27] Paulsen (1974: 604–605), for example, emphasizes the consistent close association between Spondylus and Strombus shells and oracles since the first millennium B.C. Some Strombus shells have been found modified for use as trumpets much as they still are today in the highlands. Spondylus and Conus are rarely

Figure 3.9. Moche IV vessel with cargo and bound individuals presumably being transported to an offshore island for sacrifice. Courtesy of the National Geographic Society.

Figure 3.10. Large piles of Spondylus princeps and Conus fergusoni found in the burial chamber of a Middle Sicán (ca. A.D. 1000) shafttomb at the north base of the Huaca Loro platform mound in Batán Grande, central La Leche Valley.

Fig. 3.11). These Andean camelids,[28] as with large domesticated animals of the Old World, provided a wide range of goods and services, from meat,[29] fat, wool, bone (for making implements and ornaments, such as flutes and awls for sewing and weaving), hide, sinew (for making durable cord), and stomach stones (for ritual use). The llama was also the only reliable indigenous beast of burden (large, castrated adult males capable of carrying up to 40 kg), and they also served as sacrificial offerings (including fetuses).

The question of whether or not there were viable populations of domesticated llamas on the pre-Hispanic Peruvian coast was long a subject of debate. Opinions that drew upon Mochica ceramic depictions, scattered finds of bones and skeletons in pre-Hispanic coastal sites, and observations made at coastal zoos and similar settings varied all the way from advocacy of a separate coastal breed of short-necked llamas (Horkheimer 1961, 1973) to the theory of intermittent importation of llamas for sacrificial offerings. It was, however, analyses of large volumes of camelid bones excavated at the Moche V sites of Galindo and Pampa Grande that tipped the balance in favor of the argument for the breeding and herding of llamas on the North Coast during Moche V (if not considerably earlier). The data supporting this view, as well as major economic and organizational implications, are described in Chapter 8.

E. Unpredictable Forces and Dynamic Perception of the Environment

General environmental homogeneity on the North Coast, including limited seasonal variability, can give the false impression of a stable and static environment. However, the beneficial features of the Andean cordilleras and the Pacific Ocean are juxtaposed with a variety of largely unpredictable and catastrophic natural phenomena. The Andean cordilleras are one of the most actively evolving mountain ranges in the world and part of the enormous tectonically active circum-Pacific "Circle of Fire" (e.g., James 1973). The Andes are prone to abrupt, often severe earthquakes and volcanic eruptions, as well as gradual and accretive uplift. The Pacific's "quirks,"

found depicted in Mochica art, though some specimens have been excavated from high-status ceremonial contexts, including the tomb of the "Priest-Warrior" excavated at Sipán in the Lambayeque Valley (Alva 1988). The only definite Mochica *Spondylus* workshop excavated thus far is at Pampa Grande (see Chapter 10). *Strombus,* in contrast, is found modeled in ceramics and depicted as cargo on the backs of llamas or "monsters" in paintings on Mochica vessels (Fig. 2.9). At the same

time, actual specimens are even rarer in archaeological settings than the other two shells. How these shells may have come to possess symbolic importance is considered later.

D. Llama Breeding and Herding on the North Coast

One notable difference distinguishing the modern from the pre-Hispanic North Coast landscape is the conspicuous absence of domesticated llamas (*Lama glama;*

such as *tsunami* or tidal waves and the El Niño Countercurrent, though typically infrequent and ephemeral, have extensive impact. Other changes are gradual, widespread, and longer lasting, such as deforestation and associated erosion. For both the inhabitants and investigators it is essential to properly acknowledge the dynamic qualities of the Andean environment.

Archaeological investigations of the impact of earthquakes and volcanic eruptions on pre-Hispanic Andean cultures are sparse, in spite of their known historical occurrences. The famous 1970 earthquake that rocked northern Peru with a Richter magnitude of 7.7 was responsible for some 70,000 deaths, including the 15,000 or so inhabitants of the highland town of Yungay, which was instantaneously buried by a huge ice- and mudflow (e.g., Ericksen, Plafker, and Concha 1970). On the North Coast, the multiple simultaneous breaks seen at "choke" or stress points along sharp curves on pre-Hispanic MECs may well represent severe earthquake damage (Shimada 1981: 432). *Tsunami,* which can attain the height of a several-story building and create havoc along wide stretches of littoral zone, seem to be very rare, at least in terms of recognizable physical evidence (Bird, Hyslop, and Skinner 1985; Bird 1987). But one such wave in 1873 carried a U.S. warship 3 km inland from its anchorage off Arica in northern Chile; the remains are still there.

The El Niño is a massive body of equatorial warm water (up to 31° C) some 30 m deep, low in mineral, dissolved oxygen, plankton, and saline concentrations. It originates somewhere east or northeast of the Galapagos Islands and periodically intrudes southward (over 1,200 km) into the cold and organically rich Peru Current (see Canby 1984; Cane 1986). The Spanish name, *El Niño,* refers to the nativity child and is derived from the fact that the phenomenon appears along the Peruvian coast around Christmastime.

Although its origins are still not well understood, it is now apparent that the El Niño is only one part of a highly complex and dynamic pan-Pacific phenomenon involving interaction of oceanic currents and air masses (e.g., Cane 1986; Rasmussen and Wallace 1983; Wyrtki 1975). For example, emergence of the warm El Niño Countercurrent is correlated with the chilling of waters at the western end of the Pacific. Apparently, the El Niño does not directly drive the weather but rather acts as a catalyst for prevailing conditions.

The El Niño occurs at irregular intervals, although at times for two years in a row (as in 1941–1942 and 1957–1958), and varies enormously in strength and, to a lesser extent, in duration (see, for example, Quinn, Neal, and Antúnez 1987). Because of the southerly flow of the El Niño, the North Coast is the first area to feel its effects, as well as being the area most often and severely hit. Mild countercurrents affecting Ecuador and northern Peru occur perhaps a dozen times a century. Severe events that may occur once or twice in a century are accompanied by notable climatic anomalies that affect the entire globe; they can last two years or more. Events of even more severity, with devastating impacts, may occur once in several centuries as part of a major, long-term global climatic shift toward a drier or wetter era (e.g., ones that occurred ca. 500 B.C. and A.D. 1100). A long list of past El Niño events has been identified using historical documents (e.g., Brüning 1922; Hocquenghem and Ortlieb 1992; Nials et al. 1979a; Quinn, Neal, and Antúnez 1987 [Table 1]; Ramírez-Horton 1974).

The intrusion of El Niño is accompanied by reduced winds that disrupt the normal atmospheric inversion and create conditions favorable to deep convection offshore. Convective cells laden with moisture move inland, subjecting the arid coast to localized torrential rainfall from thunderstorms. Often the adjacent highlands also receive heavy rains. The severity of the precipitation, coupled with sparse vegetation, inevitably creates widespread flooding in coastal river valleys and mudslides in the highland valleys. Dry side-valleys become impassable major rivers. The torrential rains that beset Trujillo in 1925 were severe enough (394.4 mm during March of 1925, with 226 mm in just three days; Murphy 1926; Nials et al. 1979a) to seriously damage Chimú adobe constructions at Chan Chan that had effectively withstood the test of time for 400–500 years. During March and April of the same year, the Chancay River in the Lambayeque Valley carried an estimated 2.25 billion m³ of water[30] (Portugal 1966: 22), destroying the water diversion structure at La Puntilla across the valley neck some 2 km from the site of Pampa Grande. These floodwaters enlarged the extant Lémepe Canal to form the Reque River, the present principal drainage of the Lambayeque Valley.

The historically unprecedented 1982–1983 El Niño has been blamed for upsetting worldwide weather, causing the loss of thousands of lives and billions of dollars' worth of property. The degree of its abnormality may be gauged in various ways. For example, in Piura, in contrast to average precipitation of approximately 35 mm for January to June, the corresponding 1982–1983 figure was 2,386 mm (also see Mendoza 1985). The average temperature of water along much of the Peruvian coast during the El Niño was 8°–9° C above normal.

Although El Niño rains and floods may not last long in any one locality, local leadership and institutions may be suddenly and severely tested. Supracommunal mobilization and supervision are likely to have been involved in removal of sediment left behind, repair of severed or eroded canal sections, preparation of fields and construction of new intakes and canals. Certainly these efforts are required in the rare instances when the force of a major flood eclipses its critical threshold to breach the original channel and follow a new course. Such was the case for the Reque River in the Lambayeque Valley during the 1925 El Niño flood and for the La Leche River immediately to the north during a major flood sometime around A.D. 1050–1100 (Craig and Shimada 1986; Shimada 1981, 1990a). After the severe 1578 El Niño event that extensively damaged the historic Taymi Canal, which was the MEC of the north bank of the Lambayeque Valley, inhabitants of the community of Ferreñafe did not have potable water for over a year until the canal was repaired through intercommunal efforts (Brüning 1922: 14, 28; Netherly 1984). Until recently, pre-Hispanic flood control mechanisms and disaster management on the North Coast received little attention (Vreeland 1992). Schaedel (1992) reports the rare case of a wall that may have been built to divert floodwater away from the Chimú capital of Chan Chan. The major flash flood that damaged the Huaca del Sol sometime after Moche IV will be considered in Chapter 6.

Another long-term effect of severe El Niño floods stems from the massive quantities of sand deposited at the mouths of coastal rivers. Driven constantly inland by winds off the Pacific, these deposits may result in new sand sheets that cut off irrigation canals and bury cultivation fields. One such example is found in the lower Lambayeque Valley, perhaps dating from the flood mentioned above of ca. A.D. 1100 (Shimada 1981: 434). In essence, a severe El Niño can create serious, if not long-term, problems for North Coast agriculturalists (see discussion below).

At the same time, the nature and extent of physical damage from El Niño–related rains and floods can be quite localized and, depending on local hydrology, one may see a juxtaposition of highly contrasting effects within a small region. Thus, without precise dating, it is difficult to attribute water damage in different coastal valleys to the same El Niño event (see Craig and Shimada 1986; DeVries 1987; Shimada 1990a; Wells 1987).

El Niño incursions also lead to the temporary disappearance and massive death of cold-water marine organisms. Mochica fishermen probably did not suffer to the same extent from El Niño events because of their more diversified exploitation pattern. However, species better adapted to warm water (e.g., yellowfin tuna, skipjack tuna, dolphinfish, tropical crab) soon move in to replace cold water species. During the 1982–1983 events, inhabitants of Lima were "treated" to an abundance of octopus and scallops, which were sometimes even given away free. Thus, after initial shock and confusion, there can be some dietary relief and perhaps adventure.

How cultural activities contribute to and sometimes cause deforestation is well known and documented throughout the world. Cieza de León (1554 [1984] Ch. LXVII: 204–205), who traveled throughout the former domain of the Inca Empire shortly after its downfall, marveled at the lush green forests of the contiguous valleys of Túcume (south bank of La Leche Valley)

and Cinto (north bank of Lambayeque Valley) and the abundance and diversity of wildlife. By the mid-nineteenth century, T. J. Hutchinson (1873: 220) lamented how the extensive forests of indigenous trees in Lambayeque were being depleted to make charcoal fuel for the growing demands of Lima residents. Based on her archival study, Rostworowski (1981: 15, 55–66) shows that this problem of deforestation was much more widespread on the Peruvian coast and stemmed from the Spaniards' predilection for coastal living.[31] She argues that the delicate coastal ecosystem has been consequently disturbed, resulting in desertification and loss of cultivable lands.

On the pre-Hispanic North Coast, indigenous *algarrobo, faique,* and *zapote* trees were extensively used. For example, a four- to five-room Mochica house reconstructed from excavated structural remains and modeled ceramic vessels (Fig. 3.12) is estimated to have required over two dozen *algarrobo* trunks for columns and beams. Primitive copper smelting of the sort the Mochica are believed to have carried out would have consumed an amount of charcoal fuel several times greater in weight than that of ore (see Chapter 8); if we add the fuel consumed in preheating furnaces, remelting to purify and consolidate copper, and heating for hammering and forging, production of a copper implement weighing one kilogram might have consumed as much as 25–30 kg of hardwood charcoal (Shimada 1985c, 1987b; Tylecote and Boydell 1978). The biggest consumer of hardwood fuel, however, would have been the estimated two thousand households within the city of Pampa Grande using it for cooking and heating. The urban population could have easily consumed two to three tons of hardwood fuel per day.

It is apparent that present forest coverage and associated wild fauna on the Peruvian coast have been significantly reduced in extent and number relative to preceding eras. At the same time, the argument that the pre-Hispanic inhabitants were more in harmony with their environment and consciously moderated their use of forest resources (e.g., Rostworowski 1981: 15) needs much more empirical support. We suspect that prior to the arrival of the

Figure 3.11. Drawing of a Moche I stirrup-spout bottle representing a llama carrying jars in a saddlebag. Based on an unnumbered photo in Donnan 1990: 18.

Spaniards there was a good deal of fluctuation in the extent of forest cover in response to changes in precipitation, agricultural practices, demography, and intensity of construction activities and large-scale metallurgical and ceramic production.

The last environmental change considered here is tectonic activity with extensive, long-term impacts. Although the cultural significance of the phenomenon has only recently been fully appreciated, relevant observations existed as far back as the mid-nineteenth century when Charles Darwin described a tectonically uplifted riverbed in Casma (North Coast) that caused the gradient to slope "uphill" in a downstream direction (Darwin 1962: 326). In the preceding chapter, we noted the significant reduction in cultivated land on much of the North Coast since the inferred pre-Hispanic maximum. A recent series of publications has presented a forceful argument that the primary cause for this reduction is uplift along the Peruvian continental margin related to high levels of tectonic activity in the Andes (e.g., Moseley 1983b; Moseley et al. 1983; Moseley, Feldman, and Ortloff 1981); more specifically, changes in ground slope led to river downcutting, leaving canal intakes stranded above the entrenched stream channels. Lowering of the water table is seen as another major consequence. Although the preceding situation may be remedied by reworking the intakes, it is believed that "bedrock obstacles in the valley necks [where the intakes for many MECs are situated] eventually curtail recutting, leading to . . . channel abandonment" (Moseley et al. 1983: 301). Thus, new intakes have to be established farther downstream, decreasing the amount of land that may be irrigated.

Concurrently, displacement along geological faults affects irrigation canal gradients, thereby restricting or even stopping water flow to the more distal reaches (Ortloff, Feldman, and Moseley 1985; Ortloff, Moseley, and Feldman 1983). In response, extant channels may be modified or simply abandoned, and new courses and channels may be constructed (Fig. 3.13). A secondary contributory process is believed to be erosional downcutting by flash floods

caused by rare torrential rains accompanying El Niño intrusions.

Uplift also exposes sand beds that were once under water. Though they move gradually, active sand sheets and dunes are formidable natural forces that are difficult to stabilize. They bury agricultural fields, canals, and settlements in their path, as can be seen clearly along the south margin of the Moche (e.g., around Cerros Blanco and Arena) and the Jequetepeque (Puémape, Jatanca, and Cañoncillo areas) valleys. One of the world's largest active dunes, El Pur Pur (measuring over 50 m high and 1 km across), situated between the Moche and Virú valleys to the south, is gradually but steadily encroaching on the Pan-American Highway.

These studies in the Moche Valley have established a long sequence of geophysical events and processes from ca. 1500 B.C. to the present. For the span of the Mochica culture, the studies point to a major episode of coastal uplift, perhaps of 3–6 m, around the time of Christ, with some degree of sand sheet intrusion inland, followed by a major episode of El Niño–related flash flooding and river cutting late in Moche IV (Moseley and Deeds 1982; Moseley, Feldman, and Ortloff 1981; Moseley 1987). By ca. A.D. 600 (about the beginning of Moche V) downcutting by the Moche River, which eventually reduced the total extent of irrigation, is believed to have reached some 15 km inland approaching the valley neck (Moseley and Deeds 1982). Sometime between A.D. 500 and 1100, there was at least one major El Niño–related flood.

The above studies offer a plausible alternative explanation for the significant reduction in cultivation fields, challenging conventional theories that invoke major depopulation and population resettlement such as is seen in the Incaic and Colonial eras. The efficacy of this model relative to the environmental explanation based on inferred fluctuations in precipitation remains to be explored. The latter model argues that the expansion and shrinkage of cultivation area were largely conditioned by variability in the highland precipitation that feeds coastal rivers (see Chapter 5).

Deforestation stemming from human activities noted earlier is likely to have in-

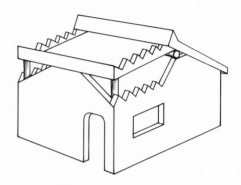

Figure 3.12. Drawing of a Mochica house based on Mochica architectural vessels.

creased the rate and extent of erosion. Half a century ago, Kroeber (1930: 57) noted that large seaward portions of North Coast valleys with evidence of pre-Hispanic occupation and cultivation were now barren or uncultivated. He suggested the water once distributed throughout the valley had been disproportionately consumed by Colonial and modern, commercial cultivation of sugarcane and rice. Certainly, sugarcane requires much water throughout its eighteen- to twenty-four-month growing period. Intense sugarcane cultivation began in the second half of the seventeenth century and now occupies over 40 percent of cultivated land in the Lambayeque region (Table 4; Ramírez-Horton 1974: 9; Shimada 1976: 45). Pumping of groundwater on a 24-hour basis during the dry months of July through November has lowered the water table as well. It is quite likely that these activities have contributed to the observed situation along with the recorded uplift.

Whatever the cause(s), it is understandable that the major sugarcane-producing agricultural cooperatives (which were landed estates before 1969) are typically situated close to the apex of the triangular-shaped valley bottomland, with ready access to fresh irrigation water and the thickest and most fertile alluvium (Ramírez-Horton 1974: 7, 9). In support of this observation, Kroeber (1930: 57) noted that on the South Coast, where cotton or grapes have largely replaced sugar as the main commercial crop, "there has been less abandonment of the seaward parts of valleys."

The geo-archaeological studies considered in this section have refined our understanding of the dynamic qualities of Andean environment and life. Yet it is quite apparent that we need more detailed studies to clarify regional differences in the magnitude, extent, timing, and nature of geophysical processes and events. Similarly, their cultural significance is difficult to determine in part due to imprecise dating and uncertainties about the rate of occurrence, orientation, and extent, not to mention our conflicting views on the relative merits of social versus physical explanations.

For example, in regard to the effect and extent of coastal uplift, we should be aware that "the net displacement we now see of hundreds of meters is an accumulation of many small events, not all being positive and upwards, often involving tilting and seldom occurring at the same rate, even for adjacent sites" (Craig 1984: 63). In fact, a notable contrast to the Moche Valley situation is seen in the Lambayeque Valley, where the Chancay-Reque River has a low gradient and there is no evidence of significant uplift at its mouth (Shimada 1981: 434). Further, the Taymi Canal, MEC of the north bank of the Lambayeque Valley, has retained the same wide "angle of reach" formed by the canal and river (approximating the theoretical maximum of 90°; Figs. 3.1, 3.4) and roughly the same intake point over the past 1,500 years or more.

Another case in point is the ongoing debate surrounding the effectiveness and abandonment of the pre-Hispanic La Cumbre Canal constructed to bring water from the Chicama River to the vicinity of the city of Chan Chan in the Moche Valley.

Figure 3.13. Airphoto showing parallel channels of the Antigua Jayanca Canal as it negotiates around the base of the western spur of Cerro Zurita, La Leche Valley. Though the canal is post-Mochica, these channels were probably dug to deal with problems such as flood damage, expanding cultivation fields, and perhaps even localized tectonic movement. Courtesy of the Servicio Aerofotográfico Nacional del Perú.

Table 4. Variety of crops cultivated today in the Lambayeque Valley and their hectarage. Taken from Table 4 in Shimada 1976: 45.

Crops	Surface	Percentage
Sugar Cane	28,886.26	40.78
Almacigo Rice	1,129.32	1.59
Transplanted Rice	15,811.34	22.32
Cotton	4,558.65	6.44
Pasture	5,387.57	7.61
Hybrid Corn	2,309.69	3.26
Indian Corn	3,105.59	4.38
Moquegua Beans	4,588.50	6.48
White Beans	253.34	0.36
Chileno Beans	34.48	0.05
Loctao	1,207.92	1.70
Broom Sorghum	118.16	0.17
Grain Sorghum	244.86	0.35
Peas	125.43	0.18
Chickpeas	1,181.10	1.67
Sweet Potato	175.31	0.25
Yuca	519.28	0.73
Tomato	258.51	0.36
Chili	88.61	0.13
Vegetables	348.67	0.49
Fruits	305.77	0.43
Tobacco	16.00	0.02
Flowers	33.66	0.05
Mint	10.00	0.01
Forestal	99.00	0.14
Soy	8.00	0.01
Barley	25.00	0.04
TOTAL	70,830.02	100.00

Competing views range from human error and technological inadequacies to changes in canal gradients stemming from tectonic activity (e.g., Farrington 1983; Ortloff, Moseley, and Feldman 1983; Pozorski and Pozorski 1982).

F. Creative Cultural Solutions to Environmental Limitations

The above section discussed the environmental potential and limitations of the North Coast and broader Central Andes, and illustrated how past and present inhabitants have dealt with them. Here, we further explore their solutions to environmental limitations and stresses.

Even El Niño floods are put to productive use. For example, thorough soaking of the normally arid coast during the 1982–1983 event blanketed the landscape with lush, impassable dense foliage. An enormous freshwater lake emerged in the Sechura Desert (see Mendoza 1985), providing a temporary home for an impressive array of waterfowl foreign to the local people. The desert became a gigantic pasture, and even farmers from the adjacent highlands brought down their animals to take advantage of the situation. Farmers of Mórrope (in the semidesert landscape of the northwestern Lambayeque Valley) were able to create short-term cultivation plots in rain-soaked higher lands for the direct sowing of indigenous crops. They gained a good harvest of a wide range of food crops such as maize, sweet potato, pumpkin, watermelon, and gourd. The cultivation technique most likely dates from the pre-Hispanic era. Their situation contrasts markedly with the devastating losses of other communities that relied on introduced crops and modern Western agricultural technology (Vreeland 1985, 1986a). Other traditional North Coast farmers elsewhere successfully planted and harvested crops in "marginal lands" higher up the valley and on mountain slopes, partially offsetting lost productivity in their normal cultivation fields (Collin 1984). Most likely, Mochica farmers similarly took advantage of some effects of ancient El Niño events. Floods also rejuvenate agricultural lands by depositing fresh alluvium and are important in reforestation of the coast. *Algarrobo* seeds depend on such thorough soaking to germinate; only when plants are established can their deep roots effectively tap underground moisture.

The 1982–1983 flood also had some interesting effects in revitalizing traditional agricultural and other subsistence-related techniques and technology. With the abundance of water and fish, traditional casting nets made with indigenous cotton once again became popular in various North Coast communities. Likewise, traditional reed fish traps set at the ends of V-shaped artificial channels came back in use (Vreeland 1986a).

Even the sand dunes and sand sheets so common on the North Coast can be used in productive manners. Eling (1987: 165) describes how modern residents of Jequetepeque Valley "still bury sacks of rice and other grains at least 20 cm deep in the sand around their houses" to protect them from insects or rodents. In earlier times storage was communal, with entire harvests stored in sand drifts while waiting for prices to rise. Eling (ibid.) suggests that "The paucity of pre-Hispanic *depositos* (storage buildings) in the valley may be attributed to this unique ubiquitous insect free underground sand storage facility." The traditional (perhaps pre-Hispanic) technique of planting or encouraging indigenous trees and shrubs such as *algarrobo, zapote,* and *chope* (*Cripto carpus piriphormis*) is effectively used to stabilize sand dunes.

In regard to heavy demand for hardwood fuel, it is likely that the Mochica alleviated this problem in part by utilizing llama dung as a fuel.[32] Llamas have a common voidance behavior, and at Moche V Pampa Grande and Galindo their dung may have been readily collected in corrals located toward the edges of the settlements. Deposits of ash with traces of a plant fiber-like substance found in kitchens, construction fill, and even in an inferred masonry ceramic kiln (in Sector D; see Chapter 8) at Pampa Grande appear to be burnt llama dung. Unburnt dung is frequently found in architectural fill, suggesting that dung as a fuel source was not exhausted.

Another pre-Hispanic solution appears to have been the conscious culling of branches. Preserved hardwood charcoal in ceramic kilns and smelting furnaces of various periods show small diameters of branches (Shimada and Merkel 1991; Shimada, Elera, and Chang 1990).

Yet another environmental problem is fluctuations in the discharge volumes of coastal rivers. Under normal conditions, there is practically no independent source of water on the coast, and the extent of cultivation is largely determined by the minimal discharge available. Though the North Coast is blessed with major perennial rivers and other key natural factors that allow for large-scale irrigation agriculture, water is always scarce; there is more cultivable land than water for its cultivation. In short, there is constant pressure to make a productive use of limited water.

One effective solution is "sunken gardens," variously known as *pukios, mahamas, huachaques,* or *hoyas,* in which the cultivation surface is lowered toward the water table by digging large depressions.[33] *Pukios* can be established well outside of irrigated areas as long as there is a relatively high, stable water table. They are commonly found in the natural topographic lows (mostly in the lower valleys and side valleys or *quebradas*) and along major waterways, allowing expansion of cultivable area. In other areas, this cultivation technique depends on a high water table that is in part maintained by intensive irrigation upstream (also see Day 1974). Perhaps the most important aspect of this technique is that it is less affected by seasonal variation in river water, extending the cultivation into the dry season (June–September) and thereby allowing continuous cropping throughout the year. Their excavation also serves to remove salt-contaminated surface soil and potentially provides soil for adobe brick making. *Pukios* are widespread along the Peruvian coast, at least from the Chicama Valley on the North Coast to the Ica on the South Coast. In contrast to the widespread opinion that sunken-field agriculture developed in late pre-Hispanic times and had only limited productive potential (e.g., Moseley 1969; Parsons and Psuty 1975), this technique was widely in use in the Virú Valley during the Puerto Moorin Phase that preceded the Moche III intrusion (West 1979, 1981).

Related to the above is the widespread practice of floodplain cultivation, particularly along seasonal or low-discharge rivers. Today local farmers extensively utilize the fertile soil of the floodplain along much of the middle portion of the La Leche River to grow one crop per year, even with the risk of its being washed away.

Another indigenous solution to water scarcity is the use of dispersed "holding ponds" or small reservoirs surrounded by cultivation plots to allow maximum and efficient local control of water use and distribution while reducing water loss during transport (Vreeland 1986a).

The main Mochica canals of the Moche and Virú valleys were situated high and closely followed natural contours to maximize the extent of irrigated fields.[34] In general these canals seem to have been established during the Gallinazo period when the maximum extent of pre-Hispanic cultivation was achieved (Moseley and Deeds 1982; Willey 1953). Mochica canals were gravity-fed; pumps or siphons were not known prior to the Colonial era. Neither artificial channelization of rivers nor the type of large-scale landscaping carried out by the Inca in and around Cusco was known on the North Coast.

Mochica canals do show certain features aimed at maintaining the proper gradient in broken terrain. For example, Eling (1978, 1987: 458; also Kosok 1965: 139) reports that an inferred late Mochica (A.D. 500–750) aqueduct (standing up to 7.5 m) of the Pampa de Cerro Colorado irrigation system on the north bank of the Jequetepeque Valley can be traced for some 10 km toward the Zaña Valley to the north.

The best-known such feature is the Ascope aqueduct on the north bank of the Chicama Valley. Kosok (1942) reported the aqueduct as 760 m in length, 12 m in height, and roughly the same in width. Mason (1968: 76) described it as having a total length of 1,400 m, a height of 15 m, and a bulk of 785,000 m³ of largely clay and adobe fill. Watson (1979: 175) emphasized that the aqueduct was only a small part of an "equally impressive irrigation system" whose main canal extended for a distance of some 45 km. Contrary to conventional opinion (e.g., Larco 1946: 162–163; Lumbreras 1974: 102), Watson (1979: 175) argued that the aqueduct in its present form probably dates to the late Middle Horizon or Late Intermediate Period. He suggested

(1979: 176) that a buried earlier canal may be of Mochica origin.

Yet another solution to maximizing limited water would have been the use of reservoirs to store excess water during floods or periods of high river discharge for release during the periods of low discharge or during the critical period of flowering and fruiting (Rodríguez 1970: 18). For example, a "reservoir" (3.4 km long and 1.0 km wide) at the east base of Cerro Ventarrón with Moche IV–V occupation in the mid-Lambayeque Valley fills up whenever water eclipses the bank of the adjacent Reque River. Though the river was a secondary drainage prior to the 1925 floods (Petersen 1956: 305), it could well have functioned the same way in Mochica times. Eling (1978) reported on dammed *quebradas* in the Jequetepeque Valley filled with canal water from the upper end. Lumbreras (1974: 102) refers to the "reservoir of San José" as "an outstanding example of Moche engineering," and Rodríguez (1970: 18) describes a number of prehistoric reservoirs of uncertain date in the Moche Valley.

Based on the relatively small size of pre-Hispanic reservoirs, Farrington (1974: 84) argues that water storage did not play an important role in ancient North Coast agriculture. Eling (1986: 141) concurs, noting that coastal reservoirs are constructed in the middle of the canal system and would have been rapidly depleted if used for irrigation. Instead, he argues for the importance of natural lakes as a possible pre-Hispanic coastal water source in the Jequetepeque Valley. Such lakes may have been formed by blocking of El Niño floodwaters or of natural drainages by sand dunes and uplifted terrain. Such lakes would have kept local water tables high.

Other expected responses to the pervasive problem of water shortage and the desire to maximize agricultural production include developing crop varieties more resistant to aridity, improving soil quality, and more effective pest control (Vreeland 1986a). We have already considered possible Mochica use of guano. In regard to crop varieties, pollen studies have provided little useful data, in part because the rains accompanying El Niño events, though rare, create an alternating cycle of wet and dry periods, unfavorable for preservation of plants and pollens. For example, analysis of soil samples from buried furrows near Huaca Soledad in the central La Leche Valley found that most of the pollen had been degraded (J. Jones, pers. com. 1991; cf. Weir and Eling 1986).

Though these solutions were probably effective in coping with short-term or minor deviations in the coastal water supply, it is doubtful they were effective against long-term or major deviations. Reliable, concrete evidence that the Mochica were subjected to severe, prolonged droughts in the sixth century emerged from a recent multidisciplinary study described in Chapter 6.

Creative solutions to the potentials and limitations of the North Coast environment must also be considered at a higher organizational level. The North Coast as a whole may be characterized by a rather homogeneous environment and repetitiveness in resources. It is argued here that this condition is partly responsible for the emergence and persistence of the principle of occupational specialization on the North Coast respected by the Chimú and the Inca. Ethnohistorians (e.g., Netherly 1977; Ramírez-Horton 1981; Rostworowski 1975) have shown that populations were organized into *parcialidades* or subdivisions by economic speciality (e.g., fishermen, metalsmiths, potters, and saltmakers; see Table 5) that resided in separate communities. In essence, occupational specialization is seen to have been a cultural means for broadening the coastal "resource" base (used here in the broadest sense) while stimulating greater regional economic interaction and interdependence (see Chapter 7).

At an even higher organizational level, the Mochicas' impressive coastwise expansion, both on land and offshore—up to a 600-km stretch from the upper Piura to the Huarmey Valley—may be seen as a conscious, concerted effort to gain access and control of diverse resources without incursion into the adjacent highlands. In other words, the impressive "horizontality" in effect is the "verticality" scheme applied to the coastal environment (see Chapter 5).

G. Highland Rains and Coastal Water

The preceding section emphasized that coastal irrigation agriculture is almost totally dependent on water carried down by rivers draining the adjacent highlands, a fact of the utmost importance to the basic tenets of this book.

Much of the Peruvian Andes is under the same tropical meteorological regime, with the southeast trade winds and equatorial easterlies dominating the windflow (Johnson 1976; Fig. 3.14). Seasonal variation is brought about by the annual southward and northward migration of the equatorial trough. Along much of the extent of the Peruvian Andes, there is only one pronounced wet season, occurring during the southern summer (November–April), when the prevailing easterlies, carrying moisture from vast Amazonia high up into the highlands, interact with the equatorial trough (Johnson 1976: 154). The dry season occurs during the southern winter (May–October). In the central and southern portions of the Peruvian Andes, most of this moisture is filtered off by the high windward escarpment of the eastern cordillera, and little falls as precipitation on the western slopes. In northern Peru, where the eastern cordillera is lower and more broken up, the western cordillera (the source of coastal rivers) acts as the major barrier to vapor-laden winds off the Amazon Basin. In both cases, the basic source of Peruvian highland precipitation is the same moisture-bearing equatorial easterlies from Amazonia. The situation changes significantly as one moves close to the equator (far north Peru and Ecuador), where two wet seasons and two dry seasons occur as the equatorial trough moves northward and later southward during the year (Fig. 3.14). The high *altiplano* south of the latitude of 15° south (Titicaca Basin, far south Peru, northern Chile, northwest Argentina, and western Bolivia), on the other hand, receives noticeably less annual rainfall than the Peruvian Andes north of this latitude.

In sum, in the absence of rare El Niño–related torrential rains, coastal irrigation agriculture is totally dependent on regular seasonal rainfall in the adjacent highlands, and thus any significant disruption of this

Table 5. List of specialists mentioned in early colonial documents. Taken from Table 1 in Ramírez-Horton 1982: 125.

Specialists	Túcume	Jayanca	Collique	Pacasmayo	Saña	Sinto	Unknown
Albañiles (bricklayers)		n.d.	1566				
Cabesteros (halter makers)		1566					
Carpinteros (carpenters)	1573	1566	1566				
Cocineros (cooks)	1566		1530's	1582		pre-1532	
Cumbicos (fine clothmakers)		1566					
Chicheros (*chicha* brewers)	1560	1540	1566		1566		
Estereros/Petateros (mat makers)		1739	1611		1549	1566	1566
Hacheros/Leñadores (woodcutters)		1540					
Hamaqueros (litter bearers)		1566	1530's		1566	pre-1532	
Huseros (spindle-whorl makers)	1566	1566					1566
Mercaderes (exchange specialists)	1560	1563	1566			1566	
Olleros (potters)	1566	1540	1566	1566		1566	
Ovejeros/Pastores (shepherds)		1540		1582		1566	
Pescadores (fishers)	1541	1540	1565	1566	1549	1566	
Pintores (de mantas) (cloth painters)	1558	1566	1558			1566	
Plateros (silversmiths)	n.d.	1566	1566			1566	
Roperos (clothes keepers)		1566				1566	
Salineros (saltmakers)	1566	n.d.			1549	n.d.	
Sapateros/Alpargateros (sandalmakers)	1566	1566					
Sastres (tailors)		1566					
Silleros (saddlers or chair/throne makers)	1566				1549	1751	
Tejedores (weavers)	1576	1540	1582			pre-1532	
Tintoreros (dyers)	1566	1566					
Venaderos (deer hunters)	1566						

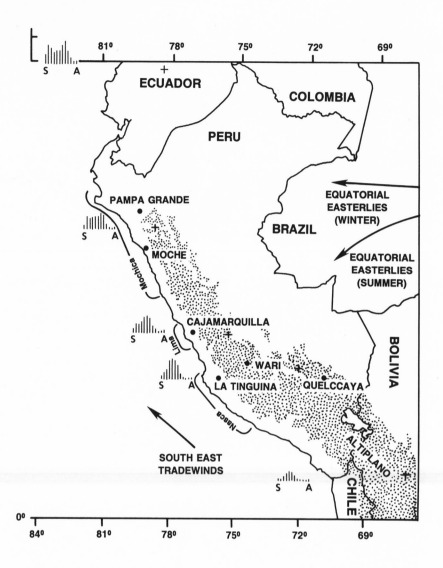

Figure 3.14. Map showing the direction of the trade winds that largely dictate precipitation patterns in the Central Andes and the locations of the Quelccaya ice cap and key archaeological sites relevant to the discussion of sixth-century droughts. Average annual rainfall at five highland sites (indicated by crosses; north to south Quito, Ecuador; Cajamarca, Huancayo, and Cuzco, Peru; and Oruro, Bolivia) is depicted by bar charts on a 200-mm scale running from September to August. The rainfall peaks show the double wet season of the equator, the low amounts of the *altiplano* wet season, the migration of the equatorial trough, and the wet season at three Peruvian locations. Topography is delineated at 2000 m. Courtesy of Crystal B. Schaaf.

pattern has immediate and widespread adverse effects on coastal populations.

3. The North Coast: A Summary Characterization

On the basis of the above data and observations we can now offer a culturally meaningful characterization of the natural environment of the North Coast of Peru, the Mochica homeland.

The twelve valleys that form the North Coast are drained by most of the largest (out of about forty) perennial rivers along the 2,400-km Peruvian coast (Table 3). The northern and southern ends are defined, respectively, by the extensive Sechura Desert and a stretch about 60 km long of numerous active sand dunes and rugged

mountains that come right down to the Pacific just south of the Casma Valley. Although the western cordillera of the Andes is a formidable physical barrier to coast-highland communication, the Casma Valley, much like the Jequetepeque to the north, provides a natural corridor linking these two areas.

The North Coast, with its tremendous economic and demographic potential, has seen the successive evolution of the powerful autonomous Mochica, Sicán, and Chimú polities, among others. This potential, as we saw above, was based on year-round access to abundant, renewable marine resources and to a set of factors that favored large-scale irrigation agriculture: perennial rivers with high annual volume and high minimum discharge, and receding Andean foothills that helped to create extensive, fertile, low-gradient alluvial plains.

Another environment, the cis-Andean *yunga*, was critical for its mineral and plant resources, as well as for the principal intakes for the coastal MECs, and was therefore a source of contention among coastal and highland populations.

Though there is no sure way of determining the pre-Hispanic language(s) of the North Coast, skeletal remains of ancient inhabitants suggest strong biological continuity in the area into the historical era (see, e.g., Larco 1939; Newman 1948; Stewart 1973).

Climatically the North Coast is blessed with abundant sun and warmth for much of the year in part due to its proximity to the equator, while the cold Peru Current stabilizes and moderates daily and annual temperature variation to a comfortable range. The upwelling nature of the current supports an immensely rich marine biotic community that can be exploited close to the shore on a year-round basis typically with simple technology and organization.

Though on a general level the North Coast environment may appear homogeneous, there is a surprisingly wide range of natural resources available to establish and maintain a high degree of economic self-sufficiency that neighboring highland polities could not hope to achieve. The agricultural, forestal, mineral, and marine riches described above were supplemented by additional resources secured by colonists outside the North Coast (Chapter 4). Thus, the more than six hundred years of Mochica cultural continuity seem to have been based largely on full exploitation of favorable natural conditions, effectively complemented by cultural strategies such as large-scale llama herding and breeding and the establishment of far-flung colonies. Locally bred and herded llamas (at least for Moche V) gave even greater stability to the economy and provided overland transport to complement marine routes.

Pre-Hispanic North Coast life was, however, by no means utopian. Its northerly latitude meant it suffered from the full impact of El Niño events. The highly specialized arid desert ecology was susceptible to short- and long-term disturbances that were sometimes irreversible.

Major ecological boundaries often coincide with cultural or ethnic boundaries. Murra (1984) argues that the extent to which the Central Andean people were able to make something positive out of a seemingly limited tropical alpine environment (e.g., "freeze-dry" food processing and the *puna* as a natural refrigerator for large-scale food storage [Morris 1981]) was crucial to the rise of highland Andean civilization. In fact, Troll (1958) and others have shown a strong correlation between the territorial extent of the Inca Empire and the *puna* zone, which supported large herds of alpacas and llamas and intensive tuber cultivation.

A similar correlation with environmental features can be discerned for the Mochica territory. With the exception of the small Chao, river valleys within its domain are quite fertile and extensive, with even, gradual gradients allowing intensive irrigation agriculture. Though annual precipitation on the cis-Andean slope anywhere along the Peruvian coast in normal years is very light, an east-west line through the Huarmey area (ca. 10° south latitude) is a prominent natural frontier. North of this line, precipitation occurs during the summer months (January–April), while south of this line precipitation is in the winter, mostly in the form of drizzle and fog with no precipitation in the summer. This north-south dichotomy is reflected in the distribution of *loma* vegetation, which depends on moisture from fog condensation.

The line through Huarmey marks other environmental changes as well. Offshore, the continental shelf dramatically broadens between 9° and 10° south latitude; the contour line 200 m below the surface widens from 40–50 km to over 100 km. This change, together with the large discharge of mineral nutrients by the Santa River (which drains the entire intermontane basin of Callejón de Huaylas), is important in sustaining the large fish population found along this particular stretch of the Peruvian coast. The port of Chimbote, well within the Mochica territory, is indeed strategically situated in this regard.

On land, the line coincides with one of the major ecological and topographical frontiers along the north-south axis of the Andes. It marks the southern end of the elongated, fertile intermontane basin of Callejón de Huaylas and the great Marañon River drainage formed by the three north-south running parallel mountain ranges (Figs. 1.1, 1.2). To the south stretches the extensive *puna* or short grassland, while to the north one finds *jalca*. In terms of both north-south and east-west movement, Huarmey is a strategic location.

The northern frontier of Mochica territory appears to have been Cerro Vicús in the upper Piura Valley, where Mochica-style metal and ceramic objects of excellent craftsmanship have been discovered from looted graves. Although in traditional thinking the difficulty of traversing the extensive Sechura Desert has been emphasized, communication between the Vicús region and the La Leche Valley could have been effectively maintained via a prehistoric inland road that passed through Olmos, Salitral, and Buenos Aires in the upper reaches of the Piura River, just as the Inca coastal trunk road did and the Pan-American Highway does today.

Inland, the Mochica reached the necks of coastal valleys and competed with the neighboring highland Cajamarca and Recuay cultures for control of the *yunga*. To the west, offshore islands were important to the Mochica as ritual settings and for guano mines and fishing.

Overall, Mochica territory encompassed a large enough area to enable access to a wide range of resources and the attainment of economic self-sufficiency, while remaining within an area that shared certain basic environmental common denominators.

4. The Lambayeque Valley Complex, the Moche V Heartland

Some of the crucial features of the North Coast are present in a much more accentuated form on the northern North Coast, composed of the five contiguous valleys between the Motupe and Jequetepeque, inclusive. In fact, over half a century ago, A. L. Kroeber (1930: 55–57) recognized that the northern North Coast possessed architectural, linguistic, and environmental unity, plus characteristics sufficiently different from the remaining valleys of the

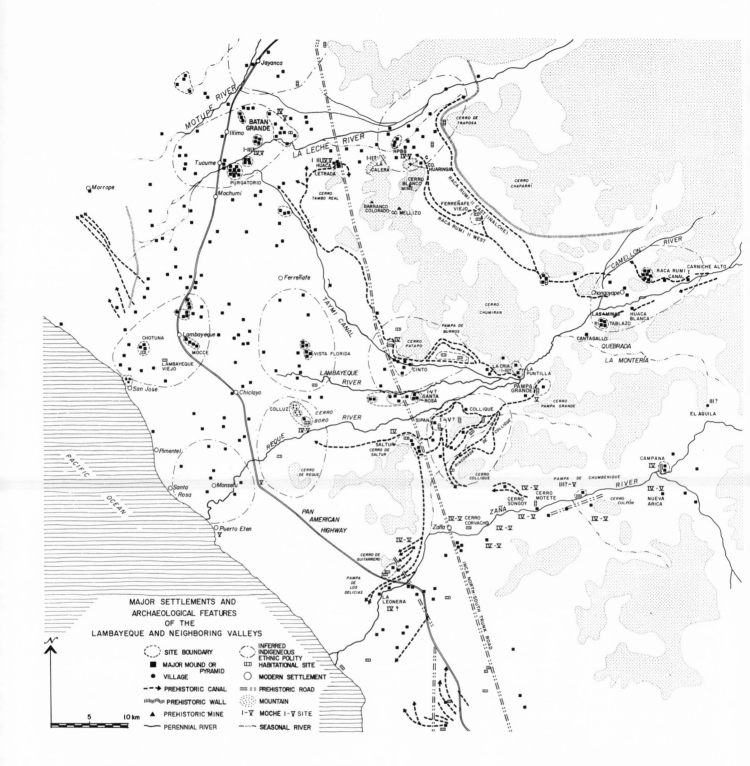

MAJOR SETTLEMENTS AND
ARCHAEOLOGICAL FEATURES
OF THE
LAMBAYEQUE AND NEIGHBORING VALLEYS

N

⊃ SITE BOUNDARY
■ MAJOR MOUND OR PYRAMID
● VILLAGE
---→ PREHISTORIC CANAL
⊪⊪⊪⊪⊪ PREHISTORIC WALL
▲ PREHISTORIC MINE
— PERENNIAL RIVER

⊃ INFERRED INDIGENEOUS ETHNIC POLITY
▥ HABITATIONAL SITE
○ MODERN SETTLEMENT
⣿ PREHISTORIC ROAD
⣿ MOUNTAIN
I–V MOCHE I–V SITE
---- SEASONAL RIVER

5   10 km

Figure 3.15. Map of the Lambayeque Valley
Complex with major pre-Hispanic canals,
sites, and roads. I–V indicate Moche phases.
Revised from an unpublished map by Paul
Kosok in the possession of Richard P.
Schaedel.

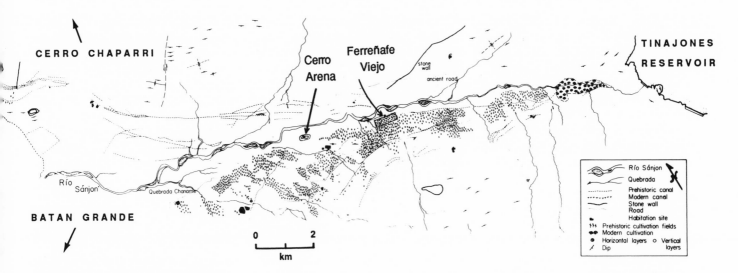

Figure 3.16. Pre-Hispanic Raca Rumi Canal and associated cultivation fields and settlements in Pampa de Chaparrí, which links the upper La Leche and Lambayeque (Chancay) valleys. Cerro de Arena has occupation spanning at least Moche V to Sicán-Inca. The main south branch of the canal carried water to Gallinazo and later settlements along the south margin of the mid–La Leche Valley. Drawn from airphoto mosaics and verified in the field by Alan K. Craig.

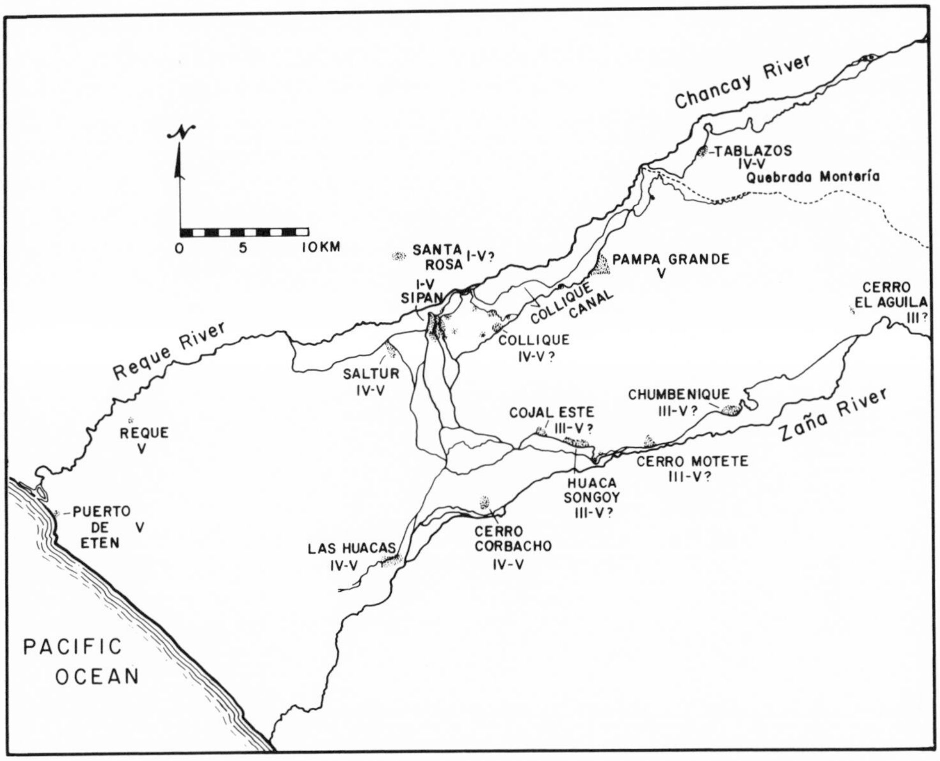

Figure 3.17. "Late Mochica" (primarily Phases IV and V) settlement and irrigation system on the south bank of the Lambayeque Valley and north bank of the adjacent Zaña Valley based on detailed surface survey and test excavations conducted by James Nolan and, to a lesser extent, the author's surface survey. Modified from Fig. 5 in Nolan 1980: 83.

North Coast to distinguish it as a geo-cultural unit.

The northern North Coast shows a significant departure from the "central and south Peruvian conditions of precipitation and valley separation" (Fig. 3.15; Kroeber 1930: 56). The southern North Coast valleys are clearly separated from each other or circumscribed and thus "still typically Peruvian" (ibid.). Those of the Northern Sector are less clearly demarcated as the mountains recede considerably further inland. Consider the necks of the Lambayeque and Moche valleys, which are situated some 50 km and 18 km inland, respectively. In Kroeber's own words (1930: 56), the "Jequetepeque is separated from the [Z]aña and this from the Lambayeque by only low swells of desert, and the plain of the Lambayeque runs imperceptibly into that of the Leche. The intensive cultivation is farther and farther from the sea to the north." The Jequetepeque Valley, which Kroeber (1930: 56; also see Kosok 1965) regarded as belonging to the Northern Sector, displays a "somewhat transitional" character as well in terms of artifact remains. This is undoubtedly due in part to the fact that the valley is a major natural corridor that probably facilitated contact between contemporaneous Mochica and Cajamarca (North Highland) cultures.

There is more record of significant rainfall in the Northern than Southern Sector due to greater proximity to the equator. Even a weak El Niño event is likely to leave some imprint in the Northern Sector, a fact dramatically reflected in regional ruins, "which are more washed and torn into gaps the more northerly they lie" (Kroeber 1930: 56).

Linguistically, several Colonial sources mention that the people of the Northern Sector spoke a dialect of *Muchik* or Mochica (called *Yunga*) distinct from that of the Southern Sector (Calancha 1638 [1976]; Rabinowitz 1983; Rivet 1949). The dialect is essentially extinct today, though early this century Brüning (1922; also see Schaedel 1988) and Kosok (1965), among others, recorded *Muchik* words from old-timers who still had partial command of the language.

Architecturally, Kroeber (1930: 63) observed that adobe platform mounds in the Northern Sector stand free either within cultivation fields or on the plains just outside, as opposed to being built against the sides or on the summits of hills, the predominant pattern in the Southern Sector. In addition, he noted steep sides, long zigzag ramps, and the frequent use of refuse-filled chambers as characteristic of northern mounds (see Schaedel 1951a,b; Shimada and Cavallaro 1986, in press).

The Northern Sector is also known as the Lambayeque Valley Complex, a name derived from the fact that the five constituent valleys were integrated into a single intervalley irrigation system, encompassing roughly a third of the total population and cultivable land on the Peruvian coast during its inferred maximum extent ca. A.D. 1000–1200 (Kosok 1959: 64, 1965: 147). The three intervalley canals out of the Chancay-Reque River of the Lambayeque Valley with its large, stable flow and relatively high elevation formed the core of this system. The interconnected La Leche–Lambayeque plain alone offers 136,000 hectares of cultivable land, of which some 90,000 hectares are under irrigation today (Fig. 3.16; see Table 25 in Collin 1984: 85).

In addition, as noted earlier, the Lambayeque Valley has the ideal topography for extensive irrigation. Although the inferred date of its maximum operation postdates the Mochica culture, recent archaeological investigations show that much of the above system (e.g., the Collique and Antigua Taymi canals) already functioned by Moche IV, if not considerably earlier (Figs. 3.15, 3.17; Nolan 1980; I. Shimada 1982).

The Collique Canal, which tapped the water of the Chancay River some 52 km from the coast, wound along the south bank of the Lambayeque Valley to the mid–Zaña Valley immediately to the south. It provided water to the major Mochica settlements of Pampa Grande, the Sipán-Collique Complex, and Pampa de Chumbenique. The Antigua Taymi Canal began near the modern water diversion point at La Puntilla opposite Pampa Grande, and closely followed the north bank contour, taking water to Mochica settlements at Cerro Patapo (or Cinto), Tres Tomas, and perhaps as far west as Cerro La Raya and El Purgatorio at the juncture of the Lambayeque and La Leche valleys to the north.

The cultural significance of the location of Pampa Grande within the Lambayeque will be examined in Chapter 5.

4

Mochica Culture before Pampa Grande

The preceding chapter elucidated the environmental conditions and forces that influenced the nature and growth of the Mochica culture and society. To understand the underlying circumstances and causes, as well as the consequences of the establishment of the Moche V capital at Pampa Grande, we must examine preceding cultural developments. What were the significant Mochica material, organizational, and ideological features, and how did they come about? Did they in some way bring about the Moche IV–V shift? Were the Mochica under pressure from rival polities?

This chapter chronicles the physical and organizational evolution of the Mochica polity up to the end of Moche IV, ca. A.D. 550. Much of the discussion pertaining to the Moche I–III situation remains speculative due to the lack of relevant fieldwork. There is much we simply do not know.

1. North Coast Antecedents of the Mochica Culture

The Mochica culture represented the primary development on the Peruvian coast during the first millennium of our era. Yet the early phases of the Mochica culture were clearly built upon the widespread an-

tecedent and contemporary North Coast cultures known as the Cupisnique, Salinar, and Gallinazo. Most likely the Mochica shared the same ethnic identity with at least one of them.

Pre-Hispanic human occupation of the North Coast dates back at least to 8000 B.C., when people subsisted on a mixed diet of small terrestrial fauna (e.g., landsnails and lizards), marine fish, and mastodons and other large extinct fauna hunted with Paiján projectile points (e.g., Chauchat 1988). Marine resources gained importance over time and were a critical factor in the emergence of permanent settlements at Huaca Prieta (Chicama Valley), Alto Salaverry (Moche Valley), and elsewhere on the North Coast by 2500–2000 B.C. (e.g., Bird, Hyslop, and Skinner 1985; Fung 1988; Moseley 1975c, 1978c; Pozorski and Pozorski 1977). By about 1800–1500 B.C., an agricultural way of life was firmly in place, and pottery-making was added to craft production and media of artistic expression that already included weaving and gourd-carving. Population growth and increasing internal complexity are suggested by larger settlements in various locations within the valleys that evinced functional and possible status differentiation as well as planned layout. Monumental ceremonial mound construction that had begun by 2000 B.C. intensified, implying greater social integration and organizational skill (e.g., Donnan 1985; Pozorski and Pozorski 1987). For example, at the site of Monte Grande in a *chaupiyunga* pocket in the upper Jequetepeque Valley, residential *quincha* (mud-covered cane walls) structures were built over an area ca. 200 by 800 m in an orderly manner around a central court, all oriented northeast-southwest (Tellenbach 1986; also Fung 1988). A multilevel platform complex overlooked the courtyard.

A. Cupisnique

Between 1500 and 1000 B.C., the art style called Cupisnique—and its local variants—that favored monochrome finish (gray to black reduced wares) and incised-line or sculptural representations of flora and fauna (including man and stylized feline) became established in most valleys of the North Coast (e.g., Alva 1986; Kaulicke 1991c; Pozorski and Pozorski 1987). Larco Hoyle (1941, 1948) defined this style and proposed a seriation based on funerary vessels found in and around the Chicama Valley. He perceived the style to be autogenous and its iconography to be the product of tribal-level societies that shared basic motifs through intense interaction and expressed them using a limited number of the same decorative techniques (Larco Hoyle 1938: 26–35, 1963: 30–37). More recently, Elera (1986: 190–195) has argued for their origin in shamanism.

Whether or not the related societies were at the tribal or chiefdom level, the Classic or Middle Cupisnique phase (ca. 1200–700 B.C.) of this stylistic tradition is associated with many monumental ceremonial structures, such as Huaca de los Reyes (Moche), Limoncarro (Jequetepeque), and Huaca Lucía (La Leche). The last is associated with over thirty habitational sites and a major pottery production center within a radius of 5 km (Shimada, Elera, and Shimada 1982; Shimada, Elera, and Chang 1990). These public structures, together with the stylistic unity of associated artifacts, seem to indicate successful social and religious integration of the valley population, at least on each bank of the river. The supracommunal effort necessary

for the construction of large irrigation canals probably contributed to such integration (e.g., Moseley 1974; T. Pozorski 1976).

Though many earlier publications have debated its cultural significance and dating vis-à-vis the better-known Chavín art style (see Burger [1988] and Kaulicke [1991c] for relevant discussions), recent investigations not only confirm Larco's view of Cupisnique's autogenous origin and temporal priority over the Chavín but also show its wide distribution throughout the northern half of Peru. For example, stylistic and iconographic antecedents can be seen at the Initial Period site of Monte Grande (e.g., compare Larco Hoyle's pre-Cupisnique [Fig. 81 in 1941: 59] with stone sculptures from Monte Grande [Fig. 7 in Tellenbach 1986: 424]) and Huaca Prieta in the Chicama Valley (Bird, Hyslop, and Skinner 1985). Available dates also support the temporal priority of Cupisnique over the Chavín (Burger 1981; also Pozorski and Pozorski 1987).

The Cupisnique style (particularly the Middle Cupisnique phase) has its clearest manifestation in the Zaña-Jequetepeque-Chicama-Moche sector of the North Coast (for valleys in the southern half of the North Coast see Daggett 1984; Proulx 1985; Wilson 1988; Pozorski and Pozorski 1987). In addition, its artifacts or influence have been documented over a much wider area, from Pandanche (Kaulicke 1975) and Pacopampa (Rosas and Shady 1970) in the North Highlands to Ancón on the Central Coast (Rosas 1970), and even Chavín de Huantar (Kaulicke 1991c; L. G. Lumbreras, pers. com. 1988), the type site of the Chavín style (e.g., Burger 1984b, 1988; Kaulicke 1991c; Rowe 1967), on the eastern side of the south end of Callejón de Huaylas. At Chavín de Huantar, many of the ritually smashed vessels found in the Ofrendas Gallery were Cupisnique in style, perhaps taken to the site by pilgrims from the North Coast (Kaulicke 1991c). It now appears that formalization of the Chavín style (expressed in its most explicit and complete form in stonework at the site of Chavín) sometime early in the first millennium B.C. was closely linked to input from the Cupisnique style centered on the North Coast.

Burger (1984b, 1988) has argued that during the Janabarriu Phase (Phase D in Rowe's [1967] classification) of the Chavín stylistic sequence (defined on the basis of his excavation at Chavín: Urabarriu, 850–500 B.C.; Chakinani, 500–400 B.C.; Janabarriu, 400–200 B.C.), the Chavín style diffused widely, covering much of the Peruvian coast. In his view, the ceramics from Morro de Eten (Elera 1986) and the cache of gold crowns and other ornaments from Chongoyape (Lothrop 1941, 1951) in the littoral and upper Lambayeque Valley, respectively, as well as recently excavated funerary ceramic and gold objects at Kuntur Wasi (Onuki 1989/1990) on the cis-Andean slope of the Jequetepeque Valley, all pertain to the Janabarriu.

However, seen from the North Coast they belong to the Late Cupisnique. In the absence of any apparent local (or even Amazonian Forest) antecedent to the innovative Janabarriu style, Elera (1986) suggests the possibility that it was derived from earlier Cupisnique influence.

B. Salinar

The emerging results of recent excavations by a Museo de la Nación team under the co-direction of Carlos Elera and José Pinilla at the desert littoral site of Puémape between the Chicama and Jequetepeque valleys (Elera and Pinilla 1990; Elera, Pinilla, and Vásquez 1992) are helpful in understanding stylistic and cultural developments on the North Coast during the second half of the first millennium B.C. They offer important stratigraphic data and large ceramic samples derived from funerary and nonfunerary settings.

The site of Puémape consists of over 20 hectares of residences, cemeteries, temples, and other structures representing superimposed occupational phases. The earliest phase, associated with Initial Period Monte Grande–style ceramics, is overlaid by an occupation containing Middle Cupisnique ceramics such as sculptural stirrup-spout bottles. In contrast to the widely held assumption that painted decorations on Cupisnique ceramics are limited to postfiring application, the latter include vessels with prefiring white zonal paint decoration. Decorative techniques and certain geometric motifs found on various bottles

Figure 4.1. Salinar-style bottle with long spout and flat handle. Naturalistic modeling and red-on-cream coloring continued into Mochica ceramic art. Raúl Apesteguía Collection, Lima. Photo by Y. Yoshii.

of the Middle Cupisnique phase are quite similar to those found on Monte Grande–phase ceramics, suggesting strong local cultural continuity (Elera and Pinilla 1990). This impression is reinforced by the local, coastal character of the floral and faunal remains recovered from the excavations.

Cupisnique-phase occupation apparently ended with a major flood (suggesting a severe El Niño event) that destroyed the inferred Late Cupisnique masonry temple (ibid.; Elera, Pinilla, and Vásquez 1992). The Puémape stratigraphy indicates a hiatus in occupation before the subsequent (final) extensive Salinar occupation.

Salinar ceramics as defined by Larco Hoyle (1944a, 1948) and the Virú Valley Project (Collier 1955; Ford 1949; Strong and Evans 1952) are a mixture of innovative and conservative features. In contrast

to the popularity of monochrome, reduced wares in Cupisnique ceramics, Salinar counterparts emphasized oxidized wares (red to buff color) much like the later Mochica (Fig. 4.1). While retaining many Cupisnique forms, notably stirrup-spout bottles, they included new forms such as the spout-and-handle bottle and modeled-figure spout-and-bridge bottle. Decorative techniques such as appliqué, incision, and patterned burnishing persisted from the Cupisnique. For example, Huacapongo Polished Plain, which was the dominant type for the Salinar (locally known as Early Puerto Moorin phase) in the Virú Valley, was characterized by a type of patterned burnishing. Though modeling of animals and humans occurred, it did not have Cupisnique's sculptural character. Cupisnique religious motifs disappeared. At the same time, geometric motifs painted in white against a reddish slipped background (white on red or the converse) emerged as a Salinar diagnostic (Larco Hoyle 1944a; Willey 1945). The Salinar ceramic sample from Puémape also includes sherds decorated with a negative painting technique more commonly found on later Gallinazo ceramics (Elera and Pinilla 1990). Daggett (1985: 44) adds "megalithic" compounds, stone-faced platform mounds, stone-lined cist tombs, and ground stone blades, among other diagnostic features, to the Salinar assemblage.

Salinar is not well defined in terms of absolute dates. In the Moche Valley, this component is dated to 450–200 B.C. (see Table 1.1 in Moseley and Day 1982: 8; Chart 1 in Donnan and Mackey 1978: 6). Brennan (1980: 3) reports a radiocarbon date of 2090 ± 110 B.P. (140 b.c.; RL-804) for the single-component Salinar site of Cerro Arena on the south margin of the Moche Valley. Three dates for the Puerto Moorin sites obtained by M. West are later than commonly *assumed* and cluster around the time of Christ.[35] This relatively late dating would pose fewer problems with the inferred Janabarriu diffusion to the North Coast sometime between 400 and 200 B.C.; i.e., Salinar would follow Chavín "diffusion."

Stratigraphic excavations by Strong and Evans in the Virú Valley and by a team from the Museo de la Nación at Puémape revealed a gap of undetermined length between the Late Guañape or Late Cupisnique and Salinar. The situation has parallels with the documented transition between Late Huacaloma (coterminous with Middle Cupisnique and sharing some stylistic and decorative features) and Layzón occupations (synchronous with Salinar) in the adjacent highlands of Cajamarca. At the sites of Huacaloma and Kuntur Wasi, the establishment of Layzón occupation was preceded by a still poorly defined, apparently short-lived "Early Layzón" phase, which was built on destroyed and buried Late Huacaloma constructions (Terada and Onuki 1985; Onuki 1989/1990).

At least in some areas of the North Highlands and Coast, the emergence of Salinar and related styles of the White-on-Red Horizon seems to have been part of a broad-spectrum cultural change. This impression is reinforced by changes in architecture and settlement patterns.

For the Chicama-Moche-Virú sector, Salinar occupation emphasized defensible locations in the upper valley (around the valley neck) in marked contrast with the preceding Cupisnique-Guañape occupation found in undefended, more evenly distributed locations on or near the lower valley floor. For the Chicama Valley, based on a preliminary survey, Russell (1990: 8) notes that Salinar settlements are "primarily located upvalley on steep hill slopes on ridge lines" (e.g., at Sausal near the neck of the valley) with narrow house terraces and steep access paths, suggesting that defense was a major factor in settlement location. He reports no Salinar occupation in the lower valley.

In the Moche Valley, the limited published data (Bankes 1972; Brennan 1980: 18; Donnan and Mackey 1978: 25, 27; T. Topic 1982: 257–259) suggest a similar Salinar settlement pattern emphasizing hillside locations in the mid- to upper valley along the south bank MEC, with small domestic settlements scattered in much of the valley down to the Pacific coast. The two largest sites, Cerro Orejas and Cerro Arena, were established along the MEC. Donnan and Mackey (1978: 25; also Moseley and Deeds 1982) observed that "it was during the Salinar phase that significant expansion of irrigation systems greatly enlarged the area of cultivation into new portions of the Moche Valley. The maximum canal line began to reach its highest elevation along the south side of the valley, where it was pushed to the limits of arable land." T. Topic (1982: 258–259) sees that during the final centuries before Christ at least the south bank of the Moche Valley was unified under the polity centered at the "urban" site of Cerro Arena.

The above is similar to the situation in the Virú Valley during the Early Puerto Moorin phase (Willey 1953: 61–101, 373–378). Though many small habitation sites have been found in the lower valley subsequent to Willey's survey (West 1979, 1981), there was clear emphasis on occupation of the Huacapongo area in the upper valley in terms of site density and the presence of the four major sites (with mounds or tem-

ples and "megalithic" enclosures). Willey (1953: 61–63, 105) described a notable decline in the number of sites from Early to Late Puerto Moorin and attendant shift in settlement pattern from upper- to lower-valley focus. He suggested (ibid., 391–392) that the shift followed implementation of large-scale irrigation agriculture of extensive valley-bottom alluvium. However, there are some questions regarding the validity of these changes and chronological differentiation (cf. Daggett 1985: 52; Wilson 1988: 149–150).

In the Santa Valley farther south, the local Salinar manifestation known as Vinzos phase is defined by its close match with the Puerto Moorin ceramic assemblage (Wilson 1988: 148–150). Forty-five Vinzos sites are found in the middle and upper valley, with some defensive features on the south bank against an inferred threat from the south (Nepeña Valley, as opposed to from the adjacent highlands).

In the Nepeña, the heaviest occupation of this time period is found in the prime agricultural land in the upper valley. Like in the Huacapongo region of the Virú Valley, "a number of centers characterized by spatially distinct megalithic compounds and aligned stone-faced platforms or platform mounds have been identified" (Daggett 1985: 41). In addition, the Nepeña sites contain most other diagnostic features of the Salinar culture.

Salinar occupation in valleys north of Jequetepeque has not been firmly established. However, there are indications of Salinar presence—if not influence—in the Lambayeque and La Leche valleys, and even as far north as the Piura Valley: for example, a stone-faced mound at Tablazos in the upper Lambayeque and diagnostic white-on-red sherds found near Pampa Grande. Some redware bowl fragments with white painted bands outlined by incision occur near the north base of Cerro Tambo Real on the south margin of the mid–La Leche Valley (cf. Donnan and Mackey 1978: 25). Ceramics of the Sechura B phase of the lower Piura Valley (Lanning 1963) and recently defined Vicús-Tamarindo A Phase (dated to the first few centuries A.D.; Kaulicke 1991a: 415) exhibit similar stylistic and technical features to those found in the Salinar ceramics of valleys farther south, including white-on-red painting in bands or spots.

As a whole, the Salinar occupation had an impressive coastal spread, spanning the Lambayeque (and perhaps Piura) to the north and the Santa and Nepeña to the south, primarily concentrated in the middle to upper valley section (Fig. 1.1; cf. Willey [1945, 1948] on the White-on-Red Horizon). The strongest Salinar presence was in the Chicama-Moche-Virú-Santa region of the North Coast. There was considerable variation in ceramics and settlement patterns from valley to valley. The ceramics were probably produced locally on a relatively small scale. Though patterned burnished pottery and "megalithic" enclosures have been reported along the coast as far south as the Central Coast (Daggett 1985: 50), it seems best to describe the area south of the Nepeña as part of the Salinar sphere of interaction.

The Salinar culture appears to have had close relationships with contemporaneous North Highland cultures. Excavation at Cerro Arena in the Moche Valley yielded decorated bowls nearly identical to the contemporaneous Layzón Red-on-White defined at Huacaloma in the Cajamarca Basin (see Plates 67 and 68 in Terada and Onuki 1985). Considering the relative abundance of this ceramic type at Layzón sites and differences in its paste from the Salinar bowls, the painted bowls at Cerro Arena appear to have been imported from the adjacent highland region. Russell (1990) also reports some Layzón ceramics at upper-valley sites in the Chicama Valley.

The above line of evidence, together with (1) the upper-valley focus of Salinar settlements, (2) concern with controlling access to the adjacent highlands (e.g., Brennan 1980: 19–20, and his Fig. 17), and (3) the popularity of the stone pillar-and-fill construction technique and "megalithic" constructions at both Layzón and Salinar sites, raises the possibility that the Salinar represented a coastward expansion of Layzón and allied cultures based in the North Highlands and the cis-Andean slopes or a hybridization with the coastal Cupisnique culture. Paleoanthropological analysis of Salinar burials should provide useful data in this regard. The good deal of

overlap or continuity in forms and decorative techniques between Cupisnique and Salinar ceramics would suggest that at least the Salinar style was a hybrid product of coastal and highland traditions. Daggett (1985: 49) also posits the possible expansion or influence of the Recuay (also known as Huaylas or Santa) culture based in the Callejón de Huaylas on the Salinar.

At the same time, Salinar innovative ceramic features such as strap handle–spout forms, well-controlled oxidation firing (evenly orangish in color), and slip decoration may have been derived from Late Chorrera (ca. 500–200 B.C.), which is often regarded as the highest technical and artistic achievement of pre-Hispanic coastal Ecuadorian ceramics (see Cummins and Holm 1991; cf. Sawyer [1966: 19] for a contrasting view emphasizing influence from the South Coast of Peru).

The upper-valley/hillside focus of Salinar occupation in most of the valleys discussed has also been attributed to endemic warfare. For example, in the Virú Valley, Willey (1953: 358) noted that the "great Hilltop Redoubt" type of fortification enclosing dwellings and major mounds was first built in the early portion of the Salinar occupation. It was interpreted as a response to intermittent hostilities among local ethnic groups that began toward the end of the Cupisnique era. Because there are several "places of refuge" and no clearcut dominant center in the valley, it is thought that the valley was not unified during Salinar times (ibid., 392, 395–396). Russell (1990) also reports that the earliest defensive structures in the Chicama Valley appear during the Salinar phase. Perhaps this endemic warfare should be seen as hostilities between an intrusive or upper-valley Salinar population and a lower-valley non-Salinar population.

Alternatively, the upper-valley focus may have related to concern with the control of water and new MEC canals (e.g., Cerro Orejas at the neck of the Moche Valley near the main intake) due to decreased runoff reaching the North Coast and/or canal damage from severe El Niño flooding (documented at Puémape).

On the strength of data from his excavations at Cerro Arena, the largest Salinar site known with over two thousand separate structures covering about 2 km², Brennan (1980: 21, 1982) argues that in terms of the urbanism, commerce, and sociopolitical administration, the Salinar occupies an "intermediate stage of development between the Cupisnique and Mochica cultures" and that it "constitute[s] the visible beginning of that distinctive north coastal cultural complex that climaxed successively in the Mochica and Chimu civilizations." He describes Cupisnique society as having achieved social ranking and theocratic leadership but no residential nucleation, settlement hierarchy, or centralized valley-wide political or economic organization (cf. Schaedel 1972: 18). Brennan (1980: 20) characterizes the Salinar as having possessed a diverse, specialized economy and social organization, as well as a complex system of social ranking ("multiplicity and intergrading social statuses"). In addition, he sees the "first indications of a hierarchy of settlements based upon their sizes and functions, and their distribution to most efficiently satisfy the requirements of commerce, irrigation, and defense on a centrally administered, valley-wide basis" (ibid., 21). He also sees signs of endemic warfare and integration of Salinar populations in the contiguous Moche and Virú valleys. On the other hand, Mochica society is characterized by Brennan as having had an elaborate settlement hierarchy, considerable population nucleation, a highly centralized state, and complex social strata.

Brennan's unilinear evolutionary views of North Coast urbanism and characterization of Salinar sociopolitical integration are not convincing, especially in light of data now available. Although Cerro Arena was probably one of the largest sites to have appeared until then, notable nucleation was already evident at the Initial Period site of Monte Grande, among others. Evidence of centralized political or economic administration at Cerro Arena is also quite tenuous. A better case may be made for political/religious centralization valley-wide or on each bank during the Middle Cupisnique phase in various valleys. Cerro Arena's unusual occupational history—"its sudden, apparently rapid foundation and expansion in an area oth-

erwise only lightly occupied, its relatively short period of occupation, and its equally rapid and permanent abandonment" (Brennan 1980: 20)—is also disturbing considering the evolutionary position that Brennan sees for it within North Coast urbanism.

Some Mochica cultural practices that were once attributed to the Salinar are now known to have existed in the Late Cupisnique. Even the impact of Salinar-Layzón-Recuay white and red slip painting on Mochica ceramic decoration may not have been as great as once thought, given the even earlier Cupisnique zonal white painting documented at Puémape. The custom of placing metal objects (e.g., copper or gold discs) in the mouth of the deceased, which continued well past Mochica times, was once thought to have started with the Salinar (Donnan and Mackey 1978: 44). Elera and Pinilla (1990: 3) report finding fragments of gilded copper sheets in the mouths accompanying Cupisnique tombs at Puémape. Mining and smelting of copper on the North Coast is likely to have started by 800–500 B.C. Copper (including *tumbaga*) gradually gained importance, becoming the foundation of the sophisticated Mochica metallurgy described later.

C. Gallinazo

Another critical piece to the jigsaw puzzle of Mochica origins is the Gallinazo style and culture. The Gallinazo was first defined in the Virú Valley, where it was tripartitioned (Early, Middle, and Late, or I through III; Bennett 1939, 1950; Larco Hoyle 1945). In their excavations at Huaca Gallinazo, Strong and Evans (1952) documented stratigraphically that the Gallinazo displaced the Salinar in the Virú Valley. On the basis of dates obtained by M. West, we may infer this to have occurred during the first century A.D.

Larco Hoyle (1948: 22–27), who used the term Virú[36] to describe Gallinazo, distinguished Virú (Early-Middle Gallinazo) and Virú de Chicama (Late Gallinazo). In the Chicama Valley, he found that Virú tombs overlay Cupisnique tombs. In addition, he observed Salinar and Virú to be contemporaneous (though no supportive data were presented; ibid., 21–22). At the same time, in a cemetery at the base of

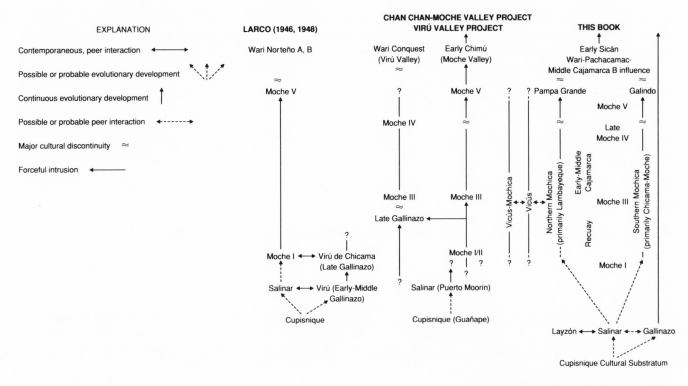

Figure 4.2. Competing evolutionary models of the origin of the Mochica.

Cerro Santa Ana, he found tombs containing both Moche I and Virú de Chicama ceramic vessels (ibid., 25–26). Thus, according to Larco, in the Chicama Valley the Salinar and Virú styles succeeded the Cupisnique, and the Virú outlived the Salinar and evolved into the Virú de Chicama, contemporaneous with Moche I. Beyond this point, the Mochica style supplanted the Virú de Chicama (Fig. 4.2).

The diagnostic forms of Gallinazo-style ceramics include pedestal-based bowls, stirrup-spout and stirrup-bridge-spout bottles (like the Salinar examples), and "corn poppers" (e.g., see Bennett 1950; Collier 1955; Larco Hoyle 1945, 1948. One of the most common forms is the unslipped jar with simple, gouged, punched, and/or incised human facial representations on the neck (Fig. 4.3). Common decorative techniques include "negative" painting much like the contemporaneous Recuay style, white-on-red painting, incision, triangular punctation or stamping, and both anthropomorphic and zoomor-

phic modeling. Late Gallinazo ceramics are better fired and more uniformly made. At least in the Chicama Valley, modeling and negative painting become rare; motifs popular in negative painting now appear in positive (black on cream; Larco Hoyle 1948: 26–27). Larco attributes these differences to strong Salinar influence.

The Gallinazo settlement pattern has a definite lower-valley emphasis in contrast to the middle- to upper-valley focus of the Salinar (Willey 1953: 102). Architectural forms and types are also different. Adobe bricks become a principal Gallinazo building material, and adobe platform mounds surrounded by dwellings emerge as ceremonial-civic centers (ibid., 109). Even at the largest Salinar site of Cerro Arena, such large corporate structures are absent. During the Late Gallinazo phase, when the maximum prehistoric population for the valley was established, much of the population resided in irregular agglutinated villages of adobe construction (ibid., 352–353, 393). There were several notable

ceremonial-civic centers, including the Gallinazo Group on the north bank of the lower valley. One estimate places thirty thousand Late Gallinazo rooms within the area of 5 or so km² covered by the eight largest sites within this group (Bennett 1950: 68–69). Huaca Gallinazo, the largest site covering some 400 by 200 m, is distinguished by a monumental adobe platform mound measuring approximately 75 m by 60 m and 25 m high (Kroeber 1930: 77; Bennett 1939: 54ff., 1950: 25–35; Willey 1953: 132–134). Local polities at the site clusters on each bank of the Virú Valley may have been unified through construction and maintenance of the MECs, with their rank reflected in the size of their associated platform mounds.

Gallinazo sites are found throughout the Moche Valley but most densely in the southern mid-valley portion toward the valley neck, much like the preceding Salinar. Cerro Orejas, stretching more than 3 km on the south bank valley neck, is the largest Gallinazo site in the valley, with nu-

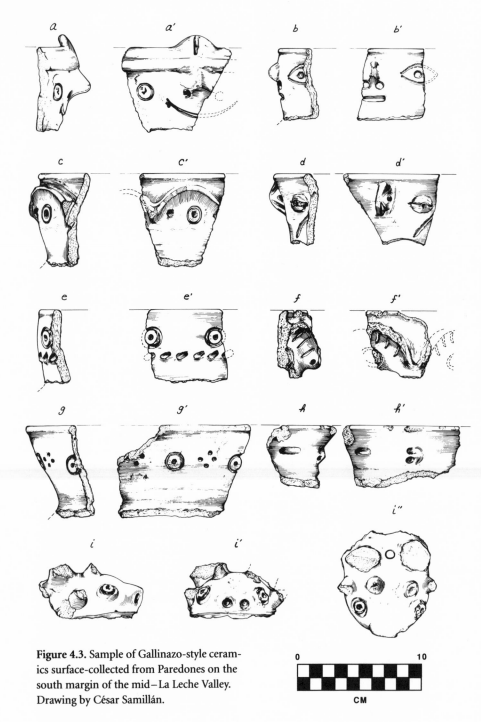

Figure 4.3. Sample of Gallinazo-style ceramics surface-collected from Paredones on the south margin of the mid–La Leche Valley. Drawing by César Samillán.

merous agglutinated masonry domestic structures and two large adobe platform mounds (Moseley and Mackey 1972). The south bank MEC that provided water to Cerro Arena was extended to its pre-Hispanic maximum during Gallinazo times, reaching Cerro Blanco overlooking the site of Moche (Moseley and Deeds 1982). In fact, a Gallinazo settlement underlays the long sequence of Mochica occupation at the west base of Cerro Blanco, and the structural core of Huaca de la Luna at Moche was probably built during Gallinazo times (Hastings and Moseley 1975).

Data from the Santa Valley in general concur with the above picture of the Gallinazo culture in its apparent heartland region of the Virú and Moche valleys. Survey data show a clear down-valley shift of settlements during the Early Suchimancillo phase (equivalent to Early and Middle Gallinazo) accompanied by larger-scale irrigation agriculture and steadily increasing population (an estimated 2.5 times the preceding Vinzos phase population; Wilson 1983, 1988: 171–172). At the same time, Wilson (1988: 172) reports the presence of forty-two "citadels" and minor defensive sites throughout the valley, indicating that warfare continued to be a major stress affecting the regional population. Also important are the presence of numerous kaolin and white-red-orange type ceramics, pointing to contact with the adjacent Callejón de Huaylas (ibid., 175). The appearance of possible llama corrals (ibid., 171) may also indicate an intensification of coast/highland interaction.

By Late Suchimancillo (Late Gallinazo) times (on the eve of Moche III intrusion), local population is estimated at thirty thousand spread among 153 recorded sites, including seven ceremonial-civic centers organized into four levels of hierarchy (Wilson 1983: 240, 256, 1988: 187, 196). Though there is no one disproportionately large corporate construction that might be seen as the symbol of valley domination or unification, it is likely that there were a number of local chiefdom-level polities within the valley.

Daggett (1985: 53–54) reports that farther south "no Gallinazo artifact assemblage can be identified for Nepeña and there are simply no Gallinazo architectural complexes to be found there." This observation may undergo revision, given that a recent settlement survey of the southern branch of the adjacent Casma Valley to the south revealed the presence of "clear Gallinazo-related diagnostics" including pottery forms and decorative techniques (e.g., negative-painted black-on-orange) documented in the Santa and Virú valleys (Wilson 1991). Associated settlements in the middle- to upper-valley section are strongly clustered with twenty-four fortress sites dispersed among them, suggesting the important processual role of warfare. Sites show little differentiation in size with only one site boasting sufficiently large, complex architecture to qualify as a possible local or regional center. At the same time, Wilson reports a conspicuous absence of Recuay-related pottery in the surveyed portion of the Casma Valley with easy access to the Callejón de Huaylas and wonders if the strong coast/highland contacts found in the Nepeña and Santa valleys did not exist in Casma.

To the north, the Gallinazo presence in the Chicama Valley is clearly documented. In addition to earlier comments on local ceramics, Larco Hoyle (1948: 25) speaks of major Late Gallinazo mounds and discoveries of gold, silver, and gilded copper in its tombs but presents no details. Russell (1990) notes a major down-valley shift in the settlement pattern during the period immediately preceding the appearance of Mochica-style ceramics and suggests that the shift may be in part related to the establishment of the mid-valley political/religious center at Mocollope, which continued to be used for the same purpose by the Mochica.

Gallinazo occupation is also relatively clear in the Jequetepeque Valley. On the basis of funerary vessels recovered from a large terraced mound designated as Huaca 31 at the coastal site of Pacatnamú (Fig. 4.4), Ubbelohde-Doering (1967: 22) attributed the terrace to a "period when Mochica and Gallinazo pottery was used concurrently as grave offering." He speaks of an associated radiocarbon date of A.D. 485 (with a possible margin of error of 50–100 years on either side; no other details given) and concludes

In the centuries before A.D. 500 [Mochica and Gallinazo] styles are found side by side at Pacatnamú, where Mochica textiles occur in their purest form. The pottery from the chamber graves . . . shows that Gallinazo ware usually predominated, even when Mochica jars were present in their classic form. . . . The impression is of a small but significant Mochica intrusion among a Gallinazo population.

This would signify that the Mochica vessels and textiles were brought for burial from elsewhere. It would then seem more likely that the [Huaca 31] terrace was constructed by a Gallinazo architect, a conclusion supported by its size and the variety of its brick forms, which at the type site of Huaca Gallinazo in the Virú Valley Wendell Bennett has designated as typical of Gallinazo II. (Ubbelohde-Doering 1967: 24)

The Gallinazo-style pottery he speaks of are unslipped jars with crude human face representations done by incision, punching, and/or pinching (see Ubbelohde-Doering 1983; cf. Strong and Evans 1952: 232, 241). He also reports the nearby presence of negative-painted ceramics at Pacatnamú. Additional Gallinazo or Gallinazo-like ceramics and constructions were found in the Tecapa-Jatanca region of mid-valley (south bank). Though many of the ceramics he illustrates would be better described as "Gallinazo-like," the data as a whole seem to indicate that at the least the Gallinazo stylistic tradition lingered on in the lower valley into the early Middle Horizon (Moche V times).

Little has been published in regard to possible Gallinazo or contemporaneous occupation of the Zaña Valley largely because no systematic valley-wide survey has been undertaken there. The situation in the Lambayeque Valley is being gradually clarified. Gallinazo-style ceramics such as unslipped jars with gouged and/or incised motifs have been found at the mid-valley site of Colluz (Kosok 1965: 149; Schaedel 1951a: 237) and in limited quantity more recently at eight sites farther inland along the north margin of the valley between La Puntilla (valley neck) and the Patapo-Pucalá area (Tschauner and Tschauner 1992). Rodríguez (1967: 3) has argued

Figure 4.4. Airphoto of the site of Pacatnamú. The City of Temples, with numerous platform mounds, is enclosed by a major wall and associated ditch that appear as a curving groove in the photo. Mochica constructions and burials appear to be concentrated in the central portion of the City of Temples. Photo Proyecto 170-36. Courtesy of the Servicio Aerofotográfico Nacional del Perú.

that the site of Cerro Ventarrón (Boró) overlooking Colluz represented the westernmost Mochica occupation (Moche IV and V) in the valley and that a contemporaneous non-Mochica (Gallinazo) lower-valley polity impeded Mochica seaward expansion.

Just to the north in the mid–La Leche Valley, however, extensive Gallinazo occupation existed, particularly along the southern margin that was apparently serviced by the south bank MEC of Raca Rumi II, which carried water from the north bank of the adjacent Chancay (upper Lambayeque) Valley through Pampa de Chaparrí (Fig. 3.16; I. Shimada 1982). For example, the top of Cerro La Calera has an impressive walled compound with internal terracing (a possible fortress), and much of the western slope is covered with additional terraces and walls (Shimada 1981: 441). Clearly the south bank center was situated at Paredones, with its impressive monumental mound complex facing north

at the base of the northwestern spur of Cerro Tambo Real (Kosok 1965: 161). The principal mound (Huaca Letrada), with approximate basal dimensions of 100 m (E-W) by 60 m (N-S) and a height of about 20 m, is flanked on the east and west by smaller but impressive platform mounds to form a U-shaped complex. These mounds are built with *tapias* (large blocks of mud) encasing loose fill, relatively small rectangular adobe bricks with cane mold-marks, and fieldstone masonry (particularly along the bases). In the Virú Valley, *tapia* blocks were used during Early Gallinazo, while cane-molded rectangular adobe characterized Middle and Late Gallinazo structures (Strong and Evans 1952: 212). It is likely that the mounds at Paredones have a complex construction history.

These mounds have an extensive associated habitational zone that includes nearby low mounds and terraced hillslopes spanning some 500–600 m east-west and over 250 m north-south. Portions of this area were built up with thick llama-dung fill, which argues for locally maintained llamas. The zone is densely covered with quite homogeneous Gallinazo ceramics, nearly all of which are plain and decorated unslipped utilitarian redwares (human and animal faces done by modeling, appliqué, incising, gouging, and/or punctating—much like Castillo Modeled and Incised types in the Virú Valley; Strong and Evans 1952; see Fig. 4.3). Pottery decorated with negative painting is quite rare.

Contemporaneous settlements, some with large platform mounds, are also found in the flatland and along the north margin (e.g., south base of Cerro Vichayal) of the mid–La Leche Valley. At Huaca Soledad, a firepit associated with an extended burial containing a Gallinazo unslipped jar with gouged face decoration has been radiocarbon dated to 1570 ± 40 B.P. (a.d. 380; calibrated date of A.D. 490 ± 60; Shimada 1981: 421). This occupational surface is overlaid by sand deposits containing Moche IV and V sherds. This date is not surprising given that a charcoal sample from a burnt storage structure that contained a large quantity of carbonized maize atop Cerro Sajino and was associated with Gallinazo-style redware ceramics yielded a date of 1680 ± 50 B.P. (a.d. 270; calibrated date of A.D. 360 ± 50; SMU-2612). In other words, throughout the mid–La Leche Valley, extensive Gallinazo occupation appears to have persisted until the Moche IV intrusion (ca. A.D. 400–500). As anticipated by Ubbelohde-Doering in his analysis of ceramics from Pacatnamú, the Gallinazo stylistic tradition as a persistent expression of the Gallinazo ethnicity outlives the Moche polity.

Even farther north, Sechura D- and E-phase ceramics from sites near the mouth of the Piura River (Lanning 1963: 172–173; Lothrop 1948b) and Vicús-Tamarindo B- (Vicús-Vicús) and C-phase pottery in the upper Piura Valley (Kaulicke 1991a: 417–418) can be subsumed within the Gallinazo stylistic tradition. The latter styles resemble Gallinazo in many respects, from paste and forms (e.g., pedestaled bottles, jars with loop handles), to surface treatment and decorative techniques that emphasized negative painting. Among the Early Intermediate Period styles on the

North Coast, Larco Hoyle (1965: 9–11) considered the Vicús style to be the most closely related to the Gallinazo. Garbanzal in Tumbes near the Ecuadorian border (Izumi and Terada 1966; Richardson et al. 1990) is "Gallinazo-like" only in some respects and is based on a small sample that is not well described.

Overall, in spite of certain ambiguities and intervalley variation, the distribution of Gallinazo-style ceramics resembles that of the Salinar and Mochica styles in covering nearly all of the North Coast (with the possible exception of the Nepeña Valley) and Piura. Areas of strong manifestation are found in the Chicama-Moche-Virú-Santa sector (like the Salinar case) and the La Leche Valley. However, Gallinazo occupation seems to have emphasized the mid-valley to the Pacific coast, in contrast to the Salinar's upper-valley focus. Gallinazo urbanism attained an impressive level in the Moche and Virú valleys, and in terms of settlement differentiation and hierarchy we may speak of individual valley unification by an extended chiefdom. Schaedel (1972: 18–20) notes that a multi-valley Gallinazo state is unlikely and that the society was characterized by "status rather than class stratification." Wilson (1988: 198) also discounts the existence of a multi-valley Gallinazo state that unified the Virú and Santa valleys, "given the strong indication of an extensive and well developed defensive system in the Santa."

2. Emergence of the Mochica Culture

With the preceding data and conclusions in mind, let us consider when, where, and how the Mochica style and associated polity emerged.

A. Emergence of the Mochica Style

Moche I style as manifested in ceramics shows strong continuities and similarities particularly with the Salinar and, to a lesser degree, with the Gallinazo, which incorporated various aspects of contemporaneous North Highland styles and the earlier Cupisnique and Chorrera stylistic and technical features. The often underestimated continuities and similarities among these styles are found in domestic or "folk" ceramics (Ford 1949). "Corporate"-style ceramics (better-made ceramics for non-domestic use that served as a vehicle for disseminating the prevalent religious beliefs and/or political dogma) show more limited similarities and selective continuities. For example, in Chapter 2, Cupisnique-Mochica continuity of the "feline fanged deity" was noted. At the same time, other well-established Cupisnique "religious motifs" were replaced by relatively simple geometric, zoomorphic, and anthropomorphic motifs that most likely reflected local subjects and values. Similarly, instead of maintaining Cupisnique emphasis on highly burnished reduced-fired wares, Mochica artisans preferred the reddish oxidized-fired wares used by Salinar potters. Mochica potters also favored Salinar white and red slip painting over the Gallinazo negative or incised/gouged decorative technique. But the total effect of the geometric motifs painted on cream slip of the Virú de Chicama vessels is strikingly similar to those of Moche I with geometric motifs. While Salinar vessels often display conventionalized animal and human forms, Moche I and II modeled vessels are closer to fine Gallinazo ceramics in being more realistic in their representations (Fig. 3.11). Berezkin (pers. com. 1992) notes that two shared ceramic features indicating strong cultural linkage between Salinar and Mochica populations are modeled representations of human sexual acts, and houses with a central entrance and overlapping gabled roof (see Donnan 1978: 79–83 for description and illustrations). These features are not shared with the Gallinazo ceramics.

At the same time, the reemergence of naturalistic full sculptural representations in Mochica-style ceramics and friezes (e.g., recently exposed painted adobe frieze near the top of Huaca de la Luna; Uceda 1992) is better explained as a case of archaic revival of the Cupisnique style. Also, the stirrup-spout bottle, which was not as popular in the Salinar and Gallinazo as in the Cupisnique, regained preeminence in the Mochica style. In other words, with the appearance of the Mochica style, what Willey (1945) labeled the North Peruvian Plastic Art Tradition was given new impetus.

Overall, it appears that the Mochica ceramic style and technology selectively tapped the coalescent regional arts of North Peru during the last few centuries before Christ, particularly the Salinar and Gallinazo styles, which seem to have been partially synchronic. Complementary processes of "archaic revival" (e.g., Cupisnique "feline" symbolism; cf. Lyon 1983), syncretism (major Recuay icon called "Moon Monster"—see below), and simple selective retention of old traits were involved during its formative era.

B. Chronological and Geographical Origins of the Style and the Associated Polities

Dating of the Moche I style relative to the Cupisnique, Salinar, and Gallinazo styles has been partially discussed. Much hinges on the confirmation of Larco's claims of Salinar-Virú (Early-Middle Gallinazo) contemporaneity, Virú–Virú de Chicama (Late Gallinazo) succession, and Virú de Chicama–Moche I synchroneity. Synthesizing relevant data from the Chicama, Moche, and Virú valleys, T. Topic (1982: 259) summarizes that "The Early and Middle Gallinazo subphases [in the Virú Valley] correlate with Gallinazo occupations in the Moche Valley, while Late Gallinazo is probably contemporary with Moche I and II in Moche and Chicama."

Excavations in 1991 in two areas of Huaca La Merced in Batán Grande provided data in support of the postulated Gallinazo–early Moche contemporaneity.[37] The excavation at the northwest corner of the site revealed an earthen floor with two intensely discolored pear-shaped pits along adobe walls, believed to be ceramic kilns (see Shimada, Elera, and Chang 1990) in association with a thick concentration of ash, llama bones, lithic cores, and sherds (Maguiña 1992; Shimada 1992). The last included Gallinazo-style modeled jars, a globular vessel with a long, slightly bulging neck, and bowls with incised and appliquéd decorations. In addition, there were distinctly Mochica-style jar neck fragments with modeled human faces, perhaps dating to Moche III.

Additional data come from Mound II, which has a 5.5-m-high stratigraphy containing some forty cultural layers and sixteen plastered floors that can be grouped into nine major phases (Maguiña 1992; Fig. 4.5). Gallinazo sherds, including some with negative painting mixed with early Moche fragments, make their first appearance in Phase 7 sandy fill (Fig. 4.6). Some finely made modeled pieces may well be as early as Moche I or II, while others such as

jars with modeled human faces on their necks appear to date to Moche III. Overlying Phase 6 fill contains late Moche III or early Moche IV sherds. Underlying Phase 8 fill contains mostly Gallinazo and some Cupisnique sherds, while Phase 9 fill has exclusively Cupisnique ceramics. Walls of Phases 6 through 8 are made with relatively small rectangular adobe bricks with cane-mold marks. Some of Phase 6 and 7 bricks bear simple geometric marks, though none were found in the Phase 8 bricks. Spacious divisions and formal layout together with ramps and clean, plastered floors suggest that Phase 6 and 7 structures had public, ceremonial character.

Though sherds from fill are often misleading, in this case the fill was sealed by a succession of floors, and a definite trend could be seen in the frequencies of different styles. The results of the two excavations at Huaca La Merced together suggest the partial contemporaneity of Gallinazo and early Moche styles. The discovery of well-made (fine off-white kaolin-like paste) Moche I (or I/II transition) modeled bottle fragments at Huaca Letrada (Fig. 4.7) further supports this argument.

Figure 4.5. Stratigraphy and adobe structures exposed by 1991 excavation by Adriana Maguiña at Huaca La Merced Mound II.

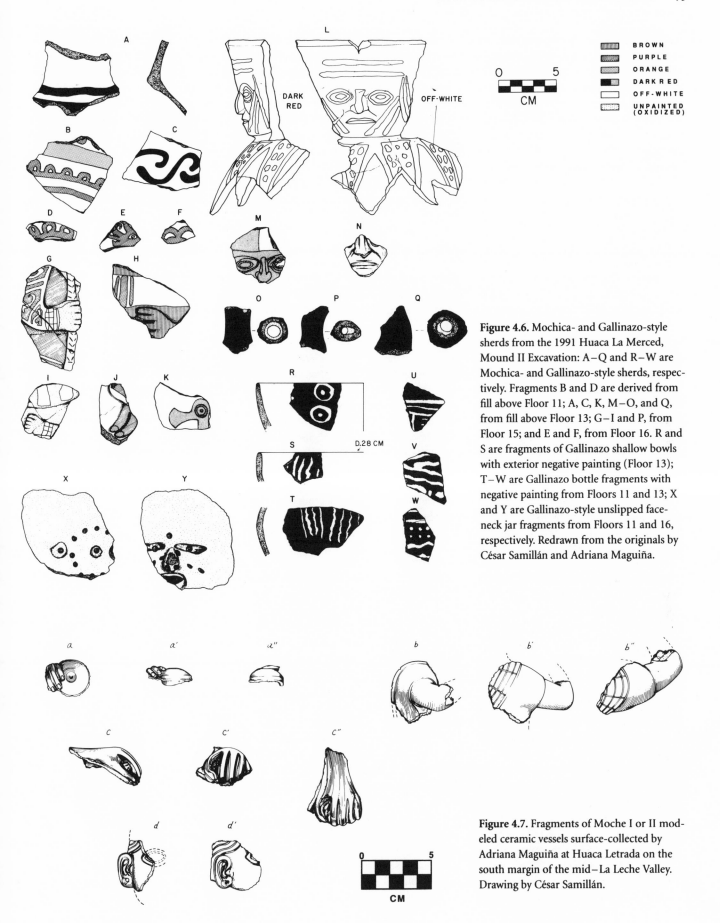

Figure 4.6. Mochica- and Gallinazo-style sherds from the 1991 Huaca La Merced, Mound II Excavation: A–Q and R–W are Mochica- and Gallinazo-style sherds, respectively. Fragments B and D are derived from fill above Floor 11; A, C, K, M–O, and Q, from fill above Floor 13; G–I and P, from Floor 15; and E and F, from Floor 16. R and S are fragments of Gallinazo shallow bowls with exterior negative painting (Floor 13); T–W are Gallinazo bottle fragments with negative painting from Floors 11 and 13; X and Y are Gallinazo-style unslipped face-neck jar fragments from Floors 11 and 16, respectively. Redrawn from the originals by César Samillán and Adriana Maguiña.

Figure 4.7. Fragments of Moche I or II modeled ceramic vessels surface-collected by Adriana Maguiña at Huaca Letrada on the south margin of the mid–La Leche Valley. Drawing by César Samillán.

The Mochica style is represented mostly by well-made bottles and jars, while the co-existent Gallinazo style is represented predominantly by simply made utilitarian wares. The emerging picture in the La Leche Valley does not point to the hostility between the Gallinazo and Mochica polities suggested by findings in the Virú Valley; rather, finely made Mochica-style ceramics seem to have been imported by the local Gallinazo elite, who may have valued them as status symbols. Other than the modeled vessels with negative painting, Gallinazo ceramics as a whole seem rather undifferentiated in quality.

Absolute dating of Moche I and II is largely a matter of extrapolation from a few rather problematical dates from Salinar, Gallinazo, and later Mochica sites (Table 1). An oft-used estimate for the emergence of Moche I is ca. A.D. 1 (Chan Chan–Moche Valley Project), though some researchers date it as early as 200–150 B.C. (e.g., Menzel 1977: 88–90 and her Table 1). If we accept radiocarbon dates for Salinar sites in the Moche and Virú valleys, then it would be difficult to place Larco's Virú de Chicama–Moche I synchroneity before A.D. 50–100. The transition to Moche II is also a matter of pure speculation. In fact, we are not even sure if the first two phases have chronological as opposed to just typological significance. In this book we use "educated guess" dates of A.D. 1–200 and A.D. 200–300 for Moche I and II, respectively. It should be clearly kept in mind that the five-phase chronology used here is based on an arbitrary judgment of some observed features.[38]

In Chapter 2, we alluded to the difficulties in determining the geographic origins of the Mochica style. Larco Hoyle (1939, 1946, 1948) argued that all five ceramic phases are found in the Chicama and Moche valleys, and thus considered the coastal region of these valleys the Mochica homeland (see below for an alternative view he himself considered). Kosok (1965: 102), impressed by the "predominance of Mochica cultural remains over those of other periods—a condition less marked in other valleys," reached the same conclusion (see also Schaedel 1985a: 448).[39] Though Larco failed to publish empirical evidence in support of this claim, more re-

cent archaeological data provide some support. Consider the following: (1) in his 1899 excavation at the site of Moche, Uhle (1913; see Donnan 1965; Kroeber 1925) unearthed one grave containing Moche I–II transition vessels and three other burials with Moche II ceramics; (2) a deep trench excavated by the Chan Chan–Moche Valley Project at the eastern base of the Huaca del Sol revealed a Moche I burial overlain by over 6 m of stratified refuse (Donnan and Mackey 1978: 59–61); (3) the stratigraphic sequence at the site of Moche shows Mochica overlying Gallinazo remains (T. Topic 1977); (4) construction of the Huaca del Sol was likely to have begun during Moche I, considering the Moche I burial noted above and given that Stage V (of the eight stages identified) of this platform mound construction is associated with a Moche III burial (Hastings and Moseley 1975: 198); (5) ongoing fieldwork by the National Institute of Culture, Trujillo Branch, at the major Huaca El Brujo mound just north of the mouth of the Chicama River has documented the presence of Moche I and II burials in the cemetery at the base of the Huaca (Correa 1992); (6) the recent discovery of a looted Moche I elite burial inside a painted adobe burial chamber at La Mina (situated between the Chicama and Jequetepeque valleys) contained many sumptuary items, including fine ceramics and gold and copper objects (Donnan 1990a: 32; A. Narváez, pers. comm. 1990); (7) the stratigraphic sequence at the site of Moche shows Mochica overlying Gallinazo remains (T. Topic 1977); and (8) in Moche III the Mochica polity forcibly intruded into the Virú Valley, conquering the Gallinazo (Strong and Evans 1952; Willey 1953).

The above suggests that the Mochica polity conquered the Gallinazo in the Moche Valley sometime during Moche I and began building what eventually became the capital of the powerful multi-valley polity at Moche. The Mochica took control of the south bank MEC and what later became the Huaca de la Luna. Embarkation on long-term construction of the monumental Huaca del Sol probably amounted to symbolic assertion of their newly established political dominance of the south bank or even the entire Moche Valley. Yet let us keep in mind that the size and complexity of Moche II occupation at Moche, as well as complementary, broader settlement-pattern data for the Chicama-Moche region, remain to be established.

Broadening the geographical scope to include areas north of the Chicama-Moche region, however, we encounter evidence that casts strong doubt on the validity of the preceding reconstruction. During the past fifteen years, various reports of looters' discoveries of Moche I and II vessels from areas north of the Chicama Valley have surfaced. For example, two Moche II bottles were looted from a burial at Cerro La Calera (with Gallinazo occupation) in the mid–La Leche valley (W. Alva, pers. comm. 1983). This is not surprising given the occurrences of similarly early Moche ceramics at nearby Huaca Letrada and Huaca La Merced as noted above. The extensive site of Sipán in mid-Lambayeque Valley (see below) also includes cemeteries with looted Moche I and II tombs. Further, a recent settlement survey of the north bank of the valley by a Sicán Archaeological Project survey team suggests that an extensive, badly looted cemetery at La Cría, just 4 km from Sipán across the Reque River, contained Moche I/II burials (Tschauner and Tschauner 1992). The nearby impressive site of Huaca Santa Rosa appears to be a major contemporaneous Mochica settlement (see below).

Overall, Moche I and II ceramics are much more widely distributed than Larco initially perceived, reaching the La Leche Valley to the north and the Moche Valley to the south.[40] The recent discoveries at Sipán and nearby sites point to the presence of a complex and powerful Mochica regional polity or polities in the Lambayeque Valley that may have provided an impetus toward the establishment of a new art style imbued with strong religious and political dogma. In fact, ceramics and metal objects attributable to Moche I and II have been reported from the Cerro Vicús–Loma Negra region of the upper Piura Valley on the Far North Coast, some 350 km north of Trujillo. These objects are examined in some depth below.

Figure 4.8. Thoroughly looted Loma Negra cemetery near Cerro Vicús in the upper Piura Valley. Hundreds of Vicús-Mochica style metal objects were looted from shaft-tombs that reached depths of 12 m or more in pure, compacted sand.

C. The Problematics of the Vicús/Mochica Style

The Vicús region remains an enigma, largely because of its distinct regional character, extensive looting, and limited archaeological attention (Fig. 4.8; e.g., see Disselhoff 1971; Guzmán and Casafranca 1964; Horkheimer 1965; Kaulicke 1991b; Larco Hoyle 1967). Ironically, the looting has brought to light a wide range of curious artifacts, including exotic ceramics and those showing a peculiar mixture of styles, techniques, and forms. They suggest contacts with areas considerably farther north[41] and south (Salinar, Gallinazo, and Mochica styles of the North Coast; e.g., Kaulicke 1991a: 381–382; Larco Hoyle 1967: 10–11).

Larco Hoyle (1967: 13–14) argued the fine "orangeware" that "antedates" Mochica ceramics in the Chicama and Virú valleys originated in the Vicús region. Though very similar in form to the common Vicús-style ceramics, the orangeware does not have negative painting. Its pres-

ence in two distant areas and inferred pre-Mochica date raised the possibility that the origin of the Mochica style should be sought there, rather than in the Chicama-Moche region. Further, he noted (1967: 18–23) that a wide range of modeled forms found in Mochica ceramics originated in the Vicús region.[42] Unfortunately, Larco offers no stratigraphic data or radiocarbon dates in support of these contentions.

Based on his study of the Domingo Seminario collection now housed at the Central Reserve Bank of Peru Museum in Lima, perhaps the largest Vicús collection, Lumbreras (1979, 1987) distinguishes Vicús/Vicús local and Vicús/Mochica styles. The latter is analogous to "Mochica A" as defined by Klein (1967; his "Mochica B" corresponds to the Mochica in the Chicama Valley). The Vicús/Mochica style includes stirrup-spout bottles with naturalistic, full sculptural representations of men and animals, plus images of supernatural beings with fangs, comparable in technical and artistic qualities to the best of the Moche I and II vessels found in the Chicama Valley (Fig. 4.9). In fact, fine Moche I vessels recently looted from an elaborate adobe chamber tomb at La Mina on the south bank of the Jequetepeque River (Donnan 1990a) can hardly be distinguished from some of the Vicús/Mochica vessels. In some ways, we can regard their coexistence as analogous to the Virú de Chicama–Moche I pairing Larco Hoyle found in the Chicama Valley. Lumbreras argues that the Vicús/Mochica ceramics were the high-quality product of a colony of selected Mochica artisans established and controlled by the North Coast Mochica polity (also see I. Shimada 1982, 1987a), while the Vicús/Vicús as well as the hybrid Vicús-Mochica ceramics were produced by local craftsmen. Based on his systematic comparison of Mochica A and B ceramics, Klein (1967: 50) concludes that the former from Vicús are artistically and technically better made and cannot be considered a derivative of the latter. Klein's view is not necessarily at odds with that of Lumbreras (1979: 118–144), who notes significant iconographic divergence between Vicús/Mochica and North Coast Mochica ceramics, an observation supported by independent studies. Iconographic representations of a trophy-head cult (Fig. 4.8) and condors (Fig. 2.5) are more prominent in Vicús-Mochica than in North Coast Mochica art (Schaffer 1983).

Though many Vicús/Mochica pieces can be straightforwardly dated using the North Coast Mochica chronology (from Phases I to V; see also Larco Hoyle 1967; Matos 1965–1966; Rowe 1942), the Seminario collection includes many others with features diagnostic of more than one Moche phase. The applicability of the North Coast Mochica stylistic chronology is thus questioned, and Lumbreras (1979: 33) accordingly assigns a wide span of 100 B.C. to A.D. 600 to the hybrid Vicús/Mochica ceramics. The puzzling mix of diagnostic features of the different Moche phases may be viewed as a reflection of frontier conservatism. Perhaps limited contact with the Mochica on the North Coast due to the relative isolation of the Vicús region led to retention of the early Mochica style and selective adoption of later changes. Greater

concordance between the "frontier" and the "heartland" would be expected for late Moche IV and V, when there was a definite shift of power to the Northern Sector of the Mochica domain.

Complicating the above situation in the Vicús region is a notable discrepancy in the relative dating of Vicús/Mochica ceramic and metal objects looted from cemeteries in the Cerro Vicús–Loma Negra area. In terms of style, form, and iconography, these ceramics (Fig. 4.9) are attributable to Moche I and II as defined by Larco Hoyle. On the other hand, numerous gold, copper, and gilded copper objects of high technical skill, many without parallel (Fig. 4.10),[43] show "artistic canons that are most similar to the fineline drawing of Moche III or IV" (Donnan, quoted by Lechtman, Erlij, and Barry [1982: 5]). Donnan (ibid.) suggests that this apparent chronological difference may be due to the possibility that "the stylistic canons of sheet metal representations were somewhat ahead of the fineline ceramic tradition."

What can we learn about the Mochica culture from the Loma Negra metal objects? Without contextual information, "[q]uestions about extraction of raw materials from the environment, the organization of production, and craft specialization" cannot be readily answered from these objects (Lechtman, Erlij, and Barry 1982: 29). Donnan (1990a: 32–33) argues that precious metal objects and ceramics found in tombs at Loma Negra, Sipán, and La Mina are "almost identical" and that they belonged to the Mochica "royalty" in each valley. Further, he suggests that because of the tradition of interring the accumulated wealth with the deceased elite, there was a continuous demand for sumptuary goods and thus "substantial numbers of skilled craftsmen" were maintained by the inferred royal courts. The observed similarities among these objects are explained as reflecting that these regional Mochica dynasties "shared insignia of power and status." Though some remains of metalworking (small copper objects) have been found near Loma Negra (Kaulicke 1991a: 413–414; Shimada 1988b), as yet no goldsmithing workshops or royal palaces have been identified in and around these tombs; in fact, we hardly know any-

thing concrete about these regional societies that sustained the inferred royalty and artisans.

One productive avenue of research would be to examine Vicús/Mochica issues from a broad Andean perspective. The mosaic or hybrid character of artifacts seen on and off in this region at least from the first millennium B.C.[44] is likely related to its intermediate location relative to a series of major cultural-environmental zones to the north and south. Kaulicke (1991a: 419) also emphasizes the strategic location of Vicús for trade with the surrounding coastal and highland regions. For example, to the north on the Far North Coast of Peru and coastal Ecuador, with such desirable resources as asphalt, *Conus, Spondylus, Strombus,* coral, emeralds, and balsa wood, there were a series of "Regional Developmental Period" chiefdoms such as the Tolita-Tumaco, Bahía, Jama-Coaque, and Guangala.

As we have already seen, some (if not all) of the above coastal Ecuadorian products were valued by the Mochica. We can readily envision mutually beneficial trade between coastal Ecuadorian polities and the Mochica. The latter, particularly the group in the Lambayeque region, could have offered products of advanced copper and gold metallurgy, including stock forms such as ingots and blanks, to their mineral-poor partners to the north. Local Piura leaders may have entered into a trading partnership (intermediary) through the threat of Mochica military conquest or in return for goods from coastal Ecuador and Mochica sumptuary objects. In fact, co-opted local leaders might have eagerly accumulated material symbols of power and status to compensate for their political inferiority and improve their image in the eyes of local populations. The Mochica would also have had a vested interest in seeing that the Piura leaders maintained a strong hold over local populations.

In this scenario, we would expect to find prestigious Mochica-style objects strictly confined to a small number of local leaders and no intrusive Mochica settlements. The quantity and quality of gold and gilt objects said to have been found at Loma Negra would not be totally unexpected. Though to date there has been no definite

Mochica settlement identified in this area, given the limited archaeological work conducted thus far, the above expectation remains untested.

D. Sociopolitical Conditions Surrounding the Emergence of the Mochica Style and Polities

Most basic to understanding the emergence of the Mochica style and polity are the prior social, economic, and political developments. The preceding survey of available data points to (1) sustained population growth in some, if not most, areas of the North Coast for at least several centuries preceding the inferred emergence of the Mochica polities, which probably occurred sometime around the time of Christ, perhaps in the Chicama-Moche and Lambayeque valleys; (2) successful irrigation agriculture that approximated, if not attained, the pre-Hispanic maximum by the Late Gallinazo (ca. A.D. 200–300); (3) the persistence and effectiveness of the

ceremonial-civic center as an institution (if not the primary one) of sociopolitical integration; (4) increasing functional differentiation, urbanization, and hierarchical ranking of settlements, suggesting that populations in various North Coast valleys attained chiefdom level by Late Gallinazo times; and (5) nearly continuous but changing interaction among "peer polities" within and/or outside the valleys (adjacent highlands and coastal valleys).[45]

Peer polities are adjacent or nearby contemporaneous, autonomous political groups that maintained some level of interaction (Renfrew 1986: 1). The term further implies that the interacting pair was on a comparable developmental level and that neither dominated the other. Thus, the interaction (whatever specific form it took—barter, administered trade, resource sharing, etc.) is seen as fundamentally creative, stimulating internal growth within both participating polities.

Figure 4.9. Vicús-Mochica stirrup-spout bottle of a fanged deity holding a *tumi* in one hand and a freshly cut head in the other. Note other decapitated heads and bodies on the base of the vessel. Compare with the style of the bottle attributed to the Chicama Valley in Figure 2.5. Museo del Banco Central de Reserva del Perú, Lima. Photo by Y. Yoshii.

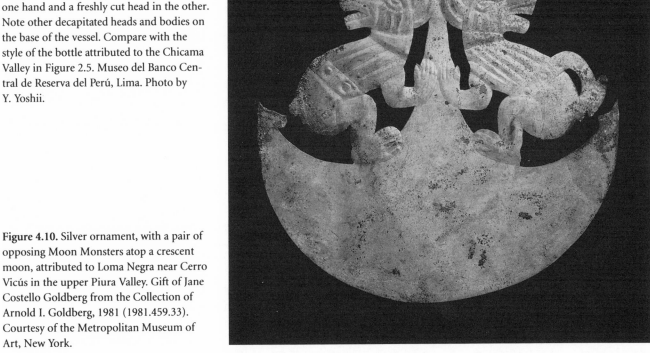

Figure 4.10. Silver ornament, with a pair of opposing Moon Monsters atop a crescent moon, attributed to Loma Negra near Cerro Vicús in the upper Piura Valley. Gift of Jane Costello Goldberg from the Collection of Arnold I. Goldberg, 1981 (1981.459.33). Courtesy of the Metropolitan Museum of Art, New York.

Though the Salinar-Gallinazo succession documented in the Virú Valley is often generalized for much of the North Coast in the literature, there is no published supportive stratigraphic evidence. Spatially segregated, these two groups of a comparable developmental level could have temporally coexisted for some time around the time of Christ in such valleys as Jequetepeque, Chicama, and Moche, maintaining creative, stimulating interaction. At least in the La Leche and Santa valleys, local Gallinazo polities persisted until the Moche III or IV intrusions, and its stylistic tradition lived on for many more years. Schaedel (1985a: 444–445) considers the Gallinazo a coastal ethnic group emphasizing "littoral-agricultural" exploitation that gradually expanded inland at least to the valley neck. He sees another inland ethnic group occupying the *chaupiyunga* and cis-Andean slope. However, considering the Salinar presence in the littoral zones of the Jequetepeque and Virú valleys, we should not overstate the upper-lower valley duality. The Salinar style and population, with their strong continuity with the preceding Cupisnique, stand as a strong indigenous base for what has come to be known as the Mochica.

Given the number of contemporaneous groups on the North Coast and adjacent North Highlands with growing populations potentially competing for resources, even a relatively ephemeral natural disaster (e.g., an El Niño–related flood) or symbiotic alliance (e.g., via elite marriages) might have provided sufficient impetus for territorial expansion. The emergence of the Mochica polity should be seen in this sort of competitive and rapidly evolving social, economic, and political setting. If art style reflects social values and processes in operation, then the emergent Mochica style that integrated selected technical and artistic features of the Cupisnique, Salinar, and Gallinazo in a new overall configuration may be seen as the symbolism of a group that was actively trying to establish its prestige. The association of early Moche and Gallinazo vessels in the Vicús, La Leche, Lambayeque, and Chicama valleys, as well as their undeniably similar domestic ceramics, suggest that this group had some political and/or social tie with what we call

Gallinazo before it established political dominance over the latter.

The emergent Mochica polities, however, were neither organizationally naive nor undeveloped. The Moche I tomb of La Mina, for example, shows not only that status differentiation was highly advanced, but that the elite had considerable power to amass sumptuary goods. Most likely, the Mochica, from their point of emergence, had knowledge of and access to the complex hierarchical sociopolitical organization and productive economy achieved by the Gallinazo. In this regard much of the territory incorporated in their hegemony was familiar ground; the oft-read description of Mochica territorial expansion as "ground breaking," incorporating new, unfamiliar regions beyond their presumed heartland in the Chicama-Moche region, is no longer tenable. From the Vicús region on the Far North Coast to Santa Valley in the south we see Cupisnique, Salinar, and Gallinazo antecedents. It is likely that the Mochica polity shared to a large extent the material, organizational, and even ideological bases of the peoples and areas they eventually subjugated.

3. Developments during Moche III (ca. A.D. 300–450)

A. Territorial Expansion to the South

What we know about the Mochica culture for the first two phases is largely limited to burials and their offerings; anything else is still highly speculative. In Moche III, with an estimated span of A.D. 300–450, we can speak confidently of a major Mochica polity centered in the Chicama-Moche region, and probably another in the Lambayeque Valley. Larco Hoyle (1948: 30) characterized Moche III as an era of cultural refinement with resultant material and artistic crystallization. Territorial expansion of the southern Mochica polity outside of the Chicama-Moche region began during this phase, if not somewhat earlier (Fig. 4.11). The Virú Valley Project documented widespread destruction of Gallinazo architecture and the seemingly sudden and total disappearance of its diagnostic material culture concurrent with the abrupt appearance of Moche III artifacts and significant valley-wide shift in settlement pattern (e.g.,

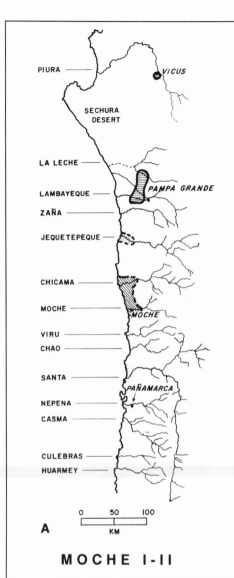

MOCHE I-II

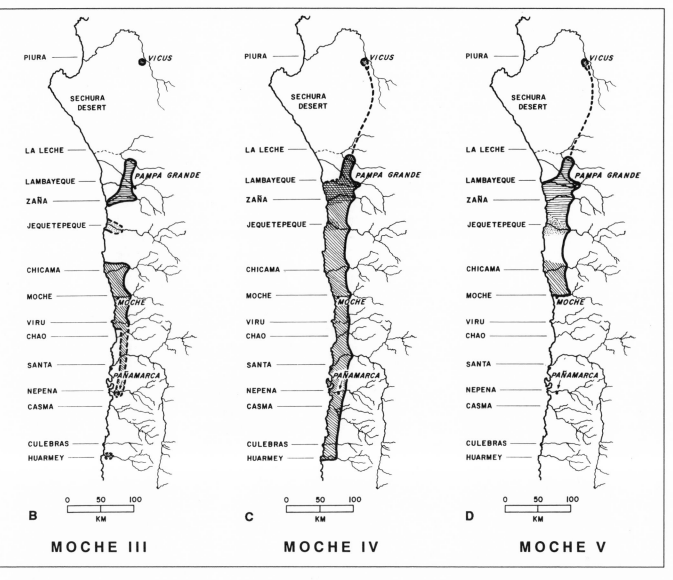

B   MOCHE III

C   MOCHE IV

D   MOCHE V

Collier 1955; Strong and Evans 1952; Willey 1953; also see Conrad 1978; Schaedel 1972).

Within the Virú Valley, the lower south bank site of Huancaco is regarded as the Mochica regional administrative-ceremonial center (Conrad 1978: 285; Schaedel 1972: 21; Willey 1953: 205–210, 382). Huancaco may have been the largest site ever established in the valley (Willey 1953: 205). Adobe constructions, including the main terraced platform adobe mound (ca. 54 by 42 by 7 m), cover an area of 300 by 200 m. Opinions differ regarding the number of levels in the regional administrative-ceremonial hierarchy imposed by the Mochica. Some see only two levels with

one secondary center (Huaca Verde, Site No. V-280; Schaedel 1972: 21), while others argue for three levels with two secondary (Huaca Verde and Santa Clara Castillo Fortification Complex, V-67) and some half-dozen tertiary centers superimposed on villages presumably inhabited by local populations (Conrad 1978: 285; T. Topic 1982: 279–280).

Moche III evidence farther south is much more limited in range, quantity, and spatial distribution. The case for physical occupation by Mochica intruders and incorporation of local populations into their emergent multi-valley administrative system is reasonably strong in the Santa but equivocal in the Nepeña, where no Mo-

Figure 4.11. Inferred territorial extent of the Northern and Southern Moche over the span of Moche I to V. Drawing (A) shows possible regional polities centered in the upper Piura, Lambayeque, Jequetepeque, and Chicama-Moche valleys. Drawing (B) shows the southward expansion of the Southern Moche polity and possible "peer interaction" of the Northern Moche with a Late Gallinazo population in the neighboring La Leche Valley. Drawing (C) depicts the Moche IV hegemony over the entire North Coast believed to have been established by the Southern Moche. Drawing (D) shows the bipolar situation during Moche V.

chica corporate construction has yet been definitely dated to this phase.

The ambiguity surrounding Moche III control of these two valleys stems from problems with the archaeological data. The apparent paucity of Moche III and IV habitation sites in the Nepeña Valley is disturbing (Proulx 1973: 39–49, 1982: 84). Of the 220 sites documented for the valley by 1971, only 22 had evidence of Mochica occupation and/or use (thirteen cemeteries, six adobe mounds, one ceremonial center [Pañamarca], and two possible habitation sites; Proulx 1973: 40). A similar paucity of Mochica habitation sites (seven out of eighty-five Mochica sites recorded) has been reported for the Santa Valley (Donnan 1973a).

Various explanations are possible: (1) Mochica habitations were located on the valley floor and have been subsequently destroyed or buried by alluviation, sand movement, and/or modern agricultural practices; (2) Mochica control of the valley was tenuous and abbreviated, with only a small number of Mochica administrators present at the regional center of Paña-marca and in the valley as a whole; (3) later occupations effectively obscure identification of earlier Mochica remains; and (4) Mochica refuse deposits have been difficult to identify.[46] One might add the possibility that Mochica administrative policy called for population aggregation at a relatively small number of large habitation sites. Most likely all these factors contributed. I suspect the available settlement pattern data underrepresent the complexity and extent of Mochica occupation.

The degree of systematization, geographical extent, and intensity of relevant survey work is also quite variable. The Virú Valley settlement-pattern study was intended to cover the total span of human occupation in the entire valley. A more recent survey suggests that the study was unintentionally skewed toward more accessible sites at the larger end of settlement size variation, perhaps missing over 50 percent of extant sites (see West 1971; Willey 1974).[47]

Similarly, comparison of two settlement pattern studies for the Santa Valley shows notable differences in sites with Moche III and/or IV ceramics. Donnan (1973a)

identified 85 sites: 60 cemeteries, 18 corresponding to adobe mounds and/or wall enclosures, and only 7 habitation sites (5 hectares total). Wilson (1988: 198), however, recorded 205 sites: 116 cemeteries and, more significantly, 84 habitation sites covering a total area of 230 hectares. The problem raised above of "habitation sites" now seems moot.

Unfortunately, Wilson did not provide detailed phase differentiation of Mochica ceramics. Donnan, on the other hand, identified a few Moche II and V ceramics, in addition to Moche III and IV. In other words, the more complete spatial patterns seen in Wilson's data must be regarded as a composite picture from the superposition of perhaps up to two hundred years of occupation.

Donnan (1973a) feels that Mochica military expansion out of the Chicama-Moche region may have begun at the end of Moche II, reaching as far south as the Santa Valley, which came under Mochica domination during Moche III. Combining data presented by Donnan and Wilson, we may tentatively conclude that sometime during Moche III, certain middle and lower valley regions were controlled by the Mochica polity. We cannot specify whether such control was intermittent or continuous throughout Moche III or intensified over the span of the phase (Shimada 1990b).

Within the Nepeña Valley, twelve of the thirty-seven sites with Moche III and/or IV ceramics lie within a 6-km radius of the Mochica regional center of Pañamarça in the mid-valley (Proulx 1982: 90; Fig. 4.12). This is close to the convergence of various ancient roads that were the most likely routes of Mochica intrusion (Proulx 1973: 84–92). We tentatively conclude that sometime late in Moche III, the Mochica came to dominate the mid-Nepeña Valley and control north-south movement. Though the nineteen Mochica sites documented by a survey of the south branch of the Casma Valley date to Moche IV (Wilson 1991; also see Tabío 1977: 62; Collier 1962b: 415), the above situation in the Nepeña, the clear, unmixed nature of Mochica symbolism found, and the presence of Moche III sites in the Huarmey Valley farther south (Shimada 1982: 151–

152) argue that Moche III southward expansion was quite forceful and proceeded relatively fast. The expansion may well have been assisted by local ethnically related (perhaps Salinar) polities.

B. Northern Sector and the Sipán Enigma

In part due to the lack of thorough valley-wide surveys, it is difficult to speak of the northward expansion of the Mochica polity centered in the Chicama-Moche region. Certainly, nothing as clear-cut as the classic case of Moche III conquest in the Virú Valley has been documented in the Northern Sector. Further, it seems that a powerful polity that shared the Mochica style was concurrently evolving in the Lambayeque Valley.

Evidence for Moche III occupation in the Jequetepeque Valley is still tenuous, with uncertain dating and limited description of evidence in publications (Eling 1987: 403; Ubbelohde-Doering 1967: 85–86). Eling (1986: 150) dated Mochica occupation in the valley as spanning A.D. 200–750. The extensive north bank Talambo irrigation and cultivation field system appears to have been used during Moche III–V (Eling 1978, 1987: 454, 456). Contemporaneous occupation has been mentioned for the lower south bank of the Zaña Valley (Alva and Meneses de Alva 1983: 336), but no details are provided. My partial survey of the Zaña Valley encountered evidence of Moche IV and V occupation of the mid-valley, notably at Cerro Cojal-Songoy, Cerro Corbacho, Las Huacas, and Pampa de Chumbenique (also see Nolan 1980; Fig. 3.15). In form, decoration, and coloration, the modeled, painted face-neck jars (Fig. 4.13) found at the east base of Cerro El Aguila some 15 km farther inland from the valley neck closely resemble those associated with the so-called "Old Lord of Sipán" burial recently unearthed at the burial mound at Sipán (see photo in Alva 1990: 4–5). Though the paste as well as the color of slip and paints are somewhat different from those of Moche III ceramics from farther south, in form these vessels appear to be from Moche III.

Mochica settlements on the north bank of the Zaña Valley may well have been functionally related to nearby ancient copper mines on the same bank and between the Zaña and Lambayeque valleys (Shimada 1984; also see Lechtman 1976: 10, 14). Pampa de Chumbenique and Cerro El Aguila sites are both within 5 km of at least two mines, and the latter may also have controlled access to the adjacent Lambayeque Valley through Quebrada de Montería. Certainly, the Moche III elite burials at Sipán are notable for the quality and quantity of copper and other metal objects.

Evidence for Moche III occupation of the Lambayeque region was minimal until 1987, when dramatic evidence surfaced at the extensive mid-valley site of Sipán (Fig. 4.14). The site has been described as the "Sipán Pyramid Complex," a major regional ceremonial center controlling the southern bank of the Lambayeque River (Kosok 1965: 153; I. Shimada 1982: 150, 1987a: 132) and the "northern provincial capital" during the period of initial Mochica expansion into the Lambayeque region (Nolan 1980: 249). Looting led to subsequent scientific excavation of burials associated with Moche III–style ceramics in a rectangular adobe platform (Fig. 4.15). The platform in question (ca. 70 by 50 by 10 m) is immediately southeast of two badly eroded large platform mounds together called Huaca Rajada.[48] The larger, rectangular platform mound (ca. 150 by 100 by 30 m) is the largest of over twenty-five major mounds found at the site.

In early April 1987, Peruvian newspapers reported the looting of a major "Mochica tomb" some 7–8 m below the surface of the highest portion of the adobe platform at the base of the Huaca Rajada. The sensation that surrounded the looting stemmed largely from the quality and quantity of the associated grave offerings.[49] Over two hundred pieces of gold, gilt, and copper objects are believed to have been removed by *huaqueros*. Scientific excavation under the direction of Walter Alva, Director of the Brüning National Archaeological Museum in the nearby city of Lambayeque, began in the early summer of 1987. In 1988, Alva and his team excavated the tomb of an adult male described as the "Lord of Sipán" near the highest part of the platform (Alva 1988; Alva et al. 1989). The many layers of sumptuary offerings

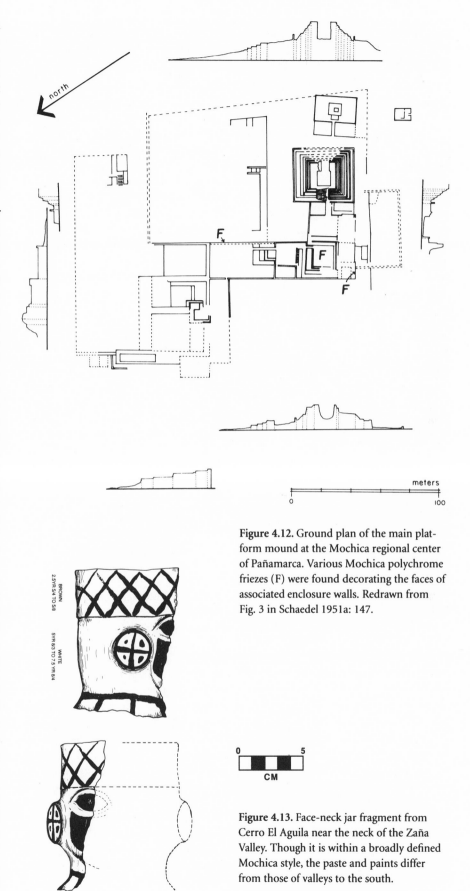

Figure 4.12. Ground plan of the main platform mound at the Mochica regional center of Pañamarca. Various Mochica polychrome friezes (F) were found decorating the faces of associated enclosure walls. Redrawn from Fig. 3 in Schaedel 1951a: 147.

Figure 4.13. Face-neck jar fragment from Cerro El Aguila near the neck of the Zaña Valley. Though it is within a broadly defined Mochica style, the paste and paints differ from those of valleys to the south.

Figure 4.14. A 1949 airphoto of the site of Sipán with indications of major mounds. M-1 and 2 correspond to Huaca Rajada, while M-3 at the south base of Huaca Rajada is the adobe platform where excavation under the direction of Walter Alva has been going on for the past several years. Numerous unlooted mounds visible in this photo were recently destroyed by looters stimulated by the discovery of gold at the mound next to Huaca Rajada. Photo Proyecto 3330-138. Courtesy of the Servicio Aerofotográfico Nacional del Perú.

found in his wooden coffin are summarized and their significance assessed in a later section. The excavation continues with exciting results (Alva 1990; Correa 1991).

The above discovery, though elucidating much about Mochica crafts and elite funerary rites, has generated a series of major questions regarding conventional views of Mochica political organization and territorial expansion, much as the earlier Loma Negra finds did. At a more specific level, it revealed a major discrepancy with the existing settlement-pattern data. Larco Hoyle (1966: 94) mentioned in passing that some Moche III, IV, and V burials existed in Lambayeque, but he presented no details. In fact, his chronological chart for the valley indicates only Moche IV and V presence. Though no one has covered the entire valley in a systematic manner, the earlier settlement-pattern studies reported only Moche IV and V ceramics and architecture (Day 1971; Kosok 1965; Nolan

1980; Rodríguez 1967; Schaedel 1951a; Shimada 1976).

In addition to the platform mound complex, the site of Sipán includes cemeteries and habitational areas (e.g., Alva 1988; Nolan 1980; Schaedel 1951a: 238) scattered around the western and southern margins of sand-covered Cerro Caballo Blanco (Fig. 4.16). West of the *cerro* lies the Mochica settlement of Collique in which cultivation fields, mounds, and habitational areas are still visible. East of the *cerro*, across the wide, flat Pampas de Ca-

Figure 4.15. An oblique-angle airphoto of the excavation by the Brüning National Archaeological Museum team at the platform mound next to Huaca Rajada.

yalti (Rinconada de Collique), there is another Mochica settlement at the west base of Cerro Saltur (Day 1971, 1975; Nolan 1980). Both Collique and Saltur have Moche IV and V occupation, but, disturbingly, no Moche III materials have been identified thus far.

The location of Sipán would have allowed control of north-south intervalley traffic through Pampas de Cayalti and control of the Collique Intervalley Canal. The latter was not only the Moche IV–V MEC for much of the south bank of the Lambayeque Valley but also carried water to the north bank of the adjacent Zaña Valley (Kosok 1965; Nolan 1980; see Figs. 3.15, 3.17). The "Inca Coastal Trunk Road" that runs north-south through Pampas de Cayalti connected the Moche IV–V sites of Cerro Corbacho (Zaña), Sipán, Patapo (north bank of the Lambayeque), and Huacas Facho and Soledad (north bank of the La Leche). Most likely the road marked the principal Mochica north-south communication route (Shimada 1987a: 132).

How could the important Mochica elite burials in Sipán exist in total isolation? Why do we have this discrepancy? That

this state of affairs in part derives from the lack of thorough settlement surveys is made clear by the recent discovery of nearby Mochica sites on the north bank of the Reque River just across (within 8 km) from the site of Sipán (Tschauner and Tschauner 1992). Huaca Santa Rosa (Fig. 4.17), with four major adobe platform mounds built atop a tell-like raised area, is particularly impressive. The best-preserved mound has basal dimensions of approximately 90 by 160 m and an L-shaped ramp. Much like the Sipán platform with elite tombs and Huaca del Sol at Moche (see below), this mound appears to be built largely of relatively small rectangular adobe bricks (a portion of which are marked with simple geometric designs) set in contiguous vertical segments. Though the sherds found at Huaca Santa Rosa are predominantly late Moche IV and V, a well-made Moche II or early III modeled face fragment was recovered in a looters' pit some 2 m deep. Given that the site has a deep stratigraphy (perhaps up to 8 m) with numerous floors, the site may well encompass the entire Moche sequence (Fig. 4.18).

In addition, we have already noted the looted cemetery at La Cría to the north that has yielded Moche I/II ceramics. Closer to Huaca Santa Rosa is another badly looted site, Algarrobal de Pucalá (also called Corral), that may have a long occupational and burial sequence spanning Middle Cupisnique to Chimú, including Middle and Late Gallinazo and Moche III–V (possibly I and II as well). Though our settlement survey continues, we are not too optimistic of finding small, early Moche sites around Huaca Santa Rosa, as it is situated in the middle of the best farming area within the valley, with a history of over four centuries of intensive sugarcane cultivation, in part with use of heavy machinery, and even longer river activity.

The "Sipán enigma," whether real or not, has forced us to reconsider the conventional view of the Mochica culture during Moche I to III as unified under a single polity centered in the Chicama-Moche area. It now seems likely that during Moche I to III, the North Coast had two major polities of the same or related ethnic iden-

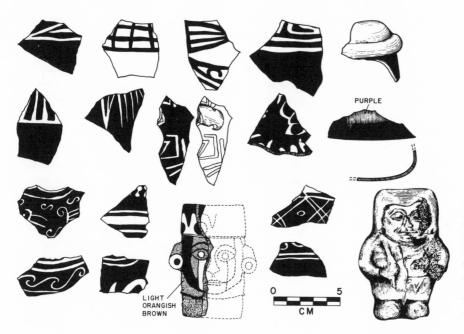

Figure 4.16. Early Moche sherds surface-collected in 1975 at a series of looted cemeteries found along the northwest base of Cerro Caballo Blanco overlooking the town of Sipán. The solid figurine probably dates to Moche V. Crude, hollow figurines also occur. Black corresponds to orangish-brown paint; white corresponds to beige color.

Figure 4.17. General view of the adobe platform mound complex at the site of Huaca Santa Rosa, Lambayeque Valley, looking south toward the site of Sipán.

tity, concurrently evolving in the Lambayeque and the Chicama-Moche regions, that shared the same stylistic tradition called Mochica.[50] By Moche III, the Lambayeque elite appear to have achieved a political-religious status and dominance that afforded them access to (or perhaps control of) a considerable amount of skilled labor and valuable material resources.[51] Numerous Chavín or Late Cupisnique–style hammered gold ornaments, small and large, recovered in Chongoyape in the upper valley (Lothrop 1941, 1951), Morro de Eten overlooking the Pacific (Elera 1986), and cemeteries in sand dunes west of Cerro Ventarrón (Boró) suggest the presence of a distinguished local gold-working tradition several centuries before Christ (Shimada 1991a: 89). The Mochica elite in Lambayeque may have enjoyed

prestige by offering gold objects or the services of their goldsmiths to the elite in other regions.[52] In fact, the impressive quantities of Mochica-style gold, *tumbaga*, and copper objects looted out of shaft-tombs at Loma Negra in the upper Piura Valley may be best explained as gifts or "rewards" from the Lambayeque-based Mochica polity to the local elite for their intermediary role in inferred trade with Ecuador. These gifts to these middlemen may have been received in the form of either finished products or on-site services of master metalworkers provided by the Mochica polity centered in Lambayeque. Through this trade, the Mochica secured tropical shells from the coast and minerals (e.g., gold nuggets, cinnabar, and turquoise from the Cañari and Cuenca basins) from the highlands of Ecuador. In

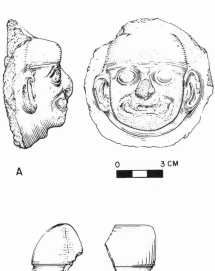

A

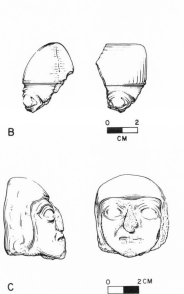

B

C

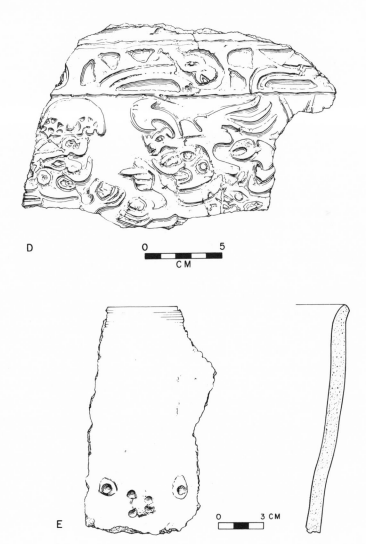

D

E

Figure 4.18. Fragments of early Moche vessels from the looted cemeteries of Huaca Santa Rosa (A; reddish brown) and Los Algarrobales (B, C; both are reddish brown except for the cream-colored eyes) near the modern town of Pucalá. B may be a part of a modeled figure, while C is the head of a solid, mold-made figurine. D is a part of a dark gray vessel with poorly executed, low-relief rendering of what appears to be the Presentation Theme. It may be Moche V in date. E is a Gallinazo face-neck jar from the looted cemetery of Los Algarrobales. Drawing by César Samillán.

turn, it is suspected that the Mochica polity offered copper products and subsistence items. Major constructions and tombs in the Lambayeque region document the organizational skills and productive power necessary for the local Mochica polity to have been a major partner in this inferred trade.

C. Summary

Following the establishment of political supremacy at least in the lower Moche Valley sometime during Moche I, the Mochica polity began its forcible southward expansion with the military conquest of the well-developed Gallinazo polity in the Virú Valley. This process may have begun as early as late Moche II—but definitely by early Moche III—and proceeded quite rapidly at least to the Santa Valley. Even if only for a relatively short time, the intrusion reached the south bank of the mid-Nepeña Valley and allowed the establishment of a Mochica colony in the Huarmey Valley. Expansion may have gained momentum in the process, with subjugated populations joining the cause. Whether intrusion occurred as a single, unified wave or as a series of aggregate waves cannot be specified given that Moche III may span as long as 150 years; in terms of military campaigns, that is a very long time.

During Moche III, thorough territorial control and integration of subjugated local populations into an emerging multi-valley hegemony centered at the site of Moche was probably confined to the five contiguous Chicama, Moche, Virú, Chao, and Santa valleys. The mid-valley portions of the Nepeña and Casma valleys may have been politically "neutralized" or the scene of intermittent conflict between the Mochica and indigenous or highland-based Recuay polity. Neutralization may have meant that, under military threat and/or for the sake of retaining some autonomy and prestige, regional populations entered into binding alliance, established trading agreements, or allowed tense but nonviolent sharing of resources, laying the groundwork for eventual annexation (Shimada 1981: 441–442). In the Nepeña and Casma valleys, the Mochica may have secured safe passage to outlying colonies in the Huarmey Valley through such an arrangement.

The situation on the northern North Coast is far from clear largely due to the lack of detailed valley-wide settlement-pattern data. For example, the lower and middle portions of the Jequetepeque Valley could well have been controlled by either a Mochica polity based in the Chicama and Moche valleys or a local Mochica polity. For either, however, control of the entire Jequetepeque Valley may have been constrained by the Early Cajamarca polity, which seems to have been expanding into the eastern and western chaupiyunga zones (Matsumoto 1988). Little can be said of the situation in the Zaña Valley. If Mochica hegemony of the North Coast was achieved through the unified action of a polity centered in the Moche-Chicama region, then the findings at Sipán would indicate a surprisingly early northward expansion (perhaps Moche I or II). However, all the facts surrounding Sipán cannot be readily explained by the "conquest state" model applied to the Southern Sector of Mochica territory. There has been too much emphasis on finding a single, powerful, expansive regional state that unified the North Coast. At least for the period of Moche I to III, the Lambayeque and Chicama-Moche regions each appear to have had a powerful ethnic polity, both of which shared seemingly homogeneous Mochica style. In general, in the Northern Sector we do not see anything as abrupt, forceful, and thorough as the domination of the Virú Valley by the intrusive Mochica.

Overall, there is an expanding list of specific features and long-term developments that distinguish early Mochica artifacts and occupations in the Northern Sector of the North Coast (in particular, the area spanning the Zaña, Lambayeque, and La Leche valleys) from the rest of the North Coast. In the preceding chapter we emphasized the significance of the topographic, hydrological, linguistic, and architectural differences. The list also includes: (1) the early establishment, sophistication, and productivity of copper and gold metallurgy (and local mining of copper ores), (2) the preferred use of orangish and purplish paint on ceramics, (3) the rarity of "portrait" vessels, and (4) possible pre–Moche III use of marked adobe bricks in public constructions (particularly at Sipán and Huaca

Santa Rosa). In addition, unlike the southern North Coast, we have no evidence of any major wave of aggressive Moche territorial expansion into the northern North Coast for the period of Moche I to III. Recent fieldwork in the mid–La Leche Valley suggests the seemingly peaceful coexistence of Gallinazo and Mochica groups in the valley. Data show the coexistence of Late Gallinazo and early Mochica ceramics (possible Moche I to III) in a ceremonial setting and a ceramic workshop excavated in 1991 at Huaca La Merced.

A similar range of contrasts in the ceramics of the Northern and Southern Sectors was observed by Klein (1967) in his rarely cited work. Klein (Table in 1967: 26–32) defined many technical and stylistic differences between Mochica ceramics from the Vicús (called Mochica A) and Chicama regions (called Mochica B). He concluded that Mochica A vessels were in general technically and artistically better made than and not derived from those of Mochica B. For example, Mochica A vessels have thinner walls and finer and more homogeneous paste. In addition, they are said to exhibit a wider range of color combinations, while Mochica B ceramics are almost always dark red-on-cream or the converse. The distinctly orangish and purplish paints distinguish early Mochica ceramics from the Vicús and Lambayeque regions (Figs. 4.15, 4.16) from those originating farther south.

In early Mochica face-neck jars from the Lambayeque region, the angle formed by the neck and shoulder is quite wide (ca. 130°), and the shoulder is frequently decorated with a lattice pattern or other simple geometric design in off-white against an orangish background or the converse.

Based on the above series of observations, as illustrated in Figure 4.11, the presence of at least one regional Mochica group is inferred for the span of Moche I to III in the Zaña–Lambayeque–La Leche region that was politically autonomous but at the same time used the style and symbolism called Mochica or Moche. In other words, during ca. A.D. 1–300, I see on the North Coast the coexistence of a series of regional polities, including the Northern Mochica centered in the Lambayeque region, Southern Mochica based in the Chicama-

Moche region, and Late Gallinazo in the La Leche and other valleys. This is akin to Donnan's conception (1990: 32–33), which posits the coexistence of "one or more [Moche] royal courts" in various valleys on the North Coast, "each having little direct contact with the common people, yet connected to one another like the royalty of Europe." In addition, based on his iconographic study, Berezkin (1978) has presented a strong argument that the five major sets of deities found in the Moche pantheon prior to late Moche IV represented five elite lineages in Moche society.

4. Developments during Moche IV (ca. A.D. 450–550)

Some scholars regard late Moche III to early Moche IV, ca. A.D. 400–500, as the Golden Age of the Mochica culture. During this span, political domination and continuous territorial control by the Mochica polity based at Moche reached its maximum from at least the north bank of the Chicama Valley to the south bank of the Huarmey Valley (Fig. 4.11). The situation in the Northern Sector is still not clear, but the Lambayeque-based Mochica polity may have suffered loss of power and prestige in late Moche III and been subsumed by its more powerful southern rival sometime in Moche IV (possibly around A.D. 500). The site of Moche appears to have been the paramount center of this impressive pan–North Coast polity (see Chapter 5). Within the central region, the Mochica controlled entire valleys from the lower reaches of cis-Andean *yunga* at 500 to 600 m above sea level, to the Pacific shore, as well as offshore islands. At the southern (Nepeña and Casma) and particularly northern peripheries (Lambayeque and La Leche), however, control was limited largely to mid-valley portions. At the same time, the Mochica sphere of influence during Moche IV was quite encompassing, reaching the Far North Coast and probably southern Ecuador, the Central and South Coast, and perhaps even some parts of the North Highlands to the west.

A. The Southern Sector

We see little change in the geographical extent of the Mochica hegemony in the south (to the Huarmey) from the preceding phase; rather there is consolidation of control through more thorough occupation of valley portions already invaded or neutralized. Integration and administration of local populations are often more difficult and time-consuming than forceful conquest. The Inca army was kept busy "reconquering" many near and distant provinces for this reason (Murra 1986), and one wonders if the same was true of the Mochica.

The impact of Mochica conquest and administration during Moche III and IV is perhaps best documented in the Santa Valley. On the basis of eighty-four habitation sites covering 230 hectares, the regional population is estimated at twenty-two thousand, a significant drop from a pre–Mochica intrusion period estimate of thirty thousand (Wilson 1983: 243). Wilson notes that

Whether or not this [population drop] is the result of the Moche incursion into the valley, it is clear . . . that a massive shift in subsistence-settlement focus has occurred. While substantial numbers of people live in the Middle Valley, over 80% of the population is now located in the Lower Valley sector. The population in this latter area is thus over five times greater than the estimate for the preceding [local Gallinazo] Late Suchimancillo Period.

This inferred population drop and the large number of cemeteries identified for Moche III–IV occupation may reflect casualties from inferred battles associated with the Mochica intrusion and subsequent imposition of heavy demands (e.g., tribute payment) and resettlement (ibid., 254). An osteological study of this population might reveal an unusually high incidence of trauma.

The population apparently shifted downvalley to occupy the edges of bottomland along the course of the north and south bank MECs. The resulting linear settlement pattern may be in part a distortion due to destruction of bottomland sites by river activities and cultivation (Donnan 1973a: 11) and in part due to the gorgelike narrow topography of the middle and upper valley. The lower-valley concentration of population and principal ceremonial-administrative sites, however, suggest that the pattern had more to do with maximizing agricultural land and productivity of the valley. In fact, 8,780 hectares of cultivable land is estimated to have been associated with Mochica settlements (estimated population of 22,020), as opposed to 5,416 hectares (estimated population of 29,765) for the preceding period (Wilson 1983: 263). The regional population appears to have been resettled from inland, hillslope, and hilltop settlements, presumably to provide a more accessible, controllable labor force for intensive irrigation agriculture directed by the Mochica polity. There is little evidence of concern with maximizing irrigation water or defending the principal intakes of the canals. This is not surprising given the Santa Valley's very high annual discharge volume from a vast watershed that includes much of the Callejón de Huaylas (Table 3), allowing year-round intensive irrigation. Additionally, available climatic records (see Chapter 6) show that the fifth century A.D. was favored with above-average precipitation, allowing expansion of agricultural cultivation.

The Mochica may have also been attracted by the excellent fishing grounds just off the mouth of the Santa River, where it discharges a tremendous quantity of silt, mineral and organic nutrients, and fresh water. As discussed in Chapter 2, the port of Chimbote has long been the center of the anchovy industry. The paucity of Mochica sites at or near the coast is disturbing. However, in northern North Coast valleys during late pre-Hispanic times, fishing "specialists" formed a caste-like class with their own subculture and were found throughout the valleys, not just on the coast (see below). This economic consideration should be weighed in considering Mochica intrusion into the Santa Valley.

The pronounced shifts in settlement location, composition, and hierarchy were accompanied by equally notable changes in ceramics. Distinctly regional Gallinazo ceramics with a wide range of types (twenty-nine and thirty-nine formal types in Early and Late Suchimancillo, respectively) were replaced by readily recognizable, "uniformly made" Mochica ceramics with only sixteen formal types (Wilson 1983: 253). Donnan (1973a) noted that, though most vessel forms found in the Mochica heartland are present in the Santa, certain forms of decoration are nearly absent (notably fineline figure painting), surface finish tends to be cruder, and some shapes are more common in the Santa sample. A study of the ceramics produced at the workshop located at Pampa de los Incas (Wilson 1988: 211) would be valuable in understanding these observations. The sample from the Nepeña exhibits a very similar character (Proulx 1973: 45). Whether intervalley similarities (perhaps representing imposition of standardized forms and decoration) or differences are emphasized is largely a matter of where one stands on the nature of the Mochica polity, as we see in Chapter 8.

These observations and conclusions on Mochica motives for expansion may not hold for the entire Southern Sector. A study of the lower and middle Virú Valley suggests that Mochica settlement pattern and hierarchy "reflect a compromise in which maintaining social and political control of the local population was the most important consideration, minimization of agricultural effort was a secondary factor, and maximization of arable land was the least important determinant of the three" (Conrad 1978: 293). However, this analysis itself was based on rather incomplete survey data that did not differentiate phases (Moche III vs. IV).

Certainly, the "agricultural maximization" explanation is difficult to apply to Moche III–IV occupation in the Nepeña Valley. Occupation is centered mid-valley, much as in the Lambayeque and La Leche valleys to the north during Moche IV and V. Competition from the contemporaneous Recuay polity, limited agricultural potential and labor force, and frontier location may have hampered efforts to conquer and administer the Nepeña Valley thoroughly (Proulx 1973: 48). As already noted, the mid-valley focus was likely to have related in part to the difficulty of traversing the sand-covered coastal terrain and securing safe passage to areas farther south.

A similar mid-valley focus is seen for the nineteen Moche IV and V sites found in the Casma branch of the Casma Valley (Wilson 1991).[53] It appears that the mid-valley administrative center of the preceding period (Gallinazo) was taken over by the Mochica for the same purpose. Historically, people traveling on foot between the Casma and Huarmey (where Mochica outposts existed) took inland (highland) routes to avoid the rugged coastal mountains and desert. This may also have been true prehistorically and in part account for the settlement preference. Fifteen sites have some indications of habitation with an estimated total area of twenty-eight hectares and three thousand or fewer persons (ibid.). These figures will undoubtedly increase when the Sechín branch of the valley is surveyed. Given that sherds found in various cemeteries consisted *entirely* of *pure* Mochica diagnostics, including those of flaring bowls (*floreros*) and stirrup-spout bottles with painted and modeled decorative motifs, Wilson (ibid., 22) argues that the Mochica style was "imposed rather abruptly by conquest" of this valley.

The situation in the Huarmey Valley farther south is described later.

B. The Northern Sector

Based on a limited number of publications, it is surmised that the situation in the Jequetepeque was that of a tenuous coexistence among Cajamarca, Mochica, and local populations.[54] Scattered evidence of Mochica presence includes a late Moche IV elite burial (Grave M XII) found in the middle of the "City of Temples" at Pacatnamú (Fig. 4.4; Ubbelohde-Doering 1967, 1983: 113–122).[55] The extensive Mochica construction and occupation within the "City" and surrounding "Suburb" (particularly the northeastern portion) referred to by German investigators (Hecker and Hecker 1985: 48–57) presumably began in Moche III and continued well into Phase V.

To date, settlement surveys in the Zaña, Lambayeque, and La Leche valleys have yielded little data on what may have happened immediately after the interment of Mochica elite (Moche III) at Sipán around A.D. 300–350. What is clear, however, is that there were late Moche IV and V settlements established in middle sections of the

Zaña, Lambayeque, and La Leche valleys, without any preceding Mochica occupation. In the Zaña, Mochica control of the north bank of the mid-valley is definite, with its extensive hillside settlements.[56] None of them, however, has what may be called "monumental" adobe structures or purely defensive character. The largest and most complex Moche IV and V occupation on the north bank of the Zaña was at Cerro Songoy, which received its water from the Lambayeque Valley via the Collique Inter-valley Canal. Cerro Corbacho was ideally situated for control of east-west intravalley and north-south intervalley traffic. Control of the south bank remains to be established. The Mochica and Cajamarca polities probably competed for control of the upper valley with its "relict rainforest" (Dillehay and Netherly 1983; Craig 1985).

The mid-valley focus of Moche IV occupation in the Lambayeque Valley has already been noted. Cerro Ventarrón (some 16 and 18 km west of the contemporaneous sites of Huaca Santa Rosa and Sipán, respectively), with a commanding view of the large reservoir at the west base and of the entire mid-valley, and with massive concentric "fortification walls," is believed to have defined the seaward limit of Moche IV control (Rodríguez 1967). However, there are Moche IV and V habitation sites farther west within the modern town of Reque and the port of Puerto Eten. For example, at the latter, modern construction activity revealed a habitational area with adobe wall remnants, a firepit, and sherds with fineline decorations on the associated floor (C. Elera, pers. com. 1991). A small Moche V occupation at Tablazos some 22 km northeast of Sipán along the south bank may have had Moche IV origins and marked the inland-most occupation of that phase. The crucial question as to the presence of a Moche IV precursor at Pampa Grande is addressed later. North bank occupation is hinted at by small quantities of bichrome Mochica ceramics in the northern sector of Cerro Patapo and Tres Tomas strategically situated in respect to the north bank MEC of the Antigua Taymi and north-south movement (Fig. 3.15).

Evidence of late Moche IV and V habitation and burials, including well-built adobe burial chambers, is found at eight sites in the mid–La Leche Valley (Fig. 4.19; I. Shimada 1981, 1982, 1987a). Radiocarbon dates from the small, stratified mound of Huaca del Pueblo Batán Grande (Table 2) suggest that the Moche IV occupation there began around A.D. 500. There was no surface clue at the site indicating the Moche IV occupation overlying sterile sand some 5 m below. Considering the many similar sites nearby, the number of mid-valley Moche IV sites may increase appreciably with future excavation. To the west, U-shaped ceremonial adobe structures with niches and murals at Huaca Soledad Mound II and Huaca La Mayanga (within Huaca Facho; Bonavia 1985; Donnan 1972) also appear to have had late Moche IV beginnings. The Huaca Soledad cemetery has Moche IV and V adobe chamber tombs (Shimada 1981, 1986; Fig. 4.16).

As with the entire Southern Sector of the Mochica hegemony since Moche III, defense of the principal intakes in the Northern Sector during Moche IV does not seem to have been a major determinant of the settlement pattern (Schaedel 1985a). However, much like the Santa Valley case, most of the Moche IV and V sites thus far identified in the Zaña and Lambayeque valleys occupy the valley edges immediately above the MECs, stabilized sand dunes, and slopes and ridges of the mountains and hills in the valley bottomland. The association of major habitation sites with these canals and cultivation fields above modern-day limits in these two valleys points to the importance of agricultural maximization. In the La Leche Valley, where there is a curious absence of agricultural activity in a large portion of the mid-valley, Moche IV and V habitation, cemetery, and ceremonial sites are found on elevated areas above the current ground level. No one specific factor emerges as the determinant of settlement pattern and hierarchy in the mid–La Leche.

Overall, when Moche IV settlements in the Northern Sector are seen as a whole, a number of important common denominators emerge: (1) intervalley ceramic similarities, (2) roughly north-south linear alignment of sites, and (3) preference for mid-valley locations without prior Mochica occupation. Their spatial character

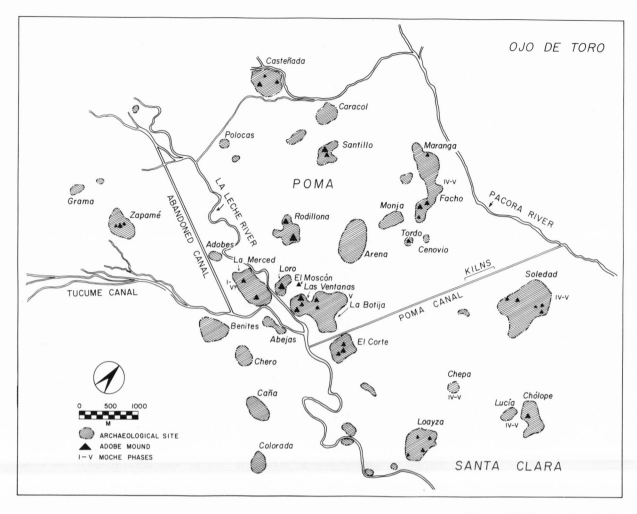

Figure 4.19. Map showing Mochica occupation in the mid–La Leche Valley.

suggests an intrusive late Moche IV wedge driven into the middle sections of these valleys. Disturbingly, we have not identified any apparent Moche IV corporate symbol of the Lambayeque-based Mochica polity posited earlier. At Sipán, to date no major Moche IV elite tomb or major structures have been identified. Did the seat of power shift from Sipán to Huaca Santa Rosa? Tentatively, we suggest that the Lambayeque-based Mochica polity lost its prestige and power sometime late in Moche III or early IV for reasons still unclear.

Given the preceding observations, we must consider the distinct possibility that these valleys may have been brought under *direct* control of the Moche IV hegemony centered at Moche. That the inferred Moche IV integration was a rapid process approximately spanning A.D. 500–550 is suggested by excavation at Huaca del Pueblo Batán Grande. Thus, early in the sixth cen-

tury the Mochica polity centered at Moche may have attained its greatest territorial extent, spanning at least the north bank of the La Leche to the south bank of the Huarmey Valley, a distance of some 470 km. The question remains, however, why the Mochica polity (whether local or Moche-centered) did not attempt to harness the tremendous agricultural potential by expanding their control into these three northern valleys. This situation may reflect the lateness of the expansion or the inferred lower-valley domination by a local Gallinazo polity. In addition, we need to consider the decrease in runoff for irrigation and/or channeling of water from the Lambayeque to the Zaña Valley. The crucial question of what caused the replacement or relocation of the capital and expansion northward so late in its history will be examined in depth in Chapter 6.

5. Mochica Horizontality

We tend to think of conquest and territorial expansion as land-based and physically continuous; however, Mochica territory appears to have included various colonies and/or confederates geographically separated from the North Coast heartland, necessitating several days on foot or by ship. Significantly, Mochica colonies have been found only along the coast and offshore islands; none is known in the highlands (cf. Rostworowski 1985) or eastern jungle. This Mochica horizontal archipelago contrasts with the highland-based vertical archipelago described in Chapter 2. Mochica expansion along much of the North Coast may be seen as a concerted effort to break away from the limitations of a homogeneous and repetitive coastal environment, what I have labeled "horizontality" (I. Shimada 1982, 1987a). Put another way, expanding sufficiently far north and south along the coast, the Mochica could approximate the resource diversity that might have been gained from vertically oriented expansion. As seen below, earlier physical evidence of trade or other forms of interaction between the Mochica and their North Highland Cajamarca, Huamachuco, and Recuay neighbors is scarce.

The Mochica outposts in Huarmey and perhaps in Vicús are significant not only for being the southern and northern frontiers, respectively, but also for the considerable distances that separate them from the nearest Mochica territory and for the transitional character of their environment. The Huarmey Valley is separated from the Casma by some 70 km of rugged sand-covered mountains and desert, while the Vicús–Loma Negra region is reachable from the La Leche through a 150-km tract of semitropical thorny forest and savanna-like vegetation.[57] The strategic location of the Loma Negra area and the possible role of the local elite have been already discussed. In respect to the mid- to lower Huarmey, seven sites on both banks have yielded Moche IV ceramics and one site had Moche III ceramics as well.[58] Cerro Campanario (also known as Fortaleza) in the lower valley is thought to be the primary site of local Mochica occupation (Y. Amano, pers. com. 1983; Conklin

1979). Much as in all the other northern and southern frontier valleys of the Mochica hegemony, littoral sites in Huarmey show no Mochica occupation. Unlike its northern counterpart in the Vicús region, Mochica ceramics in Huarmey show no apparent regional idiosyncrasies.

Why were the Mochica in Huarmey? Why did their southern expansion end there? Was the limited agricultural potential of the valley enough to attract them? As alluded to in Chapter 3, the Huarmey drainage occupies the frontier of two major cultural and environmental areas. To the north lie the productive North Coast valleys and the intermontane Callejón de Huaylas Basin. To the south one encounters lakes and extensive *puna* in the Junín highlands, along with a series of small coastal valleys. Mochica occupation of Huarmey may have both pressured the southern frontier of the rival Recuay based in Callejón de Huaylas, and procured resources and products from the Central and South Coasts and Highlands (e.g., alpaca wool, obsidian, and salt from Junín) in exchange for North Coast products such as dried and salted fish, cotton, maize, copper objects, and even Ecuadorian shells. The stylistic blending of Moche V with the Central Highland Wari and Central Coast Nievería cultures tends to support the above view (see Chapters 6 and 9).

There are tantalizing bits of evidence suggesting that the Mochica extended their sphere of influence down to Nasca territory on the South Coast. The Nasca culture was a notable contemporary that may have established an intervalley hegemony out of the Nasca Basin.[59] Scholars have long wondered if the Nasca and Mochica interacted, and if so when, why, and how. Recent studies suggest that certain Moche IV and V stylistic conventions and motifs (perhaps even themes) formed the basis of Nasca innovations, perhaps as early as Nasca Phase 6 but primarily in Phases 7–8 (ca. A.D. 550–700).[60] We are speaking of selective adoption rather than full-fledged replication. There is no definite Moche III influence on Nasca art or reciprocal Nasca influence on Mochica art.

Kubler (1948: 36) has argued that Mochica artifacts "have long been known from the South Coast of Peru [Ancón, Ca-

ñete, and Ica or Pisco valleys], although never properly evaluated as evidence for Mochica distribution."[61] He felt that the southward extent of Mochica influence had been underestimated. However, a recent study (Schaedel 1990) casts serious doubt on the provenience of the Mochica artifacts from the Chincha Islands off the South Coast that Kubler (1948) emphasized.[62]

Control of or access to these islands situated 5 to 20 km offshore raises another important facet of Mochica horizontality. Complementing land-based, llama-assisted horizontality spanning the entire North Coast, Mochica fishers based on offshore islands and using reed boats were able to establish a "marine horizontality," exploiting different fish and mammals seasonally in shallow and deep water on and off the islands. In some valleys (e.g., Nepeña to Huarmey), Mochica settlements near the shore are absent or rare, raising the possibility that marine resources were acquired by means of exchange or tribute extraction.

The Mochica economy was built first and foremost on exploitation and management of local conditions and resources, including the dual subsistence pillars of intensive irrigation cultivation and intensive marine exploitation. Even with the advent of large-scale irrigation agriculture and perhaps llama herding, marine resources remained a primary subsistence base of North Coast inhabitants (see Masuda 1985). Establishing direct control of distant resources, both on land and offshore, was in essence an extension of the above thrust—the resources becoming "local" in the cognitive map of the expansionist.

6. Mochica Verticality: Peer Polity Interaction?

The preceding adds up to a picture of a culture that successfully achieved economic self-sufficiency by intensive exploitation of diverse coastal resources (Netherly 1977; I. Shimada 1982). Territorial expansion, though perhaps initiated by population pressure on agricultural production, enabled diversification of their overall resource base for this self-sufficiency. In the latter stages of their expansion, the Mochica polity appears to have geographically and economically land-locked contemporary highland polities. Was the Mochica polity as coast-centric as the above description suggests? How can we characterize interaction between the Mochica and highland polities such as Cajamarca and Recuay? What impact, if any, did the latter have on the growth of the Mochica?

In contrast to the unrivaled political dominance and impressive territorial expansion along the coast achieved during late Moche III to early Moche IV, available evidence indicates that Mochica intrusion inland beyond the coastal *yunga* zone or highest intake points of coastal irrigation systems (500–600 m above sea level) was rare, ephemeral, and/or localized (I. Shimada 1982: 185–187; also Proulx 1982; Topic and Topic 1983); there is little concrete evidence to support the view that their inland limit reached about 1,000 m above sea level (Schaedel 1985a: 444).[63] We have no evidence of widespread, intensive, or highly organized trade between the Mochica and highland polities. Their political relationships appear to have been tenuous at best, characterized by intermittent hostilities involving raids and temporary occupations (e.g., Proulx 1982) as well as peaceful resource sharing or even trade, much like the picture painted by highland folklore recorded early in the Colonial era (e.g., Duviols 1973; Rostworowski 1985; Schaedel 1985a; Tomoeda 1985). At the same time, these peer polities seem to have respected each other's religion and principal ceremonial centers, as evinced by limited numbers of fancy Cajamarca vessel offerings at Moche (Kroeber 1925; T. Topic 1977; Uhle 1913) and Mochica vessels at the Recuay center of Cabana (Grieder 1978). Further, it is difficult to determine whether highland polities, in dealing with the Mochica, behaved as a single unified entity or whether regional constituents acted more or less on their own (Shimada 1985c, 1987a).

A. Mochica-Recuay Interaction

One line of evidence that points to contact between the Mochica and Recuay is the sharing of the related mythical animal motifs variously known as the "Moon Monster," "Crested" or "Moon Animal," or "Dragon" (Fig. 4.20).[64] These motifs occur on an appreciable number of Moche I and II vessels. Reichert (1982: 290; cf. Bankmann 1979; Nersesov 1987) sees this sharing as the result of adoption of selected aspects of "prestigious" Recuay art by Mochica artisans who misinterpreted "rigid Recuay artistic canons." Whatever the reason for this sharing, the motifs remained popular throughout the Moche sequence and beyond. Reichert (1982: 290) concludes that "contact" between these two populations was "quite limited" and "superficial." Mochica ceramics are rare in the Recuay heartland in the Callejón de Huaylas. One of the few documented cases involves two fragments in a grave offering at the temple of Pashash (Grieder 1978: 72–73).

In contrast, Recuay ceramics are found over a wide area of the Mochica Southern Sector from the Nepeña (Proulx 1982) and Santa (e.g., Gambini 1984; Larco Hoyle 1960; Wilson 1988) to Virú valleys (Bennett 1939; Strong and Evans 1952). Because of its abundance, Larco Hoyle (1960) theorized that kaolin Recuay and Recuay-influenced (what he called Santa) ceramics developed in the Santa Valley and then spread into the Callejón de Huaylas. Wilson's (1988: 175, 198) recent survey of the Santa Valley also attests to their abundance, particularly starting during the Late Suchimancillo phase (Late Gallinazo) prior to the Mochica arrival. During this period settlements are concentrated in the middle to upper reaches of the valley, suggesting the importance of socioeconomic relationships with the adjacent North Highlands.

With Moche III intrusion, however, "a sweeping reorganization of cultural priorities" took place (Wilson 1987: 68). A significant reduction in the number and extent of the kaolin Recuay ceramics was accompanied by a new settlement pattern that emphasized the lower valley and agricultural maximization.

Within the Nepeña Valley, Proulx (1982: 91) remarks that "the lack of Recuay-influenced sites in the middle and lower Nepeña Valley is even more striking than the lack of Moche sites in the upper part of the valley." Mochica concern with control of the upper Nepeña Valley and with Recuay encroachment from the adjacent highland region of Callejón de Huaylas is indicated by an eight-site cluster roughly 40–45 km inland from the Pacific (ibid.). All these sites produced minimal Moche IV ceramics. Of three sites that yielded both Mochica and Recuay ceramics, one is described as a "fortress with extremely thick fieldstone walls" located on a plateau providing an excellent view of the Nepeña River (Proulx 1982: 90). This *yunga* was clearly a zone of contention between these two polities.

Surprisingly, in spite of proximity to Callejón de Huaylas, a recent survey of the Sechín branch of the Casma Valley revealed no Recuay ceramics (Wilson 1991); apparently, the local Gallinazo polity held control of this branch.

Overall, prior to Moche III southward expansion, the Gallinazo and Recuay cultures in the Virú and Santa valleys may have had a tense coexistence, with the Gallinazo controlling the middle to lower parts of the valleys and the Recuay primarily the upper reaches. Mochica contact with the Recuay during this time was perhaps limited to rare ceremonial exchanges. With Mochica subjugation of the Gallinazo, they came into more direct conflict with the Recuay, landlocking them in the uppermost reaches of the valleys. Several scholars interpret certain Moche III and IV paintings of warriors in recognizably different costumes engaged in hand-to-hand combat as depicting battles between the Recuay and Mochica polities (e.g., Disselhoff 1956; Proulx 1982; Wilson 1987).

B. Mochica-Cajamarca Interaction

Just as the Recuay presence in the upper reaches of the southern North Coast valleys is crucial to understanding the process of Mochica southward expansion, the coeval Early and Middle Cajamarca (Table 1) presence in the *chaupiyunga* zones of various northern North Coast valleys is crucial to understanding the northward expansion process. Their distinctive decorated kaolin ceramics (Matsumoto 1988; Reichlen and Reichlen 1949; Terada and Matsumoto 1985) have been reported widely on the northern North Coast, including the Moche, Jequetepeque, and Zaña valleys (Ravi-

Figure 4.20. Recuay Moon Monster. Redrawn from Fig. 311 in Kutscher 1983.

nes 1982; I. Shimada 1982; Topic and Topic 1983). An appreciable number of Cajamarca ceramics occur among sites in the *chaupiyunga* in the upper Chicama Valley, some of which may well have been occupied by the North Highlanders (Krzanowski 1977; Russell 1990).

Recent excavations at the site of Moche recovered twenty-eight plain spoon fragments from Moche III/IV contexts (T. Topic 1977: 257–258 and her Plate 7 on 274), as well as one Early Cajamarca sherd (T. Topic 1982: 274). Homogeneity in the form and paste of these spoons, as well as their close resemblance to a well-documented, common Early Cajamarca spoon form (see Fig. 62 in Terada and Onuki 1982: 190), suggest that they were imported from a single North Highland location (Matsumoto 1988, pers. com. 1986). Early Cajamarca ceramics have also been identified from at least one location in the lower Jequetepeque Valley (Disselhoff 1958a,b).

In addition to the Cajamarca Basin and cis-Andean *chaupiyunga*, Early Cajamarca ceramics are widely found in the eastern *yunga* of the northern highlands (Lennon 1986; Matsumoto 1988; Ruíz 1985; I. Schjellerup, pers. com. 1986). In other words, concurrent with Moche III expansion, the Early Cajamarca culture was expanding into *chaupiyunga* zones on both sides of the Andes.

Subsequent Middle Cajamarca ceramics with diagnostic Floral Cursive decoration reach as far south as Cusco and the South Coast. This is particularly the case during Subphase B, which appears to overlap with Moche V and immediately post–Moche V times (Matsumoto 1988; Terada and Matsumoto 1985; see Chapter 10). Uhle (1913; Kroeber 1925) recovered a tripod vessel with such decoration at Huaca del Sol at the site of Moche. Additional Floral Cursive ceramics have been found in the La Leche and Lambayeque valleys to the north (Larco Hoyle 1948; I. Shimada 1982).

Though the sample is quite limited, the changing distribution of Cajamarca ceramics over time seems a telling barometer of the political strength of the Mochica polity, particularly for Moche V. Demise of the Moche V polity was analogous to opening the floodgates for the Cajamarca polity; evidence is quite strong for immediate post–Moche V coastward expansion of the Cajamarca population as if to reclaim lost access to the coast.

One point that emerges from the preceding discussion is that the potential or real threat of expansive Early and Middle Cajamarca (Subphase A) peer polities may have slowed or restricted effective Mochica integration of the areas north and south of the Jequetepeque River, the major corridor linking the Cajamarca Basin and the Pacific. It may well be that Moche IV northward intrusion into the mid-valley was partly an attempt to restrict the geopolitical ambition of the Cajamarca polity. Future studies may well reveal that some of the Mochica battle scenes also depict conflict with the Cajamarca polity.

Mochica artifacts in the Cajamarca region are extremely rare. In fact, the Japanese team that carried out three seasons of excavation and survey in the Cajamarca Basin found only one Mochica stirrup-spout fragment (Matsumoto 1988). Based on the presence of patronyms (names that show descent from given persons) in the now extinct coastal *Muchik* language recorded early in the Colonial era in the Cajamarca region, Rostworowski (1985) suggests that coastal polities as far back as the Mochica may have established North Highland settlements. At present, there is no physical evidence to refute or support this hypothesis. I suspect that the Mochica polity was more concerned with control (or at least sharing) of the *chaupiyunga*. Overall, a coast-centric resource base with minimal or limited vertical complementarity appears to have continued throughout the Mochica existence (I. Shimada 1982).

5 Mochica Organizational Features

This chapter focuses on the internal features and workings of the Mochica culture at its height from late Moche III to early Moche IV, particularly at Moche, the capital of the southern Mochica polity. This focus on Moche reflects the disproportionate attention the site has received.

1. Developments at the Capital of Moche

As if to keep pace with expanding territory and political power, there appears to have been increasing concern with the Mochica corporate image. Huaca del Sol at Moche underwent at least eight recognized major construction stages ending sometime in Moche IV, with five (and perhaps six) completed by the end of Moche III (Hastings and Moseley 1975). Thus, a substantial percentage of the over 143 million estimated adobe bricks used to achieve the final form must have already been in place by the end of Moche III. With estimated basal dimensions of over 342 by 159 m and a height of 40 m, the Sol mound clearly overshadows all other Mochica platform mounds, except Moche V Huaca Fortaleza at Pampa Grande.

The companion Huaca de la Luna, situated some 500 m east of the Sol mound (Fig. 2.1), consists of three mounds connected by courts and was built using over 50 million adobe bricks (ibid.). At least four to five construction stages have been documented, with adobe friezes reminiscent of Cupisnique examples and polychrome murals decorating early and late stages, respectively (Bonavia 1985; Kroeber 1926; Mackey and Hastings 1982; Uceda 1992). The main body of the platform mound measures approximately 95 by 85 by 25 m.

The claim that by the end of Moche III the site of Moche had emerged as the paramount ceremonial-political center of the southern Mochica multi-valley polity (e.g., Moseley 1983a; Schaedel 1972; T. Topic 1977, 1982) hinges on (1) the enormous investment of labor and material implied by the sheer bulk of the Sol and Luna mounds (Hastings and Moseley 1975; Moseley 1975b), (2) their persistent importance as indicated by numerous additions and modifications, (3) indications (intentional marking on constituent adobe bricks) of the requisite labor force for their construction having been drawn from within and outside of the Moche Valley (Moseley 1975b), (4) monumental mounds and associated "palaces" erected at Mochica regional centers (e.g., Huancaco, Pampa de los Incas, and Pañamarca in the Virú, Santa, and Nepeña valleys) that "echo the most important architecture at Moche in form and layout, but on a much smaller scale" (T. Topic 1977: 369; also Moseley 1983a: 219), (5) the fact that the site of Moche constitutes the largest pre–Moche V site known "by a wide margin" (T. Topic 1977: 369).

Although the present appearance of the site of Moche (Figs. 1.3, 2.1) gives the impression that it consists of only the Sol and Luna mounds, there was an associated extensive settlement serving the residential and manufacturing needs of the ceremonial-civic center. Uhle (1913, n.d.) encountered architectural and artifactual remains of what he called a "town" buried in the seemingly vacant flat area in the eastern and southern portions of the site between the platform mounds.

More recent excavations by the Chan Chan–Moche Valley Project have shed light on the nature and extent of this "town." For example, a 6-meter-deep trench in the middle of the flat area between these mounds revealed superimposed small structures built on an accumulated habitation midden containing Moche III and IV materials (Donnan and Mackey 1978: 71).

Variation in the construction, layout, and associated remains of domestic architecture excavated at Moche led to a three-part typology (T. Topic 1977, 1982: 268–270). The structures in one area (SC4; Fig. 2.1) near the east base of the Sol mound had uneven, sloping floors of packed dirt and refuse partitioned by wall foundations of cobblestones set in mud or of reused adobes.[65] The upper portions of the walls were presumably built of perishable materials. In contrast, structures found on the northwest slope of Cerro Blanco (AA1) and in the "plaza" southwest of the Luna mound had solidly built stone and adobe brick walls, well finished with mud plaster, and were relatively spacious (AA2 and AA3). Within AA2 were two domestic complexes containing sets of small storerooms, bins, and niches notable for their high-quality construction, greater elaboration, and space (Fig. 5.1). Residents here had some 8.7 m³ of storage space, suggesting control over relatively large quantities of goods (T. Topic 1982: 270). Structures

near Huaca del Sol (SC4) were associated with "many of the same kinds of artifacts" as the other excavated areas at the site, but in smaller amounts and of lower quality (T. Topic 1982: 269). Thus, T. Topic sees a three-level social stratification with the residents of AA2 as wealthy but not the highest elite.

The better-made constructions (AA1–AA3) were associated with proportionately more fine vessels, such as flaring bowls and stirrup-spout bottles, "as well as less utilitarian ware." In addition, finds included "small objects of value" (e.g., stone, copper, and ceramic beads, copper tweezers and knives, and figurine fragments) and a few "craft-related implements," such as "hammerstones and polishing stones, needles and spindle whorls, paddles and other wooden items" (T. Topic 1982: 268). These observations corroborate Uhle's (n.d.; see T. Topic 1982: 276) earlier discoveries of numerous fragments of lapis lazuli,[66] and beads of many different materials in various stages of processing on the lower slope of Cerro Blanco. He also reported broken halves of "donut-shaped" stones (possibly clod-busters or mace heads) in various stages of manufacture scattered over the northern section of the flat area between the two *huacas*. More recently, T. Topic (1977, 1982: 275) reports finding large quantities of discarded Moche IV ceramics near the southern margin of the site. Some were apparently damaged during firing but others are from large, thick storage jars that show no sign of use. In addition, "an extraordinary number of broken figurines and broken figurine molds was also found" (T. Topic 1982: 276). From these lines of evidence, Topic deduces that "the shops in this area seem to have been producing large urns, smaller-sized utilitarian ware, figurines, and low-quality fine ware."

A team from the Trujillo branch of the National Institute of Culture provides additional support for the idea of craft production in the general area. They describe what appear to be small tuyeres (ceramic blowtube tips), slag lumps, and intensely heat-discolored spots (V. Pimentel, pers. com. 1985), all of which suggest metalworking (not smelting). Surface scatters of partially worked *Spondylus* and mother-

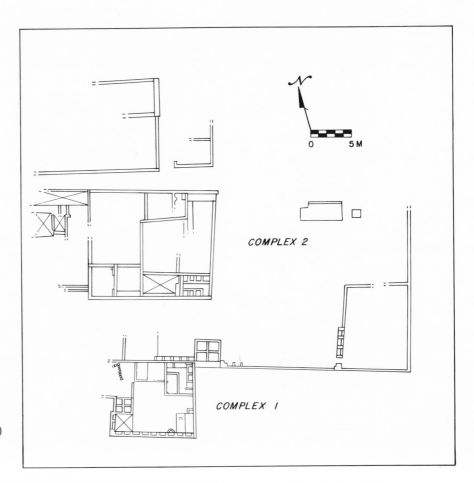

Figure 5.1. Plan of the best-preserved domestic structures at Architectural Area (AA) 2, showing niches and storage areas. Redrawn from Fig. 11.2 in Topic 1982: 271.

of-pearl have been noted near the summit of Cerro Blanco, suggesting a shell workshop or shrine offerings. However, these seem to date to late Middle Horizon, long after Mochica abandonment of the area (Menzel 1977: 40; cf. T. Topic 1982: 273–274).

These lines of evidence present a picture of the site of Moche as an important craft production center of both utilitarian and sumptuary objects.

Where the elite of the highest echelon resided is largely a matter of speculation. One possibility is that they lived in the Huaca de la Luna complex (T. Topic 1982: 270, 277–278). While polychrome murals (with up to three superimposed friezes) on the interior faces of walls partitioning the tops of the three mounds have been well studied (e.g., Bonavia 1985: 72–97; Kroeber 1930: 71–73; Mackey and Hastings 1982), our understanding of the architectural layout is far from complete. The famous "Revolt of the Artifacts" frieze, showing a battle between warriors and personified weapons, decorated the walls flanking a raised area at the southeast corner of the highest mound that may have "contained an altar, idol, or seat" (Fig. 5.2; Kroeber 1930: 72 and his Plate XXVII). Based on Mochica paintings showing a well-dressed individual seated alone on a raised platform receiving offerings and visitors, T. Topic (1982: 277–278) argues that "The dais [40 cm high] provides evidence for the existence of a Moche ruler, and suggests that he was housed at [the Luna mound], segregated from the rest of the population and viewed only on formal occasions." However, it remains to be established whether the raised area was the throne of a "hereditary king" (ibid.), or the "altar" of a sacred idol (Kroeber 1930: 72), or where the inferred king actually resided when not holding audience.

In contrast to the isolated and exclusive Luna mound, more secular and public functions are envisioned for the Huaca del Sol.[67] The presence of domestic refuse (including butchered and burnt llama bones) under, around, in, and on top of the platform mound suggests that while it "may have symbolized the power of the Moche state, everyday activities were carried out in its immediate vicinity" (T. Topic 1982: 278; also see S. Pozorski 1976: 113–118). In this view, the Sol mound was "the focus of community life, providing the actual interface between ruling class and populace" (T. Topic 1982: 278).

Overall, there are indications that by the Moche IIIB–IVA florescence, the capital of Moche was a functionally complex and differentiated settlement with a considerable resident population.

Figure 5.2. Polychrome friezes called "Revolt of the Objects" recorded by A. L. Kroeber atop the major mound of Huaca de la Luna. See Bonavia 1985: 72–85 for detailed discussion of the friezes. Courtesy of the Field Museum of Natural History, Chicago.

2. Socioeconomic Features of the Mochica Culture

A. Labor Organization and Corporate Projects

The Sol and Luna mounds at Moche have long attracted archaeological attention for their construction materials and techniques. From the days of Bishop Martínez de Compañón at the end of the eighteenth century, it was apparent that these two mounds were built by "a system of contiguously placed, abutting (not bonded) thick walls of solid adobe bricks many meters high" (Kroeber 1930: 61). Willey (1953: 206) provided additional details of the construction technique: "The usual construction unit seems to have been a wall section or oblong columns of adobes. These columns were a meter or so thick at the base, tapered somewhat toward the top, and were simply placed alongside the next columnar unit, usually without mortising the ends of the brick." The massiveness of the construction overcame the structural weakness of the plan. Kroeber (1926: 12–17, 1930: 58–66) recognized possible social ramifications of the above and initiated systematic studies of the adobe bricks and associated construction techniques. He

wondered if the reasons for this "system of adjacent thick walls," as dramatically illustrated in Figure 2.11, "may be social, each contingent of a community building its own wall or column" (Kroeber 1930: 61). The simplicity of the segmentary construction technique together with the "slovenliness" seen in execution implied "labor of population masses" (ibid.).

In his pioneering 1899–1900 excavation at Moche, Uhle (n.d.) recognized segmentary construction and discovered that many constituent bricks bore "marks of the owners" ranging from finger-drawn (e.g., crab and geometric figures) to stamped designs made before the bricks were sun-dried. He concluded that "from the masonry it may be seen that various communities (clans) contributed bricks for the construction of the temple as is shown by the different stamps or marks upon them."

More recently, members of the Chan Chan–Moche Valley Project found that adobe bricks within each vertical segment or column of the platform mounds were uniform in size, soil qualities, color, and, where applicable, mark (Hastings and Moseley 1975; Fig. 5.3). In other words, "makers' marks,"[68] as they came to be

called, were segment-specific; bricks used in individual columns were likely to have been made with the same molds at the same locales. Investigators also found that, at the Huaca del Sol, "makers' marks" appeared on 20 percent to over 50 percent of bricks in individual segments of construction stages IV–VIII (Moche II or III to IV). Further, 85–95 percent of the segments examined at the Huaca del Sol each had bricks carrying only one of the total of ninety-three distinct marks recorded (ibid., 198). Data from the Huaca de la Luna agree well with findings from the Huaca del Sol.

Building on the above observations and existing knowledge of the *mit'a* labor service demanded from able-bodied men in the Inca Empire some one thousand years later, Moseley (1975b,d) argued that each vertical adobe segment was erected by a single work crew representing a social unit (distinct community) fulfilling a labor tax levied by the Mochica polity, and that the simple marks on bricks were physical symbols of the brickmakers who either placed their adobes themselves or had them placed by selected members of the same community within their assigned segments. Thus, the few marked bricks would serve to identify the entire adobe segment as the work of a given social group.

In this interpretation, discrete labor parties drawn from different communities under Mochica control carried out all public projects such as the construction and repair of monumental "temples," major canals, and roads. The over one hundred distinct marks found on adobe bricks at the Sol and Luna mounds would have represented communities within the Moche Valley as well as from adjacent valleys (Moseley 1975b: 194–195; T. Topic 1982: 274).

In the Moche Valley proper, the segmented format for public constructions, including canals, continued well into Chimú times (Moseley 1975b,d). The segmentary format was widely employed in Mochica platform mounds outside of the Moche Valley (starting with Moche III), for example, at the Castillo mound of the Mochica regional center of Huancaco in the Virú, Huacas San José and El Brujo in the Chicama (Kroeber 1930: 61, 78, 84; Willey 1953: 206), and Pacatnamú (McClelland 1986), as well as the adobe platform with elite tombs at Sipán (Alva 1988), and Pampa Grande (Shimada 1990a, in press 1; Shimada and Cavallaro 1986, in press).

It has come to be implicitly assumed that the Mochica polity imposed this construction system and associated labor taxation on subjugated populations (Conrad 1978: 285; Moseley 1978a: 523–524, 1982: 11–12; T. Topic 1982: 272, 274; Wilson 1988: 336). Further, it has been suggested that the platform mounds built at regional administrative centers were modeled after the architectural canons of the Huaca del Sol (Moseley 1978a: 524; cf. Isbell 1986: 194).[69]

The above, though reasonable, cannot be readily assumed without extensive excavation of the mounds in question and explicit guidelines for comparison. This is a critical issue, considering that the inferred labor taxation has come to be regarded as a fundamental organizational principle of the Mochica economy (e.g., T. Topic 1982: 274).

Actually, the impressive Late Gallinazo mound of Castillo de Tomaval in the Virú Valley shows segmentary construction, suggesting that this technique may well predate the Mochica (Willey 1953: 163–164, 206; also Bennett 1939: 27–28, 1950: 68; Kroeber 1930: 78; Moseley 1975b:

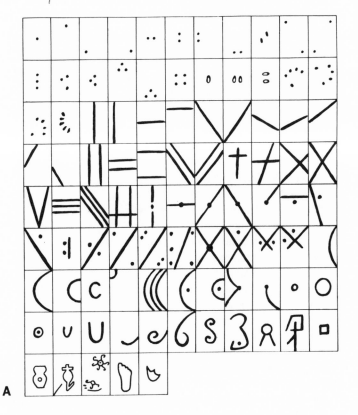

A

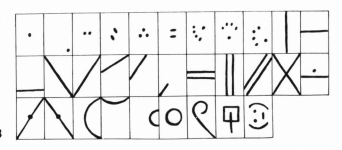

B

Figure 5.3. Compilation of adobe brick marks identified at the Huaca del Sol (A) and Huaca de la Luna (B) mounds. After Figs. 3–4 in Hastings and Moseley 1975: 199.

193). Considering the distribution of "Gallinazo" ceramics throughout the North Coast, it is quite likely that the Mochica simply followed the time-honored system of construction and labor organization with which local subjugated populations were already familiar (Shimada in press 1).

At the same time, we have no indication of marked adobe bricks in Gallinazo constructions or in the first three construction stages of the Huaca del Sol. There are two plausible scenarios for the observed situation: (1) these early stages are Gallinazo constructions, or (2) the Mochica initiated the practice of marking bricks for better "accounting" of labor forces drawn from ever widening areas (ibid.). In favor of the latter theory is the fact that stage V of the Huaca del Sol contained Moche III burials. In addition, though construction stage 1 (Moche III) bricks at the Huaca de la Luna showed no marking, 5 percent of stage II bricks were marked (Hastings and Moseley 1975). As mentioned above, the first wave of Mochica territorial expansion out of the Chicama-Moche area occurred early in Moche III, if not by the end of Moche II.

The adobe platform with early Moche elite burials in Sipán was also built with the segmentary technique (roughly one-meter-wide columns; Alva 1988). Brick marks were essentially segment-specific in excellent accord with patterns observed in the Moche Valley. A clear majority of the bricks at Huaca Rajada were marked. We need to ascertain whether the custom of marking bricks already existed along with the segmentary construction format in pre–Moche III times in Lambayeque, perhaps at Huaca Santa Rosa across the Reque River from Sipán. Given the impressive material and organizational achievements implied by elite burials at Sipán, it would not be a surprise if future studies revealed that the marking of bricks for accounting purposes was a Lambayeque innovation introduced to the Chicama-Moche area during Moche III.

In the Moche Valley proper, the use of marked bricks essentially ceased by the end of Moche IV, with very limited use at Moche V Galindo. At Moche V Pampa Grande, clearly definable segments in major corporate constructions were built with bricks of up to a half-dozen mold dimensions and a dozen marks (Shimada in press 1; Shimada and Cavallaro 1986, in press). To uphold the basic working premise that each construction segment had social significance, we would have to postulate that late in the Moche sequence or in the Lambayeque region, the composition of the labor group(s) responsible for each segment became more complex or was defined differently. These and other related issues are discussed at length in Chapter 7.

B. Social Organization

Mochica society is often described as a rigidly stratified class structure ruled by a small core of elite who provided political and religious leadership. Though architecture, burials, and iconography provide supportive data for the above characterization, we are far from having a reliable, comprehensive, and appropriately dynamic picture of Mochica social structure and organization. We are uncertain when and how class stratification (as opposed to status differentiation) emerged.

Certain artistic conventions and depictions have been interpreted as showing class stratification. The individuals in a given scene who command our attention are inevitably shown at or near the center, appreciably larger, occupying higher ground, and/or more elaborately or distinctly dressed. The converse in general holds. Systematic analysis of complex group scenes, such as public rituals, feasts, or organized deer hunting, shows at least three figure sizes and locations; for example, an organized deer hunt may show one or two large, elaborately attired personages with spear-throwers and spears, smaller figures with clubs chasing deer, and still smaller, more simply dressed individuals holding the nets to keep deer from escaping (Fig. 5.4).

Burial data provide important corroborative, but by no means clear-cut, evidence. Mochica burials of various phases documented in different regions of the North Coast show certain basic similarities such as extended bodies placed inside rectangular pits or adobe chambers, and sometimes inside cane coffins as well, the practice of placing a metal disc in the mouth, and accompanying human and animal (usually llama) extremities. At the

Figure 5.4. Moche IV fineline depiction of deer hunting scene. Well-attired individuals armed with spears and spear throwers are hunting deer within the fenced area. Note the differentiation in size and dress of hunt participants. Redrawn from Fig. 262 in Donnan 1978: 179.

same time, as burials excavated at Moche show, it is hard to discern any apparent internal correlation among the location of interment, nature of burial architecture, and quantity and quality of offerings. Some were apparently "unceremonially dumped" in middens with no accompanying grave goods (T. Topic 1982: 266–267), others carefully placed in pits dug in middens with some grave goods, and still others placed in architectural settings. For example, a disturbed burial placed under a bench in a house built on the hillside north of the Luna mound appears to have had several stirrup-spout bottles and flaring bowls (ibid., 267). A Moche IV grave placed in the adobe fill atop the Huaca del Sol contained one adult male and one adult female with disarticulated llama bones and thirty-seven ceramic vessels, some of which contained cotton seeds or "vegetal remains" (Donnan and Mackey 1978: 92).

A set of nine elite Moche IV burials was found in rectangular cells cut into a small adobe platform buried by sand in the middle of the flat area between the Sol and Luna mounds. As a group, they clearly differ from other Moche IV burials excavated at Moche in that all were "high status adult males, many of whom have large copper disc headdresses like those worn by certain individuals shown in Moche art" (Donnan and Mackey 1978: 208). In addition, most

had a large number of fine ceramic vessels, copper objects, and some exotic items such as gold flakes, coral fragments, textiles, wooden *tumis* or knives with crescent-shaped blades, *tumbaga* earspools, gilt copper objects, turquoise, and stone beads and/or discs (ibid., 102–158). In fact, the grave of one adult male (forty-five to sixty years old) had sixty-two ceramic vessels and a range of copper objects (e.g., discs, "tweezers," and needles). Though it is doubtful that the platform was originally built as a burial structure, it was reserved for "elite" interments (ibid., 208; cf. 379 of the same work).

The celebrated "Tomb of the Warrior-Priest" augments the above picture of Mochica elite burials (Strong 1947; Strong and Evans 1952: 150–167). This burial was fortuitously discovered on the last day of scheduled fieldwork in a thick deposit of refuse at the southeast base of the midden-covered dune site of Huaca de la Cruz in the Virú Valley in 1946. It contained a forty- to forty-five-year-old man wrapped in finely woven cotton cloth within a cane coffin accompanied by, among other things, (1) a sacrificed man and boy, (2) two sacrificed women, (3) two sacrificed headless "llamas," (4) numerous gourd bowls, some still containing maize, beans, and cotton bolls (seeds removed), (5) twenty-eight ceramic vessels, (6) numerous metal objects, and (7) three elaborately

carved long wooden staffs (one with an owl, another with a war mace, and the last showing a tusked "warrior-god" effigy). Notable among the metal objects were colorful animal effigy headdresses: a gilt copper fox head and two fiber-and-cloth bird heads attached to a fiber liner. Both the bird heads and the liner were covered with yellow, green, red, and blue-green feathers. The jaw of the fox head had been repaired with asphalt and thread, suggesting long use. The face of the Warrior-Priest was covered by a copper mask "held in place by cloth swathings around the entire skull. Underneath the face mask a much more elaborate mouth mask [nose ornament] of gilded copper inlaid with turquoise and polished stones partially covered the mouth" (Strong and Evans 1952: 156).

Perhaps the most publicized grave good was a wooden staff (1.74 m long) showing "a tusked deity standing on a shell-inlaid platform breaking the soil into furrows with his ceremonial digging stick. He has a small boy by his right side sowing seed into furrows" (ibid.). There is a definite similarity between the carving and grave contents. These lines of evidence suggest a man of considerable political and religious significance, perhaps a regional leader. Given that this tomb was found on the last day of fieldwork, and that recent work at the site of Sipán (see below) shows a cluster of elite tombs within a single adobe platform mound, it is quite likely that the Tomb of the Warrior-Priest was only one of a group of elite Mochica tombs at the Huaca de la Cruz mound—and not necessarily the most important.

A long-standing question about Mochica burials has been why "we do not have any that resemble the sort of 'royal' or disproportionately sumptuous burials that had been found in the consensus state-level cultures in other parts of the world" (Isbell 1979: 635). The recent discovery of sumptuous tombs near Huaca Rajada within the extensive site of Sipán[70] in the mid-Lambayeque Valley helps dispel this skepticism.

Inspection of the stratigraphy and construction of a recently looted tomb deep in the rectangular adobe platform at Sipán (Architectural Level 4) indicated the presence of undisturbed burials higher up (Architectural Level 6). One indication was a cast copper "ceremonial scepter" some 4 kg in weight and one meter in length recovered close to the above looters' pit. The head of the scepter is a miniature model of a house with balustrades in the form of war clubs on four sides (20–25 cm to a side). The house has an ornately crowned canopy, the cornice decorated with trophy heads and the back wall with two animal figures.

A repository was found near the surface containing four "crowns," a breastplate, and a mask (all of copper), numerous llama and deer bones, and over 1,200 ceramic jars grouped by size, form, and decoration. The last are believed to have contained food and drink. This cache was overlaid by four copper masks, and under the cache was an adult body (presumably sacrificial) with a bone knife in its back. Some 3.5 m below the surface was a young "warrior" (ca. twenty years old) with a gilded copper helmet and a circular copper shield on his left arm. A gold disc was placed in the youth's mouth, and both feet were reported to have been cut off.[71]

The above finds are believed to represent provisions, bodyguard, personal servants, and gear for the journey to the afterlife of the "Lord of Sipán" found below. During the summer of 1987, about a meter below the young warrior burial, Alva and his crew encountered impressions of

seventeen logs representing what remained of the roof of the principal burial chamber. Below that, a much deteriorated 1.2-by-2.2-meter wooden coffin emerged containing the remains of a 170-centimeter-tall man in his early thirties. The coffin was apparently painted red on both interior and exterior surfaces and fastened by copper clasps. The Lord was accompanied by secondary burials placed just outside his coffin: two women, both about twenty years old, at his head and feet, and one man at each side.

As expected, the Lord was accompanied by impressive quantities of sumptuary goods of all sorts. Beneath the three-plank coffin lid the excavators found, among other objects, (1) clusters of feather ornaments (fans, etc.) above and below the body, (2) fabric banners with gilt copper platelets representing a figure with turquoise bead bracelets, (3) eleven layers of pectorals, each made of numerous shell and copper beads, (4) a large gilt copper headdress, (5) some dozen each of *Conus* and *Spondylus* shells at his feet and sides, (6) a crescent-shaped gold headdress some 60 cm across below the head, (7) crescent-shaped gold bells, (8,9) two "backflaps" (presumably to protect one's posterior in battle), one gold and one copper, (10) a miniature war club and shield, (11) copper-tipped darts, (12) two conical caps of cane fiber, and (13) three shrouds that enfolded the contents of the coffin.

The Lord's garments included (1) a plain white cotton inner garment, (2) an outer shirt covered with gilt copper platelets, (3) copper sandals, (4) gold-turquoise bracelets on his forearms, (5) two necklaces of repoussé gold and silver "peanuts in the shell," and (6) a necklace of sixteen large gold discs. His face was largely covered by gold eyes, nose and chin-cheek covers, and nose ornaments. His head rested on a gold saucer. A gold slug was placed on his right hand, which held a gold rattle, and a copper ingot on the left, with a copper knife. Apparently, gold and copper placements were carefully differentiated on the right and left, respectively.

Perhaps the most artistically and technically impressive grave goods were the Lord's three pairs of gold earspools with elaborate inlaid turquoise mosaics. One

pair showed deer and another, ducks. The last depicted an elaborately dressed "warrior" holding a shield and club and wearing a helmet decorated with a crescent piece like that of the Lord of Sipán in his coffin.

Further relevant information comes from an older burial called "Old Lord of Sipán" excavated from inferred Architectural Level 1 at the same Sipán platform (Alva 1990). The quantity and quality of funerary objects found in this tomb in many ways match those of the Lord of Sipán. Objects included a gold nose ornament and backflap, silver and gold earspools and necklaces (composed of miniature human heads and those of supernatural beings with feline fangs), and a gilt copper "crab-man" figurine over 60 cm tall. A nose ornament depicting a "tiny warrior-lord" holding a gold war club and shield mounted on a silver plate represents the apex of Mochica metalworking.

The Sipán discovery, including the Lord of Sipán, the Old Lord of Sipán, and a major tomb looted from Architectural Level 4, as a whole, is without peer among documented Mochica graves, notably for its impressive accumulation of gold objects, *Conus* and *Spondylus* shells, symbolism of power and status such as miniature representations of the deceased, staffs, fanged supernatural beings, and quality and size of the tomb structures.

One possible exception to this claim of superiority is a partially documented grave, in a subterranean chamber in the west front of the Luna mound at Moche, that was looted sometime before 1910 and included (1) a well-known gilt copper mask (26 cm high) with red paint and large shell eyes (see Jones 1979: 70–72 for a photo and description), (2) two more gilt copper masks (ca. 8 and 21 cm high), and (3) a large gilt copper fox head with shell teeth, a movable tongue, and numerous spangles depending from chin and ears. All three masks either still have or show traces of inlaid shell eyes and caplike visors. Among the thirty-seven Mochica tombs excavated by Uhle at the site of Moche, gold objects were by no means rare, though all of them were relatively small in size and/or simple in manufacture (Kroeber 1944: 131–132). They contained gold bracelets, earspools, and hollow beads.

On the basis of the burial data reviewed above, what can we infer about Mochica social structure and organization? One study of Mochica burials excavated at Moche sees three groups: (1) those with no grave goods—some "unceremoniously dumped" facedown in awkward positions, (2) those with grave goods placed in middens and under floors, and (3) those with grave goods in "cemeteries" (Donnan and Mackey 1978: 59–211; T. Topic 1982: 267). These groups are believed to correspond to three distinct social classes. This reconstruction appears to be supported by the iconographic data described earlier and, to some extent, by architectural data from Moche. With the addition of the exceptional or "royal" burials, we may have a four-tiered social hierarchy, assuming the social hierarchy was similar at both Mochica centers.

The above social reconstruction is not without flaws. As with any typology, resultant groupings vary according to the defining criteria and nature of the sample. In classifying burials, if their location and dating were more finely differentiated and emphasized, the resultant grouping would be different from the three-tier typology described above. In fact, it is not certain whether the corpus of quantitative and/or qualitative burial data indeed shows the discontinuous, steplike clustering to justify the class differentiation described above. As elaborated below, there are reasons to suspect a good deal of social fluidity (upward mobility) during Moche III.

The burial data from the site of Moche are highly skewed (see Chapter 2). The "high status" cemetery in the area between the two Huacas was "excavated to exhaustion," while "less rich burials were found only by accident, in spatially restricted strata cuts which represent only a minute percentage of the total site fill" (T. Topic 1977: 22–23, 1982: 268; cf. Donnan and Mackey 1978: 101). Combined with burials from Uhle's Site F at Moche (Kroeber 1925, 1944; Menzel 1977) and atop Huaca del Sol, the resulting sample has a disproportionately high representation of Moche IV elite burials.[72] In other words, we are uncertain of the nature and range of variability in the lower tiers of the above

typology. Further, the architectural data from Moche lump Moche III and IV, a span of up to two or three hundred years, possibly masking variation due to temporal differences. This same problem applies to burials with no grave goods, which were dated to the Moche III–IV span using ceramics from the midden.

In spite of the weaknesses of the sample, certain interesting generalities emerge:

Within our burial sample from the Moche Valley, the general quality of grave goods is not higher in what appear to be high status graves than it is in simpler graves. On the contrary, the most elaborate or well made objects are found in simple graves, while objects of relatively poor quality are often found in the more elaborate graves. . . . Within the social range represented by the burials . . . however . . . it appears that high quality material is not exclusively for the consumption of the elite. (Donnan and Mackey 1978: 382)[73]

We already noted a similarly paradoxical juxtaposition of high quality metal objects accompanied by rather crudely made ceramics in the Lord of Sipán tomb.

Further, the investigators (ibid., 209) found that during Moche IV "There appears to be no clear distinction between the graves of males as opposed to females or adults as opposed to children. This suggests that there were no standards regarding an appropriate inventory of grave goods. For the most part, the variety of ceramic objects is directly proportional to the number of ceramic objects. This suggests that a variety of vessel forms in the grave was preferable to multiple examples of a limited number of forms."

These conclusions are disturbing given that archaeologists typically rely on differential distribution of goods in gauging the social and political importance of the deceased. It would be difficult to unravel the social significance of the considerable material variation seen among the twenty-one Moche III and IV burials excavated at Moche. Neither the total number of grave goods nor such labor intensive items as gilt copper objects consistently correlate with seemingly important considerations such as the location and elaboration of the tomb or quality and range of other funerary goods, with the possible exception of high-status burials placed in the buried adobe platform between the two platform mounds.[74]

It is quite possible that the inferred social stratification was expressed in perishable grave goods such as high-quality textiles (e.g., tapestries with ideologically charged motifs—see Chapter 9 for Moche IV and V examples from Pacatnamú), tattoos, face painting, and hairstyle. Though it is not known why the exceptional Sipán and Huaca de la Luna graves contained masks of various metals, sizes, forms, and appearance, some are realistic enough to represent real individuals (see Bird 1962: 206). Some of these masks are quite similar in style, technique, and overall appearance. Could the bearers of these masks have had their own exclusive symbolism and shared a small number of master metalworkers?

Another possible explanation for the absence of standardization is that the unprecedented territorial and structural growth of the southern Mochica polity and society during Moche III and IV was accompanied by new social forms and increased social mobility. For those Mochica and loyal allies who distinguished themselves in service, craft, or battle, Moche III and IV must have been an opportune time to improve their social status and prestige. Even if much of the local leadership was retained or reinstated, many capable Mochica individuals from the Chicama-Moche area would probably have been appointed to supervisory roles in the expanding administrative network and hierarchy of craft production. Also, skilled artisans from subjugated areas may have been transplanted to Moche or regional centers. Thus, the lack of apparent material differentiation in grave offerings at Moche may reflect a corresponding lack of rigidity in the evolving Mochica social, political, and economic system unique to the capital. Those who successfully attained higher status may have attempted to secure it as a hereditary position.

While available burial data from the site of Moche are inadequate to support or refute the existence of a hereditary nobility and kingship there, elite burials from Sipán may offer more conclusive data on this issue. Their stratigraphic superposition at one end of the platform mound suggests that the platform served as a sacred burial ground for generations of local elite belonging to the same lineage. Osteological analysis of these burials (see Verano 1991) may eventually show sharing of some inherited trait that would support the inference of hereditary nobility and kingship.

Bearing in mind their small number, the Sipán burials offer tentative evidence of class stratification. One important line of evidence is the differentiated use of various kinds of metal objects (gold, depletion-gilded *tumbaga*, and copper). Mochica metallurgy placed considerable importance on "goldness" (Lechtman 1979, 1984a,b). The most exclusive and the rarest is gold (placer-mined gold nuggets, ingots, and hammered gold sheets). *Tumbaga*, containing anywhere from around 12 percent to over 60 percent gold and critical to the manufacture of Mochica sheet-metal ornaments (e.g., Lechtman 1984a,b, 1988: 355), was likely to have been differentiated from pure gold. Many "pure gold" objects (e.g., "ingots") from Sipán may prove to be gold-rich *tumbaga*, just as Mochica "gold" objects that Uhle excavated at the site of Moche (including a "gold slug" weighing 214 grams) turned out to be copper-rich *tumbaga* (Kroeber 1944:131–132, 1954).[75] The "gold slug" weighing 214 grams was found to be 60 percent copper, 30 percent gold, and 10 percent silver (Patterson 1971).

The appearance of gold can be achieved with only a few microns (one thousandth of a millimeter) of gold deposited on a copper surface (electrochemical gold-plating; Lechtman 1984a; Lechtman, Erlij, and Barry 1982). The existence of such gilt copper has not yet been firmly established.

It is significant that the Lord of Sipán tombs contained gold and copper objects but no gilt copper (Alva 1988; Alva et al. 1989), while the Old Lord of Sipán was endowed with gold, *tumbaga*, and copper objects (Alva 1990). The "Priest" interred close to the Lord of Sipán in the same architectural level and the Warrior-Priest burial of the Virú Valley had only *tumbaga* and copper objects and nothing of gold. Similarly, Alva (1990:8) notes that the backflaps of the two Lords at Sipán were gold, while those of the "ordinary warriors" or "guards" were copper. We do not know where silver, silver alloys, and silver-gilt objects fit in this scheme.

The above data, along with the differentiated quality and quantity of other funerary offerings and body placement, suggest that three social classes are represented in the Mochica burials at the Sipán platform: (1) a line of hereditary lords with exclusive access to gold and *tumbaga* objects and imported *Conus* and *Spondylus* shells, buried in superimposed adobe chambers; (2) a "priest" (possibly "achieved" nobility) with *tumbaga* objects, buried flanking the lords; and (3) the lords' personal attendants from the lower class (including female attendants and warriors or guards and perhaps artisans), with copper objects. Farmers, who were not represented here, may have belonged to the third class. However, the burial data from Moche show no clear-cut differentiation of gold and gilt copper object distribution (albeit the sample is quite small) and cast doubt on the validity of the distinction between the first two classes. Though the present author favors a three-level social hierarchy for Moche III–IV times,[76] additional architectural and burial data are clearly needed.

3. The Nature of Mochica Political Organization

A. Defining the State

The preceding sections provide background to consider the long-standing debate over the nature of Mochica political organization. With the widespread adherence to neo-evolutionary thinking in American archaeology, the definition and explanation of the evolution of the state have been much debated.[77] The controversy has engulfed Andean archaeology, generating its share of archaeological literature on the topic.[78] In general, however, there has been little effort to develop independent models of state formation on the basis of internal analysis of Andean data. Rather there has been a strong tendency to apply and test the externally derived models—for example, the well-known circumscription model of R. Carneiro (1970) and the three-tiered administrative hierarchy model of Wright and Johnson (1975). An exception is the unconventional model of

a "maritime foundation of Andean civilization" (Moseley 1975c) that has stimulated much debate (e.g., Raymond 1981; Wilson 1981). Schaedel, who has been long concerned with political and urban developments on the North Coast, is also rather unique in that his discussions are closely based on North Coast archaeological and ethnohistorical data. His perspective on North Coast state formation places as much weight on economic as on political dimensions; the latter is typical of most definitions and models of the state. Schaedel's ideas will be examined in some depth later.

One of the most detailed definitions of the state is offered by Wilson (1988: 87–88), who sees it as having

[1] control of a very large and often diverse area (ranging from several thousands to several tens of thousands of square kilometers);

[2] a developed hierarchy of site size and function that includes primary centers of substantial size, regional centers, local centers, and undifferentiated habitation sites (i.e., at least four to five levels, or tiers);

[3] the rise of legally constituted coercive power or authority, usually based on the creation, maintenance, and strategic deployment of a large military force (and manifested in such features as population resettlement, massive hydraulic and land reclamation projects, monumental architecture, and large-scale trading and road networks);

[4] widespread, and often uniform, distribution of major cultural traits (including diagnostic ceramic and architectural forms, as well as iconographic themes and styles);

[5] full-time craft specialization (with mass production of pottery, textiles, and other items in specified areas of higher-order sites, as well as widespread regional uniformity of form and decorative style); and

[6] social stratification (which may be reflected in various component features of the settlement system, including internal diversification of capitals and regional centers, residence based on occupational specialization, and diverse mortuary practices).

Though Wilson's definition has various problems (e.g., numerous features that are defined in terms of an ordinal scale as opposed to nominal categories), it does represent a good effort to make the abstract concept of the state definable in the field. In this book, which draws upon both Andean and external data and models, the state is defined as a highly developed institution of sociopolitical, economic, and ideological integration, possessing (1) the power of governance based on coercive force and implemented through a centralized, hierarchical administration, (2) control and deployment of multiple modes of resource exploitation (e.g., labor service, trade monopoly, and land annexation) for the maintenance of the administrative system and its political economy, and (3) distinct social classes with differential access to goods and services.

B. Case for the Pre–Moche V State

Debate over whether the Mochica polity was a state dates back at least to the period immediately after the Virú Valley Project when some project members offered their unilineal evolutionary models of sociopolitical development (e.g., Bennett and Bird 1949; Collier 1955, 1962a; Steward 1949, 1955; cf. Rowe 1962). With an optimistic and outspoken concern for functional and evolutionary analyses at the heart of the overall conceptual scheme of the research, various members of the Virú Valley Project presented some of the earliest explicit pronouncements of the Mochica as a state. Their freshly acquired data on the Mochica conquest of the Gallinazo polity in the valley supported Larco Hoyle's (1939: 138, 1946: 167) conviction of a state-level Mochica polity.

A typical example of this generation of writing is presented by Steward, who saw the Mochica polity as a "theocratic state" with a priestly hierarchy but with an ascendant secular war complex. Kosok (1965: 111) also regarded the polity as a transitional stage between a theocratic rulership and a secular state based on classes. Steward and Faron (1959: 87) argued that "The social, political, and religious patterns that mark a fully established state are clearly disclosed by several kinds of evidence. What cannot be confidently inferred from the temples and palaces, the status burials, the forts, irrigation systems, and the settlement pattern is strikingly and convincingly illustrated in Mochica . . . ceramic and textile designs." They further saw the Mochica state as "internally structured along lines of status and occupational specialization" (ibid., 92). The prevalence of battle scenes and warrior "portraits" was interpreted as reflecting a pattern of state warfare replacing an earlier pattern of individual raids, with the Mochica culture becoming functionally dependent upon warfare (ibid., 91). The functions of the "war lords and the high priests" were said to have been combined in the same persons. This vision of Mochica populace under the strong regimentation of warrior-priest rulers was widely accepted even before the discovery of the tomb of the Warrior-Priest at Huaca de la Cruz (e.g., Larco Hoyle 1939:136–138, 1946:167; Strong and Evans 1952: 199).

Indications of military conquests, including painted battle scenes, remain key supportive evidence for modern students who also argue for the Mochica state. For example, Carneiro (1970) explained that the local warfare, which created a powerful and ever larger regional polity, was symptomatic of population pressure on the limited agricultural productivity of geographically circumscribed coastal valleys. Though the circumscription theory was meant to be a general theory of state origin, recent testing by Wilson (1983, 1988) using his survey data from the Santa Valley found that intervalley (rather than intravalley) warfare waged by the expanding Mochica polity was the critical factor in the emergence of sociopolitical complexity within the valley. Moseley (1983a: 220; Conklin and Moseley 1988: 151) also sees the Mochica polity as spreading by means of military conquests and labels it a "predatory multi-valley state" or "empire."

Specific lines of evidence offered in support of state status by various scholars[79] include the following:

(1) The abrupt appearance of Moche III occupation with full-blown Mochica corporate style directly and completely superseded local Gallinazo occupation in the Virú Valley. Concurrently, Gallinazo cor-

porate-style artifacts disappeared. In the Santa Valley, subsequent to the Mochica intrusion, a significant reduction in the range of ceramic types was noted, suggesting the imposition of a limited number of standardized types by a central authority.

(2) In conjunction with the above, the regional settlement system (and thus, population—particularly in the Virú and Santa valleys) was reorganized into a smaller number of larger settlements occupying locations strategic primarily for control of the irrigation system and agricultural fields and secondarily for control of intervalley traffic.

(3) Roughly coterminous with the above, an administrative hierarchy with a minimum of three distinct levels was imposed by the expanding Mochica polity over local populations in valleys that they intruded and presumably subjugated. It is suggested that below the hereditary king (believed to have resided at the sacrosanct Huaca de la Luna) was a high-level administrator residing atop secular Huaca del Sol who directed the administrators at the regional centers established in each valley. The regional administrators are seen in turn to have supervised local bureaucrats situated at small local administrative posts.

(4) The principal site within the individual valley administrative hierarchy boasted a monumental adobe mound that appears to have been modeled after Huaca del Sol.

(5) Such corporate architecture was built by imposed mit'a-like labor service that was presumably administered by the Mochica state bureaucrats.

(6) The notable increase in explicit depictions of the Combat Theme and warriors in Mochica art starting in Moche III suggests the increasing importance of warfare and conquest as a means or the means of political integration and territorial expansion. These iconographic representations are regarded as reflecting the rise of a legally constituted coercive authority.

(7) A minimum of three qualitatively distinguishable architectural and burial groups exist, believed to correspond to distinct social classes.

(8) The increase in estimated population and physical size of the site of Moche during Phases III and IV presumably re-

flects the influx of new wealth and rise in prestige derived from conquests.

(9) The construction and management of large scale irrigation systems, particularly intervalley canals, would have required a supralocal administrative institution empowered to mobilize considerable labor forces and resources and capable of mediating conflicting water claims within and between valleys.

C. Critical Assessment

The above lines of evidence have been used in various combinations to argue that the Mochica polity centered at Moche began a series of military conquests of the southern valleys in Moche III and in the process achieved state status. Though at first glance convincing, certain lines of evidence prove under scrutiny to be tenuous or contingent on the validity of others.

The first line of evidence pertaining to Mochica expansion is built on a largely untested assumption regarding the chronological and political significance of the apparent uniformity of the Mochica style and iconography on the North Coast. The widespread distribution of the Mochica style on the northern half of the North Coast is even more problematical due to the inferred presence of a contemporaneous powerful Mochica polity in the Lambayeque region and the lack of any definitive indications of forceful Moche III intrusion. Schaedel (1985a: 160) considers the Mochica ceramic standardization "comparable" to that found in the contemporaneous but smaller scale societies of Maranga (Lima) and Nasca on the Central and South Coasts, respectively. Similarly, he does not see any feature related to metallurgy or ceramic production that would have required state control. However, the recent discovery of ceramic production areas with quantities of molds in diagnostic Mochica styles and forms, at Moche as well as at the inferred Mochica regional centers of Mocollope in the Chicama Valley (Russell 1990) and Pampa de los Incas in the Santa Valley (Wilson 1988: 211, Appendix B), suggests a consistent, widely applied Mochica policy of large-scale production and distribution of standardized ceramics. This may reflect the central authority's interest in dissemination of its political and religious dogma for greater ideological unity. In addition, attempts at physical integration of the territory and control over the movement of goods and people are suggested by intra- and intervalley roads linking Mochica settlements (Beck 1991: 71–74; Shimada 1987a: 132; Wilson 1988: 219–220).

I concur with Schaedel (1985a: 159–160) that the lack of "exclusively administrative units" is a major weakness of the pre–Phase V Mochica state status. Commenting on the *mit'a*-like labor service proposed by Moseley (1975b,d) for the construction of Huaca del Sol and other major Mochica platform mounds, Isbell (1986: 194) echoes the same sentiment: "[What have been claimed to be] Moche administrative facilities, however, are ceremonial platforms. There is no evidence for large storage facilities, great kitchens, barrackslike quarters, or concentrations of serving utensils which are demonstrable archaeological correlates of the 'Inca Mode of Production.' . . . Moche lacks administrative facilities associated with the conspicuous generosity that permitted the Inca state to disguise its compulsory labor tax."

In Chapter 2, serious problems stemming from imprecise dating were pointed out. Lines of evidence (2), (3), and (8) should be seen in light of this warning. Objections to (3) raised by Schaedel are examined later. In regard to line of evidence (6), though the frequency of representations of warriors and combat seems to rise notably starting in Moche III, the increase coincides with the popularity of fineline drawings, particularly scenic representations, and may simply be a function of a stylistic trend. Modeled representations of individual kneeling or seated "warriors" are quite common in Moche I and II ceramics; modeled representations of pairs of combatants or battle scenes would have been much more difficult. The possible meaning of the Combat Theme and "portrait vessels" is examined in depth below.

In respect to line of evidence (5), the segmentary construction technique predates Mochica dominance of the North Coast. What seems to be a Mochica innovation is the intentional marking of constituent adobe bricks and their regulated placement, although we are still uncertain

when and where this innovation began. It could have originated in the Lambayeque Valley.

In regard to line of evidence (4), i.e., Huaca del Sol serving as the model for regional administrative centers, Pampa de los Incas in the Santa Valley provides a good case study situation. At a general level, Pampa de los Incas has a spatial and architectural organization similar to that of Moche, with the extensive habitational area (ca. 800 m by 100–150 m) on the hillslope overlooking a pair of principal mounds (separated by about 150 m) on level ground (see Fig. 101 in Wilson 1988: 203). Pampa was most likely organized as a smaller version of the paramount site of Moche. At the same time, there are various complications in comparing the forms of the principal mounds stemming from post-Mochica modifications and damage due to erosion and looting, as well as uncertainties surrounding the original configuration of the Huaca del Sol with its eight construction stages. Even for the two principal mounds at Pampa de los Incas, it is difficult to see any specific resemblance to the Huaca del Sol and Huaca de la Luna. The original form of the Pañamarca mound in the Nepeña as built by the Mochica is difficult to ascertain, as it appears to have been built over at the beginning of the Middle Horizon (Schaedel 1951c; see Fig. 4.12). Similarly, Huaca El Brujo on the Chicama coast has numerous Middle Sicán additions covering the mound. Also, the plan of the principal Mochica platform mound at Huancaco in the Virú Valley resembles the Late Gallinazo construction of Castillo Sarraque in the same valley as well as the Huaca de la Luna at Moche. Given the long-term tradition of platform mound building, it is difficult to speak of a strictly Mochica form.

The labor investment and associated managerial tasks involved in monumental mound construction are difficult to determine due to the uncertainties surrounding the original configuration and size and the duration of construction. More importantly, the solid adobe, segmentary construction technique employed allowed a gradual, accretive construction by labor gangs with a good deal of social and political autonomy (see Chapter 7).

Line of evidence (9) has been a perennial favorite, cited often since the 1940's, and raises issues of resource mobilization and administrative requirements. This argument has been weakened with the recent documentation that the impressive La Cumbre Intervalley Canal once regarded as a Mochica achievement was in reality a Chimú undertaking (see Chapter 2). Even the Ascope aqueduct may not be wholly Mochica in date. In addition, as noted in the preceding chapter, the local Gallinazo polities (not state level) had already constructed MECs in the Moche and Virú valleys that were not significantly improved by the Mochica.

Iconographic data, particularly the numerous examples of the Combat Theme in Mochica ceramic art, constitute one of the most important lines of evidence for proponents of the expansionist state (cf. Schaedel 1985b: 157). But we do not yet know the specific and broader cultural meanings of the Combat Theme. Do combat scenes depict actual secular warfare or ritual combat?

Armed combats involving human warriors, mythical or supernatural beings, and anthropomorphic animals and/or objects are one of the most frequently depicted themes during Moche III and IV. Many Moche IV depictions show a full spectrum of phases and facets of combat involving multiple pairs of opponents, as in the well-known Moche IV example described below (Fig. 5.4; also see Figs. 2.4, 5.5, 5.6).

This example clearly illustrates the wide range of symbolic elements that together compose the Combat Theme and what we assume to be typical Mochica customs. In regard to the latter, we see warriors looting weapons and clothes and pulling the hair of their defeated opponents, presumably to symbolize submission and loss of dignity (Donnan 1978: 148). Depicted in two horizontal registers, this scene shows pairs of figures confronting each other. Some figures are menacing or delivering blows, while one has successfully drawn blood from his opponent. A naked, sprawling figure with closed eyes appears dead. A running figure with an extra (star-shaped) mace, a shield, and one unidentifiable object suspended from his own mace prob-

ably represents a victor carrying looted weapons.

The costumes and weapons depicted can be differentiated into two groups: (1) figures with maces with conical ends, conical helmets, skirted tuniclike garments, and *tumi-* or axe head–shaped objects suspended from their belts in back, and (2) figures with either round or star-headed maces, collars with hanging strips, forelocks, back shields (?) suspended from shoulder straps, and, with one exception, loincloths. It is clear that the former group is winning the battle. At the same time, other combat scenes show both opposing groups armed with the same maces with round heads and conical ends.

The above description of figures identifies many symbolic elements of the Combat Theme. For example, the mace with round head and conical end is most frequently found in Moche III–V depictions of combat (see Fig. 65–66 in Donnan 1978: 46 for variability in mace head shape). The mace was most likely the principal Mochica weapon, complemented by *tumis,* shields, spears and spear-throwers, and perhaps slings. The last is rarely shown and may be associated with highland opponents (see Hocquenghem 1978: 129; Kutscher 1955a: 29). Knives are commonly associated with decapitation and sacrifice scenes involving mythical creatures and/or supernatural beings and their human victims (Schaedel 1951c: 154; see Figs. 213–262 in Kutscher 1983). Clubs shown in hunting scenes are often different in form from those depicted in the Combat Theme. Spear-throwers understandably are not shown in use in the hand-to-hand combat of these scenes.

Various scholars have suggested that the combat depicted in Mochica art was essentially ideologically motivated with the end of capturing victims for later sacrificial ceremonies, rather like the Flower War waged by the Aztecs and their contemporaries in the late pre-Hispanic highlands of Mexico. Based on Mochica depictions of combat between warriors in similar costumes, Kutscher (1955a: 28–29) suggested that, much as in ancient Greece, the Mochica were constantly entangled in civil wars: "This intertribal fighting reflects the lack of a strong authority, dominating and

Figure 5.5. Roll-out drawing of a combat scene from a Moche IV bottle. After Plate 21 in Kutscher 1954.

Figure 5.6. Roll-out drawing of two pairs of elaborately attired "warriors" in combat, from a Moche IV bottle (Peabody Museum of Archaeology and Ethnology 46-77-30/4939).

uniting all the [Mochica] groups in the different valleys, . . . [and that] neither the lust for conquest nor territorial claims, but rather the winning of captives to sacrifice seems . . . to have been the real cause of the numerous wars . . . waged among the various local groups" (see also Kutscher 1955b).

Both Donnan (1978: 182) and Hocquenghem (1978: 129) share the above view of the Combat Theme; that "the objective of the combat shown in Moche art appears to be capture of prisoners to be sacrificed later on ceremonial occasions" (Donnan 1978: 182). While Donnan does

not specify the manner or conditions in which the ritual combat was carried out, Hocquenghem presents a detailed interpretation of Mochica combat scenes based on a wide range of ethnographic ritual combat in the Ecuadorian and Peruvian highlands as well as on historically documented Inca ritual combat that was part of the annual ceremony known as *Kamay*. Using this direct historical approach, she suggests that Mochica combat scenes depict an annual ritual combat combining features of a rite of passage and an agricultural rite, fought between young members of the elite of two postulated moieties

known as *hanan* and *hurin*, occupying coastal and inland zones respectively. In Inca times, ritualized battles served specific functions: "In such battles, possibly conducted as rough games with a touch of bloodshed, different social groups settled disputes and established or confirmed their rank in the larger social order. Loss of life sometimes occurred, but massive killing was not the intent. Such battles were a ritualized way of resolving conflict and adjusting sociopolitical imbalances" (Morris 1988: 47).

These combat depictions should not be seen in isolation from those of related activities and other themes in Mochica art. When we adopt a holistic perspective, it becomes evident that combat scenes constitute only a part of the story told in segments on individual vessels. Other segments show the capture of enemy warriors, removal of arms and armor, and processions and presentations of captured, stripped prisoners (Figs. 2.4, 5.5), and finally their sacrifice, usually by decapitation. The consistent depictions of naked captives, including their sacrifice in association with supernatural beings, argues for a strong underlying ideological motive for combat. In fact, these noncombat segments are just as common as combat depictions, if not more so. In addition, combat depictions involving only supernatural creatures are quite common.

Indeed, purely on the basis of internal analysis of Mochica fineline drawings of combat, any clear secular motive is not readily forthcoming. The combatants are always shown in one-on-one confrontation, suggesting a highly regulated situation. Based on background vegetation (primarily cacti), battles seem to have consistently taken place in arid, desertlike areas rather than "desirable" agricultural fields, habitations, or fortresses. No plunder is ever depicted as being carried off other than the clothing, armor, and weapons of defeated warriors. Likewise, no depictions exist of defeated civilian populations. In addition, fineline depictions of combat scenes are essentially Moche IV and V in date, implying that the Mochica polity would have been still engaged in wars of conquest as late as Moche V. Those who argue for the formation of a multi-valley predatory state (typically dated to Moche III–IV) would face this paradox or be forced to make an anachronistic explanation. The consistent depictions of captives, including their sacrifice in association with supernatural beings, provide yet another line of supportive evidence for the religious view. Overall, combat scenes are neither convincing nor conclusive indicators of real-life secular battles for Mochica territorial expansion.

We face a similar problem in interpreting the "portrait vessels" so often heralded as realistic portraits of actual, powerful Mochica leaders (Fig. 1.4). These "portraits" are typically slightly over half life-size. Their popularity roughly coincides in stylistic phases with the realistic depictions of human warriors and their combats. R. Larco Hoyle alone amassed over three hundred Moche III and IV stirrup-spout portrait vessels (Y. Suzuki, pers. com. 1983). The importance of these vessels may be deduced not only from the great deal of care lavished upon them in manufacture to assure individuality and high quality (particularly those of Moche IV), but also from their elaborate headdresses, ornate face paintings, and nose and ear ornaments. They are so realistic and individual in appearance that many scholars have been convinced that they in fact depict real individuals of high status. Sawyer (1968: 36, 38; also Larco Hoyle 1939: 138) even suggests that the original models of these vessels may have been made from life in clay, and that the presence of these vessels in a grave "signified an honor bestowed upon the deceased." Larco Hoyle (1939: 132) claimed that he was able to identify the Great Lord (*Cie-quich* or *Gran Señor*), his young heirs, and his immediate representatives (*Alaec* or *Caciques*), as well as their activities. In addition, he observed that different "portraits" of apparently the same individuals (at different ages) were found in various valleys (Chicama, Moche, Virú, and Santa; Larco Hoyle 1939: 135 and his Figs. 192–194). Larco (ibid., 136–137) interpreted this extensive distribution as evidence of their hereditary status as the Great Lord; their portraits were distributed throughout the territory as a visible political symbol of the ruling elite. Similarly, the localized distribution (within a sector of a valley) of "portraits" of the same men is interpreted as reflecting regional lords.

A contrary view emerged out of a more recent, systematic study of five hundred "portrait vessels" (all but one depicting men; Hocquenghem 1977b). This study shows a notable shift near the end of Moche III from an earlier tendency to depict essentially the same physical traits and expressions toward the representation of strongly individualized ones. Hocquenghem's comparative study indicated that these human "portraits" were part of the more generalized Mochica tradition of depicting inhabitants of the living, dead, and supernatural worlds (in full or just heads). Besides warriors, portrait vessels depict a wide range of individuals including those with physical pathologies and various scarification (see Gantzer 1972; Pirsig 1989; Pirsig and Eisleb 1988). Thus, there are corresponding "portraits" of skulls and supernatural beings. The same physiognomy is represented more than once with varied face painting, ornaments, and coiffure, presumably for different functions. The variation, however, is not random; for example, definite correspondence can be found between a given physiognomy and hairstyle. Overall, Hocquenghem's study suggests that, contrary to Larco's assertions, these naturalistic human "portraits" do not represent specific individuals in spite of seemingly individualized features. She sees them more as symbolic representations of powerful shamans that mediated the three parallel worlds of the Mochica cosmology.

D. Alternative View: Chiefdom-Level Polity

An alternative view to state status is voiced by Schaedel. In his conception, the Mochica polity at its height during Moche IV was a "paramount chiefdom" or *macro-etnía* (Schaedel 1972: 21, 1985a: 157–158).[80] He characterizes it as having a multi-valley territorial base (spanning the La Leche to Nepeña valleys), an estimated total population of over 254,500, and political hierarchy based on dogma or sanctified propositions as opposed to the institutionalized mechanism of coercive force employed by an administratively centralized state. The secular forces are believed to have "not yet segmented themselves into a dominant class" (ibid.). He concludes that

The interpretation that suggests itself in terms of social organization and particularly political organization is that of a fairly disarticulated and undifferentiated polity. . . . Cultural evidence from grave lots and mural iconography indicates that warriors and priests were the upper class, artisans in a lower category, and probably attendants and commoner-farmers in the lower strata. There is no differentiation so far detectable in the settlement pattern to indicate that nonagricultural specialists were concentrated in great numbers permanently in any one center except the capital at Moche. The [regional] capitals seem to reflect a society unlike that described in the historical accounts of . . . chiefdoms, the more elaborate capitals of which corresponded to the domain of the paramount chiefs (with maximum populations of 10,000) where religious rites were performed and jural rights were mediated, and the smaller village centers (1,000 population) corresponded to the subject chiefs. The major capital of the Mochica polity, although it apparently enjoyed hegemony over most of the [North Coast] valleys, was simply larger, but not more differentiated than the ceremonial centers in the individual valleys. (Schaedel 1972: 23)

Schaedel (1985a: 159–160) sees the Mochica settlement hierarchy as having three levels: (1) the principal capital, seat of the highest-ranking and most powerful "paramount" chiefdom, (2) the principal settlement of each valley chiefdom subject to the paramount chiefdom, and (3) seat(s) of major political subdivisions within each valley (subchiefdoms). He considers the conquered chiefdoms of Virú, Chao, and Santa to be ethnic kindred of the paramount chiefdom situated in either the Chicama or Moche Valley (Schaedel 1985b: 448).

Overall, he argues that population estimates for the Mochica capitals and territory are within the range of chiefdoms and that the sites lack the diversification of function or "awareness of resource control by their location" expected from a state administrative hierarchy (Schaedel 1972: 17). Rather, these major Mochica settlements are seen to be primarily concerned with ideological (e.g., as attested by friezes) or military control that would be expected from a "dispersed kind of polity" at the chiefdom level.

There is some evidence supportive of the above position. The sumptuous early Moche tombs at Moche, La Mina (Jequetepeque-Chicama border), Sipán (Lambayeque), and Loma Negra (upper Piura) may imply the presence of at least four regional dynasties within the North Coast, much as Donnan (1990a: 33) has argued. In addition, based on his iconographic study, Berezkin (1978) presented a strong argument that the five major sets of deities found in the Mochica pantheon prior to late Moche IV represented five elite lineages in Mochica society. Though the geographic locations of these religious/political groups were not specified, his study supports the notion of a confederation or competing chiefdoms.

E. Summary

To summarize the above, we have seen that on the basis of the largely overlapping bodies of evidence two divergent views have been proposed regarding the nature of the Mochica polity. As there seems to be little doubt that the Mochica polity at its height attained at least chiefdom-level complexity, the burden of proof lies on the state proponents. Though the state view seems quite plausible and enjoys the support of various scholars, its case is far from unequivocal, as it suffers from imprecise, limited, and/or subjective criteria and ambivalent data, particularly those derived from straightforward interpretation of a detached segment of Mochica art.

At the same time, some of the basic arguments of the paramount chiefdom position require further clarification and empirical support. New settlement-pattern and burial data pose serious questions regarding Schaedel's position on settlement and social differentiation and hierarchies. Further, his comparative approach requires better justification. His attribution of chiefdom level may be overly dependent upon his own population and cultivated-area estimates for Mochica territory and their comparison with historically documented chiefdoms. While Schaedel's (1972: 22) population estimates for the Santa Valley under the Mochica is 32,500, some 10,000 more than the corresponding figure offered by Wilson (1988: 221), he sees fewer organizational features attributable to the state than Wilson. The discrepancy is disturbing.

The chiefdom view cannot be readily dismissed, particularly as a characterization of the pre–Moche IV situation. For the critical Moche IV–V span, Berezkin

(1978) offers an important clue based on iconographic study: that there was a notable reduction in the number of deities in the Mochica pantheon to just a dyad or triad of principal deities, each with his "retainers." He posits a concomitant major shift in modes of production and increasing consolidation and competition among two or three sociopolitical groups. In other words, the observed change may well reflect the inferred rivalry and changing power relationship between the southern (Moche-based) and northern (Lambayeque-based) Mochica polities during Moche IV–V. As detailed in the following chapter, the bipolar situation is seen to have broken down sometime in Moche IV with incorporation of the Northern Sector by the Moche-based polity, but within a relatively short span, during the Moche IV–V transition, the polity lost much of its Southern Sector and the Lambayeque-based polity reclaimed its power to dominate the Moche V domain.

4. Mochica Urbanism before Pampa Grande

Much of the above discussion pertained to the site of Moche that preceded Pampa Grande as the paramount Mochica settlement. Did the urbanism at Pampa Grande evolve out of earlier Mochica sites such as Moche?

We have seen a notable urbanization trend on the North Coast at least from the Initial Period. Besides Monte Grande, the Initial Period site of Purulén near the mouth of the Zaña River with some fifteen major platform mounds each surrounded by terraces, extensive refuse middens, and clusters of dwellings, covered an area of about 3 km² (Alva 1985). In the Casma Valley, Pozorski and Pozorski (1987; cf. Fung 1988) have argued that the monumental mound of Moxeke and the nearby Pampa de las Llamas site with its own major mound and several hundred domestic structures and over seventy small mounds formed a single, planned settlement. In fact, they have argued that Moxeke–Pampa de las Llamas, covering over 2 km², constituted the first planned city in the New World.

The Salinar site of Cerro Arena in the Moche Valley had at least two thousand separate structures of varying size along a ridge 2 km in length for a total surface area of about 2 km² (Brennan 1980: 2–3).[81] It has been characterized as "the first large, nucleated, predominantly residential north coastal site" (ibid., 21) with the diversity in architectural design, function, and quality suggesting "the presence of a wide range and complex diversity of social statuses" (ibid., 19) among its residents. Further, architectural nucleation and areas devoted to specialized functions are believed to reflect a centralized administration of the site's political and economic activities. Cerro Orejas, another Salinar site of "urban" character, was built on a terraced hillside at the strategic valley neck on the south bank of the Moche Valley (Moseley and Mackey 1972). These sites represent the first large, nucleated settlements in the valley and point to an emergent settlement hierarchy and concern with irrigation, intra- and intervalley traffic, and defense.

Among Gallinazo sites in the Virú Valley, urbanization is most notable in the "Pyramid-Dwelling-Construction Complex" type of site where the "functions of a living site and a community or ceremonial structure" were combined (Willey 1953: 109). The largest such complex, the Gallinazo Group, with a dense aggregation of dwellings (11.5 hectares in extent), had an estimated population of 2,500 that showed only status differentiation (Schaedel 1972: 19). Schaedel (ibid.) suspects that, as the capital of the regional Gallinazo polity, the site included artisans, "non-agricultural workers, . . . administrative specialists, chiefs and attendants."

Over time, the maximum extent of architectural buildup did not oscillate markedly from sites of one period to the next. However, reflecting increasing societal complexity and size, greater functional differentiation and a more complex settlement hierarchy arose. In Moche III–IV times, there were at least three levels of settlements including the capital at Moche. Regional administration in each valley was coordinated through one or two centers with disproportionately large corporate architecture in the middle or lower valley. These included Sipán (Lambayeque), Mocollope (Chicama), Huancaco (Virú), Pampa de los Incas and/or Huaca Chimbote (Santa), and Pañamarca (Nepeña). Nothing stands out in the La Leche and Zaña, though Huaca Soledad and Cerro Songoy are likely candidates as their respective regional centers. The situation in the Jequetepeque is still uncertain, though Talambo or Pacatnamú could well have been the north bank center. It would not be surprising if these regional centers were ranked in accordance with the prestige of the reigning "governors" (or even "kings") and amount of material and labor tribute.

There is no *a priori* reason to assume that all of these sites served the same functions. Recent studies point to the urban character of a number of major Mochica settlements and a considerable degree of intrasite functional differentiation, in contrast to the earlier tendency to emphasize their isolated and specialized functional character (see Schaedel 1951a, 1972). The best case is the site of Moche. For example, the Huaca del Sol and Huaca de la Luna mounds have been interpreted as serving the fundamentally different roles of civic center or "actual interface between ruling class and populace" and "residence and audience chamber of the Mochica ruler," respectively (T. Topic 1982: 278). The surrounding areas, originally covering perhaps upwards of 2 km² in area, contained workshops engaged in the production of both utilitarian and luxury goods, domestic residences, and burial grounds for various inferred social classes. Schaedel (1972: 20–22) calculates the resident population at ten thousand from an estimated carrying capacity of the Mochica territory and urban elite–rural population ratio. This figure should be regarded as a minimal estimate, as the area west of the preserved portion of the Huaca del Sol has been either washed away or destroyed by cultivation. Also, the south and west margins of the site, including much of the slopes of the Cerro Blanco and the south bank MEC that supplied water, have been covered by sand moving inland from the coast. This is exactly where one would expect to find habitational structures. In other words, during Moche IV, Moche could have covered an area of 2–3 km².

Unfortunately, the long, complex occupational history of the site and imprecise dating of relevant structures hamper attempts to better define the extent and nature of Mochica urbanism at Moche.

Pampa de los Incas in the Santa Valley and Mocollope in the Chicama are two other Mochica urban sites with extensive and diverse architecture, including major platform mounds, habitational zones, and ceramic workshops. Pampa de los Incas has the largest and most complex concentration of Mochica architecture and artifacts in the valley (Wilson 1988: 207, 211). However, much of the Complex's 2 km² area is occupied by massive adobe walls, roadways, canals, and cultivation fields. The eight associated habitation sites are estimated to have housed only 3,520 persons (ibid., 207).

The "extensive suburb" situated immediately northeast of the "City of Temples" at Pacatnamú (Fig. 4.4) displaying "careful and systematic urbanistic planning" has been attributed to the Mochica period of occupation (Hecker and Hecker 1985: 58–59). Urbanistic evidence includes cardinal orientation, delimitation by means of ditches and terraces, architectural organization around central patios or open courtyards, and differentiated configurations of land parcels. Many of the Mochica artifacts and burials cited in support of the above claim date to Moche V, but to date no excavation has been conducted in the suburb to verify the above architectural characterization, dating, and extent of synchronic occupation.

The described Mochica settlements (most notably Moche) served varied functions and had the architectural nucleation and resident population to be called "urban." Moche V Pampa Grande shared these features but in a greatly accentuated way. The clear physical separation of the crowded commoners' dwellings on the hillslopes from the monumental adobe mound and spacious elite residences was common to Pampa Grande, Moche, and Pampa de los Incas. However, the densely built and functionally differentiated architecture at Pampa Grande covered at least 5 km² and was integrated by well-defined and -controlled networks of communication and transportation. Similarly, the

common practice at Pampa Grande of placing platform mounds or terrace complexes within rectangular walled enclosures does not find apparent antecedence at earlier Mochica sites. Overall, only certain features characterizing Pampa Grande can be readily identified in earlier Mochica settlements. Critical questions regarding the factors and processes that shaped the Moche V urbanism at Pampa Grande are addressed in the following chapters.

5. Mochica Culture before Pampa Grande: A Summary Characterization

The picture that emerges of Mochica territory on the eve of the Moche IV–V transformation around A.D. 550 puts the northern and southern boundaries at the north bank of the La Leche and south bank of the Huarmey, respectively. Both northern and southern frontiers were distinctly wedge-shaped due to the mid-valley focus. Farther north, there may have been an outpost in the Vicús region of the upper Piura. The east boundary is best envisioned as an oscillating, wavy line hovering over the lower reaches of the cis-Andean *chaupiyunga* at altitudes of ca. 500–600 m. It reflects the contentious nature of interaction between the Mochica and currently poorly defined cis-Andean ethnic polities that may have been related to the Early to Middle Cajamarca or Recuay populations. The western boundary may be defined by linking offshore islands from Isla Ferrol in the south (off the Santa Valley) to perhaps Isla Lobos de Tierra in the north (off the Sechura Desert) close to the point at which the cold Peru Current turns west. The resulting totality was encircled by an uncertain but surely wider Mochica sphere of influence likely to have extended from southern Ecuador to the Central and South Coasts. In the adjacent North Highlands, only a handful of ceremonial centers manifest minimal signs of contact that could have resulted from occasional elite gift exchanges or trade.

One plausible explanation of the widespread distribution of Cajamarca ceramics on the North Coast compared to the relative dearth of Mochica ceramics in the adjoining North Highlands involves the nature of the iconography (M. Shimada, pers.

com. 1987). Cajamarca ceramics may have been deemed "decorative" pottery without threatening religious and/or political symbolism, while Mochica ceramics may have reeked too strongly of an alien religion and/or politically threatening power. Further, the representational style of Mochica ceramic art would have been more readily understood cross-culturally in contrast to the highly stylized and abstract Cajamarca motifs.

At a glance, the above summary of Mochica territorial expansion and external relationships does not seem to differ much from earlier published characterizations. However, most graphic delineations of the Mochica realm give an impression of invariable perimeters and complete control of frontier valleys. Also, interpretations heavily based on data from the Chicama-Moche-Virú area and ceramic art have been uncritically projected to the entire Mochica territory and culture with the implication of deep and comprehensive understanding.

Complete Mochica domination of the coastal valley is convincingly demonstrated only for the Chicama, Moche, Virú, and perhaps Santa valleys. Much of the Northern Sector may have been under a Lambayeque-based Mochica polity that was probably an ethnic kindred of the Moche-based southern Mochica polity. Whether these polities (and perhaps another in the Jequetepeque) were allies or rivals during Moche III and early Moche IV remains to be determined. Even after the postulated forceful incorporation of the Northern Sector into the Moche-based hegemony in Moche IV, the latter established only mid-valley control of the Lambayeque and La Leche valleys.

Overall, we have a picture of highly coast-centric expansion with no single factor able to explain the totality of Mochica expansion. Different motivations were likely to have been involved in expansion into different areas. The northward thrust of the southern Mochica polity appears to have been partly linked to the coastward thrust of the Cajamarca polity. Though the intent may have been to harness the tremendous agricultural potential of the Lambayeque Valley Complex, expansion achieved only partial control. They did,

however, landlock the Cajamarca, with the possible exception of the Jequetepeque Valley. The possibility that late Moche IV northward expansion was due to encroachment of the Wari polity into the Mochicas' Southern Sector will be examined in the following chapter. The conquest of the small Virú Valley, on the other hand, may have been motivated by peer rivalry with the Gallinazo polity, while the situation in the Santa may represent maximization of irrigation agriculture and/or control of the Recuay coastal presence. The excellent fishing grounds off the mouth of the Santa River may also have been critical. The Nepeña, together with the site of Pañamarca, remains an enigma—perhaps related to securing access to Casma and Huarmey and further landlocking the Recuay. The absence of prior occupation by a Gallinazo population may indicate that the valley was occupied by a "not-so-kindred" group (Schaedel 1985a: 448) that offered more resistance to Mochica domination. In this regard, Pañamarca may have been intended as a highly visible symbol of Mochica power and prestige in a zone of contention.

Finally, the establishment of far-flung Huarmey and upper Piura outposts is best seen as an attempt to broaden the trade network and resource base of the Mochica economy via direct colonization and alliance formation.

Though our understanding of the physical aspects of the southern Mochica realm may be reasonably complete, we are far from achieving a similar degree of understanding of attendant sociopolitical and economic organizations of the Northern Sector as a whole. Many recent publications describe the Mochica polity at its zenith as a "predatory state" or the "first true intervalley state." Yet a critical review of relevant data and arguments shows inconsistent or varied definitions and criteria, biased or incomplete sampling, subjectivity, and ambiguity. This position also projects uncritically the presumed political implications of apparent stylistic unity: that stylistic homogeneity implies political unification. It also assumes the simple scenario of a single Mochica polity based at Moche in perpetual conflict with non-Mochica groups. Review of Salinar and Gallinazo

occupations as well as data suggesting the presence of various kindred polities in the Northern Sector that shared what we call the Mochica style leads us to the much more complex scenario of Mochica territorial and organizational growth presented in this chapter. For Moche I–III, the alternative view favoring a paramount chiefdom or a confederacy of regional chiefdoms seems more plausible. At the same time, this view underplays important organizational developments that indicate that the southern Mochica polity was at least approaching state status on the eve of the Moche IV–V transformation. This view is further constrained by its rigid adherence to the concurrent formation of the city and state on the North Coast resulting from reorganization by Wari invaders.

The lack of detailed studies at Moche and other major Mochica sites hampers our search for the antecedents of urbanism at Pampa Grande. Available data show that there was a good deal of concentration of domestic occupation and multiple functions at the capital of Moche and some regional centers, in contrast to the earlier tendency to emphasize isolated, function-specific character (e.g., isolated, largely vacuous ceremonial centers). At the same time, none of these sites had the extent of architectural buildup, diversity of architectural forms, or planning apparent at Pampa Grande; Chapters 6 and 7 describe the unique circumstance and processes that shaped Moche V urbanism at Pampa Grande.

Mochica social organization is still largely inferential, but a reasonable case may be made for three classes, with some degree of upward mobility suggested for the site of Moche during expansive Moche III and early Moche IV, when administrative and diplomatic skills, not to mention military leadership, would have been highly valued. The custom of marking adobe bricks used for corporate construction, which came into use early in Moche III, may be just a hint of the emerging administrative complexity. Membership in the lowest class may have included farmers, fishers, and personal retainers, with artisans enjoying an upper category within this class. The upper strata would have been the "hereditary" nobility presumably residing within the capital, while the middle class would have been composed of those who had earned their status, e.g., low-level provincial administrators and warriors.

The artistic and technical mastery of Mochica ceramics and metal objects has long been appreciated worldwide and has given rise to the typical characterization of craft specialization. For much of the history of Mochica archaeology, little else could be said with any degree of confidence about the organizational features of the Mochica economy. Architectural studies now suggest that Mochica corporate projects such as canal and platform mound constructions were based on the preexisting tradition of standardized segmentary or modular format. Certain distributional patterns of marked adobe bricks, together with the above construction format, have, in turn, given rise to a vision that corvée labor service, much like the *mit'a* exacted of able-bodied commoners in the Inca Empire, was one of the fundamental organizational principles of the Mochica economy.

Thanks to abundant Spanish Colonial writings, we know that the *mit'a* was underwritten by the principle of reciprocity, i.e., tributaries on a rotational basis were expected to provide only their labor, while the Inca Empire provided food and drink, as well as implements, clothing, and other items necessary to perform labor service (e.g., Murra 1980, 1982). Though the above inference would imply that Mochica labor taxation was a prototype of the well-documented Incaic *mit'a*, relevant architectural data do not offer similar operational details but have certain problems and limitations. We still do not know whether participation in public construction was on a compulsory or voluntary basis. In essence, the inference is a product of the Direct Historical Approach popular since the days of the Virú Valley Project and relies too heavily on Inca analogy (Shimada in press 1; also Isbell 1986: 194–195).

One Mochica setting where we have material evidence attesting to labor service reciprocated by food and drink is at Moche V Pampa Grande (Chapter 7). Extensive excavations at Pampa Grande have also produced abundant data that have elucidated various basic organizational features of Moche V urban craft production and economy. However, in trying to determine organizational, material, and behavioral continuities, we are greatly handicapped by the lack of detailed and extensive comparative studies of both small and large pre–Moche V sites.

6

The Establishment of Moche V Pampa Grande

The previous chapters described the long-term territorial growth and organizational features of the Mochica polity and culture. The evolution, however, was by no means predictable in the sense of manifesting a constant rate or direction of change. During the florescent era of late Moche III to early Moche IV, territory expanded significantly and agricultural production and corporate projects such as monumental mound building seem to have reached their zenith. Craft goods came to exhibit an unprecedented technical mastery, artistic virtuosity, and range of subjects including complex scenes involving many real or supernatural creatures.

Late in Moche IV, however, there was a curious decline in the technical and artistic qualities of ceramics with much more conventionalized, rigid, and at times poorly executed representations of motifs and themes (Sawyer 1968: 31; also see Bawden 1978; Berezkin 1978). The care given to each object and the creative latitude artisans were allowed during Moche IIIB–IVA seemed reduced.[82] Art is an expression of the time and place in which it is produced and thus the above observation suggests that some significant changes may have occurred in the Mochica society sometime late in Moche IV.

The above presage does not adequately prepare us for the breadth and depth of cultural changes that transpired within a relatively brief time span (perhaps only fifty years or less) starting late in Moche IV, ca. A.D. 500—what is referred to here as the Moche IV–V cultural transformation. This critical period saw the nearly total abandonment of the Southern Sector of the Mochica domain (from at least the south bank of the Moche down to the Nepeña, inclusive), the virtual abandonment of the capital site of Moche, and an unprecedented population nucleation at large urban settlements situated at the necks of at least some of the valleys in the remaining Northern Sector of the Mochica domain. These and other changes discussed later were remarkable in their breadth, scale, and rapidity. This is especially true since none of them could have been anticipated readily on the basis of the long-term developmental trends and salient features of the first four phases.

During this time, there are indications at the site of Moche and elsewhere on the Peruvian coast of climatic disturbances that, taken together, appear to have been the most severe of the past fifteen hundred years. The postulated late Moche IV incorporation of the northern North Coast valleys (north of Jequetepeque) may have been related to difficulties that affected their Southern Sector. The Mochica population displaced from Moche and the Southern Sector probably constituted a major segment of the population that aggregated at the valley necks.

In this chapter, the relative merits of the two major competing explanatory models of the Moche IV–V transformation are examined in depth. One is built on recently documented severe droughts in the sixth century[83] and the other is a long-standing model positing the Wari expansion out of the Ayacucho Basin in the Central Highlands of Peru.

1. Abandonment of the Southern Sector

During Moche III and IV, we saw the powerful southern Mochica polity eliminate the Recuay coastal presence and bring about a major settlement reorganization in the Southern Sector. In contrast, corporate architecture conclusively or exclusively attributable to Moche V has yet to be found in the Southern Sector, and diagnostic Moche V ceramics are rare. Moche V fineware vessels from the site of Cenicero in the Santa Valley are actually Wari-Moche hybrids (see Plate 7 in Donnan 1973a: 134– 135) showing Wari-derived form and polychrome slip painting of essentially Mochica motifs. A settlement pattern survey of the Nepeña Valley reveals that Mochica occupation there is overwhelmingly Moche IV with no Moche V sites (Proulx 1973, 1982). The Mochica polychrome murals at the impressive regional center of Pañamarca are variously dated to "Moche Phase IV or a transition to Phase V" (Bonavia 1985: 70) or to Moche III and/or IV (Proulx 1968: 27; Fig. 310 in Rowe 1974). This divergence reflects the difficulties in cross-dating iconography and style in different media. In either interpretation, the murals are not clear-cut Moche V.

Some Moche V textile fragments have been recovered from looted cemeteries in Huarmey and farther south. Noting the widespread presence of Mochica and Mochica-derived textiles on the Central and South Coasts (Huarmey, Supe, Pachacamac, and Mala), Conklin (1979) argues

that the extent of the Mochica dominance and influence on the Peruvian coast was far greater than commonly assumed. However, most of his funerary textile sample appears to date to Moche V or even immediately post–Moche V (showing Mochica-Wari stylistic blending). Further, no Moche V settlements have been identified in the Huarmey Valley, suggesting that the Mochica polity had lost control of its colony in that valley. Given this and other indications of Mochica abandonment of the Southern Sector, we should not interpret the wide distribution of textiles in any direct way as indicative of Moche V political strength or the extent of its economic network. Rather, we should consider the distinct possibility that the technically and artistically refined Mochica textiles were valued as tribute or status items by the Wari and their coastal allies, and that their production may have persisted even after the collapse of Mochica political structure in the Southern Sector. The same argument may apply to a gravelot from Huaquerones in the Rimac Valley on the Central Coast, which contained a double-spout bottle of local form (Nievería) that had polychrome decoration whose "execution and inspiration" was "completely and authentically Mochica" (Stumer 1958: 17). This bottle has an uncanny resemblance to the double-spout Mochica-Nievería-Wari hybrid bottle from Piura (Rowe 1942; Fig. 6.1).

Overall, while the Mochica polity appears to have abandoned its Southern Sector during the Moche IV–V transition, the process may have been gradual, taking a generation or two, and in some areas, contacts may have been maintained with the Mochica to the north.

2. Abandonment of the Site of Moche

Moche V materials are also very rare at the site of Moche. In the Moche Valley itself,

there is evidence for a shift of agricultural emphasis, and population, from the southern margin of the valley to the northern margin beginning in Phase V. The area north of what was to become the Chimu [capital] site of Chan Chan was first opened to intensive irrigation during this time. On the southern margin of the

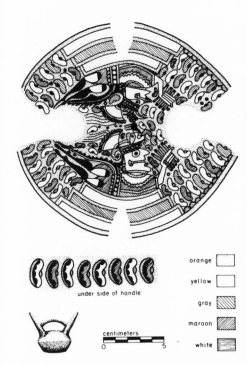

Figure 6.1. Mochica-Wari hybrid style double-spout bottle from Piura. Redrawn from the original in Rowe 1942. At least one nearly identical bottle has been looted from a cemetery at San José de Moro. Both show a personage with elaborate headdress holding sticks stretched over a multilevel platform.

valley, the Huacas at Moche were nearly abandoned, as attested to by the lack of burials and habitation refuse at the site which can be attributed to this phase. The same is true for the site of Huanchaco [overlooking the Pacific near the northern edge of the valley]. (Donnan and Mackey 1978: 210–211)

Similarly, there is not a single Moche V burial among the thirty-four Mochica burials Uhle excavated at Moche. The only Moche V ceramics reported from Moche are deliberately broken vessels recovered on the southern platform of the Huaca del Sol, where ritual offerings were made perhaps during Moche V and definitely post–Moche V (Menzel 1977: 60).[84]

Further, the final construction stage of the Sol and Luna mounds has been dated to the end of Moche IV or early Moche V based on adobe brick seriation and fre-

quency of marking (Mackey and Hastings 1982: 311; see also Hastings and Moseley 1975: 197).[85]

Moseley and Deeds (1982: 32) postulate an aeolian sand invasion of the site of Moche by or during Moche IV (Fig. 6.2) as a result of tectonic uplift that exposed a massive sand deposit along the south beach of the Moche Valley. The date is inferred from the presence of Moche IV burials in an adobe platform between the Sol and Luna mounds that had been buried by sand and abandoned (Moseley 1978b; Moseley and Deeds 1982: 37–38; T. Topic 1982: 273; cf. Donnan and Mackey 1978: 101). This platform and other sand-buried structures show little weathering and no post–Moche IV reuse. The stratigraphy observed in trenches placed between the two mounds also points to a Moche IV date for sand invasion (Moseley 1978b; Moseley and Deeds 1982: 38). Sand also invaded cultivation fields and associated canals on the south bank of the Moche Valley (including those supplying water to the site of Moche), leading to the permanent loss and widespread "agrarian collapse" of this area sometime during Moche IV (Moseley 1978b, 1983b; Moseley and Deeds 1982: 39; Moseley et al. 1983; Moseley, Feldman, and Ortloff 1981).

Overall, the available evidence indicates that the Mochica occupation of the south bank of the Moche Valley, including the site of Moche, essentially ended by the end of Moche IV. The sand-sheet invasion was apparently a significant causal factor. Given the nature of this environmental force, the abandonment of Moche may have been relatively gradual. We will consider what may have initiated this sand movement at some length later. The Moche Valley was transformed from the heart of the earlier Mochica intervalley polity to a frontier valley controlled by the emergent nucleated site of Galindo (Fig. 6.3).

3. Inland and Northward Settlement Shift

In remarkable contrast to the situation in the Southern Sector, we see an appreciable number of large late Moche IV and Moche V settlements in the Northern Sector. Associated ceramics suggest that their establishment overlapped in time with the aban-

donment of the Southern Sector. Full integration of the Northern Sector in late Moche IV may have been a move in anticipation of or motivated by the loss of the Southern Sector.

Clearly the most notable feature to emerge in the Northern Sector out of the Moche IV–V cultural transformation was the establishment of Galindo and Pampa Grande at the valley necks of the Moche and Lambayeque valleys, respectively. These urban settlements were unprecedented in abruptness of establishment, scale, and complexity. Each covered an estimated 6 km² and was the disproportionately large primary center of the Moche V settlement system in its respective valley. Moche V Pampa Grande was one of the largest sites on the Peruvian coast, with an estimated population of ten to fifteen thousand at its maximum.

Though architecture at both sites is complex, urbanism at Pampa Grande exhibits a higher degree of overall planning and is uniformly more densely built up than Galindo. In fact, important sociopolitical, ideological, and material differences between these two sites form a major line of evidence for considering these Moche V centers to have been semi-autonomous (see Chapter 7).

With Moche V occupation of the valley necks close to the principal MEC intakes (Figs. 3.4, 6.4), as noted in the preceding chapter, we see a definite concern with the control of water for the first time in Mochica settlement history. Galindo is somewhat west of the neck of the Moche Valley but also had access to the north bank MEC principal intake (Topic and Topic 1983). Pampa Grande was also in a position to control the main intakes of the Lambayeque Valley canals. The Collique Canal, the south bank MEC of the Lambayeque Valley, has its principal intake point some 7.5 km inland from the site (Fig. 3.17). The canal ran along the northern and western perimeters of Pampa Grande and also carried water to the middle portion of the north bank of the Zaña Valley. The Antigua Taymi, the north bank MEC of the Lambayeque Valley, began at the south base of La Puntilla, a rock formation across the valley neck from Pampa Grande, and carried water to Moche V settlements at Cerro

Figure 6.2. 1942 airphoto showing the site of Moche largely covered by an extensive sand sheet originating from the Pacific coast. Photo Proyecto 104-208. Courtesy of the Servicio Aerofotográfico Nacional del Perú.

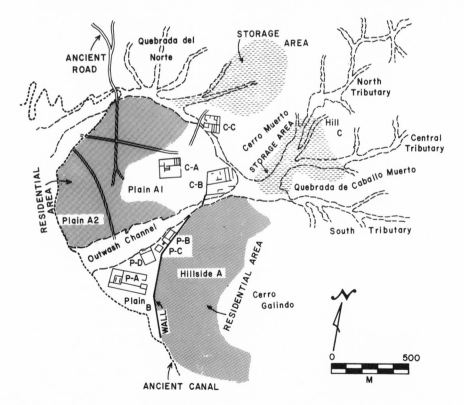

Figure 6.3. Site of Galindo on the north bank near the neck of the Moche Valley. Though there are some indications of planning in the architectural organization of the site, Galindo does not display the sort of overall cohesion seen at Pampa Grande, where centrally placed Huaca Fortaleza served as the physical and symbolic focus of site growth and organization. Redrawn from Fig. 12.1 in G. Bawden 1982: 290.

Patapo and Tres Tomas and continuing farther north and west. The Lambayeque Canal, which carries water from the Historic Taymi nearly east-west through the central portion of the Lambayeque Valley, was actually a modified river course (Kosok 1959; Portugal 1966; Reimchen 1972). It is quite likely that the Lambayeque Canal existed during Moche V occupation of Pampa Grande.

4. Moche V Domain: A General Characterization

As elucidated above, Moche V culture was essentially a northern North Coast phenomenon with the Lambayeque Valley Complex as its heartland. In the La Leche, Lambayeque, and Zaña valleys, many sites of various sizes are known, and the general settlement pattern there retains Moche IV emphasis on the mid-valley to the valley neck (Chapter 4; Figs. 3.15, 3.17, 4.19). The site of Tablazos some 12 km farther inland from Pampa Grande in the lower reaches of the *chaupiyunga* zone on the south bank of the Lambayeque appears to have been the inland-most Moche V site in the Northern Sector.

In the Jequetepeque, Moche V occupation covered both banks from the Pacific coast to the valley neck, with dispersed major settlements at Talambo, Pacatnamú, Moro Viejo, Tecapa, and Cañoncillo (see Eling 1987; Ubbelohde-Doering 1967). There was no disproportionately large urban valley neck site comparable to Pampa Grande or Galindo. However, the extensive

Figure 6.4. Location of the site of Pampa Grande in respect to the strategic valley neck.

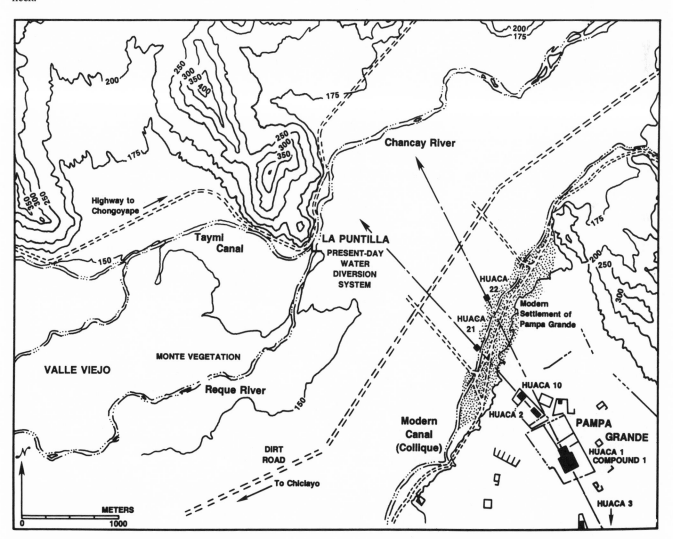

site of Cerro Talambo near the valley neck was well situated to control the principal intakes of the north bank MEC of the Jequetepeque Valley, which carried water toward the lower south bank of the neighboring Zaña Valley (Eling 1987: 250–262).[86]

The south bank Moche V occupation was centered around Cañoncillo (east of the town of San Pedro de Lloc), much of which is covered today by active sand dunes (ibid., 381). Eling's survey suggests that sand invasion began shortly before Moche V occupation and eventually forced the abandonment of associated canals and fields (ibid., 458). The sand movement thus appears to have been coeval with that noted at the site of Moche. The force responsible for sand invasion in these two valleys had a much broader scope than local uplift.

Moche V fine funerary ceramic bottles attributed to the Jequetepeque Valley, particularly to the site of Moro Viejo (Fig. 2.7; see Chapter 9), possess certain stylistic and iconographic idiosyncrasies not found at Galindo or Pampa Grande. These include fineline depictions of a funeral preparation scene and a double-stirrup spout form with a "monkey" perched at the juncture of the stirrup and the spout. The Jequetepeque Valley as a whole may have attained (or retained) a certain autonomous character within the Moche V heartland.

The situation in the Chicama Valley has not been well defined, but the collection in the British Museum of 250 vessels from the Chicama contains many fine Moche V stirrup-spout bottles (Joyce 1912: 180), suggesting the presence of a strong local Moche V polity. The site of Palenque (near Sausal) and other sites on both banks of the valley neck certainly deserve future exploration to clarify Moche V occupation. In the Moche Valley occupation was basically limited to the mid-valley portion of the north bank and dominated by the valley neck site of Galindo.

Farther afield, in the Piura region of the Far North Coast, one survey identified six sites with a total of fifty-two Moche V sherds (see Table 1 in Matos 1965–1966). Even farther north in the Cañaris region of the southern Ecuadorian highlands, we see flaring bowls with pedestal bases of Moche

V form but local decoration (Meyers 1979). Given Moche V painted ceramic depictions of llamas carrying baskets full of *Strombus* shells, it would not be surprising to learn that the Moche V polity had direct land-based trade with the south coast of Ecuador. Though it is tempting to suggest concurrent maritime trade with the same area on the basis of representations of cargo-carrying double-decked tule boats (e.g., see McClelland 1990), as seen in Chapter 4, we are still uncertain whether such boats are mythical or real.

Overall, Moche V settlements cover much of the northern North Coast, particularly mid-valley to valley neck portions. There was no significant littoral occupation, with the exception of Pacatnamú and the area around the modern town of Reque near the mouth of the Jequetepeque and Reque (Lambayeque Valley) rivers, respectively. Site location and construction do not indicate any strong preoccupation with defense. What Moche V settlement locations do indicate is concern with the control of water and north-south traffic.

5. Climatic Data

Given the above concern and indications of sand dune activity in the Moche and Jequetepeque Valleys, serious droughts had been suspected, and were confirmed by recent studies. Let us now turn our attention to the relevant evidence. Much of Peru is under the same climatic regime, and when we speak of a major drought affecting the North Coast, we should expect the same conditions elsewhere in Peru. Accordingly, we take a broad pan-Andean perspective to verify this critical test implication.

A. Central Coast

Starting around A.D. 450–500 (Early Intermediate Period Epoch 6 to 7, coeval to terminal Moche III–early Moche IV; see Table 6), when the contemporary Maranga (also called Lima) culture on the Central Coast of Peru achieved its population maximum, there was a series of related events of interest to us (MacNeish, Patterson, and Browman 1975: 52–54). Extensive irrigation networks were established throughout the middle to lower reaches of the contiguous valleys of Lurín, Rimac (where the city of Lima is situated), and

Table 6. Comparability of Mochica, Lima (Maranga), and Nasca sequences.

North Coast (Shimada)	Central Coast (Patterson 1966)	Ica Valley (Menzel 1977)	Nasca Valley (Silverman 1990)
	Lima 9		
Moche V		Nasca 9	Nasca 5
	Lima 8		
		Nasca 8	Nasca 4?
B	Lima 7		
Moche IV	Lima 6	Nasca 7	Nasca 3
A	Lima 5		

Chillón. By Epoch 7, the extent of cultivation area had surpassed that of the Lurín Valley today. Impressive adobe mound complexes, such as Maranga in the lower Rimac Valley, were associated with these irrigation networks (ibid., 53; Canziani 1987).

However, starting around A.D. 500, the earlier mound complexes and associated settlements in the lower reaches of the contiguous Chillón and Rimac valleys were abandoned (MacNeish, Patterson, and Browman 1975: 54). Concurrently, the large urban settlement of Cajamarquilla (Rimac Valley) was developed near the valley neck some 32 km from the Pacific (ibid., Patterson 1966: 112). The earlier platform mound complexes were subsequently utilized as burial grounds.

The above chain of events is believed to be causally linked to a series of fluctuations in the highland precipitation pattern starting from ca. A.D. 450. This oscillation is posited on the basis of analyses of pollen and soil samples taken from various sites within the Ayacucho region of the Central Highlands. For the period between A.D. 450 and 500, these data argue for an "interval of slightly increased precipitation" in some highland regions, "which resulted in slightly increased runoffs in the rivers of some coastal valleys." In response, "Water-control systems were expanded considerably in several coastal valleys at this time, presumably to take advantage of the increased runoff to bring formerly marginal lands under cultivation." However,

around A.D. 500, "precipitation apparently returned to normal or even subnormal levels" (MacNeish, Patterson, and Browman 1975: 52–53). An expected consequence would be the abandonment of marginal lands and canals, followed by increased wind erosion and sand movement. Destabilization of the delicate coastal ecology could have serious long-term consequences, as we saw in Chapter 3. In other words, populations that had reached maxima during the earlier favorable period now faced declining agricultural productivity. The shift to valley neck locations with ready access to water and fertile alluvium would be a logical response under such conditions. Thus, the observed settlement pattern shifts on the Central Coast (as well as the territorial expansion by the Wari polity out of the nearby highlands) are seen as systemic responses to widespread population pressure on declining agricultural productivity caused by decreasing precipitation (see Paulsen 1976).

B. South Coast

Independent support of the above data and explanation comes from Nasca Phase 7 (coeval with Moche IV; see Table 6) sites in the upper and middle Ica Valley on the South Coast of Peru. The favored location for Nasca 7 sites in the valley was dry alluvial fans or plains well above modern cultivation and habitation limits (Menzel 1971: 86). Two test pits excavated in a mound (midden over abandoned habitation structures) at La Tinguiña, the princi-

pal Nasca 7 site in the valley, yielded Phase 7 ceramics as well as plant and animal remains (ibid., 89).

The changes observed in the plant remains are particularly relevant. Plant remains from the lower strata of the excavation included various kinds of beans (*Canavalia* sp., *Phaseolus lunatus*), maize (*Zea mays*), ají peppers (*Capsicum* sp.), peanuts (*Arachis hypogaea*), and calabash (*Cucurbita moschata*) (ibid., 90). The last two were low in quantity. In the upper levels, however, maize and beans became rare and ají peppers disappeared, while calabash increased over time, representing the single largest category of cultivated plant found in the excavation. Although maize, beans, and calabash require about the same amount of moisture during their cultivation span, calabash has the shortest growth period and requires the least water overall. Today, calabash is grown in areas or times of water shortage on the coast.

Though it is not a simple matter to determine the relative economic significance of cultivated plants or prevailing climatic conditions from their preserved remains in archaeological contexts (e.g., Cohen 1972–1974), preservation was excellent and findings from both test cuts agree. Thus, the general reduction in quantities and variety of plants recovered in the excavation does not appear to be a product of biased sampling or differential preservation. The possibility of the bartering of the subsistence items cannot be ignored, but the Nasca 7 settlement-pattern data indicate a strong preference for what are today the dry valley margins.

Overall, Menzel (1971: 90–91) argues that unusually favorable pluvial conditions (above-average precipitation) at the onset of Nasca 7 allowed occupation of valley margins well beyond the limits of modern cultivation and habitation. However, water availability decreased over time, eventually forcing permanent abandonment by the end of Nasca 7. This scenario closely parallels that presented earlier for the Central Coast.

Craftsmanship of excavated Nasca 7 ceramics concurrently declines over the span of this phase; upper-level ceramics simply did not receive as much time and care as those from lower strata. Menzel (1971: 91) sees Nasca 7 ceramic art as beginning with various stylistic innovations and gradually declining as a reflection of the general impoverishment of the late Nasca 7 population due to prolonged drought conditions.

C. Quelccaya Ice Core Data

Perhaps the most convincing line of evidence attesting to major climatic disturbances during the sixth century A.D. comes from the 55 km² Quelccaya ice cap located 5,670 m above sea level (13°56' South, 70°50' West) in the south Peruvian highlands near the northern edge of the Titicaca Basin (Fig. 3.14). An annual precipitation record spanning fifteen hundred years has been derived from analyses of two deep ice cores (drilled to depths of 154.8 and 163.6 m) conducted by the Byrd Polar Research Center, Ohio State University (Thompson et al. 1979, 1984, 1985, 1986, 1988; Thompson and Mosley-Thompson 1987; Thompson, Mosley-Thompson, and Morales 1984). Microparticle concentrations, oxygen isotope ratios (δO^{18}), and conductivity were measured and found to display annual cyclical variations. However, most useful in differentiating annual wet and dry seasons is the clearly visible "layer-cake effect" in the cores (Fig. 6.5) created by alternating layers of ice and airborne dust. Much like annual tree rings, these layers can be simply counted backward in time. The annual ice layer is the most direct indication of the annual precipitation received during a highland wet season.[87] A drought condition can be recognized by the covariance of various indices: less accumulation, greater soluble and insoluble particulates, and relatively less negative δO^{18} values. The reliability of these indices has been firmly established by cross-checking with historically documented droughts.

Overall, the Quelccaya ice cores allow us to establish a reliable, long-term annual precipitation record back to ca. A.D. 470 with a ± 20 year margin of error (Fig. 6.6). The use of these annual data was highly desirable for archaeological study, since short-term environmental variations stressful to human populations could be identified (Schaaf 1988; Shimada et al. 1991a,b). With previously published decadal data, it was difficult to assess the persis-

Figure 6.5. Cliff face of the Quelccaya ice cap showing the readily visible lamination of annual ice and dust accumulations. Courtesy of Lonnie G. Thompson.

tence, severity, or abruptness of precipitation anomalies.

Looking at Figure 6.6, it is immediately apparent that one episode of subnormal precipitation spanning A.D. 562–594 stands out for its abrupt onset and the lengthy duration of extremely low precipitation, and also that this episode was preceded by a couple of shorter droughts (A.D. 524–540 and perhaps A.D. 506–512). This lengthy drought condition was followed by a pluvial period during Moche V, spanning A.D. 602–635.

Clearly the three-decade-long drought was one of the longest (another, less severe thirty-year drought began in A.D. 1020) and severest (in terms of the low precipitation) of the past fifteen hundred years (Shimada et al. 1991a,b). An idea of the potential impacts of this drought may be gained by looking at a considerably shorter

and less severe drought between A.D. 1933 and 1945 (Thompson and Mosley-Thompson 1987: 105). During this drought, the water level of Lake Titicaca dropped almost 5 m, forcing steamboat traffic to cease for several years.

An important, independent line of evidence indicating a period of severe dryness during the sixth century A.D. comes from a 2,500-year-long record of ancient precipitation revealed by changes in fossil diatoms (microscopic algae) in the sediment core of Lake Yambo (1°05' South, 78°35' West, with an elevation of 2,600 m) in the Ecuadorian highlands (Steinitz-Kannan, Nienaber, and Riedinger 1992). Observed fluctuations in the abundance of two diatom taxa are interpreted as evidence for changes in lake conductivity (concentration of dissolved ions) and water level. Changes in water chemistry (degree of sa-

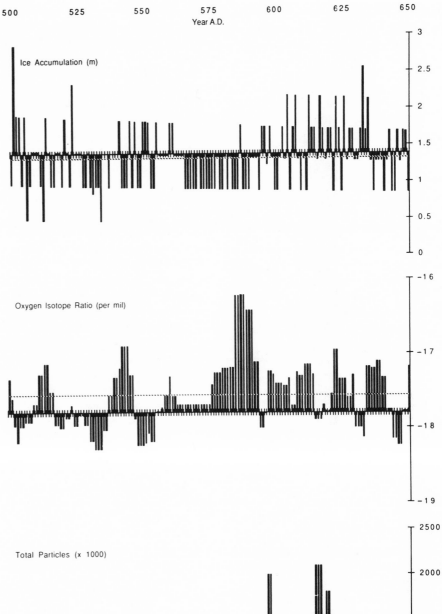

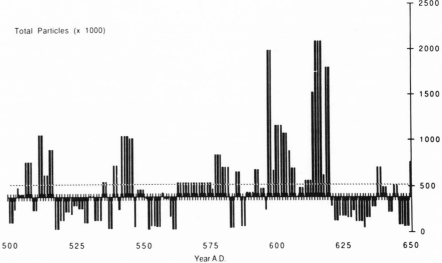

linity) correspondingly affect the diatom flora, and thus a severe drought would lower water level and increase the salinity, favoring growth of certain diatom taxa. The precipitation record thus reconstructed has been radiocarbon-dated (Fig. 6.7). Among other things, it shows two prolonged periods of severe dryness for the first half of the sixth century and eleventh century A.D., each preceded by a pluvial period. Though dating of the Lake Yambo sequence is not as precise as that of the Quelccaya, the above findings are in a very good concordance with the Quelccaya data.[88]

D. Applicability of the Quelccaya Data to the North Coast

Before elucidating the relationship between the Moche IV–V transformation and these sixth-century climatic disturbances, it is

Figure 6.6. Annual precipitation record for the central Andes (displayed around the fifteen-hundred-year mean) established from ice core samples taken from the Quelccaya ice cap. Courtesy of Crystal B. Schaaf.

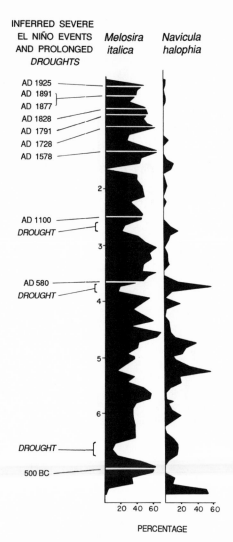

INFERRED SEVERE
EL NIÑO EVENTS
AND PROLONGED
DROUGHTS

Melosira italica   *Navicula halophia*

AD 1925
AD 1891
AD 1877
AD 1828
AD 1791
AD 1728
AD 1578

2

AD 1100
DROUGHT

3

AD 580
DROUGHT

4

5

6

DROUGHT

500 BC

20 40 60   20 40 60

PERCENTAGE

Figure 6.7. Past precipitation events in the Ecuadorian highlands reconstructed on the basis of observed changes in the fossil diatom communities of Lake Yambo. Dates shown are extrapolated from radiocarbon dates. Redrawn from Fig. 2 in Steinitz-Kannan et al. 1992: 297.

necessary to establish clearly the applicability of the Quelccaya precipitation records to the North Coast well over one thousand kilometers away and over five thousand meters lower.

This is possible since much of the Peruvian Andes is under the same tropical meteorological regime with the southeast trade winds and equatorial easterlies dominating the windflow (Johnson 1976; Schaaf 1988; Shimada et al. 1991a,b), as explained in Chapter 3. Important to our concern is the fact that annual precipitation totals across the 15° latitudinal span of the Peruvian Andes are remarkably consistent (Johnson 1970, 1976); also, the Quelccaya ice cap is situated on the eastern cordillera, well within the Peruvian Andean climatic regime that dictates the precipitation pattern of the north Peruvian highlands where North Coast rivers originate. Meteorological data collected at Quelccaya (Thompson 1980: 72) have demonstrated the same annual wet/dry season cycles occurring there as in the rest of the Peruvian Andes. Further, there is no indication of a significant shift in the basic pattern or geographical extent of this tropical climatic regime over the past fifteen hundred years. Finally, applicability of the Quelccaya data to describe the entire tropical Peruvian precipitation regime is strengthened even more by similar meteorological data and ice core records obtained at the La Garganta Glacier in the Huascarán Col in the Callejón de Huaylas in the north Peruvian highlands (9°07' South, 77°36' West, 900 km northwest of Quelccaya; Thompson et al. 1984a,b). Overall, the Quelccaya ice cores provide a reliable, precisely dated record of moisture availability on the North Coast.

6. The Moche IV–V Transformation as a Response to Severe Droughts: Archaeological Assessment

The preceding establishes the contemporaneity and pan-Peruvian Andean character of a pluvial condition sometime before A.D., 500 followed by prolonged, severe drought conditions during much of the sixth century. Does this climatic disturbance adequately account for the Moche IV–V cultural transformation? Particularly important is satisfactorily accounting for the drastic inland and northward settlement shift.

A. Chronological Consideration

One basic question that requires resolution before examining the cause/effect linkage between climatic disturbances and Moche IV–V changes is whether they were coterminous or one preceded the other. Clarification of their temporal relationship is essential in avoiding the temptation to manipulate them subjectively for a desired fit.

The five-phase Mochica ceramic chronology is by no means precise, and synchroneity between the heartland and peripheral areas has not been adequately established. However, Moche V is clearly the best radiocarbon-dated phase of the Mochica sequence, and the critical question of temporal coincidence may be partially resolved by scrutinizing Moche V dates. Excavations at Pampa Grande yielded abundant organic substances from secure primary contexts ideally suited for radiocarbon dating. Thoroughly carbonized corn kernels and unspun cotton were used for precise dating, as they were likely to have been harvested within a year of the conflagration that marked the end of Moche V Pampa Grande (see Chapter 10). The end of Moche V occupation at Pampa Grande can be put at sometime around A.D. 700, perhaps as early as 650. This assignment is supported by other reliable dates from Galindo and sites in the Batán Grande area. Claims that there may have been an "unbroken dynasty" from Moche V Pampa Grande to Chan Chan (the capital of the Chimú Kingdom; Mackey 1982: 331; T. Topic 1982: 281), or that the Moche V culture or polity lasted up to ca. A.D. 1000–1050 (Donnan 1986: 22) are not supported by available data (Shimada 1990a, in press 2).

The beginning date of Moche V occupation at Pampa Grande, on the other hand, is largely a guess. However, various lines of evidence may be adduced to show that the total span of Moche V occupation was relatively short, perhaps 150 or fewer years. The principal platform mound of Huaca Fortaleza seems to have had only two major construction phases and was built with the time- and labor-saving chamber-and-fill technique (Chapter 7).

Though many floors show replastering, dispersed deep cuts in residential and craft workshop areas typically reveal only limited architectural buildup. Many structures in the higher eastern portion of the site had hardly any refuse and, in fact, some appear to be incomplete. Associated ceramics, both excavated and surface collected, are quite homogeneous in style. Sherds recovered from the latest floor, as well as from subfloor deposits down to sterile soil in an inferred ceramic workshop in Sector D east of Huaca Fortaleza, were all quite homogeneous Moche V reduced wares.

Additional radiocarbon dates from other sites with Moche V occupation are in general agreement with those from Pampa Grande (Table 2). A sample from the hearth of a late Moche IV floor immediately above sterile sand at Huaca del Pueblo Batán Grande (mid–La Leche Valley) yielded a corrected date of A.D. 520 ± 70. This occupation is overlaid by Moche V floors with two corrected dates of A.D. 620 ± 40 and A.D. 640 ± 40 derived from charcoal samples from two hearths. Overall, the beginning of Moche V in the Lambayeque region is put at ca. A.D. 550–600.

Assignment of Moche V capital status to Pampa Grande is based on various considerations: the abundance of pure Moche V ceramics, including those decorated with traditional and innovative themes; the immense size of the Huaca Fortaleza platform mound, unmatched in the Moche V world, and its central placement; and the overall planned layout and unprecedented architectural diversity, nucleation, and expanse of the city (I. Shimada 1982: 155). It is generally assumed that the replacement of Moche by Pampa Grande as the Mochica capital coincided in time with the appearance of diagnostic features of Moche V ceramics (e.g., bottles with roughly triangular stirrups and tapering spouts). Our chronological control, however, is simply not good enough to validate this assumption. We have not yet tested the hypothesis that the replacement was direct with little hiatus between the abandonment of Moche and the establishment of Pampa Grande. Unless we envision the replacement as a prolonged affair (perhaps spanning one or two generations), the above view would have to posit either considerable foresight and

planning or Moche IV occupation of Pampa Grande.

Moche IV occupation at Pampa Grande was at best limited. Some fragments of fine painted ceramics from the surface and deep cuts made in the central portion of the site may be considered Moche IV. Similarly, the difference in the orientation of the two largest platform mounds at Pampa Grande might be construed as reflecting inferred Moche IV versus V construction dates. However, numerous deep excavations in areas of thick refuse and/or architectural buildup have failed to yield definite Moche IV ceramics.

In essence, the whole process of replacement was probably much more complex and perhaps more time-consuming than typically assumed. Equating the onset of Moche V and the establishment of Pampa Grande as the Moche V capital as a single event obscures processes of the Moche IV–V transition. It is possible that the Mochica population from Moche initially relocated to Galindo as an immediate and temporary response to problems that beset them before making the permanent and more drastic shift to Pampa Grande. Such an intermediate step within the same valley would have given the polity time to prepare for the eventual move to Pampa Grande. As yet we have not been able to identify sensitive temporal markers for differentiating one subphase that encompasses the inferred shift from Moche to Galindo and another for the span of Moche V occupation at Pampa Grande.

The above scenario assumes that the establishment of Pampa Grande was accompanied by the wholesale relocation of the Mochica elite and their retainers from the earlier capital of Moche. There is no a priori evidence that this was the case; rather we need to consider the distinct possibility that this group remained at Galindo and that the new capital was built by and for the Lambayeque-based northern Mochica polity. In this sense, it is more appropriate to speak of the replacement of the capital rather than relocation.

We have seen that there is a definite broad temporal coincidence between the Moche IV–V transformation and the thirty-two-year-long drought. Further, there is general agreement in regard to the synchroneity of drastic settlement shifts along the Peruvian coast. At the same time, we cannot specify whether these critical shifts occurred before, during, or immediately after the drought.

Though the above discussion may have emphasized the thirty-two-year drought, it must be seen within long-term trends. Importantly, it was preceded by a severe (roughly comparable to that of the thirty-two-year drought) seventeen-year-long drought (A.D. 524–540), which itself was probably preceded by a relatively short one between A.D. 506 and 512. Together with an earlier pluvial period (as suggested by the Central and South Coast data, as well as the early end of the Quelccaya record going back to ca. A.D. 450), these two earlier droughts probably accentuated the adverse effects of the three-decade drought, for example, sand movement and soil erosion by wind and El Niño–related floods. The impacts of the latter would have been considerable under hyper-arid conditions; adverse effects may well have outweighed the benefits of abundant water for a year or two.

Overall, prior to the abrupt onset of the three-decade drought, the Moche IV population was already under considerable environmental stress. When we take this long-term perspective, the issue of temporal coincidence becomes less crucial. As alluded to earlier, the Moche IV–V transformation may have spanned a generation or two. Parts of the transformation were probably a response to the environmental stress that spanned much of the sixth century rather than specifically to the three-decade drought. We cannot ignore the possibility that the transformation may have begun before that drought.

B. The Selection of Pampa Grande and the Lambayeque Valley

Why was the Moche V capital established at Pampa Grande rather than in another valley? What overriding considerations favored this particular location?

Pampa Grande is situated about 54 km inland from the Pacific on an extensive alluvial pediment ("large pampa" and thus the Spanish name *pampa grande*) on the south bank overlooking the neck of the Lambayeque Valley. The lower edges of the pediment and a major rock outcrop known as La Puntilla on the north bank constrict the Chancay River and valley bottomland to a mere 2,300 m (Fig. 6.4). As in the past, the valley neck continues to be the ideal location for water control. Today, modern concrete water-control gates bipartition and direct the water of the Chancay River to the Lambayeque River, an artificially canalized extinct riverbed that irrigates the central Lambayeque Valley (Reimchen 1972),[89] as well as to the Reque River, the modern main outlet of the valley (Figs. 3.1, 3.15). The Historic Taymi Canal drew water from the Lambayeque River just downstream of La Puntilla. The Antigua Taymi, the pre-Hispanic north bank MEC that took the water to the south bank of the La Leche Valley, had its principal intake right at La Puntilla. During Moche IV and V domination of the valley, the Collique Canal (the south bank MEC) began just inland from Pampa Grande near the village of Tablazos at an elevation of ca. 155 m (Kosok 1959: 52; Nolan 1980: 137–138).[90]

We have already seen in Chapter 3 that the Lambayeque Valley is endowed with conditions ideal for large-scale irrigation agriculture, such as a low, even gradient; thick, fertile, and wide valley bottomland; the relatively high elevation of the Chancay River; and high minimum discharge volume and high overall annual volume in part due to the large drainage area. Both the Chicama and Jequetepeque valleys have higher overall discharge volumes than the Lambayeque but are less stable, with greater differences between the minimum and maximum annual discharge volumes and much more limited cultivation areas (Kosok 1959: 50; Kroeber 1930: 75–76; see Table 3). We have already seen the widespread adverse effects of sand movement in the Jequetepeque Valley. With the Andean foothills at the southwest corner of the valley, however, the Lambayeque is relatively well-protected from sand driven by the constant winds off the Pacific. Sand movement has only affected economically marginal areas near the mouth of the Lambayeque River and to the north that chronically have suffered poor drainage and salt problems (Reimchen 1972; Shimada 1981: 434).

In addition, the valley neck location of Pampa Grande offered ready access to the principal north-south road and *chaupi-yunga* that begins slightly farther inland, fresh (low-salt) irrigation water, and the *Valle Viejo*. Historically three sectors of agricultural land were recognized in the Lambayeque Valley (Fig. 3.1). *Valle Viejo* refers to the choice area at the apex of the roughly triangular Lambayeque Valley bottomland, which has the thickest alluvium. From the Colonial era until the Agrarian Reform in 1968 this was controlled by the *haciendas* for large-scale cultivation of water-demanding sugarcane (Ramírez-Horton 1974: 7). Today, agricultural cooperatives continue sugarcane cultivation of this area. *Valle Nuevo* corresponds to the northwestern sector of valley bottomland, the lower portions of which chronically suffer from the interrelated problems of poor drainage, salinization, and water shortage (ibid.; Netherly 1984). Today, cotton which fares well under relatively dry conditions, and wet-paddy rice cultivation, which effectively deals with poor-quality soil and salinization, dominate *Valle Nuevo* agriculture. To a lesser extent, the same sorts of soil and water problems affect small plot cultivation in the lower, seaward portions of the valley known as the *Valle Bajo* (Ramírez-Horton 1974: 7; Shimada 1976: 41–54).

Overall, it is quite apparent that the valley neck location of Pampa Grande afforded easy access to the principal intakes of the pre-Hispanic north and south bank MECs for control over irrigation water and the best farming land, a critical consideration for a culture faced with or just free from prolonged drought conditions. Such control probably also meant that the Moche V polity at Pampa Grande gained a political advantage over all populations downstream. Though the Moche V settlement-pattern data point to a mid-valley focus, Pampa Grande may have exerted political control over much of the lower valley as well.

The unprecedented population nucleation at Pampa Grande (and also at Galindo) can also be readily understood as a response or solution to lengthy and severe drought conditions. Individual farmers may respond to short-term drought through a variety of strategies such as reducing the extent or intensity of irrigation or changing the composition of cultigens. However, with the extremely severe long-term droughts that beset the entire Peruvian coast during much of the sixth century A.D., their responses would have had to have been more drastic and better-coordinated, perhaps coming down from the highest levels of the society. With significantly less water reaching the coast, most likely land toward the peripheries of the irrigation networks (i.e., *Valles Nuevo* and *Bajo*) would have been abandoned first. With drought conditions persisting year after year, the groundwater level as well as the water transport efficiency of the irrigation systems would have been significantly lowered in peripheral areas. Reduction of vegetational cover would have worsened wind erosion and sand movement. Overall, the most effective strategy would have been investing the available water in cultivation of the best-quality soil close to the principal intakes (i.e., *Valle Viejo*). Even if Pampa Grande was established immediately following the thirty-two-year drought, recent experience would have directed the residents to adopt similar strategies.

The importance of maximizing every bit of water reaching the coast during the three-decade drought can be effectively illustrated by looking at modern water consumption in the Lambayeque Valley. One study that examined a span of twenty-nine years (1937–1965; Fig. 6.8) showed that about 88 percent of the water volume carried by the Chancay River (recorded at Carhuaquero some 29 km inland from Pampa Grande)[91] was consumed for agricultural purposes within the valley. In the mid-1960's, some 85 percent of the local population was engaged in some form of agricultural activity (Portugal 1966: 13, 39). Except for rare, abnormal El Niño years, only a small quantity of water volume is lost to the Pacific. Some years literally no water is discharged into the sea. The modern situation cannot be readily applied to Mochica times largely because of the currently heavy emphasis on the year-round cultivation of water-demanding sugarcane and the ever-expanding urban population. At the same time, it is esti-

mated that the Mochica cultivated about 25 to 30 percent more area than today (Kosok 1965; Moseley 1983b; Nolan 1980). Overall, modern water consumption figures do give us an approximate picture of Mochica needs, and we suspect that even a moderate 25 percent reduction in the amount of water reaching the coast could have caused a considerable hardship for North Coast farmers.

Overall, the selection of the Lambayeque, one of the largest valleys on the Peruvian coast, is readily understandable. With a reliable high minimum discharge volume, extensive fertile land, and limited sand movement, the Lambayeque offered greater agricultural potential than other large valleys in the Northern Sector of the North Coast, in particular the Jequetepeque and Chicama. Thus, we conclude that the climatic explanation accounts well for major aspects of the Moche IV–V cultural transformation, particularly the nucleation at the Lambayeque Valley neck.

It is most likely, however, that the decision to establish the new capital at Pampa Grande was not made solely on the favorable environmental conditions and factors. It is suggested here that the decision also involved political considerations related to the Lambayeque-based Mochica polity. A series of severe droughts that spanned much of the sixth century are believed to have had differential impacts on the Northern and Southern Sectors, with the former more effectively weathering the adverse effects due to its favorable conditions. Even before the onset of the three-decade drought, the southern Mochica polity centered at Moche is likely to have suffered considerable internal unrest and a decline in agricultural production from earlier droughts. As we see later, this polity, by the time it had relocated to Galindo, apparently had lost its ability to mobilize labor and resources from beyond the north bank of the Moche Valley. In addition, in this weakened state it appears to have been threatened by a nearby polity occupying the *chaupiyunga* zone of the same valley (T. Topic 1991), a stark contrast to the dominant position it held until early Moche IV. Its loss of the prestige and political control over much of its domain allowed the resurgence of the Lambayeque-based northern Mochica polity. In this sense the establishment of the city at Pampa Grande may be seen as a celebration of the regained political eminence of the northern polity as much as a solution to environmental difficulties.

C. Assessing Other Related Issues

The preceding discussion introduces the question of the possible role of a severe El Niño flood as the direct cause of the Moche IV–V transformation. A severe El Niño event, as discussed in Chapter 3, could have wreaked havoc all along the Peruvian coast. The buried adobe platform between the Huacas del Sol and de la Luna at Moche showed aeolian sand deposits capped by one to two meters of consolidated water-laid silt (Moseley 1978b; Moseley and Deeds 1982: 38). The flash flood is believed to have been responsible for damaging the Huaca del Sol and stripping several meters of soil from the site of Moche. Later intrusive burials with red-white-black tricolor ceramics that are believed to date to ca. A.D. 1000 or somewhat earlier were placed in the flood deposits (Moseley 1987: 10). Thus, "the incursion of water came after Moche Phase IV, but before the use of Red, white, black ceramics" (Moseley and Deeds 1982: 38).

For the period of A.D. 500–750, Schaaf (1988: 65) has used the Quelccaya ice core data to identify various years (A.D. 600–601, 610, 612, 650, and 681) meeting the

El Niño criteria of low ice accumulation, high total particle concentration and conductivity, and less negative oxygen isotope ratios. However, during severe El Niño events, the normal tropical climatic regime is temporarily disrupted, and the Southern Highlands (where Quelccaya is situated) typically experience short-term drought (see Antúnez de Mayolo 1992). Thus, any severe El Niño occurring within a period of lengthy drought is not easy to detect even with these criteria. Severe El Niño events are also suspected to have occurred in the years A.D. 511–512, 546, and 576, but their signals are difficult to differentiate as these fall within longer periods of drought (Schaaf 1988: 65). The Lake Yambo climatic sequence identifies A.D. 580 as a severe El Niño year (Steinitz-Kannan, Nienaber, and Riedinger 1992: 297; see Fig. 6.7).

Recently, McClelland (1990: 92) has invoked the aforementioned El Niño flood documented at Moche as the primary cause of the Moche IV–V transformation:

Widespread flooding, devastating the North Coast at the end of Phase IV, could explain the abandonment of Huacas Sol and Luna and the reorganization of Moche occupation in Phase V. This disruption may have forced them to modify their mythical world to handle these overwhelming circumstances of nature. The appearance of new marine deities [in the Moche V iconography], the new tule boat-

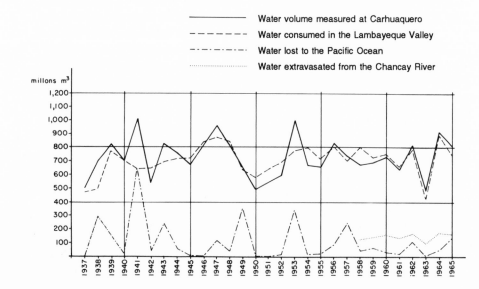

Figure 6.8. Annual discharge and utilization of the Chancay-Reque River water for the span of 1937–1965. Redrawn from Chart 1 in Portugal 1966: 37.

men and the anthropomorphized wave documents these changes. If the ocean either contributed to this stressful period or alleviated it, then the ocean and its marine deities may have acquired enlarged and new mythical roles.

This view suffers from a number of serious problems. As described above, dating of the flood is far from precise (e.g., "post-" vs. "late" Moche IV) and it could be any one of or any combination of the eight El Niño events identified during the sixth and seventh centuries. Though a recent publication places it near the end of Moche IV (Moseley 1987: 10; cf. Craig and Shimada 1986: 36), the data base for this more precise dating is not clear. Further, if an El Niño flood played any significant part in the Moche IV–V transformation, it would not make much sense to establish the new capital farther north; in general, progressively more severe and frequent damage from El Niño events occurs as one heads north along the Peruvian coast. The observed iconographic changes can be just as plausibly interpreted as reflecting a desire for a greater abundance of water. The Pacific Ocean in the Andean cosmology is the source of all water. This flood explanation also fails to account adequately for the abandonment of the Southern Sector, or for the valley neck nucleation. In other words, an El Niño event may have contributed to but does not seem to have caused the transformation.

We cannot yet fully embrace the climatic explanation. As at La Tinguiña in the upper Ica Valley, we need to look for a long-term shift in the range of cultigens and their relative proportions on the Central and North Coast. The importance of excavating Mochica habitational sites that span all of Moche IV is critical in this regard. Examination of plant remains from Pampa Grande may not be helpful given the prolonged pluvial period during Moche V and the disposal of organic refuse as animal feed and architectural fill. Obtaining representative samples of cultigens that accurately reflect their true economic significance is indeed difficult. Analysis of soil samples from pre-Hispanic cultivation fields for diagnostic pollens is useful, but such studies often suffer from poor

chronological control and pollen preservation (see Weir and Eling 1986). Interestingly, examination of pre–Moche V and Moche V canals and cultivation fields in the Jequetepeque Valley (Eling 1987) revealed that earlier small cultivation plots and canals that faithfully followed the topography gave way to larger planned cultivation fields and more streamlined canals. This observed change may indicate attempts to improve efficiency of water transport and use as necessitated by the reduction in available water. The above dating, however, is uncertain.

The Moche IV–V situation in the Chicama and Zaña valleys remains largely unknown. Was there population nucleation at the valley necks? For Moche V, I suspect that the population in the Zaña was controlled by the polity at Pampa Grande, as the latter controlled water to much of the north bank of the Zaña Valley. It is doubtful that a parallel can be drawn for the Moche-Chicama pair.

7. Assessing the "Wari Expansion" Hypothesis

A. Relevant Evidence and Arguments

We already alluded to possible effects of the looming threat of Wari expansion. The basic facts and arguments of the Wari expansion theory will be examined below.

Much has been written about the Wari culture and its expansion since it gained wide recognition in the 1950's as a distinct and important archaeological culture. The subject is complex and controversial.[92] Though varying in quality, quantity, and contexts of occurrence, Wari- and Provincial Wari–style ceramics (and, to a lesser degree, architecture) have been reported from much of the Peruvian highlands and coast, from Piura and Cajamarca in the north to Cusco and Moquegua in the south. However, the mechanisms and timing involved in their distribution and the significance of their presence to local cultures continue to be hotly debated.

Fundamental to understanding the Wari polity and the impact of its inferred expansion onto the North Coast is the work of the Virú Valley Project and Dorothy Menzel. Various members of the Virú Valley Project documented that "the sudden

break-up and disappearance of the Mochica ceramic style" during the Tomaval Phase in the valley "correlated with significant changes in both the domestic and politico-religious-military architecture" (Willey 1953: 412) and with the appearance of new intrusive ceramic styles, such as "Tomaval Three-Color" or "Coast Tiahuanaco" (today called Provincial Wari). Willey (ibid.) concluded that "One of the most important revelations in the Virú data" was that the new type of communities, called "planned enclosure" or "compound" communities, had "their inception with the arrival of the Coast Tiahuanaco" (today identified as Wari) influence or invaders. Concomitantly, he saw the "decline of interest in the great pyramids or pyramid-dwelling-palace ceremonial centers ... [and] the abandonment of the castillo-fortifications." Though placement of dwellings and ceremonial-civic structures within encircling walls was found in the earlier Puerto Moorin "Hilltop Redoubts" or in the Gallinazo "Castillo Fortification Complexes" in the valley (ibid., 111), the new types of enclosures had a clearly planned rectangular layout regardless of the topography; many of them are found on level ground. Schaedel (1951a, 1966a,b) sees the "urban lay centers," imposing dwelling-palace-temple complexes laid out within a series of rectangular enclosures, as replacing the earlier community organization throughout the North Coast. The North Coast cities are thought to have been introduced by the Wari conquerors. This position was recently restated by McEwan (1990).

Schaedel (also see Lumbreras 1974; Willey 1971) sees state and city formation as going in tandem, with their emergence on the North Coast secondary to Wari invasion. He posits (1972: 17) that restructuring of "the principal settlements so as to encompass the functions, not only of military and religious control, but of economic or resource control as well," occurred during the Middle Horizon at the hands of Wari expansionists. This change encompassed the emergence of disproportionately large urban settlements at valley necks (e.g., Galindo and Pampa Grande) and attendant diminution in the distribution of minor settlements. In addition, he argues

(Schaedel 1985b: 450) that a new system of land exploitation was installed, with restructuring of earlier field and contour canal systems. Overall, Schaedel (ibid.) attributes these major changes to "restructuring" of an overextended, "undifferentiated, loosely federated" Mochica theocratic polity and its major settlements by Wari invaders following their conquest of the North Coast early in the Middle Horizon.

According to the Wari Conquest hypothesis, the abandonment of the Mochica Southern Sector and the establishment of the new Mochica capital in the Lambayeque Valley may be seen as an attempt to seek a safe haven from the encroaching Wari threat. The large Jequetepeque Valley would have been a poor choice as it was the natural corridor linking the northern North Coast and the Cajamarca Basin, where an inferred Wari ally of the Middle Cajamarca ruled (I. Shimada 1982: 173–174). In the same vein, this explanation argues that defensive measures against the Wari threat are found in the southern Mochica frontier settlements. Indeed, the portion of Galindo that protrudes toward the valley neck has an impressive one-kilometer-long parapeted perimeter wall that stood at least 4 m high and measures some 3.5 m wide at the preserved top. Piles of small round stones, presumably for slingshots, were found at the wall top (Topic and Topic 1982: 6; T. Topic 1991: 238). The dense habitational structures built on terraces within the enclosed area thus are viewed as the "refuge area" of Galindo.

Because the inferred Wari conquest and the establishment of Galindo and Pampa Grande were sequential, accurate and precise dating of the relevant processes and events is needed.

Our understanding of Wari chronology and expansion was significantly improved by Menzel (1958, 1964, 1968, 1969). Based on detailed iconographic, stylistic, and distributional analyses of ceremonial and domestic ceramics, she argues that the polity's capital at Wari in the Ayacucho Basin was the center for the dissemination of religious ideas that eventually covered much of the Central Andes. Menzel's inferences regarding Wari political and ideological domination largely derive from her recognition that the nature and extent of Wari ceramic distribution is analogous to that of the better-understood Inca expansions. Whether Inca patterns can be directly extrapolated to the earlier Wari situation remains a major point of contention.

Specifically, Menzel sees two distinct episodes, Middle Horizon Epochs 1B (Moche V) and 2B, during which Wari-style artifacts were widely disseminated. The first (Epoch 1B) expansion is documented by the spread of three pottery styles, Robles Moqo ordinary and oversize ceremonial pottery and Chakipampa B domestic vessels. The last is a style indigenous to Ayacucho and can be traced to a pre-Wari (Late Huarpa) era. It is the widespread distribution of Chakipampa domestic ware, together with Robles Moqo vessels in ceremonial contexts, that forms the basis of her argument for religiously motivated conquest during Epoch 1B. Their distribution includes much of the highland basin of Callejón de Huaylas adjacent to the Southern Sector of the Mochica hegemony; on the coast it covered the area between the Nasca Valley on the South Coast and perhaps as far north as the Huarmey Valley on the North-Central Coast. An ordinary-sized Robles Moqo vessel, however, was looted from a grave at the site of Huaca Facho in the central La Leche Valley near the northern edge of the North Coast.

The second expansion episode during Epoch 2B is essentially based on a similar argument but can muster a greater range and quantity of supportive data. This expansion is believed to have subsumed an area at least as far north as the Lambayeque on the coast and the southern portion of the Cajamarca Basin in the highlands. Menzel saw these expansions as processes of military and political domination motivated by religious proselytizing. Lumbreras (1960, 1974) and Isbell (1978, 1986, 1988) also favor the idea of conquest but without the religious undertones. In contrast, Shady and Ruíz (1979) argue that the wide distribution of Wari-style artifacts resulted from extensive trade among dispersed major commercial centers. The divergence between Menzel's and other views largely depends on the dating and how one explains the distribution of Chakipampa domestic ware—whether it predated Middle Horizon 1B, and whether it was carried in by Wari invaders or peacefully traded in. Topic and Topic (1986; J. Topic 1991) emphasize trade and exchange of ritual goods[93] and information. We described earlier Paulsen's (1976) view that a severe drought forced the Wari polity to seek resources outside the Ayacucho Basin and thus begin its territorial expansion. Others also emphasize resource control. Isbell (1977; Isbell and Schreiber 1978) argues that the residents of the expanding site of Wari had overextended their local agricultural base and were forced to appropriate the produce of neighboring valleys (cf. Browman 1976). Lorandi (1986) sees the emergence of an increasingly centralized authority centered at Wari as a means of managing the distribution of resources procured by colonies established at various ecological zones and of countering their inherent tendency to split off and gain autonomy. She sees the creative tension between the centripetal and centrifugal tendencies of the center and colonies, respectively, as the driving force of Wari territorial and political growth.

There is no a priori reason to view Wari expansions in monolithic terms. The possibility should be entertained that different mechanisms (e.g., trade, pilgrimage/proselytism, and military threat and conquest) were employed in different areas and/or phases of the spread (Shimada 1981: 442; see Anders 1986, 1991; Schreiber 1987). A more dynamic and regionalized perspective is particularly important in examining the interaction between the Wari polity and powerful contemporary cultures such as the Mochica and Cajamarca.

B. Assessment of the Model

The "exogenous origin" theory was challenged in the 1970's by members of the Chan Chan–Moche Valley Project, which attempted to show direct cultural continuity between Moche V and the later Chimú Kingdom without any significant interruption by the inferred Wari invaders (see Table 1.1 in Moseley and Day 1982: 8; Mackey 1982; T. Topic 1982). Mackey (1982: 322) rejected the Wari introduction theory for North Coast cities in favor of an indigenous origin: "urbanism did not suddenly arise without antecedents but shows a continuous indigenous development." Her cursory survey of North Coast urban settlements, however, did not deal with the origin of the critical "planned Rectangular Enclosure Compounds."

In their zeal, these researchers did not properly assess evidence relevant to the postulated Wari influence or invasion, thereby weakening their own claims. Provincial Wari ceramics are present on the North Coast, including at Huaca del Sol in Moche (Menzel 1977). At the same time, Chakipampa B– and/or Robles Moqo-style ceramics indicative of the first Wari expansion are absent in the Southern Sector. For example, in the Santa Valley most of the diagnostic ceramics of the Early Tanguche period following local Mochica occupation (see Figs. 236–256 in Wilson 1988: 224–261) are attributable to Middle Horizon Epochs 2 and 3 (including those that Larco Hoyle [1948: 37–42] called "Northern Huari A and B");[94] some seem to date from as late as the first epochs of the Late Intermediate Period. In the Virú Valley, the critical changes in architectural forms and settlement types are dated to a single phase called Tomaval. According to diagnostic ceramics, this phase probably spanned upward of three to four hundred years (at least ca. A.D. 700 to A.D.1000). The earliest Tomaval ceramics appear to be stylistically contemporaneous with Moche V (Middle Horizon 1B). Rare Provincial Wari ceramics date to Middle Horizon Epoch 2, resembling Viñaque and Atarco styles of Epoch 2A.

Thus, given the imprecise nature of chronological control, it is not clear whether the inferred Wari invasion and attendant emergence of new community types came *before, during, or after Moche V*. The first episode of Wari expansion and Moche V are both dated stylistically to Middle Horizon Epoch 1B. But were they contemporaneous in terms of calendrical dates? If so, how long did they overlap? How long did Epoch 1B last? These questions cannot yet be answered. Meaningful and reliable radiocarbon dates for Wari sites and ceramics are still few in number,[95] and Menzel's stylistic seriation awaits refinements (see Knobloch 1991a,b). Martha Anders's work at the site of Maymi in the Pisco Valley on the South Coast is impor-

tant in refining the Wari chronology. Her study of Wari-style ceramics in ritual caches suggests the contemporaneity of Middle Horizon 1A and 1B (Anders 1990: 35) but is not fully published due to her untimely death.

What has been clearly documented is that the second wave of Wari expansion encompassed the Virú and Santa valleys *after* Mochica abandonment. Even expanding our geographical scope beyond the Virú and Santa valleys, Wari-style remains (essentially Provincial Wari) on the North Coast consistently occur in Moche V or immediately post–Moche V (Middle Horizon Epoch 2) contexts, but *not earlier*.[96] On much of the northern North Coast, Provincial Wari–style pottery of Middle Horizon Epoch 2 appears in immediately post–Moche V contexts with coastal imitations of the highland Cajamarca plates (I. Shimada 1982; Shimada and Elera 1983).

The absence of defensive features at Pampa Grande suggests that the inferred Wari intrusion into the North Coast did not pose a serious threat during Moche V occupation. Even the function of the parapeted wall at Galindo has been reinterpreted. Schaedel (1966a: 340, 1966b: 533) considered the site of Galindo a large Wari-influenced "hillside town" with boundary and defense walls delimiting and protecting it. Recently, T. Topic (1991: 240) concluded that "The defenses at Galindo do not seem to be a response to rumors of a distant, potential rival [Wari] but rather for protection against a very clearly perceived and very near menace," a cis-Andean polity concerned with the control of the *chaupiyunga* zone just inland from Galindo. There is at least one other Moche V settlement with a major parapeted wall in this contentious zone. The conspicuous absence of any Wari ceramics in this zone and the rebuilding of the parapeted wall at Galindo over a long time span are cited in rejecting the Wari Conquest model (ibid.).[97]

As seen above, a clear and critical analytical separation of the Moche IV–V transformation from the collapse of Moche V has been missing from most relevant publications. Even should Middle Horizon 1A and 1B prove to be coterminous, the Wari Conquest model will remain equivocal. For example, Schaedel (1985b: 168–

169) asserts that the "power in the Mochica society remained to the end with the priest" and that the "sudden and complete obliteration of the vase-painting tradition" (which diffused and perpetuated their dogma) at the hands of Wari expansionists signaled the end of the Mochica theocracy. Yet Pampa Grande, which has been seen as a product of "Wari restructuring," retained this artistic tradition to the end, together with the tradition of monumental platform mounds. Why would such ideologically charged and visible symbols be allowed to continue if the Wari invasion had already subjugated the North Coast? This logical inconsistency arose from rejection of the possibility of an autogenous shift from theocracy to a more secular form of governance, as Bawden (1977, 1982a, 1983) has argued for Galindo (cf. McEwan 1990; see Chapter 7).

In addition, the Wari Conquest model does not adequately explicate the unprecedented population nucleation at the valley neck. Valley-wide water control could have been achieved without such nucleation. Advantages of a localized population concentration vis-à-vis the postulated new form of economic or resource control require clarification.

8. Conclusion

At this point, there is little empirical support for the hypothesis that the first Wari expansion (Epoch 1B or even 1A) contributed to or caused the Moche IV–V transformation. There is, however, a real possibility that the expansion was a response to the same climatic disturbances, and the impact of prolonged, severe droughts in the highlands needs to be archaeologically documented. There are indications that the Moche V population maintained some contact with a Central Coast (Nievería) polity that may have served as an intermediary in spreading selected Wari traits (see Chapters 7 and 8). On the other hand, the second Wari expansion seems to have played some role in the decline and/or collapse of the Moche V polity (see Chapter 10).

The climatic hypothesis stands on a wide range of internally consistent lines of evidence, and accounts well for major features of the Moche IV–V transformation. We can conclude that the abnormal environmental stress that lasted much of the sixth century and included two long, severe droughts and possibly one or two El Niño events significantly disrupted and lowered North Coast agricultural production, particularly in the Southern Sector. This, in turn, was partially or largely responsible for the Moche IV–V cultural transformation, including the decline of the southern Mochica polity and concurrent resurgence of the northern Mochica polity. Thus, the Mochica culture was fundamentally transformed, dwindling to become a northern North Coast phenomenon. A few urban seats of power came to rule this reduced domain, which beneath its superficial stylistic unity was becoming increasingly divergent among constituent valleys.

7

Urban Landscape at Pampa Grande: Architecture and Sociopolitical Significance

One of the basic claims of this book is that Pampa Grande constituted a short-lived Moche V urban capital that emerged under unique cultural and natural conditions, and that the exigencies of its rapid establishment spawned a new sociopolitical order—the state. This chapter addresses this claim by identifying relevant material and organizational features and explaining their formative processes. More specifically, we ask what the observed variation in architectural techniques, materials, and forms tells us about Moche V society and culture at Pampa Grande. What was the nature of the urbanism that developed at Pampa Grande? Who were the urbanites of Pampa Grande, and how were they organized socially and politically? First this chapter defines what is meant by the city in this book.

1. Defining the City

Since V. Gordon Childe (1950) advanced his influential concept of "Urban Revolution," much has been written about the city by anthropologists, geographers, historians, and sociologists. Urban existence is significant in the modern world, with the transformation of social relationships brought about by permanent clustering of

large numbers of people with diverse backgrounds and interests. Yet debate surrounds the factors and conditions responsible for its emergence and growth, and even the definition of the city is disputed. Each investigator, consciously or not, brings biases stemming from his or her own cultural and intellectual background (see discussion in Wheatley 1972). Thus, many typologies have been proposed to deal with the variability in settlements that have been labeled one way or another as "cities" (e.g., Fox 1977). Marcus (1983: 196) asserts that "There are almost as many classificatory schemes for cities as there are cities."

Andean archaeology has spawned its own classifications and definitions. For example, using native North American settlements as the baseline, Rowe (1963: 3–4) defined the city in ancient Peru as an urban settlement (i.e., clustered dwellings) with over two thousand residents, including some engaged in nonsubsistence activities. The presence of rural populations associated with urban settlements ("chorism") is critical to his definition. In his "synchoritic city" some or all of the associated farmers live outside the city proper, whereas in his "achoritic city" all of the associated farmers live within the city and there is no permanent rural population. The former is seen as socially unstable due to the inevitable antagonism between urban and rural settlers. As we see later, a segment of Pampa Grande residents seems to have consisted of farmers.

Lanning (1967: 32–35) elaborated on Rowe's distinction in his comprehensive settlement typology, enumerating six criteria: resident population size, degree and nature of agglutination (population density), degree and nature of specialization (nonsubsistence occupation on a full-time basis), chorism, nucleation (presence or absence of an identifiable focus for settlement organization), and permanence of occupation.

Schaedel (1972), who has devoted much of his career to defining the origin and nature of the pre-Hispanic Andean city and state (particularly on the North Coast), sees urbanization as largely coeval with political centralization. Thus, the state, with its concentration of multiple functions (defense, religion, control of production, and differential distribution of resources) and social stratification, is crystallized in the city, a highly differentiated but integrated settlement that offers multiple functions and services.[98] His working definition of the city includes a resident population of between twenty-five and fifty thousand, a figure derived from a comparison of archaeologically and historically documented "pre-industrial cities" (Schaedel 1968: 11).

More recently, Kolata (1983) has argued that Chan Chan and Cusco (the capitals of the Chimú and Inca empires, respectively) were pre-industrial cities of *oikos* with an economy based on the needs and activities of royal households. He sees these late pre-Hispanic Andean cities as having originated and remained as "pure *oikos*-based cities," never making the transformation into market- or mixed *oikos*/market-based cities (ibid., 366–367).

While classificatory labels for cities may serve as effective shorthand descriptions of the *dominant* urban activity, use of these functionally laden terms should be bound by specific temporal and spatial parameters. They may not be appropriate if we take a long-term developmental perspective and consider their dynamic, comple-

mentary relationships with the surrounding areas. For example, a city may originate as a trade center and grow into a political center. In other words, archaeologists need to consider qualitative and quantitative changes in the form and function of the city, as well as its broader context (settlement pattern, hierarchy, and environment). Further, even if we can reach a consensus as to what constitutes a city in the abstract, archaeologists face the difficult task of applying this definition in the field. For example, identifying the occupations of urban dwellers is no easy matter. Even an expedient definition based on an arbitrary number of residents or physical extent of standing architecture poses serious problems. Estimating population size is an inexact science at best that typically involves making major assumptions regarding the correct identification of the habitational character of buildings under study, their synchronous occupation, and a conservative average number (four to five) of occupants per residence. These assumptions are usually inadequately tested, if at all, as archaeologists can typically excavate only a fraction of each site. Population estimates can only be considered at best an indication of the relative magnitude of the prehistoric population in question.

On the other hand, competing definitions do agree on certain critical features such as complex social and occupational differentiation, large permanent population, reliable water and food supply, regulated movement of goods and people, organized disposal of refuse, and symbolic landmarks. Thus, in this book the city is defined as a large, agglutinated settlement that integrates a highly differentiated resident population of over ten thousand, occupies the upper echelon of the regional settlement hierarchy, and offers a range of services and functions unavailable at any single settlement in the lower levels of the hierarchy.

We now examine how well Pampa Grande satisfies the above definition of the city and what can be said about the social and political dimensions of the urban population.

2. Physiography of Pampa Grande

The site of Pampa Grande (Figs. 1.8, 7.1, 7.2) occupies an extensive, roughly triangular pediment overlooking the neck of the Lambayeque Valley at latitude 6°45′ south and longitude 79°28′ west. Standing architecture of varying density covers nearly all of the flat pediment, which gradually slopes up toward the northwest base of Cerro de los Gentiles (Cerro Pampa Grande), a Quaternary igneous extrusion over 1,100 m high with steep, exfoliating slopes. The *cerro* provides a dramatic backdrop for the site. Over the years, water from rare El Niño rains cascading down the *cerro* has carried down sediment and large boulders and cut six major gullies in the pediment. The lower west end of the

pediment at about 100–120 m above sea level is today occupied by the village of Pampa Grande. The ancient and modern Collique canals run along here. A two-hundred-meter contour line runs through the middle of the pediment. The northern and eastern perimeters of the pediment and city are defined by Quebrada IX and the south base of Cerro Boca del Tigre (Fig. 7.3). The largest wash (ca. 50–60 m wide near the center of the site) designated Quebrada IV bisects the pediment (Southern and Northern Pediments) and provides the easiest and most direct access to the center of the site. At the upper east end of the *quebrada*, there is a small spring that could perhaps meet the daily water needs of a few families. The southern and

western edges of the site correspond to Quebrada III and the clifflike edge of the Southern Pediment. Farther west, where Cerro Campana protrudes close to the cultivation fields, the area is traversed by Quebradas I and II.

The landscape, as a whole, is not unlike the U.S. Southwest. Today, the pediment has sparse vegetation dominated by cacti (such as *Cereus macrostibas, Cactus pitajaya,* and *Melo cactus*) and occasional *zapote* (*Capparis angulata*) shrubs and *palo verde* (*Parkinsonia aculeata*) trees. Vegetation is more lush in the upper ends of the six gullies.

Figure 7.1. Architectural map of Pampa Grande based on surface survey data and airphoto interpretation. Drawing by Japhet Rosell and I. Shimada.

Figure 7.2. 1962 airphoto of Pampa Grande that shows the site's situation on an extensive, gently sloping pediment. Structures were built right up to the base of Cerro de los Gentiles. One can recognize that a major gully (Quebrada IV) running nearly east-west effectively bipartitions the site. Photo Proyecto 81-62-465. Courtesy of the Servicio Aerofotográfico Nacional del Perú, Lima.

During surface survey and mapping of the site in 1973, it became evident that the site as a whole was well preserved, with masonry walls still standing over a meter above present ground level in many areas and a seemingly undisturbed distribution of Moche V artifacts. Moche V diagnostic ceramics occurred in varying densities over much of the site, with the heaviest concentration in the central zone (a 500-meter area on both sides of the longitudi-

nal axis linking the two largest platform mounds (Huacas 1 and 2). Though construction of a dike in 1971 (and an even larger one in 1984 to protect the modern Collique Canal and the village of Pampa Grande) destroyed prehistoric architecture along the lower end of the pediment, modern residents continue to report finding artifacts and wall remnants when building houses and animal corrals within the village and the lower area of the pediment.

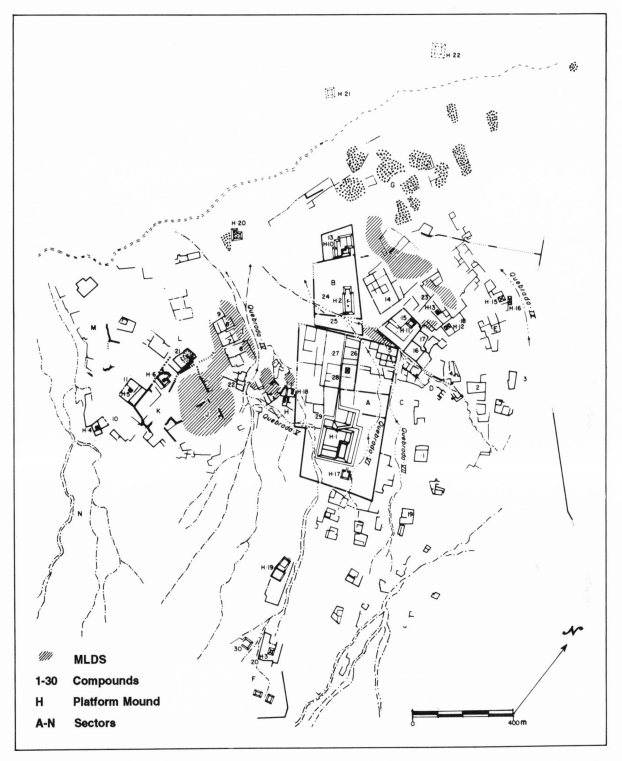

Figure 7.3. Simplified architectural map of Pampa Grande showing the locations of formal storage complexes, Sectors, *huacas,* major walled compounds, and concentrations of MLDs. Drawing by German Ocas and I. Shimada.

Examination of 1969 and earlier air photos reveals the former existence of two substantial platform mounds (Huacas 21 and 22) just east of the dike and the pre-Hispanic Collique Canal. Thus, the present-day standing architecture (ca. 4.5 km²) does not accurately reflect the pre-Hispanic extent. When we include the area occupied by the modern village, the corresponding figure is over 6 km².

3. Architectural Forms and Hierarchy

The site presents an impressive architectural diversity. Thus, a systematic analysis of architectural forms was conducted to identify basic building units and their organizational principles. The resultant codification of architectural forms (Fig. 7.4; Shimada 1978) systematized our perception of the site and helped to transform our image of the unmanageably complex site of Pampa Grande into something orderly and understandable. The following description of architectural forms is ordered from the most elemental and smallest to the most complex and largest.

A *Room (Rm)* is the smallest architectural unit, bounded on all four sides (thus quadrangular) by walls and having access limited to a single, ground-level entry (constricted opening formed by two walls). The mean width of Room entries at Pampa Grande is 75 cm with a standard deviation of 15 cm. Some have raised thresholds. Rooms may be with or without roof.

Certain specialized rooms exist and are referred to by distinct terms: a *Recessed Room (RR)* is a three-walled Room whose missing side corresponds to an entry, usually opening directly to a corridor or pathway; *Chamber (Ch)* is a Room whose access is through terraces rather than entries.

An *Anteroom (ARm)* is another elemental architectural unit, typically quadrangular in shape and bounded on all sides, as in the case of a Room, but having *two or more entries* on ground level to contiguous Room(s) and/or Anteroom(s).

Certain Anterooms are known by separate terms: *Court* designates a large Anteroom with one of its multiple entries opening directly onto a corridor, pathway, or street; and a *Plaza* is a large Anteroom

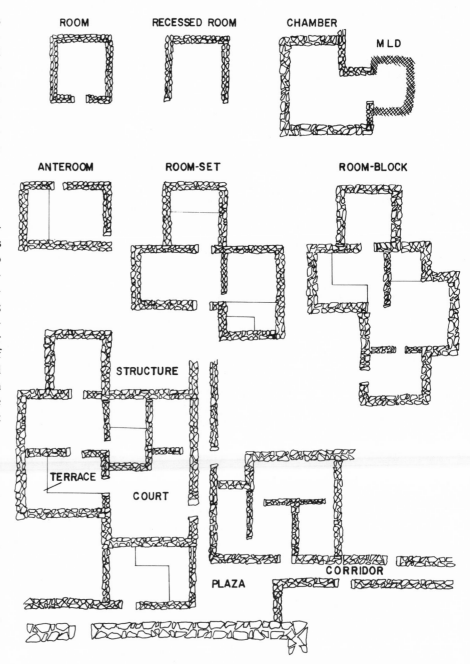

Figure 7.4. Basic construction units and their designations. Nearly all pre-Hispanic buildings at Pampa Grande can be described as simple algorithms of these basic construction units.

with all entries opening directly onto pathways and/or streets. In other words, it is the locus where pedestrian and/or llama traffic converges. This is the only case where an Anteroom occurs by itself. All other Anterooms occur in combination with other Anterooms and/or Rooms.

A *Terrace* is a construction within a Room or Anteroom that vertically differentiates the floor surface into two levels. As it is secondary to the construction of a Room or Anteroom, the wall(s) that define the outer perimeter of a Terrace abut onto the walls of a Room or Anteroom. Terraces are ubiquitous throughout the site and occur in all of the basic architectural units described earlier. Many of the Terraces within residential Rooms probably functioned as sleeping areas.

A *Room-Set (RS)* is defined as a self-contained architectural unit composed of one or more Rooms and an Anteroom (thus, xRm(s) + ARm, where x is an integer). As elaborated later, a *Room-Set is the basic household configuration.* The designation "Small Irregularly Agglutinated Rooms" (SIAR), which was popularized on the North Coast by the Chan Chan–Moche Valley Project, roughly corresponds to varied configurations of the *Room-Set.* Chimú SIARs in Chan Chan are commonly interpreted as residences and/or small-scale craft workshops of the urban proletariat (J. Topic 1982). SIARs at Pampa Grande are found in much of the Southern Pediment, Sectors C, D, and H, northern margins of the Northern Pediment, and around many of the adobe and masonry Compounds in the northern and western peripheries of the site. The population estimate for Moche V Pampa Grande was derived by applying an average household floor surface area of 80 m² (including both roofed and unroofed areas— the upper end of variation in the Southern Pediment) to the number of SIARs found throughout the site. The total surface area of SIAR suggests over 2,500 households. Multiplying this figure with a conservative family size of four to five members yields a sitewide estimate of 10,000 to 12,500. However, some SIARs in Sectors D and H are believed to have been used during the daytime by commuting laborers. At the same time, there were probably many

more SIARs at the northern edge of the site than are presently visible. Overall, it is believed a population estimate of 10,000 is conservative.

Room-Block (RB) designates an interlinked set of a Room and more than one Anteroom (Rm + xARms, where x is an integer equal to or greater than 2).

Structure (St) refers to an architectural unit composed of multiple Rooms and Anterooms, with the resultant self-contained configuration linked directly to a corridor, pathway, or street. Its shorthand description is xRm + yARms, where x and y are integers greater than 1. As seen in Chapter 8, craft workshops and associated kitchens and storage rooms are Structures or Structure/Room-Set combinations.

A *Unit (U)* is the sum total of all architectural units directly linked by a corridor.

Huaca (H) or *platform mound* refers to a freestanding raised construction standing over 3 m (arbitrary limit) above the surrounding ground.

A *Compound (C)* is essentially a rectangular enclosure with a varying degree of internal division. More specifically, it is a *Structure* or a set of *Structures* linked by a corridor whose perimeter is defined by major enclosing walls (over 30 cm in width) built in a single construction episode. Access to the *Compound* is limited to a single or few entries. Its size and form variation and its sociopolitical significance are examined later.

Sector (S) is the most inclusive architectural unit in our hierarchical classification. It is composed of a minimum of one *Unit* and a finite number of lower architectural units. Within its physical boundaries, each Sector manifests certain architectural and artifactual homogeneity and coherence. The surface survey revealed that sitewide variation in composition and distribution of artifacts and architecture, as expected in any urban setting, was not an unbroken continuum but had perceivable breaks that closely coincided with major gullies in the pediment. Each of the fourteen resultant topographical-architectural divisions or Sectors was assigned a letter (Fig. 7.3). In essence, when we speak of Sectors, we are speaking of the kind of inferred spatial segregation of different functions and services found in districts in modern major cities.

At the same time, we must recognize that Sectors were defined using only surface indications, and different Sectors, whether greatly separated in space or adjacent, may have served the same basic functions. It was in later, more detailed analyses of excavated artifacts and architecture that we found significant differences among such Sectors.

Overall, most of the architectural forms at Pampa Grande, including the SIAR, can be described using a handful of predictable configurations generated by simple arithmetic combinations of basic building units such as Rooms, Anterooms, and Terraces. Thus, a functional characterization of a large, complex urban settlement may proceed from a hierarchical architectural typology and a structured sampling of basic configurations found at different hierarchical levels. Such was the basic logic underlying my excavations in Sector H (Shimada 1978).

In addition to the above, there are certain specialized constructions that cannot be readily assigned to any one hierarchical level. The *Multilateral Depression (MLD)* refers to an enigmatic construction found individually or in clusters primarily in the Southern Pediment, Sector H, and the northern portion of the Northern Pediment (Shimada 1978: 574). A handful of MLDs excavated in Sector H and J indicate that they consisted of interconnected terraces surrounding a low, flat quadrangular area (Fig. 7.5). The uppermost terraces were often partially roofed but without enclosing walls, suggesting easy access. Collapse of walls defining the terrace edges creates an amorphous appearance and hampers excavation. The excavation of MLDs 40 and 44 in Sector H yielded no primary-context artifacts, but the cut-shell and stone fragments mixed in the secondary deposits covering the central low areas suggest possible lapidary work (Fig. 7.6; ibid., 583). Another possible function of the MLDs, given their open configuration, may have been as drying and processing areas for foods and cotton.

Given their wide distribution encompassing diverse contexts, any functional characterization of the site requires careful assessment of the MLDs. At the same time, many of what have been classified as MLDs

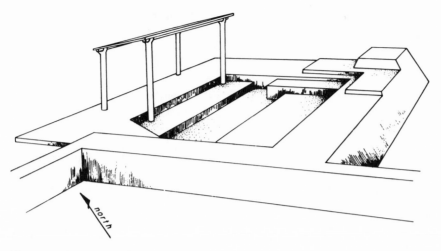

Figure 7.5. Reconstructed view of MLD 40 in Sector H.

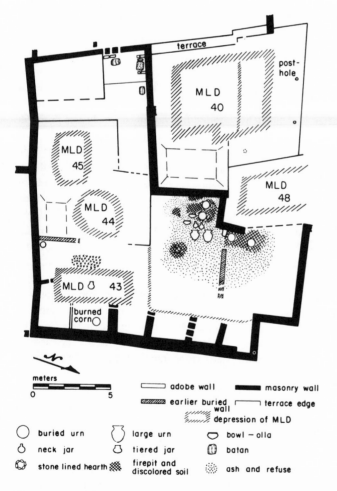

Figure 7.6. Spatial and artifactual organization in the excavated MLD cluster in Sector H.

may in reality be Rooms or Anterooms whose rubble-filled walls have collapsed, creating the appearance of MLDs.

Other specialized constructions are described in the context of broader issues.

4. Sector Characterizations

To provide some sense of how the diverse architectural forms described above are distributed at the site level, brief characterizations of Sectors are offered starting with those at the lower end of the pediment. These characterizations include observations regarding associated artifacts.

Sector G is an extensive area at the northern end of the site badly disturbed by natural and human activities. Residents of the modern village of Pampa Grande have removed stones from prehistoric constructions to build houses and corrals for their animals and "mined" the area extensively seeking prehistoric burials. The most destructive activity was the aforementioned dike construction that utilized heavy machinery. Apparently a large portion of the area did serve as a cemetery both long prior to (Early Horizon) and immediately following (Middle Horizon 2) Moche V occupation. At the juncture of Quebrada IX and Cerro Boca del Tigre (the northern corner of the site) is a thoroughly looted cemetery that, according to the few surface sherds, dates to Cupisnique times. Slightly south of the cemetery near the mouth of Quebrada IX is an area of 300 m (N-S) by 200 m (E-W) that is associated with the later Middle Sicán (A.D. 900–1100; Table 1) ceramics. This Middle Sicán occupation may have built a major southwest-northeast wall found over Moche V structures as protection from flash floods coming down Quebrada IX. More toward the center of Sector G, broken Moche V face-neck jars discarded by grave looters were noted, but almost no fineware. Though rarer, some fragments were found of unslipped face-neck jars with press-molded geometric decorations on the body (probably Middle Horizon Epoch 2) and black Chimú vessels (dating to ca. A.D. 1375–1470).

Sector A corresponds to the centrally situated Great Compound measuring 600 m (N-S) by 400 m (E-W), which enclosed the Huaca Fortaleza platform mound (Figs. 1.8, 7.7). Architecture atop the *huaca* is described later. The *huaca*, with its 290-meter ramp, bipartitioned the Compound into eastern and western halves. The larger, eastern half of the Compound was tripartitioned by two major parallel adobe walls (NE-SW). One of the few definite entries into the Compound was found in the northernmost third and offered direct access to adjacent Sector D with craft production. In general, major formal structures including storage facilities, small detached mounds, and platforms with colonnades were concentrated in the northern third of both halves. The spacious southernmost area of the eastern half is bisected by Quebrada VI. Both banks of the *quebrada* and the east corner of the Compound show numerous terraces and SIARs, as well as a considerable accumulation of dark deposits with charcoal bits, ash, sherds, and food remains, suggesting that this area may have been the main food preparation and housing area for the retainers of the elite in this Compound. There is also a low platform mound with a short central ramp at the east corner.

The smaller western half had more complex subdivisions largely due to the presence of three large formal storage facilities (Units 27, 28, and 29). Many of the walls and smaller structures in this half regulated access to these facilities. In symmetrical opposition to the eastern half, there was an opening that provided direct access to craft production areas within the adjacent Sector H (Fig. 7.8). The southwestern portion of the Compound is poorly preserved due to Quebrada V.

There may well have been a third entry near the lower end of the ramp to the *huaca* that would have provided access to traffic coming through a gap between the perimeter walls of the Great Compound and Compound 25 of Sector B. We see below that Sector A physically dominated the site and probably served as the physical and spiritual center of Moche V politics and religion.

Sector B, with overall dimensions of 430 m (NW-SE) by 180 m (NE-SW), encompassed three contiguous and interconnected adobe Compounds (13, 24, and 25) immediately northwest of the Great Compound. The largest, Compound 24, housed Huaca 2 (or Huaca Menor), the

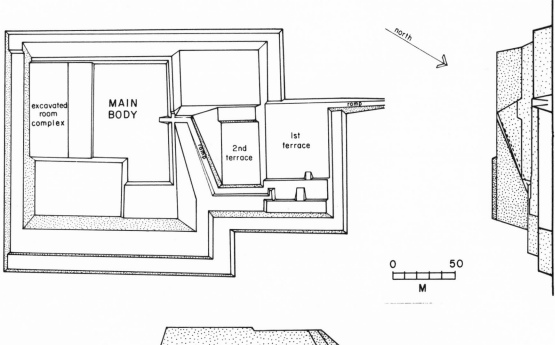

Figure 7.7. Various views of the Huaca Fortaleza platform mound based on ground measurements and airphoto interpretation.

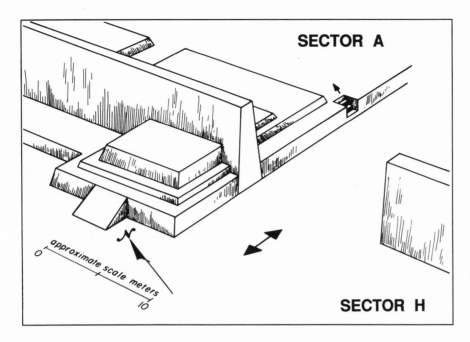

Figure 7.8. Opening along the west wall of the Great Compound (Sector A) that allowed access from adjacent Sector H to a major storage area inside.

second largest of the site (ca. 45 by 105 by 8 m), and a major formal storage facility. The top of Huaca 2 had been intensely burnt, as were all of the major *huacas* at the site. There was a U-shaped structure at the north end of the Huaca 2 top. To the north of the *huaca* lies Compound 13 with Huaca 10, which was associated with a small scatter of *Spondylus* shell fragments at the north base. The south end of the Sector was occupied by Compound 25 with the largest (twenty-four cells) formal storage complex of the site. Sector B as a whole shows little evidence of dwellings and is seen as another high-status civic-ceremonial complex.

Sectors D (ca. 300 by 60 m) and H (ca. 175 by 200 m) were loci of extensive excavations (about 10 and 15 percent of the surface area of the respective Sectors) and integrated both formal architecture and SIARs interlinked by intra-Sector streets and pathways. In Sector H, and to a lesser extent in D, many of the SIARs were loci of supervised, small-scale, compartmentalized craft production and food and beverage preparation by a diurnal labor force presumably commuting in from other Sectors (see Chapter 8). Strategically placed, formalized architecture with hierarchical terrace(s) (i.e., administrative structures) controlled access to and from craft workshops and storerooms contain-

ing beans and maize kernels. Overall, these two Sectors are seen as having provided and administered services and goods for the operation of Sectors A and B, including metal objects, textiles, food, and *chicha* (all-important "maize beer"; see Chapter 8).

Sector C, adjacent to A and D with scatters of *batanes* (large, tabular anvil stones for crushing various substances in combination with rocking stones, *chungos*) and domestic and storage vessels within relatively spacious stone structures, may well have been a residential area for those associated with activities in D. However, Sector A was not directly accessible from C; traffic from Sector C was channeled through an entry at the southeast corner of Sector D. One street led to an inferred ceramic production area in Sector D, while the other provided access to the central portion of Sector D and eventually to Sector A.

Sector I on the northern edge of the Southern Pediment is comprised of a series of five large contiguous rectangular enclosures (four central ones measuring about 50 by 75 m) with three-part internal subdivisions surrounded by SIARs (Figs. 7.1, 7.9). The easternmost, Compound 22, contained a central platform and was positioned to control traffic utilizing the Circum–Quebrada IV Street into the Northern Pediment and to and from the site itself. This street interconnected all compounds of Sector I, which are thought to have been the residences and offices of allied or conquered regional lords whose retainers were housed immediately outside of the compound, much like a microcosm of Sector A's relationship with Sectors D and H.

Sectors J through M on the Southern Pediment encompassed the most extensive zone of SIARs and thus are seen as the primary residential zones of the populace, though some scattered craft production for intra-Sector consumption may have also taken place (Fig. 7.10). Only small-scale excavations were carried out in Sectors J and K. The southern ends of Sectors K and M have relatively dense scatters of diagnostic Chimú ceramics such as black bottles with mold-made "goose-skin" texturing and carinated-rim bowls. Compound 11, with the major platform mound Huaca 5, may well have been a Chimú construction.

Sector N at the southwest corner of the site corresponds to the upper reaches of Quebrada III and has only sparse, simple stone structures. Many are crude stone enclosures several meters in diameter that may have served as llama corrals. Though no diagnostic ceramics were found here, a large boulder had a petroglyph of the head of the Middle Sicán deity. Similar roughly built stone enclosures that may also have served as llama corrals are found scattered

beyond the densely built area south of Sectors J and K, as well as along the eastern perimeter of the site. Beyond the south edge of Sector J, close to the northwest base of Cerro de los Gentiles, is a small masonry room built against a huge boulder. This isolated structure contained numerous copper objects (mostly needles) and *Spondylus* shell fragments, suggesting a workshop. Immediately behind the boulder were red-white-black geometric-style jar fragments (akin to Larco Hoyle's [1948] Wari Norteño B or Wari-Lambayeque; also see Mackey 1983). This is the only setting in Pampa Grande where this style of ceramics was found.

Sector E near the eastern edge of the site resembles Sector I in architectural appearance and organization. No excavations were carried out in Sector E. Some of the simple, essentially empty rectangular enclosures in Sector E and the large open areas in the center of Sectors D and H where streets converge may have been loading/unloading sites for llama caravans. At Galindo, at least some residences had inferred llama corrals built as part of their architectural complexes (Bawden 1982a: 314–316). As we shall see in Chapter 8, llamas were an integral part of urban subsistence and economy at Pampa Grande as well.

Sector F at the southern and upper edges of the site affords an excellent view of the entire site and of La Puntilla across

the valley. Access was provided along the ridges that separate the gullies that dissect the area. Built on these narrow ridges are two mounds atop stone-faced platforms within rectangular enclosures. A formal storage complex, Unit 30, may have kept status goods for this detached, inferred ceremonial precinct.

5. Organizational Principles of Urban Architecture

The preceding shows that the impressive architectural buildup at Pampa Grande had definite internal divisions and order. The question remains as to how these Sectors were integrated and what material and symbolic means were employed to establish and maintain the physical and social order of the city.

A. Symbolic Significance of Huaca Fortaleza

Perhaps the single most important fact in understanding the architectural organization of Pampa Grande is the central importance in every sense of the word of the gigantic Huaca Fortaleza platform mound. Its disproportionate size and central placement exerted undeniable effects on site organization.

Huaca Fortaleza had a three-tier construction (First and Second Terraces and Main Body; see Fig. 7.7) and a nearly straight, gradually ascending ramp 290 m long that provided direct (though controlled) access to the First Terrace from the northern edge of the Great Compound. The three principal parts of the *huaca* have overall basal dimensions of 270 m by 180 m and an estimated volume of ca. 1.5 million m³. The highest terrace at the southeast corner of the Main Body is some 38 m from ground level.[99] The impression of great height and volume of the *huaca* is in part due to its steep sides and long ramp.

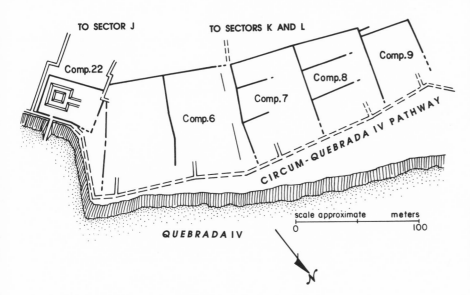

Figure 7.9. Simplified map of the contiguous rectangular compounds comprising Sector I and the associated Circum-Quebrada pathway at the east edge of the Southern Pediment.

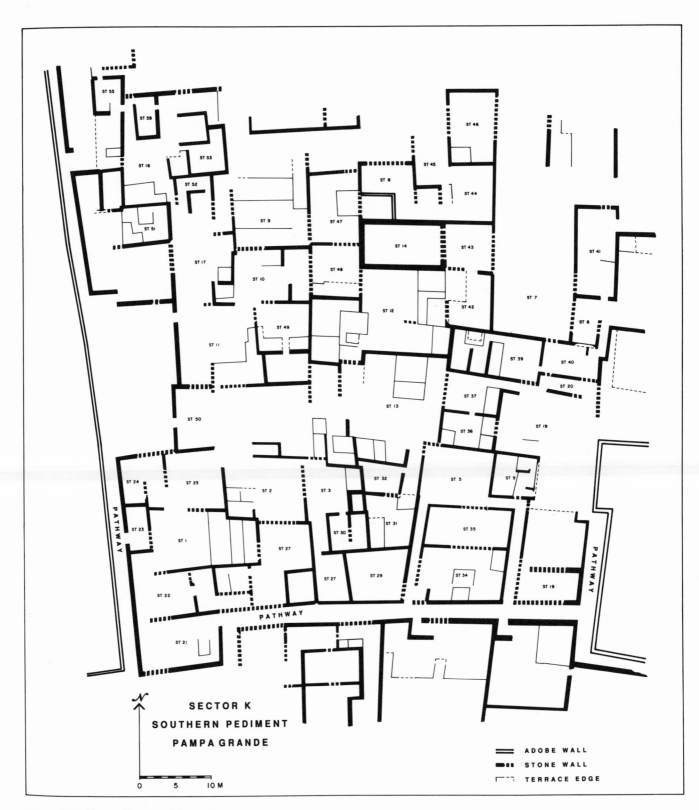

Figure 7.10. Plane-table map of Sector K.
Drawing by Charles Sternberg.

Its placement on a rising triangular pediment creates the illusion of even greater size. Huaca Fortaleza ranks as one of the largest prehistoric constructions in South America and represents the last glory of the long Mochica tradition of monumental platform mound building. Much as Huaca del Sol was disproportionately large for its time, Huaca Fortaleza had nothing comparable in the Moche V world; it simply dwarfs all contemporary mounds at Galindo and Pampa Grande. At Galindo, the importance of traditional mounds was eroded by rectangular compounds with no mounds or only small ones.

Its impressive size, achieved through a unified construction effort, and its central location and highly controlled access all point to the power and capabilities of the individuals and institutions involved. Trigger (1990: 119, 122) observes that "As the fusion of 'permanence' and 'perfection,' monumental architecture makes power visible and hence becomes power rather than merely a symbol of it.... [T]he splendour of such buildings may proclaim, and by doing so reinforce, the status of rulers, of their protective gods, and of the state."[100] He explains how monumental architecture achieves such effects in terms of the concept of conspicuous consumption of resources, particularly human labor (ibid., 125–126):

[T]he ability to expend energy, especially in the form of other people's labour, in non-utilitarian ways is the most basic and universally understood symbol of power. Monumental architecture and personal luxury goods become symbols of power because they are seen as embodiments of large amounts of human energy and hence symbolize the ability of those for whom they were made to control such energy to an unusual degree. Furthermore, by participating in erecting monuments that glorify the power of the upper classes, peasant labourers are made to acknowledge their subordinate status and their sense of their own inferiority is reinforced....

... [M]onumental architecture... constituted the most public material embodiment of the power of the upper classes. In contrast with public ceremonies, it was also the most enduring statement of power that a ruler could hope to make.

Consider, for example, the visual and psychological impact on officials and visiting dignitaries of climbing the 290-meter-long ramp of Huaca Fortaleza with various control points along the way. It would have been a highly effective way of illustrating the power commanded by the ruler who built and/or maintained the *huaca*. Any city with pretensions of being important boasts a notable landmark or symbol (e.g., Wheatley 1969, 1971).[101] Huaca Fortaleza clearly filled this critical symbolic role.

B. The Axis Mundi and Four-Tier Hierarchy of Huacas and Compounds

The presently visible Huaca Fortaleza mound and its antecedent form (the buried Phase 1 mound) was the hub of the planned physical and functional organization of the city of Pampa Grande. Huaca Fortaleza and its ramp lie along the longitudinal axis of the roughly triangular settlement. In fact, the *huaca*, which occupies the central, highest flat-topped ridge of the site, *pre-determined* the relative locations of other major architecture, as well as functionally differentiated districts. We see a concentric-ring distance-dependent zonation of inferred social classes and functions around Huaca Fortaleza (Fig. 7.11); the closer to Huaca Fortaleza, the higher the social and political importance.

The hub or first zone is the Great Compound with Huaca Fortaleza. The second zone, close to the longitudinal axis of the site and the hub, contains other major *huacas* within adobe compounds (Huaca 2/Compound 24, Huaca 3/Compound 13, Huaca 19/unnumbered compound, Huaca 11/Compound 15 [Spondylus House], and a multi-tiered adobe mound in Compound 14 [Deer House]). Farther away from the axis, in the third zone, are relatively small *huacas* within spacious masonry compounds (e.g., Huaca 13/Compound 23, Huaca 12/Compound 18). In the last zone, close to the northern and western peripheries of the site, we find less formal, smaller masonry compounds with no mounds.

It is important to note that only the structures in the first two zones were built of adobe bricks. The Compounds of the third zone, in spite of having substantial mounds, are defined by stone walls with

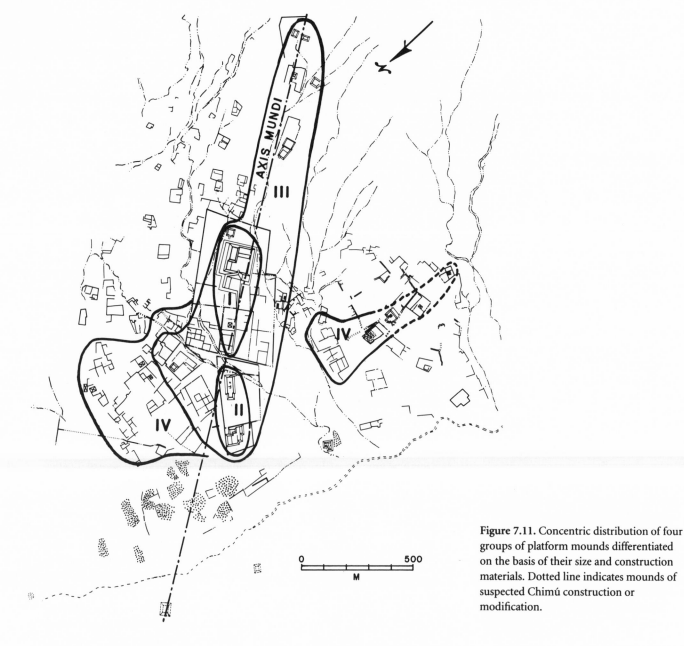

Figure 7.11. Concentric distribution of four groups of platform mounds differentiated on the basis of their size and construction materials. Dotted line indicates mounds of suspected Chimú construction or modification.

mixed stone-earthen fill. An important exception is adobe Compound 22 at the east end of Sector I, which played a critical role in control of traffic between the Southern and Northern Pediments.

Four statistically segregated groups also emerge upon examination of the surface area of some forty compounds or of the volume of associated *huacas* (twenty compounds with *huacas*; Fig. 7.12). Membership in these groups is essentially identical to the above. Huaca Fortaleza and the Great Compound overwhelm Huaca 2 and Compound 24 which, in turn, are signifi-

cantly larger than those in the third level. Membership in the third tier is the largest, with eighteen compounds. The relatively small masonry compounds in the northern and western edges, by virtue of having no mounds, occupy the fourth (lowest) level in the *huaca* volume hierarchy.

It is apparent that the longitudinal axis of the site formed by connecting *huacas* in Sectors A, B, and F (and perhaps even Huaca 21 at the lower end of the site) was the reference point not only in the physical layout of the site but also in social and functional organization of the urban

population. It is as if the axis were the *axis mundi* of the Moche V world. As seen later, the axis appears to have segregated lower-class non-Mochica populations on the Southern Pediment from elite Mochica on the Northern Pediment. Within the latter area, the greater the distance from Huaca Fortaleza, the lesser the sociopolitical significance of major constructions.

Given the inferred symbolic and organizational significance of the axis and of Huaca Fortaleza, it would not be surprising to find that the alignments of some of the major associated walls also had signifi-

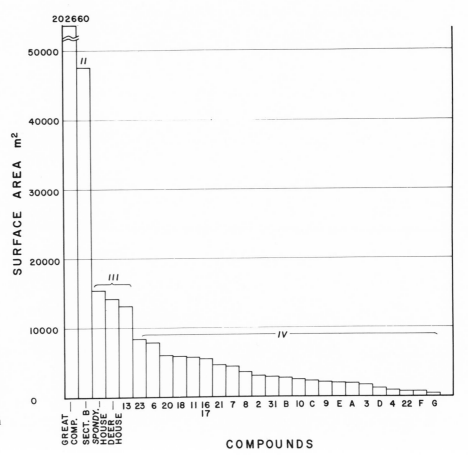

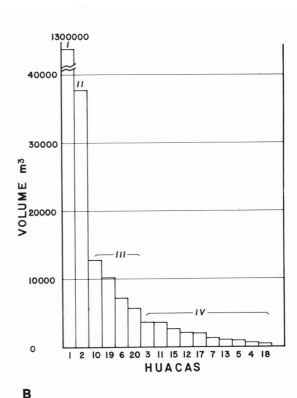

Figure 7.12. (A) Comparison of the surface area covered by principal rectangular enclosures at Pampa Grande. Sector B combines Compounds 24 and 25. Compounds 16 and 17 are contiguous and interlinked and thus treated as a single unit. Compounds A–G are unnumbered stone wall enclosures south and east of the great Compound. Those in Groups I–III all have adobe perimeter walls and platform mounds. (B) Comparison of estimated volumes of platform mounds at Pampa Grande. Relevant measurements for Huacas 7–9 are unavailable and not included. Though Groups III and IV are difficult to differentiate on a quantitative basis, those in the former are situated along or close to the central axis of the site. Huaca 6 is suspected of having later Chimú modification.

cance. In fact, the Great Compound and Sector D compounds are not rectangular, yet there are no apparent topographic barriers that might have forced compromises (Fig. 7.13). The possibility that major constructions at the site were oriented to some important celestial bodies was examined by Gary Urton (n.d.). Table 7 presents his field measurements compared to some potentially significant astronomical positions in A.D. 500. The measurements may have up to ± 2° margin of error due to various field conditions. Though suggestive, they remain inconclusive.

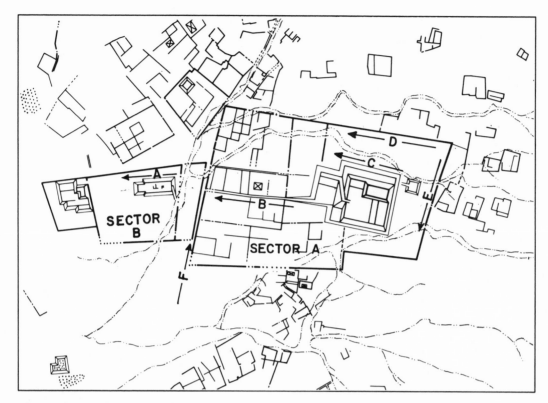

Figure 7.13. Map showing wall and platform mound alignments measured by Gary Urton and his team. See Table 7.

Table 7. Alignment orientations at Pampa Grande and their possible astronomical correlation. See Figure 7.13.

1 Alignment	2 Orientation	3 Reciprocal	4 Astronomical Correction
A	322°23′	142°23′ (hor. = 4°45′)	rise of Canopus = 142°32′ (hor. = 3°)
(perp.) A′	52°23′	232°23′	set of Fomalhous = 232°35′
B	326°35′	146°35′ (hor. = 17°55′)	rise of a Crucis = 147°20′ (hor. = 6°)
(perp.) B′	56°35′	236°35′	rise of Castor = 56°12′
D	330°37′	15°37′	—
(perp.) D′	60°37′	240°37′	rise of Pollux = 59°39′
			moon set ($-$E$-$i)* = 241°02′
E	249°37′	69°37′ (hor. = 8)	rise of Pleiades = 68°26′ (hor. = 6°; A.D. 1000)
			moon rise ($+$E$-$i)* = 70°21′ (hor. = 6°)
(perp.) E′	159°37′	339°37′	
(calc.) F	64°21′	244°21′	Venus rise ($+$E$+$i)* = 64°26′
			Venus set ($-$E$-$i)* = 244°17′

*E = ecliptic = 23°30′ north (= +E) or south (= −E) of the ecuator

hor. = horizon

i = the 5°19′ inclination of the lunar orbit north (= +i) or south (= −i) of the ecliptic

In regard to the possible significance of Huaca Fortaleza and Huaca 2 orientations, an alternative view would be that they were oriented to the principal intakes of the Lambayeque and Antigua Taymi canals at La Puntilla (Fig. 6.5). Given that the establishment of Pampa Grande was largely conditioned by the desire for water control, this is another possibility.

The ceremonial significance of Huaca Fortaleza can also be gleaned from the results of excavations carried out atop the *huaca* by J. Haas (1985). His excavation on the First Terrace revealed a dramatic and elaborate setting for ritual activities: two platforms built at the east end of a spacious (81 [E-W] by 44 [N-S] m) terrace some 14–15 m above the base of the *huaca* overlooking the eastern half of the site (Figs. 7.14, 7.15). Both platforms had colonnades supporting roofs. Various rectangular adobe-lined sockets for these columns contained llama offerings. Atop the higher platform there was a cache offering of *Spondylus* shell pendants and llama bones, as well as a badly eroded backdrop wall decorated with murals. In addition, the platform faces were decorated with polychrome murals (see Chapter 9).

Haas (ibid., 400–401) also reports finding, among the burnt, fallen roof remains on the floors of the platforms, nearly one thousand llama bones,[102] nineteen worked ceramic sherd discs and disc fragments (three of which were drilled and perforated and may have been used as spindle whorls), and a Moche V stirrup-spout bottle and effigy vessel fragments. In addition, there were abundant fragments of plainware vessels (including tall-neck jars with and without facial representations), eight reduced-ware bowls, and one highly polished blackware bowl. Though the above points to consumption of food and drink, there is nothing that suggests in situ food preparation.

The excavation of two parallel rows of carefully built adobe rooms called the Palatial Room Complex (Fig. 7.16) on a platform at the southwest corner atop the Main Body yielded additional indications of the exclusive, ceremonial character of the *huaca*. For example, "Access around the room complex and into each of the rooms was complicated and almost always indirect," and with one exception, "each room was entered from the rear, through baffled doorways" (ibid., 404). In addition, in approaching the room complex, one encountered a frieze of repetitious felines on the platform face (see Chapter 9). The central ramp that led to the room complex had a cache offering consisting of "the

Figure 7.14. Panoramic view of the excavation of the platform complex at the east end of the First Terrace of Huaca Fortaleza. Courtesy of Jonathan Haas.

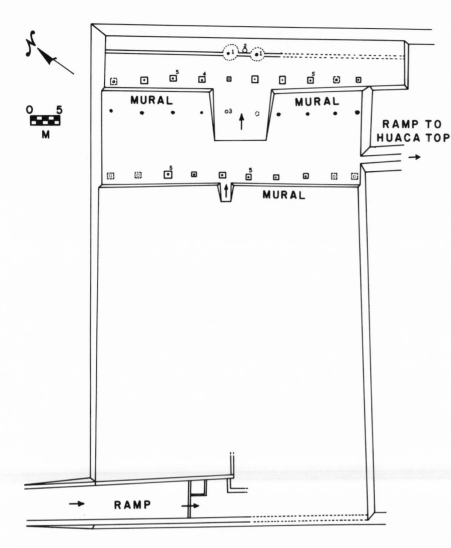

Figure 7.15. Plane view of the First Terrace of Huaca Fortaleza. Redrawn from the original by Jonathan Haas.

• Posthole

▣ Chambered posthole

• Projected posthole

1. Shallow depressions
2. *Spondylus* pendants and llama bones
3. Whole *Spondylus*
4. Llama burial in chamber
5. Partial llama burials in chambers

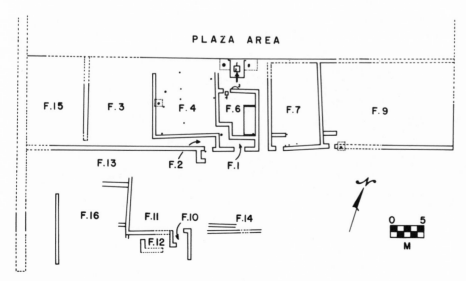

• Posthole

▣ Chambered posthole

1. Ramp
2. Llama burial with child remains covered by *Spondylus* shell necklace
3. Cached *Spondylus* shell necklace
4. Cached stone beads

Figure 7.16. Plane view of the Palatial Room Complex at the south end of the Main Body of Huaca Fortaleza. Redrawn from the original by Jonathan Haas.

Table 8. Composition, quantity, and distribution of artifacts recovered from Haas's excavation of the Palatial Room Complex at the south end of the Main Body of Huaca Fortaleza. Adapted from Table 2 in Haas 1985: 406.

Artifact	Fineware		Plain Body		Plain Neck		Face Neck		Bone*	Shell	Other
Features (F)	#	%	#	%	#	%	#	%	#	#	
3	2	0.2	717	90.5	69	8.7	4	0.5	14	0	8 quartz crystals on floor in center of entry; 1 stone mace head (handle inside) on floor immediately outside and to east of doorway
4	36	2.9	1,162	94.0	30	2.4	8	0.7	20	2 (*Donax*, mussel)	3 small polished black "tea bowl" fragments; 8 fragments of unidentifiable molded ceramic figures
6	7	1.61	393	90.6	25	5.8	9	2.1	8	0	3 fragments of thick ceramic bowl in the form of *Spondylus*
7	6	0.44	1,250	92.4	78	5.8	19	1.4	11	0	1 ceramic mace head, broken off at the handle
9	7	2.1	312	94.3	11	3.3	1	0.3	43	670**	
11	35	24.1	108	74.5	0	0	2	1.4	3	1 (unidentified)	79 large fragments of two ceramic drums; 40 fragments of large, highly polished blackware bowl
14	8	3.57	191	85.3	20	8.9	5	2.2	3	7 *Donax*	1 small polished pebble; 2 pieces of small polished black "tea bowls"; 1 fragment of ceramic *Spondylus* bowl, the same as that found in Rm/ARm 6; 1 fragment of unidentifiable molded ceramic figure

*probably llama; ***Donax* and *Thais*

bones of a child (clavicle, teeth, and a humerus) and an immature llama skeleton. Placed over these remains was a complete necklace of carved *Spondylus* sp. shell pendants and small beads of azurite, turquoise, and *Spondylus* sp. shell" (ibid., 404).[103]

Artifacts and organic remains from different *huaca* rooms and associated features are listed in Table 8. Among the more notable findings are a cluster of eight quartz crystals, a pair of copper tweezers, a stone mace head with a charred wooden handle, a ceramic vessel shaped like a mace head with handle, two ceramic drum frames, highly polished blackware bowls, and a bowl modeled as a whole *Spondylus* shell. This assemblage as a whole is singular in terms of the range and quality of artifacts found in a single context at Pampa Grande. Overall, Haas (ibid., 407) concludes that

The greatly restricted access, the formal architectural layout with adobe construction, the human and llama dedicatory remains, the concentration of luxury goods, and the complete absence of tools point to the use of the complex by a highly privileged group of people. . . . It would also appear that the rooms represented a high-status residential rather than ceremonial complex. The presence of food remains, storage vessels, eating vessels, and at least one implement of personal hygiene (the tweezers), points to habitation as at least one primary function of the complex. At the same time, the presence of ceramic drums, a stone mace, and quartz crystals indicates that other types of less mundane activities may have taken place in the complex as well. Overall, the most parsimonious interpretation of the lofty complex of spacious rooms on top of Huaca is that it probably served as the residence of some portion of the ruling elite of Pampa Grande.

The cautionary tone of the above conclusion is appropriate. The available data are not conclusive regarding residential as opposed to ceremonial function. The presence of abundant llama bones and face-neck jars (one room contained at least nineteen jars with mold-made faces) suggests consumption of food and drink but not necessarily permanent residency. A ceremonial feast should be considered as an alternative. In fact, the quartz crystals associated with shamanistic activities (Donnan 1978; Sharon 1978) and the prominent use of *Spondylus* shell in various architectural settings throughout Huaca Fortaleza (see Chapter 8) give further support to the strong ceremonial character of the *huaca*. If our reading of Mochica combat depicted on ceramic paintings is correct (Chapter 5), then even the mace head cannot be readily classified as mundane. Ceramic drum frames elsewhere at the site were associated with supervised weaving (Chapter 8). Quality cloth probably had ritual, political, and economic importance.

Haas (1985:408) recognizes the impossibility of specifying whether the privileged elite who utilized the room complex were "managers, priests, generals, or some combination thereof." The weight of the available evidence seems to tip the balance in favor of the ceremonial significance of Huaca Fortaleza, and the ruling elite in question probably embodied both a religious and political-military leadership.

C. Regulation of Movement

The network of streets, pathways, and corridors was well established and kept Sectors and their occupants segregated while simultaneously helping to achieve functional integration between Sectors. The regulated movement of people and goods characterized the entire city. *Corridors* guided pedestrian traffic within self-contained buildings such as Units or Compounds and were typically about 1 m wide. *Pathways* were roads primarily for pedestrians moving within and between *Sectors*. Though at times quite straight, they were surprisingly narrow, typically 1–2 m wide, barely enough for two adults to pass each other. Narrow ones may have been restricted to one-way traffic. Those that segregated adjacent Sectors tended to be at the wider end of the spectrum. Pathways were often built along the reinforced banks of small washes. *Streets* were roads for both pedestrian and llama traffic that connected any Sector with the outside. Major washes such as Quebrada IV served as streets.

There were additional means for controlling traffic. The principal entrance to a Sector might have been as wide as 5 m but with greatly constricted pathways or streets beyond that point (Figs. 7.8, 7.17). Many enclosures or architectural complexes had baffled or constricted entries, sometimes as small as 50 cm wide and 3 m long, that led traffic into courtyards surrounded by series of nested or "hierarchical" terraces topped by one or two altars or seats (Fig. 7.18). Alternatively, some entries were guarded by a small platform or a pair of opposing ones. Atop these terraces and platforms one often finds fine quality painted stirrup-spout bottles. Within Sectors D and H, which abutted the Great Compound, there were spacious, open plazas where three and four streets and/or pathways converged. Formal, rectangular enclosures with elaborate hierarchical terraces and/or platforms were placed next to these nodes, most likely to supervise converging traffic (Fig. 7.19). In reality, Sector D is a mosaic of irregularly shaped Structures situated at the ends of two major street networks, each dominated by a spacious hierarchical terrace complex.

Overall, one has an impression that pathways, streets, and associated supervisory terraces and platforms were intended to discourage casual inter-Sector movement of the residents; it is difficult to envision people casually strolling from one Sector to another. Traffic within the site was quite well watched and regimented.

D. Height Differentiation

Two more important organizational principles governed architecture at the site. One is height differentiation (Shimada and Cavallaro 1986:46, in press) as attested by the patterned use of platform mounds, terraces/benches, and ramps. The urban landscape clearly took advantage of topographical unevenness to create real and illusionary height. In relatively flat areas,

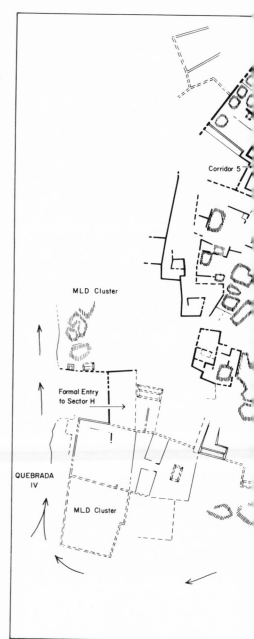

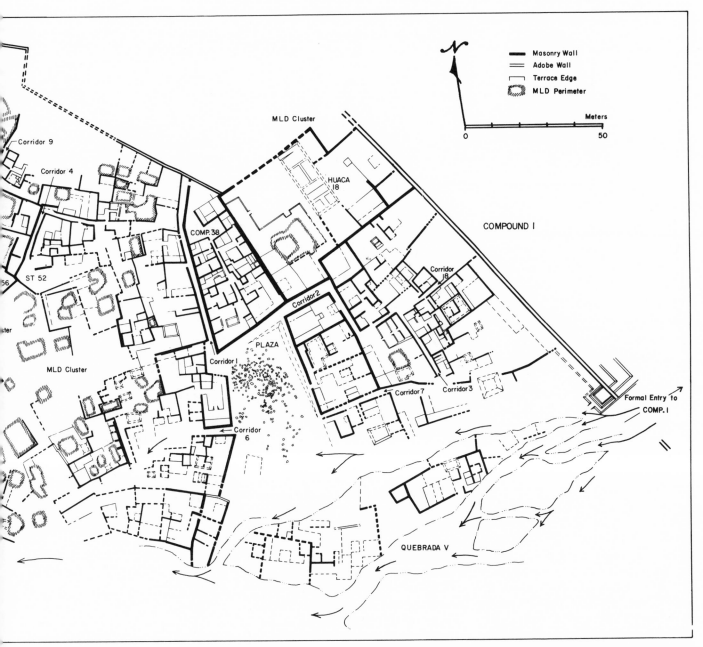

Figure 7.17. Architectural plan of Sector H. Note the network of pathways and associated plaza and entrance complexes.

terraces were created to make differences (even very subtle ones, e.g., 5 cm); in fact, such differentiation within buildings appears almost obsessive. Excavation showed some rooms with various floor levels differing as much as 50–60 cm. Thus, though there may have been no intervening wall, contiguous floor levels of different height may have functioned in effect as distinct rooms. Mochica painted and modeled vessels show how the vertical placement of personages correlates with elaborateness of dress and figure size. Figure 7.18 graphically illustrates how traffic to a storage building in Sector D was controlled by the occupants of a seat atop elaborate terraces.

Given their pervasiveness and the care with which they were constructed, terraces and the resultant vertical differentiation must have been of much importance across social boundaries. In fact, a reliable indicator of the significance of a given constructed space seems to be overall size and/ or the number of vertical levels found

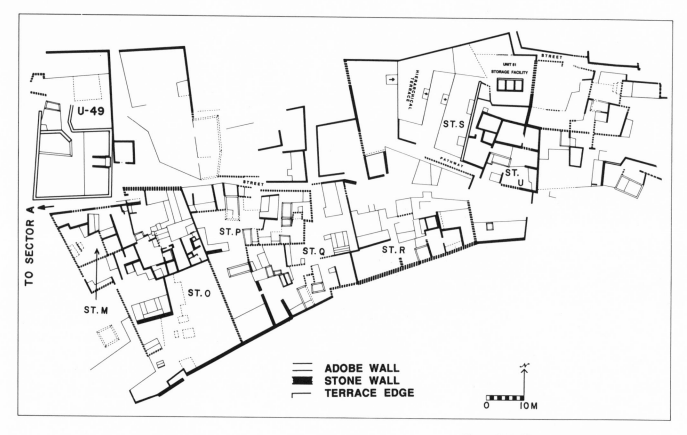

ADOBE WALL
STONE WALL
TERRACE EDGE

within (total difference between the lowest and highest points).

The Great Compound with Huaca Fortaleza is in a class by itself on both accounts. Though they are considerably smaller, substantial platform mounds are the principal features of the spacious rectangular enclosures adjoining the north end of the Great Compound. There are, in fact, over forty enclosures, with or without platform mounds, that have at least one side measuring 30 m or more. Though some are quite complex in shape, most approximate a rectangle. Nearly half of these enclosures have one major mound that was the focus of the internal layout. Topography did not affect the placement or size of these enclosures. For example, those found in Sector F occupy broken terrain, and the Great Compound walls cross two gullies. In other words, the size and relative position of these enclosures seem to have related to sociopolitical considerations.

The conspicuous consumption of built space occupied by these enclosures is in notable contrast to SIARs, which are by

and large contiguously placed, leaving only narrow pathways for movement. It is clear that built space was a valued resource differentially accessible to different social segments.

At the other end of the scale of height differentiation are platforms that measure approximately 1.5 m in height and 2–3 m to a side but have up to five terraced levels. The top level may be no more than 50 cm to a side. In other words, it would have been awkward to reach the top and, once there, one would barely have had room to perch. These small mounds are typically found at entrances to streets or architectural complexes or, conversely, set at the backs of the complexes. The settings suggest the former mounds may have served as checkpoints, while the latter may have been used as altars for the display of idols or as elevated thronelike seats. There are Mochica modeled ceramic representations of thrones atop such multilevel platforms (e.g., see Plates 29 and 60 in Willey 1953). That some of these less accessible mounds may have had some ritualistic significance

Figure 7.18. The western portion of Sector D situated contiguous to the northeast corner of Compound 1. The hierarchical terrace complex controlling access to the formal storage complex (Unit 51) is at the east end. Two thronelike seats are atop the highest terrace.

Figure 7.19. The eastern half of Sector D. Note the presence of a rectangular enclosure with a hierarchical terrace strategically placed to control access to a major intersection of pathways. The LLFA (Low Lying Flat Area) is believed to have been used as a terminal for llama caravans.

is suggested by the presence of deer antlers, quartz crystals, and/or *Spondylus* shells at the top (see Donnan 1978: 124–136).

E. Adobe Brick Construction

Another important principle of architectural organization is the use of adobe brick as the primary construction material. The site as a whole exhibits every conceivable permutation for the rather limited range of construction materials: new, recycled, and fragmentary adobe bricks; large and small fieldstones; sterile soil; clay mortar; rubble; and organic refuse, the last including llama dung, woven reed mats, ash, and animal bones. Figure 7.20 illustrates their ingenuity in making the most out of the limited range of materials.

There was definite emphasis on expedient, rapid solutions to construction tasks and maximization of the material avail-

able at the site (Shimada 1976: 476–477). Ground clearing for construction would yield abundant fieldstones. Additional stones, including boulders used in the foundations of *huacas* and major walls, were readily available in gullies. Even in situ sterile sandy soil was used extensively in making adobe bricks. The pragmatic use of other on-site materials (such as architectural rubble, kitchen refuse, and llama dung) as "fill" under new plastered floors, between masonry wall faces, and within the adobe chambers of the *huaca* body undoubtedly helped to control pests, odors, and the spread of disease, serious concerns for any city dweller.

What one must remember is that the finished construction, whether of adobe or fieldstone walls, was typically covered with one or more layers of plaster, which would have masked or "homogenized" variation

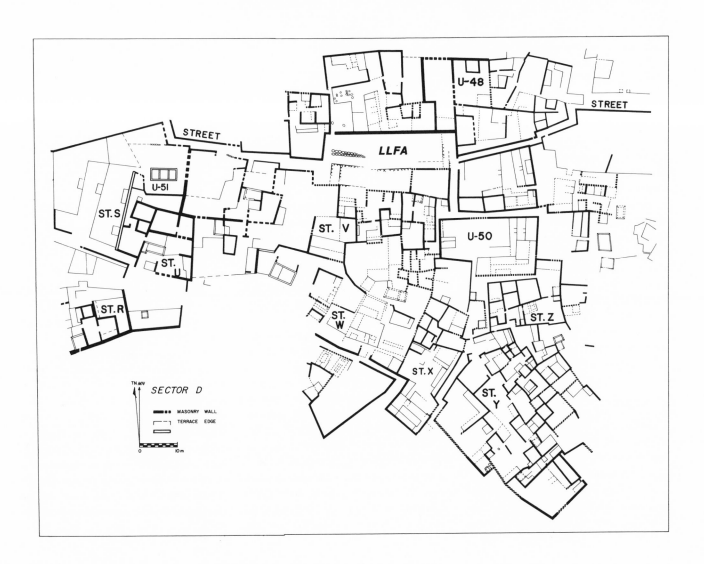

in construction techniques, styles, and materials (Shimada 1976: 477). Constructions at the site, large or small, do not in general show a high degree of technical sophistication or attention to detail (a notable exception is the formal storage facilities discussed in Chapter 8); the key seems to have been "any way that worked" with emphasis on the final, external appearance.

Large-scale use of adobe bricks was generally confined to public and elite structures. All major enclosures over 100 m to a side were defined by adobe walls built over boulder foundations. All *huacas* were similarly made with adobe bricks over rubble/refuse fill and boulder foundations. Smaller adobe structures may be found within adobe wall enclosures. All remains of Mochica murals known to date in and outside of Pampa Grande have been found on plastered adobe walls. The smooth, flat plastered surfaces, together with the "breathable" qualities of adobe walls, were ideally suited for colorful murals.

When we examine major architecture at Pampa Grande in regard to height, spaciousness, controlled access or exclusivity, and large-scale use of adobe bricks, the resultant grouping essentially duplicates the four-level hierarchy reported above. These are the qualities that reified the religious and political importance of the structures. After all, adobe bricks had qualities of considerable interest to the Mochica polity, including easy accounting (via markings) and standardization of construction format and appearance based on their mold-made, tabular block form. Large-scale use of adobe bricks was not just for the sake of appearance; it also symbolized political power over a labor force that probably encompassed various ethnic groups (Shimada in press 1). An adobe building, by extension, implied a corporate labor project (discussion below).

6. Emergence of the City and State: Factors and Processes

A. *The Traditional Ceremonial-Civic Center as the Organizational Framework*

Having defined the urban architecture and its organization, let us now turn to the question of how the city of Pampa Grande came into existence. The preceding chapter

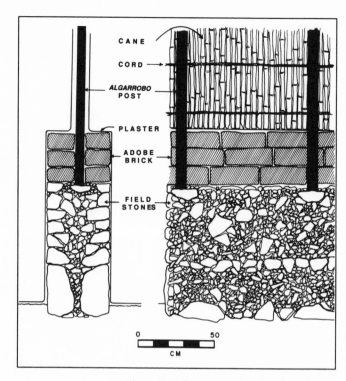

Figure 7.20. Reconstruction drawing of a wall in Sector D. Unmodified fieldstones (as well as at least one broken grinding stone) were used to build much of the masonry wall atop a large boulder foundation. The wall was then capped with adobe bricks, leaving enough space open to insert canes and/or wooden posts at the top. The entire wall surface was then plastered. Redrawn from the original by Andrew Ignatieff.

described natural and cultural factors and processes that prompted the northward shift of power and valley neck nucleation of the Moche V population. However, a viable city does not simply emerge out of population aggregation or an urbanization trend; there must have been some additional forces and organizational mechanisms that stabilized and integrated groups at Pampa Grande into a viable city.

Chapter 5 showed that no pre–Moche V settlement has presented a convincing case for city status as defined here (also see Isbell 1986, 1988; Schaedel 1985b). However, one important point that emerged in the review is that monumental platform mounds that often have been perceived as isolated ceremonial centers with small, specialized resident populations (Schaedel 1951a,b, 1972) are in some cases integral

parts of large, functionally diverse and differentiated settlements with resident populations in the thousands. What seems more important than the size of the associated resident population is the centripetal and integrative character of the center. In Schaedel's conception, largely vacant compounds with platform mounds served as the settings for occasional mass gatherings, for example, rallies before and after combat, the assumption of office by leaders, and rituals related to agricultural fertility. These sorts of gatherings were a principal vehicle for the establishment of new social conventions and messages, particularly in nonliterate societies such as the Mochica. Participation in these rituals (including pilgrimage) would have given rise to a heightened awareness of belonging to a larger whole.

Wheatley (1971: 225–226; also see 1969) offers what he regards as a cross-cultural characterization of the ceremonial center: "Operationally they were instruments for the creation of political, social and moral order. In the religious authority of the organized priesthood and divine monarchs they elaborated the redistributive aspects of the economy to a position of institutionalized regional dominance, functioned as nodes in a web of administered trade, served as foci of craft specialization." Renfrew (1975: 8) emphasized their role in redistribution of goods and information, including sanctified messages and social conventions spread through public rituals.

In other words, the time-honored Mochica ceremonial-civic center and its leaders had the social network, organizational framework, and know-how to mobilize and integrate the regional population, at least on a short-term basis. However, stressful conditions, particularly those originating abruptly and in nature, commonly bring about greater social cohesion, with the populace rallying around the traditional spiritual leaders (e.g., see Gluckman 1955). It is argued here that the abrupt onset of severe droughts (whose duration could not have been predicted) in the sixth century brought about just such stress and response. It is further suggested that the rapid and successful construction of the monumental religious-civic center (Huaca Fortaleza) as the physical and symbolic center of the new capital provided effective means for the integration of local and transplanted populations and, at the same time, demonstrated and enhanced the prestige and power of the leadership and its dogma. The prestige conferred by its successful completion, we suspect, clearly outweighed administrative and logistical problems. The legitimacy of Pampa Grande's claim to paramount status among Moche V sites on the North Coast was undoubtedly related to the monumentality of its central structure; it had to be as large as, if not larger than, any built before, perhaps eclipsing the abandoned Huaca del Sol. The continuous construction effort (documented below), entailing massive mobilization and permanence of laborers, skilled craftsmen, and other specialists, formed

the basis for the emergence of the city of Pampa Grande. Coordination and supervision of this massive corporate project involving local and regional (perhaps even some transplanted) populations is also believed to have given rise to state-level sociopolitical integration, which survived perhaps less than one hundred years.

Large-scale, long-term mobilization of the labor and resources necessary for the construction was likely to have been derived not only through the traditional institution of labor service and the self-serving elite religious-political dogma, but also through threats of possible economic and ideological sanctions. The famed oracle of Pachacamac near the city of Lima was known from early Colonial writings to have resorted occasionally to threats of bad omens or damaging earthquakes (the patron deity of Pachacamac exercising its power to shake the earth) in extracting tribute from neglecters near and far (Rostworowski 1975, 1981). In the case of Pampa Grande in the strategic valley neck location, similar sanctions could have been accompanied by threats on a water supply. For a population that had recently suffered or was still suffering from severe drought, such a threat should have been quite effective.

Though the preceding may have contributed to some extent, probably the greatest motivator of the drive to build Huaca Fortaleza was the widely shared desire to appease the forces and deities in return for an abundant and secure supply of water. Expected gains from contributing toward the unified construction effort, however difficult, were seen as more advantageous than refusing and suffering the consequences (see Haas 1982: 159–171). Though such motivation and decision-making can hardly be documented archaeologically, the abruptness, intensity, duration, and attendant adverse effects of the drought were documented in Chapter 5.

There have been justified cautions and criticisms against the hasty equation of monumental public works with certain levels of sociopolitical integration and labor force size (e.g., Cowgill 1975; Erasmus 1965; Kaplan 1963; cf. Haas 1987). In the case of Huaca Fortaleza, however, there is ample evidence that its construction was indeed rapid and necessitated mobilization and close supervision of a large labor force (Shimada in press 1).

B. Construction Techniques and History of Huaca Fortaleza

Earlier Mochica platform mounds were essentially built of series of high, thick, vertically segmented, juxtaposed walls of adobe bricks (Figs. 1.3, 2.11). Each segment was built by stacking bricks that were basically identical in soil, shape, and size (i.e., made with the same mold), suggesting that each segment was built by a relatively small number of laborers from a single community under Mochica political control. The same single mark found on bricks within each segment is believed to have identified brick makers. Moreover, Huaca del Sol and Huaca de la Luna were built through a long-term *accretive* process, the former involving at least eight major construction phases over a period of several centuries.

The construction technique and materials and the form of Huaca Fortaleza, however, differ significantly from earlier examples (Shimada in press 1; Shimada and Cavallaro 1986, in press). Available evidence indicates that the *huaca* was probably built in two stages (Haas 1985: 394–395; Shimada 1976: 407–409; Shimada and Cavallaro 1986: 59–61, in press). Little can be said about the specifics of the first stage of construction as it is buried under the subsequent construction, except where two sloping superimposed plaster layers (paralleling the natural slope) have been exposed some 6–7 m above the ground on a side of a deep gully cutting into the east side of the Second Terrace. The plaster layers were laid over a solid foundation of large, reddish, fired tiles set in clay mortar, in turn laid over courses of rectangular adobe bricks (Fig. 7.21; Shimada and Cavallaro 1986: 59–60). These rare square tiles measure 48–50 cm to a side and 4.5–5.0 cm in thickness.[104] This is the only reported case of fired tile flooring in a Mochica construction, but it seems analogous to a flagstone floor that was found in the elite sacred precinct atop Huaca de la Luna at Moche.

The function of the tile floor is not clear. Though associated with a number of plastered adobe wall faces, profiles, and corner abutments, it does not seem to be extensive; the interior of the Main Body exposed by deep erosion gullies shows no tiles or associated first-stage structures. Instead, inspection confirms an earlier observation that the second-stage construction added at least 15 m of adobe bricks over the tile floor, creating the Second Terrace and raising the height of the First Terrace by at least 5 m (Haas 1985: 395).

Critical to the discussion at hand is the fact that much of or perhaps the entire Main Body of the *huaca* was built in a unified, continuous manner using the innovative construction technique of contiguous adobe chambers filled with refuse or other loose materials (Shimada and Cavallaro 1986: 55–63). Haas (1985: 395) feels that "the entire Main Body was constructed in the first occupation phase and that the second phase involved only modifications upon the First Terrace and the addition of the Second Terrace." There are no clear Gallinazo or Mochica antecedents, as earlier platform mounds were essentially solid adobe bricks. However, monumental mounds of the contemporaneous Maranga culture in the Rimac Valley on the Central Coast, such as Huacas Aramburú, Middendorf, and San Marcos, were built using a similar chamber-and-fill technique (Agurto 1984; Jijón y Caamaño 1949; Kroeber 1954). Here, chambers built with small hand-formed rectangular bricks (on average ca. 18 by 8 cm and 13 cm high) set in clay mortar were filled with loose stone and earth. The technique, which seems to date back to pre–Moche V times on the Central Coast, may have been introduced as part of the Moche IV–V broad spectrum transformation. Such a possibility is not unexpected given the various indications of Moche V–Nievería (Central Coast) contact described in Chapters 4 and 9.

The Moche V chamber-and-fill technique entailed a definite sequence of coordinated activities. First, large boulders were placed on the gently sloping area forming the solid foundation of the Main Body of the *huaca*. This was followed by construction of discrete—but contigu-

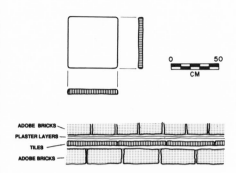

ADOBE BRICKS
PLASTER LAYERS
TILES
ADOBE BRICKS

Figure 7.21. Fired tiles that capped the first-stage construction of Huaca Fortaleza visible at the northeast corner of the mound.

ously placed—standardized square adobe-mortar walled chambers measuring about 5.0 m at the top and 1.1–1.2 m to a side on the exterior and interior, respectively (Haas 1985: 394; Shimada in press 1; Fig. 7.22). The tops of the First and Second Terraces and the platforms of the First Terrace all show this regular lattice of square chambers (Fig. 7.23). Haas (1985: 395–396) describes them as follows:

Each of these chambers appears to be surrounded by a solid rectangular block of adobe bricks laid on their sides or ends, either horizontally or vertically. Within each block there is overlap between the layers of bricks, but there is no overlap between the bricks on one block and those of adjacent blocks. Thus, each block was erected as an independent structural unit, and was not physically bonded to its neighboring blocks.

At the same time, their contiguous placement, bonded corners, and thicker wall bases provided an overall structural strength to the resultant lattice of filled chambers. Seams separating two contiguous chambers can be vertically traced for at least 25 m (Haas 1985: 397). The Main Body top that measures approximately 120 by 120 m thus may well encompass up to 484 chambers (22 by 22 chambers along the east-west and north-south axes).[105]

Huaca Fortaleza's bricks were all set in clay mortar typically 2–5 cm thick. Besides providing a strong bond between successive courses of the adobe bricks used in building the tall, fill-sustaining chambers, the mortar helped accommodate the use of adobe bricks of varying dimensions. Though these chamber walls have not been dismantled to document brick marking, it is evident from the inspection of exposed faces that the constituent bricks vary in height, width, length, soil quality, and even the presence or absence of cane-mold marks, indicating that they were produced at different locations using different molds.

Figure 7.23. Isometric reconstruction drawing of the lattice of filled chambers and buttress walls formed by standardized columns of adobe bricks that together make up the Main Body of Huaca Fortaleza.

Figure 7.22. Sand-filled adobe chamber atop the Main Body of Huaca Fortaleza exposed by 1983 rains. Note the variable size and shape of constituent bricks.

lattice of 5 x 5 m filled adobe chambers

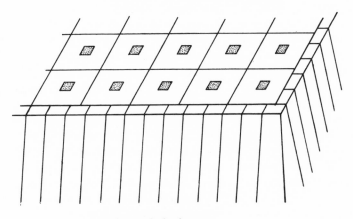

**1 x 2 m vertical columns
of adobe bricks set in clay mortar**

Once erected, the chambers were filled with readily available materials such as sand, architectural rubble, and rock, as well as kitchen refuse containing ash, charcoal, shell, and even llama bones and guinea pig dung. The alluvial sand that fills the upper portions of the chambers was readily available from the wide *quebradas* that cut through the site, and if necessary, the Chancay River, which is 3.5 km from the construction site, could have provided additional sand. Horizontally laid reed mats found within the fill may have been used to transport the fill and/or minimize the dust. Smaller Huaca 11 in Compound 15 has chambers filled with boulders and earth. Some chambers of post–Moche V platform mounds elsewhere in this region contain impressive quantities of broken ceramic vessels or llama dung (Cavallaro and Shimada 1988: 76; Shimada and Cavallaro 1986: 58).

Among some of the deeply incised erosion gullies near the northwest corner of the Main Body one can see the weathered remains of horizontally laid *algarrobo* logs several meters long and with estimated original diameters of 10–15 cm. The same phenomenon observed at post–Moche V mounds within the Lambayeque region suggests that regularly spaced logs (anywhere from ca. 20 cm to 1 m apart) were laid across the tops of at least some of the perimetric fill chambers (Cavallaro and Shimada 1988: 81; Shimada and Cavallaro 1986: 61–62).

These logs may have served various functions: (1) "to protect the adobes at the edges of narrow terraces or ledges of step pyramids" (Kroeber 1930: 61, 94), providing footing or anchoring points for the original construction as well as for anticipated periodic repairing and modifications of the exterior; (2) together with layers of clay mortar, cane, and/or woven mats, to form the solid floors/roofs for successive layers of chambers in order to counter adverse effects of subsidence resulting from compaction of loose and soft fill; (3) to stabilize and reinforce the lattice of chambers against lateral sway associated with earthquakes or buckling under the weight of additional layers of chambers and superstructures; and/or (4) to structurally bind the perimeter walls of the chamber lattice and the exterior walls of the overall platform mound (ibid.). As logs clearly span at least the outermost chambers, the first possibility was of secondary importance.

Next, the completed lattice of filled chambers was encased by slightly tapering retaining walls (at least 5 m thick at the base) built in standardized, juxtaposed vertical segments about 2 m wide and 1 m thick (Fig. 7.24), much like the traditional pattern seen at the Huaca del Sol and other Mochica platform mounds. However, the 545 bricks from seven segments examined by H. Knapp (n.d.) show that constituent bricks within each of the segments were rarely marked (24 marked bricks, with eight different marks; Fig. 7.25) and were heterogeneous in regard to mold size/shape and soil. In fact, bricks in one segment at the northwest corner of the Main Body bore five different marks.

Perhaps reflecting the single-episode construction of the Main Body core, the exterior of its retaining walls appears to have had a single steep slope, unlike the steplike profiles of Huaca del Sol. The low platform that projects out on the east base of the *huaca* may have been constructed at the same time, in part to serve as a buttress for the steep side walls. It is quite possible that the gully at the west base of the *huaca* eroded away a symmetrical basal platform.

Lastly, the top of the Main Body was capped with solid adobe flooring and protected by superstructures supported by columns set in sand-filled sockets.

D. Organizational Implications of Huaca Fortaleza and Other Major Corporate Constructions

The innovative chamber-and-fill technique presented some important advantages and idiosyncrasies crucial to the broader issues at hand. It was a cost effective way, to a limited extent, to achieve height and volume rapidly. The use of fill and clay mortar (2–5 cm thick as opposed to adobe bricks 10–12 cm thick) reduced the total number of adobe bricks required by an estimated 25–30 percent. Although the fill constitutes only about 5–6 percent of the total volume taken up by a single filled chamber at most, the chambers served as sockets for columns supporting roofs, and rapid deposition of locally available fill materials meant faster completion.

At the same time, even the small amount of clay mortar placed among adobe bricks required continuous on-site preparation and coordination with bricklaying, which, in turn, had to be coordinated with the filling of chambers. Nothing could be done about the structures atop the planned *huaca* until the lattice of chambers was filled and sealed. Overall, diversification of the material base and tasks (e.g., mortar preparation, brick making and placement, fill and water transport) necessitated a large and diversified labor force working together in a definite sequence of coordinated activities under the close supervision of a central authority. It called for an institution empowered to bring about large-scale, sustained investment of labor and material resources, as well as to integrate and administer. The organizational correlate of this project is believed to have been the emergence of a state-level central authority.

Construction details of Huaca Fortaleza and other major corporate structures at Pampa Grande, documented primarily by Hans Knapp (n.d.), provide further insights into the Moche V labor exploitation and political leadership. He found that the perimeter walls of Deer and Spondylus houses, as well as the Great Compound, were built partially or entirely in segments. For example, on the basis of three sampled segments, we deduce that the south perimeter wall of Deer House was built of thirty standardized segments roughly 6 m in length by 1.2 m in width. The enclosure walls of the nearby Great Compound and Spondylus House were each standardized to ca. 9 and 6 m in length, respectively. The former walls were massive, with a 3.0–3.5-meter basal width, and probably stood at twice their present height of 3.5–4.0 m.

At least three patterns can be distinguished (Shimada in press 1) in the distribution of marked and unmarked adobe bricks within and among these segments:

(1) Segments of standardized length each built of bricks bearing one identical mark but varying in mold size and shape, as with the perimeter walls of Deer House. The identically marked bricks of Segment 8 in Figure 7.26 clearly show at least two dis-

Figure 7.24. Standardized vertical segments of adobe bricks that form the west exterior face of Huaca Fortaleza. The photo was taken after the 1982–1983 torrential rains that exposed various heretofore unseen architectural features.

Figure 7.25. Compilation of marks found on adobe bricks sampled by Hans Knapp from various structures in Pampa Grande. Drawing based on Knapp's field notes.

"GREAT COMPOUND" (COMPOUND 1)

HUACA FORTALEZA (H-1)

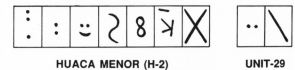

HUACA MENOR (H-2)   **UNIT-29**

"DEER HOUSE" (COMPOUND 14)

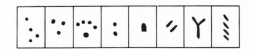

UNIT-28

tinct molds. Segments 1 and 8 had somewhat over 50 percent and 20 percent of constituent bricks marked, respectively.

(2) Segments of standardized length each built of bricks bearing various marks and varying in mold size and shape, as with the perimeter walls of Spondylus House. Here, as above, identical marks occur on bricks from different molds. The segment shown in Figure 7.27 has an estimated 15 percent of bricks marked with at least ten different marks. Though within single courses there are recognizable clusters of identical bricks, such patterning does not hold for more than two or three courses. Curiously, the perimeter wall of Deer House also includes a segment at the northern end built with heterogeneous bricks bearing seven different marks.

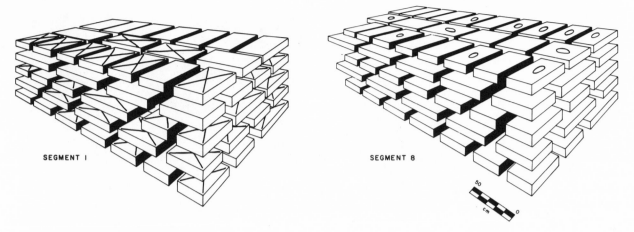

SEGMENT I   SEGMENT 8

Figure 7.26. Isometric drawing of a standardized segment of the perimeter wall of Deer House excavated by H. Knapp. Note that a few bricks of varied sizes and shapes bear the same mark. Adapted from an original drawing by H. Knapp.

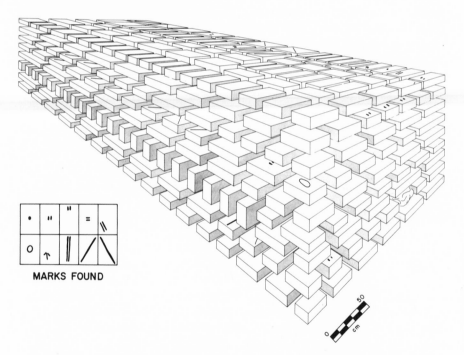

MARKS FOUND

Figure 7.27. Isometric drawing of a standardized segment of the perimeter wall of Spondylus House excavated by H. Knapp. In contrast to what is seen in Figure 7.26, here the segment was built with bricks of varied sizes and shapes bearing different marks. Adapted from an original drawing by H. Knapp.

(3) Standardized segments each built of one or a few internally homogeneous groups of unmarked bricks. Unmarked bricks may vary from one course to the next but are identical within each course. Wall segments sampled in formal storage rooms in Compounds 25 (Sector B) and 28 and 29 (both Sector A) all display this pattern. Marks are conspicuously missing from all these constructions.

What we see at Moche V Pampa Grande is a much more complex situation than that documented at the site of Moche. The first pattern resembles that observed at Huaca del Sol and Huaca de la Luna, except that the critical one-to-one correspondence between marks and mold is lacking. The second pattern is previously unreported in earlier Mochica settings. As noted before, although the exterior "skin" of Huaca Fortaleza presented standardized segments, each was built with heterogeneous bricks. In the Main Body core, adobe chambers replaced the segmented adobe columns of earlier Mochica platform mounds as the basic unit of construction, but, again, with heterogeneous bricks. Bricks exposed at the southwest corner of Huaca 2 are also heterogeneous. The third pattern is discussed in the next chapter, where the economic role of formal storage facilities is considered.

What accounts for the breakdown of the earlier Mochica tradition of segment-specific mark, mold, and soil? Why do we find three distribution patterns in contemporaneous Moche V corporate architecture? In regard to the first question, the mixed use of heterogeneous bricks is inferred to reflect centralized pooling of bricks and task differentiation (Fig. 7.28; Shimada in press 1). The Labor Tax model advocated by Moseley (see Chapter 5) sees *huaca* construction as quite simply organized, with the same group of laborers producing, transporting, and placing bricks within a specified segment of the *huaca*. In contrast, fill chambers and wall segments at Pampa Grande seem to have been built with bricks pooled at the construction site by those who were not necessarily involved in the production of bricks. Brick marking would be of importance in accounting before stockpiling. The observed limited clustering of homogeneous bricks in chamber construction may simply reflect the degree of clustering that is inevitable within a pool.

The data from Deer House also force us to question the argument that a single adobe brick mold and mark correlates with a specific social group. If the assumption that a mark identifies a social group is, in fact, valid, then the Deer House data suggest that social groups involved in segmentary construction each employed more than one mold size. Any social group with appreciable territory is likely to have had more than one *adobería* (adobe-making site) using that group's mark with different molds. Conversely, the data may be interpreted as reflecting an inclusive use of marks, i.e., each mark identified a group of related social groups. In either case, the labor organization envisioned for the site of

Moche is not applicable here.

However, explaining the coexistence of different distribution patterns in a pair of contiguous enclosures, Deer and Spondylus houses, is much more difficult.[106] The latter was a spacious enclosure with a large platform mound and an attached *Spondylus* workshop, while the former is seen primarily as a receiving, distributing, and processing center for unspun cotton (see Chapter 8). Could the divergence be related to their contrasting roles and values attached to resources managed at these two houses? For example, reflecting concern for the production of *Spondylus* objects for state-sponsored rituals and political economy, the perimeter wall of the Spondylus House may be viewed as having been built by a task-differentiated labor force under state direction. This group of laborers would be expected to use stockpiled bricks, resulting in the observed mixing of divergent bricks, both marked and unmarked. But this line of argument generates more questions than answers. Architectural expressions of high-level concern for the control of important resources, such as the placement of hierarchical terraces in traffic nodes, is more apparent in Deer House than in Spondylus House. At this point, there is no convincing explanation for the observed adobe brick patterns in Deer House wall segments.

Overall, the adobe constructions examined at Pampa Grande present both conservative and innovative features; the tradition of segmentary construction seems to have survived, but not in association with the earlier distribution pattern of marked bricks. It is likely that the traditional compartmentalized labor service and marked bricks underwent some basic transformations. Task differentiation, pooling of adobe bricks, and concomitant centralized coordination reduced the importance of the earlier community- or ethnic-level groupings of construction materials and labor force. Moreover, building Huaca Fortaleza and the city of Pampa Grande from the ground up would have been very difficult based solely or even partially on voluntary labor due to the sustained, long-term, intensive nature of the work. It is suggested that the emergent state transformed traditional labor service

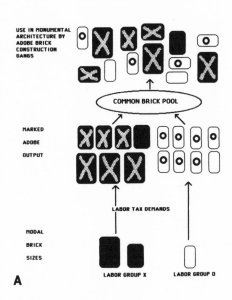

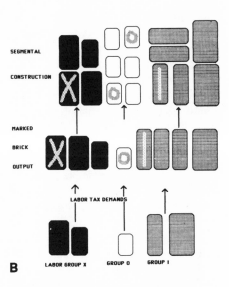

Figure 7.28. (A) Graphic model of the distribution of marked adobe bricks expected from task differentiation and centralized pooling. (B) Graphic representation of Moseley's Labor Tax Model proposed to account for the labor organization of the Huaca del Sol construction. Adapted from Figs. 11–12 in Cavallaro and Shimada 1988: 92.

to create a new centralized labor pool composed primarily of conscripted local farmers now relocated at Pampa Grande. As described in the preceding chapter, the above generalized labor force is believed to have been complemented by skillful, specialized builders (perhaps even state retainers) involved in the construction of the Group I formal storage facilities with standardized (and in many ways unique) size, shape, and construction techniques and materials. The emergent state at Pampa Grande thus seems to have established not only new forms of labor exploitation but a monopoly on them as well.

There are few marked bricks documented at Galindo, the primary Moche V site in the Moche Valley, and the practice is believed to have ceased by the end of Moche V in the Moche Valley proper (Hastings and Moseley 1975: 202). The paucity and modest scale of corporate constructions suggest that the power and economic bases of the Moche V polity there were quite limited and/or that material and labor investments were not funneled toward erecting monumental architecture to glorify or aggrandize the power of the ruling elite. In contrast to the view espoused by J. and T. Topic (see Chapter 6),[107] Bawden (1982a,b) regards the massive parapeted wall encircling the hillslopes where the lowest (and largest) class residential sector was located as an attempt to control and physically segregate them from critical, desired resources, including water.

Differences between Galindo and Pampa Grande, as well as the transformation of age-old institutions, must be seen from the perspective of Moche V as a time of major, broad-spectrum cultural transformation. As Trigger (1990: 128) emphasizes, "contextual data are essential to understand the social circumstances that influenced [the construction of the monumental architecture]." The scale and rapidity of the Huaca Fortaleza construction project were unprecedented, and in addition the cultural and natural conditions underlying the construction were exceptional. Extant institutions, customs, and priorities had been shaken to their roots by the adverse effects of severe droughts and attendant unprecedented settlement shift, with its expected internal disarray, and

perhaps by threat of incursions from highland polities. Responses varied from abandonment or entrenchment of conservative features to archaic revival, syncretism, and experimentation for inspiration, new identity, and focus (see Chapters 8 and 9). Perhaps seeking a sense of continuity and stability, Pampa Grande seems to have been at least initially organized by the time-honored social integrative institution of the ceremonial-civic center. In this sense the emergent city was a ceremonial city, as well as in the sense of the dominant role played by Huaca Fortaleza in the organization and workings of the city.

At the same time, the cultural response also included daring, experimental elements—for example, the "chamber-and-fill" technique of mound building and attendant transformation of the traditional labor services—that underwrote the political centralization to an extent unseen before. The rapid and successful completion of Huaca Fortaleza simultaneously fostered and legitimized the emergent state, which was further buttressed by the political leverage afforded by the control of the critical valley neck. As seen in Chapter 10, the Moche V city and state were short-lived, and their emergence was specific to the exceptional situation that existed during the late sixth to early seventh century.

7. The Composition and Permanence of the Pampa Grande Population

Determination of the social and ethnic composition of Pampa Grande's population is a difficult task to say the least. In this section, some tentative views derived from analyses of intrasite architectural variation and the regional settlement pattern and hierarchy are presented.

A. Establishing Permanent Residency: Demographic Correlates of the Huaca Fortaleza Construction, Agrarian Reform and Social Surplus

The preceding section laid the groundwork for consideration of the processes involved in establishing a large, diverse permanent population. Their establishment at Pampa Grande was a byproduct of the mobilization and permanence of the labor force involved in the construction of Huaca For-

taleza. Most likely, the majority of the labor force was unskilled local farmers, complemented by a smaller number of specialists in occupations such as masonry, carpentry, and wall painting. The long-term deployment of many local laborers probably meant that their families and leaders also came to Pampa Grande.

The manpower requirements of the Huaca Fortaleza construction are difficult to calculate, but a general idea may be gained by comparing modern adobe construction works. With all the necessary materials prepared ahead of time and at hand, an *adobero* (adobe-maker and builder) with an assistant can build a simple 2 by 2 m wall segment (width of 0.2 m—total of 0.8 m^3) on level ground in an hour using typical bricks measuring 0.3 by 0.2 m and 0.1 m high, plus 2–3 cm of clay mortar between courses. This yields a figure of 0.4 m^3 of adobe construction per work hour.

In other words, the second-stage construction of Huaca Fortaleza (using a conservative estimate of one million m^3 as the volume taken up by adobe bricks and clay mortar) would have required some 2.5 million work hours, or 250 ten-hour work days with one thousand laborers just to place the requisite amount of bricks and clay mortar. This is exclusive of brick manufacture. This is a very conservative figure, since the base rate of 0.4 m^3 per hour is for ground-level work, not for work 20 or 30 m above ground. In other words, if we consider all the necessary tasks, such as preparing the ground, adobe bricks, and clay mortar; setting the boulder foundation; and transporting bricks and fill materials to construction sites, even with one thousand workers laboring day after day, the second-stage construction would have taken several years. In addition, our estimate of the labor cost of the Huaca Fortaleza construction must take into account a large supporting cast, who, for example, prepared food and drink or provided on-site supervision. Though the preceding is just a rough calculation, it does provide some sense of the magnitude and complexity of the undertaking and attendant coordination and direction.

In addition, we cannot ignore the construction needs of the laborers themselves, the relocated Mochica and local elite and their retainers. Consider, for example, the labor and material demands for the construction of Deer and Spondylus houses. Pampa Grande appears to have been the scene of continuous building, perhaps right up to the time of its abandonment, judging by the considerable architectural superposition and reorganization (prehistoric "urban renewal," if you will), all associated with Moche V ceramics, in Sectors D and H. This architectural buildup in the central Sectors may relate to Huaca Fortaleza construction. In general, architectural and refuse buildup diminish as one travels from the center to the perimeters of the site. Many masonry structures, including small rectangular walled compounds, found toward the eastern and southern peripheries of the site (Sectors E, F, and G) are associated with relatively little refuse and show little or no evidence of architectural modifications. Some of them, in fact, seem never to have been finished or occupied.

The above interpretation raises a series of questions regarding provisioning, local agricultural production, and population distribution. In this regard it is important to remember that Pampa Grande not only occupied the apex of the regional Moche V settlement hierarchy (i.e., the hydraulically interlinked Lambayeque and Zaña valleys), but was disproportionately large and complex relative to secondary (Sipán and Huaca Santa Rosa for the south and north banks of the Lambayeque Valley, and Cerro Songoy for the north side of the Zaña Valley) and tertiary sites (including the "fortified" site of Cerro Ventarrón). As noted in Chapter 4, although the Sipán-Collique Complex covered upwards of 3.0 km² (Fig. 4.14), much of this area was occupied by cemeteries, cultivation fields, and canals, as was the case with Pampa de los Incas in the Santa Valley. There was no extensive architectural nucleation or integration of diverse architectural forms in any one area. Though small adobe mounds (likely Moche I–III in date) are found near Huaca Rajada in Sipán, there is no definite Moche V corporate construction found at the Sipán-Collique Complex or elsewhere in the region. In fact, there is nothing comparable in scale to Huaca Fortaleza on the entire

North Coast. The largest construction at the Sipán-Collique Complex, the rectangular mound of Huaca Rajada, probably dates to Middle Sicán (see note 13 for explanation).

Most of the relatively large Moche V sites in the region (e.g., Pampa de Chumbenique, Cerro Songoy, Sipán-Collique, Cerro Ventarrón, Cerro Patapo, Huaca Soledad) appear to have been continuously occupied since late Moche IV. Unfortunately, our limited settlement-pattern data do not allow us to specify whether their size and complexity changed during this span. In his settlement survey, Nolan (1980) examined narrow areas along the Antigua Collique and other canals that follow the edges of the south bank (from above the neck to the mid-portion) of the Lambayeque Valley and the north bank of the adjacent Zaña Valley; but he did not differentiate Moche IV from V. A preliminary settlement survey of the lower Lambayeque Valley by Kent Day (1971) that complemented Nolan's area coverage revealed only one dune site with diagnostic Moche V painted sherds. However, this survey, carried out before the initiation of our research at Pampa Grande, did not have the benefit of knowledge of Moche V domestic wares and undoubtedly underrepresented the number of contemporaneous rural settlements. During the course of an independent survey, C. Elera (pers. com. 1985) found Moche V ceramics (e.g., double-tiered and face-neck jars) exposed in a profile of a modern adobe-making pit in Reque in the southwestern portion of the valley. At the nearby site of Huaca Eten (also known as Taco) near the town of Puerto Eten, additional Moche V domestic ceramics were found.

In spite of the limitations of the above regional settlement data, it is clear that in terms of the overall extent of occupation, architectural complexity, and labor and material investments made, Pampa Grande dominated sites in the entire Zaña–Lambayeque–La Leche region.

Chapter 6 described the population shift to the valley neck and other cultural responses expected at the time of or immediately following the severe sixth-century droughts. In this respect, it is significant that Schaedel (1985a: 450; see also 1966a,b,

1986a,b) noted that the early Middle Horizon was when a new system of land exploitation was installed, with restructuring of earlier fields and contour canal systems.[108] Concurrently, he saw the emergence of disproportionately large urban settlements at valley necks and attendant diminution in the distribution of minor settlements (Schaedel 1972: 24; 1985b: 158–159). Schaedel attributed these major changes to the "restructuring" of local populations by Wari invaders. Though he favors an exogenous origin for the city and state on the North Coast, he does consider the possibility that their origins were "autogenous to the North Coast people (and research on such sites as Pampa Grande and Incapampa [Pampa de los Incas] can resolve this hypothesis)" (Schaedel 1972: 24).

Indeed, our research supports the view that Moche V Pampa Grande was an essentially autogenous city conditioned by exceptionally severe and prolonged drought and attendant cultural upheavals. We suggest that the restructuring of local agricultural production and population distribution was implemented by the Moche V state. This restructuring involved a reduction of resource redundancies and creation of a large "social surplus" by greater unification and streamlining of extant canals and by the intensification of cultivation in prime land. By taking advantage of the concentrative qualities of irrigation agriculture, inhabitants would have attempted to maximize production of crucial crops such as maize in the prime agricultural lands in the *Valle Viejo* close to Pampa Grande. The area is the most fertile (thick alluvium replenished by occasional floods) and has the easiest access to water. Historically, the *Valle Viejo* has been the focus of intensive sugarcane cultivation by large *haciendas* (Ramírez-Horton 1974). From the perspective of resource exploitation and management, populations inhabiting the *Valle Nuevo* and *Valle Bajo* would have been better employed as a labor force (social surplus) for various purposes, including city construction at Pampa Grande and intensive infield and outfield cultivation of the *Valle Viejo*.[109] This new economic organization remained in place even with the return of normal or above-normal precipi-

tation in the seventh century.

The social surplus that results from reallocation of goods and services from one use to another can be contrasted with the material surplus that results from improvement or intensification in production. Attendant centralization of authority is also seen as adaptive in reducing conflict under conditions of marked water shortage and/or population pressure on land, particularly when subsistence is largely dependent on irrigation agriculture. Population pressure in this interpretive model was not so much from the natural growth of local populations as from the reduction of agricultural production due to loss of the southern territory (primarily from the Moche Valley to the Nepeña), and water shortage. Under this situation, state-directed labor and water distribution would have been favored. The northward relocation of the Mochica capital and the contraction of the southern territory do not necessarily imply wholesale migration of the masses. Even with the limited settlement-pattern data, with the notable exception of Pampa Grande, the Moche V settlement pattern in the Lambayeque region does not seem to differ much from that of Moche IV. In fact, most sites with Moche IV components have Moche V occupation. The extensive Moche V site of Galindo also suggests major local demographic restructuring rather than massive northward movement.

Along the organizational principles defined in Chapter 8, the social surplus resulting from the above changes could have been effectively integrated into the urban economy of Pampa Grande. Chief among these principles was that of production by the masses. Each able-bodied individual had a specific role to play within the framework of segmented manufacturing or task-differentiated construction activities that emphasized maximum involvement of the available workforce.

B. Social Organization of the Urban Residents

Convinced of the importance of studying the household as the basic unit of social organization in order to understand the social dynamics within a settlement, Bawden (1977, 1982b) carried out a systematic study of thirty-eight residential structures at Galindo that varied in form, floor surface size, artifact content, and placement. Bawden estimated that over half of the ca. 5 km² expanse of the site was covered by residential architecture. He identified four major residential areas that were clearly segregated from each other and from other functional portions of the site by means of natural and manmade barriers: Area A, a large level plain fronting the cultivated zone of the Moche Valley; Area B, the lower west and south slopes of Cerro Galindo encircled by a major parapeted wall; and Areas C and D, located in the channel of the Quebrada Caballo Muerto, a major side valley that bisects that site along the northeast-southwest axis (Fig. 6.3). The first two areas are similar in size to each other and larger than the last two.

Residential architecture is defined as consisting of "a large rectangular benched enclosure (*sala*), a food preparation area (*cocina*), and one or two small rectangular storage areas (*deposito*)" (Bawden 1982b: 168–169). Its characteristic construction features are defined as follows:

Residential units were typically constructed of stout, stone-based bases with cane superstructure. Floors were mudplastered in the *salas*, of packed dirt elsewhere. Roofing of plastered cane covered *cocinas, depositos,* and the benches of *salas*, leaving the central floor of the larger areas open. A single entrance usually gave access to the *cocina*, secluding the *sala* and *deposito* from direct exterior access. The plan of the *sala* is of consistent regularity (in comparison with the other spaces) and its construction quality often surpasses that of the rest of the residential unit. (Ibid., 169)

In his excavations, Bawden found that "Specificity of componential form in the basic residential unit is repeated in the artifactual distribution," with "Each discrete spatial component contain[ing] its distinctive assemblage of domestic material remains," for example, one or two hearths associated with ash and food remains in the *cocina* or food preparation area. The *sala* typically contains a high proportion of fine ceramics relative to other sections of the residences, in addition to evidence of

domestic tasks such as copper needles and ceramic spindle whorls used in weaving. Bawden also found "Small plainware figurines representing a wide range of Moche mythical beings . . . in the *sala*, possibly indicating the existence of a domestic religious pattern." Thus, the *sala* is seen to combine the functions of the modern-day living room and bedroom (ibid.).

The above characterization is in general applicable to the households defined or inferred in Sectors D, H, I, and K at Pampa Grande (bounded Structure with single access and at least one each of a *sala, cocina,* and *deposito*). The best-documented households at Pampa Grande are found in Compound 38, Sector H (Figs. 7.29, 7.30). It is strategically situated next to the large plaza that served as the nodal point for a network of streets that linked the Great Compound on the one hand and Sector H, the Southern Pediment, and the outside (via Quebrada IV) on the other. The compound had a single narrow entrance only accessible to those coming through Pathway 1. Even before excavation began, it was apparent that the internal layout of the compound was planned. The central corridor bipartitioned the enclosure, regulated internal traffic, and served as the reference point in the construction of over twenty Rooms and Anterooms. On the basis of the strategic placement, planned internal layout, solid wall construction, and controlled access, the compound was hypothesized as the residence of the administrators of human and llama traffic through the nearby plaza and craft production area in Sector H.

In terms of access patterns and wall construction sequences (as defined by later systematic rubble clearing), four Structures (*x*Rms + *y*ARms; Fig. 7.29) were discerned. Structure A consisted of Rms 10 and 18 and ARms 12/19, 11, and 13, while Structure B encompassed Rms 23 and 31 and ARms 14, 17, 24, 30–33, 35, and 38. Rm 21, contiguous to both Structures A and B, apparently had special significance for the enclosure residents. It was built independently and with its own entry and series of low terraces subdividing the plastered floor surface. The retention walls of the terraces were adobe brick, while most other walls were built of fieldstones. Plas-

ter on an adobe wall face still retained dark red paint and traces of yellow. The room was clean and well maintained, yielding two fineware bottles and no domestic artifacts or refuse.

Subsequent contiguous-room excavation of approximately 85 percent of the compound clearly showed that the composition and distribution of artifacts and floor features had the same four groupings (Fig. 7.30). For example, we noted that each group had two kinds of storage rooms situated farthest away from the entry to the residences. Larger (ca. 9–14 m²) rooms with packed earthen floors were covered by large broken urns (ca. 65–100 cm high and 50–75 cm in diameter; locally known as *tinajas* or *porrones*) and jars that were probably used for the storage of grains, water, and *chicha* made in the nearby RRoom 8. The bases of many of these vessels were found in regularly spaced conical depressions on the floors. Such placement would have kept these vessels upright and helped preserve their contents through contact with the cool earth. Adhered to the interior of some urn bottoms was a white powdery substance suspected of being *chicha* residue.

In contrast, smaller, carefully built and plastered rooms (as small as 1.2 by 1.3 m) with clean raised floors and/or high and narrow thresholds probably held clothes or other valued perishables that required protection from moisture and/or pests.

A firepit on packed dirt floor that was associated with llama bones, maize cobs and other food remains, a *batán*, large river cobbles with battered ends, and a set of bowls and *ollas*, some with sooted exteriors—altogether indicating food preparation—was situated close to the inferred liquid/grain storerooms. Each residence also contained at least one spacious, clean, and plastered split-floor Room or Anteroom, physically and functionally equivalent to what Bawden (1982b) called the *salas*. Fineware ceramics (such as painted and reduced-ware stirrup-spout bottles, reduced-ware serving bowls, and a painted *florero*) and face-neck jars were found in these *salas*. Rm 16 even had a series of three "benches" at the east end that seemed too narrow to have provided seating and that may have functioned as an al-

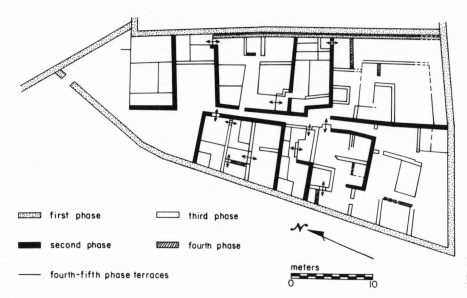

first phase   third phase

second phase   fourth phase

fourth-fifth phase terraces

N

meters
0   10

Figure 7.29. Wall abutment pattern of Compound 38, Sector H, showing four Structures.

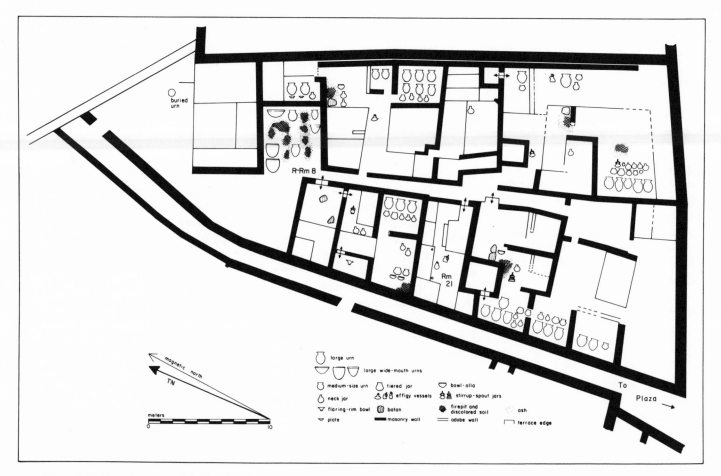

magnetic north

TN

meters
0   10

buried urn

R-Rm 8

Rm 21

To Plaza

⬭ large urn

large wide-mouth urns

medium-size urn   tiered jar   bowl-olla

neck jar   effigy vessels   stirrup-spout jars

flaring-rim bowl   batan   firepit and discolored soil   ash

plate   masonry wall   adobe wall   terrace edge

Figure 7.30. Floor features and artifacts in Compound 38, Sector H, showing four groupings that coincide with the Structures delineated in the preceding figure.

tar. Presumably, wider benches were used for sleeping and other stationary activities (e.g., eating, conversation).

Overall, as with the residences identified at Galindo, basic residential units have the same discrete components (the *depositos*, *cocina*, and *sala*), with each containing its distinctive assemblage of domestic material remains. In addition, the relatively high status of the residents hypothesized earlier on the basis of architectural and locational factors was supported by the discovery of not only a handful of high-quality ceramics but also of Rm 21 and an area dedicated to *chicha*-making, presumably for the benefit of the residents within the enclosure. Rm 21 may have been used as a formal setting for meetings between the residents and outsiders. Shared access to these specialized rooms suggests that the residents were bound together not only by their social position but perhaps even by kinship, ethnicity, and/or duties. Given the relative abundance of Mochica fineware decorated with ideologically charged motifs (even faces on jars are purely Mochica in style), residents were probably Mochica in ethnicity, while at least some of the daytime workers in the nearby workshops were not (see below and Chapter 8). As noted earlier, the residents' role in the state administrative system is suggested by the planned layout and strategic location of the compound.

Additional support for the above inference regarding the social position of the compound residents comes from examination of intrasite variation in construction quality (e.g., extent of wall and floor plastering, wall width, use of adobe brick versus fieldstone), total floor surface area, degree of formality and planning, and abundance of fineware ceramics. In this respect, it is critical that we examine the situation in the Southern Pediment.

As emphasized earlier, Quebrada IV was not only the main street connecting the center of the site with the outside, but also the single most important physical and social boundary of the site, serving as an effective physical and symbolic statement of the social gulf between the opposing banks. For the residents of the Southern Pediment, the Great Compound with its massive encircling walls and towering

Huaca Fortaleza was probably an awe-inspiring, constant reminder of their relatively low position within the existing social order.

Unfortunately, much of the Southern Pediment has not yet been mapped or excavated; our knowledge of the area is largely derived from surface inspection and mapping and test excavations in Sectors K and I (Figs. 7.9, 7.10). Nonetheless, it is quite evident that the fan-shaped Southern Pediment (ca. 650 m east-west and 400 m north-south) as a whole represents the largest expanse of architectural buildup at the site. Though the southern portion of the pediment manifests evidence of Chimú occupation, it is likely that it overlies earlier Moche V occupation. An estimated 70 percent of the pediment surface (Sectors J through M) is occupied by SIARs and MLDs, with walled-in compounds accounting for the remainder. Only the relatively small and scattered areas surrounding Compounds 11–18 (Figs. 7.1, 7.9) in the northern portion of the site are comparable in regard to the density of MLDs and SIARs.

There are both artifactual and architectural indications that the residents of the SIARs occupied the lowest social class at Pampa Grande. Relative to the central Sectors, the range of ceramic forms is limited, and fineware ceramics, such as modeled effigy vessels, painted stirrup-spout bottles, *floreros*, and reduced-ware serving bowls, are quite rare. Large oxidized storage vessels, jars decorated primarily with simple pinched and/or incised faces, and cooking *ollas* predominate the ceramic inventory. In test excavations in Sector K by M. Shimada, fineware ceramics, such as painted bottle fragments, were found only in subfloor fill.

The commonly found unslipped jars with highly simplified "human" faces, produced by pinching with fingers, reed-punched circles, crude incisions, and gouging, pertain to the Gallinazo stylistic tradition (compare Figs. 7.31 and 7.32). It is suggested that through control of the valley water supply, the Moche V polity at Pampa Grande forced relocation of mid- to lower-valley Gallinazo farmers for on-site labor service. Their exploitation may have already started with late Moche IV.

Given the abundance and distribution of these face-neck jars, the Southern Pediment seems to have been largely occupied by the Gallinazo farmers.

During surface survey in 1973 and 1975, we were struck by the relative abundance of donut-stones, chipped and ground choppers, and quartzite cobbles with battered ends in Sectors I, L, and M. The last two lithics most likely were used for food preparation, while the first may have served as the heads of clod-busters (see Chapter 8). As a generalization, SIARs and MLDs on the pediment represent the lowest-quality architecture found at the site. Architectural divisions are small; for example, the floor surfaces (both roofed and unroofed areas) of two partially excavated residences in Sector K are 68 (5.4 by 12.6 m) and 76 m² (10 by 7.6 m). These figures are only half to one-third the size of three of the four residences identified in Compound 38. Bearing in mind the small size of our sample, my impression from surface survey is that floor surfaces in Sector K residences are typical of or even at the large end of SIAR size on the Southern Pediment.

An examination of construction techniques and materials reinforces the above impression. The unmodified fieldstone walls are relatively thin, typically 30–35 cm thick, often curving or sinuous. No adobe structures have been found, though occasionally isolated bricks are found mixed among fieldstones. SIARs and MLDs show no apparent overall planning in their internal layout. But, as with the case of Sector K (Fig. 7.10), the location of SIARs and MLDs appears to have been either predetermined or influenced by the placement of rectangular walled compounds and streets. The perimeters of Sectors J and K are largely defined by straight pathways, while in Sectors L and M, pathways are quite narrow (often 70–80 cm in width) and sinuous, having been built on the banks of narrow, shallow gullies.

This difference between Sectors J and K on the one hand and L and M on the other may well be due to the possibility that at least the central portions of the former Sectors were used as the loci of small-scale craft production. Each area has an inferred small storage cell (partially built of adobe

bricks; 3.5 by 4.2 m in size) attached to a solidly built masonry building (6.9 by 11.8 m; wall width of 70–80 cm) with no apparent ground-level entry (Structures 8 and 14 in Sector K—see Fig. 7.10). In Sector J, a suspected storage structure was partially excavated, revealing a series of rectangular internal subdivisions (Fig. 7.33). Two of the cells contained large earthen urns and face-neck jars set into the earthen floor, suggesting storage of liquids. Unlike the three groups of formal storage facilities built exclusively of adobe bricks with closely supervised access in the central Sectors (Chapter 8), Sector J and K storage buildings may not have been under state management. Even with the inferred presence of craft production, on the Southern Pediment there are no readily apparent indications of high-level concern with controlling traffic, such as multilevel terraces or small platforms near pathway junctures, that we commonly see in the central Sectors. Given the inferred nature of the Southern Pediment residents, they may have been controlled by local leaders (perhaps non-Mochica) incorporated into the city.

In notable contrast to the relative freedom of movement within the pediment, communication between the pediment and the remainder of the site was evidently tightly controlled. The northern edge of the pediment, overlooking Quebrada IV, was faced with boulders to create a clifflike barrier some 3–5 m in height. The only direct access to the pediment identified thus far is a ramp situated right across from the south entrance to Sector H (Fig. 7.17), which in turn eventually allowed traffic to reach the south entry of the Great Compound. Importantly, traffic ascending the ramp immediately faced the narrow entrance to Compound 22 with its centrally placed multitiered platform mound. The compound occupied the critical point for control of the street network that covered much of the Southern Pediment. For example, the Circum–Quebrada IV street was the principal east-west route (Fig. 7.9). The strategic placement, coupled with the large-scale use of adobe bricks for the construction of the platform and enclosure walls, suggests the presence of state administrators at Compound 22. In other words,

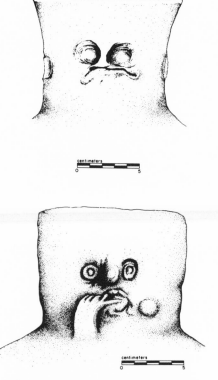

Figure 7.31. Examples of the unslipped jars with pinched, incised, and/or gouged faces common in the Southern Pediment. Though technically simple and restricted, the sizes, shapes, and nature of the faces thus made are quite diverse.

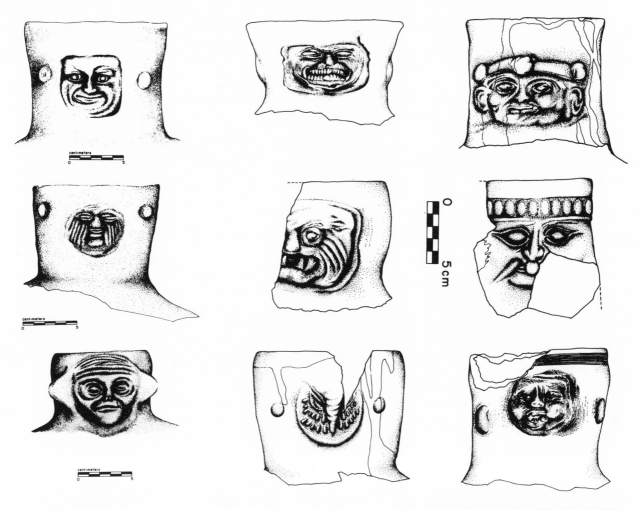

Figure 7.32. Examples of the slipped, plain, or burnished jars with press-mold–made faces common in the central Sectors of the site.

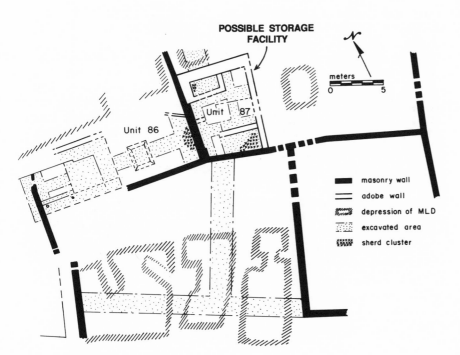

Figure 7.33. Inferred communal storage facility and surrounding structures in Sector J.

by natural and artificial means, inferred low-status, relocated farmers occupying SIARs and MLDs were clearly segregated from much of the remainder of the site and their movements controlled by the state. These commoners from the Southern Pediment are believed to have been directed by the state to serve in much of the documented craft production and related support activities (e.g., transport of raw materials and finished products, and food and drink preparation) in Sector H. Quebrada IV may have been the functional equivalent of Bawden's conception of the massive wall that encircled the base of Cerro Galindo as a means of segregating Residential Area B.

Our understanding of the social significance of the Southern Pediment would not be complete without an appreciation of Sector I with its five contiguous rectangular walled-in enclosures (Figs. 7.9, 7.34). Its placement next to Compound 22 and the Circum–Quebrada IV street seems critical in this respect. The five compounds are enclosed on three sides in the form of a U. Though their perimeters are not straight, they are substantial in size and defined by masonry walls with boulder foundation and mixed rock/earth core that originally stood at least 4–5 m high. Adobe constructions are conspicuously absent. The street served as the north perimeter of these compounds. As seen in Figures 7.9 and 7.34, each compound had three to four major subdivisions, with a relatively small platform mound occupying the center of the innermost subdivision. The mounds are largely built of rubble on stone foundations. In terms of basal dimensions (ca. 3–5 m to a side) and height (ca. 3 m), the mounds occupied the fourth and lowest tier of the intrasite platform mound hierarchy. Sector I compounds ranging in size from approximately 95 by 70 to 50 by 50 m also occupy the fourth and lowest tier of the sitewide compound hierarchy in terms of surface area occupied.

Other subdivisions are occupied by SIARs that show no apparent planning. Although no excavations have been carried out in any of these compounds, the composition and nature of surface artifacts are quite similar to those found in the SIARs

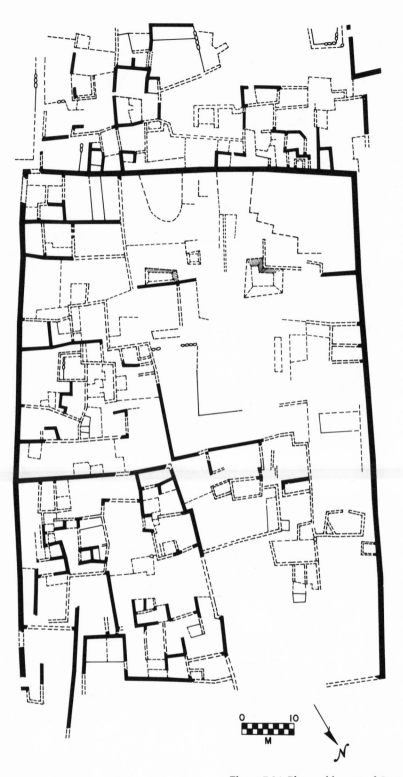

Figure 7.34. Plane-table map of Compound 7 in Sector I. Note the internal subdivisions, small platform mound, and SIARs.

and MLDs immediately outside the compounds with the important difference of having some fragments of Moche V painted fineware ceramics. These fragments show predominantly repetitious geometric motifs rather than recognizable thematic representations. Just across Quebrada IV in Sector H, Moche V painted ceramics found on the surface and in my excavations show a notably greater percentage of readily identifiable representational paintings, such as weapons-and-shield motifs and battles between mythical figures (Fig. 7.35; see Chapter 9). In fact, Moche V fineware ceramics are clearly most abundant in the central portion of the site encompassing Sectors A, B, C, D, and H, and major walled-in compounds north of Sector A.

On the basis of the observed architectural and artifactual patterns, it is hypothesized that these Sector I compounds were the residences of local, non-Mochica leaders and their retainers incorporated into the city of Pampa Grande. The situation seems akin to the Inca practice of handing out selected status items to subjugated local leaders to symbolize their status and relationship with the dominant state. The Inca state seems to have controlled the distribution of sumptuary goods such as fancy ceramics and imported shell (e.g., see D'Altroy and Earle 1985; Murra 1975). At a community near the Inca regional administrative center of Huánuco Pampa, one of the few distinguishing marks of the subjugated local leader was the presence (though quite limited in quantity) of Inca-style ceramics (e.g., see Morris and Thompson 1970; see also Earle et al. 1987).

Overall, the Southern Pediment is seen as the residential zone of relocated local (Gallinazo in ethnicity) farmers who oc-cupied the lowest social class of the society at Pampa Grande and were supervised by their traditional leaders situated in the Sector I compounds. They were physically segregated from the sources of wealth and status concentrated in the central Sector of the site by Quebrada IV and the state control of the Circum–Quebrada IV street.

Perhaps what distinguishes the society at Pampa Grande from earlier Mochica settlements is the presence of inferred intermediate-level state administrators residing in numerous roughly rectangular enclosures scattered to the west and southwest of the Great Compound, such as Compounds 1–3 and 19 (Figs. 7.36, 7.37). These enclosures share certain basic qualities: (1) they are relatively isolated by distance (not by major natural or artificial boundaries as in the case of the Southern Pediment) from the sources of wealth and status concentrated in the center of the

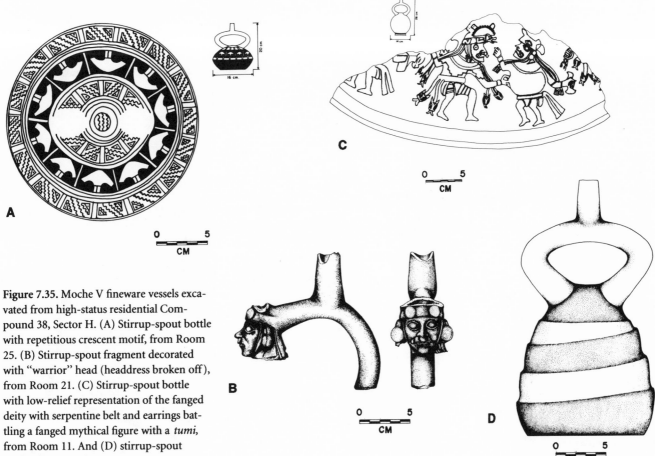

Figure 7.35. Moche V fineware vessels excavated from high-status residential Compound 38, Sector H. (A) Stirrup-spout bottle with repetitious crescent motif, from Room 25. (B) Stirrup-spout fragment decorated with "warrior" head (headdress broken off), from Room 21. (C) Stirrup-spout bottle with low-relief representation of the fanged deity with serpentine belt and earrings battling a fanged mythical figure with a *tumi*, from Room 11. And (D) stirrup-spout bottle, from Room 17.

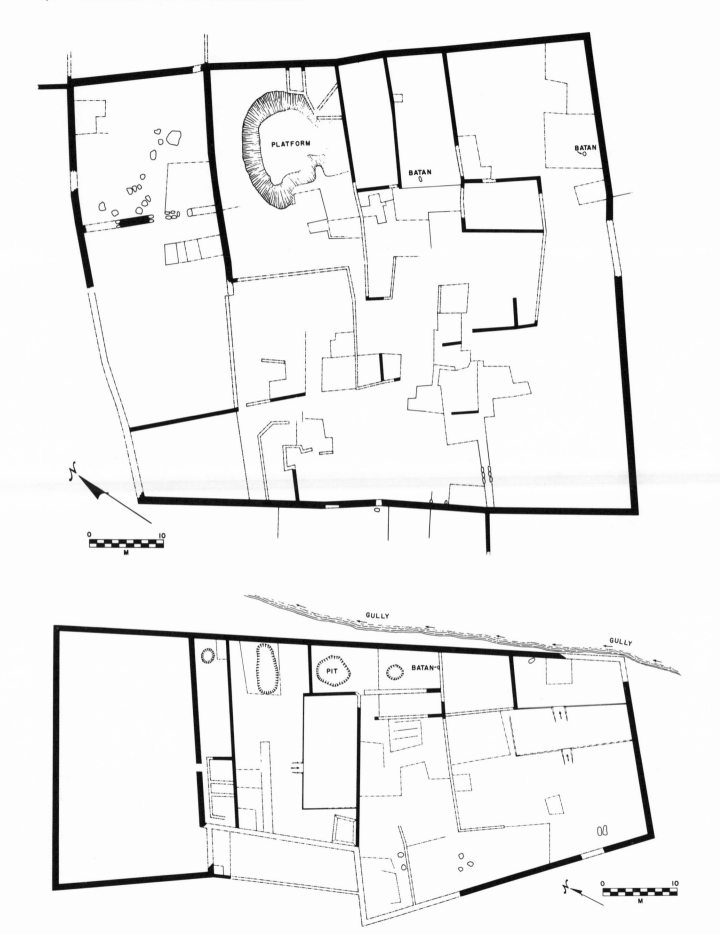

site; (2) they have typical dimensions of approximately 50–60 by 60–70 m (ca. 3,000–4,000 m²), much like the five compounds composing Sector I, and so belong to the fourth and lowest tier of the intrasite hierarchy of rectangular enclosures at Pampa Grande; (3) they are all built of fieldstone masonry, unlike the enclosures occupying the first three tiers (Great Compound, Sector B compound, and Deer and Spondylus houses); (4) they have three- to four-part internal subdivisions, often with a large hierarchical terrace dominating one such division; (5) they contain no platform mounds; (6) where perimeter walls are well preserved, only one entry is identified; (7) each is surrounded by an apparently discrete cluster of SIARs; (8) surface inspections show scatters of domestic wares (large storage urns, ollas, and face-neck jars) and some deposits of dark gray ashy soil often with tiny *Donax* shells and broken llama bones; and (9) rare Moche V painted ceramic fragments (predominantly bottles) observed on the surface are decorated with abstract geometric designs.

A partial excavation of Compound 3 (Fig. 7.37) by Luís Watanabe revealed internal subdivisions that reflect functional differences, with one area (containing two copper *tumis*) emphasizing domestic activities and another dominated by a hierarchical terrace. In addition, there is, overall, little architectural and refuse buildup. The relatively high status of the occupants is suggested by the spacious internal subdivisions and the terrace mentioned above.

Some of these features are shared by the Sector I compounds. At the same time, there are differences believed to be indicative of the nature of the occupants. In particular, we should note their placement in the northern half of the site, the conspicuous absence of platform mounds, and the absence of any major natural or artificial barrier to the center of the site. That the platform mound, a traditional religious-political emblem of the Mochica elite, is replaced by the hierarchical terrace seems to reflect broader processes of increasing political centralization and secularization.

A similar phenomenon was documented at Galindo by Bawden (1977: 41–126, 1982a: 293–304). He recognized im-

portant structural, locational, and artifactual differences between two main classes of "formal architecture," the platform mounds within or outside of walled-in enclosures, and the walled-in enclosures without platform mounds (which he calls *cercaduras*; Fig. 7.38). In regard to the platform mounds at Galindo, Bawden (1982a: 295) observed that "when the Huacas of Galindo are compared with their predecessors in Moche culture, it becomes clear that significant changes have occurred in this architectural form"; while Moche V examples at Galindo remain freestanding with a nearly identical configuration to earlier *huacas,* they are minuscule, with "mere rudimentary forms" of the preceding structures. While arguing that the *huaca* remained the symbol of Mochica social integration, he concludes that "the appearance of an elite residential complex, incorporating the huaca . . . [reflects] functional diversification associated with this architectural form . . . [and] increase in the importance of secular authority over sacred" (ibid., 296).

The inferred sharing of administrative authority is supported by the presence of a previously unseen architectural form, the *cercadura*. As seen in Figure 7.38, Cercadura A, an adobe compound measuring 170 by 135 m, shows functionally differentiated internal divisions, with one area used for cooking and another for "more formal activities associated with the terrace architecture." Many fine pottery and copper pieces, as well as some decorated textiles, were found inside. Near this compound was a cluster of "elaborate residential structures," perhaps occupied by those assisting with activities in the compound (ibid., 297, 299).

In many respects, Cercadura A closely resembles Deer House at Pampa Grande, for example, in internal components, adobe constructions, overall sizes, and the high quality of artifacts found within them.

On the other hand, the smaller masonry compounds in the northern and western peripheries of Pampa Grande are quite similar to Cercadura C at Galindo (Fig. 7.39). The latter is a masonry construction measuring 60 by 45 m that contained kitchen refuse and a large hierarchical ter-

Figure 7.36. Plane-table map of Compound 1, a masonry rectangular compound at Pampa Grande partially excavated by Luís Watanabe. Redrawn from the original map by Kent C. Day.

Figure 7.37. Plane-table map of Compound 3, a masonry rectangular compound at Pampa Grande that is inferred to have served as the residence and office of a secular administrator. Redrawn from an original map by Kent C. Day.

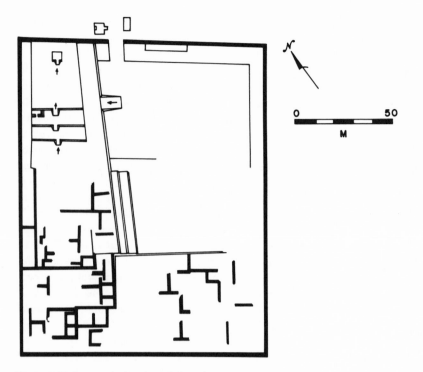

Figure 7.38. Isometric drawing of *Cercadura* A complex at Galindo. Redrawn from Fig. 12.3 in Bawden 1982a: 298.

race. Even its relative location within the site is similar. It is peripherally situated at the southwest base of Cerro Caballo Muerto (Hillside B) away from the center of the site and the inferred residential zone of the commoners on Hillside A (the west base of Cerro Galindo). Overall, Bawden (1982a: 317–318) sees the above innovative architectural forms as an expression of emergent secularized administration, an opinion shared by this author.

In summary, the evidence presented suggests that at Pampa Grande there were at least the following four social classes:

(1) The highest and probably smallest class is hypothesized to have overseen performance of exclusive rituals within the Great Compound that sanctified and dispersed elite religious and political dogma and made decisions relevant to the state political economy, both of which were underwritten by status goods believed to have been kept in the large formal storage facilities within the Compound. This group may have resided in the Palatial Room Complex atop Huaca Fortaleza, as Haas

(1985) suggested, or in the adobe structures at the northern end of the Great Compound where formal storage facilities were located and goods and services in Sector D were accessible.

(2) The second group, exemplified by the Deer and Spondylus House elite residents, were inferred to have directed the procurement of raw materials for and production of status items that allowed the operation of the state political economy. In other words, these high-level administrators were probably concerned with the overall logistics and operation of the production setup of certain status items.

(3) The third-class members are seen to have been engaged in the actual, day-to-day implementation of the decisions made by the first two classes; they carried out face-to-face supervision of dispersed workshops and their operations. It is likely that their membership may not have been as exclusive as the first two (which were perhaps hereditary), as they were hypothesized to have been largely recruited on the basis of demand, allowing upward social

mobility for individuals of Mochica and even non-Mochica ethnicities. The inferred local elite occupying the Sector I compounds, as well as the residents of Compound 38 in Sector H, are assigned to this class.

(4) The lowest and largest class recognized are the residents of the Southern Pediment, who are believed to have been primarily relocated local (probably mostly non-Mochica) farmers and, to a lesser extent, craft specialists. They are the work force that daily commuted to dispersed workshops as close as Sectors J and K and as far as Sector H and beyond.

Interestingly, Bawden (1982b) also recognized four distinct social classes present at Galindo on the basis of the systematic analysis of households described earlier. He found that floor sizes of the *salas* formed distinct and quantitatively meaningful clusters defined by the relative locations of residences within the site. *Sala* size also correlated well with differential distribution of status items such as fine ceramics and silver (ibid., 174–175). On the other hand, the *deposito* and *cocina* sizes were not good discriminants.

Thus, as with Pampa Grande, the close relationship among architectural form and content and intrasite location was the basis for the delineation of social classes at Galindo. The lowest class occupied the smallest, least carefully planned and constructed, and most crowded residences on the steep, rocky west slopes of Cerro Galindo encircled by a massive wall (Residential Area B). There is no evidence that the residents here controlled any economic activity (ibid.). Residential Area C, occupying the rough terrain in the upper reaches of the Quebrada Caballo Muerto, is characterized as intermediate between Residential Areas A and B in regard to size, construction quality, and formal regularity. Artifact composition of Area C is much like that of Area B, but with some fine ceramics. Bawden (ibid.) suggests that Area C residents may have been functionally tied to the formal storage facilities found directly above them.

Area A was occupied by a privileged class who enjoyed freedom of movement, spacious and regularly laid out quarters, relatively rich artifact content, and easy access to water. This area contained, among other structures, a specialized ceramic workshop, "re-distributive centers for subsistence items," llama corrals, and small-scale storage facilities (ibid., 176). Overall, Bawden regarded Area A residents as directly involved in the economic functioning of the settlement. Finally, Area D, occupying the mouth of the *quebrada,* possessed the largest and best constructed residences (ibid., 177), displaying an unmatched degree of internal formality and elaboration, including a small dais atop a bench in one structure. Overall, the physical connection between the finest residences and a major *cercadura* is believed to indicate that Area D residents were the ruling elite and the highest social class of the site (ibid.).

C. Summary

It is evident that findings from the contemporaneous site of Galindo effectively complement those of Pampa Grande. Intra- and intersite architectural and artifactual differences and similarities lead us to conclude that the proliferation of innovative architectural forms at both sites reflects the emergence of secular administration and attendant diversification of administrative authority. More specifically, the small rectangular masonry compounds scattered in the northern and western peripheries of Pampa Grande are believed to have been residences of low-level state administrators who emerged as a part of unprecedented state and city formation. The surrounding clusters of the SIARs may be seen as residences of their retainers. Inferred low-level administrators may well have been the ones charged with the day-to-day supervision of craft production in Sector D and other state concerns.

We are still unclear as to the origin of the compounds. However, the impressive diversity of size and associated structures, not to mention form, argue strongly against the idea of an imposition by the Wari invaders of rigidly defined architectural forms and associated sociopolitical organization. In addition, we found the tradition of Mochica monumental platform mounds clearly represented at Huaca Fortaleza inside the Great Compound,

which should force a major revision of the Virú Valley model.

The emergence of the Moche V nascent state and urban capital was a process of adaptation to stressful conditions, a rational solution to perceived needs. Yet the scale and rapidity of population and material concentration at Pampa Grande had numerous major social and political consequences; it was an unprecedented situation that required similarly unprecedented measures. The establishment of a new urban capital required not only population resettlement and shifts in land use but also the long-term massive mobilization of resources. These measures led to the permanent centralization of power and the establishment of new administrative and social norms and institutions, as well as some measures of coercion critical to the state formation. During the establishment of the capital, the traditional Mochica leadership associated with the ceremonial center was transformed into a nascent urban state, with its political power largely transferred to secular administrators. Undoubtedly many Mochica and non-Mochica individuals were recruited into the emerging state administrative apparatus, particularly in its lower levels, although data from Huaca Fortaleza suggest that some of the power remained with the traditional (more theocratic) elite. This transformation probably brought about the implementation of various measures to reinforce the power and status of the individuals who occupied higher-level positions in the form of exaggerated architectural differences as well as clear-cut bipartition of the site, with the lower-class masses largely confined to the Southern Pediment.

Pampa Grande may be seen as a ceremonial city in that institutions associated with the traditional ceremonial center provided the organizational framework for the emergence of Pampa Grande. Huaca Fortaleza was essentially a ceremonial structure. Various qualities of the *huaca,* including its immense size unmatched in the Moche V world, were critical in assigning Moche V capital status to Pampa Grande. Other features that justified this attribution include the overall planned layout of the city and the unprecedented architectural diversity, nucleation, and expanse (I. Shi-

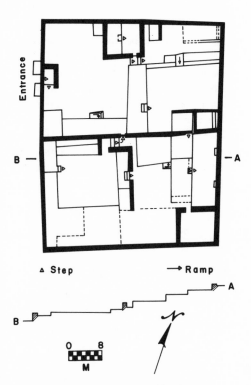

Figure 7.39. Plan map and profile of *Cercadura* C at Galindo. Redrawn from Fig. 12.4 in Bawden 1982a: 301.

mada 1982: 155). At the same time, Pampa Grande may also be envisioned as a viable "city-state" much like those seen in the contemporaneous Maya civilization of the Yucatan Peninsula. There are indications of some important differences among the valleys that shared the Moche V stylistic and ideological tradition (Chapter 9). In spite of its clear-cut dominance of the regional settlement hierarchy, it is questionable if Moche V Pampa Grande really controlled valleys beyond the Zaña–Lambayeque–La Leche region.

It should be emphasized here that the social reconstruction presented in this chapter consists of inferences that require future testing and refinement. Though independent research at the contemporaneous sites of Galindo and Pampa Grande resulted in similar reconstructions—in many ways, surprisingly so—much of the Pampa Grande data mustered here were extracted from surface surveys and coincidental findings of fieldwork that was not directed at social issues. Additional fieldwork comparable in nature to the systematic study carried out by Bawden at Galindo is needed for Pampa Grande. For now, the social reconstruction offered here serves as a working model.

It is also my impression that the social model offered in this chapter is too simplistic; for example, we cannot definitively characterize the social class of the craft workers in Sector D or the inferred retainers residing in the SIARs surrounding many walled-in compounds. There is the important possibility of dual social organization at Pampa Grande. Huacas 1 and 2 or even the north-south division of Pampa Grande may be viewed as symbolizing the inequality of upper and lower moieties that have been argued for late pre-Hispanic societies on the North Coast (e.g., Netherly 1977, 1984, 1990).

Though a suggestive lead has been offered for the identification of architectural expressions of such duality (e.g., Netherly

and Dillehay 1986; Anders 1986), the issue is quite complex. Whether explicitly acknowledged or not, the search for such architectural manifestations begins with the premise that the moiety system indeed existed in the time and place under study. By the same token, test implications of the dual social organization hypothesis are often not adequately specified and plausible alternative hypotheses not given due attention. For example, the pair of Huaca del Sol and Huaca de la Luna mounds was interpreted as having different functions, with the former being the "focus of community life" and "actual interface between ruling class and populace" and the latter "the residence and audience chambers of the ruler" (T. Topic 1982: 278). Was the inferred functional differentiation part of the dual social organization and associated dual leadership? If so, we would expect the asymmetrical political power of the upper and lower moiety leaders to be manifest in the size of the labor force and material resources that could be marshaled; that is, a more powerful upper moiety leader would have had access to laborers from both lower and upper moieties, while a lower moiety leader would have had access to only the laborers of his own moiety (Netherly 1977, 1984, 1990). This would lead us to expect a certain overlap in marks found on adobe bricks found at Huaca del Sol and Huaca de la Luna. Published marks from these two *huacas* (Hastings and Moseley 1975) show this to be the case. In other words, the possibility of archaeological identification of pre-Inca dual social organization definitely exists, but a better methodology must be developed nevertheless, such as the one employed by Cavallaro (1988) in his analysis of the *ciudadelas*, the "royal compounds" at the Chimú capital of Chan Chan. For Pampa Grande, a more extensive study of Huacas 1 and 2 and associated structures may help us clarify the issue of social duality.

8

Urban Subsistence and Economy at Moche V Pampa Grande

This chapter addresses the basic questions of how city residents lived, what they ate, what they produced in the city for their material comfort, who made these objects, and how their production and distribution were managed.

1. Subsistence Items: Riches of the Land and Sea

A. "Garbage" and the Nature of Organic Remains at Pampa Grande

Archaeologists are, in the true sense of the term, "garbage hounds," and it was in refuse and middens that we looked to find evidence of the subsistence and economic bases of Moche V Pampa Grande. Though the aridity of the North Coast allows relatively good preservation of organic remains, the task was not an easy one. For example, we searched for kitchens with primary-context food refuse and associated storerooms. Even after learning to identify and predict kitchen contexts, we found little primary refuse.

The overwhelming portion of organic refuse we examined was derived from various secondary contexts. Much of the daily refuse was apparently incorporated into construction fill, judging by its pervasive occurrence in architecture. We also had to bear in mind the refuse we did not find and ancient behaviors that may have distorted or differentially affected what we found in our excavations. For example, numerous discolored patches on floors may reflect pervasive small-scale control of garbage by burning, as is widespread today in Peru. In addition, we had to consider the key garbage-disposal role of domesticated animals such as dogs, guinea pigs, and muscovy ducks that were probably kept by numerous households and would potentially have consumed most vegetal remains as well as some bones.

Our excavations show that garbage disposal and movement was probably confined within the Sector level, with the exception of the large quantities needed for major constructions such as Huaca Fortaleza. Evidence for this localized refuse disposal is presented later.

Even carefully designed archaeological sampling and recovery employing "window" screening and flotation cannot deal with problems stemming from certain cooking and eating patterns. For example, there is the problem of identifying and assessing the importance of small fish such as anchovy that could have been slow-cooked and eaten whole, including bones. Certain seaweeds that today are still gathered seasonally by certain highland groups using llama caravans (Masuda 1985) would have been entirely consumed, leaving no remains. Coprolites (fossilized human or animal feces) that could have helped us reconstruct their diet were not found, unfortunately. Isotopic analysis (e.g., carbon and nitrogen) of human bones to determine the relative importance of different types of food was not carried out.

Other preservation problems must be considered. Most of the preserved plant remains recovered at Pampa Grande were charred. Though it often distorts shape and size, burning improves the chances for preservation. Still, preserved quantities do not reflect their real importance in the Mochica diet.[110]

To counter these difficulties stemming from the lack of preservation and identification of primary refuse, two kinds of sampling were employed at Pampa Grande: random sampling of subfloor fill within each Sector, and nonrandom, purposive sampling of contemporaneous activity areas within clearly defined architectural contexts.[111] The former provided general background information, while the latter offered in-depth understanding of specific situations. The following comments on the significance (economic or otherwise) of plants are based primarily on those found in primary contexts. Accompanying inventories of subsistence items represent both primary and secondary contexts.

B. Plant Resources

A wide range of plants was represented at the site (Table 9), including the key staple crops of maize, beans, and squash, as well as tomatoes, chili peppers, avocados, peanuts, and lúcumas (Lucuma obovata). Cultivated nonsubsistence items utilized by the urban residents included cotton, gourds, and cane (Gynerium sagittatum). However, with the exception of the concentrations of charred cotton found in Deer House and Compound 16, and maize kernels and beans found in formal storage cells in Sectors D and H, the overall quantity of recovered remains was quite small. Rather, plant remains were widely found in loose architectural fill mixed with sherds, shell, and bone, both burnt and unburnt mixed. Important root crops such as yuca

(Manihot esculenta, Fig. 8.1; also wild yuca, Apodanthera biflora), sweet potato (Ipomoea batatas; one modeled ceramic vessel found in Sector D at Pampa Grande), achira (Canna edulis), and potato (Solanum tuberosum), though often modeled or painted in Mochica ceramics (e.g., Herrera 1942; Tello 1938; Yacovleff and Herrera 1934–1935) were not identified.

There is an impressive number of ají pepper varieties, and there may have been just as diverse a range of other condiments available to please the palates of the Mochica people. As these were most likely used in small quantities, thoroughly processed (minced or pulverized), and/or digested, they are rarely found in archaeological contexts. These and other "missing" herbs were likely to have been crucial also in folk medicine, rituals, and making textile dyes.

The sweet, ripe pods of wild algarrobo trees (also rich in vitamins and protein) currently provide fodder for a wide range of domesticated animals and for making a molasses-like syrup and alcoholic beverage. At various pre-Hispanic sites in the Lambayeque region, algarrobo seeds and pods are found both mixed with and inside llama dung, which takes the form of small pellets, attesting to its widespread use as fodder (Shimada and Shimada 1985: 15). At Moche V Pampa Grande too, the algarrobo was probably used as llama fodder.

The inventory of recovered plants presented in Table 9, then, must be regarded as a minimal list.[112] Also to be kept in mind is the possibility that seeds (e.g., cotton bolls, discussed later) recovered in containers and/or in exclusive architectural settings may reflect seed keeping for planting.

Maize was an essential crop throughout the Mochica sequence. Strong and Evans (1952: 131–138; also Towle 1952, 1961) at Huaca de la Cruz in the Virú Valley encountered the abundant remains of maize stalks, cobs, and shucks in their subfloor (Moche III–IV) refuse, as well as cane, yuca roots, potato vines, peanuts, lúcumas, gourds, guayabo (Psidium pyryferum), common beans, and cotton. Maize was also quite abundant among plant remains (associated with Moche III and IV ceramics) recovered from two cuts made at

Table 9. List of cultivated and wild plants identified in sampled contexts at Pampa Grande. After Table 5 in Shimada 1982: 251.

Capparidaceae	
Capparis angulata	*Zapote*
Cucurbitaceae	
Cucurbita maxima	Squash
Cucurbita sp.	
Gramineae	
Gynerium sagittatum	Cane, *caña brava*
Zea mays	Corn
Lauraceae	
Persea americana	Avocado
Leguminosae	
Arachis hypogaea	Peanut
Canavalia sp.	Bean
Phaseolus vulgaris	Common bean
Prosopis juliflora	*Algarrobo*
Malvaceae	
Gossypium sp.	Cotton
Myrtaceae	
Campomanesia lineatifolia	*Palillo* (guavalike fruit)
Psidium guajava	*Guava*
Sapotaceae	
Lucuma bifera	*Lúcuma*
Solanaceae	
Capsicum annuum	Chili pepper

the eastern edge of the top of the Huaca del Sol mound. S. Pozorski (1976: 121 and Table 15 in her Appendix I) found almost two hundred whole cobs and fragments, a close second to squash, the most abundant plant remains by volume. Cob size was relatively large (with a range of 30–116 mm in length and a mean of 54.1 on 35 specimens), and "kernel row numbers are also large as well as varied" (eight, ten, twelve, and fourteen rows), with ten rows being most common (based on 189 specimens; ibid., 122 and Tables 59 and 61 in her Appendix I). Other cultivated plant remains were cotton, gourds, peanuts, common beans, *ají* peppers, avocados, *pacaes* (*Inga feuillei*), guayabos, cansabocas (*Bunchosia armeniaca*), and *lúcumas*. Wilson (1988: 222, 338–342; also see 1981, 1983) suspects that the Moche III–IV "revolutionary change" in the Santa Valley settlement pattern and the opening of new areas for cultivation is related to the Mochica state's attempt to make the valley a "breadbasket"—to extract tribute in the form of food and industrial products (maize and cotton).

At Pampa Grande, maize kernels and cobs were also relatively abundant. Besides the homogeneous kernels recovered in quantity from burnt formal storage facili-

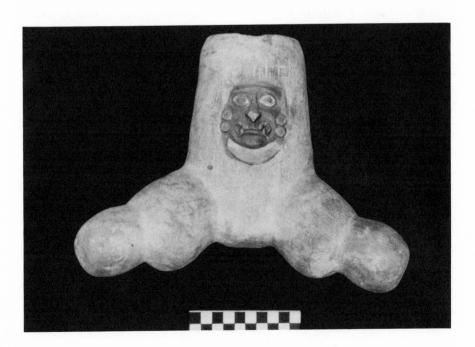

Figure 8.1. Moche IV vessel modeled as yuca. Amano Museum, Lima.

ties, cobs showing a wide range of row numbers (eight, ten, twelve, and fourteen, with about 60 percent of the fifty-one specimens showing ten rows; Fig. 8.2) and size were recovered from various contexts. This relative abundance was expected considering the importance of maize as food and as the main ingredient of chicha.

The inventory of plant remains from Pampa Grande is quite similar to those of cultivated plants recovered from the contemporaneous sites of Cañoncillo and Galindo. At Cañoncillo in the lower Jequetepeque Valley, S. Pozorski (1976: 254) identified only maize, lúcuma, and avocado. Charred maize cobs were quite common, while the fruits were rare. She reports that the "four whole burned cobs averaged 44.8 mm long by 10.5 mm in diameter, while the overall diameter of 38 cobs and fragments were 9.1 mm. The cob row number was highly variable, but most cobs had either 8 (21%), 10 (32%), or 12 (34%) rows."

Preservation of plants is poor at Galindo. Seven cuts, nonetheless, yielded a good range of plant remains, including cotton, gourds, squash, maize, common beans, lima beans, peanuts, avocados, pacae, guayabo, cansaboca, and lúcuma (ibid., 138 and tables in her Appendix I). This list essentially duplicates that of Huaca del Sol and Pampa Grande. S. Pozorski (ibid., 139) argues that "field grown cultigens are much more abundant in the sample than any of the tended fruits," and that the relative abundance of common beans and, in particular, maize may indicate "a special focus on these storable crops." In comparison with the sample from Huaca del Sol, the cob size did not differ much (sample of only six whole cobs from Galindo), while cob row numbers (based on 344 specimens) were less variable, with eight and ten rows nearly equally common and together accounting for over 90 percent of the Galindo sample (ibid., Tables 59 and 61 in her Appendix I). The limitations on plant remains discussed above make our attempt to document the expected impacts of late sixth-century severe droughts quite difficult. In addition, with precipitation returning to normal or even above-normal levels during much of the seventh century following the decades

of hardship, it is unlikely that the differently preserved plant remains would accurately reflect the impact of the droughts. Some of the Cucurbita sp. identified at Pampa Grande may well be calabash (Cucurbita moschata), which was described as having been emphasized during the drought at the South Coast site of La Tinguiña.

Overall, Moche V populations at Pampa Grande and Galindo continued to consume essentially the same variety of plants as earlier phases. The limited data on Mochica cultigens do not allow us to draw conclusions about diachronic trends or responses to drought. Similarly, a reliable projection of the relative economic importance of the constituent plants cannot yet be made.

C. Marine Resources

In spite of its inland location, a wide variety of marine resources—fish, shellfish, mammals, and birds—are represented at Pampa Grande (Table 10), affirming strong continuity in the importance of marine resources in Mochica subsistence and economy emphasized in Chapter 3. At the same time, respective quantities vary considerably, and the overall quantity in our sample of organic remains, if taken at face value, would indicate that marine resources were clearly secondary to llamas as a source of meat. It is difficult to determine the extent to which marine and freshwater resources are underrepresented in the archaeological record.

Freshwater foods such as catfish and crayfish (as big as 30–40 cm from head to tail) available from local rivers and irrigation canals would have complemented the above marine foods. Youths from the village of Pampa Grande today can still be seen fishing for them at nearby La Puntilla.

The ritual significance and hunting of sea lions and seals was discussed in Chapters 2 and 3. Penguins, sea lions, and seals, all represented by one or a few bones with definite butchering marks, occurred in mixed fill rather than specialized contexts (Shimada and Shimada 1981). Although sea lions and seals are known today mostly from southern Peru and Chile, this distribution seems more a function of intensive

hunting for hides, oil, and meat, particularly after the year 1700 (Gilmore 1950: 379). Early Colonial documents indicate that inhabitants of coastal Peru had long valued sea lions for their meat, which was boiled or charcoal broiled, and their oil, which was bottled for sale and tribute payment (Rostworowski 1981: 113).

D. Domesticated Animals

Protein from the preceding sources was supplemented by some hunting of wild game (e.g., viscacha, lizard [Holmberg 1957]; Table 11) and nearly the full range of domesticated Andean animals: dog, guinea pig, muscovy duck, and llama. In contrast to agricultural produce and marine products, these domesticated animals were easy to maintain (excepting llamas, they are all basically garbage-eaters), stable in the sense of offering year-round availability, and readily accessible, as they were probably kept on-site or close to the site (see below). With the possible exception of llama herds, these animals could be readily maintained by individual households.

Dog bones were most common after those of llamas and show butchering marks (Fig. 8.3) and several cases of modification into tools. At Galindo, dog bones were quite rare (S. Pozorski 1976: 136–137). Dogs depicted on Mochica painted ceramics are spotted. Modeled vessels excavated in Sector D (Fig. 8.4; Weiss 1976: 37) appear to depict hairless dogs with their characteristic face and body wrinkles. Ethnohistorical sources indicate that some populations within the Inca Empire still consumed dogs (including the hairless type) but that this custom was poorly regarded by the Inca (ibid., 38–39).

Muscovy ducks, which rarely take flight and fare well with minimum access to water, could have been kept by Pampa Grande households. On the North Coast and elsewhere, guinea pigs today are variously kept in cages, in room corners with grass piles, or under the ledges of split-level floors near or in kitchens where they scavenge on their own or are fed with the vegetal remains of food preparation. They were probably kept in much the same way in Moche V Pampa Grande. As their bones are quite small, they are typically not removed for cooking and are often gnawed

Table 10. List of shells identified in sampled contexts at Pampa Grande. Based on Table 7 in Shimada 1982: 252–253.

Amphineura (chiton)

Balanidae
  Balanus sp. (barnacle)

Buccinidae (whelk)
  Cantharus fusiformes
  Cantharus sp.

Cardiidae (cockles or heart clam)
  Mexicardia procera

Conidae (cone shell)
  Conus fergusoni

Donacidae (wedge clam)
  Donax peruvianus

Nassaridae (mud snail)
  Nassarius sp.

Naticidae (moon snail)
  Polinices sp.

Olividae (olive shell)
  Olivella columellaris

Pectinidae (scallop)
  Aequipecten sp.

Planorbidae
  cf. *Helisoma* pond snail

Semelidae (semele clam)
  Semele corrugata

Spondylidae (thorny oyster)
  Spondylus princeps

Thaididae (dog winkle)
  Thais chocolata
  Thais delessertiana

Trochidae (tegula top shell)
  Tegula sp.

Turbinidae (turban shell)
  Turbo sp.

Turridae (turrids)

Terrestrial gastropods
  cf. *Bostryx*   land snail
  cf. *Drymaeus*   land snail
  Scutalus sp.   land snail

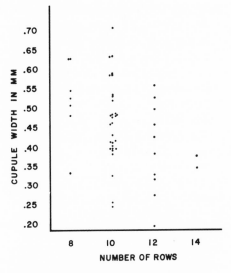

Figure 8.2. Graph showing number of rows and cupule width of maize cobs recovered at Pampa Grande. Most of the cobs recovered were burnt, and 20 percent (the estimated amount of shrinkage during carbonization) was added to the cupule width. Also, because cupule width varies on the cob, a series of measurements was taken for each specimen and the average used for the above graph.

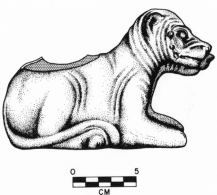

Figure 8.4. Double-chambered vessel from Sector D with realistic modeling of hairless dogs. Note their diagnostic wrinkled skin.

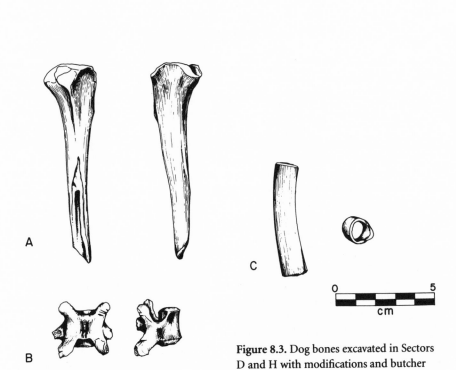

Figure 8.3. Dog bones excavated in Sectors D and H with modifications and butcher marks.

Table 11.　List of fauna identified in sampled contexts at Pampa Grande. Based on Table 6 in Shimada 1982: 252–253.

Mammals		
Marsupials		
Didelphidae		
Didelphis sp.	opossum	
Rodents		
Cricetidae		
cf. *Oryzomys* sp.	rice rat	
cf. *Sigmodon* sp.	cotton rat	
Caviidae		
Cavia porcellus	guinea pig	
Chinchillidae		
Lagidium peruanum	mountain viscacha	
Carnivores		
Canidae		
Canis familiaris	domestic dog	
Dusicyon sp.	fox	
cf. Otariidae or Phocidae	seal	
Artiodactyles		
Cervidae		
Odocoileus virginianus	white-tailed deer	
Camelidae		
Lama cf. *glama*	camelid (compare llama)	
Amphibians		
Salientia		
Bufonidae		
Bufo cf. *marinus* or *blombergi*	toad	
Ranidae		
cf. *Rana*	frog	
Reptiles		
Squamata		
Boidae		
Constrictor constrictor	boa constrictor	
Caudata		
Teidae		
Dicrodon guttulatum	lizard	

Birds	
Psittacidae	macaw
Columbidae	dove
Anatidae	duck
Cathartidae	
Coragyps atratus	black vulture
Sphenistidae	
Spheniscus humboldti	jack-ass penguin
Fish	
Carangidae	
cf. *Caranx*	pampano
Carcharhinidae	requiem shark
Clupeidae	
cf. *Sardinops*	sardine
Mugilidae	
Mugil sp.	mullet
Myliobatidae	ray
Pomadasyidae	
Anisotremus sp.	grunt
Rhinobatidae	angel shark
Sciaenidae	drum
Sciaena deliciosa	
Paralonchurus sp.	
Cynoscion sp.	
Bairdella sp.	
Sphyrnidae	
Sphyrna sp.	hammerhead shark
Syluriformes	catfish
cf. *Ariopsis*	
cf. *Rhambdia*	
cf. *Scaides*	
cf. *Eleotridae*	sleepers
Crabs	
Portunidae	
Callinectes toxotes	biquin crab
Platyanthus orbignii	purple crab

or eaten. Guinea pigs are one meat source whose importance to Mochica diet, we suspect, is greatly underrepresented in the archaeological record. At Galindo, their remains were also found from various contexts, though few in number (S. Pozorski 1976: 136).

By far the single most important terrestrial meat source was the llama (*Lama glama*).[113] They appear to have been more important than marine products in overall quantity and year-round, ready access. S. Pozorski (1976: 129, 253, 1979, 1982) reached the same conclusion for the con-temporaneous sites of Cañoncillo and Galindo. The same holds for the sample from the earlier Huaca del Sol. It became quite apparent during our surface survey of Pampa Grande—later confirmed in excavation—that llama bones occurred throughout the site (from adobe rooms atop Huaca Fortaleza to kitchens in Sectors D and H) and dominated the sampled organic remains in terms of number, volume, and weight (4,345 out of 5,007 identified bones; 10,678 g out of 12,086 g of bones; Shimada and Shimada 1981: 38, 1985: 13). Their bones represented 84, 87, and 88 percent of the total number of identified bones from Sectors D, H, and K, respectively.

The importance of llamas as a meat source is also suggested by the age structure of the sampled llama population at Pampa Grande. The age structure was about half immature and half adult (under versus over three years of age) based on qualitative and quantitative differences observed among modern comparative skeletons of llamas. Today, among Andean highland communities that maintain llamas for varied purposes, those large male animals destined to serve as beasts of burden are typically castrated at about two to three years of age (ibid., 4). For meat, young male animals are selectively killed off before reaching this age. If modern management practices are applicable here, the observed age structure at Pampa Grande suggests a diversified usage with perhaps more emphasis on food (ibid., 13).

Based on the location and frequency of cut marks found on specific elements, we can deduce how llamas were butchered (Fig. 8.5; Shimada and Shimada 1981: 38–41). For example, cut marks running across the base of the skull suggest killing by severing the spinal column. The high frequency of butchering marks on the distal ends of long bones such as the femur and humerus most likely resulted from the cutting away of the upper meatier muscles. In the highlands, to make *ch'arki* (dried meat or jerky), butchering typically occurs in the cold, dry season months of June and July (e.g., see Miller 1979: 97–100). On the North Coast, culling and butchering may have occurred year-round, with emphasis on the dry months (June–September) when there would be fewer agricultural tasks and thus fewer conflicts in labor scheduling.

2. Procurement and Distribution of Subsistence Items

A. North Coast Llama Breeding and Herding

The preceding discussion alluded to the diverse and critical role played by llamas for the viability of the urban subsistence and economy. While today there are no llamas

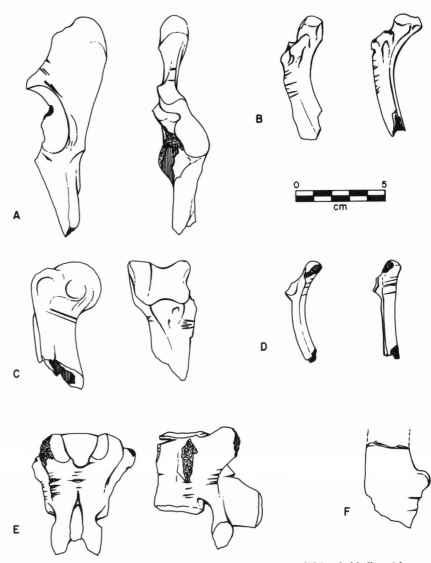

Figure 8.5. Camelid (probably llama) bones excavated in Sectors D and H with butchering marks.

on the North Coast, Moche V llama herding and breeding appears to have been an important part of the urban subsistence and economy at Pampa Grande.

With the exception of recent commercial exportation and breeding outside of the Andes, today llamas are basically found in the central and southern Peruvian highlands and neighboring Bolivian highlands, with an estimated population of some 900,000 in Peru (Franklin 1982: 473–475). Today, they still fill utilitarian and ritual roles: as meat, as important offerings (particularly the fetus), and as beasts of burden,

capable of carrying at least 25 kg. They provide wool, hides, meat, dung for fertilizer and fuel (gathering facilitated by their being corralled at night and having a common voidance pattern), and bones for artifacts (e.g., weaving implements and flutes). Even blood and kidney stones are used for rituals and folk curing, while sinews provide tough cords.

The modern distribution, population size, and cultural importance of llamas, however, is a pale reflection of their pre-Hispanic ubiquity and abundance and the reverence they commanded. On the North

Coast, several factors account for the rapid disappearance of llamas: (1) competition for fodder with imported animals, such as goats and pigs; (2) harassment and hunting by European settlers and their greyhounds; (3) introduction of wheeled vehicles and more "efficient" beasts of burden; (4) introduced diseases; and (5) European taste preferences. Paradoxically, outside of the Central Andes, for example, in Australia, England, and the United States (from Florida to New England and in most of the West), llamas have historically and recently proliferated, enjoying increased popularity as pets and pack animals due to their manageability, sturdiness, and versatility.

Llamas are capable of subsisting on an amazing range of fodder without any long-term harm, and of successfully breeding in diverse environmental settings, including the arid, sea-level North Coast of Peru. Physiological studies demonstrate high tolerance to arid conditions and low elevations, and digestive efficiency (see Shimada and Shimada 1985). In addition, sixteenth-century Spanish and native eyewitnesses attest to the presence of many llamas on the coast from southwestern Ecuador (Stahl 1988) to the South Coast of Peru.

Archaeology offers complementary data: (1) Mochica artists at least from Moche I depicted various life phases and functions of llamas on modeled and painted ceramics, including copulation, nursing, packing, and as sacrificial offerings (Figs. 3.11, 8.6); (2) in the refuse at Huaca de la Cruz, Strong and Evans (1952: 135) found not only many llama body parts but also a structure with loose cane and cornstalks together with abundant llama dung, indicating its use as a stall; and (3) excavations at the Moche V sites of Pampa Grande and Galindo yielded large numbers of bones of all body parts and age groups.[114] Further, as noted earlier, analysis of llama dung has shown that they indeed consumed local fodder such as *algarrobo* pods and leaves and maize stalks.

These lines of evidence lead us to the unescapable conclusions that llamas played an integral part in Mochica economy and religion at least from Moche I, and that in contrast to the earlier, often implicit assumption that llamas were brought down from the highlands and

only temporarily maintained on the coast, large-scale herding and breeding on the North Coast dates at least from Moche V times.

It may be that limited llama herding and breeding began much earlier on the North Coast (perhaps during the first millennium B.C.; Shimada and Shimada 1985: 8). In the adjacent North Highlands of Peru, over the first millennium B.C., there was a definite, permanent shift from deer hunting to the herding of domesticated camelids (M. Shimada 1982, 1985). This shift is seen in the increasing proportion (and thus overall significance) of camelid bones within the overall identified animal bones recovered from excavation.

Zooarchaeological data from North Coast sites dating to the first millennium B.C. suggest that a parallel development may have indeed occurred on the North Coast, although with marine resources remaining a critical component. It is clear from Moche III and IV painted and modeled vessels that deer hunting was an elite activity that probably had important ritualistic functions and took place on carefully specified occasions (Donnan 1978: 179–181). We have already noted that these vessels typically show elaborately dressed and decorated men with darts and throwing sticks or clubs with mace heads hunting deer trapped in nets or chased by dogs, plus simply dressed men drawn much smaller than the hunters (Fig. 5.4). The excavated deer (*Odocoileus virginianus*) remains—mostly antlers—show strong continuity in their association with elite ceremonialism. Significantly, the few postcranial deer bones recovered showed no butchering marks.

This continuity with earlier Moche phases suggests that any subsistence-related significance of deer on the North Coast had been long lost, perhaps in part due to their rarity from many years of prior hunting. We cannot, however, verify earlier Mochica breeding and herding of llamas, since we do not have good enough zooarchaeological data from sites of earlier phases. Testing of this proposition is an important future research task, as sixth-century droughts and the truncation of the Southern Sector would have resulted in a significant drop in agricultural produc-

tion, pressuring extant subsistence and economic systems. Stress would have been severely felt at inland urban settlements such as Pampa Grande and Galindo, unless marine products compensated. We already noted that the Moche V settlement pattern in the Lambayeque region (also in the Moche Valley) had a mid-valley focus, and that marine products were present in substantial quantity at Pampa Grande but apparently secondary to llama as a meat source. The presence of this rather impressive variety (and perhaps quantity) of marine products may have been largely due to the transport capability of llamas.

It stands to reason that under such stressful conditions, the breeding and herding in Mochica land of llamas, which in earlier phases may have served only ceremonial and perhaps limited transport functions, would have been intensified to provide a readily accessible, reliable, year-round supply of crucial protein first and foremost to urban populations.

Moche V llama herding was probably a much more labor-intensive affair than the management practices seen today or historically in the central and southern Peruvian highlands. Given the lack of the extensive natural pasture of the highland *puna* and the intensive land use on the coast, we suspect that coastal llamas were more closely supervised and confined, perhaps pastured in harvested agricultural fields, on canal banks with lush vegetation, and in side valleys beyond the margins of irrigation agriculture. These feedings were probably supplemented by food (e.g., *algarrobo* pods and maize leaves and stalks) brought to their corrals. A looter's pit in an empty, square (25 m to a side) stone enclosure in Sector G at the north end of the site exposed a 50-centimeter-thick layer of llama dung. Another looter's pit in a rectangular compound in Sector E at the east edge of the site exposed a similar accumulation of llama dung. Various roughly built rectangular enclosures with no surface artifacts in the south margins of Sectors J and N farther south are suspected of having been llama corrals. Testing of similar peripheral stone enclosures at Galindo also yielded a layer of loose organic substance believed to be crumbled llama dung (Bawden 1977: 194, 197).

In addition to providing some measure of security to urban subsistence, ready access to large numbers of llamas would have meant greater transport capability. Indeed, Mochica painted and modeled vessels illustrate llamas transporting persons, as well as goods such as baskets full of fish, jars, and *Strombus* shells as early as Moche I (Shimada and Shimada 1985; Shimada 1987a: 138–139; Figs. 3.11, 8.6, 8.7). The transport capability of llamas largely depends on their size, and large llamas (up to ca. 160 kg) bred in the United States are reported to be able to carry a person weighing over 50 kg. For the viability of "Mochica horizontality" with far-flung Mochica colonies discussed in Chapter 4, llama caravans under the control of the Mochica polity would have been critical. Rather than depending on highland traders with such caravans, the Mochica polity would have outfitted its own caravans (perhaps of specially bred large, strong llamas) for the acquisition and distribution of varied resources such as fish, copper (see below), *Spondylus*, *Strombus*, and *Conus*. Coastal llama caravans and, to a lesser extent, maritime transport using tule boats may have been critical to the economic expansion and integration of the Mochica polity.

Last, we cannot ignore the probable use of llama dung as fuel at least in ceramic firing. The common voidance of llamas (particularly those kept in corrals on or near work sites, for example in Sectors E, G, and N) would have allowed easy collection of their dung. Like dung of other domesticated herbivores, when dried, llama dung is an excellent fuel widely appreciated in highlands where other quality fuels are scarce or costly. Heavy, continuous demand for timber such as *algarrobo* and *zapote* for construction may have significantly reduced the extent of local forests and made hardwood fuels relatively scarce. In other words, llama dung may have been an important supplementary fuel at times.

In sum, the preceding discussion has demonstrated the critical role of llamas in urban subsistence as well as in the broader regional and interregional economy. This, together with the logistical complexity of maintaining large llama herds in or near

Figure 8.6. Mochica modeled vessel showing use of the llama as a beast of burden. Note that the baskets contain fish. Amano Museum, Lima.

Figure 8.7. Mochica fineline drawing of the presentation of *Strombus* (trumpet) shells. Note that the associated llama appears to be carrying sacks of additional shells. Three shells drawn near the llama may be *Conus fergusoni* rather than *Strombus*. Redrawn from Fig. 305 in Kutscher 1983.

the city, leads us to infer the involvement of officials at various levels of the Moche V administration at Pampa Grande.

B. Agricultural Produce

How and from where did Pampa Grande obtain agricultural produce? Any answer to this question at this stage of research is inferential. With political dominance over much of the Lambayeque region provided by its control of the valley neck and valley-wide water distribution, the Moche V polity at Pampa Grande probably exacted a good portion of harvests from the middle

Lambayeque and Zaña valleys as tribute to be used for redistributive ends (discussed below) inside and outside the city. As discussed in the preceding chapter, the bulk of staples for commoners in the city is believed to have been produced by farmers who were urban residents practicing intensive in-field cultivation in the *Valle Viejo*.

Nearly all of the cultivated plants identified from sampled organic remains are grown locally and throughout much of the North Coast today as they were during Mochica times (e.g., S. Pozorski 1976; Shimada 1976; Watson 1979; Weir and Eling 1986). In addition, considering contemporaneous canals (the Huaca Blanca–Tablazos and Montería systems; Nolan 1980) in the lower reaches of the *chaupiyunga* farther inland from Pampa Grande along the south bank, a wide range of fruits and crops such as coca, *molle* (*Schinus molle*; its fruits are used to make a drink), avocado, *lúcuma*, *chirimoyo* (*Annona cherimolia*), and *guayabo* were most likely cultivated there. Although coca was not identified, there is a strain of coca indigenous to the *chaupiyunga* zone of the North Coast (Plowman 1984a,b), and Mochica ceramics appear to have portrayed men chewing coca, holding a small "gourd" vessel presumably filled with lime in one hand and a spatula in the other (Benson 1976; Dobkin de Rios 1977). It is the addition of lime that releases the alkaloid, cocaine. Small rounded lumps of white powdery substance occasionally found in our excavations appear to be lime that had absorbed moisture and become chemically inert. Some painted scenes on Mochica pottery may even depict the use of hallucinogenic plants such as San Pedro cactus (Dobkin de Rios 1982; Sharon and Donnan 1977), which is available in mountains surrounding the *chaupiyunga*.

The significance of the large quantities of charred maize kernels and beans found in the formal storage facilities in Sectors H and D, respectively, will be discussed later as crucial evidence of the redistributive character of urban economy. I believe the maize kernels and beans were intended for *chicha* and food, respectively, for artisans and retainers. Cobs, while found in areas of food preparation and consumption, were not recovered from these *chicha*-making

areas. Considering the importance of uniform kernels to assure uniform germination for *chicha*-making, their selection and drying may well have been supervised in one of the major compounds at Pampa Grande. As explained later, cotton was apparently processed (at least brought together) under supervision in a central location (Deer House) for subsequent distribution to weaving workshops.

C. Marine Products

Our picture of the procurement and distribution of marine products is still hazy. One possibility is a mutually beneficial exchange between local fishers and agriculturalists. Ethnohistorical data (e.g., Netherly 1977, 1984; Ramírez 1986; Ramírez-Horton 1981, 1982; Rostworowski 1975) suggest that in the late pre-Hispanic era, when first the Chimú Kingdom and then the Inca Empire dominated the Lambayeque region, inland communities obtained marine products from their own fishing *parcialidades*[115] on the coast in exchange for agricultural produce. Occupational specialization was an age-old tradition on the Peruvian coast respected by even the mighty Chimú and Inca overlords; each specialist was expected to provide only his or her expertise and/or products. North Coast fishers formed an important castelike socioeconomic class with its own subcultural identity. They lived together in their own villages along the shore, worshiped their own gods, obeyed their own lords, married among themselves, and may have spoken their own dialect (Netherly 1977; Rabinowitz 1983). There are some indications that they also served as runners relaying messages (Rabinowitz 1983), much like the Inca *chaskis*.[116]

This symbiotic relationship between full-time coastal fishers and inland farmers may have been based originally on social ties dating back to the first millennium B.C. on the North Coast (e.g., Matsuzawa 1978). It is significant that the late pre-Hispanic fishing community of Cerro Azul in the Cañete Valley on the South Coast is known to have produced a surplus of dried fish (mostly anchovies and sardines), which were exported to nearby socially linked agricultural communities, and may have even traded with the mighty Inca Empire (Marcus 1987).

In other words, Pampa Grande may have acquired marine products indirectly, as tribute payment from various subordinate local communities in the mid-valley that had their own fishing parcialidades on the coast, or the polity may have established direct trade with coastal fishing groups. Another possibility, based on the Moche V occupation within the traditional Muchik town of Eten, is that the Moche V polity at Pampa Grande maintained its own fishing communities on the coast. The area around Eten has long been known for excellent access to fish and shellfish. Nevertheless, it is still not clear whether the presence of diagnostic Moche V ceramics indicates the presence of ethnically Mochica fishers or of a non-Mochica fishering community with a trade relationship with the Mochica population. The relative merits of these competing hypotheses remain to be determined.

D. Differential Distribution of Subsistence Items

Among areas excavated at Pampa Grande, Sector D produced the widest range of fauna as well as the greatest quantity of organic materials. This picture, however, largely derives from a few large primary-context refuse concentrations found there. For example, the central portion of Structure W, with its open layout at the southeast end of a main east-west street of Sector D (Fig. 7.19), yielded the largest single accumulation of primary refuse, including quantities of shells and bones of different animals, including humans. The floor of one room was littered with llama bones and an area approximately 2 by 4 m was covered by 30-centimeter-thick refuse. The accumulation in the above room included 419 whole and fragmentary bones. All but ten identifiable pieces belonged to llamas. Every part of the llama skeleton was represented, but long bones predominated. Most of the bones had been smashed and some had been partially burnt. Importantly, however, a handful of unifacial and bifacial basalt flakes with hard, sharp cutting edges were found with the bones. While the flakes did not show signs of preparation for a special purpose, they

would have been ideally suited for cutting the meat off bones. They showed no signs of extensive wear and are thought to have been made for specific short-term use and promptly discarded. A nearby batán with cobble pounders may have been used to crack open llama long bones for marrow.

Considering the rarity and limited quantity of primary refuse at the site level, this and the few other concentrations in Sector D are significant. These accumulations were not directly associated with hearths or other indications of cooking. The preceding, together with a notable concentration of gray- and blackware serving dishes in Sector D, suggest that the Sector was the setting for feasts. The varied classes of artifacts point to the relatively high status of the occupants there.

We have seen that llama bones represented a high proportion of the sampled organic remains from various Sectors. If the distribution of specific body parts of llamas is examined, we see no appreciable qualitative differences among sampled areas, including such elite and/or key ceremonial settings as the Palatial Room Complex atop the Main Body of Huaca Fortaleza (Chapter 7). These findings are in accord with the results of statistical tests for any significant inter-Sector differences in the range of subsistence resources, which proved negative.[117] This suggests that the city residents in the sampled areas had access to a similar range (including similar meat cuts) of food items. We wonder if their social class differences may have been manifested in the amount of a given item they were able to acquire.

At the same time, we should not underestimate uncertainties stemming from the scarcity of primary refuse. Inferred high-status occupants of Sectors A and B, for example, may have had access to exotic foods that left no traces. In addition, exotic items may have been used for ritual/shamanistic purposes as suggested by the curious contents of a medium-sized olla set into a floor in Structure Z, Sector D (Fig. 7.19). The contents included a fragmentary llama vertebra, a rectangular piece of "colonial worm" (coral), a Polinices shell, a crab pincer, a drilled hammerhead shark vertebra (perhaps for use as a bead), three caudal vertebrae from a fish of the Clupeid family

(sardine and anchovy family), and a maxillary fragment from a fish of the Sciaenid (corvina) family. Apparently, none were cooked or eaten.

3. Craft Goods and Production
A. Characterization and Differential Distribution of Ceramic Types

As elaborated in Chapter 9, Moche V fine painted funerary ceramics are stylistically rigid and iconographically less diverse, in comparison with those of the "classic" era of late Moche III–early IV. Moche V ceramics are often seen as the "post-classic" stage of Mochica art. The characterization is understandable considering the pervasive use of molds for shaping and decorating a wide range of vessels (with the exception of cooking and large storage vessels). Certainly, the time and effort saved with the use of molds were, in most cases, not invested in more thorough and careful exterior finishing.

Our sitewide ceramic vessel inventory is quite extensive (Table 12). As expected, constricted short-neck jars with or without decoration, cooking bowls with lug handles, and large storage urns dominate the inventory. The ubiquitous distribution of short-neck jars versus the localized character of reduced ware serving vessels is crucial in reconstructing Pampa Grande's social and economic organization, as seen later.

The inventory also includes new ceramic forms and decorative and manufacturing techniques derived from or inspired by the contemporaneous Nievería on the Central Coast or late Guangala on the south coast of Ecuador, and by archaic revival of Cupisnique ceramics from over a thousand years earlier.

The first group includes double-tier neck jars (both gray reduced ware and orange-colored oxidized ware) found in various Sectors (e.g., A, D, H, and J) and small jars found in Sector D with ovoid, football-shaped bodies made from two-piece vertical molds (Fig. 8.8).

The second group consists of vessels whose forms, surface finishes, and/or decorations were copied from vessels of the Cupisnique culture or inspired by them. Examples include fragments of reduced-

Table 12. Inventory of Moche V ceramics found at Pampa Grande.

I. Coarse Oxidized (Orange to Red) and Reduced (Gray to Black) Wares

  A. urns
    1. vertical rim
    2. incurving rim
    3. composite silhouette neck with flaring rim

  B. jars
    1. tall straight-neck jars
      a. unslipped
        plain
        press-mold decoration on neck
        grooved, pinched, and/or appliqué decoration on neck
      b. slipped
        plain
        press-mold decoration on neck
        grooved, pinched, and/or appliqué decoration on neck
    2. short straight-neck jars
      a. unslipped
        plain
        press-mold decoration on neck
        grooved, pinched, and/or appliqué decoration on neck
      b. slipped
        plain
        press-mold decoration on neck
        grooved, pinched, and/or appliqué decoration on neck
    3. flaring-neck jars
    4. composite silhouette neck jar
      a. unslipped
        plain
        press-mold decoration on neck
        grooved, pinched, and/or appliqué decoration on neck
      b. slipped
        plain
        press-mold decoration on neck
        grooved, pinched, and/or appliqué decoration on neck

  C. ollas
    1. incurving, short neck
    2. outcurving, composite silhouette neck with flaring rim

  D. bottles
    1. globular body
    2. cylindrical body

  E. canteens

  F. bowls
    1. incurving rim
    2. flaring rim
    3. crenulated or notched rim

  G. grater bowls
    1. incurving
    2. straight-sided
    3. slightly outflaring

  H. plates (lids? turnettes?)
    1. small to medium plates (12–40 cm diameter)
    2. large plates (50–55 cm diameter)

II. Fine Oxidized (Orange to Red) and Reduced (Gray to Black) Wares

  A. stirrup-spout vessels
    1. painted
      a. fine-line bichrome
        globular body
        squat body
      b. bichrome
        modeled effigies
    2. reduced
      a. single-chambered
      b. double-chambered

  B. bowls
    1. shallow or deep gray bowls
      a. decorated with grooved or punctate decoration
      b. undecorated
    2. crenulated and notched rim gray bowls
    3. *floreros* (flaring-rim bowls)
      a. painted—crenulated and plain rims, pedestaled and unpedestaled
      b. gray—crenulated and plain rims, pedestaled and unpedestaled
    4. small, black burnished bowls
      a. plain, sharp lip
      b. slightly flaring lip with grooved or punctate decoration
    5. composite silhouette bowls (double-tiered bowls)

III. Miscellaneous

  A. worked sherds—spindle whorls, pendants(?), and scrapers for pottery making(?)

  B. figurines
    1. solid, mold-made anthropomorphic figurines
    2. hollow, mold-made anthropomorphic figurines

  C. molds
    1. press-mold human face for tall- and short-neck jars
    2. figurine molds
    3. mold for metal

  D. *adornos*
    1. mold-made animal heads

  E. drum frame(?)

ware (possibly zoomorphic) vessels with burnished black slip and polished groove decorations found in Sector A. Though at first glance they resemble earlier Cupisnique vessels, upon closer inspection it is clear that they are mold-made and not as thoroughly burnished. Reduced-ware bowls with incurving rims and incised, punctated decorations described later may be another example of archaism (Fig. 8.9).[118]

The last group of rare vessels includes reduced-ware cooking and serving vessels that are of localized distribution, most floor-context examples coming from areas within inferred elite contexts in Sectors A, D, and H, as well as Compound 14 (Deer House). These include residences, courtyards, audience chambers (rectangular enclosures with low platform mounds), and formalized entertaining areas where drink and food were provided to guests. The largest concentration comes from Room 2 of Structure Y at the southeast end of Sector D, which appears to have been part of a ceramic workshop (Fig. 7.19). This cluster includes thirteen gray, sand-tempered shallow ollas with curving concave sides and flaring everted lips with lugs for suspension or carrying (Fig. 8.9). Most are 20 cm in diameter and 9–10 cm deep. While identical in overall form and probably in size, decoration varies, consisting of punctated rosettes and other similar simple designs. The concentration also includes two bowls with punctate designs, a small bottle with undulating sides and a

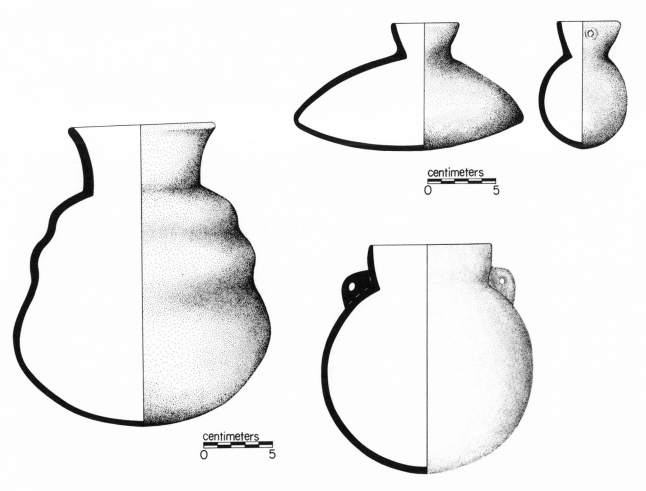

centimeters
0   5

centimeters
0   5

Figure 8.8. Three new ceramic forms perhaps introduced from the Central Coast. The ovoid vessel was made using two vertical molds.

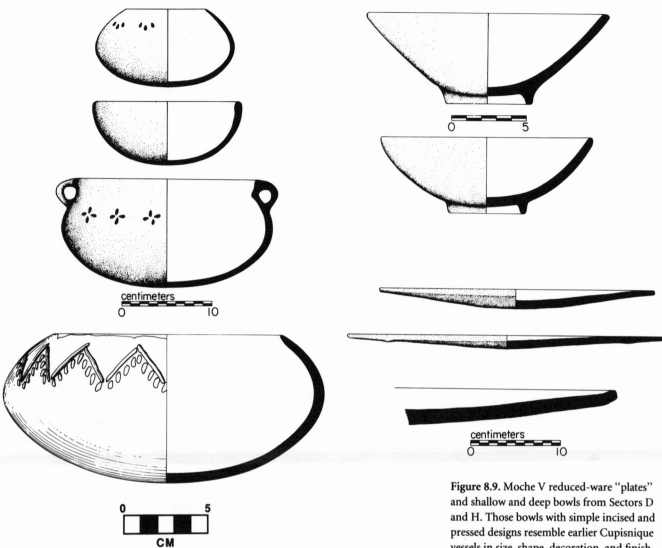

centimeters
0   10

0   5
CM

Figure 8.9. Moche V reduced-ware "plates" and shallow and deep bowls from Sectors D and H. Those bowls with simple incised and pressed designs resemble earlier Cupisnique vessels in size, shape, decoration, and finish. These "plates" were recovered near a ceramic workshop in Structure Y, Sector D. Some of them may have been used by potters as a turntable upon which vessels could be placed for working.

rounded bottom, and two castellated *floreros* (one plain blackware and the other with an incised step motif on the underside of its castellated lip). In addition, this cluster contains "pierced discs," plain ceramic discs with holes of varying bores in the middle, that may have been used as lids for bottles and jars. The last is unique to Structure Y.

Bowls at Pampa Grande are typically gray reduced ware with coarse burnishing. Shallow bowls with low ring bases have flaring rims and typical diameters of about 13–16 cm, a comfortable size for holding in one hand (Fig. 8.9). Bowls without ring bases have nearly vertical or incurving rims (diameters of ca. 8–18 cm) and are some-

times decorated with impressed simple geometric or incised linear designs (Fig. 8.10). Their basic shape resembles the well-known *tecomates* of Mesoamerica, and they may have replaced or been inspired by cut gourd bowls that are still used today in rural communities on the North Coast to serve *chicha* or soup. In fact, numerous gourd fragments were found in refuse.

There are, at the same time, a few examples of small (ca. 12–13 cm in diameter), highly burnished, black slip reduced-ware bowls that have fine paste and very thin well-fired walls (Fig. 8.10). One example was recovered from Deer House and another from Sector D. Clearly, the rarity, high technical quality, and architectural setting of their use suggest that these small, exquisite black bowls were highly valued. Based on their distribution, it might be argued that gray bowls were imitations of the black bowls but that most of the site residents probably utilized perishable gourd vessels for serving and eating.

"Plates" are another rare group of ceramic vessels (Fig. 8.9). They are gray reduced-ware discs, slightly concave and smoothly finished on both faces. Some have flattened bottoms, while others are slightly rounded. There is only one example with a pedestal base (ca. 20 cm in diameter, with the base 6 cm in diameter and 2.5 cm in height). The larger plates without ring bases may have served as large lids, for example, for storage urns. There is yet another possible function. Given various lines of evidence indicating the presence of a ceramic workshop within Structure Y, these plates are more likely to have served as turntables to facilitate detail work.

The distribution of other fine-quality vessels, such as painted stirrup-spout bottles and modeled effigy vessels (bichrome painted and blackware; Figs. 8.11, 8.12), closely overlaps that of gray and black bowls, and extends to other architectural settings that are predictable based on floor size and the extent of vertical differentiation (terracing) described in the preceding chapter. Thus, excavations of the spacious, hierarchical terraces commonly found at traffic nodes have yielded one or more of these fine vessels atop the highest terrace, as if to reinforce the architectural symbolism of power.

B. Ceramic Production and Workshops

In spite of our understanding of the distribution patterns of different ceramic types and their social and economic significance, we have identified few physical remains to tell us where and how they were manufactured. In fact, until quite recently there was a real dearth of sites identified as definite pre-Hispanic ceramic workshops and kilns not only on the North Coast of Peru but in all of the New World. Dispersed, small-scale ceramic production using coils and slabs (as opposed to durable ceramic molds) and open-air firing is not as easy to identify in archaeological settings. Unless preservation is exceptional, such production leaves surprisingly few diagnostic material remains (e.g., see Stark 1985). Those few workshops and kilns that have been archaeologically identified, including those just at the edge of Mocollope in the Chicama Valley (Russell 1990) and Pampa de los Incas in the Santa Valley (Wilson 1988: 211), were involved in relatively large-scale production of mold-shaped, standardized ceramics that left behind sizable piles of wasters (discolored, deformed, cracked, or broken pieces), molds, and/or durable kilns.

The best body of evidence for on-site ceramic production at Pampa Grande comes from a cluster of tightly packed rooms, some unusually small (less than 10 m² of floor space), together designated as Structure Y at the southeast end of Sector D (Fig. 7.19). We noted earlier a large concentration of reduced-ware vessels in Room 2 of Structure Y, including thirteen identical cooking ollas with no signs of use and no associated hearth. In addition, Room 2 had a stone burnisher, and adjacent Room 11 yielded a stone burnisher and a pointed, polished bone tool fashioned out of a llama or deer tibia.

More direct evidence of ceramic production comes from partially excavated Room 13 (adjacent to Rooms 2 and 11), where an impressive variety and quantity of ceramic remains were recovered from a thick homogeneous layer of dark gray ash subfloor fill. Most were sand-tempered reduced grayware showing varying degrees of burnishing. The grayware included plates, open and incurving bowls, castellated *floreros*, constricted neck ollas, pierced discs, and cut sherds. Importantly, some were nearly identical in size, shape, and manufacturing to those found on the floor of Room 2. The remains of mold-made, fineline painted stirrup-spout bottles and *floreros* painted with fineline geometric designs were also found in the fill. In addition, there were several mold-made figurine fragments.

The specific artifacts of ceramic production and finishing were (1) fragments of molds, including one of a llama head with harness straps; (2) five small, smooth rounded river cobbles, all with parallel

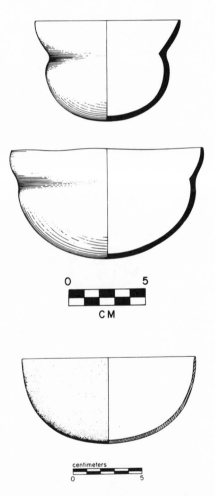

Figure 8.10. Small, well-burnished blackware bowls from Sector D. They have thin walls with fine, well- and evenly fired paste. Similar bowls were found in Deer House. Drawing by César Samillán and I. Shimada.

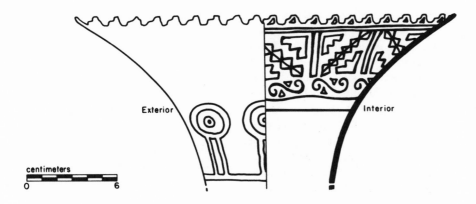

Figure 8.11. Bichrome *florero* or flaring-rim bowl from the top of Huaca 18, Sector H.

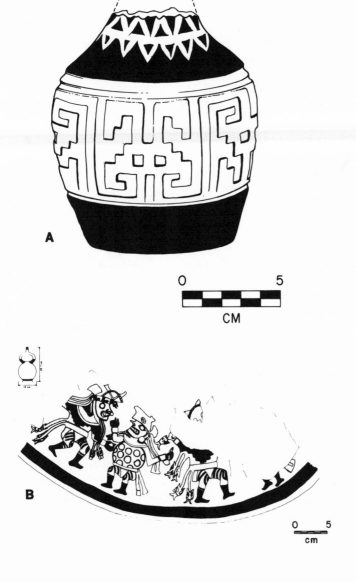

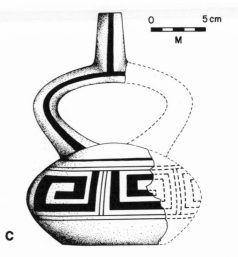

Figure 8.12. Moche V fineware vessels excavated from Deer House and Sectors D and H. (A) Broken, mold-made bottle with low relief of highly abstracted motifs in square panels, from Sector D. The bottom and top of the vessel body are painted dark red. (B) Stirrup-spout bottle from Deer House— nearly identical to that illustrated in Figure 7.35. On this bottle, the low relief was painted. (C) Stirrup-spout bottle from Sector H.

scratches believed to have been used to polish the exteriors of ceramic vessels; and (3) a stamp fragment, the flat face of which had a molded representation of a skull, while the reverse had the stub of an oblong grip. Excavation of the same fill containing this stamp turned up a face-neck jar fragment with a press-molded representation of a skull that fit the stamp loosely but perfectly, taking into account shrinkage through firing.

The homogeneous dark ash, mold fragments, and stone ceramic polishers, as well as the predominance of a single ceramic type (reduced ware), all argue that the fill derived from pottery production. The large quantity and very loose quality of the fine powdery ash make it unlikely that the fill was moved very far. Examination of the ash reveals some charcoal bits but mostly carbonized fine material that readily crumbles in the hand. While the charcoal may represent the remains of hardwood fuel for a lasting fire, the ash may well be remains of burnt llama dung employed to attain a lasting high heat and a reducing atmosphere.

Considering the lengthy droughts that spanned much of the sixth century and the expected reduction of forest areas, local hardwood fuel might have become scarce during Moche V occupation of Pampa Grande. Under such conditions, llama dung would be particularly valuable. However, evidence is too scant at this point to demonstrate any cause/effect relationship between drought-induced emphasis on llama dung as a major fuel for ceramic firing and the notable increase in black and gray reduced wares produced in Moche V in comparison with earlier phases. On the other hand, the popularity of reduced-ware ceramics may simply have been an aspect of the archaic revival of fine Cupisnique reduced wares or influence of late Guangala ceramics from the south coast of Ecuador, where reduced wares were more common and had a longer tradition (Paulsen 1970, 1982).

Sherds in the Structure Y fill do not seem to be wasters; the larger pieces may have been used to cover open-air kilns as refractories and to hold fuel in place, and/ or to regulate air circulation and thus the temperature gradient, as still widely prac-

ticed by the traditional pottery makers of coastal Peru (e.g., see Bankes 1985; Camino 1982; Sabogal 1982; Shimada 1985d; see Fig. 8.13).

In sum, the first and second (also the last) phase of occupation of the northern half of Structure Y may have been involved in the manufacture of a wide range of relatively small reduced-ware ceramics. Considering the limited distribution and quantity of reduced-ware vessels at the site, a handful of workshops may have met on-site demand.

Complementing the above picture of Moche V reduced-ware ceramic production is a Moche V workshop involved in oxidized-ware ceramic production (at least the firing stage) that was excavated at the northern fringe of Galindo (Bawden 1977: 187–198). The roughly 15 m² workshop had a packed earth floor and included a roughly circular (ca. 7 m in diameter) shallow pit filled with ash containing wood, camelid dung, and rough pottery fragments. The pit was apparently an open-air pit kiln.[119] Sixty-five ceramic mold fragments representing a wide range of forms (neck jars, double-bodied jars, human form figurines) were recovered in and around the pit. Near the kiln was a storage pit (1.5 m in diameter and 1 m deep) con-

taining cane and wood mixed with llama dung, apparently fuel destined for use in firing. The vessels to be fired are thought to have been packed with wood and manure and, after ignition, covered by a layer of earth (Bawden 1977: 193). Alternatively, in place of the layer of earth, the large fragments of coarse redware utilitarian vessels (mostly storage jars and cooking vessels) littering the surrounding floor could well have been used for control of airflow and temperature.

Given the need to bring in bulky fuel for firing and heavy clay for pottery, it makes good sense that the workshop was situated to have easy access to and from the valley and the main road to the site as well as being adjacent to a llama corral, an enclosure (18 by 13 m) with a deposit of llama dung 15–25 cm thick. The refuse, heat, and smoke generated by firing would favor locating ceramic workshops near the edges of the site. Traditional potters of Mórrope and Chulucana on the northern coast of Peru today are situated at the edges of their respective communities with ready access to ample space.

The ceramic workshop at Moche V Galindo is not separated from surrounding residential structures, and this has been interpreted to mean that "it did not play a

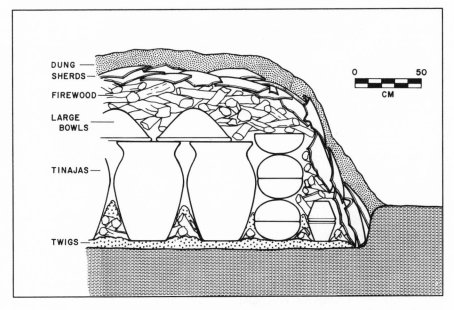

Figure 8.13. Cross-sectional drawing of modern open-air (shallow circular pit) kiln in Mórrope, lower Lambayeque Valley.

role in primary social integrative systems" and that there was no direct supervision of ceramic production by the ruling authority (Bawden 1977: 200). The absence of molds or fragments of fine-quality ceramics also supports the view that ceramic production here did not have "formal state function" (ibid.). Thus, the Galindo workshop contrasts with the Sector D case, which appears to have been involved in production of valued reduced-ware ceramics near the center of Pampa Grande. However, in both cases the entire ceramic production, spanning initial clay preparation to final firing, is assumed to have occurred more or less in the same locales.

Workshops that produced the fine, painted stirrup-spout and effigy vessels have yet to be identified in or outside of Pampa Grande or Galindo. In contrast to notable changes in form and iconography, the technique and technology of Moche V finewares did not differ much from those of "classic" late Moche III–early IV vessels. Paste is fine (Table 13), and the vessel is covered with cream-colored slip. Some stirrup-spout bottles have rather thick slip. Polishing is not as thorough as on the "classic" vessels, and at times the exterior has a matte finish. The degree of fracturing of quartz grains observed in thin section samples of the Moche V *floreros* and stirrup-spouts from Pampa Grande suggests that these vessels were fired at a relatively low temperature of about 750°–850° C (S. Fleming, pers. com. 1985).

There must have been heavy, continuous demand for cooking and storage vessels. Consider, for example, findings from a residential complex of Compound 38, Sector H. All but one residence there had one small and three large storerooms, each containing at least a dozen large urns, plus constricted-neck and tiered, large-mouth jars. Given that we did not locate any reliable water source within the site except a small spring at the head of Quebrada IV, potable water presumably had to be regularly brought in from the Collique Canal, which skirted around the lower end of the site some 1 km away from the center. Most likely, there was widespread household and communal storage of potable water at Pampa Grande. Many of these large vessels in Compound 38 probably contained wa-

Table 13. (A) Prevalence of mineral inclusions in Moche V painted sherds surface-collected in Sector H, Pampa Grande. (B) Modal analysis of petrographic data obtained from mineralogical thin sections. Analyses were carried out at the MASCA, University Museum, University of Pennsylvania.

A

Mineral Type[a]	#PG 83-59	#PG 83-60
Plagioclase	***	**
Rock fragments	***	***
Slag remnants	.	.
Microcline	.	.
Muscovite	**	**
Biotite	**	**
Hornblende	***	***
Pyroxene	.	.
Magnetite	***	***
Ilmenite	*	.
Haematite	**	.
Apatite	*	.
Garnet	.	.
Monazite	*	.
Zircon	*	.
Andalusite	.	.
Actinolite	.	.
Chlorite	.	.
Epidote	.	.

[a]Quartz occurred in abundance in all the wares studied here. The symbols key to these data for the qualitative frequency of other minerals is as follows:

**** abundant
*** common
** minor
* rare
. not found

B

Ref. #	Matrix	Quartz	Others*	Voids	Degree of Quartz Fracture
PG83-59	49.9	13.1	15.1	21.9	moderate
PG83-60	57.2	22.2	10.5	10.1	little

* Primarily plagioclase inclusions and rock fragments.

ter for cooking, drinking, and washing, while others were probably used for grain and *chicha* storage. Together with varied vessels in the *chicha*-making room (over five thousand sherds), we are speaking of nearly one hundred utilitarian vessels just within this compound. We can readily project a figure of tens of thousands of utilitarian vessels for the whole site.

Fieldwork has yielded little to clarify the loci and organization of production of utilitarian vessels. What can be said is confined to manufacturing and decorative techniques. Although the telltale signs of techniques used for vessel formation are typically erased or obscured by subsequent trimming, smoothing, and polishing, X-ray photos or even simple visual and tactile examination often provide sufficient data for reconstruction. The undulation commonly found on the interior surface of body sherds suggests that large storage vessels were formed from superimposed coils built atop a semispherical, apparently mold-made base. Certain shallow oval depressions sometimes found on the interior surface may indicate use of a hand-held stone anvil (e.g., cobblestone) in conjunction with a wooden or ceramic undecorated paddle to bond, flatten, and strengthen clay slabs and/or coils used for the body walls.

On the shoulder of many excavated storage vessels, we found a small appliquéd, incised, grooved, or stamped mark, such as a cross, squatting toad, or "owl" face (Fig. 8.14). Molded, naturalistic representations of birds, bats, and monkeys are also found on the shoulders of small- to medium-sized storage jars and cooking ollas. Did these marks identify potters as do ethnographic examples from the Peruvian highlands (Donnan 1971) or even relate in some way to accounting, as we infer for marked adobe bricks?

Perhaps the most commonly found utilitarian vessels are constricted-neck jars, which are believed to have been primarily used for transport and temporary storage of food and drink, including *chicha*. Body form ranges from globular and elongated globular to almost tear-shaped and occurs both with and without neck decoration. Typically, these jars measure ca. 25–30 cm in diameter and 30–40 cm in height, with a roughly 5–7-liter (gallon to gallon and a half) capacity. The neck constriction is narrow and high enough to prevent spillage and to allow easy coverage with a lid but barely allows an adult hand to reach in. Overall, the size and shape of these constricted-neck jars are well suited for transport, and the shoulder adornments may have facilitated transport by providing something to tie onto. These jars are ubiquitous throughout the site, including examples at the Platform Complex on the First Terrace and at the Palatial Room Complex atop the Main Body of Huaca Fortaleza. In particular, large numbers are found in *chicha*-making areas. More generally, they are associated with areas of food and/or drink preparation or consumption throughout the site.

Most whole or reconstructable jars with constricted necks have animal, bird, or human face decoration done in a variety of techniques (pinching, incising, modeling appliqué, press-molding, and painting; see Figs. 7.31, 7.32). Unlike earlier modeled or molded Mochica jars painted to represent people or animals, decoration on Moche V neck jars is largely confined to the neck and a few splashes of white slip. Possible social significance of face-neck jars with incised or gouged eyes was discussed in Chapter 7.

Molds imposed certain limitations on artistic creativity and variation. However, Moche V artisans at Pampa Grande produced an impressive number of face molds; over twenty-five human and animal faces can be differentiated among jars excavated and surface collected from Sector H alone (Fig. 7.32). Many other different faces come from other Sectors. In fact, these molded faces are far more Mochica in appearance than those made with other techniques.

If workshops in Sectors D and H were supplied with food and drink from particular kitchens using these neck jars, one wonders if each group responsible for food and drink preparation had its own diagnostic set of face-neck jars (both Gallinazo and Mochica style). This is an interesting hypothesis that remains to be tested.

Some ideas on the production of these utilitarian ceramics may be gained from ethno-archaeological studies of modern

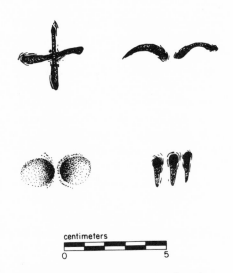

centimeters

0   5

Figure 8.14. Some of the intentional marks found on large storage vessels excavated in Sector H at Pampa Grande and at Huaca del Pueblo Batán Grande in the La Leche Valley.

kin-based pottery making in Mórrope, Simbilá, and Chulucana. Some dozen families in Mórrope, utilizing the ancient paddle-and-anvil technique (perhaps up to twelve hundred years old), produce a variety of earthenware vessels, including cooking bowls, flower pots, and 5-, 10-, and 20-gallon urns traditionally used for water storage and *chicha* making.

Typically, an adult male, assisted by male kinsmen (usually sons), carries out all three major stages of pottery production (procurement and preparation of clay, actual pottery making, and firing). Clay is obtained from one's own land and/or bought or bartered from another member of the community whose land yields good clay. Burros transport the clay to workshops.

In the densely built town of Mórrope, the workshop is a spacious, well-lit room within the potter's residence (Fig. 8.15). This room is often used for other activities (e.g., dining) that vary according to the time of day. In the surrounding countryside where there are fewer constraints on space, the workshop is a partially enclosed roofed area adjacent to the potter's residence (Fig. 8.16) used exclusively for pottery making.

Vessel formation begins with the placement of clay slabs on the exterior of an inverted, stationary mold, followed by systematic beating with hands and wooden paddles for good form fit and overall strength. Once the body is formed, it is removed from the mold and placed upright. The exterior of the body is once again paddled against a relatively flat, oval cobble held inside the body to serve as an anvil. Paddling assures strong bonding of clay slabs, removes any residual air bubbles from the clay, and evens out vessel walls. Then the body is air-dried in a cool, shady area adjacent to the workshop. When the body walls have solidified somewhat, a coil is placed at the top to form the neck and rim. A skilled potter in Mórrope, working from about 6 A.M. to 4 P.M. and utilizing the above combination of mold and paddle-anvil technique, can form some twelve to fifteen 20-gallon *tinaja* bodies per day. With the neck and rim added, typical weekly production comes down to some three to four dozen completed *tinajas*.

After two or more weeks of drying, the *tinajas* are fired. Firing is a major event requiring a good deal of preparation and planning. Relatives are often called upon to help (1) gather sufficient fuel, including desiccated animal dung, dried grasses, and firewood; (2) prepare open-air pits, typically by digging shallow depressions (some 40 cm deep) 3 to 5 m in diameter; (3) preheat vessels to be fired by rolling them in hot ash; (4) load the oven (Fig. 8.13); and (5) keep an eye on the oven once the fire is set. Through breakage and cracking, typically some 5 percent of the fired vessels are lost.

Within and outside of the town of Mórrope, the oven is placed in an open area close to the workshop. At the completion of firing, the large sherds used to cover the oven, as well as ashes from thoroughly burnt fuel, are removed, leaving a lightly discolored, shallow pit as the only apparent physical evidence of firing.

Many potters in and around Mórrope are not full-time; many engage in pottery making during lulls (usually during the cold, dry months of June to September or somewhat longer) in the subsistence-oriented activities of farming or fishing

and shellfish gathering. In fact, most potters identify themselves as farmers or fishers. Yet when they are making pottery, they devote most of their waking hours to this task and might be described as "part-time craft specialists." Before Mórrope potters began aggressively marketing their vessels in the urban markets of Lambayeque, Chiclayo, and beyond, they traveled the countryside with their burros bartering their products.

Overall, in spite of some important differences between modern Mórrope and Moche V production of utilitarian vessels, the above provides important insights. It is quite possible that during our surface surveys or even in excavations, we simply failed to identify dispersed ceramic workshops integrated within the small, agglutinated residences in the Southern Pediment. That is to say, we cannot discount the possibility of dispersed on-site household production manned by kinsmen. It is unlikely that there was significant seasonal variation in the demand for utilitarian vessels. On-site or not, full-time production is likely to have occurred given the level of demand placed by the estimated ten to fifteen thousand residents at Pampa Grande.

C. Metal Objects and Metalworking

Perhaps the best-known metal objects attributed to Moche V Pampa Grande (or for that matter to the entire Moche V culture) are "seven matched hollow, gold jaguars" with embossed pelage markings (Lechtman, Parson, and Young 1975). Each one of this set is about 11 cm long and 3 cm wide. These jaguars fashioned out of sheet gold are excellent examples of the technical mastery attained by Mochica metalsmiths. This sweat-welding of sheet gold is "as elegant as any goldsmithing techniques in the ancient or for that matter the modern world" (Lechtman 1980: 294).

Though our fieldwork at Pampa Grande failed to elucidate where such sumptuous objects were made, something can be said about their probable provenience.[120] According to the former owner of the Hacienda Pampa Grande, Víctor Baca (pers. com. 1978; I. Shimada 1982: 165; also see Shimada 1976: 99), these "jaguars" were found among the rubble of the southern end (highest part) of the Main Body of

Huaca Fortaleza that had been weakened by the 1925 torrential rains and subsequently fell down at the time of the 1931 earthquake. The jaguars may have been yet another ritual cache offering within the Palatial Room Complex atop the Main Body. More recent discoveries of gold objects in the Lambayeque Valley further suggest a distinguished local goldworking tradition (see Chapter 4).

With the exceptions of one heavy, dark gray spindle whorl from Sector D, believed to be galena (lead sulfide), and tiny fragments of gilded copper sheet (together with cut shell and stone fragments) from Sector H (Shimada 1978: 583), all other metal objects recovered in our fieldwork are essentially small copper implements (such as *tumis* [Fig. 8.17], needles, and spindle whorls) and ornaments.

We anticipated finding supervised metal workshops in Sectors D and H that were hypothesized as providing food and drink, as well as craft goods for the Sector A elite. Indeed, surface surveys and excavations in these Sectors yielded appreciable numbers of utilitarian copper implements, as well as hammer stones presumably used for making and shaping sheet metal. Structure 52 in Sector H was a definite metal workshop involved in forging, i.e., the forming or shaping of metal by alternate annealing and hammering. Metallurgical remains from Structure R in Sector D probably represent another workshop.

These are the only Mochica metal workshops excavated to date, representing only one component of a complex metallurgical production system. Thus the workshops and excavated copper objects are discussed within the context of our current understanding of the broader production setup.[121]

Copper formed the backbone of Mochica metallurgy (Lechtman 1979, 1980) and was most likely locally smelted from copper oxide ore mined in a small-scale, labor-intensive manner from localized shallow deposits dispersed among the Andean foothills defining the margins of North Coast valleys. Within easy reach of Pampa Grande there are various abandoned ancient copper mines.[122] These mines apparently exploited zones of heavy mineralization derived from the formation of Cerro de los Gentiles (Pampa Grande)

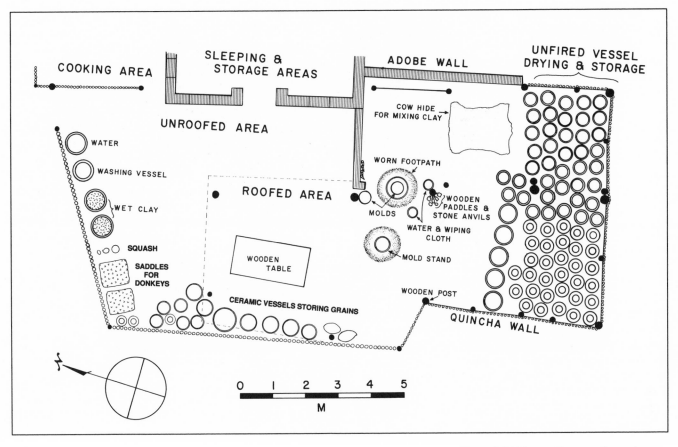

Figure 8.15. Plane-table map of a modern paddle-anvil pottery workshop in Mórrope (household-level production).

Figure 8.16. Photo of a modern paddle-anvil pottery workshop (household-level production) in Romero outside of Mórrope.

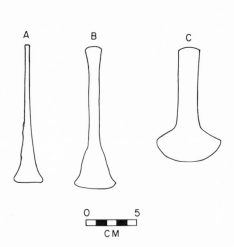

Figure 8.17. Copper implements found clustered in Structure R, Sector D. Rather than being all-purpose "knives," A and B may have been used for graving or other activities in metalworking.

Figure 8.18. Scene from a replicative copper smelting experiment at Cerro Huaringa in Batán Grande illustrating the use of tuyere-tipped cane blowtubes placed at the mouth of the smelter.

and/or Cerro Alumbral, the highest mountain of this general area at 1,533 m above sea level. All these mines have certain common characteristics: (1) direct association with definite or probable pre-Hispanic architecture, ceramics, and/or roughly triangular, nonlocal stones with battered ends that appear to have been used as picks, and (2) narrow, irregularly shaped workings that closely followed the highest-grade ore vein. Though the associated ceramics are often not informative as to their age and cultural affiliation, those that are diagnostic belong to coastal cultures from Mochica to Chimú. In spite of imprecise dating, we can infer that the mountainous area around Pampa Grande was important to Mochica mining, which was in general small-scale but highly selective and labor-intensive. Though each mine's output was small, simultaneous mining at dispersed local mines would have yielded a large overall output at the regional level.

Thus far, at Pampa Grande we have no material remains of on-site copper (or any other metal) smelting, i.e., primary extraction of usable metal from ore. The absence

is not unexpected. Sicán metallurgical centers in nearby Batán Grande indicate that smelting loci are largely dictated by their proximity to ore and fuel sources.

Smelting of copper was a dirty task that demanded much time, labor, ore, and fuel. It probably utilized (1) a charge that combined roughly equal amounts of crushed, hand-sorted copper oxide ore and high-grade hematite (red iron oxide ore) or some other locally available flux;[123] (2) high-quality fuel such as lumps of charcoal made from local *algarrobo* trees; (3) simple, bowl-shaped furnaces (probably ca. 1.5–2.0 liters in capacity); and (4) blowtubes such as locally available cane shafts with ceramic tuyere tips. Bellows were apparently unknown, and draft to power the smelters was supplied by human lung power through the aforementioned blowtubes (Fig. 8.18).

Attaining and maintaining copper melting temperature (1083° C) posed a serious challenge. In our replicative smelting experiments, even with simultaneous use of three or four blowtubes we were unable to melt the entire furnace charge thoroughly even for a brief moment. Slag must be thoroughly molten for metallic copper to sink to the furnace bottom to form a crude ingot. Rather, what resulted in our experiments after three hours of continuous blowing were prills or droplets of metallic copper trapped in viscous slag. This brittle slag had to be crushed to free the prills so they could be gathered and remelted to form ingots. Figure 8.19 illustrates a thin crude convex ingot of pure copper looted from a possible Mochica grave around Cerro Pan de Azúcar in the upper Zaña Valley.

It is apparent that the material and human costs of copper smelting were considerable. To operate a single furnace necessitated (1) preheating of the furnace, (2) preparation of the charge, (3) preparation and repair of blowtubes with tuyeres, as they do not last long, (4) up to three or four persons to provide continuous drafts, (5) at least one person to supervise them and charge the furnace, (6) slag crushing on *batanes* and *chungos* to release trapped prills, and (7) remelting of prills to consolidate them into an ingot. In other words, it took a team of at least four people much of one day to produce one moderate-sized copper ingot weighing a few hundred grams.[124]

The metal workshop excavated in Structure 52, Sector H, apparently depended on ingots and blanks produced at smelting site(s) not yet identified.[125] The workshop was situated at one end of a narrow street that also provided access to an apparent residence at the other end and to RS 65, with a spacious hierarchical terrace positioned to control traffic to and from the street (Fig. 8.20). The workshop consisted of four interlinked but functionally differentiated areas involved in (1) annealing and melting, (2) forming, cutting, and shaping sheet metal(s), (3) food and drink storage and consumption, and (4) possible food preparation and refuse disposal.

In the spacious, partially walled-in area closest to the street, there were two unusually large, thoroughly discolored planoconvex hearths (70–80 cm in diameter, over 20 cm deep) with clay-lined bottoms and walls built of fieldstones set in clay mortar. In contrast to their solid construction, the packed earth floor surrounding the hearths was relatively uneven and covered by a thick deposit of ash and silt with charcoal inclusions. On the floor close to the hearths was a broken but complete miniature rectangular ceramic trough (4 by 6.5 cm and 4 cm high with a maximum capacity of ca. 50–60 cc) with distinct greenish encrustations on the interior surface. The vessel, made out of fine clay, was quickly produced; the smooth trough was probably made with a mold, while the base was formed by simply pressing it against something flat and hard. Electron microprobe analysis of a sample indicates that the encrustation is largely copper oxide. The top of the encrustation formed a horizontal line, perhaps reflecting the waterline of copper slag. The vessel probably served as a mold for making a small copper ingot.[126]

Artifacts from nearby ARm 61, a small room with a well-preserved, clean plastered floor, a bench, and two tables, complement the above picture. The room contained two sets of faceted stones (Fig. 8.21) that apparently served different but related functions. One set from the bench top consisted of two highly polished basalt cobbles, each with various flat working surfaces, and two ellipsoid quartzite cobbles with partial polish. The second set consisted of a highly polished basalt cobble with numerous flat faces, and two rectangular blocks of fissile shale. One can discern fine striations on the faces of these blocks, as if something was cut on them. In addition, a large (20 by 18 by 5 cm) tabular andesite slab with a flat, polished surface was found leaning against the base of a small, square "worktable" (35 cm high) built in the corner of the room using hard, fine-grained adobe bricks. It appeared as if this stone had slid off the table top.

It is easy to imagine kneeling metalworkers using stone hammers to shape metal pieces against an andesite anvil placed atop the adobe table. Together with nearby braziers for annealing, these handheld stone hammers were most likely used for forging sheet metal, with one face slightly domed for stretching the metal and the other face flat for planishing (smoothing blows) the sheet after it had been stretch-hammered to near the size and

Figure 8.19. Copper ingot looted from a cemetery at Cerro Pan de Azúcar near Oyotún, upper Zaña Valley. It is not well refined or consolidated. According to proton-induced X-ray emission analysis, it is essentially pure copper, containing no arsenic. It probably dates to the early Mochica occupation of the area.

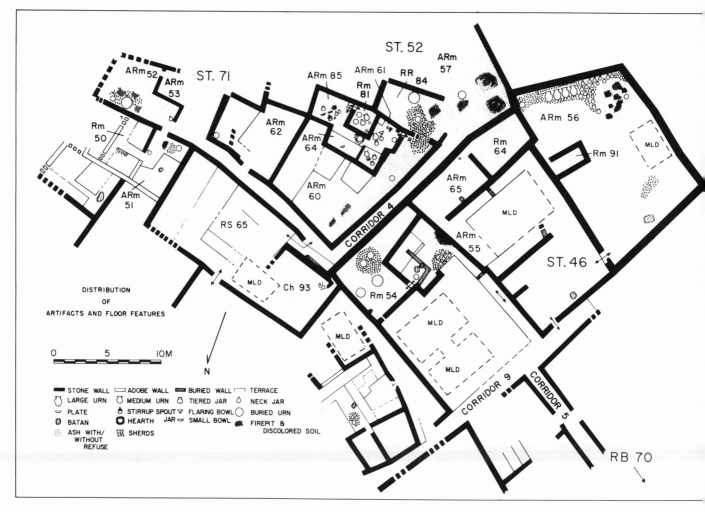

Figure 8.20. The broader architectural setting of the metalworking area in Structure 52, Sector H.

thickness desired (J. A. Griffin, pers. com. 1992). The shale blocks with their sharp, right-angle corners would have been effective for bending, cutting, or otherwise shaping sheet metal. Altogether, we seem to have quite a complete tool kit for making and working sheet metal. The only metal object found in association with the tool kit, a narrow perforated copper strip with a U-shaped cross section, could well have been made within this workshop.

Independent lines of evidence provide strong collaboration for the above reconstruction. For example, findings from ARm 57 call to mind an annealing scene depicted on a Mochica vessel.[127] Similarly, descriptions and drawings of Inca metalworking tools by sixteenth- and seventeenth-century writers are surprisingly

similar to those found in ARm 61 (e.g., Benzoni 1572 [1967]: 62; Garcilaso 1609 [1960], Book 2, Chapter 28: 82; see also Bray 1972; Lothrop 1938: 12–19).

The nature of pottery found on the floors of small ARms 64 and 85 was rather unexpected. These rooms yielded fine pottery, including a painted stirrup-spout bottle, a painted *florero*, and a small bowl with a press-molded decoration, as well as gray serving dishes and two sooted cooking pots. These fine ceramics probably signify the presence of high-status supervisory personnel, or are symbolic of the high status accorded to valued master metalworkers. What can be said with some confidence is that access to the workshop was closely controlled through the terrace complex in RS 65.

There is no evidence of food preparation among these rooms, and the plastered floor was kept refuse-free and in good repair. Tiny Rm 81, with its narrow entry and high threshold, had jars firmly set in the floor, probably for storage of drinks. Various firepits associated with thick deposits of ash, charcoal, and food remains in the adjacent spacious ARm 60 and RR 84 suggest regular food and drink preparation. The latter room even had an intact storage urn nearly 1 m high. Neither room yielded metallurgical remains.

Structure 52 was a self-contained workshop equipped to deal with major (perhaps all) component phases and facets of the metalworking stage (which follows smelting) of copper metallurgy, perhaps with on-site supervision. These compo-

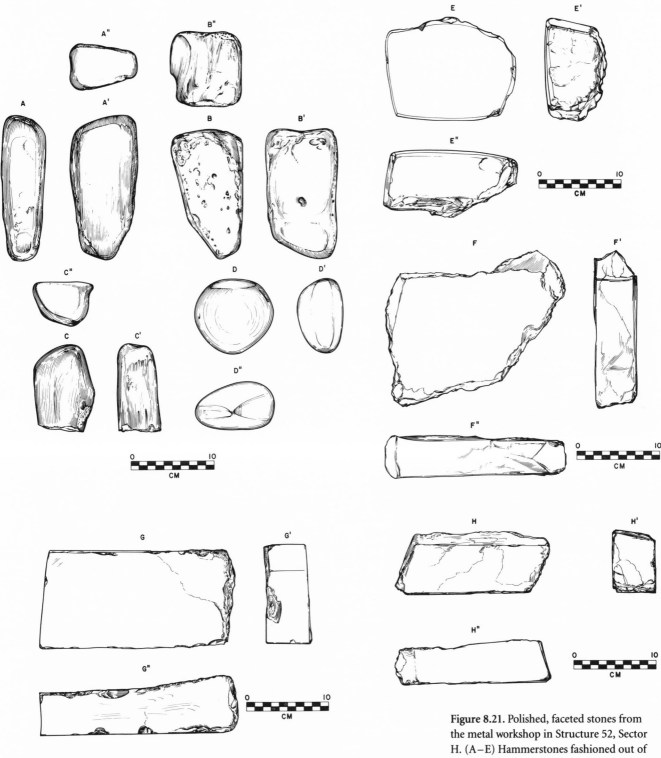

Figure 8.21. Polished, faceted stones from the metal workshop in Structure 52, Sector H. (A–E) Hammerstones fashioned out of quartzite, basalt, and diorite. (F–H) Relatively soft shale with perfectly flat surfaces and 90° corners. They may have been used for bending and cutting.

nents were clearly manifested in the differential distribution of relevant artifacts, each within a clearly demarcated architectural setting. The smelting that provided ingots and blanks was carried out in spatially segregated loci. Though the workers were apparently fed by food prepared within the workshop, they commuted in from elsewhere, and their movements, as well as those of the metal products, were tightly controlled. Whether the workshop indeed produced "finished" objects (in the sense of requiring no further processing and being ready to use) or components to be assembled into final form elsewhere cannot be said. Certainly, we do not see small chisels and punches, templates, and other tools expected for fine decorative work (e.g., repoussé) and soldering. At the same time, the recovered tools seem complete enough to produce simpler utilitarian objects (such as pins, tweezers, and needles) fashioned out of sheet metal and utilizing mechanical joinings (e.g., staples and wires). Likewise, we do not know where casting occurred. The one or two isolated faceted stones occasionally found in households (possibly metalworkers' homes) at Pampa Grande were probably used by city dwellers to repair simple household copper implements or to recycle them for other purposes. As discussed below, availability of copper objects to the general populace of the city seems to have been limited to small, utilitarian implements.

Data from Galindo complement what has been described thus far. A group of stone rooms close to a major platform (Platform A), the inferred residence of "a paramount ruler" of Galindo, revealed firepits for possible annealing, two large hammer stones, several small smoothed and polished stones, and several hundred small fragments of copper. This scatter of debitage included ceremonial and ornamental objects such as axes, small pierced discs, and a single bell, but no utilitarian implements such as needles or hooks. Overall, the evidence argues that these rooms were involved in metalworking (no smelting), under close supervision, of high status, ceremonial copper objects. This production and supervision setup is quite similar to that defined for a *Spondylus*

workshop at Pampa Grande that is discussed later.

D. Weaving and Textiles

The pre-Hispanic Andes, together with ancient Persia, have been deservingly called the two major weaving centers of the world in terms of the antiquity, technical originality, and sophistication of their textiles, as well as their artistic beauty and overall cultural significance. Though only a handful of Moche III and V textile pieces are known, they clearly show that Mochica weavers contributed to this distinguished tradition.[128]

As with other craft goods, the best examples of Moche V textiles come from elite burials. For example, a young adult female with tattooed right hand and forearm in Coffin "b" in a subterranean burial chamber (E-1) in the City of Temples at Pacatnamú was wrapped in loosely woven cloth embroidered with stepped volutes and covered by a head veil embroidered with large, bright flowers. An adult male in cane Coffin "a" in the same burial chamber, in addition to wearing a blue feather cloak, had two fine slit tapestries (Ubbelohde-Doering 1967: 27–29; also see Hecker and Hecker 1983: 53). Under a layer of white, unspun cotton covering the head, excavators found a "pictorial cloth" (not an article of clothing) that was carefully folded and stitched in a few places so that it would not unfold. A second pictorial cloth was worn as a short skirt. Both pieces are rich in iconography and thought to be "religious codices" (believed related to a water and fertility cult; see Chapter 9) that graphically illustrated important structural, temporal, and functional relationships within the Mochica cosmology.

Though no textile fragment was found in our fieldwork, excavations uncovered a possible weaving workshop in RB 70 in Sector H and evidence of large-scale cotton processing in Deer House (Compound 14).

A fire that razed Deer House, a large rectangular adobe enclosure (ca. 95 by 155 m; Figs. 8.22, 8.23) immediately north of Sector A and east of Sector B, charred and helped to preserve a layer of cotton fiber (up to 10 cm thick) that covered much of the plastered floor of a large open court-

Figure 8.22. Well-built adobe walls, one with niches, surrounding a terrace that overlooked a courtyard with burnt cotton remains within Deer House Compound. Photo by Kent C. Day.

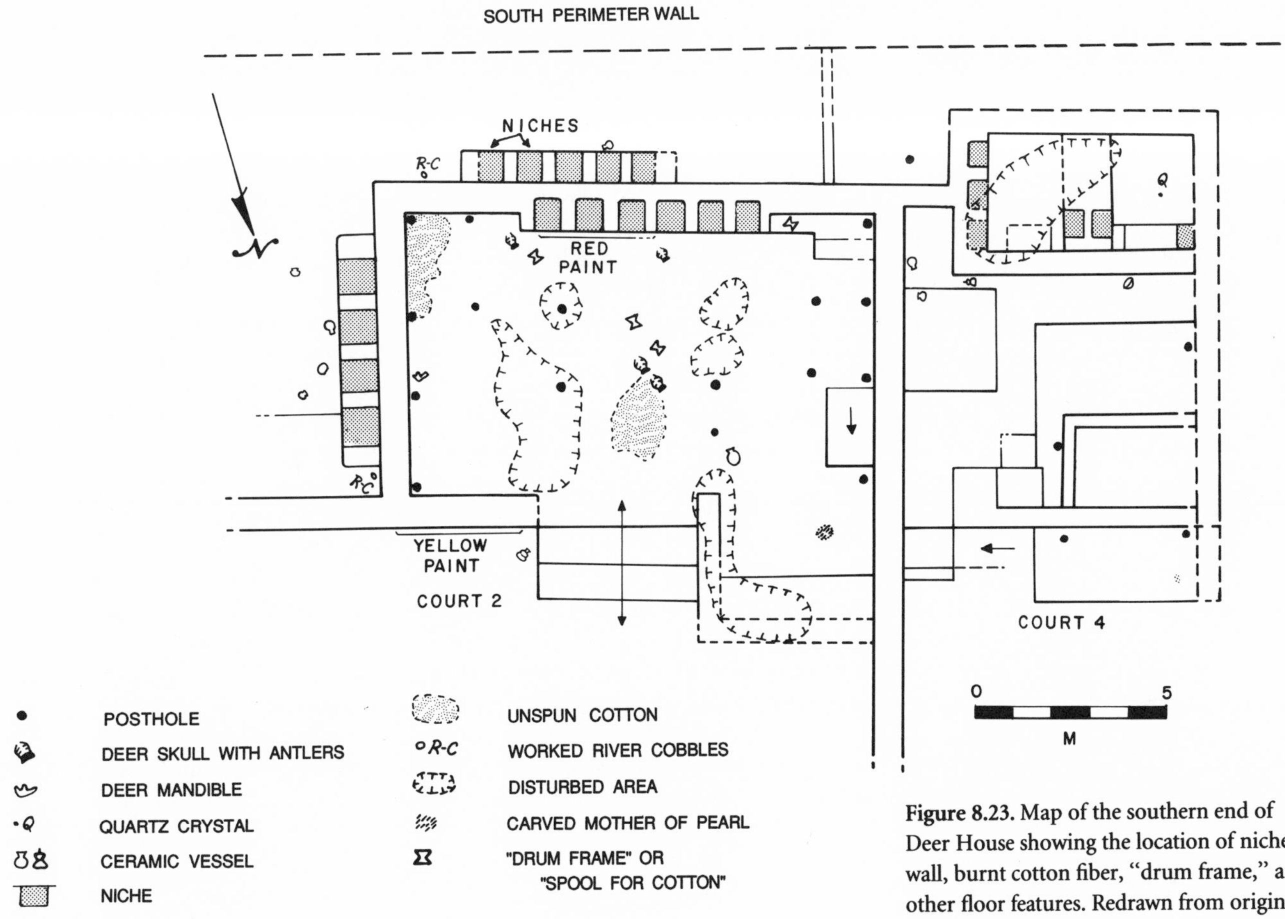

SOUTH PERIMETER WALL

NICHES

R-C

RED PAINT

R-C

YELLOW PAINT

COURT 2

COURT 4

	POSTHOLE			UNSPUN COTTON
	DEER SKULL WITH ANTLERS	R-C		WORKED RIVER COBBLES
	DEER MANDIBLE			DISTURBED AREA
Q	QUARTZ CRYSTAL			CARVED MOTHER OF PEARL
	CERAMIC VESSEL			"DRUM FRAME" OR "SPOOL FOR COTTON"
	NICHE			

0   5

M

Figure 8.23. Map of the southern end of Deer House showing the location of niched wall, burnt cotton fiber, "drum frame," and other floor features. Redrawn from original map by Kent C. Day.

yard that occupied the southern end of the enclosure. Seeds had been removed from the fiber. In the village of Mórrope and nearby communities, indigenous cotton (*Gossypium barbadense* as opposed to modern hybrid cotton) is still grown even in the face of a government ban (Vreeland 1978, 1982). The bolls are opened out, lock by lock, and the seeds removed by hand. The resulting fiber locks are stacked in a conical pile that is then thoroughly beaten with switches to form a thin, homogeneous, compacted layer (Fig. 8.24). This pancakelike layer is then folded and rolled for spinning (Vreeland 1986b: 367). If this processing sequence applies to Mochica times, the cotton fiber in Deer House may have been prepared for spinning.[129]

To gain access to the courtyard where the cotton was found, one first passed through the enclosure's single entry, near its northwest corner, and then through the central platform complex, which included a raised courtyard with a niched wall on its west side (Figs. 8.22, 8.23). Two wide steps on the east side of the raised courtyard led down to the inferred cotton processing area.

Figure 8.24. A Mórrope woman beating out ginned cotton fiber into a large, thin bundle in preparation for spinning. Courtesy of James M. Vreeland.

The architectural features and artifacts associated with the upper courtyard are unique. The west wall actually has six niches on its interior and four on its exterior, all of which are roughly symmetrical when viewed from above. Two steps appear to have provided access across the top of the niched wall. The original function of these niches is difficult to ascertain, but they should be considered within a broader setting that included a heavy ceramic object thought to be a drum frame (Fig. 8.25) and two large, complete sets of deer antlers still attached to their skulls near the niches.[130] Though their specific significance eludes us, the association of deer with elite rituals is quite clear in Mochica art. Another deer antler associated with a quartz crystal was found on the floor atop a small platform that guarded an entry (intersection of Corridors 3 and 7) to a room complex in Sector H. Overall, the association of the antlers, drum frame, and niched wall suggests a strong ritual significance for this setting.

Did the "drum" help create a solemn or, conversely, festive atmosphere for the delivery and processing of cotton? Alternatively, K. Day (pers. com. 1989) suggests that the drum frames were in reality large spools for cotton that were filled for delivery to dispersed weaving workshops. A spool or drum frame of roughly the same size and shape was found in an inferred weaving workshop in Structure 78 in Sector H described below.

Whatever the answer, cotton processing probably took place under elite supervision. Considering the lack of evidence of spinning or weaving activity within this compound, the processed cotton was probably distributed to dispersed workshops.

A substantial amount of cotton was recovered from one other context, a small two-tiered and roofed adobe platform in Compound 16 that was also burnt. Burnt seed cotton spilling out of a broken storage jar covered a narrow passage between the back perimeter wall of the lower platform and the base of the upper platform. It may be significant that the cotton here still had seeds and was kept in a vessel placed away from sun and traffic. Today, in Lambayeque, "Artisans never store de-seeded cotton for long periods of time, but keep

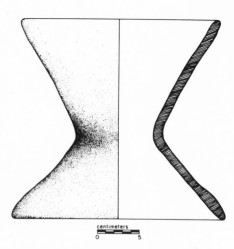

Figure 8.25. A ceramic "drum frame" excavated in ARm 78, Sector H. A nearly identical piece was found on a terrace overlooking a courtyard with burnt cotton remains in Deer House.

seedcotton for several years without damage in fabric sacks, gourds, and large ceramic vessels" (Vreeland 1986b: 367). Some seed cotton (mixed with beans) was also preserved in two constricted-neck jars in a corner of the walled-in top of a small platform mound (Huaca 18) overlooking all of Sector H. Perhaps the storage of seed cotton and beans in such formal settings reflects a high-level concern over the quality of seeds and harvest or their use in rituals related to agricultural success.[131]

Little is known about what happened to the prepared cotton fiber. The only inferred weaving workshop thus far found is within the rectangular RB 70 at the west end of Corridor 5 in Sector H (Fig. 8.26). This is one of various architectural settings interlinked by Corridor 5 that were tested for functional interdependence. Prior excavation had shown that Structure 46 at the east end of the corridor had the basic function of food and *chicha* preparation and storage.

Excavation of a largely undisturbed area at the northeast end of the Room-Block revealed an unusual array of architecture, artifacts, and floor features. A small, low, three-tiered platform was built close to a partially enclosed adobe room (RR 79). The platform, in spite of its low height, had a well-built ramp on the southwest side, and a solid clay mortar-lined roof with cane and wooden beams supported by at least one pair of posts on opposing sides of the platform. One of the postholes had a dedicatory macaw (*Psittacidae*) burial.

The adobe room had a low bench along the northeast and northwest sides, and a low one-adobe-brick-wide wall on the remaining sides that probably served more to demarcate the sunken interior floor than to impede physical and visual access. Although burnt straw and cane partially covered the plastered floor of this room, there was nothing that suggested a heavy, solid roof.

Just south of RR 79, on a well-maintained plastered floor also lightly covered by burnt roofing materials, excavation uncovered (1) a ceramic drum frame or spool tightly fitting within a small three-sided adobe brick enclosure (possibly to stabilize the spool or drum to improve its resonance),[132] (2) a broken but whole painted *florero,* (3) a sherd cluster representing at least two whole constricted-neck jars, (4) ten postholes within an area of ca. 2.5 by 3.0 m, (5) a buried flaring-neck jar whose rim was level with the floor surface, and (6) a large fragment of a carefully shaped and highly polished hardwood implement.

The last is of particular interest, as it closely resembles the traditional batten (also known as sword or beater), one of the most cherished and basic weaving tools used to open sheds so a weft may be inserted. Whether in European, Navajo, Andean, or other traditional, nonmechanized weaving, the batten is typically hardwood and has a basic knife-blade shape (long and flat, but in cross section one end is somewhat rounder and wider). The material must be hard, as the batten separates tight warp threads, and it must be polished to a very smooth finish so as not to snag threads. The preceding is a precise and accurate description of the excavated wooden object.

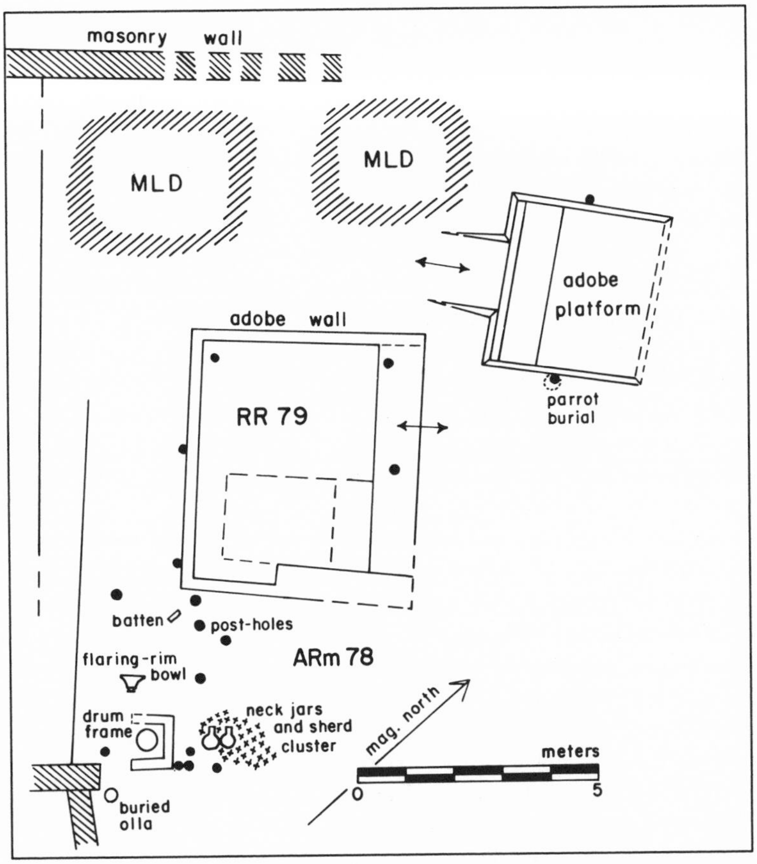

The number and configuration of postholes in RR 79 and around the drum frame are curious. There are more than would seem necessary considering the relatively light roofing suggested by the excavated materials. Did they serve functions other than supporting roofs?

A detailed scene of supervised weaving painted on a Moche IV *florero* now in the British Museum (Fig. 8.27) may be the key to interpreting the significance of the posthole pattern. Various weavers (all but one seem to be women) are shown in simple, roofed, open-air structures operating back-strap looms anchored to posts. Contiguous to the weavers and drawn at a larger scale are two elaborately dressed men seated on raised platforms. One of these men is apparently entertaining two visitors. Two constricted-neck jars nearby probably hold some drink. The weavers are associated with stirrup-spout bottles, *floreros,* and various shuttles, as well as cloth pieces whose patterns they are replicating on the looms. The elaborate dress, larger scale, and architectural setting all argue that the two seated men are in control of the weaving. Close elite supervision of high-quality textile production is indeed what we would expect from the clearly differentiated distribution of such products

Figure 8.26. Floor plan of inferred weaving workshop in ARm 78, Sector H.

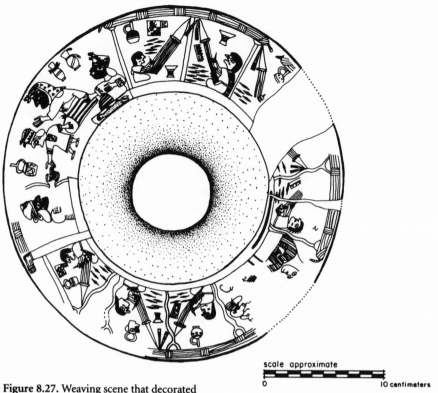

scale approximate

0   10 centimeters

Figure 8.27. Weaving scene that decorated Moche IV *florero* (flaring bowl) now in the British Museum. Drawing by Charles Sternberg.

depicted in Mochica paintings and found in burials.

Although we have found little direct physical evidence of weaving at Pampa Grande, there are definite architectural and artifactual similarities between the painted scene and RB 70. The platform in RB 70 would have been ideally positioned to supervise activity in adjoining RR 79, which, like the workshop in the painted scene, had many posts available to anchor looms and an open layout that would have offered good lighting. Thus, we infer that RR 79 was a setting for daytime weaving activity and physically detached from other domestic activities. It is also significant that another context where a ceramic drum frame or spool was found (Deer House) was also related to weaving (cotton processing). The presence of a macaw offering also affirms the importance attached to the workshop and its products.

Overall, the *florero* scene provides a basis for inferring that RR 79 and the immediate vicinity within RB 70 was an important weaving workshop manned by commuting artisans supervised by a high-status occupant of the nearby platform.

E. Bone and Stone Artifacts

A range of bones (llama, dog, human, deer, and bird) and stones (turquoise, basalt, magnetite, onyx, quartz crystals, etc.) were fashioned into various tools, personal ornaments, and ritual paraphernalia. The tibia, radius, ulna, and metapodial of llamas were popular for making tools. In modifying long bones, most commonly one or both ends were first sawed off the shaft (Fig. 8.28), although for awls, spatulas, and similar tools, one articulating end of the bone was often left unmodified to provide a handle (Fig. 8.29). Metapodials were often grooved longitudinally and split to make pointed tools such as awls. Relatively round, long shafts such as deer and llama femora were sometimes made into flutes or cut into rings (Fig. 8.30). These techniques originated well over a thousand years earlier and were widely shared by both highland and coastal cultures (e.g., see M. Shimada 1982, 1985; Wing 1972). Considering the abundance and relatively even distribution of llama bones at Pampa Grande, plus the simplicity of the techniques involved, tools were most likely manufactured at the individual or household level as the need arose. Deer bones were rare and may have had ceremonial significance and been reserved for elite use. The base of a shed antler recovered from a refuse deposit in Sector A had been hollowed out to form a small container, perhaps to hold lime for the coca leaf chewing shown in Mochica paintings (Fig. 8.31).

Some tools must have been cherished for durability, ease of use, and multifunctional character—for example, the so-called awls, which may have been used variously for shelling maize, picking wefts in weaving, decorating ceramics, or working with leather. However, many of the cutting, scraping, and puncturing tasks were performed with casual or improvised bone and stone tools. These are whole or fragmentary bones or stones "used without prior modification, apparently for short-term use and inferred limited function," discarded just as casually as they were made (M. Shimada 1982: 315). Casual tools are not the most obvious because of the minimal amount of modification. For example, long bones broken for marrow may yield fragments suitable for casual tool use. We already noted flakes with sharp cutting edges struck off basalt cobbles as part of what may be the remains of a large feast in Sector D.

Besides the metalworking stone and *batán-chungo* set described earlier, permanent stone tools include tabular pieces of fine-grained stones such as shale that were ground on one or both faces to produce smooth, straight scraping and cutting edges. Along with onyx, turquoise, and quartz crystals, slate was also used for making beads and elaborately worked pieces of unknown function. There are also large, tabular teardrop- (so-called handaxes) and disc-shaped bifacially flaked tools (Fig. 8.32) of diorite and basalt. These rocks do not readily yield sharp cutting edges like flint or obsidian. A chertlike stone was, however, used in making a borer that was surface-collected from Sector I. The only examples of imported obsidian (presumably from Quispisisa in the Central Highlands of Peru) were two tiny flakes recovered from subfloor fill. The paucity of obsidian artifacts on the Central and North Coast is believed to reflect their distribution along highland routes (Burger and Asaro 1979).

Relatively flat, perforated circular cobbles (typically quartzite) were noted on the surface along the perimeter of the site, particularly on the Southern Pediment. The hole was drilled from both sides, giving an hourglass shape in cross section. These donut stones presumably were used in conjunction with wooden hafts and have been variously interpreted as mace heads, clod-breakers, weights for fishing nets or drilling instruments, water flow regulators in canals, and so on (Eling 1987: 168–171). The size, weight, and battered perimeters of many examples, as well as their occurrence in agricultural fields, tend to support the clod-breaker thesis and the argument that many of the Southern Pediment residents were farmers.

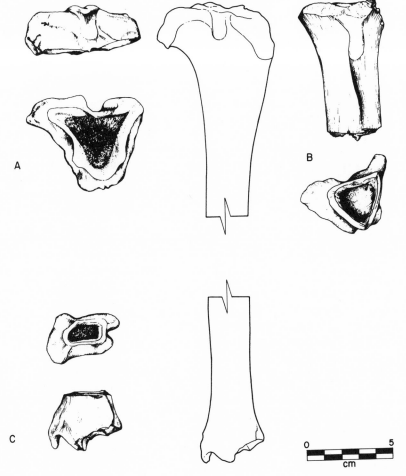

Figure 8.28. Drawings illustrating how the ends of llama long bones were removed so that the shafts could be modified for the making of implements, including flutes and awls. Bones were recovered from Sectors D and H.

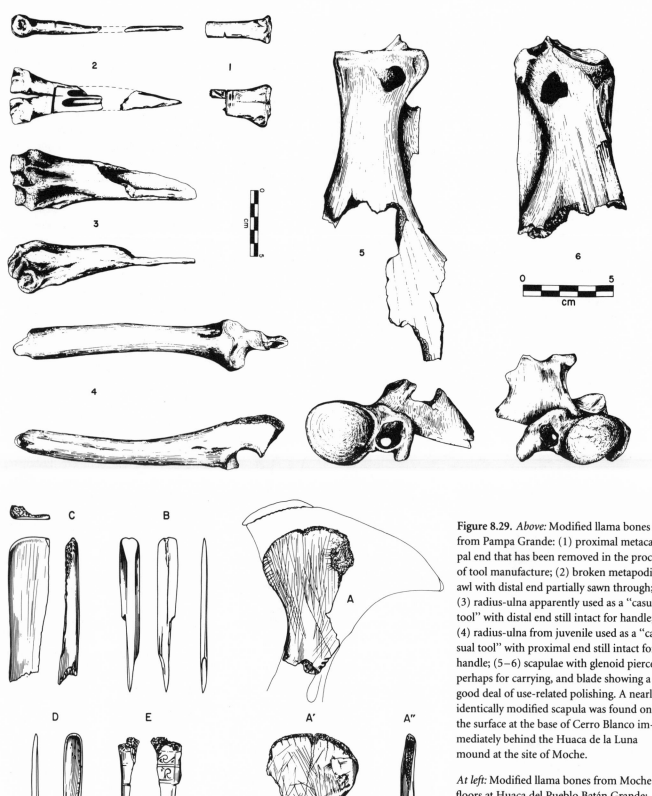

Figure 8.29. *Above:* Modified llama bones from Pampa Grande: (1) proximal metacarpal end that has been removed in the process of tool manufacture; (2) broken metapodial awl with distal end partially sawn through; (3) radius-ulna apparently used as a "casual tool" with distal end still intact for handle; (4) radius-ulna from juvenile used as a "casual tool" with proximal end still intact for handle; (5–6) scapulae with glenoid pierced, perhaps for carrying, and blade showing a good deal of use-related polishing. A nearly identically modified scapula was found on the surface at the base of Cerro Blanco immediately behind the Huaca de la Luna mound at the site of Moche.

At left: Modified llama bones from Moche V floors at Huaca del Pueblo Batán Grande: (A) modified ilium showing shaping and extensive grinding on all surfaces; (B–E) broken spatulas from the Moche V level at Huaca del Pueblo Batán Grande, probably made of camelid long bone shafts.

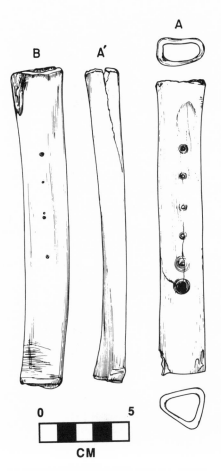

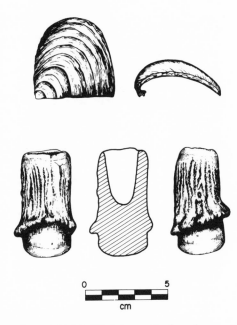

Figure 8.31. Modified deer antler base (possibly a lime container) and cut shell from Pampa Grande.

Figure 8.30. Flutes made out of camelid long bone shafts excavated from Moche V floors at Huaca del Pueblo Batán Grande, La Leche Valley. Similar, broken flutes were found in Sectors D and H at Pampa Grande. Drawn by César Samillán from originals by I. Shimada.

In general, because of their relative rarity in excavated primary contexts, it is difficult to characterize the functions of many of the stone tools at Pampa Grande. Use-wear analysis has not yet been carried out. Surface survey and collection, however, indicate that stone tools are most common in Sectors D, H, and much of the Southern Pediment—i.e., inferred areas of habitation and dispersed craft production of utilitarian objects. The densely built

areas at the north and south ends of the Sector I compounds, for example, have yielded a wide range of stone tools such as donut stones, borers, handaxes, and hammer stones.

On the basis of this differential distribution, one wonders if stone and bone implements were the "commoners'" equivalents of tempered copper implements that had a more restricted distribution. The only instances of sets of copper implements (tumis and spatulas) come from inferred craft (metal, bone, and ceramic) workshops in Structures O and R, Sector D, and nearby spacious Compound 2 just to the east of Sector D. We also noted the association of high-status ceramics with copper working in Structure 52, Sector H. However, it should be kept in mind that our sampling of the Southern Pediment as a whole was quite limited, and the resultant data are not readily comparable to those from the central Sectors of the site. The possible dichotomy between copper tools on the one hand and stone and bone tools on the other is one line of study well worth pursuing.

F. Spondylus *and Other Shell Objects*

A remarkable contrast to the above is seen in respect to the procurement, supervised manufacture, distribution, and use of exotic *Spondylus*, *Strombus*, and *Conus* shells, which were all imported from warm tropical waters off the Ecuadorian coast. While *Strombus* often appear in Mochica art as trumpets, stylized monsters, and the cargo of llamas—and are even shown in Moche V Burial Theme scenes—*Spondylus* and *Conus* are quite rare in pre–Moche V art and actual specimens found.[133]

Spondylus shells were available in an appreciable number and used in a variety of contexts at Pampa Grande. A significant increase in the use and distribution of *Spondylus* among Middle Horizon and subsequent cultures of the North Coast seems to originate with the Moche V power shift to the northern end of the North Coast and the inferred intensification of trade with coastal Ecuador.

At Pampa Grande, there is no documented use of *Strombus*. The only examples of *Conus* come from subfloor fill of the square courtyard just off the entry to

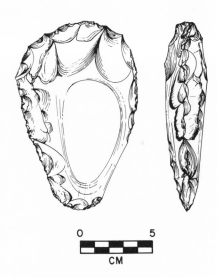

Figure 8.32. Bifacially flaked and ground "handaxe" excavated in Sector H.

Structure R in Sector D. Two possible pendants made by sculpting the solid innermost spiral of *Conus* were recovered; one seems to represent an anthropomorphized *Strombus* creature, the other a monkey (Fig. 8.33). The latter is similar to monkeys found perched on the stirrup-and-spout joint of Moche V bottles from the Jequetepeque Valley, while the former resembles the *Strombus* Monster found on a Moche V tapestry excavated at Pacatnamú in the same valley (see Chapter 9).

Supportive evidence for the increased use of *Spondylus* comes from our fieldwork at Pampa Grande. Whole and worked *Spondylus* were recovered from several primary-use contexts at Pampa Grande, attesting to its ceremonial importance: (1) a whole *Spondylus* shell was found at the base of each of an opposing pair of walls constricting the corridor atop the 290-meter-long ramp; (2) a dedicatory offering of a whole *Spondylus* was found in the central ramp to the Second Platform at

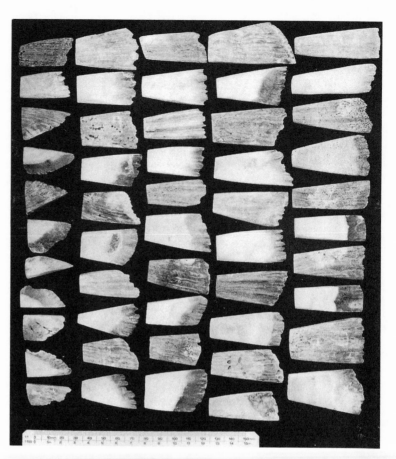

Figure 8.34. Cut, polished *Spondylus* pieces that were interred in a subfloor pit as an offering at the First Terrace of Huaca Fortaleza.

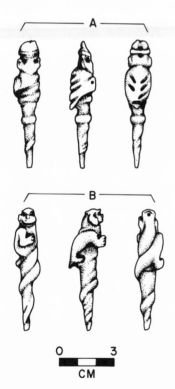

Figure 8.33. Spiral shell (probably *Conus fergusoni*) cores with carved (A) *Strombus* monster and (B) monkey, recovered from Sector D.

the east end of the First Terrace of Huaca Fortaleza; (3) a carved and polished *Spondylus* shell necklace and a cluster of llama bones were recovered in a cache immediately behind the center of the backdrop wall of the Second Platform; and (4–5) a complete carved and polished *Spondylus* necklace, shell pendants, and small beads of "azurite" (more likely to be sodalite), turquoise, and whole *Spondylus* were placed over a few bones and teeth of a child, and over an immature llama skeleton (Haas 1985: 404). These sacrificial offerings were found in a plastered, sealed chamber built inside the main access ramp (2.7 m long by 2.3 m wide) to the Palatial Room Complex at the southwest corner of the Main Body top. The necklace had forty-six trapezoid pendants of graduated size (Fig. 8.34); there were twenty tiny turquoise beads, five tubular *Spondylus* shell beads, and two tubular "azurite" beads. Just beyond the top of the ramp in a shallow subfloor pit was a second, matching *Spondylus* shell necklace with fifty-two pendants, twenty-five turquoise beads, and ten "azurite" beads.

There is definite evidence for the working of *Spondylus* at Pampa Grande. The 1978 excavation confirmed the hypothesis that the surface scatters of *Spondylus* fragments found next to a series of small platform mounds (Huacas 10, 11, and 13) represented small dispersed *Spondylus* workshops (I. Shimada 1982; Shimada and Shimada 1981). A surface scatter at the southeast corner of Huaca 11 within the spacious, terraced adobe Compound 15, known as Spondylus House (130 by 125 m), was selected for excavation (Fig. 8.35).

The scatter was within Rm 1, which had one entry and a multilevel terrace built against the north wall. The room excavation yielded thirty-two whole *Spondylus* shells, as well as hundreds of small spines that had been broken off the shell and numerous tiny shell splinters and roughly trapezoidal pieces some with spines systematically removed and others with spines still intact (Fig. 8.36). The overwhelming portion of broken spines, splinters, and trapezoidal pieces were found in three clusters on and near the floor (Fig. 8.35). The more scattered distribution of whole shells is clearly related to the burning of the roof and to the stones and adobe bricks that washed in more or less as a single mass, probably during the torrential rains and associated floods that attacked the site close in time to its abandonment (see Chapter 10).

As expected, we also found fragments of constricted-neck jars that were probably used to bring food and drink to artisans in the room. A fist-sized cobble with partially battered ends found with the above rubble fill was the only implement found.

This room represents the only documented Mochica *Spondylus* workshop. The composition of the *Spondylus* remains allows us to offer a tentative reconstruction of activities within the room and gain some perspective on the scale of production. The whole shells were first broken into roughly trapezoidal pieces, typically 5–6 cm long and 3.0–3.5 cm wide, perhaps using simple tools such as a copper chisel and a stone hammer. These dimensions match those of the pendants found at Huaca Fortaleza. Spines were then struck off, probably with the same simple tools, and the fragments collected, perhaps to make tiny beads or powder or to use in inlay work. Worked pieces recovered from the top of Huaca Fortaleza indicate that the next step was to smooth and polish surfaces and straighten edges. Long surface scratches suggest smoothing with something like coarse-grained sandstone, preshaped coral blocks, or coarse-tempered sherds, perhaps followed by polishing with finer-grained sherds or stones.

The above inferred *Spondylus* craft is remarkably simple in the techniques and tools involved. If all the observed scatters

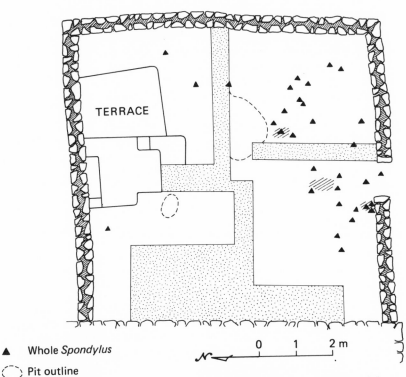

▲ Whole *Spondylus*
⬭ Pit outline
▦ Unexcavated area
▨ Cluster of *Spondylus* fragments

0   1   2 m

Figure 8.35. Excavated *Spondylus* workshop at the southeast corner of Huaca 11 within Spondylus House (Compound 15).

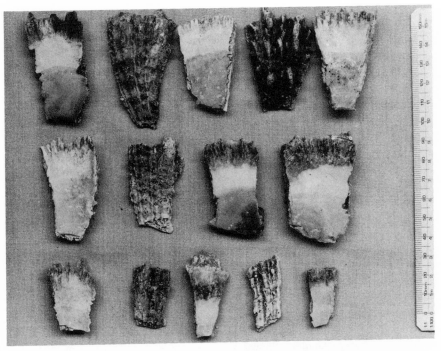

Figure 8.36. Roughly shaped *Spondylus* pieces recovered at the workshop in Spondylus House. Compare these pieces with those shown in Figure 8.34.

represent the same sort of *Spondylus* work-shops, then we are once again dealing with craft production in dispersed locations manned by commuting artisans, much as posited for the other products we examined earlier.

However, *Spondylus* working was distinguished from other crafts by isolated production loci and the high-status or ceremonial value of the products. Spondylus House is dominated by extensive terraces and a sizable platform mound, and no associated residential structures have been identified. The contexts are quite similar for the two possible workshops next to Huacas 10 and 13. The physical isolation of the *Spondylus* workshops and their association with *huacas* probably reinforced their importance. Overall, we see exclusive, tightly controlled production and use of *Spondylus* products.[134]

Considering the sizes of *Spondylus* caches found at Huaca Fortaleza, a concentration of thirty-two whole shells in one workshop is quite impressive. Whole *Spondylus* shells recovered from the workshop had circular valves measuring ca. 6 cm to over 11 cm from hinge to perimeter.[135] Each shell could potentially have yielded four to twelve trapezoidal pieces of the above dimensions. Thus, the two largest caches of *Spondylus* pendants (ninety-eight pieces) from Huaca Fortaleza may represent the investment of somewhere between nine and twenty-five whole shells.

Considering the overall rarity of *Spondylus* reported for Mochica sites, *Spondylus* findings from Pampa Grande represent an impressive quantity.[136] Productive output would be even more impressive if all three *Spondylus* scatters at Pampa Grande indeed represented the same sort of simple, redundant production seen in Rm 1. However, the scatters next to Huacas 10 and 13 may represent workshops involved in the complementary tasks of making shell inlays and beads under the supervision of the central authority.

It remains to be determined whether the appearance of various inferred *Spondylus* workshops at Pampa Grande reflected a significant upsurge in demand for *Spondylus* stemming from Moche V shifts in religious ideology and rituals (see Chapter 9), changes in trading partners in coastal Ecuador, or something else. Resolution of these questions requires future excavation of other *Spondylus* scatters at Pampa Grande as well as a better understanding of earlier Mochica use and distribution of *Spondylus* products.

4. Redistributive Nature of the Moche V Urban Economy

One of the key features of the Moche V urban economy was that craft production was underwritten by the principle of redistribution. Below, we examine the data that form the basis for this characterization.

A. Centralized, Differentiated, Large-Scale Storage

The basic cornerstone of a large-scale redistributive economy is the centrally administered storage and distribution of goods (e.g., see D'Altroy and Hastorf 1984; Day 1982a,b; Isbell 1978; Morris 1981, 1986; Murra 1980). No large-scale, formalized, corporate storage system has yet been documented for pre–Phase V Mochica sites. For example, at the site of Moche, only small domestic storerooms have been identified thus far (T. Topic 1982: 274).

At Moche V Pampa Grande, however, there were at least three classes of storage: (1) unprecedented large-scale storage, under centralized administration, of comestibles and noncomestibles (raw materials and finished craft goods probably differentiated) for state-sponsored craft production, rituals, feasts and other redistributive activities, as well as for the support of elite households; (2) communal storage of food and drink for workers engaged in inferred dispersed production of mundane, utilitarian goods in the Southern Pediment under traditional local authority; and (3) household storage. All were relatively isolated, and each storeroom had restricted access through a single entrance often with a high threshold. The first two groups in particular have floors and walls that were well built and plastered. The first group even displays standardization of forms, dimensions, and construction materials and techniques, as well as careful ground preparation for even floors and good drainage (Anders 1977, 1981).

Household storage encompasses masonry storerooms with series of large storage vessels set directly in the dirt floors as well as in quite small but well-built plastered rooms. The elite residences in Compound 38 in Sector H described earlier present good examples of household storage.

The second group is the least known. A storage facility occupying the southwest corner of a rectangular masonry enclosure in Unit 87, Sector J, on the Southern Pediment (Fig. 7.33) is regarded as an example of communal storage. Its capacity (a floor area of ca. 32 m²) is respectable even relative to the first group and clearly exceeds any household storerooms defined thus far. There is no apparent doorway; a ladder was probably used to gain access. Its irregular internal divisions into three rooms and peculiar construction (adobe abutting onto thick masonry walls) also deviate from the standards of the first and third groups. Two storerooms contained various large storage vessels but the third yielded no clue as to its original contents. The plastered floors of these rooms were lower (by about 30 cm) than those of surrounding structures. These construction features suggest that the intent was to keep the inside as cool as possible. We suspect that this type of storage is likely to be found in other areas of the Southern Pediment, perhaps including the five contiguous enclosures that together form Sector I.

What concerns us most here is the first group, consisting of nine structures built exclusively of mortared adobe bricks in areas with elaborate, tightly controlled access in the central Sectors of A, B, D, F, and H and their immediate vicinity. All but one were comprised of one or two rows of contiguously built rectangular or square cells (anywhere from three to twenty-four cells). Cells within each complex were standardized in shape, size, and construction technique and materials.

Excavation of sampled cells and their broader settings yielded few clues about their original contents (Anders 1977, 1981). The cells were essentially void of floor features and artifacts. However, in addition to the characteristics described above, there are several important details and observations about their construction that provide the basis for attributing storage function to these complexes: (1) high, inconvenient thresholds (70 cm high or more) integrated as part of the continuous coursed walls; (2) solid, thick, mortar-sealed roofs;[137] (3) thorough interior and exterior plastering; (4) thick (up to 80 cm), mortared (at times chinked with sherds and stones) adobe brick walls with bonded corners that were apparently built in a single episode; and (5) carefully prepared foundations (e.g., adobe-lined, limestone gravel, and/or ash-charcoal fill; Anders 1981: 395–396; H. Knapp, pers. com. 1988).

All bespeak a concern with the control of natural elements (pests, dust, humidity, light, and temperature) that is the key to any long-term storage. Further, the contiguous placement and cubic or rectangular shape of the cells would minimize surface area exposed to natural forces.[138]

Four groups were recognized within the first class of storage facilities on the basis of significant variation in the number and arrangement of constituent storerooms, inferred or documented contents, associated structures and broader architectural contexts, and relative locations within the site (Table 14; Anders 1981: 395–399).

Group I consists of the three largest complexes (Unit 25, with twenty-four storerooms; Unit 29, with twenty cells; and Unit 30, with fourteen cells; Figs. 8.37, 8.38), all with the same two-row lattice layout and large adjacent court areas. The individual storerooms of this group are up to five or more times larger than those of other complexes just in horizontal dimensions. These complexes are secluded, with access controlled by multiple security points at the Sector and Unit levels. Yet they are spatially close to Huacas Fortaleza, 2, and 3, and their contents were most likely related to the functions of these *huacas*. Group II contains the three smaller complexes of Units 26–28, all found in Sector A, each closely associated with a colonnaded platform with a central ramp and spacious court (Fig. 8.39). Perhaps reflecting their smaller size, their foundations are not as solid or carefully prepared as those of the first group.

Group III within the centrally administered storage system corresponds to two complexes found in Sectors H (Unit 32) and D (Structure S, Unit 51). As elaborated below, they are the smallest complexes, with five and three cells, respectively. They both had been burnt, thus preserving their original contents, the former containing four cells with maize kernels and one with beans, and the latter containing two cells of maize kernels and one of beans. The complexes are situated in the midst of craft-production and service-oriented areas that are contiguous and readily accessible to Sectors A and B. In regard to the last characteristic, the complexes, though small, are exclusively of adobe-mortar construction, in contrast to the surrounding small agglutinated masonry domestic constructions.

Group IV is a tentative category composed of only one example: a possible formal adobe storage structure situated within an annex conjoined to the east wall of Deer House and accessible only through a single narrow entry. The regular undulations on the surface suggest that it may have three standardized cells.

The original contents of Group I are a matter of speculation. Given the external and internal forces and conditions that brought about the establishment of Pampa Grande, large-scale food storage would

Table 14. Comparison of capacities of storage complexes at Pampa Grande. Taken from Table 8 in Shimada 1982: 205.

Provenience	Number of cells	Computed storage capacity using a standardized height of 2m
Unit 25	24	1242.2 m³
Unit 29	20	570.4
Unit 30	14	487.2
Unit 28	6	131.7
Unit 27	7	237.3
Unit 26	5	111.0
Unit 32	4 or 5	185.3 (computed as five cells)
Unit 51	3	30.6

Figures based on Anders (1975)

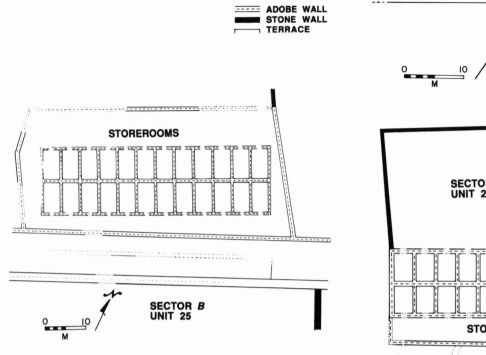

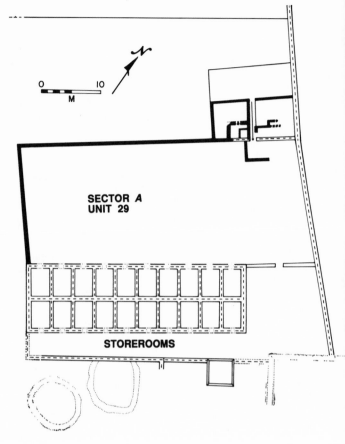

Figure 8.37. Group I storage complexes in Units 25 (Sector B) and 29 (Sector A). Redrawn by César Samillán from original field maps by Martha Anders.

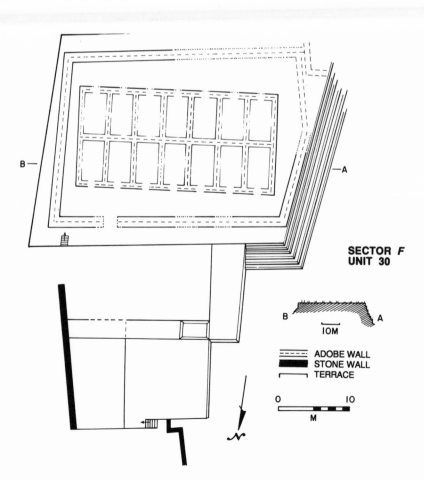

Figure 8.38. Storage complex in Unit 30, Sector F. Redrawn by César Samillán from original field maps by Martha Anders.

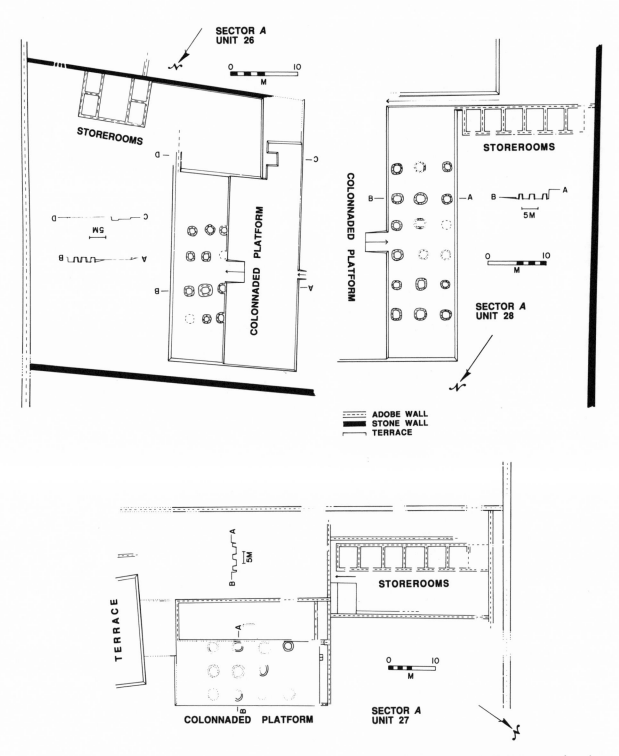

Figure 8.39. Group II storage complexes in Units 26–28, all in Sector A. Redrawn by César Samillán from original field maps by Martha Anders.

seem logical. However, it is doubtful whether we can formulate such a simple equation (cf. Isbell 1978). Andean cultural responses to droughts have not been well studied (Shimada et al. 1991a: 265). Logically, we would expect that responses would be shaped by the abruptness, duration, and severity of droughts, as well as by the subsistence and other resource basis, size, and organizational capabilities of the affected populations. They are creative processes that are situation-specific. In our case, the establishment of Pampa Grande appears to have been preceded by at least some of the series of severe droughts and El Niño events that spanned much of the sixth century, and was soon followed by a prolonged pluvial period between A.D. 602 and 635 that surely led to increased agricultural production. An important question is whether the Moche V polity learned and planned ahead for future unpredictable climatic anomalies by incorporating large-scale food storage as an integral part of the original urban planning.

The storage facilities of Group I failed to yield clues about their former contents.[139] Also, we have the nagging question of why Group I complexes were not burnt along with those of Group III if the former also contained food. It is just as plausible to argue that they served for the storage of valued craft goods produced in Sectors D and H and exotic raw materials and sumptuary tribute brought to the site. Sectors A and H were accessible to each other through a formal gate at the southeast corner of Sector H. Unit 29, one of the largest storage complexes at the site, is located just inside the gate. On the east side of the Great Compound, there is a symmetrically placed gate that provided direct access to the northeast portion of the Compound from Sector D. Craft goods may well have been stored in Sector A for later use in accordance with the political economy and ritual calendar controlled by the central authority. The circumstances surrounding the end of Moche V occupation at Pampa Grande (see Chapter 10) also suggest that at least a portion (if not much) of the contents of the first storage group was highly valued craft goods.

Our picture of the timing of the construction of storage buildings is not clear.

The largest storage facility, Unit 25 in Compound 2, appears to have been built over a specially prepared surface on sterile soil. No repair or resurfacing of the floor was noted, suggesting a late construction date. In Unit 29 near the northwest corner of Huaca Fortaleza, however, storerooms were located over the remains of two earlier construction phases that do not appear to have served for storage. At this point, we can only conclude that at least some of the large formal storage facilities were constructed relatively late in time. Alternatively, they could have been built originally at the time of the establishment of Moche V Pampa Grande and their locations subsequently changed as part of the evolving urban landscape. Overall, we find insufficient support for the argument that large-scale, centrally administered storage at Pampa Grande was a buffer against future environmental stress.

In the case of Group II, the contents were likely to have been goods used by participants of ceremonies atop the nearby colonnaded platforms. The low height of the platforms, the absence of perimeter walls that would have shielded the platform top, and the spacious surrounding courts all suggest that such activities were meant to be widely seen. Indeed, Mochica art is replete with scenes of apparent ceremonies centered atop roofed platforms.

Group III facilities (Units 32 and 51) were more accessible, with perhaps only one low-level authority controlling access. As discussed below, the maize and beans in these storerooms seem to have been used on a frequent, regular basis. In other words, this group supported more regular and mundane activities involving low-level officials and artisans, in contrast to the second group, which seems to have been related to more sporadic elite-oriented ceremonies.

Group IV may also have stored grain. The surrounding structures with utilitarian ceramics and evidence of fire use may have been the kitchens for preparing food and drink for the elite residents and commuting workers engaged in the cotton fiber distribution and processing coordinated through Deer House.

In spite of the variation observed above, these storage groups (particularly I–III) all manifest high-level concern with access, protection of contents, differentiation of contents, standardization of the quality and quantity of stored goods, and uniformity of architecture. The first and final two points need some elaboration. The first includes the supervision and accounting of ingress and egress, particularly in Unit 51, Sector D, with its hierarchical terrace with a thronelike seat, and in the multiroom building in Unit 29, Sector A (Figs. 7.18, 7.19).[140] The quality standardization of stored goods is highly evident in maize kernels, as explained below. Quantitative standardization is inferred from the uniform dimensions of the component storerooms within each complex. Consistent use and careful bonding of adobe bricks, as well as standardized dimensions, imply close, high-level supervision of the labor force and construction materials (Shimada in press 1). These storage complexes were built as well as or perhaps better than any other corporate adobe architecture at Pampa Grande. On these bases we argue for the centralized administration of large, formal storage facilities and their contents at Pampa Grande.

Formal storage facilities documented at the contemporary site of Galindo in the Moche Valley (Bawden 1977: 148–186) are pale reflections of the degree of formality, architectural unity, and perhaps even functional differentiation seen at Pampa Grande. Access was indirect via a single path and controlled by isolated hillside placement and the presence of major supervisory compounds. There was virtually no evidence of domestic or any other activity but storage. Two functionally differentiated masonry storage constructions were found on extensive walled-in Hillsides B and C overlooking the site (Fig. 6.3). Masonry structures on Hillside B were quite variable in form and size, built directly on the sloping terrain without any apparent order, and stored large crude jars. Hillside C featured storage structures of greater regularity and quality built on well-prepared terraces. Like those of Hillside B, these structures also had stone benches and stone-lined sunken pits. However, the coarse plainware vessels found on the benches within were generally smaller than those found in Hillside B structures. Some

structures in Hillside C contained no vessels. Though no indications of the original contents of these vessels were found, Hillside C is believed to have been an area of "more exclusive and elite storage" than Hillside B because of its greater topographical isolation and cultural measures (walls and complexes) for controlling access, as well as its orderly layout and better-quality architecture (ibid., 175).

Those Galindo masonry structures with internal subdivisions and plainware jars resemble communal storage at Pampa Grande. In fact, the extensive use of ceramic vessels for storage presumably under the central authority at Galindo is curious. Galindo does not have anything like the highly standardized and elaborately constructed adobe storage structures found at Pampa Grande. Could this mean that traditional Mochica labor conscription was in disarray? We already noted the paucity of marked adobe bricks. Was large-scale storage at Galindo more concerned with water and food items? Was there less demand for sumptuary goods for the political economy at the frontier center of Galindo? Bawden (ibid., 181–182) argues that "Redistribution at Galindo must thus be viewed in localized terms with the settlement marking a secondary center of authority, the prime direction of policy probably emanating from Pampa Grande. This situation obviates the necessity for such quantities of highly valued commodities as would have been necessary at the center of the [Mochica] state." However, as discussed in the preceding chapter, it is questionable whether Galindo and Pampa Grande were linked into a single Moche V political economy.

B. The Redistributive Economy in Operation: Chicha and Craft Production

It has become quite common to attribute a redistributive character to the economy of pre-Inca Andean cultures. However, too often evidence is meager and there is implicit but heavy dependence on analogy to the Inca redistributive economy.[141] My excavations at Pampa Grande were an attempt to reconstruct Moche V urban economy on its own terms proceeding from the characterization of individual activity areas to their articulation at progres-

sively higher levels of organization. The final section of this chapter thus presents my empirical characterization of the redistributive urban economy at Pampa Grande.

Provisioning of workers engaged in craft production with chicha and food is seen in a number of locations within Sectors D and H (I. Shimada 1978, 1982). But let us begin by first examining the cultural significance and production of chicha.

It would not be an exaggeration to state that the most widely consumed and important traditional beverage in the Andes has been chicha, a mildly fermented drink made out of various crops such as maize, yuca, and peanuts. Clearly, the most important is maize chicha. In the Inca Empire, an abundant supply of maize chicha was essential in the proper operation of its political economy and performance of religious ceremonies. The generous offer of chicha was critical in establishing and perpetuating the image of the Inca's "chiefly generosity" to his guests and those rendering services to him (e.g., see Murra 1960; Morris 1974, 1979, 1986). At the same time, sharing of chicha also helped to establish and reinforce the unwritten but binding reciprocal relationship between ruler and ruled. Aside from these symbolic gestures and significance, chicha consumption and attendant intoxication, even to a mild degree, undoubtedly helped to create an "affirmative" image of imposed tasks that might otherwise be onerous. Recently, Moore (1989) presented archaeological and ethnohistorical data attesting to similar roles of chicha in the Chimú Kingdom. Below, we see that at least some of the importance the Inca and the Chimú attached to chicha dates back to Moche V times.

In spite of some regional variation, chicha making in the Andes, past and present, has certain shared basic steps, with each step requiring vessels of different size and shape (e.g., Camino 1987: 30–32, 39–42; Cobo 1653 [1964]: 242; Morris 1979; Shimada 1976: 215–218). Ethnographically, uniform kernels are germinated, dried, and crushed with a wooden or stone batán-chungo set, and then mixed with cold water in a large open bowl or basin. The resultant milky white liquid is then slowly cooked in large, tall urns. While the liquid cools, some kernels are masticated by women, mixed in as a fermentation agent, and left overnight. When the desired balance of acidity, sweetness, and alcoholic strength is achieved, the liquid is strained and cooked again. Finally, it is decanted into smaller vessels with constricted necks for distribution and consumption or storage for a higher alcohol level. Figure 8.40 illustrates a typical *chicha*-making scene in the village of Vicús. Note the range of vessel forms present and compare it with the above description and Figure 8.41, a Moche III vessel believed to depict *chicha* preparation.

Now, consider findings from large spacious ARm 56, Structure 46 (Fig. 8.20), which was readily accessible from the weaving workshop in RB 70 via Streets 5 and 9. Various lines of evidence suggest large-scale *chicha* making was carried out in the room: (1) numerous burnt patches on the floor associated with ash, charcoal, and lumps of carbonized maize kernels, but no food remains; (2) an in situ *batán*; (3) a wide range of vessel types and sizes, including one large basin (ca. 50 cm in diameter and over 25 cm deep; estimated functional capacity of ca. 12–15 liters) and at least four large broken urns showing fire-blackened bottoms; and (4) an unusual concentration of over thirty constricted neck jars with no indication of use over fire.

Nearby ARm 55, on the other hand, yielded a hearth and various blackened cooking vessels, as well as a *batán-chungo* set in direct association with primary organic refuse, including whole and fragmentary maize cobs. Food preparation is clearly indicated. That ARm 56 had only kernels and no cobs in contraposition to the findings from the above kitchen (ARm 55) is quite important. Here and elsewhere in Pampa Grande, cobs were associated with food preparation or consumption and not with *chicha* making.

In his study of *chicha* making in three regions of Peru, Nicholson (1960: 298) observes that the careful choice of maize type is of primary importance, since "uniformity of type, with reference to the types of maize used for *chicha*, means uniformity of germination rate," which is crucial. Significantly, large numbers of kernels of highly uniform size and form were found

in the burnt five-cell storage facility in Unit 32, Sector H. Four contiguous cells contained maize kernels, and the last, beans with some maize kernels mixed in perhaps as a result of the post-abandonment collapse of the cells (Anders 1977, 1981; Shimada and Shimada 1981).

The provisioning of workers engaged in craft production with *chicha* and food is also suggested by data from strategically situated Structures R and S near the center of Sector D (Fig. 7.19). These structures straddle one of the main east-west streets of the Sector at the point where a north-south street branches off.

Structure R as a whole was built on a gentle slope along an east-west running street (corresponding to a present-day gully) and was buried deep in flood deposits shortly after the abandonment of the site. One such buried construction was Rm 5 (with interior measurements of 5.3 by 5.5 m), which contained a wide range of ceramic vessels and a mixture of ash, charcoal bits, and carbonized kernels. Ceramics included several large coarse redware storage vessels, including one measuring 61 cm in diameter and originally standing over a meter high, a complete basin with everted rim (45 cm across and 27 cm deep; an estimated functional capacity of ca. 15 liters), several constricted-neck jars, some with animal or human face decorations, and fragments of a fineline-painted stirrup-spout bottle.

Testing of low areas immediately around Rm 5 yielded an impressive range and quantity of constricted-neck jars to the near exclusion of other vessel types. For example, based on differences in form and painted, modeled, and molded decoration, at least seventeen reconstructable vessels of one constricted-neck jar subtype can be recognized. There must have been literally dozens of constricted-neck jars in this area. Coupled with the proximity to storerooms with maize (Unit 51), the above findings suggest that this part of Structure R was involved in *chicha* making and distribution.

Water for *chicha* making, as well as finished *chicha*, may have been stored in a small (2.5 by 2.8 m) solidly built room (Rm 3; Fig. 8.42) with a high threshold and a three-step interior stairway situated

across the terraced area from Rm 5. Most of the sherds that literally covered the entire floor belonged to constricted-neck jars and storage vessels that were set in six shallow conical depressions (33–43 cm in diameter and 7–8 cm deep) in the floor.

Food consumption is indicated by considerable accumulations of organic refuse within Structure R. The organic debris near Rm 3 included bird, dog, guinea pig, deer, and llama bones, various shellfish, corn cobs, and an avocado seed. Rm 4 also yielded a concentration of *Donax* shells (some seven hundred), and fragments of crab shells and llama bones. At the same time, excavations yielded no ceramic serving dishes or definite food preparation areas. Food may have been served in perishable gourd vessels.

There are various lines of evidence that point to small-scale copper working within Structure R. First, a faceted stone showing long, fine scratches and three fragments of a small concave crucible (6.9 cm across and 1.9 cm high) were recovered from refuse north of Rm 3. The crucible, made of a coarse, unfired sand/clay mixture, had a thick, grayish slag interior coating and may have been used to melt or purify copper ingots or blanks. Second, a short rectangular piece of slate with one beveled side of the type posited for use in shaping copper sheets was found on the floor of nearby Rm 2. Finally, a group of four copper needles of various lengths and fashioned out of copper sheets was encountered on the adjacent Rm 4 floor.

Adjoining Structure S, Unit 51 (Figs. 7.18, 7.19), provides strong evidence that the above activities, including *chicha* making, were closely supervised and provisioned by the same supervisory group. Structure S is dominated by an impressive terrace complex with three ramps bridging three levels. The orientation and layout of this complex indicates that it was designed to control the key intersection of north-south and east-west streets plus access to storerooms in the adjacent courtyard to the northeast. In both cases, one had to pass in front of two substantial bench-thrones (4.6 by 2.0 m by 0.3 m high, and 2.6 by 2.6 m and 0.3 m high) built atop the highest terrace against a solid adobe back wall spanning the entire terrace.

Figure 8.40. Photo showing *chicha* preparation in a rural house in Vicús, upper Piura Valley, a region long known for large production and consumption of *chicha*. Here, a mixture of water, mashed maize, and some cane sugar and yeast is slowly cooked in large earthen vessels made using the traditional paddle-anvil technique. Note the many gourd and ceramic vessels of varied shape and size used in different stages of *chicha* making.

Figure 8.41. Moche III vessel believed to show *chicha* making in progress. Brüning National Archaeological Museum, Lambayeque.

The fire that beset the storerooms (as well as the adjacent highest terrace) preserved their architectural details and contents. The storage facility (ca. 3.35 by 7 m on the exterior), built on a low terrace, consisted of three contiguous cells of uniform dimensions (interior measurements of ca. 2.55 by 2 m) that had a solid roof. The walls were preserved all around to a height of about 20–35 cm. The amount of associated rubble suggests that their original height was perhaps close to 1.5 m. The typical storage capacity of each cell may have been around 5 m³.

The central and west cells contained a layer 8–10 cm thick of carbonized kernels of uniform size (length of 0.5–0.7 cm) and shape. The east cell contained a layer about 4–6 cm thick of carbonized beans of various size (0.5–1.7 cm in length). As in Unit 32 storerooms, maize kernels predominate here. It is not clear why the ratio of maize

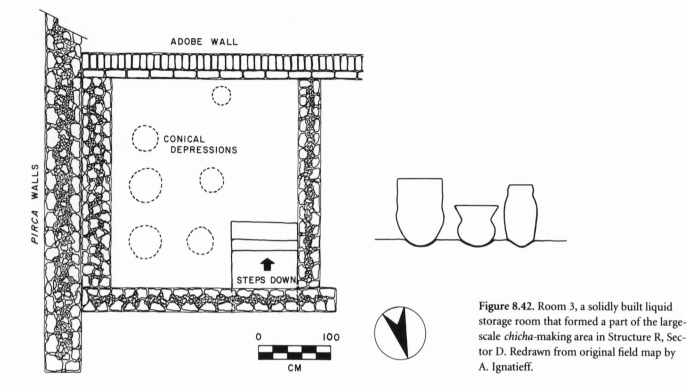

Figure 8.42. Room 3, a solidly built liquid storage room that formed a part of the large-scale *chicha*-making area in Structure R, Sector D. Redrawn from original field map by A. Ignatieff.

to beans (2:1 vs. 4:1) represented in these two storage complexes differs.

Overall, we see indications in Sectors D and H of a commuting work force involved in various supervised service and manufacturing activities who were provided with food and drink, particularly *chicha*. Whether some of the work force was specifically assigned the task of food and drink preparation[142] or the responsibility fell on family members of artisans or on other, unrelated workers we cannot say. Considering the documented and inferred supervision of materials procurement for craft goods, it is quite likely that elite benefactors also provided the materials.

Though the activities described in this chapter subsume only a portion of the urban economy and population, they are, nonetheless, a significant part. Sector H, for example, is where some of the populace from the Southern Pediment seems to have come on a daily basis to serve the state. That the inferred artisan/state relationship was underwritten by the principle of reciprocity goes a long way in characterizing much of the Moche V urban economy at Pampa Grande as being redistributive in

nature. Structures R and S in Sector D provide perhaps the clearest evidence of functional articulation between centrally administered storage (maize and beans) on the one hand and craft production and *chicha* making and consumption on the other.

5. Organization of Craft Production: Summary

Reviewing the data and observations presented here, craft production at Pampa Grande can be characterized as follows: (1) spatially dispersed, with typically a single workshop per Structure; (2) organizationally "compartmentalized" or "modular" in the sense that each workshop was responsible for a certain stage(s) of more complex production; (3) carried out in small, compact workshops, perhaps each manned by only a handful of artisans who diurnally commuted from residences perhaps within the same Structure or outside of the Sector; and (4) clearly supervised within the workshop and in some cases at the Structure or Unit level. In addition, some of the goods thus produced appear to have been deposited in tightly controlled formal storage complexes in the Great Compound. Craft workers were provided with *chicha* and food prepared at nearby interlinked areas using maize and beans from large storage facilities under the control of the central authority, the benefactors of craft production. A succinct characterization, then, would be *dispersed, supervised, modular craft production underwritten by the redistributive principle and manned by a commuting labor force.*

It seems the Moche V urban economy at Pampa Grande was in certain ways antithetical to modern Western mass production that typically brings together many workers at a single location for high productive efficiency (Shimada 1978; Shimada, Epstein, and Craig 1983). Though the segmented nature and small size of each workshop may give an impression of low potential output and organizational unity, the total output may have been surprisingly high. Further, when one considers the complementary personnel involved in provisioning the artisans, the whole setup may even be considered holistic.

Dispersed workshops may have been inefficient in terms of the time and effort involved in moving from one stage or one component to the next, and in terms of redundancy in support personnel. However, it is argued that this organizational setup reflected the basic character of the labor force integrated at Pampa Grande, i.e., nonoverlapping craft specialists perhaps from various North Coast valleys under different leaders (much like late preHispanic *parcialidades*) who were relocated to the city. Under such conditions, this setup would facilitate the integration of not only the artisans but also their sociopolitical leaders and families into the emergent urban economy by assuring continuity in their roles and internal organization. In other words, what we have is closer to production by the masses than to modern mass production.

Though the preceding characterization is appropriate for what we know about most craft production at Pampa Grande, it only partially "fits" *Spondylus* working. The entire production process of shell pendants seems to have been carried out in one single workshop. In addition, the locations of the excavated and inferred *Spondylus* workshops contiguous to platform mounds within major compounds imply that elite benefactors were directly involved in supervision, and it is plausible that the associated artisans had acquired status as full-time "state" retainers as opposed to being under the control of the leaders of *parcialidad*-like groups. The central authority would also have been involved in the procurement of *Spondylus* shell from coastal Ecuador, either controlling trade specialists or participating in pan-coastal long-distance maritime trade (see Murra 1975; Rostworowski 1975; Schaedel 1990; Shimada 1985c, 1990a, in press 2).

In other words, in terms of supervision and the culturally defined value of products, we can differentiate at least three levels of craft production: (1) limited production of ceremonial and sumptuary goods (for example, *Spondylus* at Pampa Grande and gilt copper at Galindo) by a small number of skilled artisans at a few locations (elite compounds) directly and tightly controlled by the central authority; (2) production of valued utilitarian objects (reduced-ware ceramics, certain copper objects such as *tumis* and armor, and perhaps fine cotton cloth) by a commuting labor force at small, dispersed workshops in the central Sectors under mid-level supervision; and (3) dispersed production of mundane, utilitarian goods (e.g., copper implements such as needles, fishhooks, and tweezers, plain cotton cloth, and cooking and storage vessels) in the Southern Pediment.

Clearly, ceremonial, sumptuary goods were relatively limited in quantity and distribution. Most were probably for special-ized contexts and occasions, and taken out of circulation in the form of grave and ritual offerings. The second production yielded utilitarian goods used on a regular basis by the elite. The scarcity of artifactual and architectural symbols of central authority at production loci scattered across the Southern Pediment suggests that the last class of production was under the supervision of low-level administrators who may well have been the traditional leaders of the artisans. Products of the last form of production were basically available to all members of the city of Pampa Grande.

These forms of production were supported by different groups of storage facilities described earlier. The communal-level storage may have held raw materials and food provided to those involved in the dispersed low-level production of mundane, utilitarian goods. The production of valued utilitarian objects, on the other hand, was supported by dispersed, small-scale, formal storage facilities under direct state control. We suspect that the state also cared for those workers engaged in the closely supervised production of ritual and sumptuary items. In reality, goods subsumed in these three categories may have been culturally classified into even more subdivisions and thus had correspondingly greater differentiation in supervision and production.

Together with the forceful shift in land use described in Chapter 7, the economic system presented in this chapter provides strong support for the view that Pampa Grande was at the core of the Moche V redistributive state. The state controlled various forms of interdependence and exploitation, including monopoly over valued goods such as shells from coastal Ecuador (cf. Schaedel 1985b: 163–165); the Moche V urban economy subsumed three levels of production and integrated labor forces and material resources from near and far.

9   Art and Religion

Art is an expression of the time and place in which it is produced. As an integral part of the culture, art reflects its immediate and long-term concerns, as well as internal and external processes at work. In nonliterate cultures, including the Mochica, art serves as a highly effective means of informing and legitimizing the religious and political dogma of the ruling elite. Rituals complement art in disseminating prescribed or approved social conventions and messages. In this chapter, through analyses of iconography, rituals, and funerary practices, we hope to gain some understanding of Moche V art and religion and to elucidate processes and conditions that shaped them. The analyses emphasize examples from Pampa Grande but also present complementary cases from other sites, particularly Galindo.

1. Moche V Art Style and Iconography
A. Skewed Data Base and Basic Features

Certain basic features of Moche V art and its data base should be clearly kept in mind.

(1) Moche V art is largely known from elaborately painted and/or modeled stirrup-spout ceramic bottles, complemented by some metal and carved shell objects and incomplete textiles and murals. Most of these specimens were apparently looted from Moche V tombs in the Lambayeque Valley Complex. There are fewer than a dozen scientifically excavated and published Moche V burials.

(2) Comparison of the form and iconography of vessels with good provenience information indicates certain regional idiosyncrasies (probably at the workshop level), the Jequetepeque Valley being particularly notable. In fact, regionalism in Mochica art is accentuated during Moche V.

(3) In part reflecting the preceding facts, there are notable differences in the range and popularity of iconographic themes and motifs found on bottles from nonfunerary contexts at Pampa Grande and Galindo versus those from tombs. As we see below, funerary art may have become much more specialized during Moche V than in any preceding phases.

(4) As the last bastions of the Mochica culture, painted ceramics at Galindo and Pampa Grande show definite similarities in artistic canons and fineline representations to those of Moche IV. At the same time, reflecting the divergent roles and characters of Galindo and Pampa Grande, their ceramics present different pictures of the popularity and distribution of fine painted

ceramics with mythical and real-world motifs.

(5) Moche V ceramics evince both innovative and conservative characteristics. The former include innovations through archaism and selective adoption of forms and finish introduced from the Central Coast and perhaps the south coast of Ecuador. There is a notable surge in the popularity of press-molded decoration and black and gray finish (reduced ware), particularly in plates with annular bases, small thin bowls, and double-chambered bottles.

(6) The tradition of fineline scenic representation continues into Moche V with some important changes. The trend toward rigid control over subject matter and style that became evident during late Moche IV is accentuated. Fineline drawings become highly conventionalized, at times careless. There is a strong compulsion to fill all available surface. Solid dark painted features are extensively used as well.

(7) The Moche V iconography is characterized by the appearance of a new theme, notable transformations of existent themes, and a reduction in the overall range of themes. On at least two stirrup-spout bottles, iconographic themes that earlier appeared individually are presented sequentially, implying that each theme represents only a segment of a longer narrative.

(8) The naturalistic style and sculptural art of the earlier phases is largely replaced by geometric designs and conventionalized style. "Portrait vessels" that flourished in Moche IV are no longer found. Mold-made human and animal faces commonly found on jars are, in general, faint reminders of the earlier naturalistic modeling.

(9) Lastly, some of the observed variation in form and iconography may reflect temporal differences. For example, we are still uncertain as to the chronological position of the Mochica-Wari or Mochica-Nievería-Wari hybrid ceramics vis-à-vis Moche V ceramics at Galindo and Pampa Grande. The hybrid ceramics are decorated with striking Wari-derived polychrome slip painting of essentially Mochica motifs (Larco Hoyle's [1948] Mochica-Wari; see Disselhoff 1957; Rowe 1942; Stumer 1956, 1958; Fig. 9.1) and/or display exogenous forms (e.g., Nievería double-spout-bridge bottles, Fig. 9.2; cylindrical bottles with an opposing pair of lug handles on shoulders, Fig. 9.3). Such sherds have been found at Huacas Facho, Soledad, and Lucía in Batán Grande (La Leche Valley) and at San José de Moro (Jequetepeque Valley) but not at Galindo or Pampa Grande. This discrepancy may simply reflect the fact that other major centers were rapidly deserted at the time of the abandonment of Moche V Pampa Grande (see Chapter 10), while the Moche V artistic tradition lingered in the more peripheral areas. In the remainder of this chapter we examine some of these features in depth.

B. Characteristics of Moche V Ceramic Art

In Moche V ceramic art, themes are drawn in a highly conventionalized style to fill much of the available space. Any remaining space, including stirrup and spout, is thoroughly filled in with simple motifs and geometric fillers (e.g., points, wavy lines, triangles, concentric circles, volutes, steps, etc.; Figs. 2.7, 9.4). Repetition of secondary motifs also accentuates this tendency. The compulsion to fill space and the use of curvilinear fillers reminds us of the contemporaneous Floral Cursive style of the Middle Cajamarca culture (see Terada and Matsumoto 1985). Larco Hoyle (1948: 35) described Moche V ceramic art as "without vitality or character" in contrast to earlier "vigorous sculptural art." In these senses, Moche V art was a baroque art. At the same time, the appreciable variation seen in details of painted scenes implies that Moche V painters still had a good deal of artistic freedom. In fact, they were quite adept at adjusting the thematic layout and proportions of its components to fill space evenly.

Technically speaking, Moche V ceramics are comparable with those from Moche III and IV, being well made and fired. But given the Moche V emphasis on fineline painting, examples of the most elaborate and careful work are found on stirrup-spout bottles of plain globular body form. These bottles were "showcase" pieces for master painters. Examining a large enough group of such bottles, certain consistencies are discerned in the execution of details, layout of the principal motifs of the given themes, color tone and shade, and other variables that suggest tentative subgroup-

Figure 9.1. Wari-Mochica hybrid style double-stirrup-spout bottle, possibly from the site of San José de Moro in the Jequetepeque Valley. (The scale at the bottom is 10 cm.) It shows a major figure with rays emanating from his back. He is usually found in the Presentation Theme receiving a goblet presumably containing the blood of a sacrificed prisoner. Amano Museum, Lima.

Figure 9.2. Double-spout Moche V bottle from the site of San José de Moro in the Jequetepeque Valley. Though the vessel form is believed to derive from the Central Coast, the decoration is Mochica in style and iconography. The spouts are connected by the double-headed, arching "Sky Serpent."

Figure 9.3. A rare cylindrical bottle with Mochica style bichrome designs. Their symmetry and placement in square panels are reminiscent of the polychrome mural designs at Huaca de la Luna. Museo de la Nación, Lima. Photo by Y. Yoshii.

ings that may well reflect idiosyncrasies of master painters and/or their workshops. For example, bichrome stirrup-spout bottles (also polychrome double-stirrup-spout bottles; Figs. 2.7, 9.1) with low pedestal base and an opposing pair of monkeys on the stirrup, believed to have been looted from the Jequetepeque Valley, show such coherence. That this coherence is in part chronological is suggested by a microseriation of Moche V bottles, which depicts the monkey ornaments as a late addition (Donnan and McClelland 1979: 10). The preceding inferences might be tested, for example, by detailed physical and chemical analyses of paste.

Just as notable as the rigidity of style and the compulsion to fill space is the reduction and modification of traditional themes and deities found in these funerary painted bottles. As noted in Chapter 5, Berezkin (1978, 1980, 1987), for example, observes that the majority of polymorphic humans and supernaturals that became identifiable for the first time in Moche III art disappear in Moche V (perhaps as early as late Moche IV). The "Rayed God," the principal figure in the Presentation Theme (see below) and what Berezkin (ibid.) infers to have been the "supreme patron deity" of the Moche IV dynasty (upper

Figure 9.4. A rare-shaped stirrup-spout bottle with typical Moche V intricate, fine-line decoration. The flat top shows a radiant sunlike motif, while the body is decorated with highly conventionalized sea lion–like creatures with elaborate headdresses. This vessel form is also known from the San José de Moro site. Museo de la Nación, Lima. Photo by Y. Yoshii.

Figure 9.5. A Moche V stirrup-spout bottle decorated with the Rayed God on a tule boat. Many Moche V bottles show variants of this scene that McClelland (1990) calls the Tule Boat Theme. Museo de la Nación, Lima. Photo courtesy of the National Geographic Society.

moiety) was shown in a limited number of settings with precise iconographic and social characteristics in Moche IV. In Moche V art, the Rayed God is "radically" altered and commonly associated with the Navigation Theme (Fig. 9.5). These changes, he feels, do not imply necessarily a significant change in underlying beliefs. He argues that the Mochica pantheon reflects the existing sociopolitical order—that the reduction in the range of deities represented suggests a consolidation of power among fewer groups at the apex of the Mochica social hierarchy. As argued in Chapter 6, this is in general accord with our view of the Moche IV–V transformation and the inferred emergence of the Moche V state.

In contrast to over one dozen themes found in Moche IV, Moche V art is largely confined to the "Presentation" (Fig. 2.10), "Burial" (Fig. 9.6), "Combat," and "Navigation" (more generally marine scenes; Figs. 9.5, 9.7) themes.

The Burial Theme appears for the first time on Moche V funerary bottles. It is not known on ceramics from nonfunerary contexts. The focus of the theme is the "burial scene," which shows a high-status individual apparently encased in a rectangular bundle (possibly a coffin) "being lowered into his grave with ropes manipulated by two figures standing at the edge of the grave" (Donnan 1976: 82; also Donnan and McClelland 1979; Fig. 9.6).[143] Often one of these attendants is shown holding one end of a rope tied to the neck of a llama presumably about to be sacrificed. The face (perhaps with protective coverings) is shown at one end of the bundle. *Strombus* shells surround the coffin, together with jars, bottles, and/or crescent-shaped objects believed to be gourd vessels filled with a variety of food, drink, and other offerings.

Interpretations of the depicted objects are undoubtedly influenced by extant information on Mochica burials, such as those at the Huaca de la Cruz and Pacatnamú. However, there is also undeniable correspondence between excavated materials and the painted depictions, e.g., shells surrounding the Lord of Sipán (in this case, *Conus*), rectangular cane coffins at Pacatnamú and the Huaca de la Cruz, abundant offerings such as food in gourd

Figure 9.6. Three fragments of a Moche V stirrup-spout bottle with the Burial Theme. The top left photo shows the inferred "curer" being eaten, while the top right photo illustrates rows of well-dressed figures. The wrapped body guarded by an anthropomorphized vulture is seen at the bottom of the last photo. The bottle was looted from the site of San José de Moro. Private collection.

and ceramic vessels, and cotton bundles at all these and other Mochica elite burials.

Depictions of three secondary activities constitute the remainder of the burial theme: (1) the "assembly" comprised of separate groups of elaborately attired human, animal, and anthropomorphic figures in orderly alignment on two sides of the burial pit, presumably witnessing the lowering of the coffin; (2) the "conch-shell transfer" scene, which shows a *Strombus* shell being transferred between an elaborately dressed, kneeling figure atop an ornately decorated gabled and roofed mound and a smaller figure who ascends the stair of the mound; (3) the "sacrifice" scene, placed above the preceding, showing at least two figures, one with a *tumi* and another with spears, as well as what could be buzzards, some of which are pecking at an apparently dead, naked female figure interpreted as the unsuccessful curer.

Figure 9.7. Fish (possibly bonito) monsters, each holding a *tumi* and a trophy head, on a Moche V stirrup-spout bottle excavated in Sector D.

The last view is based on a seventeenth-century written account by Fray Antonio de la Calancha on the special role and status of pre-Hispanic curers, who "prior to the arrival of Europeans, . . . were privileged public officials who were paid a regular wage by the state. Their curing was done largely with herbs. If a curer lost a patient through ignorance, he was put to death by beating and stoning, and his body was tied to the patient's corpse. The patient was buried, but the curer's body was left above ground to be eaten by birds" (Calancha 1638 [1976]: 556; Donnan 1978: 87). The interpretation is plausible, not only because of good correspondence between what was written and painted but also because Calancha derived much of his information from the Jequetepeque Valley, precisely the region that seems to have yielded most of the bottles with painted funerary scenes. Nevertheless, for this interpretation to be accepted one must demonstrate that there was cultural continuity during the intervening one thousand years before Calancha's recording and that the above practice was specific to this area.

We cannot tell whether each bottle bearing the Burial Theme represented the burial of a separate high-status individual or the burial of a particularly important individual who left various legacies, including the establishment of the theme. Further, we cannot be sure that the Burial Theme depicts a Moche V burial scene. Exclusive use of *Strombus* (as opposed to *Spondylus*, which became more common during Moche V) and the extended burial position shown in the theme may mean that it was based on a pre–Moche V burial. The complexity and formality of the burial scene argue for its evolution over a period of time. At the same time, much like the case of the "portrait vessel," the Burial Theme may have been inspired by a specific historical case but intended to be generic in significance.

Interestingly, Menzel (as quoted in note 5 in Donnan and McClelland 1979: 7) observed that the two sets of three rows of figures drawn in profile oriented toward a central "grave shaft" overall resemble the composition of the famed carving on the Gateway of the Sun at the site of Tiwanaku in the Bolivian *altiplano*. The latter also shows three rows of "feline-headed angels," drawn in profile, oriented toward the central deity and holding staffs. Though the Burial Theme and its configuration are new, the style and constituent motifs seem to be Mochica.

Unlike the preceding theme, Moche V examples of the Presentation Theme show strong continuity with those of Moche IV. Presumably, the basic sociopolitical and religious orders and principles embodied in this traditional theme remained viable into Moche V. The Presentation Theme involves "the presentation of a goblet to a major figure" with a serpent belt and "spikes" radiating out of his back (Donnan 1976: 117). The personage is drawn relatively large and occupies a high (e.g., platform top), central position within the entire scene. In the Pañamarca mural, the most impressive example of this theme, the goblet is presented by an elaborately dressed "Great Priestess" (Bonavia 1985: 59).[144] The goblet is believed to contain blood from a nearby naked, bound sacrificial victim whose throat was cut by anthropomorphic animal assistants.

The theme, including component symbolic elements and Moche IV and V examples, has been described at length elsewhere (Donnan 1976: 117–129, 1978: 158–173). Here, relevant comments are confined to the only definite example of the theme recovered from Pampa Grande, shown in Figure 2.10. Though the scene is incomplete, one can clearly identify all the main features of the Presentation Theme. For example, the primary figure with rays (which end in snakelike heads with protruding forked tongues) emanating from his head and shoulders is drinking from a goblet presented by an anthropomorphic bird wearing a distinctive headdress and having highly conventionalized wings. To the left of the primary figure an anthropomorphized feline figure (with what may be wings) is cutting the throat of a kneeling figure whose arms are extended behind him. Blood flows from the throat in the form of a stylized serpent.

We briefly remarked on the major Moche IV–V transformation of the Navigation (Tule Boat) Theme[145] and its popularity in Moche V. McClelland (1990), for example, notes a two-fold increase in the

Figure 9.8. Example of Moche V Tule Boat Theme. Here a mythical, double-decked boat carries a cargo of jars and bound "prisoners" or "sacrificial victims." Compare this to Fig. 9.5. Redrawn from Fig. 318A in Kutscher 1983.

depiction of marine scenes and deities during Moche V over the preceding phase, when less than a quarter of the documented fineline drawings related to them. Moche V versions (Figs. 9.5, 9.8) usually depict one of two set deities (with or without surrounding rays) riding or paddling a large two-tiered and/or two-bowed tule boat. The boat carries a cargo of jars, sometimes together with several human figures with their hands tied behind their backs. Typically these two deities appear on opposite sides of the bottle body. Though no example of tule-boat sailing has yet been found at Galindo or Pampa Grande, the continued importance of marine motifs and scenes such as anthropomorphic fish monsters with decapitated heads and *tumi,* fishing, and supernatural combat with sea monsters is apparent in fineline representations found at these sites (Fig. 9.7).

Hocquenghem (1979a,b, 1987: 124–131) interprets the Navigation Theme and all scenes related to water, whether in real or mythical worlds, as representing myths and rites, as mythical beings play out the creative acts that enable people in the real world to continue to live, or as people

recreate these acts to assure fertility. Thus, tule boats carrying prisoners and cargo (Fig. 3.9) are described as taking offerings to the offshore islands at the opening of the fishing season in exchange for an abundance of fish and fertility of guano for crops.[146] At another interpretive level, the boats are likened to a lunar crossing as a rite of passage from life to death.

The importance of rituals and calendars related to agricultural fertility is also reflected in scenes depicted on two fine tapestries found in Coffin "a" excavated at Pacatnamú, which contained a body with a deformed head and tattooed right arm (Hecker and Hecker 1983: 53).[147]

The first tapestry was carefully folded and laid over the deformed head but was not an item of clothing. The textile is thought to have been religious codices or "texts" to accompany the dead person in the world of the gods (Ubbelohde-Doering 1967: 28–29). What was preserved of the central area of the cloth shows a "deity" with a raised arm inside a gabled building with serpent-headed beams and a border of clubs on the roof. Behind him stands a little foxlike figure with his rattle-topped staff raised like a banner before him. The

motifs on the decorative strip overlying the central temple are interpreted as a row of growing maize that "Placed . . . in the heavens over the temple roof . . . could have a symbolic significance since rainfall was essential for the growth of maize, the subsistence crop of ancient Peru" (ibid.).

Preserved portions of the cloth show two "secondary" gabled temples at two corners of the overall roughly square layout. It seems that there were originally four secondary temples, one in each corner of the square, that corresponded to the cardinal directions and "stood in some relation to the calendar year, which in ancient Peru . . . played a decisive role in religious affairs. Sacred wisdom derived from the calendar. It was not just a basis for historical reckoning, but was directed by the gods" (ibid.).

The second tapestry, a short "skirt" around the hips of the body, shows a row of snail monsters with anthropomorphic demons lying on their furrowed surfaces (Fig. 9.9). Following the reasoning outlined above, this tapestry as a whole is believed to show the "adjuration of water, i.e., a fertility rite in which the sacred calendar would have played a decisive role" (ibid., 29).

C. Thematic Sequence

In addition to the above peculiarities, Moche V iconography presents an important sequence of themes. Paintings on a few Moche V bottles present new thematic compositions by placing scenes or personages side by side or one above the other that in earlier phases were presented as parts of isolated themes. For example, a painting done in a spiral covering the entire body of a bottle (Fig. 9.10) shows the main scene of the Presentation Theme (goblet being carried and a seated figure drinking from it) placed next to the Navigation Theme (a row of three double-decker tule boats) and what appear to be components of the Combat Theme. War club and shield motifs are also important components. There is at least one other Moche V bottle showing essentially the same thematic configuration and components.

Figure 9.9. Reconstruction drawing of a slit tapestry fragment excavated by Ubbelohde-Doering from Mochica Tomb E-1 at Pacatnamú. At the center of the drawing are four *Strombus* monsters each accompanied by an anthropomorphic deity who grasps the eye stalk of the monster and threatens it with a *tumi*. See Conklin 1979 and Ubbelohde-Doering 1967 and 1983 for additional details and divergent views of the textile motif. Drawing courtesy of William J. Conklin.

The three tule boats on each of these two bottles show three different figures aboard. As part of the transformation of the Navigation Theme noted earlier, deities associated with other themes in earlier phases are at times added to this theme (McClelland 1990). One of the bottles even shows a tule boat with arms dragging a "warrior" by his hair.

How can we interpret the observed thematic sequence? Certainly, it sheds some light on interrelationships among themes recognized thus far. Were earlier strictures governing isolated or partial representa-

tions of themes lifted during the Moche IV–V shift, and if so, why? Presumably, in areas that share the same cultural tradition, even scaled-down depictions of thematic elements would be enough to evoke images of the complete themes in the minds of observers. Whether or not Moche IV and V scenic paintings are visualizations of an extant oral tradition (Berezkin 1980; Lyon 1989), the appearance of more complete (or integrated) thematic representations may reflect the fragmentation and disarray of the Mochica culture and society; artisans no longer assumed certain basic

shared cultural knowledge among the beholders and felt the need to reinforce their cultural value and identity. A general impression that emerges here is that Moche V culture and society was under stress (both externally and internally generated) and in a state of flux. As seen below, a shift in burial position, from extended to flexed, and notable changes in ritual activity during Moche V both reinforce this sense of transiency.

D. Moche V Murals at Pampa Grande

Prior to excavation at and around Huaca Fortaleza and Huaca 2 in Pampa Grande, there was the expectation of finding impressive murals much like those of Pañamarca and the Huaca de la Luna. Unfortunately, rain had badly eroded the adobe walls, including those atop the Main Body of Huaca Fortaleza where spectacular murals would be expected. Only four fragmentary murals have been recorded at Pampa Grande. However, traces of paint observed on many excavated adobe walls suggest that most adobe walls of the elite and/or ceremonial architecture were once decorated with murals.

One fresco decorated the east wall of a large adobe room west of an enigmatic building that contained a possible accounting area associated with a large storage facility in Unit 24, Sector B.[148] Both ends of the fresco as well as part of the center and top are incomplete. The best-preserved, south end (ca. 2.1 m long and 60 cm high) painted above a small 10-centimeter-high terrace showed "an anthropomorphic figure . . . with yellow legs (with black boots

and a deep pink circle on the ankle) and fan-shaped plumage of varying colors [black, deep pink, light and dark blue] issuing from a circular red center. A black spike projects from the center of the plumage. Flanking this figure are two sets of two vertical, deep pink bands with light blue circles. These bands rest on light blue lenticular bases with wavy tops" (Bonavia 1985: 97; also see Anders 1977: 267; Fig. 9.11). To the right of this figure is a "warrior" with yellow face and extremities, wearing a black and dark blue nose plug, a red shirt with a blue collar, and a short red skirt outlined in black. In his left hand, he holds a light blue club with a round black head and a small circular black and red shield. The black object in his right hand is unidentifiable. A blue *tumi*-shaped backflap hangs from his waist.

Judging by the remaining traces of white background paint, the fresco must have originally covered the entire 7.5-meter-long wall. The style and component motifs are clearly Mochica, "though somewhat removed from classic Moche canons" (Bonavia 1985: 99). Unlike the better-known earlier Mochica examples, motifs are painted directly without incised outlines.

One of the two other preserved frescoes encountered in our 1975 excavations was associated with the platforms (Figs. 7.14, 7.15) at the east end of the First Terrace of Huaca Fortaleza. The west face of the retaining wall of the first platform (including ramps, approximately 1.5 m high and 40 m long) had traces of "a red, orange and blue-gray mural," but no figures could be distinguished (Haas 1985: 398). The west face of the second platform (ca. 50 m long, height not specified) had similar paint traces.

Figure 9.10. A Moche V bottle (with broken stirrup-spout) with Animated Objects, Navigation, and Presentation Themes drawn in a spiral sequence from the bottle base to the top. Only one other Moche V bottle has been found with a similar sequential drawing of different themes. See McClelland 1990 and Shimada 1991a for additional comments. Private collection, Lima. Photo by Y. Yoshii.

The best-preserved fresco appeared on the east walls of a pair of symmetrically opposed three-sided rooms (16 m by 16.5 m, opening to the west) occupying the southeast and northeast corners of the first platform and separated by a central ramp (10.3 m wide by 8.5 m long; Haas 1985: 399–400). Although only the lower 60 cm of the murals remains, the many fragments of painted wall plaster recovered from the fill at the base of the wall faces suggest that the murals extended much higher. The preserved portions of the murals (Fig. 9.12) all showed "a series of repeated orange and red reptiles on a white background" (ibid.). The rows of reptiles on both sides of the ramp are mirror images of each other; i.e., those on the southern halves faced north and vice versa. These creatures "have uniform teeth and dorsal scales, and each is ca. 105 cm long and 32 cm high," and "Unless the mural has hidden complexity, there are probably processual lines of 16 reptiles facing each other on each side of the ramp" (ibid.). There was some variation in representation of the eye, one having a round eye with no pupil, another a diamond-shaped eye with an oval pupil. Originally the entire exterior face of the east wall was painted. It is also quite likely that the poorly preserved backdrop wall (40 cm wide and 25 cm high) at the upper east end of this platform complex had an even more elaborate mural.

The serrated backs and general form suggest that the "reptiles" may be iguanas (*Iguana tuberculata;* Fig. 3.6), which most commonly appear anthropomorphized in Mochica art (cf. Fig. 10 and 13–17 in Kutscher 1983). The circular appendages above the eye in Figure 9.12 may be poorly executed ears or the spiraling antennas seen on earlier Mochica painted vessels. The same iguana motif is also found painted on a number of stirrup-spout bottles from Sector D. The motif remains popular on the northern North Coast well into the end of the Middle Horizon.

Though iguanas are typically thought to be confined to the Far North Coast of Peru and coastal Ecuador, they are relatively common in the semitropical thorny forests of Batán Grande and surrounding regions, where they attain lengths of up to 1.5 m or more and are treasured for their medicinal oil, tough skin, and savory meat. At another level, like the toads that emerge from hibernation with the coming of summer rains (El Niño–related or otherwise), the iguana's appearance is related to the arrival of summer and water.

The last mural remains come from the lower part of the front wall of a low (60 cm) platform (where the Palatial Room Complex is situated) at the rear of the Main Body. Excavation of the eastern half of the wall revealed faint traces of a row of nine repetitive animal figures facing west, each with a long curled tail, large front paws, and a straight tongue sticking out between large serrated teeth (Haas 1985: 402–404; Fig. 9.13), painted in red on a white background (as with all other known Mochica murals). Much like the murals on the First Terrace, the unexcavated western half of the front wall is likely to be decorated by the mirror image of the eastern half.

Though pelage markings are absent (or at least not visible), these are feline features. The animals seem to be seated in the same position as the "Moon Animal" within the narrow sickle of the young crescent moon or under the arching mythical Sky Serpent (Menzel 1977: 34). The seated feline becomes quite popular in post–Moche V coastal styles and iconographies. It appears alone or as an opposing pair below the arching Sky Serpent, decorating many Provincial Wari ceramic vessels of Middle Horizon Epochs 2 and 3 (see Figs. 55 and 61 in Menzel 1977: 39). According to Menzel (ibid., 34), the "curled snout projection is the marking of an ancient sky spirit of the religious tradition of northern Peru." Unfortunately, the critical snout portion is not preserved in the case under consideration.

Overall, in terms of style, motifs, and layout, the murals recorded thus far at Pampa Grande are Mochica with no readily apparent Wari influence. The murals were clearly associated with Moche V jars and stirrup-spout bottles. Still, they are not the finest examples of Mochica mural art, being poorly executed, repetitious, and simple in conception and color usage.

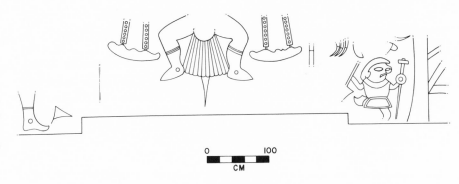

Figure 9.11. Remnants of a polychrome mural decorating an adobe wall near a storage complex in Unit 24, Sector B. Redrawn from the original by Martha Anders.

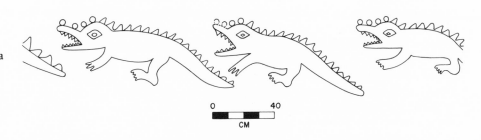

Figure 9.12. Remnants of a mural showing a line of "iguanas" decorating the upper terrace walls of the First Terrace of Huaca Fortaleza. Redrawn from the original by Hans Knapp.

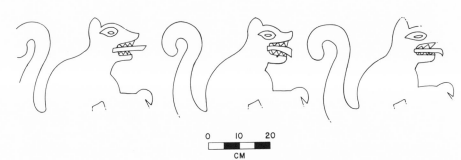

Figure 9.13. Remnants of a mural showing a line of "felines" decorating the front wall of a Room Complex toward the south end of the top of Huaca Fortaleza. Redrawn from the original by Hans Knapp.

Outside of Pampa Grande, we have already discussed possible Moche V murals at Huaca de la Luna and Pañamarca. Polychrome murals decorating niches within the main wall of a relatively small, possibly three-sided adobe construction with a central courtyard at Huaca La Mayanga in Batán Grande (Bonavia 1985: 99–104; Donnan 1972) deserve mention.

On the back wall of each roughly cubical niche[149] was a polychrome mural showing a winged figure in a running position, holding in its hand a gobletlike object. All figures were drawn in profile and faced a central sector of the wall. The winged figures were essentially an anthropomorphized version of the common Mochica club-and-shield motif. Like most Mochica murals, these figures were first drawn freehand with light incisions and then painted (red, black, white, and yellow) ending with outlining of the colored areas with black paint (Bonavia 1985: 101). Overall, the technique of execution and motifs are Mochica in character.

At the same time, there are some Wari-derived features: (1) the systematic red-yellow color contrast seen between the facade (the central sector of the main wall was red while the flanking sides were yellow) and niche interiors (yellow for central niches and red for peripheral ones) holds for the figures inside the niches; figures in the central niches were painted predominantly red against a yellow background; (2) the isolation of the individual figures from the overall scene by placing them in clearly demarcated, square areas (niches), much like the pattern seen in Wari textiles; (3) the use of a background color other than the white that is typical for Mochica murals; (4) the reduced range of colors; and (5) the overall organization of the murals, oriented toward a central axis where some unknown central figure presumably existed (ibid.). The central figure was likely to have been a staffed deity as seen in the "Central Deity Theme" (Cook 1983) of Wari iconography and the "Gateway of the Sun" carving at Tiwanaku (Donnan 1972).

Based on the presence of seven superimposed floors at the Huaca La Mayanga construction (Donnan 1972), Moche V bichrome and polychrome bottle fragments, and a looted tomb with a Wari Robles Moqo–style (Middle Horizon Epoch 1B) bottle all in the immediate vicinity, this construction had a complex construction and occupation spanning part of Moche V and periods immediately post–Moche V. It is significant that the mural is found on the final phase wall at the site built immediately above the rubble of the preceding phase wall (see profile in Donnan 1972: 86). The razed wall likely had another Mochica mural. The Wari-Mochica hybrid mural may have been painted immediately after the demise of Moche V Pampa Grande, when the Mochica religion had lost much of its long-standing prestige. As with the cases of Huaca del Sol and Pañamarca, reuse of the prestigious Mochica ceremonial structures would have effectively symbolized the dominance of the Wari-derived religion.

2. Ritual and Mortuary Practices

A. Spondylus *Shells and Moche V Rituals*

The transformations and/or innovations in Moche V art described thus far find important parallels in religious rituals and paraphernalia at Pampa Grande and other Moche V sites.

Llama sacrifices found inside four of the fourteen excavated sand-filled column sockets on the First Terrace of Huaca Fortaleza provide a glimpse into the changing nature of Moche V rituals. The practice of offering entire or partial llamas was widespread both before and during Moche V. For example, Moche V burials at Pacatnamú were associated with carefully placed llama extremities and whole skulls. Llama extremities were a frequent grave offering in elite burials at the site of Moche as well.

What distinguishes the Huaca Fortaleza offerings is that some juvenile llama bones recovered from the sockets showed seemingly casual placement and definite signs of weathering and carnivore (most likely dog) gnawing, suggesting that the bones were exposed for some period (Shimada and Shimada 1981: 52). This leads us to infer that the performance of sacrificial rituals may have been more important than the form and/or substance of the sacrifice.

Perhaps the most notable shift in the Mochica rituals and associated paraphernalia is the remarkable surge in *Spondylus* shells, presumably imported from Ecuador, where divers gather them from reefs deep off the coast. *Spondylus princeps* apparently held considerable ceremonial significance on the Central Andean coast and highlands at least from the first millennium B.C. (Paulsen 1974). However, starting in Middle Horizon Epoch 1B (Moche V) the thorny oyster seems to appear in greater abundance and in a wider range of contexts (e.g., workshops, art, tombs, and ceremonial architecture) throughout much of the Central Andes.[150]

Though *Spondylus* shell is rarely shown in pre–Phase V Mochica art, Moche V ceramics present explicit representations, as seen in Figure 9.14. At Pampa Grande, Haas (1985: 406) found fragments of bowls with their exteriors studded to imitate *Spondylus* shell spines in two rooms of the Palatial Room Complex atop Huaca Fortaleza. In fact, with the exception of two ritual objects representing a *Strombus* monster and a monkey carved from the spiral cores of *Conus* shells found in subfloor fill, ritual offerings made atop Huaca Fortaleza (see Chapter 8) and Huaca 2 (necklace in an offering pit) were exclusively *Spondylus*.

In the late pre-Hispanic highlands, *Spondylus* carried symbolic importance associated with water. For example, Murra (1975: 257) cites Bernabé Cobo's 1653 account that shells were sacrificed whole, broken, or as powder, primarily at the start of the planting season, to ensure an abundance of vital water. Zuidema (1977–1978: 135) also points out that the Incas offered *mullu* ("round objects" in Quechua, in this case tropical seashells such as *Spondylus*) to lakes toward the same end. The *mullu* was also considered the favorite food of the gods; Quechua folklore recorded at Huarochirí relates how Macahuisa, son of the powerful deity Pariacaca, rejected food offered him by the Incas, demanding that *mullu* be brought to him (Murra 1975: 258).

Earlier Chavín depictions of *Spondylus* and *Strombus* (see, for example, their depictions in the Tello Obelisk; Kaulicke 1991a; Paulsen 1974; Rowe 1967) attest to

these shells' persistent association with water and agricultural fertility. One theory explains the symbolic importance of these shells as an extension of the Andean worldview that the Pacific is the source of all water (Chapter 3). But one wonders why these particular shells attained such importance.

What is clear is that the special symbolic importance of *Spondylus princeps* shell is found primarily in the Central Andes, south of their native habitat along coastal Ecuador where it seems to have had no particular religious importance. For example, though *Spondylus* processing on a regular basis began during the Chorrera phase (first millennium B.C.) on the island of Salango, along the south coast of the Manabí region of Ecuador, efforts focused more on bead making (Norton, Lunnis, and Nailing 1984). Further, Marcos and Norton (1981) noted that while *Spondylus princeps* was found by the hundreds in late pre-Hispanic contexts in their excavation on the Isla de la Plata, *Spondylus calcifer* was practically absent. They note that it was the more valuable *Spondylus princeps* that was collected on the island, and that the processing centers along the Ecuadorian coast are mostly for the working of *Spondylus calcifer*, which was not valued in Peru.

The preceding pattern raises the possibility that the symbolic importance of *Spondylus* in the Peruvian Andes somehow relates to the southward intrusion of the El Niño Countercurrent along the Peruvian coast. *Spondylus* shells may appear along the Peruvian coast as far south as the Central Coast as a result of particularly severe and persistent El Niño events (effects lasting two to three years) as warm currents carry the larvae southward and allow growth (Sandweiss and Rodríguez 1991). For example, at the coastal site of Puémape (Jequetepeque Valley), *Spondylus* is found with numerous warm-water shells that excavators believe together derive from a major El Niño event (Elera, Pinilla, and Vásquez 1992). The simple fact of its appearance along the Peruvian coast would not account for its importance (Díaz and Ortlieb 1992). Though it may take transplanted larvae a few years to grow to a recognizable size, their appearance along the

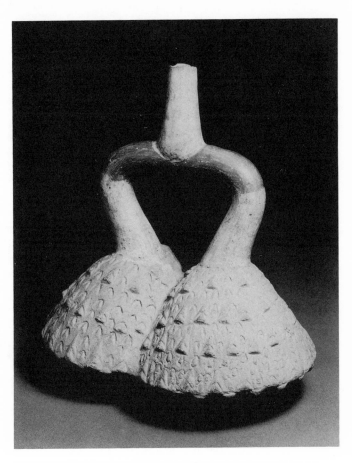

Figure 9.14. A rare Moche V stirrup-spout bottle with its body representing two *Spondylus* shells. Museo de la Nación, Lima. Photo by Y. Yoshii.

Peruvian coast may have come to be associated with the arrival of heat and abundant water. Ritual offerings of imported *Spondylus* may have thus begun as a way of seeking water without destructive El Niño–related torrential rains.

Conversely, its striking reddish- to orangish-colored shell and meat, as well as its periodic toxicity, may have been perceived as somehow related to "red tides" that often appear during severe El Niño events with accompanying rains. Also, the powerful neurotoxin produced by a microorganism residing in *Spondylus* shells in the late spring or early fall (Davidson 1980) may have been used in rituals related to the agricultural cycle.

The importance of *Strombus* and *Conus* shells remains a puzzle, though the distinct sound produced by the use of the former as trumpet surely played some role. Conch shells were used to call forth the rainbow from *ushñu,* a centrally situated ritual setting that included a drain, basin, and platform within Inca settlements (Zuidema 1977–1978).

If we may extrapolate the above symbolic significance of *Spondylus* to Moche V times, a logical question is why the apparent surge in its importance (or at least in its number) occurred at that particular time. It is argued here that the surge was conditioned by a series of severe droughts in the sixth century—that its use was intensified in rituals to assure abundance of water (Shimada et al. 1991b: 51–52). One wonders if the late pre-Hispanic *mollo casqui camayoc* that Rostworowski (1975) identifies as the coastal group in charge of distributing *Spondylus* to sanctuaries originated in Moche V times, or if the Moche V polity at Pampa Grande controlled such a group.

The inferred *Spondylus* trade seems to have been accompanied by the introduction of new technical features from coastal Ecuador. For example, the popularity during Moche V of figurines made with single-piece press molds with flat undecorated back and rigid expression and form (Fig. 9.15) is interesting in light of the long, widespread antecedent tradition (since the Chorrera times, 1000–500 B.C.) of similarly made and posed figurines on coastal Ecuador (Cummins 1991, in press; Cummins and Holm 1991). Conceptually and technically, Moche V and contemporaneous coastal Ecuadorian figurines (e.g., Jama-Coaque) are clearly related. In both, the basic physiognomy and costume elements on the front were mold-made, while the back was built up by hand and left as an undecorated smooth surface. Similarly, the notable rise in reduced-ware ceramics, particularly bowls, in Moche V may well reflect possible imitation of Guangala Phase 4 ceramics (A. Paulsen 1970, 1982, pers. com. 1988).[151] The last are known for fine blackware bowls, and the relevant technical information could have been conveyed by those involved in the *Spondylus* trade.

B. Human Sacrifice and Trophy Heads

Earlier discussion of ritualized combat (Chapter 5) raised the issue of human sacrifice and trophy heads. Mochica art is replete with explicit and implicit depictions of human sacrifice, decapitation, and trophy heads, as well as dismemberment of lower limbs. Mountain scenes, for example, often show sprawled, naked individuals, dismembered bodies, and naked prisoners with ropes around their necks, presumably destined for sacrifice. We already noted a common association between supernatural beings with *tumis* and acts of decapitation or decapitated heads, human and otherwise (Figs. 4.9, 9.7). One Moche IV fineline painting shows a decapitated human head lying on a combat field along with a victorious warrior leading a bound, naked prisoner (see Figs. 213–223 in Kutscher 1983). Though rare, there are clear representations of trophy heads with rope passed through the mouth (see Figs. 273–274 in Donnan 1978: 189). Overall, the frequent depictions of human sacrifices, decapitated heads, and their association with supernatural creatures attest to their considerable religious significance.

The custom of taking trophy heads was shared by Mochica contemporaries and neighbors. Well-preserved examples from the Nasca culture on the South Coast have been long and widely known (e.g., Proulx 1971, 1989; Silverman 1988). Recuay art of Callejón de Huaylas in the North Highlands also has many explicit representations. For example, Aija-style stone sculptures of warriors typically carry a club and rectangular shield, as well as a trophy head on their backs (e.g., see Lumbreras 1974: 116; Schaedel 1948: 67). Heads are shown with or without straps passing through the mouth.

Excavated human remains at Pampa Grande provide some physical evidence for trophy heads as well as the possibility of their use in rituals and even cannibalism. Human bones, burnt and unburnt mixed, were recovered from all three Sectors (D, H, and K) sampled for subfloor fill and in considerable number from Sector D (Shimada and Shimada 1981: 42; Fig. 9.16). None were derived from graves. Carnivore (probably dog) gnawing was observed in a number of cases, but no butchering marks were observed on these bones. Figure 9.16 shows skull bones with apparently cut and smoothed edges. In terms of number,

skulls are highly represented, while no bones from the trunk were recovered from the fill sample. This curious composition raises the possibility that heads were selectively valued and retrieved from combat or sacrifice sites, which would account for the absence of trunk bones. Frequent use of extremities as funerary offerings in Mochica elite burials would also help account for this particular composition at a living site such as Pampa Grande. This custom is likely to be an extension of the taking of limbs as part of the loot from combat, perhaps to signify the valor of the victorious warriors (Fig. 2.4).

C. Moche V Burials

One of the major unresolved puzzles surrounding Moche V Pampa Grande is the whereabouts of burials of both the populace and the elite. In 1973, when we began systematic surface survey and mapping of the site, local residents who had occasionally engaged in illicit excavations confided that there were no tombs with fine Mochica ceramic and metal objects. For any archaeologist who has worked many years in Peru and been frustrated by looters who always seem to find the cemeteries first, this information was difficult to swallow. At this point, however, we have to accept this observation as an accurate assessment of the situation.

In general, looters' pits at the site are relatively sparse, small, and shallow. Our inspection of the heavily pitted northern (lower) margin of the site that borders the modern village of Pampa Grande revealed broken vessels and human bones, but none that could be reliably dated to Moche V occupation of the site. In fact, the well-burnished blackware, *paleteada* (paddled) redware, press-molded grayware, and other recognizable remains are overwhelmingly post–Moche V.

Our excavations in various Sectors failed to locate a single burial. This is all the more curious given that human bones are recovered occasionally from fill, sacrificial burials occurred atop the Huaca Fortaleza, and Moche V burials of various status, plus cemeteries, have been located at contemporaneous sites near and far.

Among Moche V tombs found at Pacatnamú the most impressive is E-1, which

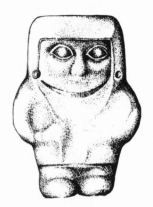

Figure 9.15. Moche V mold-made figurine surface-collected in Sector H, Pampa Grande. Nearly identical figurines were found in a looted cemetery at Sipán and other Moche V sites in the Lambayeque Valley Complex. Drawing by Genaro Barr and I. Shimada.

contained a group of extended burials in cane coffins. Elaborate embroidered cloth (see Chapter 5) and other luxurious adornments were found in this subterranean chamber, the entrance to which was sealed with standing hardwood logs and mortared adobe bricks.

The Batán Grande region has Moche V cemeteries of appreciable size but no major Moche V population center. At the south end of the large Huaca Soledad mound (over 800 m long), looters exposed numerous nearly contiguous rectangular adobe chambers, some with undisturbed human remains (extended position) accompanied by utilitarian Moche V vessels (Fig. 9.17). Some chambers had a narrow adobe brick-lined access shaft and well-worn threshold. One chamber even had a complete but somewhat disjointed human skeleton that was apparently pushed aside to create space for a later interment. Remains of fine painted Moche V stirrup-spout bottles and buried adobe chambers at the nearby sites of Huacas Lucía, Facho, and La Mayanga suggest additional Moche V cemeteries, perhaps for those of relatively high status.

At Galindo, the situation seems quite different. Burials were found in and around residential structures in various areas of the site (Bawden 1977: 364–365).[152] Several burials were found within the confines of domestic residences while excavating high-status architecture in the southern portion of the extensive floodplain (Plain A2; see Fig. 6.3). In this same area, there were also "several apparently formal burials in the open ground near the residential architecture." Lastly, there were badly looted remains of additional burials in or next to low-status residential structures inside the walled-in western hillslope of Cerro Galindo.

The first group in general "were not elaborate, contained few grave goods, and did not possess a formal burial chamber" (Bawden 1977: 364–365). One exception was a young adult male within a simple rectangular burial chamber (defined by walls the width of one adobe brick) placed inside one of the benches in a large residential structure. The body was in an extended position, three-quarters turned, and apparently covered with a coarse textile. The only grave offerings were two small pieces of copper placed between the feet. Within the same bench, an infant body wrapped in plain cloth and laid on its side in a slightly flexed position was found at the feet of the above burial just outside the chamber. The bench had been carefully reconstructed after the latter interment. Of other burials of the first group, various child burials are in a fully flexed position, while the two adult burials were extended on their sides.

Observations on the third group from the hillslope indicate that, much like the first group, they were associated with residential structures, had no formal chambers, and were accompanied by plain textiles and copper. Information on their burial position is not available because of looting and poor preservation.

In contrast to the preceding, the second group of burials in the general vicinity of the residential structure consistently manifested definite grave preparation and were accompanied by fine, decorated stirrup-

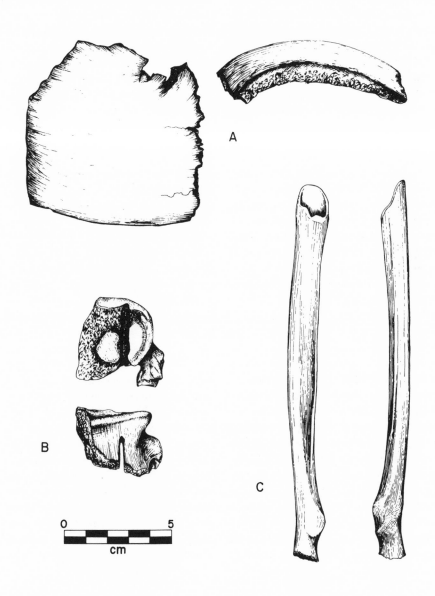

Figure 9.16. Human bones recovered from fill in Sectors D and H showing modification. (A) Cut, polished skull fragment. (B) Vertebra showing deep cut. (C) Tibia with distal end showing polishing from casual use.

spout bottles, suggesting relatively high status. In fact, the clustering of roughly eight burials, all badly damaged from looting, in one area may merit the designation of cemetery.

Apparently these eight burials were placed inside rectangular chambers (1.8 m deep, larger in length than breadth) built of regular courses of bricks set in clay mortar. The form and size of the chambers suggest that the burials were in extended position. Many fragments of fine, painted Moche V stirrup-spout bottles and flaring bowls, as well as figurines, were found around the chambers.

A cluster of three partially looted burials was also found nearby in the southern margin of the floodplain. Extended adult bodies (at least two lying on their right sides) were placed within adobe burial chambers that were not as well made or deep (being only up to 1 m) as the preceding cluster. Fragments of copper discs, chain links, and at least twenty-four ceramic vessels of varied form were recovered from these damaged graves. The vessels included "six stirrup-spout forms, all of them of typically Moche V shape and decoration, a grayware double-chambered vessel, and various necked jar and flask forms" (ibid., 371; Fig. 9.18).

Overall, in contrast to earlier Mochica burial patterns, there was no large formal cemetery at Galindo, and at least some of the site's lower-status population disposed of their dead in the form of residential burial. At the same time, some elite were buried in the traditional extended position within adobe burial chambers.

How can we explain the Pampa Grande situation in light of Moche V burial patterns documented at Galindo? Could our excavation loci at Pampa Grande, which were determined by research problems unrelated to recovering burials, simply have missed the Moche V residential burial pattern documented at Galindo? For example, because of limited excavations of residential structures and subfloor deposits, residential burials could have been missed in Sector H. Yet residential structures and subfloor were extensively excavated in Sector D without encountering burials. Though future testing of residential benches at Pampa Grande is clearly rec-

ommended, differences in research interests and attendant field methodologies do not adequately explain the Galindo–Pampa Grande discrepancies, given the total amount of excavation carried out at Pampa Grande.

Did the inhabitants of Pampa Grande, fearing desecration of their cemeteries and ancestors' bodies by Wari and Cajamarca intruders, bury their deceased in more secure locations? If so, why did Galindo and Pacatnamú residents bury their dead within their settlements? Were relocated populations of Mochica and Gallinazo ethnicities interred in their home communities away from Pampa Grande? Devastating erosion from the 1983 El Niño–related heavy rains thoroughly exposed the interior of the Main Body of Huaca Fortaleza as well as Huaca 2 down to the base in places. No evidence was revealed of any burials inside these *huacas*, other than sacrificial offerings inside the sand fill of adobe columns. Dissociation of burials from adobe platform mounds at Galindo and Pampa Grande itself represents a major break from the earlier Mochica tradition of interment in adobe mounds, for example at Moche and Sipán. Even if burials were placed around the bases of the mounds, they were usually aligned with the mounds. A major ideological break between the Moche V mounds and burial rituals is suggested.

There are some areas that deserve excavation testing, for example the slightly raised area without any standing architecture at the east base of the Huaca Fortaleza. At this point, however, we simply do not have any plausible explanation for the situation at hand.

D. Changes in Mochica Burial Practices

The overwhelming majority of published Moche I–IV burials throughout the North Coast are oriented to a cardinal direction in fully extended position, lying on the back, legs straight and arms at the sides. The few pre–Moche V flexed burials seem to have been sacrificial, hastily done, or ethnically "foreign" (possibly related to the Recuay). For example, the Warrior-Priest at Huaca de la Cruz (Strong and Evans 1952: 152) and an elite adult male at Huanchaco (Donnan and Mackey 1978:

Figure 9.17. Moche V adobe burial chamber excavated at Huaca Soledad, Batán Grande. One of the two extended adult burials found inside had been moved in ancient times, apparently to make space for additional bodies. Note how the adobe bricks on the threshold of a short entry shaft have been worn down. Photo by James Vreeland.

206) had two flexed, sacrificed women and a flexed, partially dismembered woman, respectively.

Though the number of published Moche V burials is still small, sometime during late Moche V there seems to have been a gradual shift in burial position. Only some burials from Galindo displayed this traditional position, while others were either fully flexed or extended on their sides. One of the seventeen tombs excavated by Disselhoff (1941) at a cemetery near El Brujo, a major Mochica site in the lower Chicama Valley, contained one extended and one flexed burial associated with Moche V ceramics.

A tightly flexed adult burial excavated at Huaca Lucía in Batán Grande (Fig. 9.19; Shimada 1981) was accompanied by eight ceramic vessels of varied form and character, as well as a black stone disc 5 cm in diameter that covered and was covered by

what appears to be yellow ochre, a small quartz crystal, a semitransparent fluorite crystal, ten copper sticks about 10 cm long of indeterminate function, and scattered turquoise and black stone beads, all on the chest. A stirrup-spout bottle from this burial, representing four gourds bound together, clearly has Moche V form but atypical decoration; fine black line painting depicts spiders (each with eight pairs of legs) within eight panels demarcated by bands of cream paint outlined by fine black lines on an orangish red slip background (Fig. 9.20). Other vessels include a Wari Norteño B–style jar (also popularly called "Cachaco style"; Larco Hoyle 1948) with a pair of opposing shoulder lug handles and curvilinear cream paint designs on an orangish brown slip, and a pair of face-neck jars (one is a poor imitation of the other), resembling Middle Horizon Epoch 2 Provincial Wari–style jars. It is clear that the

Moche V stylistic tradition lingered on long after the demise of the Moche V polity at Pampa Grande but perhaps with significantly different cultural meaning. Continuities in form do not necessarily imply similar continuity in meaning.

The preceding discussion shows that the tradition of extended burials, which lasted over a thousand years, was replaced first by flexed burials on side or back and eventually by flexed and seated or seated, crosslegged burials. The last position was firmly established during the Early Sicán culture of Middle Horizon Epoch 2A, which immediately succeeded Moche V in the Batán Grande region. That the flexed position, earlier associated with burials of those with special qualities, was widely adopted by the end of Moche V and immediately succeeding times implies a rather significant change in religious beliefs governing funerary customs.

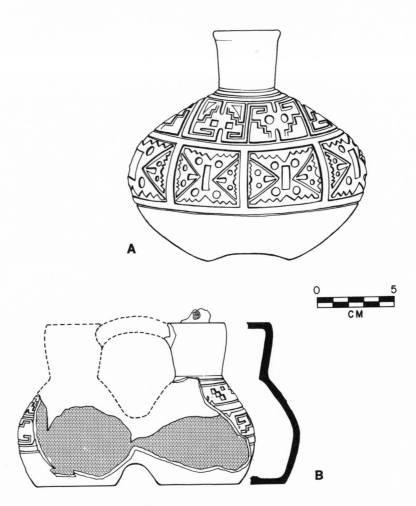

Figure 9.18. (A) Jar with mold-made geometric designs excavated at Galindo. Redrawn from Fig. 109 in Bawden 1977: 334. (B) Double-chamber bottle with mold-made geometric designs excavated at Galindo. Redrawn from Fig. 114 in Bawden 1977: 342.

Figure 9.19. Photo of a tightly flexed Moche V burial excavated at Huaca Lucía, Batán Grande. The scale at the top of the photo is 1 m.

Parallel to what was described for the North Coast, the transition from extended to flexed burial position on the Central Coast also occurred gradually (Middle Horizon Epochs 1B to 2A).

At Ancón the shape of the burial chambers, as well as the style of the contents, changed almost with every phase, so that burial structures are good indicators of the date of the burial. Most burials of Epoch 1B are long and shallow, with the dead buried in extended positions. This pattern reflects the burial custom of the people of this area before the time of the [Wari] Empire. With the empire came a new burial custom in which the dead were buried seated, with their knees drawn up. Some graves of Epoch 1B contained more than one dead, and sometimes one of these was seated while the other was extended on his (her) back. These graves reflect the fact that the cultural impact of the [Wari] Empire was not as all-embracing in its beginning stage as it became after its reorganization in Epoch 2. (Menzel 1977: 44; also see 1964: 21–22, 70)

The situation is quite similar for burials excavated at the Nievería cemetery in the Rimac Valley (Menzel 1964: 31, 1977: 46; Figs. 1–3 in Muelle 1935; Fig. 10 in Uhle 1910); extended and flexed burials were associated with Epoch 1B and Epoch 2 ceramics, respectively. The coastwide diffusion of the flexed burial sometime during Middle Horizon Epoch 1B may well have been rooted in the Paracas-Nasca tradition of the South Coast, where the flexed burial position was widespread and had a long history.

The shift in burial position seems to coincide with selective adoption of some new ceramic features such as symmetrically placed shoulder lug handles and press-mold decorated ceramics (e.g., associated with Galindo burials) with little or vague religious significance. Much as Kroeber (1925) suggested earlier, Schaedel (1979) has argued that press-molded decoration spread northward from the North-Central Coast sometime in the early Middle Horizon. Moche V burials at Pacatnamú are extended within similarly traditional cane coffins, but some are accompanied by jars with lug handles or mold-made faces on the necks, together with stirrup-spout bottles. One interesting cache (looted from Cenicero in the Santa Valley and known as PV28–97 Cache 2; Donnan 1973a: 134–135) that included a Moche V fineline painted bottle and four Wari double-tiered polychrome jars (apparently imported) is said to have been associated with an extended burial. The individual had its arms at the sides and its head oriented west.

Overall, if the aforementioned innovations indeed derive from the Wari culture, the data suggest that Mochica-Wari contact may have begun sometime late in Moche V and involved various mechanisms and personnel (e.g., trade, military threat, missionaries-cum-traders, and usurpation of Mochica ceremonial centers as Wari regional dissemination points). Perhaps more mundane Wari features were first selectively adopted by the Mochica population prior to widespread acceptance or tolerance of religious beliefs and attendant iconography and funerary custom. It is proposed here that the observed mortuary shift occurred primarily after the abandonment of Huaca Fortaleza at Pampa Grande,

which symbolized the power and prestige of the Moche V polity and religion. In this view, receptivity to a new custom most likely disseminated by Wari-affiliated peoples followed the loss of credibility and prestige of the Mochica religion in the eyes of the local population. Nevertheless, we should not assume that the shift in burial position occurred simultaneously throughout the North Coast; rather, the little evidence we have suggests a good deal of variation from one area to another.

3. Understanding Moche V Art and Religion

Reconstructing iconography and religion is challenging to archaeologists who work primarily with preserved material remains; our interpretations are often untestable and remain circumstantial. However, in our examination of the interrelated phenomena of art, rituals, and burials, we see certain parallels that together appear to point to important societal concerns and the broader processes and conditions that gave rise to them.

It is evident that the Moche V culture embodied both traditional and innovative features. In general, Moche V fineline drawings and murals exhibit undeniable technical, stylistic, and iconographic linkage with those of prior phases. At the same time, the reduction in the range of iconographic themes and supernaturals represented, the appearance of the Burial Theme, major modifications of the Navigation Theme, emphasis on water-related (including maritime) scenes, and the sequential presentation of themes are uniquely Moche V. In fact, the breadth and magnitude of the observed iconographic changes within the long Mochica cultural tradition seems unprecedented.

A similar eclectic, expedient, and transitory character emerges whether we take ceramic forms and techniques or ritual and mortuary practices. Conservative and innovative trends existed side by side. Innovative features were often expedient in terms of labor and material investment in achieving a certain outward appearance or impression; the facade was just as important as the contents, if not more so. Concurrent with showpiece stirrup-spout bottles with elaborate fineline drawings, we find bottles with abstract or conventionalized press-mold decorations that are clearly inferior in artisanship and limited in ideological significance. Details no longer received the attention such bottles once merited. In this regard, the seemingly haphazard disposition of sacrificial llamas and infants found atop Huaca Fortaleza is not an exception. Perhaps certain sacrificial rituals had become primarily a formality.

Explanations put forth for pre–Moche V developments and characteristics are not readily applicable to the situation at hand. For example, the reduction in the pantheon and range of iconographic themes depicted, as well as the concurrent rise in conventionalized and geometric motifs,

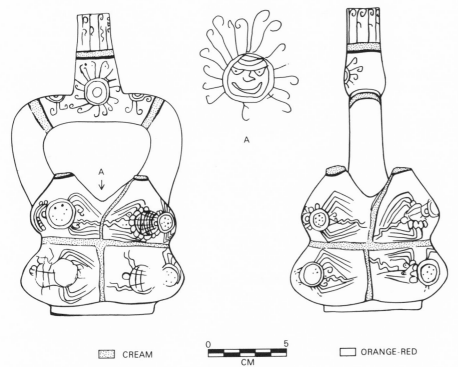

CREAM   0   5   CM   ORANGE-RED

Figure 9.20. Stirrup-spout bottle associated with a flexed Moche V burial excavated at Huaca Lucía, Batán Grande.

probably reflects a trend toward centralization and secularization of the Mochica power structure. While some argue that the Mochica theocracy held sway until the very end, data and observations presented in this book argue otherwise. The Moche IV–V transformation also broadened or, at the least, intensified peer polity interaction, particularly with the Central Coast and coastal Ecuador. The popularity of new vessel forms, mold-made figurines, fine blackware vessels, and press-molded decoration seems to relate to these newly defined external relationships. The notable surge in the depiction and ritual use of *Spondylus* shells, as well as the popularity of water-related scenes in Moche V art, may well relate to the prolonged, severe droughts that beset the Mochica population during much of the sixth century (Chapter 6). This view, however, hinges on the difficult task of extracting the cultural meanings underlying these drawings. We are speaking of changes that occurred or were initiated at the time of the Moche IV–V transition, not during Moche V. The change in burial position, however, appears to have begun sometime late in Moche V and is likely related to northward diffusion of the Wari-related religion. Whether the inferred introduction of the chamber-and-fill construction and press-mold decoration techniques occurred together with the preceding changes remains to be determined. Stylistically dated, Epoch 1B as it stands is simply too imprecise and long for meaningful discussion of various relevant processes.

Overall, results of our analysis of Moche V art and architecture concurs with the conclusion drawn in the preceding chapters; that, under externally and internally generated stresses, the Moche V culture remained in a state of flux throughout its existence. It strived to achieve some sense of normality through deliberate and organized experimentation or the adoption of new features, while retaining some traditional values and institutions.

10 The Demise of Moche V Pampa Grande

The focus of this chapter is to clarify the processes and conditions responsible for the collapse[153] of the Moche V state centered at Pampa Grande and the abandonment of this city. To the extent possible, a clear analytical and chronological differentiation needs to be made among the demise of the polity, the abandonment of the city, and the end of the Mochica culture. There is no a priori reason to assume their contemporaneity. Even after the collapse of the central government, the city could well have lingered on as a viable settlement. Similarly, constituent regional polities on the northern North Coast that were formerly aligned with Pampa Grande may have selectively perpetuated Mochica institutions, style, and material culture for some time.

The task at hand also requires that we consider both immediate and long-term, as well as internal and external, factors: actual abandonment may have been quite abrupt and thorough, but this event may have been conditioned by long-term internal and/or externally imposed stresses.

1. Demise of the Moche V Polity and Mochica Abandonment of Pampa Grande

A. Intentional, Synchronic, Selective Burning of Key Structures

Available evidence points to a rather abrupt, violent, and simultaneous end to both the Moche V polity and occupation at least in the central portion of the city of Pampa Grande.

Adobe architecture, particularly structures with elaborate vertical differentiation (such as *huacas* and nested terraces), denoted political and religious power and prestige. It is precisely these constructions that were partially or entirely burnt. That the burning of these structures was intentional, synchronic, and coinciding with (if not causing) Mochica abandonment of the site is indicated by various lines of evidence:

(1) Patterned, selective burning: Of the some thirty adobe mounds and terraces excavated or mapped mostly in the central portion of the site, over three-quarters show clear evidence of intense fire, usually at the highest portions and sometimes more extensively. The burnt structures do not form any apparent spatial pattern; i.e., any formal structure symbolizing the ex-

tant sociopolitical and/or religious order was indiscriminately targeted. The most impressive evidence of the fire is seen atop the Main Body of Huaca Fortaleza. Along much of the top, one can readily identify a more or less uniformly baked, discolored, 1–3-centimeter-thick horizon of a single plastered floor in the profiles of erosional gullies. Haas (1985: 398) observed that "The intensity of the fire is expressed by the fact that much of the roof plaster was vitrified, and the plaster on the walls and floor was fired to ceramic hardness." The same striking situation prevails on the First Terrace of the *huaca* and atop Huaca 2. None of the burnt structures that were excavated showed any indication of repair or reoccupation. Burnt floors were directly covered by similarly fire-reddened roofing materials, with no intervening deposits to suggest a hiatus between fire-hardening of the floor and roof collapse. Burnt and collapsed structures were simply deserted, marking the end of their occupation.

In fact, we found no indication of squatter occupation in excavated Moche V structures at Pampa Grande, as was perhaps the case with the Huaca Galindo compound at Galindo (Conrad 1974). Abandonment of at least the central portion of Pampa Grande was likely to have been rapid and thorough. Data for peripheral Sectors are inadequate to speak confidently of the nature of the abandonment process. Evidence for post–Moche V occupation, such as paddled wares, as well as highly diagnostic Middle Sicán blackware bottles and Imperial Chimú bowls, were localized in the northern and western perimeters of the site.

Both adobe buildings and evidence of fire seem to taper off as one travels out from the city center. In contrast, several dozen stone constructions excavated in Sectors D, H, J, and K showed no evidence of fire. In other words, we are not speaking of a huge conflagration that indiscriminately engulfed a large part of the site burning both large and small adobe and stone constructions.

(2) Sociopolitical and religious significance of the burnt structures: Fire attacked only those formal constructions that represented the existing sociopolitical leadership and religious order. Many of the burnt structures, particularly those at the larger end of size variation, were built with marked and unmarked bricks of varied size and shape in segments of set dimensions; that is to say, they were examples of corporate architecture built with bricks from multiple sources by various labor gangs.

(3) Excellent condition of burnt structures and their contents: The presence of large quantities of maize and beans still in adobe storage complexes in Sectors D and H, and ginned, beaten cotton in Deer House, both covered so directly by burnt roofing materials, suggests that they were being used or worked on until shortly before the fire. A neat cluster of quartz crystals and a mace head with a charred wooden handle on the floor give a similar impression that the Palatial Room Complex atop Huaca Fortaleza was abandoned just before or immediately after the onset of fire. There is no evidence of pillage or spoilage from pests, moisture, and mold. Burning solidified or preserved the stored items. Largely intact stirrup-spout bottles and storage vessels found in unburnt rooms inside elite residential Compound 38 in Sector H, plus neat piles of llama bones undisturbed by dogs in kitchens in various Sectors, point to a hasty and thorough abandonment of the city. It is not clear, however, why the large storage complexes escaped burning and whether or not the contents were plundered.

Overall, the above lines of evidence suggest a rather abrupt and violent end to the Moche V state and urban capital at Pampa Grande.

B. Explaining the Collapse and Abandonment: General Considerations

While much has been written on the origins of the state in the Andes, its collapse has received comparatively little attention other than cursory remarks in general textbooks (e.g., Lanning 1967: 140) and the controversial argument for the Wari invasion of the North Coast dating back to the time of the Virú Valley Project. In interesting contrast, Maya archaeologists as a group have proposed a whole gamut of theories for the explanation of the Classic Maya collapse.[154] In a major cross-cultural study, Tainter (1988: 42–90) identified ten major themes commonly invoked to explain the collapse of complex societies: (1) depletion or cessation of vital resource(s) on which the society depends; (2) the establishment of a new resource base; (3) the occurrence of some insurmountable catastrophe; (4) insufficient response to circumstances, with basic limitations of social, political, and economic systems preventing an appropriate response to circumstances; (5) conflict or competition with other complex societies; (6) intruders; (7) class conflict, societal contradictions, or elite mismanagement or misbehavior that may lead to such problems as peasant revolts; (8) social dysfunction (vaguely defined internal processes); (9) mythical factors or subjective judgment on the state of individual societies (e.g., loss of vigor, or decadence); (10) chance concatenation of events or concurrent outbreaks of problems. Tainter's (1988) own position invokes economic explanations based on the related concepts of declining advantages of complexity, increasing disadvantages of complexity, and increasing costliness of complexity.

With the exception of the mythical argument, which Tainter (ibid., 90) regards as having no scientific merit, the remaining themes are judged to illuminate relevant variables and processes, but are ultimately based on unwarranted or tenuous assumptions and logic and thus "inadequate as presently formulated." His general explanation of collapse, which "should provide a framework under which these explanatory themes can be subsumed," is based on the economic theme, which was seen to be most satisfactory among those considered (ibid.). Critical to an understanding of collapse, according to Tainter (ibid., 93, 118–123), is the idea that investment in sociopolitical complexity as a problem-solving response breeds diminishing returns ("declining marginal productivity").[155]

In essence, Tainter's interest is to define the preconditions of eventual collapse brought about by the theme(s) outlined above. His explanatory framework is basically a variant of the dictum that *growth of a given system in size and complexity creates new forms within, which in turn constrain further growth of the system as a whole by placing their own demands.* This proposition guided our earlier discussion of the

emergence of the city and state at Pampa Grande and what was to follow.

We argue that processes that preconditioned the eventual collapse of the Moche V polity and abandonment of Pampa Grande were inherent in their formation under stressful conditions. The emergence of the Moche V nascent state and urban capital was in essence seen as the result of a process of adaptation to a series of severe environmental disturbances in the sixth century that required greater centralization and nucleation to better deal with society-wide needs. However, as Tainter (ibid., 195) puts it succinctly, "while initial investment by a society in growing complexity may be a rational solution to perceived needs, that happy state of affairs cannot last." For the elite who sought to integrate disparate subgroups brought together at Pampa Grande and to demonstrate the viability and legitimacy of their leadership, the construction of gigantic Huaca Fortaleza served the end well. Construction, however, necessitated not only a tremendous investment of material resources but also on-site permanence of a labor force and the establishment of new administrative norms and institutions. This effort to establish the new capital and to maintain and legitimize the organizational byproducts that it spawned required constant high-level mobilization of resources. Much of this burden must have been borne by the masses. With amelioration of the water supply from a prolonged pluvial period between A.D. 602–635, shouldering the burden of urban existence and the state-level authority may have become increasingly onerous; that is, what initially led to the population nucleation at the valley neck and legitimized the establishment of the state largely disappeared. In addition, the completion of Huaca Fortaleza would have freed numerous workers/farmers.

Moche V leadership was most likely in a state of flux, with ongoing secularization and segmentation during much of its existence. Given such a dynamic situation, the inferred low-level bureaucrats occupying small, rectangular masonry enclosures were probably constantly jostling to gain the upper hand. It is doubtful whether the leadership was capable of effectively resolv-

ing the conflicting claims of the constituent sociopolitical groups brought together at the city.

According to this scenario, then, by around the mid- to late seventh century, the level of discontent among various sectors of the Moche V society at Pampa Grande was seriously high, and the society was in danger of collapse from internal decomposition or external threat.

C. Specific Causes of the Collapse and Abandonment

Given the general conditions described above, what were the specific causes of the observed destruction of corporate architecture and the inferred collapse of the Moche V polity and capital at Pampa Grande?

A logical extension of the above scenario is a revolt of urban residents. It may have begun when members of the society in and/or outside of Pampa Grande perceived extant conditions as critically maladaptive and felt that their organized, goal-oriented actions would yield a positive, systemic impact on their culture as a whole. Their ire would have been directed toward the ruling elite and their physical representations, formal adobe structures.

What role might environmental disturbances have played? A ten-year drought between A.D. 636 and 645, as well as a period of considerable year-to-year precipitation fluctuation between A.D. 646 and 692, followed by a moderate dry spell ca. A.D. 701–715, may have created sufficient anxiety and hardship for the populace to lose confidence in the existing leadership. Agriculturalists were already forced to bear the burden of sustaining a large number of nonfarming residents of Pampa Grande with no way of predicting the length and severity of drought. Perhaps psychologically more stressful were memories of the tremendous hardship experienced during the thirty-two-year drought at the end of the sixth century.

A number of severe El Niño events have been identified in the Quelccaya data during the span of Moche V (A.D. 600–601, 610, 612, 650, and 681; Schaaf 1988: 60–61), and the adverse effects of a severe El Niño may well have been what eclipsed the threshold of popular tolerance and set the stage for revolt.

However, it is too easy to juggle the imprecisely dated abandonment of Pampa Grande with precisely and reliably dated El Niño events or droughts in the Quelccaya sequence for an ideal match. We must guard against the temptation to invoke climatic factors as the omnipotent causal explanation. El Niño events and short-term droughts were undoubtedly experienced by earlier Mochica polities without leading to collapse. Certainly, the seventh- and eighth-century droughts were nothing like the three-decade drought in regard to duration, abruptness, and severity (ibid., 62). Available evidence (see below) indicates that a severe flash flood associated with an El Niño event occurred sometime after the fire that marked the end of Moche V occupation of the city, and *not* before. In fact, other than the El Niño event of A.D. 681, there are no independently derived indications of climatic stress during the late seventh and early eighth centuries. As noted in Chapter 5, subsistence remains recovered from Pampa Grande do not, in either quality or quantity, readily suggest such stresses.

We should also consider the possibility of a military conquest by a Wari (Middle Horizon Epoch 2A expansion) or combined Wari-Cajamarca force. As explained in the preceding chapter, Wari and Wari-derived features on the North Coast date to sometime during late Moche V (Middle Horizon Epoch 1B—the first Wari expansion) or immediately post–Moche V (Epoch 2A—the second expansion). At Pampa Grande and Galindo, we saw evidence of selective incorporation of various features that originated in the area south of the North Coast. These features appear to be part of a generalized Moche V reassessment of existent values that led to revision of traditional institutions, archaic revivals, and assimilation of new foreign traits and ideas.

Both imported Wari ceramics and their provincial imitations are widely found on the North Coast (Fig. 10.1), including Site A on the Southern Platform of the Huaca del Sol at the site of Moche. We have already seen a wide distribution of ceramics (and one mural) that show blending of Moche V and Middle Horizon Epoch 1B Wari art along the coast between the Piura

on the Far North Coast and the Rimac Valley on the Central Coast.

Wari or Wari-derived materials at Site A are mostly fragments of painted ceramic vessels depicting Wari religious themes and deities intentionally smashed as part of sacred offerings. That Wari religious rituals involved human and animal sacrifice and music is indicated by bones and broken ceramic whistles and trumpets scattered over areas of up to 20 m across at Site A (Menzel 1977: 38). These remains are largely religious in character and numerous, not just one or two offerings but many, spanning Middle Horizon Epoch 1B to 2B. Usurpation of Huaca del Sol by followers of the Wari religion for their rituals is a dramatic and highly symbolic assertion of their ideological and political dominance over the Mochica. The act at the same time underscores the continuing reverence the *huaca* commanded from the local population. This symbolic use of the *huaca*, as argued below, is a critical point in understanding the possible role of the Wari polity and religion in the downfall of Moche V Pampa Grande.

Epoch 2 Provincial Wari ceramics (Wari Norteño A) have been noted throughout the northern North Coast. Closer to Pampa Grande at the site of Sausal in the Chicama Valley, there is an Epoch 2A cache offering consisting of a set of three cups, which were apparently ritually smashed, and a gold spindle whorl (Donnan 1968). The Epoch 2A Provincial Wari ceramics illustrated in Figure 10.1 were part of a looted burial at San José de Moro in the Jequetepeque Valley. A well-burnished, smoked blackware bottle showing an opposing pair of seated feline creatures stylistically attributable to Epoch 2A was recovered from an immediately post–Moche V floor nearly 4 m below the top of the Huaca del Pueblo Batán Grande mound in the La Leche Valley (Fig. 10.2; Shimada 1985a, 1990a; Shimada and Elera 1983).

In comparison with the southern regions of the North Highlands (Huamachuco and Callejón de Huaylas), evidence of Wari intrusion and dominance of the adjacent Cajamarca Basin on the North Highlands is quite limited (T. Topic 1991). Various surveys and excavations have recovered only a handful of Epoch 1B and 2

Wari and Wari-derived ceramics within the basin (Julien 1988; Matsumoto 1988; Reichlen and Reichlen 1949; Terada and Matsumoto 1985). Two relatively small rectangular enclosures at Ichabamba (120 by 75 m) and Yamobamba (130 by 210 m) near the southern end of the Cajamarca Basin have been interpreted as intrusive Wari administrative settlements (Williams and Pineda 1985: 59, 61; cf. Hyslop 1984; Schreiber 1987). However, ceramics in support of Wari attribution (as opposed to Inca, for example) have yet to be presented.

In the adjacent Huamachuco region to the south, evidence of Wari presence is strongest for Epoch 1B and scant for Epoch 2A (Thatcher 1975, 1977; J. Topic 1991; T. Topic 1991; Topic and Topic 1984). The site of Cerro Amaru, with probable workshops of obsidian projectile points, is believed to have been the center of Epoch 1B Wari presence in Huamachuco, with inferred emphasis on the trading of exotic, sumptuary goods (Topic and Topic 1984: 56). The nearby Wari intrusive site of Viracochapampa was never completed and was abandoned sometime in Epoch 2A (ibid., 58; J. Topic 1991).

On the other hand, the distribution of contemporaneous, highly distinct kaolin Middle Cajamarca B ceramics calls our attention. Basically they correspond to what was earlier called Floral Cursive (Thatcher 1975), which seems to have first appeared in Epoch 1B and attained its widest distribution in Epoch 2 (Matsumoto 1988; Terada and Matsumoto 1985). Kaolin ceramics are found in appreciable quantities at the site of Wari and scattered in the Wari heartland (e.g., at Ayapata [Ravines 1969, 1977] and at Jargampata [Isbell 1971, 1977]) and hegemony, such as the South Coast (Ica Valley [Menzel 1969]) and near Cusco (Curahuasi [Menzel 1964, 1969]).[156] At the site of Wari, abundant imported Cajamarca ceramics are found, as well as what appear to be local imitations variously called Geometric on Light (Bennett 1953) and Wari Cursive (Lumbreras 1960).

Significant to the issues at hand is the fact that Floral Cursive ceramics are found on much of the North Coast, from a tripod vessel excavated by Uhle (1913; also Kroeber 1925) at Moche to those found at sites

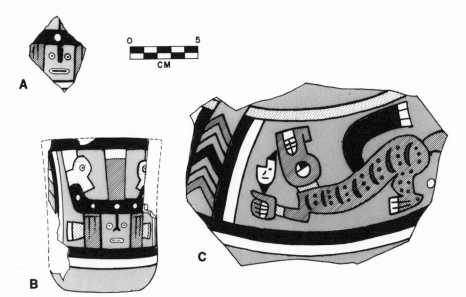

Figure 10.1. (A) Middle Horizon Epoch 2 Provincial Wari lyre cup fragment surface-collected at Huaca Soledad, Batán Grande. (B) Middle Horizon Epoch 2 Provincial Wari lyre cup looted from San José de Moro, Jequetepeque Valley. Private collection. (C) Fragment of a Middle Horizon Epoch 2 (possibly B) Provincial Wari vessel looted from San José de Moro. It shows a mythical feline like the Atarco B style of the South Coast. Private collection.

Figure 10.2. An opposing pair of seated felines decorating an Early Sicán blackware bottle (Middle Horizon Epoch 2A) excavated from an immediately post–Moche V floor at Huaca del Pueblo Batán Grande, La Leche Valley.

in the Jequetepeque, Lambayeque, and La Leche valleys (Eling 1987; Larco Hoyle 1948; I. Shimada 1982, 1990a; Shimada and Elera 1983). Chronologically, they appear to partially overlap the rather abrupt appearance of "Coastal Cajamarca" plates (together with Epoch 2 Provincial Wari–style blackware ceramics) found abundantly throughout the Lambayeque Valley Complex (Shimada and Elera 1983; also Ravines 1982). These bichrome (red-on-cream) or tricolor (red outlined by black on cream) plates are locally manufactured and in general resemble the better-made (kaolin paste) North Highland Cajamarca plates.[157] The localized distribution of imported Floral Cursive ceramics and the more extensive distribution of locally manufactured Coastal Cajamarca ceramics raise the distinct possibility of scattered Cajamarca colonies and their long-term integration in these northern North Coast valleys (Eling 1987; I. Shimada 1982, 1990a; Shimada and Elera 1983).

Overall, the data and observations presented thus far concerning the nature and distribution of Wari and Cajamarca materials argue that some nonbelligerent form of contact (perhaps involving traders-cum-missionaries) between the Moche V and Wari cultures occurred during Middle Horizon Epoch 1B. The Wari may well have formed an alliance with the Caja-marca polity sometime during Epoch 1B to conquer the northern North Coast or for the latter to carry out inferred conquest and administration with the former's backing during Epoch 2A. That the Cajamarca polity served as the North Peruvian Wari agent during Epoch 2A is suggested by the presence of both imported Floral Cursive and locally manufactured Coastal Cajamarca ceramic styles. In contrast, the only Wari-style ceramics found in the same region are locally manufactured Provincial Wari. Definite Wari intrusive settlement (in terms of architectural style and form, as well as associated artifacts) has not yet been found on the northern North Coast. Though some suggest that the Middle Cajamarca polity remained largely autonomous during the height of Wari hegemony (Shady and Rosas 1977), it is difficult to account for the co-occurrence of Middle Cajamarca B and Epoch 2A Provincial Wari style ceramics. Easy transit to the northern North Coast through the productive Cajamarca Basin and Jequetepeque Valley would make very good tactical sense for the Wari polity. In fact, available evidence pertaining to the distribution of Provincial Wari materials argues that Wari expansion emphasized highland corridors, with coastal intrusion through a handful of selected valleys (e.g., Huarmey, Jequetepeque, and perhaps Santa), probably with the assistance of local highland powers.

One basic issue regarding the Wari Conquest model is whether the second or Epoch 2A expansion preceded or followed the collapse of the Moche V capital of Pampa Grande. The ambiguities surrounding the correspondence between stylistic and absolute (calendrical) dates of Wari ceramics is quite relevant here. Also, the distinct possibility of the temporal coexistence of Epoch 1B and 2A ceramics suggested by Anders's (1990) work at Maymi on the South Coast has direct bearing on the discussion at hand. If widespread Epoch 2A Provincial Wari in northern Peru overlaps (in calendrical dates) with the latter portion of Moche V (Epoch 1B), Wari-Cajamarca expansion onto the northern North Coast could be seen as in some way responsible for the Moche V demise. If they are sequential with minimum overlap, the Epoch 2A expansion may have simply filled the political vacuum left by the Moche V demise. Chronological refinement and additional absolute dating of Epoch 1B and 2A are urgently needed.

D. Assessing the Models of Specific Causes

Let us scrutinize these competing models in terms of data from Pampa Grande. The Internal Revolt model would posit a systematic attack on and rejection of the material symbols of power and order, such as *huacas* and iconography charged with the elite dogma. The highly selective destruction stipulated by the model is exactly what we have noted. At the same time, those carrying out the revolt would carefully avoid harming their own property. The fact that all adobe enclosures and at least three-quarters of the adobe mounds examined had been indiscriminately burnt argues against the idea that the revolt was led by someone of a major Mochica lineage or some other corporate group residing within the city. By the same token, the absence of fire or other forms of destruction in the relatively small masonry enclosures and residences supports the notion of a popular uprising (i.e., primarily the urban populace).

However, this does not explain the burning food items such as maize kernels and beans. This is a matter for speculation.

The destruction of stored foods may have been an attempt to dislodge urban residents and remove the heavy burden of their support from the hinterland agricultural sector. Alternatively, they may have been perceived as being too intimately linked to imposed labor services for the elite.

The few murals that remain show no sign of intentional defacing. Incisions found on the plastered face of a niched adobe wall overlooking the inferred cotton processing area in the Deer House seem to show a rather regular lattice and are not associated with any traces of paint. Similarly, the breakage pattern of many fine ceramic vessels found in burnt structures does not appear to reflect intentional smashing but rather the collapse of roofs and/or walls.

The Wari Conquest model would also posit selective destruction of the material symbols of the Moche V religion and state. We would expect plundering of stored valuables and human casualties, similar expectations to those of the Internal Revolt model. The fact that large storage facilities were empty of their contents may signify Wari plunder or removal by fleeing Mochica elite. Further, other than sacrificial burials, we have not located a single Moche V burial or cemetery within the site or in the immediate vicinity. No human remains that could be interpreted as casualties of violence associated with either the postulated internal rebellion or foreign invasion (e.g., hastily prepared mass burials, skeletons with severe traumas) have been found.

One expectation that distinguishes the Wari Conquest model from the other is the presence of defensive features, such as parapeted walls and deep ditches. A straight ditch dug into sterile soil at the eastern margin of the site is not only narrow and shallow (about 1.0–1.5 m in width and depth), but seems to be quite recent given that it has little waterlaid fill and erosion.

On the other hand, two major walls (1–2 m high today; ca. 1.5 m wide at the base; adobes atop a stone foundation) that intersect at the northeast corner of the site are clearly ancient (see Fig. 7.1). The walls cut through Moche V structures and are believed to have protected Middle Sicán occupations from flash floods.

Competing hypotheses as to the function of the parapeted wall at Galindo were discussed in Chapters 6 and 7. The presence or absence of defensive features on their own by no means constitutes a conclusive line of evidence in support of or refuting the Wari Conquest model.

Depending on the size of the invading force and how long they were present, we would also expect to find some imported Wari artifacts. Yet we identified no foreign weapons or armor. Earlier, we noted a small post–Moche V metal workshop in the south margin of the site[158] in association with three-color Geometric jar fragments. This localized discovery is the only example of Middle Horizon Epoch 2 Wari-inspired ceramics recorded thus far at Pampa Grande.

A sherd of an imported Floral Cursive kaolin plate was recovered from a floor pit in the Palatial Room Complex atop the Main Body of Huaca Fortaleza (Haas 1985: 405; Fig. 10.3). No other Cajamarca ceramics were recovered during our fieldwork. Though the location is quite intriguing, we can say little about the broader significance of the ceramics.

The above expectation of finding appreciable amounts of Wari style or other foreign artifacts may not be realistic. Victories in battles away from Pampa Grande and consequent *blitzkrieg*-type attack and destruction of the site would probably leave few material remains. It would be difficult to document a transitory presence archaeologically, a conclusion Tainter (1988: 89) also reached. What can be said with confidence is that there is no material evidence of the prolonged presence of Wari or Wari-affiliated groups at Pampa Grande.

If their use of Huaca del Sol at Moche for religious ceremonies is instructive of Wari behavior in subjugated portions of Mochica land, we would expect Huaca Fortaleza at Pampa Grande to have been similarly used. However, with the possible exception of the Floral Cursive sherd mentioned above, there is no evidence at all of post–Moche V use of Huaca Fortaleza.

That Wari rituals and offerings were not made at Huaca Fortaleza suggests that it permanently lost its importance among the local populace without Wari intervention, which tends to support the Internal

Revolt model. Is it possible that by the time of the abandonment of Pampa Grande, Huaca Fortaleza had become more of a political symbol than a religious one? On the other hand, Wari-Mochica polychrome murals at Huaca La Mayanga and Epoch 2A Provincial Wari ceramics at Huaca Soledad and on immediately post–Moche V floors at Huaca del Pueblo Batán Grande, all in the mid–La Leche Valley, seem to indicate that Wari influence (at least stylistic and religious) was indeed felt in the Lambayeque region shortly after the demise of the Moche V polity at Pampa Grande.

Relatively soon after the selective burning that forced abandonment around A.D. 700, the deserted city of Pampa Grande was beset by torrential rains and associated flash flooding, which preserved standing structures and their contents by burying them in thick deposits of sand and silt (Craig and Shimada 1986). A case in point is the "*Porrón* Room" in Structure S in Sector D that lies just off a dry riverbed, which was modified to function as one of the Sector's principal east-west streets. Examination of the deposits that completely buried the room indicates that up to 70 cm of alluvial materials resulted from a single flood.

This flood was probably quite powerful, as it swept up most of the burnt organic material and caused substantial collapse of the stone walls of the room. In the west side of the room there was a large accumulation of adobe melt and broken adobes. The water flow also turned one nearly complete *porrón*, 61 cm in diameter and at least 87 cm high, upside down some 20 cm off the floor of the room. The flood deposits preserved another large broken *porrón*; many jar fragments, some with face-necks; and one complete coarse redware basin 45 cm in diameter and 27 cm deep.

The deep stratigraphy at Huaca del Pueblo Batán Grande provides a similar picture. Up to 30 cm of rather uniform water-laid deposits of silt and sand separate Moche V from succeeding Early Sicán floors (ibid.).

That the flood occurred after the fire is clearly seen in the excavated stratigraphy. In his excavation of room complexes atop the Main Body of Huaca Fortaleza, Haas

(1985: 398) observed that "burned roofing material was found directly on the floor with no intervening natural or cultural deposit," an observation independently confirmed by excavations at other burnt adobe structures such as Huaca 2 and Deer House. The excavated floors and wall faces showed no waterlaid deposits or damage (e.g., melting). A flash flood associated with a severe El Niño cannot be considered as a factor in the abandonment of the city.

In sum, sometime around A.D. 700 the Moche V polity centered at Pampa Grande met its demise, and at least the central portion of the city was rapidly and permanently abandoned. Though some residents who cultivated nearby prime land may have lingered on in the peripheries of the city (or more likely used the northern edge of the site as a burial ground), there is no evidence of any serious effort to resuscitate it as a major settlement or to establish yet another capital in or outside of Lambayeque.

Available evidence tends to favor the Internal Revolt explanation as the immediate cause of the rapid and violent end of the Moche V polity at Pampa Grande. The Wari Conquest model is not easy to prove or disprove due to inadequate dating, the limited amount of relevant data, and uncertainties surrounding the diagnostic material indicators of their conquests. What is clear is that the Wari culture did not play

Figure 10.3. Imported kaolin Middle Cajamarca B Floral Cursive sherd recovered atop the Main Body of Huaca Fortaleza in Pampa Grande.

any significant role in the Moche IV–V transformation. At the same time, perhaps through the agency of a contemporaneous Central Coast culture such as Nievería or Pachacamac, initial Wari-Mochica contact may have been made sometime during Moche V. If the Wari or Wari-Cajamarca military force actually intruded into the North Coast at all, it may have occurred shortly after the demise of the Moche V state centered at Pampa Grande to fill the political vacuum that it left behind.

It should be emphasized that the issues related to Moche V collapse are far from satisfactorily resolved. We may never learn with certainty what triggered the selective burning of the material symbols of the existent power and order. We can say, however, that the unique cultural and natural conditions and forces that underlay the rapid establishment and growth of the Moche V city and state had, at the same time, built-in tendencies toward destabilization, or what Tainter (1988) has called "declining marginal returns."

2. Disintegration of the Moche V Culture on the Northern North Coast

Did the disintegration of the Moche V city and state really create a major political vacuum for many years on the northern North Coast? The collapse discussed above was concerned only with Pampa Grande. Though the term *collapse* may suggest a rapidly spreading domino effect, we cannot assume a simultaneous or similar destructive end for the entire Moche V domain, particularly in light of certain regional differences we have observed thus far.

Little can be said about the final days of the frontier city of Galindo. The radiocarbon dates from Moche V Galindo (Table 2) are less precise than those of Pampa Grande but, with the exception of one date, are internally consistent and suggest that much, perhaps the totality, of the site was abandoned at roughly the same time as Pampa Grande (ca. A.D. 700–750).[159] Ceramics independently support this dating. Though there are some vessel forms with antecedents in areas south of the Mochica domain, Bawden (1977: 398) asserts that "The vast majority of ceramic fragments

recovered [at Galindo] fall entirely within the bounds of traditional [Mochica] pottery, both structurally and decoratively." No Provincial or imported highland Wari ceramics dating to Middle Horizon Epoch 1B or 2A have been reported at the site. In contrast to Pampa Grande, there seems to be little indication of widespread physical destruction of structures that symbolized Moche V power and ideology.

The situation elsewhere on the northern North Coast is even less known. As noted earlier, Donnan's (1986: 22) claim of the Moche V occupation at Pacatnamú lasting until ca. A.D. 1000 is quite problematical. Such dating would be contemporaneous with the Late Cajamarca and Middle Sicán cultures, which have been securely dated. Ceramics of the latter two cultures have been found at various sites within the Jequetepeque Valley (Eling 1987; Shimada 1990a, 1991b, in press 2). In fact, Middle Sicán ceramics and textiles have been found just outside the "city wall" at Pacatnamú (Eling 1987: 349; also see Flores 1984). Cotton textiles bearing strong stylistic and iconographic resemblance to those found at the famed ceremonial center of Pachacamac near Lima (probably Middle Horizon Epoch 2) have also been found at Pacatnamú (Keatinge 1978; Shimada 1991b; Ubbelohde-Doering 1967, 1983). Without the support of independent dating and clarification of the nature of the inferred Moche V occupation and its articulation with Provincial Wari, Pachacamac, Middle Sicán, and Late Cajamarca encompassed within its inferred period of occupation, we cannot accept this late dating.

Evidence presented above suggests that if the Wari polity (perhaps in consort with the Middle Cajamarca polity) did indeed establish political hegemony over the North Coast, it was ephemeral in character, essentially spanning the final portion of Epoch 1B and early Epoch 2A, ca. A.D. 700. Evidence of the physical presence of a Wari population on the North Coast is minimal. There is little that suggests commerce (e.g., very limited distribution of imported obsidian) as a significant motive for expansion into the North Coast. Yet Wari religious proselytizing, which began during Epoch 1B, was widespread. Ritual offerings at the Huaca del Sol, Wari-Mochica murals

at the Huaca La Mayanga, and perhaps modifications to the Pañamarca mound (Schaedel 1951c) all suggest a strategy of taking over and modifying prestigious local ceremonial centers without investing much labor and time during Middle Horizon Epoch 1B (Shimada 1981: 441–442). Huaca del Sol continued to be important as an Epoch 2A ritual site. The site of San José de Moro (Moro Viejo) in the Jequetepeque Valley contains burials with Epoch 2A Provincial Wari ceramics.[160] A ritual cache of Epoch 2A Provincial Wari ceramics was found at Sausal in the Chicama Valley. This strategy is an efficient way of demonstrating the domination of the Mochica religion by its Wari counterpart. Participation in rituals at these ceremonial centers would have served to disseminate new beliefs as well as create and strengthen bonds among the participants. These religious activities during late Epoch 1B and early Epoch 2A may well have been accompanied by tribute demands to take advantage of the impressive productivity of the North Coast agriculture, metallurgy, fishing, and trade with coastal Ecuador.

Before we can conclusively resolve the dating and causal processes of Moche V political demise and the abandonment of Moche V cities, we need a better understanding of the nature, timing, and causes of Wari and Cajamarca expansions. For example, how did these two highland polities react to the prolonged period of environmental stress during much of the sixth century? Some (e.g., Cardich 1980; Paulsen 1976) have argued that territorial expansion was their response to prolonged droughts. It is plausible that the first wave of Wari expansion was at least in part conditioned by the late sixth-century drought (Shimada et al. 1991a,b). In some ways, highland agriculturalists practicing both dry and irrigation farming would have felt the adverse effects of the drought more strongly than their coastal counterparts. However, the second wave of expansion (Middle Horizon Epoch 2B), which may have had some relationship with the demise of the Moche V polity, may have been motivated by internal factors (Menzel 1964). Overall, the end of Moche V culture cannot be understood only from a North Coast perspective.

11

Moche V Legacies and Conclusion

In concluding this book we define the long-term impacts and the broader significance of the Moche V culture and the city of Pampa Grande within Andean civilization. Though there was no temporal hiatus between Moche IV and V, in substance there were notable disjunctures. Moche V was not a simple extension of the Mochica cultural tradition. It was a time of rapid, drastic, and in many ways innovative cultural changes. Some were internally generated as the rapid establishment and growth of the city of Pampa Grande was accompanied by a variety of new institutions and compromises. Others can be traced to external processes such as the severe three-decade drought in the late sixth century and perhaps Wari expansion. Below we examine these changes and the question of whether they represented ephemeral or permanent shifts.

1. Legacies of the Mochica Culture and Pampa Grande

A. Art and Religion

Perhaps the most often heard comment regarding Mochica legacies is the lasting role of its ceramic art as an inspirational source for later counterparts. Detailed studies of this archaism (Burger 1976) are rare. As noted in Chapter 2, the persistent use of the terms "Proto-" and "Early Chimú" to designate what came to be called Mochica in the 1930's with Larco Hoyle's insistence and clarification attests to the readily apparent similarities between Mochica and the later Imperial Chimú ceramics that are separated by over five hundred years. Though examples are rare, some Chimú effigy vessels were apparently made with molds taken from Mochica originals. Many others that seem to be imitations of Mochica originals may actually be the final results of a long-term process by which specific Mochica motifs and themes were first accurately and faithfully copied, then gradually modified, often deleting details, and ultimately transformed to the aesthetic taste of the Chimú (ibid.). Eventually these changes became established and standardized. Typical of Chimú ceramic art, the scene became simple and static, probably having lost much, if not all, of its original symbolic meaning. Chimú potters were indifferent to the representational fineline painting so crucial to the Mochica in disseminating their political and religious dogma. Though Larco Hoyle (1946, 1948) adopted the name of a Chimú deity, *Ai-apaec*, to describe the Mochica feline-fanged deity, it is not certain whether they are indeed the same or originated among the Mochica.

Certain motifs and forms on Chimú vessels that appear to be archaic revivals may have been in continuous use since their first appearance in Mochica art or even earlier. Within Chimú ceramics, we can recognize motifs and forms of antecedent Cupisnique, Mochica, Wari, and Sicán examples. There is little in the Chimú archaism that is based on specifically Moche V forms or iconography. A monkey perched on the stirrup of a bottle, which is widely seen in Chimú ceramics, is actually quite common in Moche V (Fig. 2.7) and Middle (A.D. 900–1100) and Late (A.D. 1100–1375) Sicán stirrup-spout bottles (Shimada 1990a, notes 5 and 7).

In general, Chimú copies and imitations are mass produced with two-piece vertical molds and have a black or gray finish. Typically, they do not show attention to detail, and burnishing is often cursory or lacking. Modeling is relatively crude, and much of the decorative detail is press-molded. Though press-mold decoration and gray or black finish did exist in pre–Moche V ceramics, these two features gained considerable importance in Moche V ceramics and persisted until the Chimú times. Middle Horizon Epoch 2 and 3 ceramics from the site of Moche, for example, show press-mold decorations on Wari-derived forms (Menzel 1977).

In general, Chimú use of Mochica ceramic art does not appear to have been dictated by ideological concerns. Thus, we see continuity in form and manufacturing technique but with the original meaning probably altered or to a large extent lost.

Imitations and continuities in Mochica ceramic forms and motifs are by no means restricted to the Chimú. The best example of the fusion of Mochica and Wari features is seen in Middle Sicán art which is dominated by representations of the Sicán Deity (Fig. 11.1) who is believed to represent syncretism of "Mochica Lords" (major deities) with the "single male Wari deity" (Menzel 1977: 61–62). Menzel (ibid., 61) argues that, though the organization of the religious concepts differed, "The mythical beings of Moche religion were not dissimilar to those of [Wari] religion," and similarities between particular mythical beings

of these religions "provided the basis for the rapid but selective syncretism," probably during Middle Horizon Epoch 2B. The distinctive comma-shaped eyes of the Sicán Deity are a development out of the "painted Moche eye form of mythical beings and some humans appearing in religious scenes," while the pairs of vertical lines below the eyes of the Sicán Deity are a Wari trait (ibid.). The Sicán Deity is shown at times with wings and other avian qualities. He was presumably endowed with all the esteemed qualities of the Mochica and Wari deities and controlled celestial forces fundamental to life and abundance.

In addition to the above Mochica-Wari syncretism, there are Middle Sicán blackware ceramics that depict recognizable Mochica scenes in their entirety, retaining the same structural relationships among the constituent motifs. These ceramic representations are consistently well made and appear to have been used as elite grave offerings, suggesting that Mochica religious concepts and mythical beings, even after some one hundred fifty years or more, still commanded respect among local populations. Integration of the two prestigious Mochica and Wari art styles with local iconographies and ideologies known to all, then, gave legitimacy and clout to the Sicán Deity and religion and helped assure acceptance by local populations. Menzel (ibid., 59) concludes that "Moche traditions were not extinguished in the time of the [Wari] Empire, but only became mingled to some extent with [Wari] ideas. Moreover, under the stimulation of [Wari] ideas, particularly in the realms of religion and aggrandizement of power, north coast culture [Sicán] appears to have undergone a new flowering in slightly altered form, a form in which it was spread far more widely than before." At the same time, the observed Mochica imitations and revival may stem in part from a conscious effort on the part of a local population under the Sicán polity to reassert its ethnic identity following a prolonged period of foreign influence (Early Sicán).

Evidence of the lasting impacts of Mochica art outside of the North Coast is limited.[161] We noted that the distribution of artistically and technically sophisticated Moche V textiles on the Central and South Coasts of Peru may reflect an appreciation of these textiles by the Wari and Wari-affiliated coastal elite who may have conscribed them as tribute or even relocated Mochica weavers to their home communities. Farther afield on the South Coast, late Nasca (Phase 7) ceramic art displays some motifs and stylistic conventions likely to have been derived from that of Moche IV (Knobloch 1991a). In general, Nasca and Mochica, the two most prominent pre-Hispanic art styles of the Peruvian coast, show surprisingly little stylistic or iconographic influence on each other in spite of their contemporaneity and relative proximity (Shimada 1991a).

Beyond the northern edge of Mochica territory, one sometimes hears comments about Mochica ceramics in local collections on the Ecuadorian coast, but there is little published evidence (Collier 1948). Given the importance of tropical seashells for the Mochica elite and religion, and the popularity of single-mold-made hollow figurines and reduced wares that probably reflect the adoption of coastal Ecuadorian technical features, the presence of Moche V ceramics would not come as a surprise.

Overall, the long-term impacts of Mochica art outside of Mochica territory were limited in scope and quite diffused. For the art that some regard as one of the major ancient narrative styles of the world, this conclusion seems surprising. However, it is not unexpected, given the minimal indications of Mochica interaction with the contemporary cultures surrounding its territory. The iconography was strongly bound up with the unique historical and cultural contexts of the North Coast. Also, perhaps it was too strongly charged with the powerful Mochica elite dogma to be willingly assimilated into other styles and iconographies.

Turning our attention to religious beliefs and rituals, flexed, seated burials appear during Moche V and coexist with the traditional extended position. Moche V burials, examined in Chapter 9, suggest that the shift neither uniformly nor rapidly spread through the North Coast. This duality continued in the subsequent Sicán phases, and presently available data suggest

that the seated position represented elite status.[162]

The increased use of *Spondylus* noted at Pampa Grande is one lasting Moche V legacy. The water/agricultural fertility symbolism of *Spondylus* documented for Inca times seems to be an age-old Andean belief, perhaps going back to the Early Horizon or earlier. It was argued that the surge in *Spondylus* at the onset of or during Moche V reflected a desire to counter the adverse effects of the severe thirty-two-year drought that beset the Central Andes. The Moche V polity may have controlled *Spondylus* trade with coastal Ecuador. *Spondylus* offerings appear in various dispersed Middle Horizon Epoch 1B and 2 Wari sites on the coast and highlands. Wari expansion to the north may have been in part motivated by the desire to secure a *Spondylus* supply and to take over this trade in immediately post–Moche V times. *Spondylus* use became even more extensive and intensive after Moche V. *Spondylus* collection by diving from boats and its regular use in rituals are amply shown in later Middle Sicán ceramics and metal objects (Cordy-Collins 1990; Shimada 1990a, in press 2), and a recently excavated elite tomb alone contained 179 *Spondylus* and 141 *Conus* shells (Shimada 1992). Chimú elite may have eclipsed everyone in their generous use of whole, cut, and pulverized *Spondylus* found in the inferred royal burial platforms in Chan Chan (Conrad 1982: 99). The Sicán and later Chimú polities may well have taken over and expanded the inferred shell trade with coastal Ecuador (Shimada 1991b, in press 2).

B. Territorial Expansion, Cultural Interaction, and Human-Environment Interplay

With increasing research into the nature of Early Intermediate Period cultures on the North Coast over the past several years, our conception of their interrelationships and political organization has undergone considerable revision.

It is quite apparent that a Gallinazo ethnic population occupied nearly the entire North Coast, favoring the mid- to lower valley zones. Though our knowledge of the Salinar culture is still limited, it appears to have had an upper-valley focus in most

Figure 11.1. A typical Middle Sicán blackware bottle with the Sicán Lord face at the base of the spout. Brüning National Archaeological Museum.

North Coast valleys and stands as a strong candidate for the ethnic precursor of the Mochica. In addition, recent discoveries of early Mochica elite tombs at Loma Negra, Sipán, and La Mina have raised the strong possibility that within the first few centuries of our era, each of the larger northern North Coast valleys supported a regional polity that shared a new art style and symbolism that we call Mochica. The Mochica polity centered at Moche probably started out as just one of such regional polities.

With successful domination of the contemporaneous Gallinazo polity in the Moche Valley, this southern Mochica polity began its southward expansion as early as late Moche II. By Moche IV, it had established a hegemony that stretched to the Huarmey Valley. The Moche-based polity defeated contemporaneous regional Gallinazo polities and came to control the entire area between the Chicama and Santa valleys. The Nepeña, Casma, and Huarmey show later primarily Moche IV mid-valley occupation, suggesting that either incorporation of this area into the Mochica hegemony was quite late or that the southern Mochica polity may have established alliances with local polities who paid tribute in return for continued autonomy and neutralizing of the coastward Recuay expansion. The oft-heard view of the Mochicas' single-minded aim of agricultural maximization seems valid only for certain valleys.

The concurrent situation on the northern North Coast is still unclear. However, data from Sipán, together with the recent discovery of early Mochica sites in the mid-Lambayeque Valley, suggest that this area was the base for another powerful Mochica polity that held sway until early Moche IV. It is likely that during Moche I–IV there were at least two powerful Mochica polities on the North Coast. The simple, conventional equation of a presumably uniform Mochica style and distribution with political unification requires major revision. It is argued in this book that such unification did not take place until late Moche IV (ca. A.D. 500). It is interesting that Berezkin's (1978) study of the Mochica pantheon also suggests concurrent consolidation of political power.

Our scrutiny of relevant evidence pertaining to the nature of pre-Moche V political organization of either the northern or southern polity finds state status quite tenuous in spite of its popularity in recent publications. The case for such status suffers from imprecise, limited, and/or subjective criteria and ambivalent data, particularly those derived from straightforward interpretation of combat scenes and "portrait" vessels. There is no one line of conclusive evidence, and the view of superchiefdom is just as plausible. We need better documentation of the "integration of functionally disparate units" and the complementarity and monopoly over various forms of resource exploitation expected for a state-level polity (Schaedel 1985b).

There is surprisingly little material evidence of interaction between the Mochica and polities in adjacent cis-Andean and North Highland regions until Moche V. Most interaction in northern Peru apparently took the form of tense coexistence and resource sharing in the *chaupiyunga* zone and occasional elite/ceremonial gift exchange. This is believed to reflect the ba-

sically competitive and even antagonistic relationships among them, as well as the economic self-sufficiency attained by the Mochica and the dynamic, autonomous, and advanced character of Mochica cultural developments. The impressive horizontal expansion of the Mochica both on and off the coast gave control over agricultural production and maritime exploitation; landlocked the Cajamarca and Recuay cultures, or at least constricted their access to the Pacific; and allowed them to break away from the homogeneous environment of repetitive coastal valleys by providing access to a wide range of resources.

At the same time, Mochica economic self-sufficiency based on large-scale irrigation agriculture and intensive exploitation of marine resources essentially continued what had been achieved by the time of Christ. In fact, some regions of the North Coast reached their prehistoric maxima for total land surface under irrigation and population size under the Late Gallinazo (ca. A.D. 200). Mochica refinements and innovations to this dual subsistence system included control of offshore islands and intensification (though not initiation) of large-scale coastal llama breeding and herding. The former was both economic and spiritual in nature; though guano mining has often been mentioned in the literature, control of offshore islands also meant control of sea mammals, fishing grounds, and sacred places, all crucial to the well-being of coastal populations.

Large-scale local breeding and herding of llamas effectively complemented the traditional subsistence base of marine resources and agricultural produce. Their local, year-round availability, manageability, and diversity of use added stability and flexibility to Mochica subsistence and economy and made it less dependent on maritime resources, both important considerations for Moche V inland urban centers such as Galindo and Pampa Grande. Llamas appear to have supplanted marine products as the single most important source of meat protein at both Galindo and Pampa Grande. These reliable beasts of burden also provided mobility for the Moche V population. Whether or not this emphasis on llamas is a response to the decreased and/or unreliable agricultural

production during the stressful sixth century remains to be determined. Large-scale herding and breeding on the North Coast lasted until the Spanish Conquest.

These underpinnings of the Mochica polities and culture were shaken to their foundation at the time of the Moche IV–V transition. Economic self-sufficiency became quite tenuous with the thirty-two-year drought that abruptly began in A.D. 562. Not just another catastrophe, this was the severest drought in the fifteen-hundred-year precipitation record established on the basis of ice cores from the Quelccaya Ice Sheet south of Cusco. Much of the Peruvian coast probably experienced a prolonged significant reduction in available water, preconditioning the major northward shift of Mochica geopolitics and unprecedented valley neck population nucleation. The selection of Pampa Grande as the setting for the Moche V capital was probably based on two major considerations: favorable natural conditions that assured residents of relatively high agricultural production in spite of the drought, and the prominence of the Lambayeque-based northern Mochica polity, which probably saw this moment as an opportunity to reclaim its own former power. During this same time, the North Highland Recuay and Cajamarca polities may have begun their own coastward expansion in response to drought conditions. Such expansion, perhaps in conjunction with the Wari response to these same drought conditions, may have contributed to the Mochica abandonment of the Southern Sector of the North Coast. Having lost much of its economic and political power base, the Moche-based southern Mochica polity relocated to Galindo, which held only regional importance during Moche V. The situation at Pampa Grande is summarized below.

The Moche IV–V transformation also marked an end to the long-standing North Coast–centric orientation of the Mochica population. Although two waves of Wari expansion are commonly emphasized, the beginning of the Middle Horizon was a period of considerable interregional movement. During Moche V we see indications of interactions with their Nievería, Guangala, Wari, and Cajamarca counterparts.

We have seen that the changing distribution of Cajamarca and Recuay ceramics over time is a telling barometer of the political strength of the Mochica and other North Coast polities. During Moche IV, their coastal distribution was quite limited. However, the demise of the Moche V polity was analogous to opening the floodgates for the Cajamarca polity; evidence is quite strong for immediately post–Moche V coastward expansion of the Cajamarca population, as if to reclaim lost access to the Pacific and the coast. The art of the Early Sicán culture that succeeded Moche V shows ample evidence of Cajamarca, Pachacamac, and Wari stylistic and iconographic influence (Shimada 1990a, 1991b). Concurrently, the Middle Cajamarca polity may have established coastal colonies in the Lambayeque region. However, by around A.D. 850–900, following the demise of the Wari polity, the Middle Sicán polity began to reclaim regional autonomy and soon established control over the northern North Coast, curtailing coeval Late Cajamarca influence on the coast.

In a basic sense, during the first millennium of our era the North Coast witnessed a series of changes in political balance between the two polities centered in the Lambayeque and Moche-Chicama regions. The latter eclipsed the former sometime in Moche IV, only to lose its grip at the time of the Moche IV–V transition. The Moche V northern focus preconditioned subsequent Middle Sicán hegemony over the same area. In turn, the Chimú Kingdom, based in the Moche Valley, conquered the Lambayeque area around A.D. 1375. Overall, the divergence between the two cultural subareas within the North Coast became more apparent during the first millennium of our era.

C. Redistributive Economy and the State

Moche V Pampa Grande provides ample material evidence of a redistributive economy or "institutionalized hospitality," i.e., labor services in craft production reciprocated with food and *chicha* prepared in spatially distinct kitchens with grains kept in nearby small, state-controlled storage facilities. Though a redistributive economy is often invoked for pre-Inca periods in the archaeological literature, there are only a few case studies that provide sufficient material evidence for that claim. The nature and size of labor forces involved must be defined in addition to demonstrating that food/drink preparation was for nonhousehold consumption with ingredients under the control of the beneficiaries. Work at Pampa Grande and various Wari sites in and around Ayacucho (e.g., Anders 1986; Isbell 1977) suggests that the reciprocal relationship between worker and state extensively documented for the Inca Empire can be traced at least back to the beginning of the Middle Horizon. The importance of *chicha* in this reciprocal exchange and feasting is quite clear at Pampa Grande.

Labor service underwritten by "institutionalized hospitality" seems to have formed the core of the Moche V urban economy at Pampa Grande. Much of the labor service is believed to have been provided by non-Mochica residents (inferred Gallinazo ethnicity) resettled to the Southern Pediment largely from agriculturally marginal lands in the Lambayeque and adjacent valleys. It was not a simple matter of exacting labor service or tribute from a local population. The establishment of a viable urban economy at Pampa Grande is believed to have necessitated population resettlement and shifts in land use. Significant and prolonged reduction in water reaching the coast accentuated an existing inequality in the distribution of water and land, and led to population nucleation at the optimal valley neck location. The strategic and productive valley neck was taken over by the newly established Moche V polity. Control of the valley neck and hence of all the regional canal intakes provided the Moche V polity at Pampa Grande with enough clout to institute these changes.

The Moche V urban economy integrated other modes of production. As noted earlier, an ample supply of *Spondylus*, for example, depended on long-distance trade with coastal Ecuador. The close association of *Spondylus* shells with major *huacas* suggests that the shell was closely related to the basic survival of the extant religious and political order. Its processing and use may have been closely controlled by the ruling elite, and the former charged to a small group of artisans retained by the state.

Overall, the continuing viability of Moche V Pampa Grande was dependent upon various forms of complementary exploitation. Thus, in the sense of redistributing resources gained through multiple exploitation systems at intrasite, regional, and interregional levels, and forceful usurpation of lands and an attendant shift in their use, we may characterize the Moche V polity centered at Pampa Grande as a short-lived redistributive state.

Evidence for the post–Moche V redistributive state on the North Coast said to have been installed by the Wari invaders (Schaedel 1966a,b, 1972, 1985b) is limited and tenuous. A stronger case can be made for a Middle Sicán state that monopolized regional copper alloy production and trade with coastal Ecuador (Shimada in press 2). The Chimú Kingdom that emerged in the Moche valley sometime around A.D. 1100–1200 came to possess features that also merit the label redistributive state during its 250–350-year existence (e.g., see Day 1982a; Schaedel 1978, 1985b; J. Topic 1990).

Any summary of Moche V economy cannot exclude large-scale storage found at both Galindo and Pampa Grande. At the latter, management by the central authority is indicated by (1) tightly controlled access, (2) strategic placement, (3) formal layout not seen in other types of architecture, and (4) standardized forms, dimensions, and construction materials (adobe bricks). At Galindo, the two areas of large-scale storage also feature highly controlled access, but the masonry storage structures are not as standardized in construction and dimensions or as formal in layout as the adobe storerooms at Pampa Grande. Though it is tempting to relate the appearance of large-scale storage to stresses stemming from the late sixth-century drought, we still do not have adequate data from pre–Moche V sites to determine whether it was peculiarly Moche V. In addition, at both sites we have only a partial glimpse of the nature of stored goods. At Pampa Grande, circumstantial evidence argues that these storage facilities held craft goods produced in supervised workshops essential for the Moche V political economy and

trade. Valuable raw materials used in these workshops were probably stored there as well.

Large-scale storage facilities, though expected at the Middle Sicán capital of Sicán in Batán Grande, have not been definitely documented. At the Chimú capital of Chan Chan, large-scale storage of goods is believed to have been a critical function of the *ciudadelas* (e.g., Day 1982a,b). Each *ciudadela* has rows of small, well-made storerooms with standardized dimensions, high thresholds, and controlled access, much like those at Pampa Grande. Though none of the excavated storeroom cells yielded clues as to the original contents, their architectural features and contexts, as well as the proximity to the craft workshops outside the *ciudadelas*, argue that they were used for the storage of manufactured goods and agricultural produce needed for imperial political economy.

D. Monumental Architecture and Attendant Institutions

Huaca Fortaleza was the last of the Mochica monumental mounds and ceremonial centers, a tradition going back to the second millennium B.C. While the idea of building an awe-inspiring gigantic mound was retained through Moche V, the construction techniques involved and the actual form diverge from pre–Moche V mounds. What has been documented, like many other aspects of the Moche V culture, is a mixture of innovative and conservative trends. The innovative chamber-and-fill technique was used in conjunction with the traditional segmentary format. The former technique was already in use on the Central Coast, where the Maranga culture employed it for their monumental mound constructions. Thus, the filled-chamber technique may well have been derived from areas south of the North Coast along with a number of other nonreligious features (e.g., new ceramic forms) early in Moche V.

This technique, together with abundant use of clay mortar and mixing of bricks of varied size and shape, allowed rapid construction of tall, massive mounds with steep sides, unlike earlier mounds that had to be built in many stages by stacking platforms of increasingly smaller size. These qualities of Huaca Fortaleza construction suggest that much of the mound was erected in a highly unified, continuous mode under close supervision, involving a large labor force at the construction site and the pooling of construction materials from diverse sources.

The tradition of constructing steep-sided truncated platform mounds using this technique was resurrected by the Middle Sicán culture around A.D. 900. In the Middle Sicán examples, however, standardized chambers are considerably larger in size, and various tiers of bonded chamber lattice walls are superimposed. Though the marking technique and many of the simpler marks are identical to those found on Moche V or pre–Moche V bricks, there is no longer consistent one-to-one correspondence between mark on the one hand and brick size and shape, mold size, soil color, and texture on the other, such as is found at Huaca del Sol and Huaca de la Luna.

Many of the above qualities of Middle Sicán mounds cannot be adequately explained by the models of labor organization considered in Chapter 7. That is to say, we may be witnessing continuity in the tradition of marking bricks but with different meaning attached to the marks; e.g., identification of patrons voluntarily donating materials and perhaps even labor for the construction of public temples. The use of marked bricks continues at least into the fifteenth century A.D. and probably up to the time of Spanish Conquest (1532–1535) in the Lambayeque region. Continuity of segmentary construction beyond the Middle Sicán in the region remains to be documented.

Clearly, the innovative qualities of the filled-chamber format for rapidly erecting massive buildings while minimizing labor and material investment were widely appreciated. This format also had an important effect of encouraging the centralization of political power. These features probably explain its persistence and widespread acceptance on the post–Moche V North Coast.

E. City and State Formation

The preceding picture from the Lambayeque Valley Complex is in sharp contrast with that from the Moche Valley. The Mochica tradition of marked bricks is poorly represented at Moche V Galindo and seems to disappear permanently thereafter. The segmentary technique, however, is once again seen in Chimú state constructions at Chan Chan and even surviving into the early Colonial period (Moseley 1975b). In addition, it has been long known that in the Moche and valleys to the south on the North Coast monumental mound construction went out of fashion with the demise of the Mochica polity, or perhaps from the Moche IV–V transition, and that subsequent corporate architecture typically took the form of large rectangular walled-in compounds (e.g., *ciudadelas* at Chan Chan). At Chan Chan, several monumental mounds are built detached from the *ciudadelas,* apparently with the chamber-and-fill technique that was probably introduced from the northern North Coast.

This mound/rectangular compound or sacred/secular dichotomy stems from Moche V. At Galindo, traditional Mochica platform mounds are small in size and peripheral in location while rectangular compounds are relatively large in size and centrally placed within the site. This difference is believed to reflect a transfer of authority from the sacred to the secular at Galindo.

At Pampa Grande, the traditional religious leaders of the northern Mochica polity attempted to reestablish eminence. Pampa Grande was planned around the centrally placed, disproportionately large Huaca Fortaleza mound. Its construction probably began from the very beginning of Moche V Pampa Grande. Second-stage construction of the *huaca* was most likely completed within a single generation. Its rapid and successful construction was essential for strengthening the struggling leadership and for the sociopolitical integration of a society that had just experienced unprecedented upheaval. This impressive *huaca* was intended to symbolize the viability of the Moche V religion and polity.

Together with the stressful conditions that led to valley neck nucleation, the organizational ramifications of the continuous, unified effort required with the chamber-and-fill construction format are critical in understanding the formation of the Moche V city and state at Pampa Grande. They brought together a large labor force and a wide range of supportive crafts and services in Pampa Grande, necessitating their permanence at the site. At the same time, the long-term, massive mobilization of resources led to permanent centralization of power, new administrative norms and institutions, and some measure of coercion critical to state formation. Thus, time-honored Mochica religious institutions provided the rallying point and organizational framework in establishing the new capital but in that process were ultimately transformed into a nascent secular state. The seeds of discontent that preconditioned the collapse of this polity were sown during this formative stage. The emergence of the Moche V nascent state and urban capital was a process of adaptation to stressful conditions, a rational solution to perceived needs. But with the completion of Huaca Fortaleza and concurrent improvement in the water supply, the high cost of their maintenance and legitimization became increasingly burdensome for the masses. It is questionable whether the Moche V leadership in its transformation from sacred to secular achieved any long-lasting stability in the city, and by around the mid- to late seventh century, Moche V society at Pampa Grande was in danger of collapse from internal decomposition or external threat.

The demise of the city and state was probably rapid and violent, with major corporate architecture showing systematic, intentional fire. Available evidence favors an internal revolt as the immediate cause of the collapse, though threats of encroaching Wari and Cajamarca polities may have contributed as well. Physical occupation of the site by external groups is not indicated.

We can also characterize Pampa Grande as a ceremonial city in the sense that the construction of Huaca Fortaleza provided the basis for its sociopolitical and physical integration and since the *huaca* was the hub of the growth and social organization of the city. On the northern North Coast, monumental mounds made an impressive comeback in Middle Sicán times and apparently retained their importance until the Spanish Conquest. However, there are some notable differences between Moche V Pampa Grande and post–Moche V ceremonial cities. The resident population attached to the Middle Sicán mound cluster (some dozen monumental mounds) within the Sicán Precinct appears to have been quite small. As with the other major coastal ceremonial cities of Pachacamac and Pacatnamú, most residents lived in clustered quarters close to but physically segregated from the ceremonial zone with monumental constructions (Shimada 1991b). In other words, these ceremonial cities did not have the unified, densely and continuously built appearance of Pampa Grande.

During Late Sicán, large settlements emerged along the hillside flanks of the Lambayeque Valley Complex (see Schaedel 1951a, 1966a,b, 1972). While some are extensive, we do not see the physical and functional integration of a massive ceremonial center within an urban setting as at Pampa Grande.

The site of El Purgatorio, with over a dozen monumental mounds clustered around a conical hill at the juncture of the La Leche and Lambayeque valleys, for the most part reached its impressive size sometime during Late Sicán. Largely on the strength of a cluster of regularly laid out roomlike constructions atop Huaca Larga, Schaedel (1951a,b, 1972, 1985a; cf. Trimborn 1979) argues that El Purgatorio constituted the urban capital of a late pre-Hispanic secular state. However, the function and dating of these "apartment-like" structures remain uncertain (Shimada and Cavallaro 1986, in press). It is doubtful that they are comparable to the architectural nucleation seen at Moche V Pampa Grande in extent, density, or multifunctional character.

Overall, one of the distinctive qualities of Moche V Pampa Grande, the physical and functional integration of ceremonialism and urbanism, was apparently ephemeral. Though a strong case for the autochthonous origin of Moche V urbanism (as opposed to Wari introduction) can be made, the cultural and natural forces that promoted its emergence were extraordinary. What transformed the population aggregated at the valley neck into a functioning city was the massive public labor project to erect Huaca Fortaleza. Such a collective goal-oriented approach has the seeds of self-destruction built in for the time when the goal is achieved, becomes irrelevant, or proves to be ineffectual (e.g., amelioration of climatic conditions). In addition, there is the challenging task of managing the complex sociopolitical dynamics resulting from the multiethnic population at the city. It appears that external pressure was a necessary condition of Moche V urbanism. It is likely that these considerations apply to other cities that emerged about the same time (for example, Cajamarquilla, near the neck of the Rimac Valley on the Central Coast and Wari in the Ayacucho Basin). However, it is debatable if they can be widely applied to the understanding of other urbanism in the Andes and elsewhere.

F. Mochica and Chimú Dynastic Continuity?

It has been suggested that there was an "unbroken dynasty from Moche to Pampa Grande to Chan Chan" (T. Topic 1982: 281). Though indeed provocative, this proposition has various problems. Similarities in architectural forms between Moche V Galindo and Chan Chan identified thus far (e.g., rectangular walled-in compounds, standardized storerooms, "burial platforms," and U-shaped "audiencia" or "administrative" structures [see Bawden 1982a; Conrad 1982; Moseley 1975e; T. Topic 1982]) would favor the idea of dynastic continuity within the Moche Valley. However, a scrutiny of available evidence indicates that it is difficult to date the founding of the Chimú Kingdom earlier than A.D. 1100–1200 (e.g., Cavallaro 1988; Conrad 1990; Rowe 1948a,b; Shimada in press 2; cf. Kolata 1990), leaving at least a four-hundred-year gap after the demise of the Moche V polity at Galindo. Thus, this hypothesis faces the difficult task of identifying the capitals during this span and explaining the significance of Huaca El Dragón (a major platform mound north of Chan Chan; Donnan 1990b; Schaedel 1966c; cf. Kolata 1990) and the appreciable number of Provincial Wari and Middle and Late Sicán artifacts within the valley (e.g., Donnan and Mackey 1978; Larco Hoyle 1948; Menzel 1977; Shimada in press 2). Though archaeologists who work in the North Coast region inherently tend to seek evidence of its cultural autonomy and primacy, the five hundred years or so that separate the end of Moche V Pampa Grande and Galindo and the beginning of the Chimú Kingdom saw complex cultural development that simply cannot be dismissed as transitory or insignificant.

One alternative that has not been adequately explored is the idea that Taycanamu, the founder of the Chimú Kingdom, came from the Lambayeque region (Kosok 1965: 180; cf. Moseley 1990) sometime after a drought that lasted thirty years, the violent destruction of the Middle Sicán monuments in Batán Grande (ca. A.D. 1050), and a subsequent major El Niño event, all occurring during the eleventh century (Shimada 1990a, in press 2).

In sum, the Mochica culture, which persisted for over six hundred years, controlled or influenced a section of the coast of over 1000 km and maintained an intimate and creative relationship with its environment for self-sufficiency and beyond. It initiated and promoted technological and organizational innovations and established new standards of artistic and technical excellence, leaving lasting impacts of its presence well into the final centuries before the Spanish Conquest.

Notes

Chapter 1
The Mochica and Pampa Grande
in Andean Prehistory

1. We do not know the original names of this and the adjacent mound to the east at the site, popularly called Pyramid of the Moon or Huaca de la Luna. There is nothing that proves or disproves their relationship to the sun and moon. A sixteenth-century document refers to Huaca del Sol as the temple of Pachacamac, indicating that it was a branch of the famous oracle center of Pachacamac near Lima (Netherly 1977: 321–322). Even to this day local people visit the site, suggesting its lingering religious importance.

2. It is believed to have established an empire covering much of Peru during the seventh and eighth centuries. See Isbell and McEwan (1991) for a recent synthesis on the Wari Empire.

Chapter 2
Archaeology of the Mochica Culture

3. Stübel excavated, together with Wilhelm Reiss, the Ancón cemetery near Lima, and inspected the impressive site of Tiwanaku (Tiahuanaco) near the south shore of Lake Titicaca in the Bolivian highlands.

4. Planned publication of his "Final Report" (Uhle n.d.) by the Ibero-Amerikanisches Institut in Berlin is eagerly awaited.

5. For example, see Collier 1955; Disselhoff 1958a,b; Ford 1949; Larco Hoyle 1948, 1963; Strong and Evans 1952; J. Rowe as described in Menzel 1977: 59; Shimada 1981, 1990a.

6. Actually, Uhle did not use the term *Mochica* but rather *Proto-Chimú*. Initially, Kroeber (1925, 1926) adopted Uhle's term *Proto-Chimú* in his publications, but later (1930: 54) switched to *Early Chimú* as *Proto* implies "a formative stage and the culture in question is already fully formed." However, starting in the 1940's, following Larco Hoyle's publications (1938, 1939; see below), Kroeber (1944) and other scholars adopted the term *Mochica*. The usage of the term *Proto-Chimú* is understandable because of stylistic similarity to the later Chimú. In addition, a substantial portion of the territory controlled by the Chimú overlapped that of the Mochica. We now know that Chimú artisans often used Mochica ceramics for artistic inspiration. They not only replicated Mochica forms in black or gray reduced wares, but also imitated the diagnostic red-on-cream finish. This "archaism"

confused early students of North Coast prehistory.

7. Larco Hoyle's attempt at Mochica ethnography encompassed a diverse range of topics and views including sexual habits and beans as ideograms. He argued (1943, 1944b) that the "beans" of various color patterns frequently depicted in Mochica ceramic art served as ideograms among the Mochica. Beans are shown in natural, anthropomorphic, and zoomorphic forms, and are often associated with runners carrying small bags of beans (thus "messages"). Beans are also shown frequently with sticks held by pairs of opposing figures, raising the possibility of their use in a game or for accounting (Figs. 2.2, 2.3). These beans and sticks may have been used much like dice and gridded tablets that some ethnohistorical sources indicate were used in divination or determining the duration and order of funerary rituals (Jiménez Borja 1985: 50–51).

8. Occasionally orange paint was also applied to accentuate certain features (Fig. 2.4). Similarly, fugitive organic black paint was employed to show details such as mustaches. Additional discussion of Mochica art is found in Chapter 10.

9. Kroeber (1944: 53) clearly noted that "full records" of Larco Hoyle's excavations were kept.

10. Scholars have included A. Baessler (1902–1903), M. Schmidt (1929), G. Kutscher (e.g., 1955a, 1983), and more recently U. Bankmann (1979) and I. von Schuler-Schömig (1979, 1981).

11. The themes underlying the complex pictorial scenes she has identified are (1) throwing of flowers as an act of purification, (2) sexual union between a woman and a mythical being, (3) punishment, (4) craft manufacture (weaving), (5) hunting of deer and other animals related to the dead, (6) dance of the dead, (7) running race, (8) offering and consumption of coca leaves, (9) combat and capture of prisoners, (10) dance of warriors with rope, (11) sacrifice, (12) transport by boats of prisoners to guano islands, (13) preparation of prisoners' bodies and hunting of seals on the guano islands, (14) entrance of the sacrificed body into the world of the dead, (15) rebellion of objects (arms), (16) game

playing, (17) presentation of cultivated plants (harvesting), (18) passage through a rope bridge (childbirth), and (19) feasting. As explained in the text, these themes are seen to relate to astrological, agricultural/seasonal life cycles and calendars that regulated the activities and roles of inhabitants in the natural and supernatural worlds.

12. See, for example, Anders 1977; Bonavia 1985; Donnan 1972; Kroeber 1930; Mackey and Hastings 1982; Schaedel 1951c.

13. Critiques of the Virú Valley Project and the settlement-pattern study by Willey are found in Rowe 1962, Schaedel and Shimada 1982, Willey 1974, and Willey and Sabloff 1980.

14. The value of airphotographs for Peruvian archaeology was already shown by the Shippee-Johnson Peruvian Expedition (Shippee 1932, 1933).

15. The effort to document Mochica presence in this area is seen in Christensen 1951; Guffroy, Kaulicke, and Makowski 1989; Guzman and Casafranca 1964, 1967; Kaulicke 1987/88, 1988/89, 1990, 1991b; Lanning 1963; Larco Hoyle 1965, 1967; Richardson et al. 1990; and Tolstoy 1971.

16. One find that brought a large number of Loma Negra Mochica metal objects to the illegal American antiquities market is said to have been looted in 1969. These objects include small copper and gold masks (many with bedangled visors, repoussé and inlaid head and nose ornaments) and ornamented staffs and knives that illustrate mastery of copper casting, and realistic, repoussé copper miniatures of shrimp, scorpions, and crabs, all measuring less than 1.5 cm in length (e.g., Disselhoff 1972; Jones 1979; Lapiner 1976; Lavalle 1985; Schaffer 1981).

17. These studies include Alva 1988; Cavallaro and Shimada 1988; Mackey and Klymyshyn 1981; McClelland 1986; Shimada in press 1; Wilson 1988.

18. Publications resulting from this valuable effort include Schaedel 1986a,b, 1987 and Vreeland 1978, 1982, 1985.

19. Cis-Andean refers to the western slope of the Andes facing the Pacific.

Chapter 3
Mochica Land and Culture

20. For this book, the North Coast is defined as the twelve contiguous river valleys from the Motupe in the north to the Casma in the south, inclusive.

21. Some major publications in this genre include Dollfus 1981; Drewes and Drewes 1966; H. Koepcke 1952; M. Koepcke 1954; Pearson and Ralph 1968; Pulgar Vidal 1987; Robinson 1964; Tosi 1960; Troll 1958; and Weberbauer 1945.

22. The *jalca* is the lush tall grassland characteristic of the Ecuadorian and Colombian highlands and is transitional between the *puna* and the *páramo;* e.g., see Brush 1982; Pulgar Vidal 1987.

23. The iguanas and toads that emerge from hibernation in spring at the same time may have similarly symbolized the coming of spring and water in pre-Hispanic North Coast iconography and religion.

24. Freeze-drying is an indigenous food processing technique that takes full advantage of the local climate in preserving anything from potatoes to duck meat. Moisture is crystallized by nocturnal temperatures and sublimated by the intense semitropical sun. Several days of alternate freezing and drying are sufficient to keep the processed food comestibles for up to a year or more (Murra 1984). Raised fields are formed by scraping thin topsoil into regularly laid linear or even concentric circular ridges or low platform mounds, with resultant troughs serving to drain and/or water the cultivation area. In pre-Hispanic times, the technique created thousands of hectares of productive cultivation around the shores of Lake Titicaca (e.g., Denevan 1982; Erickson 1988; Kolata 1986; Smith, Denevan, and Hamilton 1968; Torre and Burga 1986). In the *altiplano,* these indigenous techniques persist or are being revived today, while on the coast, the indigenous lifestyle has largely disappeared since the Colonial era.

25. *Loma* usually refers to coastal vegetation supported by condensation of winter fog or *garúa* that moves inland from the cold Pacific and comes into contact with the slopes of nearby Andean foothills (Craig 1985; Kautz 1976).

26. The word *guano* is a hispanization of the Quechua word *wanu* signifying "dung [sea bird droppings] for fertilizer" (Julien 1985: 189).

27. *Spondylus* has two Pacific species, *Spondylus princeps* and *Spondylus calcifer.* The former, which was the most highly valued by pre-Hispanic Andeans (including the Mochica), is characterized by long, curving spines and a bright red band around its interior edge (Olsson 1961). It is normally found only as far south as the point of the Santa Elena Peninsula in Ecuador (Marcos 1980: 125). The latter is larger and thicker and has short spines and a purple interior band. It is said to be found as far south as Punta Pariña in Peru (ibid.). Given that *Spondylus princeps* is found at greater depths (15–50 m) than *Spondylus calcifer* (5–10 m), its harvesting was probably done by specialists who were permanent residents of coastal Ecuador.

28. Besides llamas and alpacas, pre-Hispanic Andean domesticates included dogs, muscovy ducks, and guinea pigs.

29. The dried form is known in Quechua as *ch'arki,* which gave rise to the English word *jerky.*

30. Typical annual discharge volume of the Chancay is ca. 700 million m^3.

31. Today, demand for *algarrobo* charcoal for cooking by urban dwellers and restaurateurs remains unabated, and efforts continue to protect the Poma National Archaeological and Ecological Reserve in Batán Grande, mid–La Leche Valley, the only remaining extensive indigenous semitropical thorny forest on the Peruvian coast, against the onslaught of clandestine charcoal making.

32. A recent sociological study of rural stock raisers in highland Peru found that production emphasis was not so much on meat, fiber, or cash but rather on manure for fertilizer and fuel (McCorkle 1991; also see Winterhalder, Larsen, and Thomas 1974).

33. See, for example, Moseley 1969; Parsons 1968; Parsons and Psuty 1975; Regal 1970; Rodríguez 1970; Rowe 1969; R. T. Smith 1979; Soldi 1979; West 1979, 1981; cf. Knapp 1982.

34. See Eling 1987 and Nolan 1980, who describe similar situations in the Jequetepeque and Lambayeque valleys, respectively.

Chapter 4
Mochica Culture before Pampa Grande

35. 1965 ± 70 B.P., 15 b.c.; 1899 ± 79, a.d. 51; 1876 ± 79 B.P., a.d. 74—Late Puerto Moorin–Early Gallinazo (Watson 1979:15). Laboratory numbers as well as the quality and/or contexts of samples are not specified for all these Salinar dates.

36. Larco Hoyle (1945, 1948: 20) independently defined it in 1933 as the Virú Culture in recognition of its importance in the Virú Valley.

37. Due to the fact that excavations were completed in January 1992 and no detailed analysis has yet been carried out, the description of ceramics that follows is necessarily sketchy and should be regarded as tentative.

38. One phase was not replaced overnight by a succeeding phase, and the synchronicity and slow process of changes across time and space are more assumed than demonstrated (Chapter 2). While fourteen of the Mochica burials Uhle excavated at Moche were associated exclusively with Moche III ceramics, two contained both Moche II and III vessels (Donnan 1965; Kroeber 1925). The absolute dates assigned to the first two phases should be thought of as quite tentative and approximate.

39. In Chapter 2, Schaedel's observation on the potential importance of the pairing of small and large valleys in respect to the emergence of political centralization was emphasized. However, if the Moche polity proves to have originated in the larger Chicama Valley, this would contradict the observation.

40. One grave (No. V–VII) excavated at the site of Pacatnamú was accompanied by a Moche I highly polished modeled bottle depicting an owl (Ubbelohde-Doering 1983: 126 and Plate 63). Curiously, all nearby graves dated to Moche IV, V, or immediately post–Moche V when potters were faithfully "reviving" archaic forms, often in blackware.

41. The northern contacts include Bahía and other Regional Development period cultures (Lumbreras 1979; Matos 1965–1966) of coastal Ecuador and the Tolita-Tumaco culture of the Ecuadorian-Colombian border area, some 800 km north of Loma Negra.

42. Impressed by the diversity of ceramic forms and techniques found in the Vicús region, Larco Hoyle (1967: 69) saw the region as the point of origin for numerous artistic and technological innovations. However, one can conversely argue that the region was more of a recipient to external innovations and influences, including those emanating from the southern and central coasts of Ecuador (e.g., late Chorrera culture and Guangala cultures).

43. These objects display impressive technological sophistication and virtuosity, as well as artistic mastery in many ways unmatched in pre-Columbian America. The masterful synthesis of artistic and technological constraints and potentials merits the label "Mastercraftsmen" (Bennett and Bird 1949) sometimes used to describe the Mochica. Although Mochica metal objects have always been highly esteemed for their outstanding quality, it was the influx of looted Vicús/Mochica objects into the antiquities market during the 1970's and concurrent attention they received from scholars that clearly established their singular place in pre-Columbian metallurgy.

44. These include discoveries of Tolita-Tumaco style ceramics in the Vicús region and gold idols at Frias, inland from Loma Negra (Kaulicke 1991a: 382–384). The idols are now housed in the Brüning National Archaeological Museum in Lambayeque. See Jones (1979) for illustrations and description of one of the idols, as well as its problematical provenience data.

45. There are similar, roughly coterminous, developmental trends in the adjacent North Highlands where we see the emergence of the Cajamarca and Recuay styles and polities. In the Cajamarca Basin, the Layzón culture, with its hilltop "megalithic" ceremonial centers and possible trading ties with the North Coast Salinar culture, was succeeded around the time of Christ by the Cajamarca culture. The latter became the contemporary force to be reck-

oned with in the northern sector of the Mochica hegemony (Terada and Matsumoto 1985; see below). The Recuay culture based in the fertile Callejón de Huaylas (Fig. 1.1) appears to have been a contemporary of the Gallinazo and persisted to become the highland peer polity for the Southern Sector of the Mochica hegemony (Proulx 1982; Reichert 1982; Grieder 1978; J. W. Smith 1979).

46. Much of the data has been garnered from settlement surveys. Identification of Mochica presence or contact is overly based on diagnostic fineware. Without large fragments of diagnostic stirrup-spouts and/or fineline painting, critical distinction between Moche III and IV (or among Moche III subphases) is not a simple matter. A similar difficulty exists in respect to differentiation of Mochica utilitarian vessels from those of local style(s) without concurrent stratigraphic excavations and intensive, systematic comparative studies (Collier 1955; Ford 1949; Strong and Evans 1952).

47. This estimate is based on a comparison of the numbers of Puerto Moorin or Salinar Phase sites identified and recorded by G. R. Willey and later by M. West.

48. It is unlikely that the Huaca Rajada mounds are of Moche III construction (cf. Alva 1988: 532). Their placement on flat valley land, their steep-sided form, and the multilevel chamber-and-fill construction technique used for the larger, rectangular mounds all point to Middle Sicán (A.D. 900–1100) dates (Cavallaro and Shimada 1988; Shimada and Cavallaro 1986, in press). As explained in Chapter 7, the chamber-and-fill technique appeared for the first time on the North Coast during Moche V and was utilized for nearly one thousand years. The Sipán Complex has both Moche V and Middle Sicán occupation. In fact, the platform where burial excavation continues has yielded Moche III, Early and Middle Sicán, Chimú, and Chimú-Inca burials. The adjacent, badly eroded conical mound is more difficult to date. The erosion pattern is unlike that of solid adobe mounds and may also have been built with the chamber-and-fill technique. Pairing of rectangular and conical mounds is also seen in the Middle Sicán

monumental mounds of Huacas La Merced and Loro in Batán Grande. Functional and chronological relationships among the Huaca Rajada mounds and the platform remain to be defined.

49. A recent article (Nagin 1990) reconstructs how looted objects from Sipán may have been illegally imported to the United States and discusses various difficult ethical and legal questions regarding looting and the protection of archaeological remains.

50. The situation seems akin to the current view of the Classic Maya culture. Largely on the basis of deciphered hieroglyphic writings, Maya archaeologists (e.g., Culbert 1988, 1991; Willey 1990) have come to realize that the Classic Maya culture of the lower Petén region of the Yucatan Peninsula, in spite of its stylistic coherence, may not have ever been politically unified. Instead, hieroglyphic data point to the coexistence of a series of autonomous city-states and to the importance of networks of kinship, alliance, and ceremony among elite of different centers established and maintained by means of "royal visits and marriages" (see Mathews 1991; Schele and Mathews 1991). Donnan (1990a: 32–33) has drawn a similar conclusion regarding early Mochica political scenes. However, it seems still premature to posit another dynasty in the Jequetepeque Valley on the basis of one looted tomb at La Mina.

51. Interestingly, at Sipán, the superior technical and artistic quality of metal objects associated with the Lord of Sipán and other elite burials (Alva et al. 1989) contrasts with that of ceramic objects. The overwhelming portion of ceramics is mold-made jars that do not show the balance, polishing, and details seen in Moche III funerary vessels from the Chicama-Moche region. The paste used in Sipán vessels seems different from that of Moche III ceramics from the Chicama-Moche area, suggesting a local origin. In contrast, Moche I and II style ceramics believed to have been associated with the precious metal objects looted from Loma Negra are technically and artistically very well made.

52. In general, even the most elaborate Mochica burials documented from areas south of Lambayeque are relatively poor in

gold objects. However, tombs looted in front of the Huaca de la Luna at the site of Moche early in this century may have been accompanied by many gold objects (see Jones 1979: 70–72). Copper was clearly of importance. While we still do not know the source of Mochica gold, at least half a dozen pre-Hispanic copper mines (Shimada 1984; also see Lechtman 1976) and three pre-Hispanic smelting sites have been identified in the Zaña Valley. I concur with H. Lechtman's assessment of metallurgical remains at Cerro Songoy dating back to Mochica times (most likely Moche IV–V).

53. The nineteen sites break into the following categories: one habitation/fort (minor reoccupation of the well-known site of Chankillo), two habitation sites, eleven habitation/cemetery sites, four cemeteries, and one administration/habitation/cemetery site (D. Wilson, pers. com. 1992).

54. See Disselhoff 1958a,b; Eling 1987; Ravines 1982; Schaedel 1972, 1985a,b; Ubbelohde-Doering 1967.

55. The nature of occupation and the function of Pacatnamú has been a controversial issue. Ubbelohde-Doering (1960, 1967) and Keatinge (1977, 1978) see the site as a ceremonial-pilgrimage center that attracted devotees from various cultural and social backgrounds. Schaedel (1985a: 161) makes an analogy to the Vatican. Eling (1987: 348–349) argues that a prehistoric drainage trench 1,315 m long on the pampa outside the walled-in portion (the "City of Temples") of the site protected graves placed in the pampa. More recently, Donnan (1986: 23) has voiced his opposition to the "pilgrimage center" interpretation, arguing that there is no material evidence to "clearly indicate that anyone other than members of the local valley population is buried at Pacatnamú" (cf. Eling 1987: 349).

56. These sites include Cerros Corbacho, Songoy (Cojal East and West), and Molete; Pampa de Chumbenique; and Las Huacas.

57. The importance of llamas bred and maintained on the coast as beasts of burden for this horizontality is considered in Chapter 8.

58. D. Bonavia, pers. com. 1981. The diagnostic ceramics and textiles were exam-ined by I. Shimada in 1980 in Lima. Also see Tabío 1977: 112–113.

59. It is best known for its polychrome ceramics (up to a dozen slip paint colors on a vessel) that display technical mastery, impressive stylistic complexity, and an iconography emphasizing representations of mythical creatures and shamans involved in the perpetuation and abundance of life. Unlike Mochica representational art, the Nasca style has been characterized variously as "referential" (Roark 1965: 56–57), "metaphorical," or "paradigmatic" (Allen 1981: 48), as it does not seem to be based on significant historical events or individuals and instead emphasizes the fundamental and unchanging natural and supernatural order.

60. Gayton and Kroeber 1927: 16; L. Dawson as described by Knobloch 1991a; Lyon 1991.

61. The Farrabee Collection of Peruvian ceramics in the Peabody Museum at Harvard University contains a Moche III vessel attributed to either the Ica or Pisco Valley on the South Coast. Unfortunately not much can be said about it without contextual data.

62. Since the publication of G. Kubler's (1948) article on the archaeology of the guano islands of Peru, it has been believed that the Mochica controlled the largest guano deposit on the Chincha Islands off the South Coast (e.g., I. Shimada 1982, 1987a). Kubler described Moche III and IV artifacts (ceramic vessels and wooden scepters and figures depicting nude, seated "prisoners" with hands tied behind their backs) attributed to the Chincha Islands (see also Hutchinson 1873). Recent reexamination of documents pertaining to these objects by R. Schaedel (pers. com. 1987) reveals that the wrong provenience was given to these artifacts in the confusion following their exhibition in England. Most likely, they were recovered from guano deposits on Macabí or other islands off the North Coast. Nonetheless, as Kubler (1948) emphasized, it is quite surprising and significant that evidence attesting to the exploitation of guano on the Chincha Islands by contemporary South and Central Coast populations is conspicuously absent.

63. Based on the distribution of primary copper-, silver-, and gold-bearing ores, Netherly (1977: 26, 38) claims that "while an ecological definition of the North Coast would surely end at 1000 m or below, in terms of resource control, a cultural boundary at 2000 m is justified." She does not provide adequate supportive data for her claims; rather, my surveys of coastal mines indicate that at least copper and silver ores were available in coastal foothills below 500 m or so (Shimada 1984, 1985c, 1987b; cf. Lechtman 1991).

64. They are also known as "Moon Monster" (Bruhns 1977) or "Plumed Puma" (Sawyer 1968).

Chapter 5
Mochica Organizational Features

65. These structures may well have been temporary housing for laborers involved in mound construction. Similar poorly made structures were found at the north base of the Middle Sicán monumental platform mound of Huaca Las Ventanas in the mid–La Leche Valley.

66. Blue stone beads found in archaeological contexts are commonly assumed to be lapis lazuli imported from northern Chile. However, such identification is not based on specific analytical data. Recent X-ray diffraction analysis and specific gravity measurements of various blue stone beads from Cupisnique and Middle Sicán tombs in Batán Grande have proven to be high-grade sodalite. Future analysis of Mochica blue beads, I suspect, will identify them as sodalite. Given the widespread distribution of igneous rock in the Peruvian Andes, sodalite could have been mined from a closer source than lapis lazuli. Lumbreras (1974: 199) mentions a possible source of this mineral in the North Highlands.

67. Similarities and divergences found between the two principal platform mounds at Moche V Pampa Grande and Moche will be considered later. One alternative to T. Topic's view is that Huaca de la Luna was a temple for worshiping the patron deities of the local elite, including the deceased. Another possibility is to view the pairs as corporate symbols of asymmetrical upper and lower moieties (dual social divisions).

68. The designation *marked brick* is preferred since it simply describes the physical appearance without attaching any functional significance (Shimada in press 1).

69. Some marked adobe bricks were found at a mound believed to be Mochica in affiliation at Pampa de los Incas in the Santa Valley. Mochica "state-organized corporate labor construction" has consequently been suggested (Wilson 1988: 336). The inference is tenuous, considering the fact that marked adobes occur in non-Mochica constructions with or without segmentation (e.g., Middle Sicán and Chimú; see Shimada and Cavallaro in press; Mackey and Klymyshyn 1981; Shimada and Cavallaro 1986). For reconstruction of labor organization, evidence of construction units is at least as critical as the presence of marked adobe bricks.

70. The following description of the recent discovery at an adobe platform at the south base of Huaca Rajada is based on Alva (1988) and various Peruvian newspaper and magazine articles published during 1987. I was fortunate to witness ongoing Huaca Rajada excavation at various times during 1987–1991.

71. There is no information regarding the presence or absence of cut marks on this body that would indicate when and how the feet were removed, i.e., at the time of death or long after burial. Critical information on cut marks is also lacking for the extra llama and human bones of extremities that often turn up in Mochica burials (e.g., Donnan and Mackey 1978).

72. Some of the burials Uhle excavated in front of Huaca de la Luna are curious in that they were in seated position rather than the typical extended Moche position. Menzel (1977: 60) suggests that these burials may have had special ritual significance. Alternatively, they may belong to a non-Mochica ethnic group or date to Moche V or immediately after V, when the seated burial position dominated (see Chapter 9).

73. The criteria and their relative weights used for determining social status are not explicitly stated. Also, we simply do not know the relative value of various categories of funerary goods (e.g., fineline painted stirrup-spout bottle vs. hammered gold object).

74. There is ongoing debate as to what funerary goods represent. Were they the personal possessions of the deceased placed in the grave for use in the afterlife, or do they reflect the regard held by relatives and friends living near and far? In the latter case, a well-esteemed individual in theory might have received a large number and wide variety of sumptuary goods at death. Thus, grave offerings may not accurately reflect the role and status held by the deceased, and a straightforward interpretation of social position, wealth, and political power based on the quantity and variety of funerary offerings could be highly misleading (see Hodder 1978, 1979, 1982 for cautionary tales).

75. The surface of *tumbaga* objects may be "pickled" with acid to remove copper, thereby increasing the surface gold content (called depletion gilding). Well-polished depletion-gilded *tumbaga* objects cannot be readily differentiated from solid gold objects.

76. Schaedel (1972: 23) espouses a two-class structure with priests and warriors in the upper class and attendants and farmers in the lower.

77. For example, see Claessen and Skalnik 1978; Cohen 1978; Cohen and Service 1978; Friedman and Rowlands 1977; Johnson and Earle 1987; Jones and Kautz 1981; Renfrew and Cherry 1986; Service 1975; and Wright 1977, 1978.

78. For example, see Browman 1978; Haas 1982; Haas, Pozorski, and Pozorski 1987; Isbell 1978, 1986; Isbell and Cook 1987; Isbell and Schreiber 1978; Schaedel 1972, 1985b; Steward 1949; Steward and Faron 1959; and Wilson 1983, 1988.

79. For example, see Conrad 1978; Larco Hoyle 1939: 132–138; Moseley 1983a: 219–220; Strong and Evans 1952: 216–218; T. Topic 1982: 270–273; and Wilson 1988: 332–342.

80. Schaedel (1985a: 443) defines the *etnia* as "a supra-community aggregation with a range of societal complexity that corresponds to the *señorío* (chiefdom) level polities, having the cultural peculiarities that lead to their recognition as distinct from others by state administrators of the Inca and Spanish viceroyalty and therefore as significant basic subdivisions in their re-

spective administrative hierarchies." Thus, the *macro-etnia* represents the maximum end of the aggregation of *etnías:* i.e., super- or paramount chiefdom.

81. The unusual occupational history of this site—sudden, rapid foundation and expansion, and equally rapid and permanent abandonment—resembles that of Pampa Grande. Similar nucleation at these sites was likely to have been conditioned by the sudden and rapid growth.

Chapter 6
The Establishment of Moche V Pampa Grande

82. Unfortunately, this observation is based on looted funerary vessels, and consequently we cannot specify whether the decline was geographically confined to certain areas.

83. A deterministic model of pan-Andean climatic fluctuation and its cultural impact has been offered on the basis of the number, regularity, and chronology of seemingly parallel cultural changes on the Santa Elena Peninsula of coastal Ecuador and the South Coast of Peru. The alternation of periods of increased precipitation and drought inferred from changes in land-use and settlement patterns on the peninsula is said to coincide in time with geographical shifts in the "locus of political power and cultural vigour" in southern Peru (Paulsen 1976: 127). The severe drought that began ca. A.D. 600, following a prolonged pluvial period, is believed to have been pan-Andean in scope and the underlying cause of the rise of the Wari Empire. Though similar in part to what is presented here, Paulsen's model is much more encompassing in its spatial and temporal parameters and deterministic in the causal role of climatic disturbances. The data base and the chronological precision also differ.

84. The Huaca del Sol, particularly its southern platform, continued to be used by non-Mochica populations as an important site of religious offerings and burials at least through Middle Horizon Epoch 3 (ca. A.D. 900–1000), as is apparent from Uhle's excavation (Menzel 1977: 37–40). Thus, when we speak of the abandonment of the

site of Moche at the end of Moche IV or early Moche V, we are referring to Mochica occupation and use.

85. Dating of the mural associated with the final remodeling of the principal platform of the Huaca de la Luna is also controversial. Though Mackey and Hastings (1982: 311) date it to late Moche IV or early Moche V based on stylistic analysis, it is not clear to what extent this conclusion was preconditioned by architectural dating of the *huaca*. Rowe (Plate XXXV in 1974) assigns it to Moche V. However, Bonavia (1985: 95–96) dates it to Middle Horizon Epoch 3, arguing that it is characterized by the syncretism of foreign and local (primarily Wari and Mochica) iconographies and styles.

86. The extensive site of Ventanilla farther inland deserves future exploration as a possible Moche V/Middle Cajamarca frontier settlement (see also Eling 1987: 363–372). It is situated at the juncture of the Jequetepeque and a major side valley some 36 km from the coast and is dominated by a large truncated pyramid apparently built with the chamber-and-fill technique, much like Huaca Fortaleza at Pampa Grande. Yet the site is not particularly close to the north or south bank MEC, and Moche V ceramics are rare, at least on the surface. Considering the fact that the site literally sits atop a major ancient road going up the valley (presumably to the Cajamarca Basin), Ventanilla appears to have been an important site controlling traffic between the coast and adjacent North Highlands at least since Moche V times (Eling 1987).

87. Meteorological data obtained at Quelccaya indicate that the mean annual temperature is below freezing (minus 3° C; Shimada et al. 1991a,b). Therefore, the ice layer formed annually is not affected by significant melting and percolation; in other words, the ice cores accurately represent annual precipitation. The long-term δO^{18} records as well as the consistency between the two cores suggest that this has been the case throughout the fifteen-hundred-year period (Thompson et al. 1985).

88. The Ecuadorian and Peruvian highlands differ in that the former has two wet seasons and two dry seasons per year as the

equatorial trough moves northward and later southward during the year. However, severe climatic episodes such as these droughts would be expected to have had pan-Andean scope and impacts. Though a strong case for the pan-Andean nature of the drought has been made here, we await the collection or publication of relevant data from different regions not discussed here.

89. The Lambayeque River was the main drainage of the valley below the La Puntilla water gate prior to the destructive 1925 flood, which blocked the river and diverted the entire flow through the (previously secondary) Reque River (Petersen 1956: 305).

90. Nolan (1980: 133–135) calls the South Bank MEC "Huaca Blanca-Tablazos." During what he refers to as Late Mochica times (Moche IV and V), the system is estimated to have irrigated an area of 1,360 hectares.

91. Carhuaquero is just below where the Chancay and Cumbil rivers merge. It is the last major confluence before the first major water intake for irrigation. Thus water volumes measured there accurately reflect the overall quantity available for irrigation in the valley.

92. The publication (Isbell and McEwan 1991) resulting from a Wari Round Table held at Dumbarton Oaks, Washington, D.C., in 1984 offers recent assessments on the subject.

93. For example, T. Topic (1991: 162) lists obsidian, ceramics, and possibly lapis lazuli from the south, and Cajamarca pottery and *Spondylus* shells from the north.

94. Reliable dating of the earliest Wari occupation in the adjacent Callejón de Huaylas is needed. The Wari presence in the nearby Huamachuco area (headwater region of the Moche Valley) dated to Epoch 1B is believed to have been motivated by the production and exchange of exotic commodities (e.g., obsidian) rather than political domination (Topic and Topic 1984: 56; J. Topic 1991; T. Topic 1991). Similarly, North Coast Epoch 1B Wari-style remains do not suggest a belligerent state of affairs.

95. Various chapters in a recent volume on the Wari culture and sites (Isbell and McEwan 1991) present some radiocarbon dates, but we still need a comprehensive compilation (with details on samples, contexts, calibration, etc.) and critique of relevant dates.

96. For example, see Collier 1955: 185; Donnan 1968, 1972, 1973a; Donnan and Mackey 1978; Kroeber 1926; Larco Hoyle 1948; Mackey 1982; and Menzel 1977.

97. Bawden (1982a,b), however, believes that the wall was built to physically segregate and control the lowest class (see Chapter 7).

Chapter 7
Urban Landscape at Pampa Grande

98. Contrast this view with that of Service (1975) who sees the urbanism as following the emergence of the state.

99. In my earlier publications (e.g., I. Shimada 1978, 1982, 1987a), the height of the Huaca Fortaleza was incorrectly given as ca. 55 m.

100. Trigger (1990: 119) defines monumental architecture as having scale and elaboration that "exceed the requirements of any practical functions that a building is intended to perform."

101. Benson (1972: 98) suggests that the monumental Mochica mounds symbolized sacred mountains.

102. Given the paucity of primary context garbage elsewhere at the site, it seems strange that garbage from a ritual feast in such an exclusive setting would have been left to decompose. The refuse was directly covered by the remains of the burnt, fallen roof, raising the possibility that the feast occurred close in time to the burning.

103. The blue stone may well be sodalite rather than azurite.

104. They are in some respects like flat, oversized fired adobe bricks; i.e., they were probably made with molds, with the top surface smoothed flat and corners carefully rounded but the bottom left rough and uneven. They have coarse sand temper much like large redware storage vessels found at the site.

105. The most dramatic illustration of the fact that the Huaca Fortaleza core consists of a lattice of discrete filled chambers is the extent and manner in which the huaca has eroded. Water tends to erode along the vertical seams separating chambers. Once any part of a chamber is breached, water readily removes the fill, leaving pinnacles and ridges of the more solid adobe chamber walls.

106. The observed differences between adobe bricks from the Deer House and Spondylus House perimeter walls may well be spurious due to the small number of wall segments sampled by Knapp.

107. The Topics base their interpretation largely on findings from their excavation of the wall, including the discovery of piles of inferred slingstones on the wall top and evidence of various repairs presumably done over a considerable span of time. The original wall was ca. 3 m thick and stone faced with stone and dirt fill (T. Topic 1991: 238). Whether or not the original wall functioned as a defensive feature has not been established, nor has the length of time the wall was maintained. Information on the nature of occupation within the walled area presented by Bawden, however, cannot be readily explained by the Topics' refuge-area hypothesis.

108. The Antigua Collique Canal had two roughly parallel channels during the Late Mochica period (as defined by Nolan [1980]). The upper channel faithfully followed the natural contour of the valley edge, while the lower one cut through the flat valley bottomland away from the valley edge. The latter may represent streamlining. Precise dating of these channels is not easy. We face the same problem in respect to dating various channels of the Antigua Taymi Canal, the MEC of the north bank. At Cerro Patapo, with Moche IV and V occupation (and possibly earlier at the base of the *cerro*), as well as immediately post–Moche V occupation, the highest and most massive channel faithfully follows the contour of the *cerro*. But we have not yet determined at what point in time the much more streamlined Historic Taymi came into existence. A thorough study of the Taymi Canal and associated settlements is currently being conducted (Tschauner and Tschauner 1992). Eling (1987), working in the Jequetepeque Valley to the south, also encountered the same problem. Canals be-

lieved to have been in use during the Mochica occupation of the valley are thus dated to a 250-year period called "Period 2."

109. In terms of Rowe's differentiation between the "synchoritic" and "achoritic" cities, Pampa Grande was becoming increasingly achoritic.

Chapter 8
Urban Subsistence and Economy at Moche V Pampa Grande

110. While it is important to extract as much information as possible from the plant remains we recover, statistical analyses to determine their relative significance too often disregard how unrepresentative the samples are in most cases. Consider Cohen's (1972–1974) criticisms of MacNeish's (1967) methods and how they may apply to Pozorski's (1979) "percent of plant diet" table for the Moche Valley.

111. For detailed discussion of our sampling strategy, see Shimada and Shimada 1981.

112. Also see Table 7.1 in Weir and Eling 1986 for a list of pollen identified in soil samples from late Mochica cultivation fields in the Jequetepeque Valley.

113. It should be noted that, in spite of general size differences, llamas and alpacas are difficult to differentiate on the basis of postcranial bones. Primarily on the basis of varied functions they served and bone measurements (Shimada and Shimada 1985, 1987), we speculate that camelid remains from Pampa Grande are llamas. At the same time, we cannot conclusively reject the possible presence of alpacas.

114. This implies that the llama was butchered locally and that there was a local breeding llama population. If the llama was imported from elsewhere alive or in processed parts, a significantly different bone and age composition would result. We would not expect to find a range of ages if llamas were brought down from the highlands as beasts of burden.

115. The term refers to indigenous sociopolitical units each with a distinct economic role and certain recognized obligations that originally had lineage ties with inland populations (see Chapter 4).

116. See note 7 describing Larco Hoyle's view on messengers carrying beans. Though his view has not won wide support, other recurring motifs (e.g., frets) in Mochica ceramic paintings and textiles may carry certain conventionalized meanings, for example, related to status and seasons.

117. It should be kept in mind, however, that samples from certain Sectors were quite small. See Shimada and Shimada 1981 for details.

118. Archaism as a source of inspiration is also seen elsewhere. Blackware ceramics accompanying Moche V burials in subterranean chambers in the City of the Temples at Pacatnamú (Ubbelohde-Doering 1967: 26–27 and Plates 68–69; Hecker and Hecker 1985: 52–122) imitate Moche III and Cupisnique forms.

119. We do not know much about Mochica ceramic kilns. Excavations of superimposed kilns in Batán Grande spanning ca. 800 B.C. (Middle Cupisnique) to A.D. 400 (Gallinazo) indicate that relatively small, double-chambered, semi-closed kilns dug into the ground were used to fire bowls, jars, and other small- to medium-sized vessels (Shimada, Elera, and Chang 1990). Replicative firing experiments revealed that these kilns are quite fuel efficient and easy to control, allowing firing under either oxidized or reduced atmospheres and assuring a high rate of successful firing. However, the number of vessels that can be fired at a time is quite low due to their small size. With the increased use of molds in vessel formation and demand for corporate style ceramics during Mochica times, one would expect a corresponding rise in standardization and overall production. Concurrently, we would expect changes in firing techniques and/or kiln designs. Another factor that may have contributed to these changes is the use of slip paint on Mochica pottery, which would have reduced the necessity of carefully firing to produce certain surface colors. One of the small masonry rooms in Structure Y, Sector D, at Pampa Grande may well have been a large, semi-closed kiln (see photo in Schaedel 1988: 116 for an ethnographic example of such a kiln in Monsefú in the lower Lambayeque Valley).

The inferred open-air kiln at Galindo is surprising given the poor fuel economy and limited temperature and air control such a kiln would have afforded.

120. There has been some debate as to their provenience and cultural assignation (Chavín culture of the first millennium B.C. vs. Mochica) on the basis of either style or iconography. Jones (1979: 65–67) offers a succinct summary of the debate. Information provided here supports the view that the jaguars are Moche V in style and date (cf. note 6 in Jones 1979: 66; note 74 in Lechtman 1980: 328; Shimada 1976: 495).

121. Much of the discussion here is based on (1) our understanding of the copper mining and copper-alloy metallurgy of the Sicán culture that succeeded the Mochica, including data gathered from a series of replicative smelting experiments; and (2) a possible metal workshop found at the site of Moche (V. Pimentel, pers. com. 1985). See Merkel and Shimada 1988; Shimada 1987b; Shimada, Epstein, and Craig 1983; and Shimada and Merkel 1991 for additional data.

122. These mines include one on the south slope of Cerro Las Minas to the northeast (ca. 20 km away) and another to the east (ca. 15 km away) atop Cerro Las Palomitas, both in the upper Lambayeque Valley, as well as one other southeast (8 km) in Quebrada de Agua Salada behind the site of Pampa Grande. There are at least three others on the north bank of the Zaña Valley.

123. *Flux* refers to an additive that helps separate metal and slag during smelting.

124. Fifteen oval copper slugs were found in association with the Mochica burials that Max Uhle excavated at the site of Moche (Site F). Their weight and length range from ca. 80–450 g and ca. 6–10 cm (Kroeber 1944: 129).

125. In terms of proximity to Pampa Grande, Cerro Songoy on the north bank of the Zaña Valley is a likely candidate.

126. In earlier publications on Pampa Grande, I noted that no evidence of blowtubes had been found in this excavation. However, more recently acquired knowledge of ancient North Coast tuyeres raises the distinct possibility that what I identified

before as a weathered, broken bottle spout fragment from an ash-silt deposit was in fact a broken ceramic tuyere.

127. Although originally described as a "smelting" scene (Donnan 1973b), the open circular form of the hearth and the presence of what appear to be a T-shaped axe head and a circular crucible atop the hearth suggest that this vessel shows the melting of an ingot or blank and annealing of certain implements. My original identification of the ARm 57 hearths as having been used for copper smelting (Shimada 1978: 581–582) is also corrected here.

128. Overall, five distinct Mochica weave structures have been identified: (1) a plain weave, (2) a compound weave, (3–4) two forms of slit tapestry weave, and (5) weft wrapping. These structures are described in detail by Conklin (1979). All known samples of Mochica textiles utilize the concept of discontinuous weft inherited from Chavín precursors and are woven with cotton warp and camelid wool weft.

129. Kent Day (pers. com. 1989), who excavated Deer House, independently reached the same conclusion regarding cotton. The small ramp (ca. 1 m high) built in the courtyard leads nowhere, and Day suggests that it was probably a dock for unloading bundles of cotton.

130. Niched walls at the site of La Mayanga in Batán Grande were painted with Mochica-Wari polychrome murals. See Chapter 9.

131. While it is plausible that maize and beans found within formal storage facilities in Sectors H and D were kept as seeds for the next sowing, the available data, elaborated below, favor the view that they were intended for consumption and *chicha* making.

132. Another drum frame placed within a small adobe-lined square enclosure was found in Rm 6, which is set at the back of a Structure (possibly a large residence) at the eastern edge of Sector H. Neither the architectural setting nor the associated artifacts readily clarify the true function of the drum frame.

133. *Conus* and *Spondylus* are both used for inlay work. The Lord of Sipán was flanked on both sides by *Conus* and *Spon-*

dylus shells. These same two shells were found at the shrines at Huaca El Dragón and atop Cerro Blanco, overlooking the site of Moche (Schaedel 1966c; cf. Menzel 1977: 41).

134. A small excavation by Melody Shimada at the southwest corner of Sector K yielded forty-five *Spondylus* fragments on and above a floor similar in composition and appearance to those from Rm 1. This inferred *Spondylus* workshop, however, may well be Chimú in date, as shell fragments were found in close proximity to a handful of Chimú sherds and only one Moche V sherd. Unfortunately, the critical stratigraphy had been disturbed by water coming down the small gully that passed through the workshop. Should this workshop prove to be Moche V, we would have to revise our view of Moche V *Spondylus* working and output at Pampa Grande. Its location outside of a major compound and dissociation from a major mound would imply a different mode of supervision than suggested here.

135. Mean, mode, and standard deviation values of ca. 9, 9, and 1 cm, respectively. See Table 10 in Shimada and Shimada 1981: 58.

136. These figures pale next to the scale of *Spondylus* offerings documented in Middle Sicán (ca. A.D. 1000) platform mounds and elite shafttombs in nearby Batán Grande (Shimada 1990a: 341, 1992, in press 2; Shimada and Cavallaro in press; also Cordy-Collins 1990).

137. Cane (*Gynerium sagittatum*), bamboo (*Guadua angustifolia*), straw, and two-ply cord were interwoven and bound as a mat 30 cm or more thick to form the basis of the roof.

138. Though there is heavy reliance on "negative" evidence, this combination of particular architectural context, form, and other qualities cannot readily be accounted for by alternative explanations. See Day 1973 for a detailed discussion of this logic.

139. Pollen analysis proved of limited value. Pollen samples recovered from two excavated cells in Groups I and II suggest that they may have stored nonlocal ferns and some plants of the *Bromeliaceae* family, perhaps for medicinal purposes (Anders 1981: 401). On the other hand,

rains accompanying the 1972–1973 El Niño intrusion brought about lush and diverse vegetation that thoroughly blanketed the site. This "nonlocal" plant pollen may well derive from such ephemeral growth following the major flood that beset the site shortly after its abandonment (Chapter 10).

140. Anders (1977: 271) proposed a possible accounting function for an opposing pair of contiguous rooms, each with a thronelike seat and large number of small, round cobbles.

141. Recent studies have shown that the model of Inca redistributive economy as envisioned by J. V. Murra (1980) requires some major revisions, and that it may be most applicable to the early stages and heartland of the Inca state (e.g., see D'Altroy 1987; Morris and Thompson 1970; Schaedel 1978). Certainly the Inca economy was undergoing a significant transformation at the time of the Spanish Conquest, including the rapid expansion of the non-taxpaying sector and the rise of individual ownership.

142. We may think of people much like Incaic *acllacunas,* popularly known as the "chosen women" or "Virgins of the Sun," whose primary tasks included *chicha* making for ceremonies, weaving of fine cloth, and service in the state church.

Chapter 9
Art and Religion

143. Kutscher (Fig. 161 in 1983) illustrates a vessel that seems to show two figures with their hands on a coffin and a third playing a drum. Hocquenghem (Fig. 18 in 1979b) believes it depicts a preburial "purification rite."

144. Hocquenghem and Lyon (1981) present a fine discussion of the significance of women in Mochica rituals.

145. See Hocquenghem 1987 for a good compilation of navigation scenes.

146. Lumbreras (1969: 159–160, 1974: 103) suggests that naked captives were slaves sent to offshore islands to mine guano. T. Topic (1977: 380) echoes a similar sentiment in suggesting that these islands were penal colonies.

147. Age and sex are unspecified.

148. The following description of the mural and its setting differs in specifics from those in the two preceding citations.

149. There may have been over thirty niches, each ca. 80 cm wide, 70 cm high, and 80 cm deep.

150. Recorded cases include Middle Horizon 2 caches from Pikillacta near Cusco (Menzel 1969: 51) and from Pinilla near Ica (Paulsen 1968, 1974: 603), and *Spondylus/Conus* shell workshops at Huaca El Dragón near Trujillo (Schaedel 1966c: 434, 436) and atop Cerro Blanco overlooking the site of Moche (Menzel 1977: 41).

151. As noted in the preceding chapter, the popularity of the reduced wares may reflect in part increased use of llama dung as fuel in firing. Also see Stumer 1957 for a possible late Maranga (Central Coast) source for the Moche V blackware.

152. This section summarizes a detailed description found in Bawden 1977: 363–376.

Chapter 10
The Demise of Moche V Pampa Grande

153. *Collapse* here is understood to mean "a rapid, significant loss of an established level of sociopolitical complexity" (Tainter 1988: 4).

154. For example, see Culbert 1973, 1988; Lowe 1985; Sabloff and Willey 1967; Sharer 1977; Willey and Shimkin 1971.

155. This proposition is based on three basic premises: (1) human societies are problem-solving organizations; (2) sociopolitical systems require energy for their maintenance; and (3) increased complexity carries with it increased costs per capita (Tainter 1988: 93).

156. For a summary of relevant data, including findings from sites in the eastern *yunga* (Kuelap near Chachapoya), the North Coast, and as far north as the southern highland of Ecuador, see Matsumoto 1988 and Terada and Matsumoto 1985.

157. Eling (1987: 415–417) notes certain regional stylistic differences in what are described here as Coastal Cajamarca.

158. The workshop is a room 3.5 by 5.0 m with a compacted dirt floor delineated by

crudely built stone walls on the north and by a huge rock on the downslope side.

159. In some publications (e.g., Bawden 1977: 403; Table 1.1 in Moseley and Day 1982), the end of Moche V in the Moche Valley is put at about A.D. 850. This is based on margins of error of approximately one hundred fifty years associated with some radiocarbon dates. Some population could possibly have lingered on at the site of Galindo until that late date, but it is quite doubtful that the Moche V polity and style remained viable (see Shimada 1990a: 312, 329).

160. It has been rumored that some local collectors have pure, highland Wari-style, imported polychrome effigy jars looted from this site.

Chapter 11
Moche V Legacies and Conclusion

161. One curious case is various objects dating to Middle Horizon Epochs 2 to 4 found on the Far North Coast of Chile. They show definite similarities to certain recurrent Mochica representations (Berenguer 1986). Some artifacts resemble Mochica objects displaying "hand in half fist" form. This position may be related to certain mythical qualities of mountains, which clearly held an important place in Mochica cosmology (Donnan 1978: 144–155). These Chilean objects appear to be poorly made local imitations of Mochica originals that the local potters probably did not possess. However, it is not clear why just these scenes were imitated and what sorts of mechanisms were involved in the distribution of the Mochica originals.

162. There is as yet no evidence of large-scale migration out of or onto the North Coast between Moche V and Middle Sicán. The biological population of the Mochica culture appears to have continued in the same regions, following their long cultural tradition but with the changed political and religious elite symbolism called Middle Sicán. Thus, Middle Sicán extended burials may pertain to lower-class descendants of the Mochica. Given the strong continuation of the Gallinazo stylistic tradition well into the Sicán periods, some of the extended burials may belong to the Gallinazo ethnicity.

Bibliography

Agurto, Santiago
  1984   *Lima prehispánica.* Municipali-
         dad de Lima Metropolitana,
         Lima.

Allen, Catherine J.
  1981   The Nasca creatures: Some prob-
         lems of iconography. *Anthropol-
         ogy* 5: 43–70. State University of
         New York, Stony Brook.

Alva, Walter
  1985   Tempranas manifestaciones cul-
         turales en la región de Lamba-
         yeque. In *Presencia histórica de
         Lambayeque,* compiled by Eric
         Mendoza, pp. 53–75. Editorial y
         Imprenta DESA, Lima.
  1986   *Cerámica temprana en el valle de
         Jequetepeque, norte del Perú.*
         Materialien zur Allgemeinen
         und Vergleichenden Archäologie,
         Band 32. Verlag C. H. Beck,
         Munich.
  1988   Discovering the New World's
         richest unlooted tomb. *National
         Geographic Magazine* 174 (4):
         510–550.
  1990   New tomb of royal splendor.
         National Geographic Magazine
         177 (6): 2–15.

Alva, Walter, and Susana Meneses de Alva
  1983   Los murales de Ucupe en el Valle
         de Zaña. *Beiträge zur Allge-
         meinen und Vergleichenden Ar-
         chäologie* 5: 335–360.

Alva, Walter, Maiken Fecht, Peter Schauer,
   and Michael Tellenbach
  1989   *La tumba del Señor de Sipán:
         Descubrimiento y restauración.*
         Verlag des Römisch German-
         ischen Zentralmuseums, Mainz.

Anders, Martha B.
  1977   Sistema de depósitos en Pampa
         Grande, Lambayeque. *Revista del
         Museo Nacional* 43: 243–279.
         Lima.
  1981   Investigation of state storage fa-
         cilities in Pampa Grande, Peru.
         Journal of Field Archaeology 8:
         391–404.
  1986   Wari experiments in statecraft: A
         view from Azángaro. In *Andean
         archaeology: Papers in memory of
         Clifford Evans,* edited by R. Ma-
         tos, S. Turpin, and H. Eling, pp.
         163–188. Monograph 27 of the
         Institute of Archaeology, Univer-
         sity of California, Los Angeles.
  1990   Maymi: Un sitio del Horizonte
         Medio en el Valle de Pisco. *Gac-
         eta Arqueológica Andina* 5 (17):
         27–39. Lima.

Antúnez de Mayolo, Santiago E.
1992   Recurrencia del fenómeno "El Niño" y el Titicaca. In *Paleo ENSO records, international symposium: Extended abstracts*, edited by L. Ortlieb and J. Macharé, pp. 15–20. ORSTOM, Lima, and CONCYTEC, Lima.

Baessler, Arthur
1902–   *Ancient Peruvian art: Contribu-*
1903   *tions to the archaeology of the empire of the Incas*. Translated by A. H. Keane. 4 vols. A. Asher Co., Berlin, and Dodd, Mead & Co., New York.

Bankes, George H. A.
1971   Some aspects of the Moche culture. Ph.D. dissertation, Institute of Archaeology, University of London, London.
1972   Settlement patterns in the lower Moche Valley, north Peru, with special reference to the Early Horizon and Early Intermediate Period. In *Man, settlement, and urbanism*, edited by P. J. Ucko, R. Tringham, and G. W. Dimbleby, pp. 903–908. Schenkman, Cambridge.
1985   The manufacture and circulation of paddle and anvil pottery on the north coast of Peru. *World Archaeology* 17: 269–277.

Bankmann, Ulf
1979   Moche und Recuay. *Baessler-Archiv* 27: 253–271.

Barnes, Monica, and David Fleming
1991   Filtration gallery irrigation in the Spanish New World. *Latin American Antiquity* 2: 48–68.

Barr, Genaro
1991   "La Poza Alta"—Un proyecto de rescate arqueológico en Huanchaco. *Revista del Museo de Arqueología* 2: 39–48. Universidad Nacional de Trujillo.

Bawden, Garth L.
1977   Galindo and the nature of the Middle Horizon in northern coastal Peru. Ph.D. dissertation, Department of Anthropology, Harvard University, Cambridge, MA.
1978   Life in the pre-Columbian town of Galindo. *Field Museum of Natural History Bulletin* 3: 16–23. Chicago.
1982a   Galindo: A study in cultural transition during the Middle Horizon. In *Chan Chan: Andean desert city*, edited by Michael E. Moseley and Kent C. Day, pp. 285–320. University of New Mexico Press, Albuquerque.
1982b   Community organization reflected by the household: A study of pre-Columbian social dynamics. *Journal of Field Archaeology* 9: 165–183.
1983   Cultural reconstitution in the late Moche period: A case study in multidimensional stylistic analysis. In *Civilization in the ancient Americas: Essays in honor of Gordon R. Willey*, edited by R. M. Leventhal and A. L. Kolata, pp. 211–235. University of New Mexico Press, Albuquerque, and Peabody Museum of Archaeology and Ethnology, Harvard University, Cambridge, MA.

Beck, Colleen M.
1991   Cross-cutting relationships: The relative dating of ancient roads on the north coast of Peru. In *Ancient road networks and settlement hierarchies in the New World*, edited by Charles D. Trombold, pp. 66–79. Cambridge University Press, Cambridge.

Bennett, Wendell C.
1939   *Archaeology of the North Coast of Peru: An account of exploration and excavation in Viru and Lambayeque valleys*. Anthropological Papers, Vol. 37 (Part 1). American Museum of Natural History, New York.
1948   The Peruvian Co-Tradition. In *A reappraisal of Peruvian archaeology*, assembled by Wendell C. Bennett, pp. 1–7. Memoir of the Society for American Archaeology, No. 4. Society for American Archaeology and Institute of Andean Research, Menasha, WI.

1950   *The Gallinazo group, Viru Valley, Peru.* Yale University Publications in Anthropology, No. 43. Yale University Press, New Haven.

1953   *Excavations at Wari, Ayacucho, Peru.* Yale University Publications in Anthropology, No. 49. Yale University Press, New Haven.

Bennett, Wendell C., and Junius Bird

1949   *Andean culture history.* American Museum of Natural History, Garden City, NY.

Benson, Elizabeth P.

1972   *The Mochica: A culture of Peru.* Praeger Publishers, New York.

1974   *A man and a feline in Mochica art.* Studies in Pre-Columbian Art and Archaeology, No. 14. Dumbarton Oaks, Washington, D.C.

1976   "Salesmen" and "sleeping" warriors in Mochica art. In *Actas del 41 Congreso Internacional de Americanistas* 2: 26–34. Mexico City.

Benzoni, Jerónimo

1572   *La historia del Mundo Nuevo.*
[1967]   Translated and edited by Carlos Radicati di Primeglio. Universidad Nacional Mayor de San Marcos, Lima.

Berenguer, José

1986   Relaciones iconográficas de larga distancia en los Andes: Nuevos ejemplos para un viejo problema. *Boletín del Museo de Arte Precolombino* 1: 55–78. Santiago, Chile.

Berezkin, Yuri

1978   The social structure of the Mochica through the prism of mythology (ancient Peru). Written in Russian with an English summary. *Vestnik drevnei istorii* 3: 38–59. Izd-vo Akademii nauk SSSR, Moscow.

1980   An identification of anthropomorphic mythological personages in Moche representations. *Ñawpa Pacha* 18: 1–26.

1983   *Mochika.* Akademiia "Nauka," Leningradskoe otd-nie, Leningrad.

1987   Moche society and iconography. In *Pre-Columbian collections in European museums*, edited by A. M. Hocquenghem, P. Tamási, and C. Villain-Gandossi, pp. 270–277. Akadémiai Kiado, Budapest.

1990   Estructura social de la civilización Mochica y su reflejo en la iconografía. Written in Russian with a Spanish abstract. In *Problemy arkheologii i drevnei istorii stran Latinskoi Ameriki*, edited by V. A. Bashilov, pp. 223–247. Nauka, Moscow.

Bergsøe, Paul

1937   *The metallurgy and technology of gold and platinum among the pre-Columbian Indians.* Translated from Danish by C. F. Reynolds. Danmarks Naturvidenskabelige Samfund, i Kommission hos G.E.C. Grad, Copenhagen.

1938   *The gilding process and the metallurgy of copper and lead among the pre-Columbian Indians.* Translated from Danish by C. F. Reynolds. Danmarks Naturvidenskabelige Samfund, i Kommission hos G.E.C. Grad, Copenhagen.

Bird, Junius B.

1962   Art and life in old Peru: An exhibition. *Curator* 5: 145–210. American Museum of Natural History, New York.

Bird, Junius B., John Hyslop, and Milica D. Skinner

1985   *The preceramic excavations at the Huaca Prieta, Chicama Valley, Peru.* Anthropological Papers, Vol. 62 (Part 1). American Museum of Natural History, New York.

Bird, Robert

1987   A postulated *tsunami* and its effects on cultural development in the Peruvian Early Horizon. *American Antiquity* 52: 285–303.

Blanchard, Peter (editor)

1991   *Markham in Peru: The travels of Clements R. Markham, 1852–1853.* University of Texas Press, Austin.

Bock, Edward K. de

1988   *Moche: Gods, warriors, priests.* Spruyt, Van Mantgem & De Does, Leiden.

Bonavia, Duccio

1968   *Las ruinas del Abiseo.* Universidad Peruana de Ciencias y Tecnología, Lima.

1985   *Mural painting in ancient Peru.* Translated by Patricia Lyon. Indiana University Press, Bloomington.

Bowman, Isaiah

1938   *Los Andes del Sur del Perú.* Translated by Carlos Nicholson. Universidad Católica de Arequipa, Arequipa.

Braun-Blanquet, J.

1950   *Sociología vegetal, estudio de las comunidades vegetales.* Acme Agency, Buenos Aires.

Bray, Warwick

1972   Ancient American metal-smiths. In *Proceedings of the Royal Anthropological Institute for 1971*, pp. 25–43. London.

Brennan, Curtiss T.

1980   Cerro Arena: Early cultural complexity and nucleation in north coastal Peru. *Journal of Field Archaeology* 7: 1–22.

1982   Origins of the urban tradition on the Peruvian north coast. *Current Anthropology* 23: 247–254.

Browman, David L.

1976   Demographic correlations of the Wari conquest of Junín. *American Antiquity* 41: 465–477.

1978   Toward the development of the Tiahuanaco (Tiwanaku) state. In *Advances in Andean archaeology*, edited by David L. Browman, pp. 327–349. Mouton, The Hague.

1980   Tiwanaku expansion and altiplano economic patterns. *Estudios Arqueológicos* 5: 107–120.

Bruhns, Karen O.

1977   The moon animal in northern Peruvian art and culture. *Ñawpa Pacha* 14: 21–39.

Brüning, Enrique (Hans Heinrich)
1922   *Estudios monográficos del Departamento de Lambayeque, Tomo 1: Lambayeque.* Dionisio Mendoza, Chiclayo.

Brush, Stephen
1977   *Mountain, field, and family: The economy and human ecology of an Andean village.* University of Pennsylvania Press, Philadelphia.
1982   The natural and human environment of the Central Andes. *Mountain Research and Development* 2: 19–38.

Burger, Richard L.
1976   The Moche sources of archaism in Chimu ceramics. *Ñawpa Pacha* 14: 95–104.
1981   The radiocarbon evidence for the temporal priority of Chavín de Huantar. *American Antiquity* 46: 592–602.
1984a   Archaeological areas and prehistoric frontiers: The case of formative Peru and Ecuador. In *Social and economic organization in the prehistoric Andes*, edited by D. L. Browman, R. L. Burger, and M. A. Rivera, pp. 37–71. BAR International Series, 194. Oxford.
1984b   *The prehistoric occupation of Chavín de Huantar, Peru.* University of California Publications in Anthropology, Vol. 14. University of California Press, Berkeley.
1988   Unity and heterogeneity within the Chavín horizon. In *Peruvian prehistory*, edited by Richard Keatinge, pp. 99–144. Cambridge University Press, Cambridge.

Burger, Richard L., and Frank Asaro
1979   Análisis de rasgos significativos en la obsidiana de los Andes Centrales. *Revista del Museo Nacional* 43: 281–325. Lima.

Calancha, Antonio de la
1638   *Corónica moralizada del Orden*
[1976] *de San Agustín en el Perú con sucesos egemplares vistos en esta monarquía.* P. Lacavallería, Barcelona.

Caley, Earle R.
1973   Chemical composition of ancient copper objects of South America. In *The application of science in examination of works of art*, edited by W. J. Young, pp. 53–61. Museum of Fine Art, Boston.

Caley, Earle R., and Lowell W. Shank
1971   Composition of ancient Peruvian copper. *Ohio Journal of Science* 71 (3): 181–187. Columbus.

Camino, Lupe
1982   *Los que vencieron al tiempo, Simbilá, costa norte: Perfil etnográfico de un centro alfarero.* Centro de Investigación y Promoción del Campesinado, Piura.
1987   *Chicha de maíz: Bebida y vida del pueblo Catacaos.* Centro de Investigación y Promoción del Campesinado, Piura.

Camino, Alejandro, Jorge Recharte, and Pedro Bidegaray
1981   Flexibilidad calendárica en la agricultura tradicional de las vertientes orientales de los Andes. In *La tecnología en el mundo andino: Runakunap Kawsayninkupaq Rurasqan Kunanqa*, edited by Heather Lechtman and Ana María Soldi, pp. 169–94. Universidad Nacional Autónoma de México, Mexico City.

Canby, T. Y. (editor)
1984   El Niño's ill wind. *National Geographic Magazine* 165 (2): 144–183.

Cane, M. A.
1983   Oceanographic events during El Niño. *Science* 222: 1189–1195.
1986   El Niño. *Annual Review of Earth and Planetary Sciences* 14: 43–70.

Canziani, José
1987   Análisis del complejo urbano Maranga Chayavilca. *Gaceta Arqueológica Andina* 4 (14): 10–17.

Cardich, A.
1979   Cultivation in the Andes. In *National Geographic Research Report, 1979 Projects*, pp. 85–98. Washington, D.C.
1980   El fenómeno de las fluctuaciones de los límites superiores del cultivo en los Andes: Su importancia. *Relaciones de la Sociedad Argentina de Antropología* 14: 7–31. Buenos Aires.
1984/   La agricultura nativa en las tierras
1985   altas de los Andes peruanos. *Relaciones de la Sociedad Argentina de Antropología* 16: 63–96. Buenos Aires.
1985   The fluctuating upper limits of cultivation in the Central Andes and their impact on Peruvian prehistory. *Advances in World Archaeology* 4: 293–333.

Carneiro, Robert L.
1970   A theory of the origin of the state. *Science* 169: 733–738.

Carrera, Fernando de la
1644   *Arte de la lengua yunga.* Edited
[1939] by R. A. Altieri. Publicaciones Especiales del Instituto de Antropología, No. 3. Universidad Nacional de Tucumán.

Cavallaro, Raffael
1988   *Architectural analysis and dual organization in the Andes.* Ph.D. dissertation, Department of Anthropology, Harvard University, Cambridge, MA. University Microfilms International, Ann Arbor.

Cavallaro, Raffael, and Izumi Shimada
1988   Some thoughts on Sicán marked adobes and labor organization. *American Antiquity* 53: 75–101.

Chauchat, Claude
1988   Early hunter-gatherers on the Peruvian coast. In *Peruvian prehistory*, edited by Richard Keatinge, pp. 41–66. Cambridge University Press, Cambridge.

Childe, V. Gordon
1950   The urban revolution. *The Town Planning Review* 21: 3–17.

Christensen, R. T.
1951   Preliminary report of excavations in the Piura Valley, Peru. *Bulletin of the University Archaeological Society* 2: 35–53. Brigham Young University, Provo.
1955   A modern ceramic industry at

Simbila near Piura, Peru. *Chimor* 3: 10–20. Trujillo.

Cieza de León, Pedro

1554 *La crónica del Perú.* Espasa-
[1932] Calpe, Madrid.

1554 *Crónica del Perú.* Pontificia
[1984] Universidad Católica del Perú, Fondo Editorial, Lima.

Claessen, Henri J. M., and Peter Skalnik (editors)

1978 *The early state.* Mouton, The Hague.

Cleland, Kate M., and Izumi Shimada

1991 *Paleteada* potters: Technology, production sphere and sub-culture in ancient Peru. Paper presented at the 56th Annual Meeting of the Society for American Archaeology, New Orleans.

Cobo, Bernabé

1653 *Historia del Nuevo Mundo,* To-
[1964] mos 1–2. Biblioteca de Autores Españoles, 91–92. Aldus Velarde, Madrid.

Cohen, Mark N.

1972– Some problems in the quantita-
1974 tive analysis of vegetable refuse illustrated by a Late Horizon site of the Peruvian coast. *Ñawpa Pacha* 10–12: 49–60.

Cohen, Ronald

1978 State origins: A reappraisal. In *The early state,* edited by Henri J. M. Claessen and Peter Skalnik, pp. 30–76. Mouton, The Hague.

Cohen, Ronald, and Elman R. Service (editors)

1978 *Origins of the state: The anthropology of political evolution.* Institute for the Study of Human Issues, Philadelphia.

Collier, Donald

1948 Peruvian stylistic influences in Ecuador. In *A reappraisal of Peruvian archeology,* assembled by Wendell C. Bennett, pp. 80–86. Memoirs of the Society for American Archaeology, 4. Society for American Archaeology and Institute of Andean Research, Menasha, WI.

1955 *Cultural chronology and change as reflected in the ceramics of*
the Virú Valley, Peru. Fieldiana: Anthropology, Vol. 43. Field Museum of Natural History, Chicago.

1959 Pottery stamping and molding on the North Coast of Peru. In *Actas del 33 Congreso Internacional de Americanistas* 2: 421–431. San José, Costa Rica.

1962a The Central Andes. In *Course towards Urban Life,* edited by R. J. Braidwood and G. R. Willey, pp. 165–176. Viking Fund Publications in Anthropology, No. 32. Wenner-Gren Foundation for Anthropological Research, New York.

1962b Archaeological investigations in the Casma valley, Peru. In *Akten des 34 Internationalen Amerikanistenkongress, Wien, 1960,* pp. 411–417. Vienna.

Collin Delavaud, Claude

1984 *Las regiones costeñas del Perú septentrional.* Pontificia Universidad Católica del Perú, Lima.

Conklin, William J.

1979 Moche textile structures. In *The Junius B. Bird Pre-Columbian Textile Conference, May 19th and 20th, 1973,* edited by A. P. Rowe, E. P. Benson, and A. Schaffer, pp. 165–184. The Textile Museum and Dumbarton Oaks, Washington, D.C.

Conklin, William J., and Michael E. Moseley

1988 The patterns of art and power in the Early Intermediate Period. In *Peruvian prehistory,* edited by Richard Keatinge, pp. 145–163. Cambridge University Press, Cambridge.

Conrad, Geoffrey W.

1974 Burial platforms and related structures on the North Coast of Peru. Ph.D. dissertation, Department of Anthropology, Harvard University, Cambridge, MA.

1978 Models of compromise in settlement pattern studies: An example from coastal Peru. *World Archaeology* 9: 281–298.

1982 Burial platforms of Chan Chan:

Some social and political implications. In *Chan Chan: Andean desert city*, edited by Michael E. Moseley and Kent C. Day, pp. 87–117. University of New Mexico Press, Albuquerque.

1990   Farfán, General Pacatnamú, and the dynastic history of Chimor. In *The northern dynasties: Kingship and statecraft in Chimor*, edited by Michael E. Moseley and Alana Cordy-Collins, pp. 227–242. Dumbarton Oaks, Washington, D.C.

Cook, Anita G.

1983   Aspects of state ideology in Huari and Tiahuanaco iconography: The Central Deity and the Sacrificer. In *Papers from the first annual Northeast Conference on Andean Archaeology and Ethnohistory*, edited by D. H. Sandweiss, pp. 161–185. Cornell Latin American Studies Program, Ithaca.

Cordy-Collins, Alana

1990   Fonga Sigde, shell purveyor of the Chimu kings. In *The northern dynasties: Kingship and statecraft in Chimor*, edited by Michael E. Moseley and Alana Cordy-Collins, pp. 393–417. Dumbarton Oaks, Washington, D.C.

Correa, Segundo

1991   Sipán: Nuevas tumbas guerreras. *Pulso Norteño* 6 (51): 2–4, 80. Chiclayo.

1992   "El Brujo": Resumen cultural de 5 mil años. *Pulso Norteño* 6 (53): 2–6. Chiclayo.

Cowgill, George

1975   On causes and consequences of ancient and modern population changes. *American Anthropologist* 77: 505–525.

Craig, Alan K.

1973   Placer gold in eastern Peru: The great strike of 1942. *Revista Geográfica* 79: 117–128.

1984   On the persistence of error in paleoenvironmental studies of western South America. In *Simposio Culturas Atacameñas, XLIV Congreso Internacional de Americanistas, Manchester*, pp. 57–69. Universidad del Norte, Antofagasta, Chile.

1985   Cis-Andean environmental transects: Late Quaternary ecology of northern and southern Peru. In *Andean ecology and civilization*, edited by Shozo Masuda, Izumi Shimada, and Craig Morris, pp. 23–44. University of Tokyo Press, Tokyo.

Craig, Alan K., and Izumi Shimada

1986   El Niño flood deposits at Batán Grande, northern Peru. *Geoarchaeology* 1: 29–38.

Culbert, T. Patrick

1988   Political history and the decipherment of Maya glyphs. *Antiquity* 62 (234): 135–152.

Culbert, T. Patrick (editor)

1973   *The Classic Maya collapse.* University of New Mexico Press, Albuquerque.

1991   *Classic Maya political history: Hieroglyphic and archaeological evidence.* Cambridge University Press, Cambridge.

Cummins, Thomas B. F.

1991   The figurine tradition of coastal Ecuador: Technological styles. Paper presented at the 56th Annual Meeting of the Society for American Archaeology, New Orleans.

In Press   Los figurinas de Jama-Coaque. *Miscelánea Antropológica Ecuatoriana* 8. Guayaquil.

Cummins, Thomas B. F., and Olaf Holms

1991   The pre-Hispanic art of Ecuador. In *Ancient art of the Andean world*, edited by Shozo Masuda and Izumi Shimada, pp. 167–184. Iwanami Shoten, Tokyo.

Daggett, Richard E.

1984   *The Early Horizon occupation of the Nepeña Valley, north central coast of Peru.* Ph.D. dissertation, Department of Anthropology, University of Massachusetts, Amherst. University Microfilms International, Ann Arbor.

1985   The Early Horizon–Early Intermediate Period transition: A view from the Nepeña and Viru valleys. In *Recent studies in Andean prehistory and protohistory: Papers from the Second Annual Northeast Conference on Andean Archaeology and Ethnohistory*, edited by D. Peter Kvietok and Daniel H. Sandweiss, pp. 41–65. Latin American Studies Program, Cornell University, Ithaca.

D'Altroy, Terence N.
1987   Introduction to the special issue: Inca ethnohistory. *Ethnohistory* 34: 1–13.

D'Altroy, Terence, and Timothy K. Earle
1985   Staple finance, wealth finance, and storage in the Inca political economy. *Current Anthropology* 26: 187–206.

D'Altroy, Terence, and Christine Hastorf
1984   The distribution and contents of Inca state storehouses in the Xauxa region of Peru. *American Antiquity* 49: 334–349.

Darwin, Charles R.
1962   *The voyage of the Beagle.* Annotation and introduction by Leonard Engel. American Museum of Natural History, Garden City, NY, and Doubleday & Co., New York.

Davidson, J. R.
1980   The *Spondylus*: An instrument of ecological regulation. Paper presented at the 79th Annual Meeting of the American Anthropological Association, Washington, D.C.

Day, Kent C.
1971   Quarterly report of the Royal Ontario Museum Lambayeque Valley (Peru) Expedition. Report submitted to the Office of the Chief Archaeologist, Royal Ontario Museum, Toronto.
1973   Architecture of Ciudadela Rivero, Chan Chan, Peru. Ph.D. dissertation, Department of Anthropology, Harvard University, Cambridge, MA.
1974   Walk-in wells and water management at Chan Chan, Peru. In *The rise and fall of civilizations*, edited by J. Sabloff and C. Lamberg-Karlovsky, pp. 182–190. Cummings Publications, Menlo Park.
1975   Mid-season report, Royal Ontario Museum Lambayeque Project. Report submitted to the Office of the Chief Archaeologist, Royal Ontario Museum, Toronto.
1982a Storage and labor service. In *Chan Chan: Andean desert city*, edited by Michael E. Moseley and Kent C. Day, pp. 333–349. University of New Mexico Press, Albuquerque.
1982b Ciudadelas: Their form and function. In *Chan Chan: Andean desert city*, edited by Michael E. Moseley and Kent C. Day, pp. 55–66. University of New Mexico Press, Albuquerque.

Denevan, William M.
1982   Hydraulic agriculture in the American tropics: Forms, measures and recent research. In *Maya subsistence*, edited by Kent Flannery, pp. 181–203. Academic Press, New York.

DeVries, Thomas J.
1987   A review of geological evidence for ancient El Niño activity in Peru. *Journal of Geophysical Research* 92 (C13): 14,471–14,479.

Díaz, Amanda, and Luc Ortlieb
1992   El fenómeno "El Niño" y los moluscos de la costa peruana. In *Paleo ENSO records, international symposium: Extended abstracts*, edited by L. Ortlieb and J. Macharé, pp. 73–79. ORSTOM, Lima, and CONCYTEC, Lima.

Diez de San Miguel, Garci
1964   Visita hecha a la provincia de Chucuito por Garci Diez de San Miguel en el año 1567. In *Documentos regionales para la etnología y etnohistoria andina, Tomo 1*, edited by Waldemar Espinoza, pp. 3–287. Ediciones de la Casa de la Cultura del Perú, Lima.

Dillehay, Tom D., and Patricia J. Netherly
1983   Exploring the upper Zaña Valley in Peru: A unique tropical forest setting offers insights into the Andean past. *Archaeology* 36 (4): 22–30.

Disselhoff, Hans D.
1941   Acerca del problema de estilo Chimú medio. *Revista del Museo Nacional* 10: 51–62.
1956   Hand und Kopftrophaen in plastischen Darstellungen der Recuay-Keramik. *Baessler Archiv* N.F. 3 (2): 55–73.
1957   Polychrome keramik in der nordperuanischen Küstenzone. *Baessler Archiv* N.F. 5 (2): 203–207.
1958a Tumbas de San José de Moro (Provincia de Pacasmayo, Perú). In *Proceedings of the 32nd International Congress of Americanists*, pp. 364–367. Copenhagen.
1958b Cajamarca Keramik von der Pampa von San José de Moro, Provincia Pacasmayo. *Baessler Archiv* N.F. 6 (1): 181–193.
1969   Seis fechas radiocarbónicas de Vicús. *Actas del 38 Congreso Internacional de Americanistas* 1: 341–345. Stuttgart, Munich.
1971   *Vicús: Eine neuen entdeckte altperuanische Kultur.* Monumenta Americana, VII. Gebr. Mann Verlag, Berlin.
1972   Metalleschmuck aus der Loma Negra, Vicús. *Antike Welt, Zeitschrift für Archäologie und Urgeschichte* 3 (2): 43–53. Raggi-Verlag, Küsnacht, Zurich.

Dobkin de Rios, Marlene
1977   Plant hallucinogens and the religion of the Mochica—an ancient Peruvian people. *Economic Botany* 31: 189–203.
1982   Plant hallucinogens, sexuality and shamanism in the ceramic art of ancient Peru. *Journal of Psychoactive Drugs* 14: 81–90.

Dollfus, Olivier
1981   *El reto del espacio andino.* Instituto de Estudios Peruanos, Lima.

Donnan, Christopher B.
1965   Moche ceramic technology. *Ñawpa Pacha* 3: 115–138.
1968   An association of Middle Horizon Epoch 2A specimens from the Chicama Valley, Peru. *Ñawpa Pacha* 6: 47–113.

1971 Ancient Peruvian potter's marks and their interpretation through ethnographic analogy. *American Antiquity* 36: 460–466.

1972 Moche-Huari murals from northern Peru. *Archaeology* 25 (2): 85–95.

1973a *Moche occupation of the Santa Valley, Peru.* University of California Publications in Anthropology, Vol. 8. University of California Press, Berkeley.

1973b A pre-Columbian smelter from northern Peru. *Archaeology* 26: 289–297.

1976 *Moche art and iconography.* UCLA Latin American Center Publications. University of California, Los Angeles.

1978 *Moche art of Peru.* Museum of Cultural History, University of California, Los Angeles.

1986 Introduction. In *The Pacatnamú papers*, Vol. 1, edited by C. B. Donnan and G. A. Cock, pp. 19–22. Museum of Cultural History, University of California, Los Angeles.

1990a Masterworks of art reveal a remarkable pre-Inca world. *National Geographic Magazine* 177 (6): 17–33.

1990b The Chotuna friezes and the Chotuna-Dragón connection. In *The northern dynasties: Kingship and statecraft in Chimor*, edited by Michael E. Moseley and Alana Cordy-Collins, pp. 275–296. Dumbarton Oaks, Washington, D.C.

Donnan, Christopher B. (editor)

1985 *Early ceremonial architecture in the Andes.* Dumbarton Oaks, Washington, D.C.

Donnan, Christopher B., and Guillermo A. Cock (editors)

1986 *The Pacatnamú papers*, Vol. 1. Museum of Cultural History, University of California, Los Angeles.

Donnan, Christopher B., and Carol Mackey

1978 *Ancient burial patterns of the Moche Valley, Peru.* University of Texas Press, Austin.

Donnan, Christopher B., and Donna McClelland

1979 *The burial theme in Moche iconography.* Studies in PreColumbian Art and Archaeology, No. 21. Dumbarton Oaks, Washington, D.C.

D'Orbigny, Alcides

1839 *L'homme américain (de l'Amérique méridionale) considéré sous ses rapports physiologiques et moraux.* F.G. Levrault, Paris.

Drewes, Wolfram U., and Arlene T. Drewes

1966 *Clima y fenómenos relacionados de las laderas orientales andinas del Perú Central.* Serie Traducciones, No. 6. Universidad Nacional Federico Villarreal, Facultad de Educación y Ciencias Humanas, Lima.

Dunn, Mary E.

1979 Ceramic depictions of maize: A basis for classification of prehistoric races. *American Antiquity* 44: 757–774.

Duviols, Pierre

1973 Huari y llacuaz. *Revista del Museo Nacional* 39: 153–187. Lima.

Earle, Timothy K., T. N. D'Altroy, C. Hastorf, C. Scott, C. Costin, G. Russell, and E. Sandefur

1987 *Archaeological field research in the upper Mantaro, Peru, 1982–1983: Investigations of Inka expansion and exchange.* Monograph 28 of the Institute of Archaeology, University of California, Los Angeles.

Elera, Carlos G.

1986 *Investigaciones sobre patrones funerarios en el sitio formativo del Morro de Eten, Valle de Lambayeque* (two volumes). Bachelor's thesis, Especialidad de Arqueología, Pontificia Universidad Católica del Perú, Lima.

Elera, Carlos, and José Pinilla

1990 Research summary of the Proyecto Arqueológico Puémape (1987–1989). *Willay* 34: 2–4. Cambridge, MA.

Elera, Carlos, José Pinilla, and Victor Vásquez

1992 Bioindicadores zoológicos de eventos ENSO para formativo medio y tardío de Puémape, Perú. In *Paleo ENSO records, international symposium: Extended abstracts*, edited by L. Ortlieb and J. Macharé, pp. 93–97. ORSTOM, Lima, and CONCYTEC, Lima.

Eling, Herbert

1978 Interpretaciones preliminares del sistema de riego antiguo de Talambo en el Valle de Jequetepeque, Perú. In *Actas y Trabajos del III Congreso Peruano, el Hombre y la Cultura Andina* 2: 401–419. Lima.

1986 Pre-Hispanic irrigation sources and systems in the Jequetepeque Valley, northern Peru. In *Andean archaeology: Papers in memory of Clifford Evans*, edited by R. Matos, S. Turpin, and H. Eling, pp. 130–149. Monograph 27 of the Institute of Archaeology, University of California, Los Angeles.

1987 *The role of irrigation networks in emerging societal complexity during late prehispanic times, Jequetepeque Valley, North Coast, Peru.* Ph.D. dissertation, Department of Anthropology, University of Texas, Austin. University Microfilms International, Ann Arbor.

Erasmus, Charles

1965 Monument building: Some field experiments. *Southwestern Journal of Anthropology* 21: 277–301.

Ericksen, G. E., G. Plafker, and J. F. Concha

1970 Preliminary report on the geological events associated with the May 31, 1970, earthquake. *United States Geological Survey Circular* 6: 66–82.

Erickson, Clark L.

1988 Raised field agriculture in the Lake Titicaca basin: Putting ancient agriculture back to work. *Expedition* 30 (3): 8–16.

Evans, Clifford
  1968   Obituary: Rafael Larco Hoyle, 1901–1966. *American Antiquity* 33: 233–236.

Farrington, Ian S.
  1974   Irrigation and settlement pattern: Preliminary research results from the North Coast of Peru. In *Irrigation's impact on society*, edited by T. E. Downing and M. Gibson, pp. 83–94. Anthropological Papers of the University of Arizona, No. 25. Tucson.
  1983   The design and function of the intervalley canal: Comments on a paper by Ortloff, Moseley, and Feldman. *American Antiquity* 48: 360–375.

Flores, Isabel
  1984   Telas Pintadas de Pampa de Fáclo, Pacatnamú. *Gaceta Arqueológica Andina* 3 (12): 6–7.

Ford, James A.
  1949   *Cultural dating of prehistoric sites in Virú Valley, Peru.* Anthropological Papers of the American Museum of Natural History, Vol. 43, Part 1. New York.

Fox, Richard G.
  1977   *Urban anthropology.* Prentice-Hall, Englewood Cliffs, NJ.

Franklin, W. L.
  1982   Biology, ecology, and relationship to man of the South American camelids. In *Mammalian biology in South America*, edited by M. A. Mares and H. H. Genoways, pp. 457–489. Pymatuning Laboratory of Ecology, University of Pittsburgh, Linesville, PA.

Friedman, Jonathan, and M. J. Rowlands (editors)
  1977   *The evolution of social systems.* Duckworth, London.

Fung, Rosa
  1988   The Late Preceramic and Initial Period. In *Peruvian prehistory*, edited by Richard Keatinge, pp. 67–96. Cambridge University Press, Cambridge.

Gambini, Wilfredo
  1984   *Santa y Nepeña: Dos valles, dos culturas.* M. Castillo R., Lima.

Gantzer, J.
  1972   Die Gesichtsverstümmelungen auf den Keramiken der Mochica-Kultur. *Med Welt* 23: 137–141.

Garcilaso de la Vega, El Inca
  1609   *Los comentarios reales, primera*
  [1960] *parte.* Biblioteca de Autores Españoles, 133. Editorial Atlas, Madrid.

Gayton, A. H., and A. L. Kroeber
  1927   *The Uhle Collections from Nievería.* University of California Publications in American Archaeology and Ethnology, 21 (8): 305–329. Berkeley.

Gillin, John
  1947   *Moche, a Peruvian coastal community.* Institute of Social Anthropology Publication, No. 5. Smithsonian Institution, Washington, D.C.

Gilmore, Raymond M.
  1950   Fauna and zooarchaeology of South America. In *Handbook of South American Indians*, Vol. 6, edited by J. H. Steward, pp. 345–464. Bureau of American Ethnology, Bulletin 143. Washington, D.C.

Gluckman, Max
  1955   *Custom and conflict in Africa.* The Free Press, Glencoe, IL.

Grieder, Terence
  1978   *The art and archaeology of Pashash.* University of Texas Press, Austin.

Guffroy, Jean, Peter Kaulicke, and Krzysztof Makowski
  1989   La prehistoria del Departamento de Piura: Estado de los conocimientos y problemática. *Boletín del Instituto Francés de Estudios Andinos* 18: 117–142. Lima.

Guzmán Carlos, and José Casafranca
  1964   Vicús: Informe preliminar de excavaciones. Comisión Nacional de Cultura, Lima.
  1967   Vicús, enigma para arqueólogos. *Fanal* 83: 21–26. Lima.

Haas, Jonathan
  1982   *The evolution of the prehistoric state.* Columbia University Press, New York.

1985   Excavations on Huaca Grande: An initial view of the elite at Pampa Grande. *Journal of Field Archaeology* 12: 391–409.

1987   The exercise of power in early Andean state development. In *The origins and development of the Andean state*, edited by Jonathan Haas, Shelia G. Pozorski, and Thomas Pozorski, pp. 31–35. Cambridge University Press, Cambridge.

Haas, Jonathan, Shelia G. Pozorski, and Thomas Pozorski (editors)

1987   *The origins and development of the Andean state.* Cambridge University Press, Cambridge.

Hastings, Charles M., and Michael E. Moseley

1975   The adobes of Huaca del Sol and Huaca de la Luna. *American Antiquity* 40: 196–203.

Hecker, Giesela, and Wolfgang Hecker

1983   Gräberbeschreibung. In *Vorspanische Gräber von Pacatnamú, Nordperu*, compiled by Heinrich Ubbelohde-Doering, pp. 39–131. Materialien zur Allgemeinen und Vergleichenden Archäologie, Band 26. Verlag C. H. Beck, Munich.

1984   Erläuterung von Beigaben und Zeitstellung vorspanisher Gräber von Pacatnamú, Nordperu. *Baessler Archiv* N.F. 32: 159–212.

1985   *Pacatnamú y sus construcciones: Centro religioso prehispánico en la costa norte peruano.* Verlag Klaus Dieter Vervuert, Frankfurt.

1987   Pacanga: Eine Keramik der nordperuanischen Küstenregion aus der Zeit des Mittleren Horizontes. *Baessler Archiv* N.F. 35: 45–107.

Herrera, Fortunato L.

1942   Plantas endémicas domesticadas por los antiguos peruanos. *Revista del Museo Nacional* 11: 179–195. Lima.

Hocquenghem, Anne Marie

1977a   Les représentations de chamans sur les vases mochicas. *Ñawpa Pacha* 15: 123–130.

1977b   Une interprétation des vases portraits mochicas. *Ñawpa Pacha* 15: 131–146.

1978   Les combats mochicas: Essai d'interprétation d'un matériel archéologique à l'aide de l'iconologie, de l'ethnohistoire et de l'ethnologie. *Baessler-Archiv* 26: 127–157.

1979a   L'iconographie mochica et les rites de purification. *Baessler-Archiv* 27: 211–252.

1979b   Rapports entre les morts et les vivants dans la cosmovision mochica. *Objet et Mondes* 19: 85–95. Paris.

1981a   Les mouches et les morts dans l'iconographie mochica. *Ñawpa Pacha* 19: 63–70.

1981b   Les vases mochicas: Formes et sujets. *Ñawpa Pacha* 19: 71–78.

1984a   *El orden andino.* Lateinamerika-Institut der Freie Universität, Berlin.

1984b   Moche: Mito, rito y actualidad. *Allpanchis Phuturinqa* 23: 145–160.

1987   *Iconografía Mochica.* Fondo Editorial de la Universidad Católica del Perú, Lima.

Hocquenghem, Anne Marie, and Patricia J. Lyon

1981   A class of anthropomorphic supernatural females in Moche iconography. *Ñawpa Pacha* 18: 27–48.

Hocquenghem, Anne Marie, and L. Ortlieb

1992   Historical record of El Niño events in Peru (XVI–XVIIth centuries): The Quinn et al. (1987) chronology revisited. In *Paleo ENSO records, international symposium: Extended abstracts*, edited by L. Ortlieb and J. Macharé, pp. 143–149. ORSTOM, Lima, and CONCYTEC, Lima.

Hodder, Ian

1978   Simple correlations between material culture and society: A review. In *The spatial organization of culture*, edited by I. R. Hodder, pp. 3–24. University of Pittsburgh Press, Pittsburgh.

1979   Economic and social stress and material culture patterning. *American Antiquity* 44: 446–454.

1982   *Symbols in action.* Cambridge University Press, Cambridge.

Holmberg, Allan R.

1957   Lizard hunts on the North Coast of Peru. *Fieldiana: Anthropology* 36: 203–220.

Holstein, Otto

1927   Chan Chan: Capital of the great Chimu. *Geographical Review* 17: 36–61.

Horkheimer, Hans

1944   *Vistas arqueológicas del noroeste del Perú.* Instituto Arqueológico de la Universidad Nacional de Trujillo.

1961   *La cultura Mochica.* Las grandes civilizaciones del antiguo Peru, Tomo 1. Peruano Suiza, Lima.

1965   *Vicús.* Ediciones del Instituto de Arte Contemporáneo de Lima.

1973   *Alimentación y obtención de alimentos en el Perú prehispánico.* Universidad Nacional Mayor de San Marcos, Lima.

Howell, W. E.

1954   Local weather of the Chicama Valley (Peru). In *Archiv für Meteorologie, Geophysik, und Bioklimatologie,* Serie B, 5: 41–51.

Humboldt, Alexander von

1814   *Researches concerning the institutions and monuments of the ancient inhabitants of America.* Translated by H. M. Williams. Longmans, London.

Hutchinson, Thomas

1873   *Two years in Peru with exploration of its antiquities.* Sampson Low, Marston, Low and Searle, London.

Hyslop, John

1984   *The Inka road system.* Academic Press, New York.

Idyll, C. P.

1973   The anchovy crisis. *Scientific American* 228: 22–29.

Isbell, William H.

1971   Un pueblo rural ayacuchano durante el imperio Huari. In *Actas y Memorias del XXXIX Congreso Internacional de Americanistas* 3: 89–105. Lima.

1977   *The rural foundation for urbanism: Economic and stylistic interaction between rural and urban communities in eighth century Peru.* University of Illinois Press, Urbana.

1978   Environmental perturbations and the origin of the Andean state. In *Social archaeology: Beyond subsistence and dating,* edited by C. L. Redman, M. J. Berman, E. V. Curtin, W. T. Langhorne, Jr., N. W. Versaggi, and J. C. Wanser, pp. 303–313. Academic Press, New York.

1979   Review of *Ancient burial patterns of the Moche Valley, Peru* by C. B. Donnan and C. Mackey. *American Antiquity* 44: 634–635.

1986   Emergence of city and state at Wari, Ayacucho, Peru, during the Middle Horizon. In *Andean archaeology: Papers in memory of Clifford Evans,* edited by R. Matos, S. Turpin, and H. Eling, pp. 164–189. Monograph 27 of the Institute of Archaeology, University of California, Los Angeles.

1988   City and state in Middle Horizon Huari. In *Peruvian prehistory,* edited by Richard Keatinge, pp. 164–189. Cambridge University Press, Cambridge.

Isbell, William H., and Anita Cook

1987   Ideological origins of an Andean conquest state. *Archaeology* 40 (4): 26–33.

Isbell, William H., and Gordon F. McEwan

1991   A history of Huari studies and introduction to current interpretations. In *Huari administrative structure: Prehistoric monumental architecture and state government,* edited by William H. Isbell and Gordon F. McEwan, pp. 1–17. Dumbarton Oaks, Washington, D.C.

Isbell, William H., and Gordon F. McEwan (editors)

1991   *Huari administrative structure: Prehistoric monumental architec-ture and state government.* Dumbarton Oaks, Washington, D.C.

Isbell, W. H., and K. J. Schreiber

1978   Was Huari a state? *American Antiquity* 43: 372–89.

Ishida, Eiichiro (editor)

1960   *Andes 1: Report of the Tokyo University Scientific Expedition to the Andes in 1958.* Bijutsu-shuppan-sha, Tokyo.

Izumi, Seiichi, and Kazuo Terada

1966   *Andes 3: Excavations at Pechiche and Garbanzal, Tumbes Valley, Peru.* Kadokawa Publishing, Tokyo.

James, D. E.

1973   The evolution of the Andes. *Scientific American* 229 (2): 60–69.

Jijón y Caamaño, Jacinto

1949   *Maranga, contribución al conocimiento de los aborígenes del valle del Rímac, Perú.* La Prensa Católica, Quito.

Jiménez Borja, Arturo

1985   Pachacamac. *Boletín de Lima* 7 (38): 40–54.

Johnson, A. M.

1970   One year in the Peruvian Andes. *Weather* 25 (11): 487–494.

1976   The climate of Peru, Bolivia and Ecuador. In *Climates of Central and South America,* edited by W. Schwerdtfeger, pp. 147–201. World Survey of Climatology, 12. Elsevier, Amsterdam and New York.

Johnson, Allen W., and Timothy Earle (editors)

1987   *The evolution of human societies: From foraging group to agrarian state.* Stanford University Press, Palo Alto.

Jones, Grant D., and Robert Kautz (editors)

1981   *The transition to statehood in the New World.* Cambridge University Press, Cambridge.

Jones, Julie

1979   Mochica works of art in metal: A review. In *Pre-Columbian metallurgy of South America,* edited by E. P. Benson, pp. 53–104. Dumbarton Oaks, Washington, D.C.

Joyce, Thomas A.
1912   *South American archaeology*. Putnam, London.

Julien, Catherine J.
1985   Guano and resource control in sixteenth-century Arequipa. In *Andean ecology and civilization*, edited by Shozo Masuda, Izumi Shimada, and Craig Morris, pp. 185–231. University of Tokyo Press, Tokyo.

Julien, Daniel J.
1988   *Ancient Cuismancu: Settlement and cultural dynamics in the Cajamarca region of the North Highlands of Peru 200 B.C.–A.D. 1532*. Ph.D. dissertation, Department of Anthropology, University of Texas, Austin. University Microfilms International, Ann Arbor.

Kaplan, David
1963   Men, monuments, and political systems. *Southwestern Journal of Anthropology* 19: 397–410.

Kaulicke, Peter
1975   *Pandanche: Un caso del Formativo en los Andes Centrales*. Seminario de Historia Rural Andina, Universidad Nacional Mayor de San Marcos, Lima.
1987/
1988   First two seasons of the Proyecto Arqueológico "Alto Piura": Preliminary report. *Willay* 26/27: 15–19. Cambridge, MA.
1988/
1989   Research summary of the 1988 season of the Proyecto Arqueológico "Alto Piura." *Willay* 29/30: 13–15. Cambridge, MA.
1990   Research summary of the 1989 season of the Proyecto Arqueológico "Alto Piura." *Willay* 34: 12–15. Cambridge, MA.
1991a   El Período Intermedio Temprano en el Alto Piura: Avances del Proyecto Arqueológico "Alto Piura" (1987–1990). *Boletín del Instituto Francés de Estudios Andinos* 20: 381–422. Lima.
1991b   Research summary of the 1990 season of the Proyecto Arqueológico "Alto Piura." *Willay* 35/36: 5–7. Cambridge, MA.
1991c   Chavín art and iconography. In *Ancient art of the Andean world*,

edited by Shozo Masuda and Izumi Shimada, pp. 47–69. Iwanami Shoten, Tokyo.

Kautz, Robert R.
1976   *Late Pleistocene paleoclimates and human adaptations on the western flank of the Peruvian Andes*. Ph.D. dissertation, Department of Anthropology, University of California, Davis. University Microfilms International, Ann Arbor.

Keatinge, Richard W.
1977   Religious forms and social functions: The expansion of state bureaucracies as reflected in prehistoric architecture on the Peruvian north coast. *Annals of the New York Academy of Sciences* 293: 229–245.
1978   The Pacatnamú textiles. *Archaeology* 31 (2): 30–41.
1982   The Chimú empire in a regional perspective: Cultural antecedents and continuities. In *Chan Chan: Andean desert city*, edited by Michael E. Moseley and Kent C. Day, pp. 197–224. University of New Mexico Press, Albuquerque.

Keatinge, Richard W., David Chodoff, Deborah Phillips Chodoff, Murray Marvin, and Helaine Silverman
1975   From the sacred to the secular: First report on a prehistoric architectural transition on the North Coast of Peru. *Archaeology* 28 (2): 128–129.

Keatinge, Richard W., and Geoffrey W. Conrad
1983   Imperialist expansion in Peruvian prehistory: Chimu administration of a conquered territory. *Journal of Field Archaeology* 10: 255–283.

Klein, Otto
1967   *La cerámica Mochica: Carácteres estilísticos y conceptos*. Scientia, No. 131. Universidad Técnica "Féderico Santa María," Valparaíso.

Knapp, Gregory
1982   Prehistoric flood management on the Peruvian coast: Reinterpreting the "sunken fields" of

Chilca. *American Antiquity* 47: 144–154.

Knapp, Hans
n.d.   Unpublished fieldnotes on the adobe brick constructions at Pampa Grande. Donated to Izumi Shimada.

Knobloch, Patricia
1991a   Artisans of the realm: Art of the Wari empire and its contemporaries. In *Ancient art of the Andean world*, edited by Shozo Masuda and Izumi Shimada, pp. 107–123. Iwanami Shoten, Tokyo.
1991b   Stylistic date of ceramics from the Huari centers. In *Huari administrative structure: Prehistoric monumental architecture and state government*, edited by William H. Isbell and Gordon F. McEwan, pp. 247–258. Dumbarton Oaks, Washington, D.C.

Koepcke, Hans-Wilhelm
1952   División ecológica de la costa peruana. *Pesca y Caza* 3: 3–23. Lima.

Koepcke, María
1954   *Corte ecológica transversal en los Andes del Perú Central con especial consideración de los aves*. Memorias del Museo de Historia Nacional "Javier Prado," No. 3. Universidad Nacional Mayor de San Marcos, Lima.

Kolata, Alan L.
1983   Chan Chan and Cuzco: On the nature of the ancient Andean city. In *Civilization in the ancient Americas: Essays in honor of Gordon R. Willey*, edited by R. M. Leventhal and A. L. Kolata, pp. 345–371. University of New Mexico Press, Albuquerque, and Peabody Museum of Archaeology and Ethnology, Harvard University, Cambridge, MA.
1986   The foundations of the Tiwanaku state: A view from the heartland. *American Antiquity* 51: 748–762.
1990   The urban concept of Chan Chan. In *The northern dynasties: Kingship and statecraft in Chimor*, edited by Michael E. Mose-

ley and Alana Cordy-Collins, pp. 107–144. Dumbarton Oaks, Washington, D.C.

Kosok, Paul
1942   The role of irrigation in ancient Peru. In *Proceedings of the Eighth American Scientific Congress,* Vol. 2: *Anthropological Sciences,* pp. 169–178. U.S. Government Printing Office, Washington, D.C.
1959   El valle de Lambayeque. In *Actas y Trabajos del II Congreso Nacional de Historia del Perú: Epoca Pre-Hispánica* 1: 69–76. Lima.
1965   *Life, land, and water in ancient Peru.* Long Island University Press, New York.

Kroeber, A. L.
1925   *The Uhle pottery collections from Moche.* University of California Publications in American Archaeology and Ethnology 21 (5): 191–234.
1926   *Archaeological explorations in Peru,* Part I: *Ancient pottery from Trujillo.* Field Museum of Natural History, Anthropology Memoirs, 2 (1). Chicago.
1930   *Archaeological explorations in Peru,* Part II: *The northern coast.* Field Museum of Natural History, Anthropology Memoirs, 2 (2). Chicago.
1944   *Peruvian archaeology in 1942.* Viking Fund Publications in Anthropology, No. 4. Wenner-Gren Foundation for Anthropological Research, New York.
1954   *Proto-Lima: A Middle period culture of Peru.* Fieldiana: Anthropology, Vol. 44. Chicago Natural History Museum, Chicago.
1963   The methods of Peruvian archaeology. *Ñawpa Pacha* 1: 61–71.

Krzanowski, Andrzej
1977   *Yuraccama: The settlement complex in the Alto Chicama region (northern Peru).* Polish Contributions in the New World Archaeology, 16. Prace Komisji Archeologiczne, Kraków.

Kubler, George
1948   Towards absolute time: Guano archaeology. In *A reappraisal of Peruvian archeology,* assembled by Wendell C. Bennett, pp. 29–50. Memoirs of the Society for American Archaeology, 4. Society for American Archaeology and Institute of Andean Research, Menasha, WI.
1967   Style and the representation of historical time. *Annals of the New York Academy of Sciences* 138: 849–855.
1970   Period, style, and meaning in ancient American art. *New Literary History* 1: 127–144.

Kus, James S.
1972   *Selected aspects of irrigation agriculture in the Chimu heartland, Peru.* Ph.D. dissertation, Department of Geography, University of California, Los Angeles. University Microfilms International, Ann Arbor.

Kutscher, Gerdt
1954   *Nordperuanische Keramik.* Monumenta Americana, I. Gebr. Mann, Berlin.
1955a   *Ancient art of the Peruvian North Coast.* Translated by W. H. Bell. Gebr. Mann, Berlin.
1955b   Sacrifices et prières dans l'ancienne civilisation de Moche (Pérou du nord). *Anais do XXI Congreso Internacional de Americanistas, São Paulo, 1955* 2: 763–776. São Paulo.
1967   Iconographic studies as an aid in the reconstruction of Early Chimu civilization. In *Peruvian archaeology: Selected readings,* compiled by John H. Rowe and Dorothy Menzel, pp. 115–124. Peek Publications, Palo Alto.
1983   *Nordperuanische Gefässmalereien des Moche-Stils.* Indexing by Ulf Bankmann. Verlag C. H. Beck, Munich.

Lanning, Edward P.
1963   *A ceramic sequence for the Piura and Chira coast.* University of California Publications in American Archaeology and Ethnology, 46 (2): 135–284.
1967   *Peru before the Incas.* Prentice-Hall, Englewood Cliffs, NJ.

Lapiner, Alan

1976 *Pre-Columbian art of South America.* Harry N. Abrams, New York.

Larco Hoyle, Rafael

1938 *Los Mochicas, tomo 1.* La Crónica y Variedades, Lima.

1939 *Los Mochicas, tomo 2.* Rimac, Lima.

1941 *Los Cupisniques.* La Crónica y Variedades, Lima.

1943 La escritura peruana sobre pallares. *Revista Geográfica Americana* 20: 277–292. Buenos Aires.

1944a *La cultura Salinar.* Sociedad Geográfica Americana, Buenos Aires.

1944b La escritura peruana sobre pallares. *Relaciones de la Sociedad Argentina de Antropología* 4: 57–63. Buenos Aires.

1944c *Los Mochicas.* Sociedad Geográfica Americana, Buenos Aires.

1945 *La cultura Virú.* Sociedad Geográfica Americana, Buenos Aires.

1946 A culture sequence for the North Coast of Peru. In *Handbook of South American Indians*, Vol. 2, edited by Julian H. Steward, pp. 149–175. Bureau of American Ethnology, Bulletin 143. Washington, D.C.

1948 *Cronología arqueológica del norte del Perú.* Sociedad Geográfica Americana, Buenos Aires.

1960 La cultura Santa. In *Antiguo Perú: Espacio y tiempo*, edited by Ramiro Matos, pp. 235–239. Editorial Mejía Baca, Lima.

1963 *Las épocas peruanas.* Santiago Valverde, Lima.

1965 *La cerámica de Vicús.* Santiago Valverde, Lima.

1966 *Peru.* Frederick Miller, London.

1967 *La cerámica de Vicús y sus nexos con las demás culturas, 2.* Santiago Valverde, Lima.

Lavalle, José Antonio de (editor)

1985 *Arte y tesoros del Perú: Moche.* Banco de Credito del Perú, Lima.

Lechtman, Heather N.

1973 The gilding of metals in pre-Columbian Peru. In *The application of science in examination of works of art*, edited by W. J. Young, pp. 38–52. Museum of Fine Art, Boston.

1976 A metallurgical site survey in the Peruvian Andes. *Journal of Field Archaeology* 3: 1–42.

1979 Issues in Andean metallurgy. In *Pre-Columbian metallurgy of South America*, edited by E. P. Benson, pp. 1–40. Dumbarton Oaks, Washington, D.C.

1980 The Central Andes: Metallurgy without iron. In *The coming of the Age of Iron*, edited by T. A. Wertime and J. D. Muhly, pp. 267–334. Yale University, New Haven.

1984a Pre-Columbian surface metallurgy. *Scientific American* 250 (6): 56–63.

1984b Andean value system and the development of prehistoric metallurgy. *Technology and Culture* 25: 1–36.

1988 Traditions and styles in Central Andean metalworking. In *The beginning of the use of metals and alloys*, edited by Robert Maddin, pp. 344–378. MIT Press, Cambridge, MA.

1991 The production of copper-arsenic alloys in the Central Andes: Highland ores and coastal smelter? *Journal of Field Archaeology* 18: 43–76.

Lechtman, Heather N., Antonieta Erlij, and Edward J. Barry, Jr.

1982 New perspectives on Moche metallurgy: Techniques of gilding copper at Loma Negra, northern Peru. *American Antiquity* 47: 3–30.

Lechtman, Heather N., L. E. Parson, and W. J. Young

1975 *Seven matched hollow gold jaguars from Peru's Early Horizon.* Studies in Pre-Columbian Art and Archaeology, No. 16. Dumbarton Oaks, Washington, D.C.

Lennon, Tom

1986 Research summary of the 1986 season of the Río Abiseo National Park Research Project. *Willay* 23/24: 7–8. Cambridge, MA.

Lorandi, Ana María
1986 "Horizons" in Andean archaeology. In *Anthropological history of Andean polities*, edited by J. V. Murra, N. Wachtel, and J. Revel, pp. 35–46. Cambridge University Press, Cambridge.

Lorenzo, José L.
1981 Archaeology south of the Río Grande. *World Archaeology* 13: 190–208.

Lothrop, Samuel K.
1938 *Inca treasure as depicted by Spanish historians*. The Southwest Museum, Los Angeles.
1941 Gold ornaments of Chavin style from Chongoyape, Peru. *American Antiquity* 6: 250–262.
1948a Julio C. Tello, 1880–1947. *American Antiquity* 14: 51–56.
1948b Pariñas-Chira archaeology: A preliminary report. In *A reappraisal of Peruvian archeology*, assembled by Wendell C. Bennett, pp. 29–50. Memoirs of the Society for American Archaeology, 4. Society for American Archaeology and Institute of Andean Research, Menasha, WI.
1951 Gold artifacts of Chavín style. *American Antiquity* 16: 226–240.

Lowe, John W. G.
1985 *The dynamics of apocalypse: A systems simulation of the Classic Maya collapse*. University of New Mexico Press, Albuquerque.

Lumbreras, Luis G.
1960 La cultura de Wari, Ayacucho. *Etnología y Arqueología* 1: 130–226. Universidad Nacional Mayor de San Marcos, Lima.
1969 *De los pueblos, las culturas y las artes del antiguo Perú*. Editorial Moncloa, Lima.
1974 *The peoples and cultures of ancient Peru*. Translated by Betty J. Meggers. Smithsonian Institution Press, Washington, D.C.
1979 *El arte y la vida Vicús*. Banco Popular del Perú, Lima.
1987 *Vicús: colección arqueológica*. Museo Banco Central de Reserva del Perú, Lima.

Lyon, Patricia J.
1983 Hacia una interpretación rigurosa del arte antiguo peruano. *Historia y Cultura* 16: 160–173. Lima.
1989 Archaeology and mythology II: A re-consideration of the Animated Objects Theme in Moche art. In *Culture in conflict: Current archaeological perspectives*, edited by D. Tkaczuk and B. Vivian, pp. 62–68. The Archaeological Association of the University of Calgary.
1991 Andean art and its cultural implications. In *Ancient art of the Andean world*, edited by Shozo Masuda and Izumi Shimada, pp. 27–45. Iwanami Shoten, Tokyo.

Mackey, Carol J.
1982 The Middle Horizon as viewed from the Moche Valley. In *Chan Chan: Andean desert city*, edited by Michael E. Moseley and Kent C. Day, pp. 321–331. University of New Mexico Press, Albuquerque.
1983 La cerámica chimú a fines del Horizonte Medio. *Revista del Museo Nacional* 47: 73–92. Lima.

Mackey, Carol J., and Charles M. Hastings
1982 Moche murals from the Huaca de la Luna. In *Pre-Columbian art history: Selected readings*, edited by Alana Cordy-Collins, pp. 293–312. Peek Publications, Palo Alto.

Mackey, Carol J., and A. M. Ulana Klymyshyn
1981 Construction and labor organization in the Chimu empire. *Ñawpa Pacha* 19: 99–114.

MacNeish, Richard S.
1967 A summary of the subsistence. In *The prehistory of the Tehuacan Valley*, Vol. 1: *Environment and subsistence*, edited by Douglas S. Byers, pp. 290–309. University of Texas Press, Austin.

MacNeish, Richard S., T. C. Patterson, and D. L. Browman
1975 *The central Peruvian prehistoric interaction sphere*. Philips Academy, Andover, MA.

Maguiña, Adriana
1992 Informe de los trabajos realizados en Huaca La Merced del complejo arqueológico Batán Grande. In *Informe de la temporada de los años 1991–1992 del Proyecto Arqueológico de Sicán*, edited by Izumi Shimada. Report submitted to the Instituto Nacional de Cultura, Lima.

Marcos, Jorge
1980 Intercambio a larga distancia en América: El caso del *Spondylus*. *Boletín de Antropología* 1: 124–129. Mexico City.

Marcos, Jorge, and Presley Norton
1981 Interpretación sobre la arqueología de la Isla de La Plata. *Miscelánea Antropológica Ecuatoriana* 1: 136–154. Cuenca.

Marcus, Joyce
1983 On the nature of the Mesoamerican city. In *Prehistoric settlement patterns: Essays in honor of Gordon R. Willey*, edited by Evon Z. Vogt and Richard M. Leventhal, pp. 195–242. University of New Mexico Press, Albuquerque, and Peabody Museum of Archaeology and Ethnology, Harvard University, Cambridge, MA.
1987 *Late Intermediate occupation at Cerro Azul, Peru: A preliminary report*. University of Michigan Museum of Anthropology Technical Report, No. 20. Ann Arbor.

Markham, Clements R.
1892 *A history of Peru*. Charles H. Siegel, Chicago.

Martínez de Compañón y Bujanda, Baltazar Jaime
1782– *Trujillo del Perú a fines del siglo XVIII*. 9 vols. Ediciones Cultura Hispánica, Madrid. [1978–1991]

Mason, J. Alden
1968 *The ancient civilization of Peru*. Penguin Books, Harmondsworth, Middlesex, Eng.

Masuda, Shozo
1985 Algae collectors and *lomas*. In *Andean ecology and civilization*, edited by Shozo Masuda, Izumi Shimada, and Craig Morris, pp.

233–250. University of Tokyo Press, Tokyo.

Mathews, Peter
1991   Classic Maya emblem glyphs. In *Classic Maya political history: Hieroglyphic and archaeological evidence*, edited by T. Patrick Culbert, pp. 19–29. Cambridge University Press, Cambridge.

Matos, Ramiro
1965– Algunas consideraciones sobre el
1966   estilo de Vicús. *Revista del Museo Nacional* 34: 89–130. Lima.

Matsumoto, Ryozo
1988   The Cajamarca culture: Its evolution and interaction with coastal peer polities. Paper presented at the 53rd Annual Meeting of the Society for American Archaeology, Phoenix.

Matsumoto, Ryozo, and Reiko Kimura
1991   Reconocimiento del Valle de Chancay-Maichil. In *Informe de la temporada del año 1990 del Proyecto Arqueológico de Sicán*, edited by Izumi Shimada. Report submitted to the Instituto Nacional de Cultura, Lima.
1992   Reconocimiento y excavaciones en la zona de Chongoyape, valle de Chancay. In *Informe de la temporada de los años 1991–1992 del Proyecto Arqueológico de Sicán*, edited by Izumi Shimada. Report submitted to the Instituto Nacional de Cultura, Lima.

Matsuzawa, Tsugio
1978   The Formative site of Las Haldas, Peru: Architecture, chronology and economy. Edited and translated by I. Shimada. *American Antiquity* 43: 652–673.

McClelland, Donald
1986   Brick seriation at Pacatnamú. In *The Pacatnamú papers*, Vol. 1, edited by C. B. Donnan and G. A. Cock, pp. 27–46. Museum of Cultural History, University of California, Los Angeles.

McClelland, Donna
1990   A maritime passage from Moche to Chimu. In *The northern dynasties: Kingship and statecraft in Chimor*, edited by Michael E.

Moseley and Alana Cordy-Collins, pp. 75–106. Dumbarton Oaks, Washington, D.C.

McCorkle, Constance M.
1991   Major achievements of the SR-CRSP/Peru, 1980–1990. *Willay* 35/36: 7–9.

McEwan, Gordon F.
1990   Some formal correspondences between the imperial architecture of the Wari and Chimu cultures of ancient Peru. *Latin American Antiquity* 1: 97–116.

Mendoza, Eric
1985   Daños ocasionados por las lluvias de 1983 en Lambayeque. In *Presencia histórica de Lambayeque*, assembled by Eric Mendoza, pp. 224–229. Editorial e Imprenta DESA, Lima.

Menzel, Dorothy
1958   Problemas en el estudio del Horizonte Medio en la arqueología peruana. *Revista del Museo Regional de Ica* 9/10: 24–57.
1964   Style and time in the Middle Horizon. *Ñawpa Pacha* 2: 1–105.
1968   *La cultura huari*. Peruano-Suiza, Lima.
1969   New data on the Huari empire in Middle Horizon Epoch 2A. *Ñawpa Pacha* 6: 47–114.
1971   Estudios arqueológicos en los valles de Ica, Pisco, Chincha y Cañete. *Arqueología y Sociedad* 6: 1–158. Universidad Nacional Mayor de San Marcos, Lima.
1977   *The archaeology of ancient Peru and the work of Max Uhle*. R. H. Lowie Museum of Anthropology, University of California, Berkeley.

Merkel, John F., and Izumi Shimada
1988   Arsenical copper smelting at Batán Grande, Peru. *Newsletter of the Institute for Archaeo-Metallurgical Studies* 12: 4–7. London.

Meyers, Albert
1979   Arqueología de los Cañaris: evidencias cronológicas y relaciones interregionales. Paper presented at the XLIII Congreso Internacional de Americanistas, Vancouver.

Middendorf, E. W.
1893– *Peru: Boebachtungen und Studien*
1895   *über das Land und seine Bewohnet während eines 25 jährigen Aufenthaltes*. 3 vols. Robert Oppenheim, Berlin.

Miller, George R.
1979   *An introduction to the ethnoarchaeology of the Andean camelids*. Ph.D. dissertation, Department of Anthropology, University of California, Berkeley. University Microfilms International, Ann Arbor.

Moore, Jerry
1989   Pre-Hispanic beer in coastal Peru: technology and social context of prehistoric production. *American Anthropologist* 91: 682–695.

Morris, Craig
1967   *Storage in Tawantinsuyu*. Ph.D. dissertation, Department of Anthropology, University of Chicago.
1974   Non-agricultural production in the Inka economy: An institutional analysis. In *Reconstructing complex societies*, edited by Charlotte Moore, pp. 49–60. American School of Oriental Research, Cambridge, MA.
1979   Maize beer in the economics, politics, and religion of the Inca empire. In *Fermented beverage foods in nutrition*, edited by C. Gastineau, W. Darby, and T. Turner, pp. 21–34. Academic Press, New York.
1981   Tecnología y organización inca del almacenamiento de viveres en la sierra. In *La tecnología en el mundo andino*, Vol. 1, edited by H. N. Lechtman and A. M. Soldi, pp. 327–375. Universidad Autónoma de México, Mexico City.
1986   Storage, supply, and redistribution in the economy of the Inka state. In *Anthropological history of Andean polities*, edited by J. Murra, N. Wachtel, and J. Revel, pp. 59–68. Cambridge University Press, Cambridge.
1988   A city fit for an Inka. In *Archaeology* 41 (5): 43–49.

Morris, Craig, and Donald Thompson
1970   Huánuco Viejo: An Inca administrative center. *American Antiquity* 35: 334–362.

Moseley, Michael E.
1969   Assessing the archaeological significance of *mahamaes*. *American Antiquity* 34: 485–487.

1974   Organizational preadaptation to irrigation: The evolution of early water management systems in coastal Peru. In *Irrigation's impact on society*, edited by T. E. Downing and McGuire Gibson, pp. 77–82. University of Arizona Press, Tucson.

1975a   Review of *Archaeological investigations in the Nepeña Valley* by Donald Proulx. *American Anthropologist* 77: 691–692.

1975b   Prehistoric principles of labor organization in the Moche valley, Peru. *American Antiquity* 40: 191–196.

1975c   *Maritime foundations of Andean civilization.* Cummings Publishing, Menlo Park.

1975d   Secrets of Peru's ancient walls. *Natural History* 84: 34–41.

1975e   Chan Chan: Andean alternative of the pre-industrial city. *Science* 187: 219–225.

1978a   The evolution of Andean civilization. In *Ancient native Americans*, edited by Jesse D. Jennings, pp. 491–541. W. H. Freeman, San Francisco.

1978b   An empirical approach to prehistoric agrarian collapse: The case of the Moche Valley. In *Social and technological management in dry lands*, edited by Nancy L. Gonzalez, pp. 9–43. AAAS Selected Symposium, 10. Westview Press, Boulder.

1978c   *Pre-agricultural coastal civilizations in Peru.* Carolina Biological Readers, 90. Carolina Biological Supply Co., Burlington.

1982   Introduction: Human exploitation and organization on the north Andean coast. In *Chan Chan: Andean desert city*, edited by Micheal E. Moseley and Kent C. Day, pp. 1–24. University of New Mexico Press, Albuquerque.

1983a   Central Andean civilization. In *Ancient South Americans*, edited by J. D. Jennings, pp.179–239. W. H. Freeman, San Francisco.

1983b   The good old days were better: Agrarian collapse and tectonics. *American Anthropologist* 85: 773–99.

1987   Punctuated equilibrium: searching the ancient record for El Niño. *The Quarterly Review of Archaeology* 8 (3): 7–10.

1990   Structure and history in the dynastic lore of Chimor. In *The northern dynasties: Kingship and statecraft in Chimor*, edited by Michael E. Moseley and Alana Cordy-Collins, pp. 1–41. Dumbarton Oaks, Washington, D.C.

Moseley, Michael E., and Kent C. Day (editors)
1982   *Chan Chan: Andean desert city.* University of New Mexico Press, Albuquerque.

Moseley, Michael E., and Eric Deeds
1982   The land in front of Chan Chan: Agrarian expansion, reform, and collapse in the Moche Valley. In *Chan Chan: Andean desert city*, edited by Michael E. Moseley and Kent C. Day, pp. 25–53. University of New Mexico Press, Albuquerque.

Moseley, Michael E., and Carol J. Mackey
1972   Peruvian settlement pattern studies and small site methodology. *American Antiquity* 37: 67–81.

Moseley, Michael E., Robert A. Feldman, and Charles R. Ortloff
1981   Living with crises: Human perception of process and time. In *Biotic crises in ecological and evolutionary times*, edited by M. Nitecki, pp. 231–267. Academic Press, New York.

Moseley, Michael E., Robert A. Feldman, Charles R. Ortloff, and Alfredo Narvaez
1983   Principles of agrarian collapse in the Cordillera Negra, Peru. *Annals of the Carnegie Museum* 52: 299–327.

Muelle, Jorge C.
1935 Restos hallados en una tumba en Nievería. *Revista del Museo Nacional* 4: 135–151. Lima.

Mujica, Elias
1985 Altiplano-coast relationships in the South-Central Andes: From indirect to direct complementarity. In *Andean ecology and civilization*, edited by Shozo Masuda, Izumi Shimada, and Craig Morris, pp. 103–140. University of Tokyo Press, Tokyo.

Murphy, Robert C.
1925 *Bird islands of Peru*. G. Putnam's Sons, New York.
1926 Oceanic and climatic phenomena along the western coast of South America during 1925. *Geographical Review* 16: 26–53.

Murra, John V.
1960 Rite and crop in the Inca state. In *Culture in history*, edited by S. Diamond, pp. 393–407. Columbia University Press, New York.
1968 An Aymara kingdom in 1567. *Ethnohistory* 15: 115–151.
1972 El "control vertical" de un máximo de pisos ecológicos en la economía de las sociedades andinas. In *Visita de la provincia de León de Huánuco 1562*, Tomo 2, edited by John V. Murra, pp. 429–476. Universidad Nacional Hermilio Valdizán, Huánuco.
1975 El tráfico de *mullu* en la costa del Pacífico. In *Formaciones económicas y políticas del mundo andino*, pp. 255–267. Instituto de Estudios Peruanos, Lima.
1980 *The economic organization of the Inka state*. JAI Press, Greenwich, CT.
1982 The *mit'a* obligations of ethnic groups to the Inka state. In *The Inca and Aztec states, 1400–1800: Anthropology and history*, edited by G. Collier, R. I. Rosaldo, and J. D. Wirth, pp. 237–262. Academic Press, New York.
1984 Andean societies. *Annual Review of Anthropology* 13: 119–41.
1986 The expansion of the Inka state: armies, war, and rebellions. In *Anthropological history of Andean polities*, edited by J. V. Murra, N. Wachtel, and J. Revel, pp. 49–58. Cambridge University Press, Cambridge.

Nagin, Carl
1990 The Peruvian gold rush. *Art and Antiques* 7 (5): 98–105.

Nersesov, Y. A. N.
1987 *Pre-Columbian collections in European museums*, edited by A. M. Hocquenghem, P. Tamási, and C. Villain-Gandossi, pp. 240–251. Akadémiai Kiadó, Budapest.

Netherly, Patricia
1977 *Local level lords on the North Coast of Peru*. Ph.D. dissertation, Department of Anthropology, Cornell University, Ithaca, NY. University Microfilms International, Ann Arbor.
1984 The management of late Andean irrigation systems on the North Coast of Peru. *American Antiquity* 49: 227–254.
1990 Out of many, one: The organization of rule in the North Coast polities. In *The northern dynasties: Kingship and statecraft in Chimor*, edited by Michael E. Moseley and Alana Cordy-Collins, pp. 461–487. Dumbarton Oaks, Washington, D.C.

Netherly, Patricia, and Tom D. Dillehay
1986 Duality in public architecture in the upper Zaña Valley, northern Peru. In *Perspectives on Andean prehistory and protohistory*, edited by D. H. Sandweiss and D. P. Kvietok, pp. 85–114. Cornell Latin American Studies Program, Ithaca, NY.

Newman, Marshall T.
1948 A summary of the racial history of the Peruvian area. In *A reappraisal of Peruvian archaeology*, assembled by Wendell C. Bennett, pp. 16–19. Memoir of the Society for American Archaeology, No. 4. Society for American Archaeology and Institute of Andean Research, Menasha, WI.

Nials, Fred L., E. E. Deeds, M. E. Moseley, S. G. Pozorski, T. Pozorski, and R. A. Feldman
1979 El Niño: the catastrophic flood-
a,b ing of coastal Peru. *Field Museum of Natural History Bulletin* 50 (7): 4–14; 50 (8): 4–10.

Nicholson, G. Edward
1960 *Chicha* maize types and *chicha* manufacture in Peru. *Economic Botany* 14: 290–299.

Nolan, James L.
1980 *Pre-Hispanic irrigation and polity in the Lambayeque sphere, Peru.* Ph.D. dissertation, Department of Anthropology, Columbia University, New York. University Microfilms International, Ann Arbor.

Norton, Presley, Richard Lunnis, and Nigel Nailing
1984 Excavaciones en Salango, Provincia de Manabí, Ecuador. *Miscelánea Antropológica Ecuatoriana* 3: 9–72. Guayaquil.

Olsson, Axel Adolf
1961 *Mollusks of the tropical eastern Pacific, particularly from the southern half of the Panamic-Pacific faunal province (Panama to Peru).* Paleontological Research Institution, Ithaca, NY.

O'Neil, John P.
1984 Feather identification. In *Costumes and featherwork of the lords of Chimor: Textiles from Peru's North Coast* by A. P. Rowe, pp. 145–150. The Textile Museum, Washington, D.C.

Onuki, Yoshio
1989/ Research summary of the 1989
1990 fieldwork of the Misión Arqueológica de la Universidad de Tokio at Huacaloma and Kuntur Wasi. *Willay* 32/33: 9–15. Cambridge, MA.

Ortloff, Charles R., Robert A. Feldman, and Michael E. Moseley
1985 Hydraulic engineering and historical aspects of the pre-Columbian intravalley canal systems of the Moche Valley, Peru. *Journal of Field Archaeology* 12: 77–98.

Ortloff, Charles R., M. E. Moseley, and Robert A. Feldman
1982 Hydraulic engineering aspects of the Chimú Chicama-Moche intervalley canal. *American Antiquity* 47: 572–595.
1983 The Chicama-Moche intervalley canal: Social explanations and physical paradigms. *American Antiquity* 48: 375–389.

Panofsky, Erwin
1955 *Meaning in the visual arts: Papers in and on art history.* Doubleday, Garden City.
1962 *Studies in iconology: Humanistic themes in the art of the Renaissance.* Harper and Row, New York.

Parsons, Jeffrey R.
1968 The archaeological significance of *mahamaes* cultivation on the coast of Peru. *American Antiquity* 33: 80–85.

Parsons, Jeffrey R., and Nobert P. Psuty
1975 Sunken fields and prehispanic subsistence on the Peruvian coast. *American Antiquity* 40: 259–282.

Patterson, Clair C.
1971 Native copper, silver, and gold accessible to early metallurgists. *American Antiquity* 36: 286–321.

Patterson, Thomas C.
1966 *Pattern and process in the Early Intermediate Period pottery of the Central Coast of Peru.* University of California Publications in Anthropology, 3. Berkeley.
1973 *America's past: A New World archaeology.* Scott, Foresman and Co., Glenview, IL.

Paulsen, Allison C.
1968 A Middle Horizon tomb, Pinilla, Ica Valley, Peru. *Ñawpa Pacha* 6: 1–6.
1970 A chronology of Guangala and Libertad ceramics of the Santa Elena Peninsula in south coastal Ecuador. Ph.D. thesis, Department of Anthropology, Columbia University, New York.
1974 The thorny oyster and the voice of God: *Spondylus* and *Strombus*

in Andean prehistory. *American Antiquity* 39: 597–607.
1976 Environment and empire: Climatic factors in prehistoric Andean culture change. *World Archaeology* 8: 121–32.
1982 La sequencia de la cerámica de Guangala de la Península de Santa Elena y sus implicaciones para un contacto prehistórico entre el Ecuador y América Central. In *Primer Simposio de Correlaciones Antropológicas Andino-Americano*, edited by Jorge G. Marcos and Presley Norton, pp. 203–212. Escuela Superior Politécnica del Littoral, Guayaquil.
1988 Prehistoric relationships between Ecuador and the North Coast of Peru. Paper presented at the 53rd Annual Meeting of the Society for American Archaeology, Phoenix.

Pearson, O. P., and C. P. Ralph
1978 The diversity and abundance of vertebrates along an altitudinal gradient in Peru. *Memorias del Museo de Historia Nacional "Javier Prado"* 18: 1–97. Universidad Nacional Mayor de San Marcos, Lima.

Pearson, Gordon W., and Minze Stuiver
1986 High-precision calibration of the radiocarbon time scale, 500–2500 B.C. *Radiocarbon* 28 (2B): 839–862.

Petersen, George
1956 Hidrología del Río Chancay, Lambayeque. In *Primer Congreso Nacional de la Geología, Sociedad Geológica del Perú, Anales—Parte I*, pp. 297–322. Lima.

Petrie, W. M. Flinder
1904 *Methods and aims in archaeology.* Macmillan, London.

Pinder, David, Izumi Shimada, and David Gregory
1979 The nearest-neighbor statistic: Archaeological application and new developments. *American Antiquity* 44: 430–445.

Pirsig, Wolfgang
1989 Diseases of the nasal region on ceramics of the Moche-culture in

ancient Peru. *Rhinology,* Supplement No. 9, pp. 27–36.

Pirsig, Wolfgang, and Dieter Eisleb
1988   Severed noses and nosebleed on earthenware vessels from the Moche period. *Baessler-Archiv* N.F. 36: 109–116.

Plowman, Timothy
1984a   The origin, evolution, and diffusion of coca, *Erythroxylum spp.,* in South and Central America. In *Pre-Columbian plant migration,* edited by Doris Stone, pp. 125–163. Papers of the Peabody Museum of Archaeology and Ethnology, Harvard University, Vol. 76. Cambridge, MA.
1984b   The ethnobotany of coca (*Erythroxylum spp., Erythroxylaceae*). In *Ethnobotany in the Neotropics,* edited by G. T. Prance and J. A. Kallunki, pp. 62–111. Advances in Economic Botany, 1. New York Botanical Garden, Bronx.

Porras, Raúl
1963   *Fuentes históricas peruanas: Apuntes de un curso universitario.* Universidad Nacional Mayor de San Marcos, Lima.

Portugal, José A.
1966   *Influencia de Proyecto Tinajones.* Editorial Huascarán, Lima.

Posner, Gerlad S.
1954   The Peru Current. *Scientific American* 190: 66–71.

Pozorski, Shelia
1976   *Prehistoric subsistence patterns and site economics in the Moche Valley, Peru.* Ph.D. dissertation, Department of Anthropology, University of Texas, Austin. University Microfilms International, Ann Arbor.
1979   Prehistoric diet and subsistence of the Moche Valley, Peru. *World Archaeology* 11: 413–432.
1982   Subsistence systems in the Chimú state. In *Chan Chan: Andean desert city,* edited by Michael E. Moseley and Kent C. Day, pp. 177–196. University of New Mexico, Albuquerque.

Pozorski, Thomas
1976   *Caballo Muerto: A complex of early ceramic sites in the Moche valley, Peru.* Ph.D. dissertation, Department of Anthropology, University of Texas, Austin. University Microfilms International, Ann Arbor.

Pozorski, Shelia, and Thomas Pozorski
1977   Alto Salaverry: Un sitio precerámico de la costa peruana. *Revista del Museo Nacional* 43: 27–60. Lima.
1982   Reassessing the Chicama-Moche intervalley canal: Comments on "Hydraulic engineering aspects of the Chimú Chicama-Moche intervalley canal." *American Antiquity* 47: 851–868.
1987   *Early settlement and subsistence in the Casma Valley, Peru.* University of Iowa Press, Iowa City.

Proulx, Donald A.
1968   *An archaeological survey of the Nepeña Valley, Peru.* Department of Anthropology, Research Report 2. University of Massachusetts, Amherst.
1971   Headhunting in ancient Peru. *Archaeology* 24 (1): 16–21.
1973   *Archaeological investigations in the Nepeña Valley, Peru.* Department of Anthropology, Research Report 13. University of Massachusetts, Amherst.
1982   Territoriality in the Early Intermediate Period: The case of Moche and Recuay. *Ñawpa Pacha* 20: 83–96.
1985   *An analysis of the early cultural sequence in the Nepeña Valley, Peru.* Department of Anthropology, Research Report 25. University of Massachusetts, Amherst.
1989   Nasca trophy heads: Victims of warfare or ritual sacrifice? In *Cultures in conflict: Current archaeological perspectives,* edited by Diana C. Tkaczuk and Brian C. Vivian, pp. 73–85. Proceedings of the 20th Annual Chacmool Conference, University of Calgary. Archaeological Association, Calgary.

Pulgar Vidal, Javier
1987   *Geografía del Perú.* 9th ed. Promoción Editorial Inca, Lima.

Quinn, W. H., V. T. Neal, and S. E. Antúnez de Mayolo
1987   El Niño occurrences over the past four and a half centuries. *Journal of Geophysical Research* 92 (C13): 14, 449–61.

Rabinowitz, Joel
1983   La lengua pescadora: The lost dialect of Chimu fishermen. In *Investigations of the Andean past,* edited by Daniel H. Sandweiss, pp. 243–267. Cornell Latin American Studies Program, Ithaca, NY.

Ramírez, Susan
1985a   Social frontiers and the territorial base of *curacazgos.* In *Andean ecology and civilization,* edited by Shozo Masuda, Izumi Shimada, and Craig Morris, pp. 423–442. University of Tokyo Press, Tokyo.
1985b   *Provincial patriarchs, land tenure and the economics of power in Colonial Peru.* University of New Mexico Press, Albuquerque.
1986   Notes on ancient exchange: A plea for collaboration. In *Andean archaeology: Papers in memory of Clifford Evans,* edited by R. Matos and S. Turpin, pp. 225–238. Monograph 27 of the Institute of Archaeology, University of California, Los Angeles.

Ramirez-Horton, Susan
1974   *The sugar estates of the Lambayeque Valley, 1670–1800: a contribution to Peruvian agrarian history.* University of Wisconsin Land Tenure Center Research Papers, 58. Madison.
1981   La organización económica de la costa norte: Un análisis preliminar del período prehispánico tardío. In *Etnohistoria y antropología andina,* edited by A. Castelli, M. Koth de Paredes, and M. Mould de Pease, pp. 281–297. Instituto de Estudios Peruanos, Lima.
1982   Retainers of the lords or merchants: A case of mistaken iden-

tity? In *El hombre y su ambiente en los Andes Centrales*, edited by Luis Millones and Hiroyasu Tomoeda, pp. 123–136. National Museum of Ethnology, Suita, Japan.

Rasmussen, E. M., and J. M. Wallace
1983 Meteorological aspects of the El Niño/Southern Oscillation. *Science* 222: 1195–1202.

Ravines, Rogger
1969 Un depósito de ofrendas del Horizonte Medio en la sierra central del Perú. *Ñawpa Pacha* 6: 19–45.
1970 Introducción. *100 años de arqueología en el Perú*, compiled by Rogger Ravines, pp. 11–28. Instituto de Estudios Peruanos, Lima, and Petróleos del Perú, Lima.
1977 Excavaciones en Ayapata, Huancavelica, Perú. *Ñawpa Pacha* 15: 49–100.

Ravines, Rogger (compiler)
1982 *Arqueología del valle medio del Jequetepeque.* Instituto Nacional de Cultura, Lima.

Raymond, J. Scott
1981 The maritime foundations of Andean civilization: A reconsideration of the evidence. *American Antiquity* 46: 806–821.

Regal, Alberto
1970 *Los trabajos hidráulicos del Inca en el antiguo Perú.* Gráficos Industrial, Lima.

Reichert, Raphael X.
1982 Moche iconography—the highland connection. In *pre-Columbian art history: Selected readings*, edited by Alana Cordy-Collins, pp. 279–291. Peek Publications, Palo Alto.

Reichlen, Henry, and Paule Reichlen
1949 Recherches archéologiques dans les Andes de Cajamarca: Premier rapport de la Mision Ethnologique Française au Peróu Septentrional. *Journal de la Société des Américanistes* 38: 137–174. Paris.

Reid, James
1988 Arte textil del Perú. In *Arte textil del Perú*, edited by J. A. de Lavalle

and J. A. González, pp. 28–291. Industria Textil Piura, Lima.

Reimchen, Theodore H.
1972 A geological and geomorphological survey of the Lambayeque Valley, Peru. Report submitted to the Office of the Chief Archaeologist, Royal Ontario Museum, Toronto.

Reinhard, Johan
1985 Chavín and Tiahuanaco: A new look at two Andean ceremonial centers. *National Geographic Research* 1: 395–422.

Renfrew, Colin
1975 Trade as action at a distance: Questions of integration and communication. In *Ancient civilizations and trade*, edited by J. A. Sabloff and C. C. Lamberg-Karlovsky, pp. 3–59. University of New Mexico Press, Albuquerque.
1986 Introduction. In *Peer polity interaction and sociopolitical change*, edited by Colin Renfrew and John F. Cherry, pp. 1–18. Cambridge University Press, Cambridge.

Renfrew, Colin, and John F. Cherry (editors)
1986 *Peer polity interaction and sociopolitical change.* Cambridge University Press, Cambridge.

Rhoades, R. E., and S. I. Thompson
1975 Adaptive strategies in alpine environments: Beyond ecological particularism. *American Ethnologist* 2: 535–551.

Richardson, James B. III, Mark A. McConaughy, Allison Heaps de Peña, and Elena B. Décima Zamecnik
1990 The northern frontier of the Kingdom of Chimor: The Piura, Chira, and Tumbez valleys. In *The northern dynasties: Kingship and statecraft in Chimor*, edited by Michael E. Moseley and Alana Cordy-Collins, pp. 419–445. Dumbarton Oaks, Washington, D.C.

Rivero, Mariano Eduardo, and Johann J. von Tschudi
1855 *Peruvian antiquities.* Translated

by F. L. Hawks. A. S. Barnes and Co., New York.

Rivet, Paul

1949 Les langues de l'ancien Diocèse de Trujillo. *Journal de la Société des Américanistes* n.s. 38: 3–51.

Roark, Richard

1965 From Monumental to Proliferous in Nasca pottery. *Ñawpa Pacha* 3: 1–92. Berkeley.

Robinson, David A.

1964 *Peru in four dimensions.* American Studies Press, Lima.

Rodríguez, Victor Antonio

1967 Secuencia cultural en el valle de Lambayeque. Paper presented at the Primer Simposio de Arqueología de Lambayeque, Chiclayo, Peru.

1970 Irrigación prehistórica en el valle de Moche. Paper presented at the 39th International Congress of Americanists, Lima. Mimeo.

Root, William C.

1949 Metallurgy. In *Handbook of South American Indians,* Vol. 5, edited by Julian H. Steward, pp. 205–225. Bureau of American Ethnology, Bulletin 143. Smithsonian Institution, Washington, D.C.

1951 Gold-copper alloys in ancient America. *Journal of Chemical Education* 28 (2): 76–78.

Rosas, Hermilio

1970 La secuencia cultural del período formativo en Ancón. Bachelor's thesis, Programa de Psicología y Ciencias Sociales, Universidad Nacional Mayor de San Marcos, Lima.

Rosas, Hermilio, and Ruth Shady

1970 Pacopampa: Un complejo temprano del período formativo peruano. *Arqueología y Sociedad* 3: 3–16. Lima.

Rostworowski, María

1975 Pescadores, artesanos y mercaderes costeños en el Perú prehispánico. *Revista del Museo Nacional* 41: 311–349. Lima.

1981 *Recursos naturales renovables y pesca, siglos XVI y XVII.* Instituto de Estudios Peruanos, Lima.

1985 Patronyms with the consonant F in the *Guarangas* of Cajamarca. In *Andean ecology and civilization,* edited by Shozo Masuda, Izumi Shimada, and Craig Morris, pp. 401–421. University of Tokyo Press, Tokyo.

Rowe, John H.

1942 A new pottery style from the Department of Piura, Peru. *Notes on Middle American Archaeology and Ethnology* 1 (8): 30–34. Carnegie Institution Division of Historical Research, Washington, D.C.

1945 Absolute chronology in the Andean area. *American Antiquity* 10: 265–284.

1948a The Kingdom of Chimor. *Acta Americana* 6: 26–59.

1948b On absolute dating and North Coast history. In *A reappraisal of Peruvian archaeology,* assembled by Wendell C. Bennett, pp. 51–52. Memoir of the Society for American Archaeology, No. 4. Society for American Archaeology and Institute of Andean Research, Menasha, WI.

1954 *Max Uhle, 1856–1944, a memoir of the father of Peruvian archaeology.* University of California Publications in American Archaeology and Ethnology, 46 (1). Berkeley.

1962 Stages and periods in archaeological interpretation. *Southwestern Journal of Anthropology* 18 (1): 40–54.

1963 Urban settlements in ancient Peru. *Ñawpa Pacha* 1: 1–28.

1967 Form and meaning in Chavin art. In *Peruvian archeology: Selected readings,* compiled by John H. Rowe and Dorothy Menzel, pp. 72–103. Peek Publications, Palo Alto.

1969 The sunken gardens of the Peruvian coast. *American Antiquity* 34: 320–325.

1974 Kunst in Peru und Bolivien. In *Das alte Amerika,* edited by Gordon R. Willey, pp. 285–350. Propyläen Kunst Geschichte, Band 18. Propyläen Verlag, Berlin.

Ruíz, Arturo

1985   Los monumentos arqueológicos de Leimebamba. *Boletín de Lima* 7 (42): 69–82.

Russell, Glenn S.

1990   Preceramic through Moche settlement pattern change in the Chicama Valley, Peru. Paper presented at the 55th Annual Meeting of the Society for American Archaeology, Las Vegas.

Sabloff, Jeremy A., and Gordon R. Willey

1967   The collapse of Maya civilization in the Southern Lowlands: A consideration of history and process. *Southwestern Journal of Anthropology* 23: 311–336.

Sabogal, José R.

1982   *La cerámica de Piura, Tomos I y II.* Instituto Andino de Artes Populares, Quito.

Salinas, Máximo

1991   El Castillo de Tomabal: Una fortificación del período Gallinazo en el valle de Virú. *Revista del Museo de Arqueología* 1: 66–82. Universidad Nacional de Trujillo, Trujillo.

Sandweiss, Daniel, and María del Carmen Rodríguez

1991   Moluscos marinos en la prehistoria peruana: Breve ensayo. *Boletín de Lima* 13 (75): 55–63.

Sawyer, Alan R.

1966   *Ancient Peruvian ceramics: The Nathan Cummings Collection.* Metropolitan Museum of Fine Art, New York.

1968   *The mastercraftsmen of ancient Peru.* S. R. Guggenheim Foundation, New York.

Schaaf, Crystal B.

1988   Establishment and demise of Moche V: Assessment of the climatic impact. Master's thesis, Harvard University Extension School, Cambridge, MA.

Schaedel, Richard P.

1948   Stone sculpture in the Callejón de Huaylas. In *A reappraisal of Peruvian archaeology*, assembled by Wendell C. Bennett, pp. 66–79. Memoir of the Society for American Archaeology, No. 4. Society for American Archaeology and Institute of Andean Research, Menasha, WI.

1949   Martínez de Compañón, founder of Peruvian archaeology. *American Antiquity* 15: 161–163.

1951a   Major ceremonial and population centers in northern Peru. In *The civilizations of ancient America: Selected papers of the 29th International Congress of Americanists*, edited by Sol Tax, pp. 232–243. University of Chicago Press, Chicago.

1951b   The lost cities of Peru. *Scientific American* 185: 18–23.

1951c   Mochica murals at Pañamarca. *Archaeology* 4 (3): 145–154.

1966a   Incipient urbanization and secularization in Tiahuanacoid Peru. *American Antiquity* 31: 338–344.

1966b   Urban growth and ekistics on the Peruvian coast. In *Proceedings of the 36th International Congress of Americanists* 2: 531–539. Buenos Aires.

1966c   The Huaca El Dragon. *Journal de la Société des Américanistes* 55 (2): 383–496.

1968   On the definition of civilization, urban, city and town in prehistoric America. In *Actas y Memorias del 37th Congreso Internacional de Americanistas* 1: 5–13. Buenos Aires.

1972   The city and the origin of the state in America. In *Actas y Memorias del 39 Congreso Internacional de Americanistas* 2: 15–33. Lima.

1978   Early state of the Incas. In *The early state*, edited by Henri J. M. Claessen and Peter Skalnik, pp. 289–320. The Hague, Mouton.

1979   The confluence of the pressed ware and paddle ware traditions in coastal Peru. In *Estudios Americanistas II: Homenaje a H. Trimborn*, edited by Rothwith Hartmann and Udo Oberem, pp. 231–239. Haus Völker und Kulturen-Anthropos Institut, St. Augustin, Germany.

1985a   Coast-highland interrelationships and ethnic groups in northern Peru (500 B.C.–A.D. 1980). In *Andean ecology and civilization*, edited by Shozo Masuda, Izumi Shimada, and Craig Morris, pp. 443–473. University of Tokyo Press, Tokyo.

1985b   The transition from chiefdom to state in northern Peru. In *Development and decline: The evolution of sociopolitical organization*, edited by Henri J. M. Claessen, Pieter van de Velde, and M. Estellie Smith, pp. 156–169. Bergin and Garvey, South Hadley, MA.

1986a   Control de agua y control social. In *La heterodoxia recuperada en torno a Angel Palerm*, edited by Susan Glantz, pp. 126–146. Fondo de Cultura Económica, Mexico City.

1986b   Paleohidrología y política agraria en el Perú. *América Indígena* 46: 319–330.

1987   2000 años de la continuidad cultural de los Muchik en la costa norte del Perú. *Ibero-Amerikanisches Archiv* N.F. 13: 117–128. Berlin.

1989   *La etnografía muchik en las fotografías de H. Brüning, 1886–1925.* Ediciones COFIDE, Corporación Financiera de Desarrollo, Lima.

1990   El comercio en el antiguo Perú. In *Historia, antropología y política: Homenaje a Angel Palerm*, edited by Modesto Suárez, pp. 163–189. Alianza Editorial Mexicana, Universidad Iberoamericana, Mexico City.

1992   Paleotechnology and flood control on the Peruvian north coast. In *Paleo ENSO records, international symposium: Extended abstracts*, edited by L. Ortlieb and J. Macharé, pp. 285–286. ORSTOM, Lima, and CONCYTEC, Lima.

Schaedel, Richard P., and Izumi Shimada

1982   Peruvian archaeology, 1946–80: An analytical overview. *World Archaeology* 13: 359–371.

Schaffer, Anne-Louise
1981   A monster-headed complex of mythical creatures in the Loma Negra metalwork. Paper presented at the 21st Annual Meeting of the Institute of Andean Studies, Berkeley.

Schele, Linda, and Peter Mathews
1991   Royal visits and other intersite relationships among the Classic Maya. In *Classic Maya political history: Hieroglyphic and archaeological evidence*, edited by T. Patrick Culbert, pp. 226–252. Cambridge University Press, Cambridge.

Schmidt, Max
1929   *Kunst und Kultur von Peru*. Propyläen Verlag, Berlin.

Schreiber, Katharina J.
1987   From state to empire: The expansion of Wari outside the Ayacucho Basin. In *The origins and development of the Andean state*, edited by Jonathan Haas, Shelia G. Pozorski, and Thomas Pozorski, pp. 91–96. Cambridge University Press, Cambridge.

Schreiber, K. J., and J. Lancho
1988   Los puquios de Nasca: Un sistema de galerías filtrantes. *Boletín de Lima* 10 (59): 51–62.

Schuler-Schömig, Immima von
1979   Die "Fremdkrieger" in Darstellungen der Moche-Keramik. *Baessler-Archiv* 27: 135–213.
1981   Die sogenannten Fremdkrieger und ihre weiteren ikonographischen Bezüge in der Moche-Keramik. *Baessler-Archiv* 29: 207–239.

Service, Elman R.
1975   *Origins of the state and civilization: The process of cultural evolution*. Norton, New York.

Shady, Ruth, and Hermilio Rosas
1977   *El Horizonte Medio en Chota: Prestigio de la Cultura Cajamarca y su relación con el "Imperio Huari."* Arqueológicas, 16. Lima.

Shady, Ruth, and Arturo Ruíz
1979   Evidence for interregional relationships during the Middle Horizon on the North-Central coast of Peru. *American Antiquity* 44: 676–684.

Sharer, Robert J.
1977   The Maya collapse revisited: Internal and external perspectives. In *Social process in Maya prehistory: Studies in honour of Sir Eric Thompson*, edited by Norman Hammond, pp. 531–552. Academic Press, London.

Sharon, Douglas
1978   *Wizard of the four winds: A shaman's story*. The Free Press, New York.

Sharon, Douglas, and Christopher B. Donnan
1977   The magic cactus: Ethnoarchaeological continuity in Peru. *Archaeology* 30 (6): 374–381.

Shimada, Izumi
1976   *Socioeconomic organization at Moche V Pampa Grande, Peru: Prelude to a major transformation to come*. Ph.D. dissertation, Department of Anthropology, University of Arizona. Microfilms International, Ann Arbor.
1978   Economy of prehistoric urban context: Commodity and labor flow in Moche V Pampa Grande, Peru. *American Antiquity* 43: 569–592.
1981   The Batán Grande–La Leche Archaeological Project: The first two seasons. *Journal of Field Archaeology* 8: 405–446.
1982   Horizontal archipelago and coast-highland interaction in north Peru: Archaeological models. In *El hombre y su ambiente en los Andes Centrales*, edited by Luis Millones and Hiroyasu Tomoeda, pp. 185–257. National Museum of Ethnology, Suita, Japan.
1984   Ancient mining and metallurgy on the northern North Coast of Peru. Paper presented at the 3rd Annual Meeting of the Northeast Conference on Andean Archaeology and Ethnohistory, Amherst.
1985a La Cultura Sicán: una caracterización arqueológica. In *Presencia histórica de Lambayeque*, compiled by Eric Mendoza, pp. 76–133. Editorial y Imprenta DESA, Lima.
1985b Introduction. In *Andean ecology and civilization*, edited by Shozo Masuda, Izumi Shimada, and Craig Morris, pp. xi–xxxii. University of Tokyo Press, Tokyo.
1985c Perception, procurement and management of resources: Archaeological perspective. In *Andean ecology and civilization*, edited by Shozo Masuda, Izumi Shimada, and Craig Morris, pp. 357–399. University of Tokyo Press, Tokyo.
1985d Productivity, specialization and space as resources: An ethnoarchaeology of Mórrope potters. Paper presented at the 50th Annual Meeting of the Society for American Archaeology, Denver.
1986   Batán Grande and cosmological unity in the Andes. In *Andean archaeology: Papers in memory of Clifford Evans*, edited by R. Matos and S. Turpin, pp. 163–188. Monograph 27 of the Institute of Archaeology, University of California, Los Angeles.
1987a Horizontal and vertical dimensions of prehistoric states in north Peru. In *The origins and development of the Andean state*, edited by Jonathan Haas, Shelia G. Pozorski and Thomas Pozorski, pp. 130–144. Cambridge University Press, Cambridge.
1987b Aspectos tecnológicos y productivos de la metalurgia Sicán, costa norte del Perú. *Gaceta Arqueológica Andina* 4 (13): 15–21. Lima.
1988a The Sicán and their neighbors: An overview of issues and data. Paper presented at the 53rd Annual Meeting of the Society for American Archaeology, Phoenix.
1988b A metallurgical survey in the Vicús region of the Far North Coast of Peru. Paper presented at the 7th Northeast Conference on Andean Archaeology and Ethnohistory, Amherst.

1990a Cultural continuities and discontinuities on the northern North Coast, Middle-Late Horizons. In *The northern dynasties: Kingship and statecraft in Chimor*, edited by Michael E. Moseley and Alana Cordy-Collins, pp. 297–392. Dumbarton Oaks, Washington, D.C.

1990b Andean archaeology in the 1980's: An assessment. *Journal of Field Archaeology* 17: 221–229.

1991a The flowering of regional art: Mochica and Nasca. In *Ancient art of the Andean world*, edited by Shozo Masuda and Izumi Shimada, pp. 71–105. Iwanami Shoten, Tokyo.

1991b Pachacamac archaeology: Retrospect and prospect. Introduction to a new edition of *Pachacamac* by Max Uhle, originally published in 1913, pp. xv–lxvi. University Museum Press, University of Pennsylvania, Philadelphia.

1992 Research summary on the 1991–1992 season of the Sicán Archaeological Project. *Willay* 37/38: 13–19. Cambridge, MA.

In press Organizational significance of marked bricks and associated construction features on the north Peruvian coast. In *Arquitectura y civilizaciones en los Andes prehispánicos*, edited by Elisabeth Bonnier. Instituto Francés de Estudios Andinos, Lima.

In press The regional states of the coast during the Late Intermediate Period: Archaeological evidence, ethnohistorical record and art outline. In *Pre-Inca regional states and the Inca empire*, edited by Laura Laurencich-Minelli, JACA Book, Milan, Italy.

Shimada, Izumi, and Raffael Cavallaro
1986 Monumental adobe architecture of the late pre-Hispanic northern North Coast of Peru. *Journal de la Société des Américanistes* 71: 41–78.

In press Monumental adobe architecture of the late pre-Hispanic northern North Coast of Peru: A holistic perspective. In *La tecnología en el mundo andino*, Vol. 2, edited by H. N. Lechtman and A. M. Soldi. Universidad Autónoma de México, Mexico City.

Shimada, Izumi, and Carlos G. Elera
1983 Batán Grande y la emergente complejidad cultural emergente en el norte del Perú durante el Horizonte Medio: Datos y modelos. *Boletín del Museo Nacional* 8: 41–47. Lima.

Shimada, Izumi, Carlos Elera, and Victor Chang
1990 Excavaciones en hornos de cerámica de la época formativa en Batán Grande, Costa Norte del Perú. *Gaceta Arqueológica Andina* 5: 19–43. Lima.

Shimada, Izumi, Carlos G. Elera, and Melody Shimada
1982 Excavaciones efectuadas en el centro ceremonial de Huaca Lucía-Chólope del Horizonte Temprano, Batán Grande, Costa Norte del Perú: 1979–1981. *Arqueológicas* 19: 109–210. Lima.

Shimada, Izumi, Stephen M. Epstein, and Alan K. Craig
1983 The metallurgical process in ancient north Peru. *Archaeology* 36 (5): 38–45.

Shimada, Izumi, and John F. Merkel
1991 Copper alloy metallurgy in ancient Peru. *Scientific American* 265: 80–86.

Shimada, Izumi, C. B. Schaaf, Lonnie G. Thompson, and E. Mosley-Thompson
1991a Cultural impacts of severe droughts in the prehistoric Andes: Application of a 1,500-year ice core precipitation record. *World Archaeology* 22: 247–270.

1991b Implicaciones culturales de una gran sequía del siglo VI d.C. en los Andes peruanos. *Boletín de Lima* 13 (33): 33–56.

Shimada, Melody
1982 Zooarchaeology of Huacaloma: Behavioral and cultural implications. In *Excavations at Huacaloma in the Cajamarca valley, Peru*, edited by Kazuo Terada and Yoshio Onuki, pp. 303–336. University of Tokyo Press, Tokyo.

1985   Continuities and changes in patterns of faunal resource utilization: Formative through Cajamarca periods. In *The Formative Period in the Cajamarca Basin*, edited by Kazuo Terada and Yoshio Onuki, pp. 289–310. University of Tokyo Press, Tokyo.

Shimada, Melody J., and Izumi Shimada

1981   Explotación y manejo de los recursos naturales en Pampa Grande, sitio Moche V: Significado del análisis orgánico. *Revista del Museo Nacional* 45: 19–73. Lima.

1985   Prehistoric llama breeding and herding on the North Coast of Peru. *American Antiquity* 50: 3–26.

1987   Comments on the functions, husbandry and osteological identification of alpaca. *American Antiquity* 52: 836–839.

Shippee, Robert

1932   The "great wall of Peru" and other aerial photographic studies by the Shippee-Johnson Peruvian Expedition. *Geographical Review* 22: 1–29.

1933   Air adventures in Peru. *National Geographic Magazine* 63: 81–120.

Silverman, Helaine

1988   De la historia del Perú antiguo: La obtención de cabezas trofeo. *Boletín de Lima* 58: 49–56.

Smith, Clifford, William Denevan, and Patrick Hamilton

1968   Ancient ridged fields in the region of Lake Titicaca. *Geographical Journal* 134: 353–367.

Smith, John W.

1979   *The Recuay culture: A reconstruction based on artistic motifs.* Ph.D. dissertation, Department of Anthropology, University of Texas at Austin. Microfilms International, Ann Arbor.

Smith, Richard T.

1979   The development and role of sunken field agriculture on the Peruvian coast. *Geographical Journal* 145: 387–400.

Soldi, Ana María

1979   *Chacras excavadas en el desierto.* Seminario de Historia Rural Andina, Universidad Nacional Mayor de San Marcos, Lima.

Squier, Ephraim G.

1877   *Incidents of travel and exploration in the land of the Incas.* Harper and Brothers, New York.

Stahl, Peter W.

1988   Prehistoric camelids in the lowlands of western Ecuador. *Journal of Archaeological Science* 15: 355–365.

Stark, Barbara

1985   Archaeological identification of pottery production locations: Ethnoarchaeological and archaeological data in Mesoamerica. In *Decoding prehistoric ceramics*, edited by B. C. Nelson, pp. 158–194. Southern Illinois Press, Carbondale.

Steinitz-Kannan, Miriam, Mark A. Nienaber, and Melanie A. Riedinger

1992   The fossil diatoms of Lake Yambo, Ecuador: A 2500-year record on intense El Niño events. In *Paleo ENSO records, international symposium: Extended abstracts*, edited by L. Ortlieb and J. Macharé, pp. 295–298. ORSTOM, Lima and CONCYTEC, Lima.

Steward, Julian H.

1949   Cultural causality and law: A trial formulation of the development of early civilizations. *American Anthropologist* 51: 1–27.

Steward, Julian H. (editor)

1955   *Irrigation civilizations: A comparative symposium.* Pan American Union, Washington, D.C.

Steward, Julian H., and L. C. Faron

1959   *Native peoples of South America.* McGraw-Hill, New York.

Stewart, Thomas D.

1973   *The people of America.* Charles Scribner's Sons, New York.

Strong, William D.

1947   Finding the tomb of a warrior-god. *National Geographic Magazine* 91: 453–482.

Strong, William D., and Clifford Evans
1952   *Cultural stratigraphy in the Virú Valley, northern Peru.* Columbia University Studies in Archaeology and Ethnology, Vol. 4. Columbia University, New York.

Stuiver, Minze, and Gordon W. Pearson
1986   High-precision calibration of the radiocarbon time scale, A.D. 1950–500 B.C. *Radiocarbon* 28 (2B): 805–838.

Stuiver, Minze, and P. J. Reimer
1986   A computer program for radiocarbon age calibration. *Radiocarbon* 28 (2B): 1022–1030.

Stumer, Louis M.
1956   Development of Peruvian coastal Tiahuanacoid styles. *American Antiquity* 22: 59–69.
1957   Cerámica negra del Estilo Maranga. *Revista del Museo Nacional* 26: 272–289. Lima.
1958   Contactos foráneos en la arquitectura de la costa central del Perú. *Revista del Museo Nacional* 27: 11–30. Lima.

Suárez, Hermes
1985   Algunas consideraciones sobre la fauna del Departamento de Lambayeque. In *Presencia histórica de Lambayeque*, compiled by Eric Mendoza, pp. 37–48. Editorial y Imprenta DESA, Lima.

Tabío, Ernesto E.
1977   *Prehistoria de la costa del Perú.* Instituto de Ciencias Sociales de la Academia de Ciencias de Cuba, La Habana.

Tainter, Joseph
1988   *The collapse of complex societies.* Cambridge University Press, Cambridge.

Tellenbach, Michael
1986   *Die Ausgrabungen in der formativzeitlichen Siedlung Montegrande, Jequetepeque-Tal, Nord-Peru.* Materialien zur Allgemeinen und Vergleichenden Archäologie, Band 39. Verlag C. H. Beck, Munich.

Tello, Julio C.
1938   Arte antiguo peruano: Album fotográfico de las principales especies arqueológicas de cerámica muchik existentes en los museos de Lima, primera parte: Tecnología y morfología. *Inca* 2: vii–lxii, 1–280. Lima.
1942   Origen y desarrollo de las civilizaciones prehistóricas andinas. In *Actas y trabajos científicos del XVII Congreso Internacional de Americanistas, Lima, 1939* 1: 589–720. Lima.

Terada, Kazuo, and Ryozo Matsumoto
1985   Sobre la cronología de la tradición Cajamarca. In *Historia de Cajamarca, 1: Arqueología*, edited by F. Silva, W. Espinoza, and R. Ravines, pp. 67–92. Instituto Nacional de Cultura, Cajamarca, and Corporación de Desarrollo de Cajamarca, Cajamarca.

Terada, Kazuo, and Yoshio Onuki (editors)
1982   *Excavations at Huacaloma in the Cajamarca valley, Peru, 1979.* Japanese Scientific Expedition to Nuclear America, Report 2. University of Tokyo Press, Tokyo.
1985   *The Formative period in the Cajamarca Basin, Peru: Excavations at Huacaloma and Layzón, 1982.* Japanese Scientific Expedition to Nuclear America, Report 3. University of Tokyo Press, Tokyo.

Thatcher, John P. L., Jr.
1975   Early Intermediate Period and Middle Horizon 1B ceramic assemblages of Huamachuco, North Highlands, Peru. *Ñawpa Pacha* 10–12: 109–127.
1977   A Middle Horizon 1B cache from Huamachuco, North Highlands, Peru. *Ñawpa Pacha* 15: 101–110.

Thompson, Donald E.
1976   Prehistory of the Uchucmarca Valley in the North Highlands of Peru. In *Actas del 41 Congreso Internacional de Americanistas* 2: 99–106. Mexico City.

Thompson, L. G.
1980   Glaciological investigations of the tropical Quelccaya ice cap, Peru. *Journal of Glaciology* 25 (91): 69–84.

Thompson, L. G., M. E. Davis, E. Moseley-Thompson, and K-B. Liu
1988   Pre-Incan agricultural activity recorded in dust layers in two tropical ice cores. *Nature* 336: 763–765.

Thompson, L. G., S. Hastenrath, and B. Morales
1979   Climatic ice core records from the tropical Quelccaya ice cap. *Science* 203: 1240–1243.

Thompson, L. G., and E. Mosley-Thompson
1987   Evidence of abrupt climatic change during the last 1,500 years recorded in ice cores from the tropical Quelccaya ice cap, Peru. In *Abrupt climatic change*, edited by W. H. Berger and L. D. Labeyrie, pp. 99–110. NATO ASI Series C, Vol. 216. D. Reidel, Norwell, MA.

Thompson, L. G., E. Mosley-Thompson, J. F. Bolzan, and B. R. Koci
1985   A 1500-year record of tropical precipitation in ice cores from the Quelccaya ice cap, Peru. *Science* 229: 971–973.

Thompson, L. G., E. Mosley-Thompson, W. Dansgaard, and P. Grootes
1986   The Little Ice Age as recorded in the stratigraphy of the tropical Quelccaya ice cap. *Science* 234: 361–364.

Thompson, L. G., E. Mosley-Thompson, P. Grootes, M. Pourchet, and S. Hastenrath
1984   Tropical glaciers: Potential for ice core paleoclimatic reconstructions. *Journal of Geophysical Research* 89 (D3): 4638–4646.

Thompson, L. G., E. Mosley-Thompson, and B. Morales
1984   El Niño–Southern Oscillation events recorded in the stratigraphy of the tropical Quelccaya ice cap, Peru. *Science* 203: 50–53.

Tolstoy, Paul
1971   Reconocimientos arqueológicos en el valle de Piura. *Arqueología y Sociedad* 5: 17–22. Universidad Nacional Mayor de San Marcos, Lima.

Tomoeda, Hiroyasu

1985   The llama is my *chacra*: Metaphor of Andean pastoralists. In *Andean ecology and civilization,* edited by Shozo Masuda, Izumi Shimada, and Craig Morris, pp. 277–299. University of Tokyo Press, Tokyo.

Topic, John R., Jr.

1982   Lower-class social and economic organization at Chan Chan. In *Chan Chan: Andean desert city,* edited by Michael E. Moseley and Kent C. Day, pp. 145–175. University of New Mexico Press, Albuquerque.

1990   Craft production in the Kingdom of Chimor. In *The northern dynasties: Kingship and statecraft in Chimor,* edited by Michael E. Moseley and Alana Cordy-Collins, pp. 145–176. Dumbarton Oaks, Washington, D.C.

1991   Huari and Huamachuco. In *Huari administrative structure: Prehistoric monumental architecture and state government,* edited by W. H. Isbell and G. F. McEwan, pp. 141–164. Dumbarton Oaks, Washington, D.C.

Topic, John R., and Theresa L. Topic

1983   Coast-highland relations in northern Peru: Some observations on routes, networks, and scales of interaction. In *Civilization in the ancient Americas,* edited by R. M. Leventhal and A. L. Kolata, pp. 237–259. University of New Mexico Press, Albuquerque.

1986   El Horizonte Medio en Huamachuco. *Revista del Museo Nacional* 47: 13–52. Lima.

Topic, Theresa L.

1977   Excavations at Moche. Ph.D. dissertation, Department of Anthropology, Harvard University, Cambridge, MA.

1982   The Early Intermediate Period and its legacy. In *Chan Chan: Andean desert city,* edited by Michael E. Moseley and Kent C. Day, pp. 255–284. University of New Mexico Press, Albuquerque.

1991   The Middle Horizon in northern Peru. In *Huari administrative structure: Prehistoric monumental architecture and state government,* edited by W. H. Isbell and G. F. McEwan, pp. 233–246. Dumbarton Oaks, Washington, D.C.

Topic, Theresa L., and John R. Topic

1982   Preliminary report on the final season (1980) of the Prehistoric Fortification Systems of Northern Peru Project. Department of Anthropology, Trent University, Peterborough, Canada.

1984   Huamachuco Archaeological Project: Preliminary report on the third season, June–August 1983. Trent University Occasional Papers in Anthropology, No. 1. Peterborough, Canada.

Torre, Carlos de la, and Manuel Burga (editors/compilers)

1986   *Andenes y camellones en el Perú andino.* CONCYTEC, Lima.

Tosi, Joseph A., Jr.

1960   *Zonas de vida natural en el Perú: Memoria explicativa sobre el mapa ecológica del Perú.* Boletín Técnico, No. 5. Instituto Interamericano de Ciencias Agrícolas de la OEA, Zona Andina, Lima.

Towle, Margaret

1952   Descriptions and identifications of the Virú plant remains. Appendix to *Cultural stratigraphy in the Virú Valley, northern Peru* by William D. Strong and C. Evans, pp. 352–356. Columbia Studies in Archaeology and Ethnology, 1 (1). Columbia University, New York.

1961   *The ethnobotany of pre-columbian Peru.* Viking Fund Publications in Anthropology, 30. Aldine, Chicago.

Trigger, Bruce G.

1990   Monumental architecture: A thermodynamic explanation of symbolic behaviour. *World Archaeology* 22: 120–131.

Trimborn, Hermann

1979   *El reino de Lambayeque en el antiguo Perú.* Collectanea Instituti Anthropos, No. 19. Haus Völker und Kulturen-Anthropos Institut, St. Augustin, Germany.

Troll, Carl

1958   *Las culturas superiores andinas y el medio geográfico.* Translation from the German original by Carlos Nicholson. *Revista del Instituto de Geografía* 5: 3–55. Lima.

Troll, Carl (editor)

1968   *Geo-ecology of the mountainous regions of the tropical Americas.* Colloquium Geographicum, Band 9. Dümmlers Verlag, Bonn.

Tschauner, Hartmut, and Marianne Tschauner

1992   Prospección a lo largo del antiguo canal Taymi, Valle de Lambayeque, temporada de 1991. In *Informe de la temporada de los años 1991–1992 del Proyecto Arqueológico de Sicán,* edited by Izumi Shimada. Report submitted to the Instituto Nacional de Cultura, Lima.

Tylecote, Ronald F., and P. J. Boydell

1978   *Experiments on copper smelting based on early furnaces found at Timna.* Archaeo-Metallurgy Monograph Vol. 1, pp. 27–49. Institute for Archaeo-Metallurgical Studies, London.

Ubbelohde-Doering, Heinrich

1949   Ceramic comparisons of two North Coast Peruvian valleys. In *Proceedings of the 29th International Congress of Americanists, New York, 5–12 September* 1: 224–231.

1957   Der Gallinazo-Stil und die Chronologie der altperuanischen Fruhkulturen. *Bayerischen Akademie der Wissenschaften, Philosophisch Historische Klasse, Sitzungsberichte* 9: 1–8. Munich.

1958   Bericht über archäologische Feldarbeiten in Peru. *Ethnos* 23: 67–99. Stockholm.

1960   Bericht über archäologische Feldarbeiten in Peru, III. *Ethnos* 25: 153–182. Stockholm.

1967   *On the royal highways of the Inca.* Thames and Hudson, London.

1983   *Vorspanische Gräber von Pacat-namú, Nordperu.* Materialien zur Allgemeinen und Vergleichenden Archäologie, Band 26. Verlag C. H. Beck, Munich.

Uceda, Santiago

1988   *Catastro de los sitios arqueológicos del área de influencia del canal de irrigación Chavinmochic: Valles de Santa y Chao.* Patrimonio Arqueológico Zona Norte/1. Instituto Departamental de Cultura – La Libertad, Trujillo.

1990   Huaca Choloque: Sitio fortificado Moche en el valle del Santa. *Revista del Museo de Arqueología* 1: 37–65. Universidad Nacional de Trujillo, Trujillo.

1992   Evidencias de grandes precipitaciones en diversas etapas constructivas de la Huaca de la Luna, costa norte del Perú. In *Paleo-ENSO records, international symposium: Extended abstracts*, edited by L. Ortlieb and J. Macharé, pp. 315–318. ORSTOM, Lima, and CONCYTEC, Lima.

Uceda, Santiago, José Carcelen, and Víctor Pimentel

1990   *Catastro de los sitios arqueológicos del área de influencia del canal de irrigación Chavinmochic: Valles de Santa (Palo Redondo y Virú).* Patrimonio Arqueológico Zona Norte/2. Instituto Departamental de Cultura – La Libertad and Proyecto Especial de Irrigación Chavinmochic, Trujillo.

Uhle, Friedrich Max

1903   *Pachacamac: Report of the William Pepper, M.D., LL.D. Peruvian Expedition of 1896.* Department of Archaeology, University of Pennsylvania, Philadelphia.

1910   Über die Frühkulturen in der Umgebung von Lima. In *Proceedings of the 16th International Congress of Americanists* 2: 347–370. A. Hartleben's Verlag, Vienna and Leipzig.

1913   Die Ruinen von Moche. *Journal de la Société des Américanistes de Paris*, n.s. 10: 95–117.

1915   Las ruinas de Moche. *Boletín de la Sociedad Geográfica de Lima* 30 (3–4): 57–71.

n.d.   Final report on the excavation at the site of Moche in 1899. Deposited in the Ibero-Amerikanisches Institut, Preussischer Kulturbesitz, Berlin.

Urton, Gary

n.d.   Report on archaeoastronomical fieldwork at Pampa Grande. September, 1985. Manuscript in possession of Izumi Shimada.

Verano, John

1991   Moche: Perfil de un antiguo pueblo peruano. *Revista del Museo de Arqueología* 2: 104–113. Universidad Nacional de Trujillo, Trujillo.

Vreeland, James M.

1978   Algodón "País": Un cultivo milenario olvidado. *Boletín de la Sociedad Geográfica de Lima* 97: 19–26.

1982   The ethnoarchaeology of ancient Peruvian cotton crafts. *Archaeology* 35 (3): 64–66.

1985   Agricultura tradicional en el desierto de Lambayeque durante un año aluviónico. In *Ciencia, tecnología y agresión ambiental: El fenómeno El Niño*, pp. 579–621. CONCYTEC, Lima.

1986a   Una perspectiva antropológica de la paleotecnología en el desarrollo agrario del norte de Perú. *América Indígena* 46: 275–318.

1986b   Cotton spinning and processing on the Peruvian North Coast. In *The Junius B. Bird Conference on Andean textiles, April 7th and 8th, 1984*, edited by Ann P. Rowe, pp. 363–383. The Textile Museum, Washington, D.C.

1992   Indigenous response mechanisms to periodic climatic disasters on the Peruvian North Coast: Paleotechnological repertory in 1578. In *Paleo ENSO records, international symposium: Extended abstracts*, edited by L. Ortlieb and J. Macharé, pp. 329–330. ORSTOM, Lima, and CONCYTEC, Lima.

Watson, Richard P.
1979 Water control and land use on the arid North Coast of Peru: Prehispanic agricultural systems in the Chicama Valley. M.A. thesis, Department of Anthropology, University of Texas, Austin.

Weberbauer, August
1945 *El mundo vegetal de los Andes peruanos.* Ministerio de Agricultura, Lima.

Webster, Steven S.
1971 An indigenous Quechua community in exploitation of multiple ecological zones. *Revista del Museo Nacional* 37: 174–183. Lima.

Weir, Glendon H., and Herbert H. Eling, Jr.
1986 Pollen evidence for economic plant utilization in prehistoric agricultural fields of Jequetepeque Valley, northern Peru. In *Andean archaeology: Papers in memory of Clifford Evans,* edited by R. Matos M., S. A. Turpin, and H. H. Eling, Jr., pp. 150–162. Monograph 27 of the Institute of Archaeology, University of California, Los Angeles.

Weiss, Pedro
1976 *El perro peruano sin pelo.* Publicaciones del Museo Nacional de Antropología y Arqueología, Serie: Paleobiología, 1. Lima.

Wells, Lisa E.
1987 An alluvial record of El Niño events from northern coastal Peru. *Journal of Geophysical Research* 92 (C13): 14463–14470.

West, Michael
1971 Prehistoric human ecology in the Viru valley. *California Anthropologist* 1: 47–56. Los Angeles.
1979 Early watertable farming on the North Coast of Peru. *American Antiquity* 44: 138–144.
1981 Agricultural resource use in an Andean coastal ecosystem. *Human Ecology* 9: 47–77.

Wheatley, Paul
1969 *City as symbol.* H. K. Lewis and Co., London.

1971 *The pivot of the four quarters: A preliminary enquiry into the origins and character of the ancient Chinese city.* Aldine Press, Chicago.
1972 The concept of urbanism. In *Man, settlement and urbanism,* edited by P. J. Ucko, R. Tringham, and G. W. Dimbleby, pp. 601–637. Duckworth, London.

Wiener, Charles
1880 *Pérou et Bolivie, récit du voyage.* Librairie Hachette, Paris.

Willey, Gordon R.
1945 Horizon styles and pottery traditions in Peruvian archaeology. *American Antiquity* 11: 49–56.
1946 The Virú Valley program in northern Peru. *Acta Americana* 4 (4): 224–238.
1948 Functional analysis of "horizon styles" in Peruvian archaeology. In *A reappraisal of Peruvian archaeology,* assembled by Wendell C. Bennett, pp. 8–15. Memoirs of the Society for American Archaeology, No. 4. Society for American Archaeology and Institute of Andean Research, Menasha, WI.
1953 *Prehistoric settlement patterns in the Viru Valley, Peru.* Bureau of American Ethnology, Bulletin 155. Smithsonian Institution, Washington, D.C.
1971 *An introduction to American archaeology, Vol. 2: South America.* Prentice Hall, Englewood Cliffs, NJ.
1974 The Virú Valley settlement pattern study. In *Archaeological researches in retrospect,* edited by Gordon R. Willey, pp. 149–179. Winthrop, Cambridge, MA.
1990 Ancient Maya politics. *Proceedings of the American Philosophical Society* 134: 1–9.

Willey, Gordon R., and Jeremy A. Sabloff
1980 *A history of American archaeology.* Second edition. W. H. Freeman, San Francisco.

Willey, Gordon R., and Demitri B. Shimkin

1971   The collapse of Classic Maya civilization in the Southern Lowlands: A symposium summary statement. *Southwestern Journal of Anthropology* 27: 1–18.

Williams, Carlos, and José Pineda

1985   Desde Ayacucho hasta Cajamarca: Formas arquitectónicas con filiación Wari. *Boletín de Lima* 7 (40): 55–61.

Wilson, David L.

1981   Of maize and men: A critique of the maritime hypothesis of state origins on the coast of Peru. *American Anthropologist* 83: 93–120.

1983   The origins and development of complex prehispanic society in the lower Santa Valley, Peru: Implications for theories of state origins. *Journal of Anthropological Archaeology* 2: 209–276.

1987   Reconstructing patterns of early warfare in the lower Santa Valley: New data on the role of conflict in the origins of complex north-coast society. In *The origins and development of the Andean state*, edited by Jonathan Haas, Shelia G. Pozorski, and Thomas Pozorski, pp. 56–69. Cambridge University Press, Cambridge.

1988   *Prehispanic settlement patterns in the lower Santa Valley, Peru: A regional perspective on the origins and development of complex North Coast society.* Smithsonian Institution Press, Washington, D.C.

1991   Prehispanic settlement patterns in the Casma Valley, North Coast of Peru: Preliminary results of the 1989–1990 seasons in the Casma branch of the valley. Second report to the Committee for Research and Exploration, National Geographic Society, Washington, D.C.

Wing, Elizabeth S.

1972   Utilization of animal resources in the Peruvian Andes. Appendix 4 to *Andes 4: Excavations at Kotosh, Peru*, edited by S. Izumi and K. Terada, pp. 327–352. University of Tokyo Press, Tokyo.

Winterhalder, Bruce, Robert Larsen, and R. Brook Thomas

1974   Dung as an essential resource in a highland Peruvian community. *Human Ecology* 2 (2): 43–55.

Wittfogel, Karl A.

1957   *Oriental despotism: A comparative study of total power.* Yale University Press, New Haven.

Wright, Henry T.

1977   Recent research on the origin of the state. *Annual Review of Anthropology* 6: 379–397.

1978   Toward an explanation of the origin of the state. In *Origins of the state: The anthropology of political evolution*, edited by Ronald Cohen and Elman R. Service, pp. 49–68. Institute for the Study of Human Issues, Philadelphia.

Wright, Henry T., and Gregory A. Johnson

1975   Population, exchange and early state formation in southwestern Iran. *American Anthropologist* 77: 267–289.

Wyrtki, K.

1975   El Niño—the dynamic response of the equatorial Pacific Ocean to atmospheric forcing. *Journal of Physical Oceanography* 5: 572–584.

Yacovleff, Eugenio N., and Fortunato L. Herrera

1934–   El mundo vegetal de los antiguos
1935   peruanos. *Revista del Museo Nacional* 3: 241–322; 4: 29–102. Lima.

Yamamoto, Norio

1982   A food production system in the southern Central Andes. In *El hombre y su ambiente en los Andes centrales*, edited by Luis Millones and Hiroyasu Tomoeda, pp. 39–62. National Museum of Ethnology, Suita, Japan.

Zuidema, Tom

1977–   Shafttombs and the Inca empire.
1978   *Journal of the Steward Anthropological Society* 9: 133–178.

Index